Design Innovation and Network Architecture for the Future Internet

Mohamed Boucadair
Orange S.A., France

Christian Jacquenet
Orange S.A., France

A volume in the Advances in Web Technologies and Engineering (AWTE) Book Series

Published in the United States of America by
  IGI Global
  Engineering Science Reference (an imprint of IGI Global)
  701 E. Chocolate Avenue
  Hershey PA, USA 17033
  Tel: 717-533-8845
  Fax: 717-533-8661
  E-mail: cust@igi-global.com
  Web site: http://www.igi-global.com

Library of Congress Cataloging-in-Publication Data

Names: Boucadair, Mohamed, editor. | Jacquenet, Christian, editor.
Title: Design innovation and network architecture for the future internet / Mohamed Boucadair,
    and Christian Jacquenet, editors.
Description: Hershey, PA : Engineering Science Reference, [2021] | Includes
    bibliographical references and index. | Summary: "This edited book
    offers a comprehensive overview on the recent advances in networking
    techniques that are likely to shape the future Internet and which also
    mitigate currently known issues of architecture, security and
    networking"-- Provided by publisher.
Identifiers: LCCN 2020055546 (print) | LCCN 2020055547 (ebook) | ISBN
    9781799876465 (h/c) | ISBN 9781799876472 (ebook)
Subjects: LCSH: Computer networks--Technological innovations. | Computer
    networks--Research. | Internetworking (Telecommunication)--Forecasting.
Classification: LCC TK5105.5 .H367 2021 (print) | LCC TK5105.5 (ebook) |
    DDC 004.67/8--dc23
LC record available at https://lccn.loc.gov/2020055546
LC ebook record available at https://lccn.loc.gov/2020055547

This book is published in the IGI Global book series Advances in Web Technologies and Engineering (AWTE) (ISSN:
2328-2762; eISSN: 2328-2754)

British Cataloguing in Publication Data
A Cataloguing in Publication record for this book is available from the British Library.

All work contributed to this book is new, previously-unpublished material. The views expressed in this book are those of the
authors, but not necessarily of the publisher.

For electronic access to this publication, please contact: eresources@igi-global.com.

Advances in Web Technologies and Engineering (AWTE) Book Series

Ghazi I. Alkhatib
The Hashemite University, Jordan
David C. Rine
George Mason University, USA

ISSN:2328-2762
EISSN:2328-2754

MISSION

The **Advances in Web Technologies and Engineering (AWTE) Book Series** aims to provide a platform for research in the area of Information Technology (IT) concepts, tools, methodologies, and ethnography, in the contexts of global communication systems and Web engineered applications. Organizations are continuously overwhelmed by a variety of new information technologies, many are Web based. These new technologies are capitalizing on the widespread use of network and communication technologies for seamless integration of various issues in information and knowledge sharing within and among organizations. This emphasis on integrated approaches is unique to this book series and dictates cross platform and multidisciplinary strategy to research and practice.

The **Advances in Web Technologies and Engineering (AWTE) Book Series** seeks to create a stage where comprehensive publications are distributed for the objective of bettering and expanding the field of web systems, knowledge capture, and communication technologies. The series will provide researchers and practitioners with solutions for improving how technology is utilized for the purpose of a growing awareness of the importance of web applications and engineering.

COVERAGE

- Data and knowledge validation and verification
- Data and knowledge capture and quality issues
- Competitive/intelligent information systems
- Web Systems Architectures, Including Distributed, Grid Computer, and Communication Systems Processing
- Data analytics for business and government organizations
- IT readiness and technology transfer studies
- Mobile, location-aware, and ubiquitous computing
- Radio Frequency Identification (RFID) research and applications in Web engineered systems
- Integrated user profile, provisioning, and context-based processing
- Web systems performance engineering studies

IGI Global is currently accepting manuscripts for publication within this series. To submit a proposal for a volume in this series, please contact our Acquisition Editors at Acquisitions@igi-global.com or visit: http://www.igi-global.com/publish/.

Titles in this Series

For a list of additional titles in this series, please visit:
http://www.igi-global.com/book-series/advances-web-technologies-engineering/37158

Challenges and Opportunities for the Convergence of IoT, Big Data, and CloudComputing
Sathiyamoorthi Velayutham (Sona College of Technology, India)
Engineering Science Reference • © 2021 • 350pp • H/C (ISBN: 9781799831112) • US $215.00

Examining the Impact of Deep Learning and IoT on Multi-Industry Applications
Roshani Raut (Pimpri Chinchwad College of Engineering (PCCOE), Pune, India) and Albena Dimitrova Mihovska (CTIF Global Capsule (CGC),Denmark)
Engineering Science Reference • © 2021 • 304pp • H/C (ISBN: 9781799875116) • US $245.00

Emerging Trends in IoT and Integration With Data Science
Petar V. Kocovic (Nikola Tesla University, Serbia) and Muthu Ramachandran (Leeds Beckett University, UK)
Information Science Reference • © 2021 • 340pp • H/C (ISBN: 9781799841869) • US $225.00

Result Page Generation for Web Searching Emerging Research and Opportunities
Mostafa Alli (Tsinghua University, China)
Engineering Science Reference • © 2021 • 126pp • H/C (ISBN: 9781799809616) • US $165.00

Building Smart and Secure Environments Through the Fusion of Virtual Reality, Augmented Reality, and the IoT
Nadesh RK (Vellore Institute of Technology, India) Shynu PG (Vellore Institute of Technology, India) and Chiranji Lal Chowdhary (School of Information Technology and Engineering, VIT University, Vellore, India)
Engineering Science Reference • © 2020 • 300pp • H/C (ISBN: 9781799831839) • US $245.00

The IoT and the Next Revolutions Automating the World
Dinesh Goyal (Poornima Institute of Engineering & Technology, India) S. Balamurugan (QUANTS Investment Strategy & Consultancy Services, India) Sheng-Lung Peng (National Dong Hwa University, Taiwan) and Dharm Singh Jat (Namibia University of Science and Technology, Namibia)
Engineering Science Reference • © 2019 • 340pp • H/C (ISBN: 9781522592464) • US $255.00

Integrating and Streamlining Event-Driven IoT Services
Yang Zhang (Beijing University of Posts and Telecommunications, China) and Yanmeng Guo (Chinese Academy of Sciences, China)
Engineering Science Reference • © 2019 • 309pp • H/C (ISBN: 9781522576228) • US $205.00

701 East Chocolate Avenue, Hershey, PA 17033, USA
Tel: 717-533-8845 x100 • Fax: 717-533-8661
E-Mail: cust@igi-global.com • www.igi-global.com

Table of Contents

Section 1
New Network Designs

    Richard Li, Futurewei Technologies, Inc., USA
    Uma S. Chunduri, Futurewei Technologies, Inc., USA
    Alexander Clemm, Futurewei Technologies, Inc., USA
    Lijun Dong, Futurewei Technologies, Inc., USA

    Tirumaleswar Reddy Konda, McAfee, India

    Yannick Le Louédec, Orange S.A., France
    Gaëlle Yven, Orange S.A., France
    Valéry Bastide, Orange S.A., France
    Yiping Chen, Orange S.A., France
    Gwenaëlle Delsart, Orange S.A., France
    Mateusz Dzida, Orange S.A., France
    Frédéric Fieau, Orange S.A., France
    Patrick Fleming, Orange S.A., France
    Ivan Froger, Orange S.A., France
    Lahcene Haddak, Orange S.A., France
    Nathalie Labidurie Omnes, Orange S.A., France
    Vincent Thiebaut, Orange S.A., France

Section 2
Latest Developments in Network Automation

Section 3
Towards "Attack-Proof" Network Security Frameworks

Detailed Table of Contents

Section 1
New Network Designs

Chapter 1
    Richard Li, Futurewei Technologies, Inc., USA
    Uma S. Chunduri, Futurewei Technologies, Inc., USA
    Alexander Clemm, Futurewei Technologies, Inc., USA
    Lijun Dong, Futurewei Technologies, Inc., USA

Industrial machine-type communications (e.g., industrial internet), emerging applications such as holographic type communications, IP mobile backhaul transport for 5G/B5G (beyond 5G) for ultra-reliable low latency communications and massive machine-type communications, emerging industry verticals such as driverless vehicles, and future networking use cases as called out by ITU-T's focus group on network 2030 all require new networking capabilities and services. This chapter introduces "New IP," a new data communication protocol that extends packet networking with new capabilities to support future applications that go beyond the capabilities that are provided by internetworking protocol (IP) today. New IP is designed to allow the user to specify requirements, such as expectations for key performance indicators' (KPIs) service levels, and other guidance for packet processing and forwarding purposes. New IP is designed to interoperate with existing networks in a straightforward manner and thus to facilitate its incremental deployment that leverages existing investment.

Chapter 2
    Tirumaleswar Reddy Konda, McAfee, India

Application-aware networking (AAN) is a framework in which applications can discover services offered by a network and explicitly signal their flow characteristics and requirements to the network. Such framework provides network nodes with knowledge of the application flow characteristics, which enables them to apply the correct flow treatment (e.g., bind the flow to a network slice, bind the flow to a service function chaining, set appropriate quality of service marking, invoke policing and shaping rules) and provide feedback to applications accordingly. This chapter describes how an application enabled collaborative networking framework contributes to solve the encountered problems. The chapter also describes recent proposals such as the PAN (path-aware networking) framework discussed within the IRTF and the APN (application-aware networking) framework that is meant to convey application identification and its network performance in-band.

Yannick Le Louédec, Orange S.A., France
Gaëlle Yven, Orange S.A., France
Valéry Bastide, Orange S.A., France
Yiping Chen, Orange S.A., France
Gwenaëlle Delsart, Orange S.A., France
Mateusz Dzida, Orange S.A., France
Frédéric Fieau, Orange S.A., France
Patrick Fleming, Orange S.A., France
Ivan Froger, Orange S.A., France
Lahcene Haddak, Orange S.A., France
Nathalie Labidurie Omnes, Orange S.A., France
Vincent Thiebaut, Orange S.A., France

This chapter provides an overview on the recent advances and perspectives on content delivery networks (CDNs). After a reminder on the definition and core features of CDNs, the first section highlights their importance with quantitative illustrations. The second section identifies the various types of CDNs which have been deployed to address different markets. The growth of the CDNs has been driven primarily by video streaming. Next to media content, CDNs have evolved to deliver always more demanding social networks and applications. Security solutions are now fully integrated into CDNs and marketed as flagship products. The third, fourth, and fifth sections outline the challenges and technical evolutions of the CDNs to keep up with their customers' hunger for media content, web performance, and security. The sixth section focuses on the convergence of CDNs and clouds. The seventh section reviews the status and perspectives of different approaches for using multiple CDNs. The last section presents the current positioning and future perspectives of the CDNs in the mobile domain.

Joël Penhoat, Orange S.A., France
Mikko Samuli Vaija, Orange S.A., France
Dinh-Thuy Phan-Huy, Orange S.A., France
Guillaume Gérard, Orange S.A., France
Zakaria Ournani, Orange S.A., France
Dominique Nussbaum, Orange S.A., France
Gilles Dretsch, Orange S.A., France
Quentin Fousson, Bouygues Telecom, France
Marc Vautier, Orange S.A., France

The Intergovernmental Panel on Climate Change claims that global warming can be avoided by "reaching net zero carbon dioxide emissions globally around 2050 and concurrent deep reductions in emissions of non-carbon dioxide forcers, particularly methane." To protect the planet and guarantee prosperity for all,

The United Nations has set up a sustainable development program made up of 17 goals. Among them, Goal 12 establishes sustainable consumption and production patterns so that a social and economic growth does not increase the pressure on Earth's resources, and Goal 13 constrains global warming. This chapter explores some actions the telecommunication companies have implemented: assessing the issues of mineral resources on network equipment, improving data centre energy consumption, reducing the average electricity intensity of the transmitting data, contributing to the energy transition.

Section 2
Latest Developments in Network Automation

Chapter 5

The goal of this chapter is to provide a clear view of SDN, its origin, and its possible future. This chapter starts by taking a step backwards and looks at SDN in a historic perspective by visiting the history of network programmability and identifies how it helped pave the way and shape SDN. This historic journey will provide a general context of SDN and put SDN into perspective. Then the authors show the current view of SDN as defined by standard development organizations (SDOs), provide a sense of SDN's malleability, explore SDN interactions with different networking architectures, and finally, provide a vision of a possible SDN future.

Chapter 6

Network functions virtualization (NFV) is consolidating as one of the base technologies for the design, deployment, and operation of network services. NFV can be seen as a natural evolution of the trend to cloud technologies in IT, and hence perceived as bringing them to the network provider environments. While this can be true for the simplest cases, focused on the IT services network providers rely on, the nature of network services raises unique requirements on the overall virtualization process. NFV aims to provide at the same time an opportunity to network providers, not only in reducing operational costs but also in bringing the promise of easing the development and activation of new services, thereby reducing their time-to-market and opening new approaches for service provisioning and operation, in general. In this chapter, the authors analyse these requirements and opportunities, reviewing the state of the art in this new way of dealing with network services. Also, the chapter presents some NFV deployments endorsed by some network operators and identifies some remaining challenges.

Samier Said Barguil, Universidad Autonoma de Madrid, Spain
Oscar Gonzalez de Dios, Telefonica I+D, Spain
Victor Lopez, Telefonica I+D, Spain
Kellow Pardini, Vivo (Telefonica Brasil), Brazil
Ricard Vilalta, Centre Tecnològic de Telecomunicacions de Catalunya (CTTC/CERCA),
    Spain

Internet service providers are shifting to an open, modern, software-based architecture that enables both new operating and business models. The target architecture is loosely coupled, cloud-native, data and artificial intelligence-driven, and relies on traffic engineering-related protocols to get the full potential of the network capabilities. The components need to use standard interfaces to be easily procured and deployed without the need for customization. Achieving these goals will require a significant change in how the network resources are architected, built, procured, licensed, and maintained. Some levers to drive this transformation rely on adopting open protocols such as NETCONF/RESTCONF or gNMI to operate the network and use standard data models to interact with the network more programmatically. This chapter presents such architecture, including service provider experiences.

Eric Debeau, Orange S.A., France
Veronica Quintuna-Rodriguez, Orange S.A., France

The ever-increasing complexity of networks and services advocates for the introduction of automation techniques to facilitate the design, the delivery, and the operation of such networks and services. The emergence of both network function virtualization (NFV) and software-defined networks (SDN) enable network flexibility and adaptability which open the door to on-demand services requiring automation. In aim of holding the increasing number of customized services and the evolved capabilities of public networks, the open network automation platform (ONAP), which is in open source, particularly addresses automation techniques while enabling dynamic orchestration, optimal resource allocation capabilities, and end-to-end service lifecycle management. This chapter addresses the key ONAP features that can be used by industrials and operators to automatically manage and orchestrate a wide set of services ranging from elementary network functions (e.g., firewalls) to more complex services (e.g., 5G network slices).

Zhaohui Huang, King's College London, UK
Vasilis Friderikos, King's College London, UK
Mischa Dohler, King's College London, UK
Hamid Aghvami, King's College London, UK

The dawn of the 5G commercialization era brings the proliferation of advanced capabilities within the triptych of radio access network, end user devices, and edge cloud computing which hopefully propel the introduction of novel, complex multimodal services such as those that enlarge the physical world around us like mobile augmented reality. Managing such advanced services in a granular manner through the emerging architectures of microservices within a network functions virtualization (NFV) framework allows for several benefits but also raises some challenges. The aim of this chapter is to shed light into the architectural aspects of the above-envisioned virtualized mobile network ecosystem. More specifically, and as an example of advanced services, the authors discuss how augmented reality applications can be decomposed into several service components that can be located either at the end-user terminal or at the edge cloud.

Chapter 10

Jorge Proença, CISUC, DEI, University of Coimbra, Portugal
Tiago Cruz, CISUC, DEI, University of Coimbra, Portugal
Paulo Simões, CISUC, DEI, University of Coimbra, Portugal
Edmundo Monteiro, CISUC, DEI, University of Coimbra, Portugal

A diversity of technical advances in the field of network and systems virtualization have made it possible to consolidate and manage resources in an unprecedented scale. These advances have started to come out of the data centers, spreading towards the network service provider (NSP) and telecommunications operator infrastructure foundations, from the core to the edge networks, the access network, and the customer premises LAN (local area network). In this context, the residential gateway (RGW) constitutes an ideal candidate for virtualization, as it stands between the home LAN and the access network, imposing a considerable cost for the NSP while constituting a single point of failure for all the services offered to residential customers. This chapter presents the rationale for the virtual RGW (vRGW) concept, providing an overview of past and current implementation proposals and discussing how recent technological developments in key areas such as networking and virtualization have given a competitive edge to a RGW virtualization scenario, when compared with traditional deployments.

Chapter 11

Rinki Sharma, Ramaiah University of Applied Sciences, Bangalore, India

Vehicular communication is going to play a significant role in the future intelligent transportation systems (ITS). Due to the highly dynamic nature of vehicular networks (VNs) and need for efficient real-time communication, the traditional networking paradigm is not suitable for VNs. Incorporating the SDN technology in VNs provides benefits in network programmability, heterogeneity, connectivity, resource utility, safety and security, routing, and traffic management. However, there are still several challenges and open research issues due to network dynamicity, scalability, heterogeneity, interference, latency, and security that need to be addressed. This chapter presents the importance of vehicular communication in future ITS, the significance of incorporating the SDN paradigm in VNs, taxonomy for the role of SDVN, the software-defined vehicular network (SDVN) architecture, and open research issues in SDVN.

Section 3
Towards "Attack-Proof" Network Security Frameworks

Chapter 12

Mohamed Boucadair, Orange S.A., France
Christian Jacquenet, Orange S.A., France

Security has always been a major concern of network operators. Despite a pretty rich security toolbox that never ceased to improve over the years (filters, traffic wells, encryption techniques, and intrusion detection systems to name a few), attacks keep on increasing from both a numerical and amplitude standpoints. Such protean attacks demand an adapted security toolkit that should include techniques capable of not only detecting these attacks but also anticipating them even before they reach their target. Strengthening future networking infrastructures so that they become protective, instead of being "just" protected must thus become one of the key strategic objectives of network operators and service providers who ambition to rely upon robust, dynamic, security policy enforcement schemes to develop their business while retaining their existing customers. This chapter discusses the various security challenges that may be further exacerbated by future networking infrastructures. It also presents some of the techniques that are very likely to become cornerstones of protective networking.

Chapter 13

Marc Lacoste, Orange S.A., France
David Armand, Orange S.A., France
Fanny Parzysz, Orange S.A., France
Loïc Ferreira, Orange S.A., France
Ghada Arfaoui, Orange S.A., France
Yvan Rafflé, Orange S.A., France
Yvon Gourhant, Orange S.A., France
Nicolas Bihannic, Orange S.A., France
Sébastien Roché, Orange S.A., France

This chapter explores the security challenges of the drone ecosystem. Drones raise significant security and safety concerns, both design-time and run-time (e.g., supply-chain, technical design, standardization). Two broad classes of threats are considered, on drones and using drones (e.g., to attack critical infrastructures or vehicles). They involve both professional and non-professional drones and lead to various types of attacks (e.g., IoT-type vulnerabilities, GPS spoofing, spying, kinetic attacks). Trade-offs involving hardware and software solutions to meet efficiency, resource limitations, and real-time constraints are notably hard to find. So far, protection solutions remain elementary compared to the impact of attacks. Advances in technologies, new use cases (e.g., enhancing network connectivity), and a regulatory framework to overcome existing barriers are decisive factors for sustainable drone security market growth.

Chapter 14

Hamid Asgari, Thales UK Research, Technology, and Innovation, UK

Methodologically-sound security assessments are crucial for understanding a system in fulfilling the requirements, realizing its behavior, and identifying implications. A system is made resilient if and only if there is enduring confidence that it will function as expected. It is cyber secure if it displays this property in the face of an adversary. This chapter provides an explanation of various static security risk assessment methodologies (SSRAM) having long epochs for assessing and revisiting the risks and explains their strengths and weaknesses. The SSRAM will form the basis for elaborating on dynamic security risk assessment methodologies that must have very short epochs depending on the emergent threats and vulnerabilities to combat new or evolving threats. This is essential for handling cyber security of dynamic complex systems including future networks having a number of self-managing properties including self-protection for defending against malicious attacks.

Preface

A POSSIBLE HISTORY OF THE FUTURE

The red light kept on blinking. It was too late. The Russians? Moscow was hit first. Beijing came next. The Yankees, then? After all, the failed assault on the Capitol a couple of decades ago should have been taken as a serious warning. The new President-elect always entertained her reputation of a hell raiser, and social networks of all kinds were flooded by her daily anger, followed by millions of haters. The Internet had gone truly global since 2035: anyone and anything was globally reachable.

Although SpaceX failed to secure trips to Mars because of a malicious malware that jeopardized the operation of their recyclable space shuttles, they did manage to bring NASA staff to the Moon in 2027. And they also launched so many satellite constellations that night on Earth had become a nice souvenir: circumnavigation at 500 km high inevitably affected sleep cycles. But everyone was connected: wasn't it the ultimate objective? 13 billion people, several hundred times more of connected objects eventually made the Internet the only communication network that was left.

Data lakes bloomed in all continents, starting with the old, pioneering Gaia-X European project three decades ago, immediately followed by countless American, Chinese, Indian, and Brazilian initiatives that transformed the digital world into a vast data space. Spreading over all continents (Antarctica included for its obvious cooling capacities), telco cloud infrastructures were operated by the so-called GAFAM at the expense of incumbent operators that soon became history.

"Tomorrow never dies" as a well-known British spy would have put back in the 20th century: the truth was no longer the truth. The truth is that fake news ruled the world, but very few were concerned about it. Because everybody was connected and that was all that mattered for most.

Teleworking, when compatible with the actual work to accomplish, had become the rule since the World Health Organization failed to convince governments to eliminate the Covid-19 virus and its innumerable variants. Tele-education was also the rule, at least for those who could afford the price for accessing reliable teaching and support material with decent network access conditions.

For most of the population, social networks had indeed become the only source of information and education with enough bandwidth to post their 200-character questions wherever they may connect to the Internet. And these networks kept control over what their users were entitled to share or not. Of course, books had become history too (and were considered the new gold for smugglers at the risk of being part of the burnings if ever they were caught by the henchmen from the Ministry of Information). The global library had gone virtual.

But Washington DC went down too. Erased from the surface of the Earth in the blink of an eye.

So, who takes the blame?

Despite all the efforts made to achieve digital inclusion at a global scale while developing energy-aware networking techniques for the benefit of the planet (and mankind for that matter), the small population of the Vanuatu islands became desperate. Yes, they were connected. Yes, they used solar cells to supply the energy required to communicate with the global Village. But they couldn't prevent the waters to rise. They became the very first climatic refugees of the Anthropocene age. They had lost their homes and were forced to embark on an erratic journey, destination nowhere.

And this really pissed them off.

With all the online tutorials available (from "how to cook a banana pie?" to "how to dismantle an atomic bomb?") and the tech expertise they had acquired over decades of social networking, they managed to create a lethal variant of the Mirai virus that first infected the aforementioned satellite constellations.

The descendants of the survivors of Monsieur de la Pérouse's "Astrolabe" shipwreck then made sure the malware propagated at the speed of light so that all the shiny boxes that stupidly circled the globe for the sake of global, reportedly safe communication, were used as amplifiers of solar winds that literally torched the Earth.

Science fiction? Maybe. Maybe not.

A SHORT STORY OF THE FUTURE: NEW DESIGNS FOR THE FUTURE INTERNET

The Internet as we know it is the privileged infrastructure for global communications. It never ceased to evolve from the very first mail that was exchanged between a couple of terminals back in the seventies of the last century to the current blooming of a set of techniques that are meant to achieve various goals, including a few that somewhat echo the societal and environmental stakes that have been elaborated by the United Nations. Such goals include (but are not limited to):

- Access to content with a decent level of quality regardless of where the end-user connects to the network by means of environmentally adaptive connectivity schemes.
- Make sure the network is instrumental in the struggle against climate change by means of energy-efficient designs that include devices, networks, and data centers.
- Facilitate the production and the allocation of whatever resource (network, CPU, storage) involved in the provisioning of the aforementioned connectivity services by means of network automation techniques.
- Protect communications, end-user premises and individuals from any kind of attack and make the Internet a safer place by means of proper risk assessment and advanced attack mitigation schemes.

THE NETWORK IS INSTRUMENTAL TO FOSTER DIGITAL INCLUSION

The Covid-19 pandemic dramatically affects our everyday life. Confinement and curfews measures question working procedures and access to education and culture. The pandemic also reveals that not everybody accesses the Internet equally, i.e., those who live in rural, possibly deserted areas are having hard times to go online because of poor coverage conditions, whereas others enjoy several hundred Mbit/s access rates thanks to their fiber connection.

Of course, the closer the content, the better the experience. Local and customized content would be even better. Nevertheless, it is not available everywhere. Centralization remains a concern of the current Internet design. Indeed, a few platforms exploit data (including privacy data) that they do not share and they prevent others from accessing such data. One iconic example is the recent evolution of a popular app's General Conditions of Use that literally allow a popular company that owns a big social network to exploit that app users' data for whatever purpose (target advertisement, customer profiling, etc.). Such centralization must be questioned for the benefit of end-users. And it stimulates the need for more distributed platforms, thereby revisiting the current Internet architecture.

The pandemic also reveals the critical importance of network designs that can accommodate the most constraining delay and latency requirements. The massive use of videoconferencing, sometimes deployed at large scale to compensate restrictions that forbid the physical attendance of students in amphitheaters for example, is one iconic example of the extreme solicitation of network resources. Access to video footage or live streaming thus questions current Content Delivery Network (CDN) designs, as cache servers currently hosted in Points of Presence may prove to be inefficient in accommodating an ever-growing demand raised by end-users whose network access conditions can be extremely different one from another.

Likewise, the development of immersive services based upon virtual and augmented reality techniques for various usages (e.g., industrial 3D modeling, immersive experiences in various yet virtual environments) are likely to solicit the network and companion resources like computational and storage resources, at the cost of revisiting access to content, especially when the end-user is in motion.

In addition, the foreseeable yet massive development of the Internet of Things (IoT) raises new network challenges. Not only the dimensioning figures have no equivalent in today's IP networks as several of thousands objects may be networked, the very nature of the constraints that pertain to some of these network objects question current network designs: CPU and energy limitations now become critical in the route computation process, especially when the connected objects are used to collect biometric data, such as the blood pressure or heartbeat.

The IP forwarding scheme that has been enforced for the past three decades (and counting) proved its long time efficiency that can be summarized by the following observation: anything can be carried in IP packets and IP packets can be carried over anything. The evolution of the TCP/IP protocol suite has led to a pretty rich toolkit that includes (but is far from being limited to) traffic encryption capabilities, advanced traffic engineering techniques including schemes based upon the manipulation of information that is additional to the destination address carried in the IP packet header, resource signaling and reservation capabilities, etc.

A strength of the TCP/IP model is that there's always room for improvement as new demands, constraints, or requirements appear, which therefore stimulates innovation. Some communities questioned the validity of the model over the years and came up with a new protocol that would replace IP at the risk of ignoring 30 years of Internet evolution (and counting). Others rather focus on advanced capabilities where IP could still play a key role for forwarding different kinds of traffic, but would also be distorted to carry specific traffic that is poorly tolerant to delay, inter-packet delay variation, latency, let alone packet loss.

Questioning the future of IP is only natural and must remain a primary incentive for network innovation. Challenging IP is also part of the aforementioned innovation which may take its share in reshaping the Internet.

FUTURE CONNECTIVITY SERVICES SHOULD BE ENERGY-EFFICIENT, ENVIRONMENTALLY FRIENDLY, AND USER-CENTRIC

Energy-efficient techniques are a key challenge for network operators. Besides sourcing policies that usually take care of power supply and energy consumption considerations, additional techniques are required to automatically control the energy consumption during the lifetime of a network: this is what we call "energy-aware networking". Energy-efficient networking thus became a pillar of some of network operators' strategies. Besides marketing motivations, "Greener" designs are endorsed. Such designs rely upon the combination of energy-efficient networking and components that embark only the functions that are strictly required. Even if important progress was accomplished to support tools to better control the energy efficiency of some network elements, more effort is required to socialize these tools to users so that they can enable them (e.g., control WLAN activation, support of the "energy economy" mode).

From frugal innovation concepts that usually target the market of developing countries to the use of energy information as a means to compute energy-efficient routes, the panel of techniques that contribute to the development of energy-efficient network designs is broad. Duty cycle management that used to apply to the radio components of sensors could for example expand to Wide Area Network (WAN) resources, where traffic patterns and peak hours would better dictate how traffic should be forwarded overnight, and whether putting some network components (nodes, line cards) into an idle state progressively becomes a common practice.

Energy-aware designs also aim at reducing the carbon footprint as well as the pollution generated by fossil energy, among other sources.

One networking example where pollution greatly matters is the Intelligent Transport Service (ITS) that relies upon so-called autonomous vehicles, and which is meant to better master car traffic and its dreadful consequences in terms of air pollution, among others. It is thus envisioned by some vendors that chained, driver-less, vehicles that ride in specific lanes will improve the efficiency of car transportation while limiting car accidents, thereby improving passenger's safety. However, more effort is still required to reach such objectives as some studies revealed that autonomous cars may increase pollution.

From a networking perspective, ITS services raise very stringent constraints that include the need to detect and anticipate the presence of obstacles on the road, the need to dynamically manage traffic lights to ensure the best possible traffic fluidity, the need for inter-vehicle communication for various purposes – access to the Internet, management of car breakdown, speed mastering as a function of the traffic, etc.

Of course, the dynamic management of ITS service resources can take advantage of network automation techniques.

SET THE CONTROLS FOR THE HEART OF THE AUTOMATED NETWORK

The expansion of the service portfolios proposed by network operators and service providers is further exacerbated by the deployment of new infrastructures, such as 5G networks. Even better (or worse, for that matter), 5G infrastructure deployments and forthcoming telco-cloud architectures have just started but the community already investigates what more could be brought by the next generations of networks. Also, communication services become more sophisticated as their composition relies upon a complex alchemy of functions that are meant to accommodate various requirements and constraints.

The configuration of such functions is complex and therefore prone to errors. In addition, the time it takes to complete execution tasks and assess their conformance against the target service further extends the time for a customer to access the service he/she has subscribed to.

The basic motivation for introducing network automation techniques in service design, delivery, and operational procedures is to shorten such production times, while significantly reducing the risk of making errors at every stage of the service production, from the exposure of service parameters to service-inferred resource allocation, fulfillment and assurance.

Network automation techniques have attracted the interest of the network operators' community for quite some time. The advent and the progressive mastering of Software-Defined Networking (SDN) techniques in the early 2010's was an important marker: SDN computation logics facilitate dynamic resource allocation and policy enforcement, regardless of the underlying networking infrastructure and its companion vendor technologies.

In addition, the past few years have been the opportunity to publish several standard data models from which the SDN computation logics have the ability to dynamically instantiate network functions and service-inferred policies in a technology-agnostic manner, thereby alleviating the risk of tedious vendor lock-ins.

In the meantime, virtualization techniques that have been applied to flexibly manage resources in data centers can now apply to a whole set of "core" network functions, such as the functions that pertain to the core of a 4G or a 5G network. Open source communities bloomed too, to facilitate access to running codes and let network operators hope that the physical gear they have been deploying for the past three decades in their networks would eventually become history. And be replaced by commodity hardware that would only be responsible to switch packets at (almost) the speed of light, while open source software would become the privileged placeholder for developing advanced capabilities in a Continuous Integration/Continuous Deployment (CI/CD) fashion.

With this concept of disaggregation where networking software is broken down into functions whose placement can be optimized, network operators enter a world of virtualized capabilities whose 5G deployment is likely to be one of its most iconic representatives. Virtual Customer Premises Equipment (vCPE) are among the Virtual Network Functions (VNFs) that claim to hold the promises of flexibility and adaptability that have long been cherished by service providers who are not only concerned with the optimization of the Operational Expenditure (OpEx) budgets, but also with their ability to exactly address the requirements of their customers while optimizing network resource usage, their global footprint, and the number of calls discontent customers may place to their hotline support.

With a slice of (service) orchestration on top of network automation frameworks and the progressive mastering of Artificial Intelligence techniques, the service delivery journey should be able to alleviate the risk of bumps in the road that may compromise the quality of the service. From the dynamic service parameter exposure and negotiation to service fulfillment and compliance, network automation becomes global and systemic.

Orchestration plays a key role in such an idyllic environment, as outcomes of the aforementioned negotiation would feed the orchestration's computation logic so that it can dynamically structure the service requested by the customer, identify the elementary functions that will compose such service, and then forward instructions to the SDN computation logic so that it can reliably locate the most relevant instances of such functions and proceed with resource allocation and configuration.

The Open Network Automation Platform (ONAP) project hosted by the Linux Foundation is one emblematic example of an open, programmable, orchestration platform that is conceived to process service orders and instructs an embedded SDN computation logic to deliver the service that has been requested. Partners of the ONAP project are numerous and includes several, yet major incumbent operators and legacy vendors from around the world.

Regretfully enough, the network automation journey has only started. It is still a long way before holding the promises of network automation, as current experience still confirms the need for a set of declarative configuration tasks, while feedback mechanisms and control loops to be activated at every stage of the service delivery procedure remain areas that have been hardly investigated so far, let alone commercially implemented.

A SAFER INTERNET?

Quite inevitably, the pandemic also highlights the weaknesses of current network designs. Besides poor network connectivity conditions in some areas as previously mentioned, the attack surface due to tele-working procedures has dramatically increased. Indeed, tunnels are established between the CPE and the enterprise's intranet and tunnels are quite well-known as privileged attack vectors.

Generally speaking, attacks of all sorts (denial of service, identity spoofing, ransomware, malware) have never ceased to expand over the years. Their number expanded, but also did their amplitude (number of victims, up to several of Tbit/s of traffic), scope (up to the scale of the global Internet) and duration (up to several weeks). Security has always been a major concern of network operators and service providers. Despite a pretty efficient toolkit (traffic filters, traffic encryption, robust authentication schemes, etc.), security policies have always been enforced in a reactive mode: the detection of an attack triggers specific mitigation actions, but experience shows that they can never prevent some damage.

In other words, the question is: how to move from three decades of protected infrastructures to a future where the network becomes truly protective if not collaborative with other partnering peers? The basic motivation for this radical change in conceiving security policies is (1) to anticipate attacks (regardless of their nature) way before they cause damage and (2) to mitigate attacks as close to their source as possible.

Some progress has been recently achieved in this direction, with the publication of a couple of standards that detail how the detection of a potentially suspect traffic by an agent that would be hosted in the network can lead to the signaling of a request that would be sent to a mitigation server whose computation logic would then proceed with the definition of a mitigation plan. This mitigation plan would then be enforced by all the relevant components to redirect and discard the attack traffic for example. Even better, such a mitigation plan could be forwarded to partnering networks so that they can anticipate the attack before it reaches them.

A slice of artificial intelligence would also assist the aforementioned agents in the attack traffic detection process, by means of predictive traffic analysis techniques that would help them compare what they observe with a set of traffic patterns the agents would maintain in a local library.

This protective networking framework can be applied to any kind of infrastructure. Networking unmanned aerial vehicles (UAV) is no exception, and albeit such drone networking raises specific security issues, protective networking can provide guarantees to preserve service continuity where UAVs would be used to redirect traffic to and from the Internet whenever the CPE connection to the network is lost, for example.

Also, assessing the security risk is an important task when considering the deployment of new networks, new features or new services. Such assessment may look, but it is important to develop and enforce rigorous security risk assessment methodologies for improving the efficiency of security policies, hence network robustness.

Of course, the bloody virus is not the only incentive for reconsidering how networks are designed, deployed and operated. But experience shows that major crises are the opportunity to shed a different light on issues that may have been investigated for quite some time and others that may have been overlooked until now (e.g., network connectivity with an adequate level of quality).

WHAT THIS BOOK IS ABOUT

This book explores some of the techniques that have been highlighted earlier in this foreword. The book is organized into three main areas:

- **Section 1: New Network Designs** for improved content delivery, better environmental and energy consumption footprint, and advanced packet forwarding techniques. This part includes the following chapters:
  - New IP: Enabling the Next Wave of Networking Innovation
  - Collaborative Networking Towards Application-Aware Networking
  - Content Delivery Networks: On the Path Towards Secure Cloud-Native Platforms at the Edge
  - Green by Design
- **Section 2: Latest Developments in Network Automation**, including orchestration, virtualization and SDN. This part includes these chapters:
  - Future SDN-Based Network Architectures
  - Network Functions Virtualization (NFV): Challenges and Deployment Update
  - Automation of Network Services for the Future Internet
  - ONAP: An Open Source Toolkit for Zero Touch Automation
  - Granular VNF-Based Microservices: Advanced Service Decomposition and the Role of Machine Learning Techniques
  - Revisiting the Concept of Virtualized Residential Gateways
  - Software-Defined Vehicular Networks (SDVN) for Intelligent Transportation Systems (ITS)
- **Section 3: Towards "Attack-Proof" Network Security Frameworks**. This part includes the following chapters:
  - From Protected Networks to Protective and Collaborative Networking: An Approach to a Globally Anticipative Attack Mitigation Framework for the Future Internet
  - Drone Security: Threats and Challenges
  - Security Risk Assessments and Shortfalls for Evaluating and Protecting Dynamic Autonomic Systems in Future Internet

The techniques presented in this book may not limit the slide of social networks into hatred. They may not be able to refrain mankind from launching satellite constellations. They may not prevent rising waters, let alone solar winds.

But the techniques presented in this book are likely to be instrumental for the development of a truly global, energy-efficient, and safer Internet.

This is why we believe that the future of networking has never been so bright.
Enjoy the ride.

Acknowledgment

Many thanks to the following reviewers for their thoughtful insights and constructive comments:

- Adam Wiethuechter
- Akbar Rahman
- Alex Galis
- Amelia Andersdotter
- Amina Boubendir
- Anoop Ghanwani
- Artur Hecker
- Brian Carpenter
- Bruno Chatras
- Daniel Migault
- Dirk Hugo
- Italo Busi
- Jon Shallow
- Markus Amend
- Meiling Chen
- Michael Boc
- Morgan Richomme
- Nabil Benamar
- Nagendra Kumar Nainar
- Nathalie Labidurie

Acknowledgment

- Ning Wang

- Pedro Aranda

- Prosper Chemouil

- Qin Wu

- Robert Moskowitz

- Roque Gagliano

- Shuai Zhao

- Stefano Secci

- Stuart Card

- Theresa Enghardt

- Valery Smyslov

- Wei Pan

- Nour El Houda Yellas

Thanks also to the following individuals for their availability:

- Alexandre Petrescu

- Luis Miguel Contreras Murillo

- Mohamed Faten Zhani

Section 1
New Network Designs

Chapter 1
New IP:
Enabling the Next Wave of Networking Innovation

Richard Li
Futurewei Technologies, Inc., USA

Uma S. Chunduri
Futurewei Technologies, Inc., USA

Alexander Clemm
Futurewei Technologies, Inc., USA

Lijun Dong
Futurewei Technologies, Inc., USA

ABSTRACT

Industrial machine-type communications (e.g., industrial internet), emerging applications such as holographic type communications, IP mobile backhaul transport for 5G/B5G (beyond 5G) for ultra-reliable low latency communications and massive machine-type communications, emerging industry verticals such as driverless vehicles, and future networking use cases as called out by ITU-T's focus group on network 2030 all require new networking capabilities and services. This chapter introduces "New IP," a new data communication protocol that extends packet networking with new capabilities to support future applications that go beyond the capabilities that are provided by internetworking protocol (IP) today. New IP is designed to allow the user to specify requirements, such as expectations for key performance indicators' (KPIs) service levels, and other guidance for packet processing and forwarding purposes. New IP is designed to interoperate with existing networks in a straightforward manner and thus to facilitate its incremental deployment that leverages existing investment.

DOI: 10.4018/978-1-7998-7646-5.ch001

INTRODUCTION

Current Internet technologies, with the Internet Protocol (IP) as its bedrock, have been a tremendous success. Originally devised as a way to interconnect computers over long distances in a highly resilient, decentralized manner that would be able to withstand outages of links and nodes, IP has evolved in a breathtaking fashion ever since. Today, the Internet interconnects not just a handful of computers but billions of devices (including "Things") with an exorbitant volume of traffic growing at a breakneck pace. In addition, the Internet is able to support services that did not exist at the time of its conception – such as the World Wide Web or Social Media – and that would have been deemed impossible to support at the time – such as "real time" services like voice and interactive video. Throughout its evolution, the Internet has also been a driving force enabling network convergence, allowing previously separate custom networks to be integrated into a single infrastructure providing significant economies of scale. This made networks much more economical to operate, further contributing to their increasing pervasiveness.

It is thus fair to say that the Internet has come a long way, morphing from a niche novelty into a societal backbone that supports an ever-expanding set of services. Internet technology centers on IP (Internet Protocol) and the TCP/IP protocol suite in the data plane, as well as related mechanisms such as Quality of Service (QoS). While Internet technology has seen many extensions, at the core of its success are still its original principles based on best-effort, hop-by-hop forwarding. These principles do not provide any hard guarantees about whether packets will arrive within a certain time, or even in their original order, or even arrive at all, but they offer simplicity in terms of their implementation and resilience to perturbations experienced in the network. This does not mean that there have not been plenty of advances. Switching technologies like MPLS provide enforcement of homogenous traffic forwarding policies for each and every packet of a given flow. Traffic Engineering (TE) techniques like MPLS-TE with Path Computation Element (PCE) provide some guarantees about the compliance of a path with traffic requirements and fast-reroute capabilities at the network layer. However, none of these technologies is able to provide actual end-to-end latency gurantees or in general more Service Level Agreement (SLA) aware connectivity. In general it is left up to other layers to deal with any fallout of, for example, lost packets.

However, the question is whether the same principles will be applied forever, able to support any and all technical requirements of an ever-growing array of services and converging even more networks until all networking infrastructure can be consolidated, or whether foundational barriers will eventually be encountered that will prove hard if not impossible to overcome. As laid out later in this chapter, in recent years, a number of new requirements and networking use cases have begun to appear which cannot be readily supported by today's Internet technologies. This is because they exhibit properties that cannot be remedied by simply layering new capabilities on top, even assuming that the issue of Internet ossification can be overcome. Note that Internet ossification refers to the increasing inability to add new services, capabilities, and functions to the existing Internet, due to a variety of factors from adversarial impact of middleboxes to standardization hurdles. The fact that many of these use cases open up the possibility for a whole new wave of innovation for networked applications and connected industries adds to the pressure for answers to the question of how the required capabilities might be supported in the future.

Many of the new networking use cases involve applications that require a very high degree of precision in sending data from one place to another, for example, with regards to end-to-end service-level guarantees such as end-to-end latency or reliability with low packet loss ratio. These requirements are compounded by that many of those applications are mission-critical and are highly sensitive to any violations of required service guarantee. Existing Internet applications might experience a gradual deterioration of the Quality of Experience (QoE) when underlying network service levels are degraded. For example, audio quality may degrade, or Web page load times become more sluggish, but the application as a whole may fundamentally still be usable. In contrast, many future applications may break down completely even when slight degradation occurs. For example, the ability to safely operate remote machinery may be lost completely when network latency or loss cause an operator to lose their sense of haptic control due to timing requirements of control loops being exceeded.

It should be noted that "precision" with regards to latency is not to the same as latency that is simply "ultra-low", and the two should not be confused. Precision latency simply means that a given quantified latency target (not necessarily ultra-low) will be met, as it is required for an application of a networking service to function. Clearly, a network will not be able to deliver on arbitrary latency targets. Targets for ultra-low latency in particular will be challenging as physical limitations apply; in such cases realities will dictate that some guarantees simply cannot be given and some use cases cannot be supported when they necessitate communication that extends beyond certain distances.

These characteristics (e.g., need for high precision and low latency) coupled with low tolerance for any degradations are not a good match for the best-effort Internet principles. Given very tight bounds for tolerance, traditional techniques to compensate at upper layers for any deficiencies, such as retransmission (to compensate for loss) or buffering (to smoothen variations in experienced service levels) may no longer be sufficient. In addition, challenges abound with regards to security and how to maintain privacy in an increasingly interconnected world. New answers are likely to be needed and are worth the investigation.

One possible answer for this is "New IP" (Li et al., 2020), a networking technology that is designed to address those issues. To be clear, New IP is not intended as a complete replacement for existing Internet Technology. Instead, it is designed (1) to progressively connect more networks and systems that require support for new services (many of which may not be connected to the Internet today) and (2) to be easily interoperable with the legacy networks to leverage the investments that have been made. This way, it will allow for incremental addition of new services and applications where they need to be supported and gradual migration over time.

This chapter will take a look at the proposed "New IP" and how we got here. To this end, we will start with an overview of some of the applications and use cases which are emerging. We will describe their associated network requirements which need to be addressed to make them a reality and unleash a whole new wave of innovation. Subsequently, the particular technical issues that need to be addressed and foundational hurdles that need to be overcome with existing technology are analyzed. With this background, we will present the fundamentals of New IP. We will also describe how New IP addresses some of the requirements and use cases that are of interest to the Industry. This is followed by a discussion of how New IP can be incrementally deployed. A brief discussion of related work as well as an outlook for future work will conclude the chapter.

Use Cases and Requirements

In order to better understand the requirements that Internet Technology will be increasingly confronted with, let us take a look at some of the networking applications and use cases that are emerging and that will need to be supported in the future. Many of those use cases are running into limitations in network technology. This creates bottlenecks for innovation that is waiting to happen but that can only be fully unleashed once the bottlenecks are removed.

As we will show, many of these bottlenecks relate to the ability to deliver network service levels with very high precision and extremely high reliability as required for mission-critical services. In addition, other more traditional requirements still apply. These include aspects such as support for higher bandwidth and low latency, advances in operational efficiency in order to increase profitability, greater security while at the same time ensuring privacy, as well as agility to rapidly adapt networks and networking services to new requirements and deployment needs while continuing to support existing services without any negative impact or disruption.

Several industry consortia and standards bodies have been considering emerging networking applications, including the IETF, the ITU-T Focus Group on Network 2030, the 5G Alliance for Connected Industries and Automation, the 5G Automotive Association, and the 3GPP. The following will present sample use cases and applications deemed particularly representative and illustrative of the challenges being posed. Many additional examples can be found in documents produced by those respective organizations, e.g., in ITU-T FG-NET2030 (2020), 5GACIA (2020), 5GAA (2017), and 3GPP (2018).

Industrial Control and Automation

Industry 4.0 refers to the next step in control and automation of traditional manufacturing and industrial practices using smart technology. Much has been made of the emergence of Industry 4.0 as the next step in the industrial revolution. In many cases, this involves machine-to-machine communications in which the control logic is separated from the industrial machinery (including robots) that it controls. This allows holistic control and coordination of sets of machines that need to be operated together instead of independent of each other, in many cases involving precisely synchronized and choreographed work sequences. By placing the control logic into separate integrated controllers, coordinating those work sequences become much easier and less error-prone than if each machine were integrated with its own local controller. Controllers might be hosted in a single location on a factory floor or might even be hosted remotely in the central/edge cloud.

A prerequisite for this use case to work is a network that is able to deliver packets within very precise latency bounds and with extremely high reliability. Packets that arrive late can have a detrimental effect and cause machinery to spin out of control. As an illustrative example one can picture a gyroscopic controller like those that might be found in a Segway scooter, adjusting the balance in a tight control loop using data from sensors that detect velocity and tilt. Any sluggishness or uneven delay in sensor readings would rapidly put the equipment off-balance, putting a rider at risk. Due to the real-time nature of gyroscopic control, controllers and sensors today are collocated and no one would dream of separating them and having them communicate over a network, as latency and delay variations would yield such a solution ineffective. However, similar requirements apply to controllers of robotic arms, where positioning and control of actuators occurs using control loops that feedback locational awareness from robotic arm sensors, involving latency in the range of a few milliseconds or even sub- milliseconds.

As another example, consider the need for safety precautions on a factory floor where equipment may need to be shut off rapidly using circuit breakers in case of an emergency (5GACIA, 2020). For this purpose, heavy and dangerous machinery (e.g., rotating saws, laser beams, welding equipment) can be placed in a perimeter that is protected by a light curtain. A light curtain consists of a transmitter and a receiver. The transmitter emits multiple parallel light beams towards the receiver. If one of the beams is interrupted by an object, for example a hand that is getting too close, the light curtain generates a signal. The chosen distance between light beams is determined by the smallest object requiring detection (e.g., a human finger). Typically, a light curtain system will periodically poll safety equipment in order to elicit a response within a specified time or subscribe to a continuous stream of sensor data to confirm the safety equipment is operational. The required response time for a light curtain is generally based on the specific industrial use case, e.g., the proximity of the nearest worker to a potential danger, the walking speed of the worker, and the total reaction time (sensors plus controller plus time required to halt the machine) that is needed to place the machine in a safe state. Certain safety functions may require a very short response time, sometimes as short as 1 ms, which places a corresponding upper bound on the maximum acceptable network latency for a remote controller (and thus its location).

If the response is delayed or not received within this interval, the machine is placed in a safe state, i.e., stopped, brakes activated, power cut off, etc. In order to restart operations, manual intervention may be required, such as acknowledging and canceling a safety message on the operator panel. The cost for such interruptions increases drastically when not just a single machine, but interlinked machines are impacted.

The assembly of automobile parts is another example in which the joining of chassis and car body, requires precise communication between the conveyor carrying the chassis and the conveyor carrying the body to move them both in synchronous manner to allow them to be bolted together. Printed circuit board assembly lines typically operate entirely autonomously, but can be remotely controlled to implement product changes in real-time or to capture in-process data. Again, communication is required between the multiple controllers for the various components/devices on the assembly line and the central control unit. Similarly, chemical manufacturing involves tightly controlled processes involving continuous adjustments based on data reported from multitudes of sensors measuring flow rates, temperature, and pressure occurring at pumps, valves, stirrers, and other components. Some applications also involve video feeds that must be continuously monitored, resulting in high demands also in terms of required bandwidth.

There are several common themes to all these industrial applications. If they are to be controlled from remote controllers, the interconnecting network must provide connectivity services with very tight latency guarantees. This includes very low end-to-end latency, generally in the order of very few milliseconds. As a side note, this of course rules out control over very long geographic distances due to the limited propagation speed of light. However, remote control across an area that is significantly larger than a factory floor is still possible, for example across an urban area with control logic placed near the edge. Likewise, latency variations must be tightly controlled. In many cases, packets must be evenly spaced due to additional synchronization requirements. Generally, it is not sufficient for communication services to merely optimize end-to-end latency and have applications accept whatever outcome can be delivered. Instead, precisely quantified bounds must be guaranteed that satisfy the requirements as determined by the nature of the application.

It goes without saying that networks must also be very reliable and avoid packet loss. Due to tight timing requirements, having the sender retransmit packets after they are determined as lost by the receiver is simply not an option. Likewise, very high data rates must be supported due to the myriads of sensor readings occurring at very high velocity.

Perhaps it is worth mentioning that there is, however, one aspect in which industrial applications can be arguably a bit more benevolent than other applications. This concerns that data traffic and traffic matrix in many such applications and their deployments tend to be fairly stable over time: the same data rates between the same sources and sinks need to be continuously supported, with the same service level objectives, across deployments that are "reasonably" stable. In other words, traffic tends to be more predictable and less bursty compared with other scenarios.

All of the above requirements make industrial applications quite distinct from other scenarios. Accordingly, we refer to the technology that is able to operate in those settings as "Operational Technology" (OT), as opposed to "IT" (Information Technology). Due to its unique and extremely stringent requirements, OT is today largely based on networking technology that is separate from IP and that is in many cases limited to very small physical distances, for example a factory floor (Industrial Internet Consortium, 2017). Those same requirements have until today been preventing network convergence based on IP as has happened with so many other network services.

Holographic-Type Communications

The use of holograms as a means for users to interact with computing systems has long captured people's imagination, as evidenced in movies such as "Star Wars" or "Minority Report". Holographic display technology has made significant advances in recent years. As a result, holographic applications are well on their way to becoming a reality. Many such applications will involve network aspects, specifically the ability to transmit and stream holographic data from remote locations across the network to render it on a local holographic or light field display.

Far from constituting mere gimmicks, useful examples of such applications abound. For example, Holographic Telepresence will be used to project remote participants as lifelike holograms to local meeting participants in a room. Conversely, immersive spaces may project holograms resembling artefacts from a distant location into a room to immerse the user into that space. Remote troubleshooting and repair applications will allow technicians to interact with holographic renderings of artefacts located in a remote location that would be difficult to reach otherwise, such as an oil-drilling platform. Training and education can provide users with the ability to dynamically interact from remote with ultra-realistic holographic objects for teaching purposes. Then there is immersive entertainment, gaming, sports, and much more.

It is easy to foresee that the majority of those applications will involve holographic-type communications (HTC), i.e., the ability to transmit and stream holographic data across networks. This raises the question what makes holograms unique and how they differ from other media types. What is it about holograms that would pose significant challenges to a network? An excellent analysis is provided in Clemm et al. (2020); some of its findings are summarized here.

One aspect that makes a hologram different from other types of images is the fact that it interacts with the viewer, changing what the eyes perceive depending on how and from where it is being looked at. A viewer's position may change along six degrees of freedom (6DoF): up/down, left/right, forward/backward, roll, pitch, and yaw. As the viewpoint changes, objects that appeared to be in the foreground and that perhaps even obstructed parts of other objects may move into the background, with other objects coming more prominently into the picture. In effect, a hologram thus contains multiple images at the same time. This is one intuitive reason why the amount of data to represent a hologram can be very large, depending on size and resolution. Accordingly, the transmission of an uncompressed human-size hologram may require hundreds of Gbit/s or even several Tbit/s (Xu et al., 2011). Compression and viewpoint prediction techniques are making significant advances and can reduce data volumes significantly (Schwarz et al, 2019). However, even when compressed, the data volumes involved are still significant and their transmission may incur significant latency that is unacceptable for highly interactive applications.

Hence, other schemes need to be devised that minimize the volume of data to be transmitted while maintaining acceptable image quality. This means focusing on the data that will likely have the highest effect on quality first, for example, transmitting image data that is in focus at the highest quality, while transmitting other portions of the image at lesser quality (e.g., reducing resolution, frame rate) or not at all (e.g., dropping certain tilts and angles). To allow for transmission at such differentiated qualities, images are often partitioned into three-dimensional (3D) tiles, building on the concept of two-dimensional tiles that are used for analogous reasons in virtual reality applications. Alternatively, a point cloud could be partitioned in a set of objects, each represented by a separate smaller point cloud. Depending on viewpoint, some aspects of the image or objects in the point cloud might be obscured in their entirety or be outside the field of view and may not have to be transmitted at all, a fact that is exploited by smart solutions.

3D tiles and point cloud objects can be streamed independently of one another, each with its own custom quality parameter settings. These settings may vary in aspects such as color depth, resolution, and frame rate, with the highest settings applied to the objects or tiles at the center of focus. On the receiver, the original image is assembled from these different components arriving over different streams. These streams must be synchronized in order to avoid additional delay for buffering while waiting for components of image data to arrive.

Table 1 summarizes the parameters that might vary for different types of media, adding more dimensions as media becomes more advanced: from color depth and resolution for a single image, via frame rates for video and numbers of tiles in Virtual Reality (VR) or Augmented Reality (AR) applications, towards variation of angles and viewpoints for volumetric media.

Table 1. Various types of media and parameters

Artefact	Parameters
Still image	Resolution, Color depth
Video	Frame rate
VR/AR	Tiles
HTC	Viewpoints per 6DoF: up/down, left/right, forward/backward

Determining the user focus in order to select which portions of the image data to prioritize depends on how the user interacts with the media, for example, what the user wants to look at next. To maintain a high quality, it would be unacceptable to experience deteriorations in image quality every time the user refocuses or moves while waiting for image streams to adjust and new image data to load. Delays of 20 milliseconds until an image adjusts will be noticeable, even more so when the user is moving continuously, and hence not be acceptable. Therefore, determination of which portions of image data will be needed next needs to be done proactively in advance. This is commonly referred to as the "user interactivity problem". Addressing the user interactivity problem involves user movement prediction schemes that allow to proactively adapt contents to be streamed to ensure the right image content is already being served up just when it is needed. As changes in user position are predicted (or detected), the receiver communicates those changes back to the server, which allows the server to subsequently adjust its image data streams accordingly.

Supporting such schemes requires highly adaptive and ultra-low latency control schemes to be able to adapt streamed holographic contents as needed. The shorter the round-trip delay, the better the experience of the user will be due to avoidance of quality fluctuations during user movement. A frame rate of

60 frames per second would require a round-trip time of approximately 15 ms to allow for reactions in real time, which also needs to include required time for processing required for capture and rendering. However, in realistic scenarios, a time budget of 15 ms turns out to be insufficient to accomplish this. User movement prediction allows to mitigate this. However, the further the time horizon moves into the future, the more difficult it becomes to perform accurate prediction. To some degree, the effects of longer round-trip latency can also be mitigated by transmitting additional image data beyond the one being in focus in case it becomes needed if sufficient bandwidth is available. However, even in the case where such redundancy is an option, doing so will result in the waste of bandwidth that could be put to better use by transmitting image data in higher quality.

It is important to realize that all these considerations apply even in the case where the application does not involve interaction with a live remote party, such as in the case of a holographic video call. Instead, they apply even in the case of canned contents by virtue of user interactivity affecting the data needing to be streamed at any particular instant. This makes streaming of holographic content different from streaming video contents, where an initial delay incurred by video buffering might be acceptable.

Vehicular Networks

A lot of progress has been made of the rise of self-driving vehicles in recent years. Much of the attention has been given to technology that allows vehicles to drive autonomously, relying on feeds from a multitude of sensors being processed on-board the vehicle. Advances have indeed been impressive, even if technical and regulatory hurdles remain.

However, at the same time other variants of driverless vehicle technology are emerging that may have not received as much attention as autonomous vehicles but that are just as exciting and that constitute an enormous potential. This concerns remote driving, in which vehicles are not truly autonomous but can be remotely controlled and operated, for example a driver who operates from a remote pod in similar ways that unmanned aerial vehicles (a.k.a., drones) might be. Remote operations require networking services to carry everything from vehicle-driving commands to continuous remote feeds of video and telemetry data in order to provide visibility to the remote operator.

As a minimum goal, the remote operator should be able to see the same that a driver inside the car would be able to see, and possibly more. For one, feeds can be pre-processed and enhanced to direct attention to potentially hazardous conditions such as wet or icy surfaces, presence of pedestrians, and enhanced for better visibility, e.g., cutting through fog or poor illumination. In addition, feeds from the car can be augmented with feeds from other sources, for example feeds from other cars that are ahead or feeds from roadside infrastructure, such as a feed about the traffic situation of an upcoming intersection from sensors mounted as part of traffic lights or street lights.

Remote driving enables driverless vehicles where autonomous driving falls short and can also be used to complement it. For example, it is easy to conceive driverless vehicles that drive for the most part autonomously (such as on highways that are well-marked, have dedicated lanes, without needing to be concerned for erratic pedestrians), but that allow a remote driver to take over under certain conditions, for example, in residential settings for the "last mile". In addition, regulatory environments may prohibit the use of autonomous driving technology in some scenarios where remote driving would be permissible. Other factors to consider include economics and customer acceptance.

Remotely operated vehicles may also be of interest to personal transportation services, providing a safe work environment for drivers. Other uses of remotely operated vehicles involve environments that are both difficult to navigate in (precluding autonomous driving) and that would be hazardous or unsafe for humans to operate in, for example construction vehicles in remote sites or emergency service vehicles in areas that are affected by chemical spills, by active wildfires, or by hurricane conditions.

Obviously, safety is of utmost importance for any such applications. Unexpected obstacles or events can occur at any point in time, from erratic pedestrians coming out of "nowhere" to garbage falling from a truck. At a speed of 60 km/h, a vehicle travels roughly 16 meters per second. Any latency incurred by the network adds to the latency already incurred by human (or automated) reaction times as well as processing time required for rendering, adding to the distance required for the vehicle to come to a stop (or to take other evasive action in scenarios where stopping is either not feasible or not possible). It would be clearly unacceptable to lose visibility from or control over a vehicle at any point in time. The ramifications for the network are thus clear: in addition to having to support significant data volumes, end-to-end latency must be very low and indeed guaranteed to ensure safe operating conditions. High reliability and avoidance of packet loss are critical as retransmissions would result in unacceptable increases in delay. Due to the mission-critical nature of the application, any deterioration results not only in a mere deterioration of the QoE but makes the application unfeasible and hazardous to operate, putting lives at risk.

Other interesting applications for vehicular networks involve vehicle-to-vehicle (V2V) and vehicle-to-infrastructure (V2X) communications, benefitting even regular driving application. For example, a problem today concerns scenarios in which visibility is restricted by a truck in front. A video feed from the vehicle up front will provide a driver with greater visibility, allowing to anticipate e.g. hazards that allow stopping in time without rear-ending the vehicle in front. Likewise, passing assistants could make passing safer by analyzing data feeds from the vehicle in front regarding its speed and acceleration, oncoming traffic, and road conditions.

Summary of Inferred Requirements

The common themes in the above listed, and other, applications include the need for networking services that offer very low latency and that are able to support multiple concurrent data streams with very high velocity and high data rates. In that regard, the resulting requirements simply extrapolate the same trajectory that networking applications have been following for many years: applications will require greater transmission rates to be able to communicate growing volumes of data. At the same time, they demand ever-lower latency, often to the point where it is clear that they can only be offered within a given geographical span due to inherent physical limitations.

However, the requirements go further. Beyond low latency and high bandwidth, there is a need for high precision: networks must deliver services with service level objectives, specifically latency objectives, that are not just "optimized" but quantifiable, that can be guaranteed, and that are highly reliable. In addition, networking services must be able to support multiple concurrent data streams whose service levels are highly synchronized, to support applications relying increasingly on many concurrent feeds of interdependent data. Of course, some applications and deployment scenarios can arguably be addressed by special-purpose networks that bypass Internet Technology and Layer 3 altogether, such as private 5G on a factory floor for industrial IoT applications. While viable in certain niches, those solutions do not benefit from network convergence and the ability to utilize the same networking infrastructure for a multitude of services and deployments, resulting in a wide range of benefits including lower cost due to economies of scale associated with commodity networking equipment, improved operational efficiencies, and greater Return on Investment (RoI).

The need for high-precision also reflects the lack of tolerance of any degradation or fluctuation of service levels that are delivered by the network. Another common theme of the presented applications concerns the fact that they are not tolerant of missed guarantees of end-to-end latency or packet loss. Rather than degrading gracefully with a slightly reduced QoE, any misses result quickly in a complete breakdown of the application. Solutions at the application layer or by applications themselves, such as clever buffering or encoding schemes, are often possible for applications that have greater tolerance for service level misses or less stringent service level needs. However, they are simply not an option for many of those new applications. At the same time, many of the intended applications are mission-critical, with any failures posing significant dangers in the real world. It is one thing if network conditions result in deteriorating quality of a video call, but a different thing entirely if it causes a remotely-controlled emergency vehicle to spin out of control. While there are significant benefits and business potential of the envisioned applications, the realization of those applications will be utterly unfeasible without networks to support those requirements.

For this reason, it makes sense to revisit the foundations the current Internet is built on and to explore what modifications/additions may be needed to prepare networks that will be able to support the anticipated next wave of networking applications. This will be further discussed in the following section.

Motivation and Gap Analysis

Now that we have introduced some of the emerging networking use cases and their implied requirements for networking services, let us turn to the question of why the existing Internet technology may not be sufficient and what foundational challenges need to be overcome to result in successful solutions. The answers to this will pave the way to New IP, make it clear why it is needed, motivate its underlying design principles, and explain how it can be used to address those challenges.

Connectivity Vs. Service-Level Guarantee

Current Internet technology has connectivity service as its essential networking goal and allows users to send packetized data between any source and destination using IP transfer capabilities. IP provides basic forwarding service as a protocol of the data plane. It is complemented with additional protocols on the control plane to provide services such as domain name resolution and maintenance of dynamic routing tables. However, as far as forwarding is concerned, any additional capabilities or functional gaps need to be addressed by protocols that are layered on top of IP, starting with the transport layer and extending to the application layer.

IP itself has been deliberately governed in ways that make extensions extremely difficult. IPv4 is sunsetting and all further standardization has ended. IPv6 per RFC 8200 permits extension headers that can be processed by the destination but that is not allowed to affect packet per-hop behavior. Hop-by-hop option headers can be inspected (but not modified) by intermediate nodes but may not be supported by every deployment or node. This has resulted in the "hourglass" design of the Internet with its widely recognized benefits (for example, universal interoperability, high scalability and high stability). There are also a few notable associated shortcomings, for example ossification, i.e., the hurdles to evolve its design to support new requirements in the data plane). While many overlays and Layer 2/Layer 2.5

enhancements have been made to augment networking capabilities that cannot be provided in IP, there is need for extensibility in IP layer itself. To that regard, one notable recent effort has been the work on IPv6 Segment Routing (SRv6), resurrecting source routing principles in the context of IP. Despite its successes, even this effort has shown the limitations of IPv6 extensibility and the difficulties in enhancing it. It is therefore up to protocols at upper layers to devise and apply extra schemes that address any additional requirements that are not supported by IP itself.

For example, video streaming required ways to deliver video continuously in the best possible quality without disruptions due to the need to wait for subsequent video frames to load. This resulted in the introduction of DASH (Dynamic Adaptive Streaming over HTTP) (ISO/IEC 23009-1, 2019), based on the idea of breaking contents into small parts encoded in different quality that would be requested incrementally depending on current network conditions. The combination of clever buffering and transcoding schemes and multiple protocol layers over IP (TCP, HTTP, and DASH) was able to adapt shortcomings such as the possibility of packet loss, packet reordering, and variations in bandwidth in order to deliver a smooth QoE.

In some cases, requirements can be addressed through physical deployment. For example, Content Delivery Networks (CDNs) places frequently requested content in servers and systems close to clients in order to reduce distance and latency to result in a better acceptable user experience (in addition to reducing load on network and servers). Edge computing and fog computing are more recent incarnations of the similar idea to work around the issue that TCP/IP cannot guarantee predictably short latency. Likewise, specialized deployments of Internet Technology with dedicated circuits in controlled environments may be able provide guarantees in special cases, such as described in (Wikipedia, 2021). However, the challenge remains to provide the same support across general networking infrastructure that carries a multitude of converged services for many users and applications simultaneously without imposing prohibitive constraints on deployments.

The belief in each case is that as long as access to network connectivity is granted and clients show some ability to adapt, whatever QoS is inherently provided by the network will prove sufficient as the basis for overlaid services. And truth be told, this belief has turned out to be correct for the vast variety of services supported today over the Internet. This development was fueled further by simultaneous breathtaking advances in transmission technologies which provide vast increases in networking bandwidth coupled with hugely improved loss characteristics, offering leaps in service quality "for free".

However, for all its advances, providing connectivity is different from providing actual guarantees as demanded by mission-critical applications of the type that were described earlier. While service levels are optimized and become acceptable for services that degrade gracefully, resulting in slightly reduced QoE by users when network service levels deteriorate, their deterioration is always a very real possibility. Fundamentally, access to connectivity amounts to access to service that, at their core, remain by nature "best effort". But sometimes, best effort, despite all the best intentions, is not sufficient. What is needed are services that are guaranteed to provide a certain level of service, that can be relied on by mission-critical applications, and simply do not allow for glitches that might result in catastrophic failure. For example, when networks are used to connect machine tools and industrial controllers, some automation functions require the maximal communication latency to be 10 ms. Some of the deployments may involve interconnected components across different sites or even in the cloud. If the network does not provide 10 ms latency, it does not operate correctly and may even cause an accident.

The reason why those mission-critical applications are not a reality over the Internet today is that Internet Technology has not been able to deliver the connectivity services that must be able to adhere to stringent service level requirements with a high degree of precision. At the end of the day, an application will not care whether or not its traffic has "higher priority" than that of other applications, or whether networking resources have been reserved for it. What is will instead care about is whether its service level requirements have been met, which ultimately enables their ability to deliver the user experience that is expected from them.

What is required in particular are "in-time services" and "on-time services" as explained in ITU-T FG-NET2030 (2019):

"In-time services" are services that ensure delivery of packets with a required latency that is not to be exceeded. Packets may be delivered at any time before or until the latency deadline. A client application requesting an in-time service will specify the required maximum latency that is not to be exceeded. In addition, any constraints under which the required latency is to be delivered must also be specified – specifically, the expected bandwidth (e.g., bit rate, possibly differentiated by sustained and burst rates) as well as the acceptable miss rate (i.e., the ratio of packets that are dropped or do not meet the required latency versus the total number of packets).

"On-time services" are services that ensure the arrival of data within a specific time window. Like in-time services, they impose a maximum latency that is not to be exceeded. In addition, they indicate a minimum latency. A packet must be delivered no later than upper bound of the time window, but also no earlier than the lower bound of the time window. The window can be specified either in terms of specifying lower and upper bounds, or in terms of a latency target representing the midpoint of the window and the size of the window. A special case of an on-time service is the case when the time window is nominally "0" (with the lower bound equaling the upper bound), resulting in latency which is deterministic within the bounds of the clock uncertainty. A client application requesting an on-time-service will thus specify the required latency (for example, using a target latency midpoint and acceptable time window, or using lower and upper latency bounds). As with in-time services, constraints under which the required latency is to be delivered (expected bandwidth, acceptable miss rate) must also be specified. Figure 1 summarizes the difference between in-time and on-time data delivery and shows the latency with which a packet is expected to be received. Packets whose actual latency falls outside the range that is depicted in green (i.e., packets that are too late or too early) are considered out of compliance with the service level objective and contribute to the miss rate. The miss rate specifies the ratio of packets that fail to be delivered per the required latency, i.e., whose actual latency falls outside the required latency range, or that are lost entirely. The miss rate must approach "0" as close as possible.

An "in-time service" can be considered as a special case of an on-time service in which the acceptable latency window extends all the way from zero. However, solutions that support an on-time service involve additional challenges beyond solutions that support merely an in-time service: because packets must not be delivered earlier than a minimum latency, the network can give the forwarding preference to other packets or send the packet along a slower path when needed.

The need for the definition of parameters and constraints to qualify expectations and capture requirements for instances of connectivity has been recognized before, for example described in RFC 7297 for IP Connectivity Provisioning Profiles. Both In-time and On-time services can be thought of as instances of such profiles, provided and guaranteed as part of a dynamic service offering. Likewise, there have of course been many attempts to improve the ability of the network to provide better quality of service. IETF has defined two complementary QoS architectures in order to facilitate delivery of networking services whose QoS requires certain guarantees.

Figure 1. In-time vs on-time services (from ITU-T FG-NET2030 (2019))

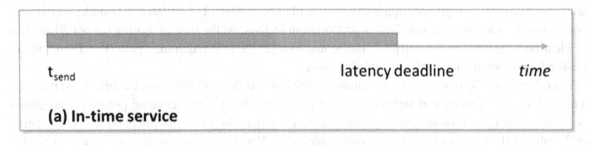

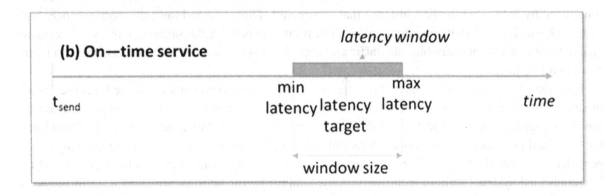

The first QoS architecture, IntServ, includes two services: Controlled Load Service (Wroclawski, 1997) and Guaranteed Service (GS) (Shenker et al., 1997). The latter is of particular relevance as it provides per-flow fixed bandwidth guarantees based on the concept of reserving resources in advance for a given flow. GS traffic is shaped at the ingress network edge as necessary so the flow does not consume more resources than have been reserved. To support latency guarantees, flows need to be re-shaped on every hop as collisions and resource contention between packets could still occur, which in turn might lead to the possibility of loss and unpredictable variations in latency. GS does not support flows to dynamically adjust the bitrate. It also offers no mechanisms to slow down packets in case a minimum latency is desired, as might be required for applications requiring fairness such as gaming or financial trading. Furthermore, queueing does not prioritize packets on their desired service level.

The second QoS architecture, DiffServ (Blake et al., 1998), is a multiplexing technique that is used to manage resources such as bandwidth and queuing buffers on a per-hop basis between different classes of traffic. This allows to separate traffic into different classes which can be assigned different priority. This allows traffic of applications that may be more sensitive to latency or loss to be given preference over traffic of applications that are more tolerant, for example applications that can afford retransmission and do not require remote communications in near-real time. While being given preference is better than not being given preference at all, it does not eliminate the possibility of degraded service levels or packet drops due to collisions with other traffic. It constitutes a per-hop optimization but no path-level guarantee.

More recently, the IETF DetNet Working Group has proposed the Deterministic Networking Architecture (DetNet) (Finn et al., 2019). The DetNet architecture intends to provide per-flow service guarantees in terms of maximum end-to-end latency, as well as packet loss ratio and upper bounds on out-of-order packet delivery. The most fundamental limitation of DetNet, similar to GS, is in its targeted scope of

Constant Bit Rate (CBR) reservations, whereas many future applications may have highly variable bitrates (for example, holographic applications as explained earlier). Lower latency bounds, as required for on-time services, are also not directly supported in DetNet. At the time of writing (as per 2020), it is not clear how exactly DetNet will be implemented to meet the said requirements in IPv4/IPv6 without causing foundational backward compatibility issues.

Time-Sensitive Networking (TSN) (Time-Sensitive Networking (TSN) Task Group, 2020) provides in effect a Layer 2 variation of IntServ with two enhancements: Cyclic queueing (async mode) allows for traffic shaping and avoids the need for time synchronization. Frame Replication and Elimination for Reliability (FRER) introduces "1:n" path protection, allowing to send replicated packets across different paths that should be provisioned to be disjoint. Replicas are eliminated on egress and latency is minimized by delivering the first instance that is received. TSN is geared towards short distances and essentially for Layer 2 switching domains, i.e. not routing capable. Like IntServ, TSN is furthermore geared towards CBR, not variable-rate traffic and does not support slowdown of packets based on minimum required latency.

It should be noted that the lacking ability to provide service level guarantees also reduces the ability of service providers to monetize their services. While they can monetize access to services, monetizing of guarantees becomes much more difficult because the guarantees given may not be "absolute" but statistical by nature. This leaves a substantial portion of the networking business opportunity to the providers of "over the top" services and services that rely on upper-layer protocols, implemented by interconnected systems without requiring specific support by the network which as a result provides little added value and opportunity.

Loss and Retransmission Vs Lossless Networking

Another aspect of the current "best effort" Internet is that it is prone to packet loss that can occur due to, for example, congestion. As explained earlier, many emerging use cases (such as teleoperation of critical machinery) involve mission critical applications that are not tolerant for any Service Level Objective (SLO) violations, let alone packet loss.

Of course, loss can be mitigated by retransmission. For example, a sender can resend packets when an acknowledgment for packets is not received in time, as in the case of TCP. However, doing so leads to further delay, typically at least tripling one-way latency. This would simply be unacceptable to many of the same emerging applications that are also sensitive to packet loss. As one mitigation approach, senders could decide to proactively resend critical data packets repeatedly in short succession without awaiting their acknowledgment first. This might result in a smaller delay penalty in case of loss; however, doing so would be wasteful and substantially increase network load, resulting in further congestion and even more collisions and thus loss. In turn, this could require networks to be substantially larger dimensioned to begin with, adding more bandwidth and forwarding capacity. Even in deployments where this is technically feasible, it would however lead to a substantial increase in cost while still falling short on being able to guarantee avoidance of congestion loss.

To be clear, loss can have many causes and the possibility of loss can never be ruled out completely. For example, bit errors may occur as a result of an unstable transmission medium, a line failure such as a fiber cut might occur mid-transmission, a natural disaster such as a tsunami causes flooding which knocks forwarding equipment offline, a burst of cosmic rays interferes with wireless transmission. Of course, in most cases networks might be protected against such events by using concurrent protective plans, but even then multiple failures might occur simultaneously and cause packet loss.

A far more common cause for loss, and the one to be therefore most concerned about, is congestion. The possibility of congestion occurring is rooted in and explained by queueing theory, and by the fact how queuing theory applies to packet-based network technology. Congestion typically occurs when packets arrive simultaneously from multiple incoming interfaces and need to be forwarded over the same outgoing interface, causing them to collide. As a result, packets need to be queued. However, memory that would be needed to implement buffers and queues at network nodes is expensive. This limits for practical purposes the number of packets that can queued, and any queue size has its limits. Once the queue is full, there is no space to put any additional packets and let the queue build up further, requiring them to be dropped.

Congestion loss is an issue inherent to IP which has not been overcome despite decades of QoS research. As described in the previous section, IntServ and DiffServ are the two foundational QoS architectures. DiffServ allows to differentiate packets in order to allow more critical (or loss-sensitive) packets to be given preference over other packets. This is an important optimization but does not eliminate the possibility of packet drops, as collisions with other traffic (of the same, or higher) priority can still occur. IntServ allows to reserve resources sufficient for a given flow, but does not fare well in the face of highly variable traffic rates. One mitigation would be to reserve enough resources that collisions can never occur even at peak rates, but doing so would be extremely wasteful and make networks prohibitively expensive.

What is needed is a technology that is able to rule out the possibility of loss due to congestion and, more generally, loss other than due to "Acts of God". The current IP is fundamentally limited here. However, other technologies have proven that solutions do exist. For example, circuit switching does not suffer the same type of issues but operates on a set of different principles. While it is highly desirable to preserve the wealth of attractive properties of IP and packet switching, such as resilience, efficiency, and avoidance of connection establishment handshakes, IP's inability to support more effective solutions that avoids congestion loss needs to be addressed.

Diversity In Addressing

Another observation IS that different application domains rely on different types of addressing. While IP networks are of course built around IP addresses, the same cannot be said for other types of networks. Plenty of other addressing schemes are in use, including E.164 addresses for telephone service (ITU-T, 2010), 16-bit Zigbee addresses in Zigbee (IoT) networks (ZigBee Alliance, 2015), MAC addresses at layer 2, or numeric ID in some industrial networks. Each of these addressing schemes comes with its own peculiarities but also has its own reason for being so. Some of those reasons may be historical but others are technical as well.

For example, E.164 addresses allow for easy distributed administration by separate authorities using hierarchical schemes (which can also be used to route calls between administrative domains). An interesting feature is that, where endpoints are within the same domain (for example, the same area code, country code, or even the same private branch exchange network), only the portion of the address within that same domain needs to be included. For example, on the same branch exchange, only the other party's extension number needs to be dialed, not the part of the globally unique number such as country code and area code that would be shared between both endpoints. As a result, it is possible to dial much shorter numbers when global disambiguation is not required.

Zigbee addresses are very short, consisting of only 16 bits, targeted at low-power devices in domains where transmission of every bit comes at a premium in terms of its energy cost. As a result, Zigbee networks are very local in nature and addresses are only unique within the scope of their particular network. Addressing Zigbee devices globally is not possible within the Zigbee architecture itself. Instead, it requires the addition of a globally addressable proxy that goes beyond the Zigbee framework. MAC addresses are not targeted at routing at all, but at unique identification of hardware devices connected to a network. Unlike other addresses, they are generally assigned not by operators of a network but often by manufacturers and intended to be permanently bound to a specific piece of equipment.

For a device to be directly connected to an IP network, it needs to have an IP address – consisting of 32 bits in the case of IPv4 or 128 bits in the case of IPv6. Without it, it can neither send nor receive any data, as both the source and the destination address must be included in any IP data packet. Any network that is supposed to converge on IP but that uses non-IP address has therefore to define a solution to translate between address spaces. This requires the introduction of address translation functions along with various types of data stores to maintain the corresponding mappings – whether ARP tables in the case of MAC and IPv4, proxies maintaining port mappings to Zigbee addresses, or directory functions to translate between E.164 and IP. This sets out to complexity. Additional complexity is involved when an address does not merely refer to a single endpoint, for example in case of multicast addresses.

The reality is that the diversity of different types of devices that need to be interconnected across different domains will continue to grow. Increasingly, this will not only include classical IT systems (servers, computers, client devices) and user devices (tablets, phones, smart TVs) but IoT devices, including low-power devices, and OT – operational technology such as found in industrial applications. Today, accommodating all these may require translation functions and gateways if a common federative layer is not used (e.g., IP). However, for networks to be truly convergent, the goal would be not only for different types of networks to be interconnected, but for different types of systems and end devices to be interconnected using the same network technology and the same internetworking architecture. However, doing so will require an underlying network protocol that is able to accommodate different types of addressing and address architectures. Systems interconnecting via IP are required to have an IP address today. What will be required instead to accomplish true convergence is free choice in the type of addresses being used, allowing endpoints to be addressed in a manner of their choosing, not IP i.e., not 32-bit or 128-bit addresses as the only option. This capability is referred to as "Free Choice Addressing".

Embedded Security (Intrinsic Security) and Other Aspects

There are many other aspects in which the current state-of-the-art of Internet technology needs improvements to meet the requirements for future networking applications. These include aspects such as:

● Support for very agile network service lifecycles: As the number of emerging networking applications, many with unique requirements, continues to explode, network providers need to be able to rapidly introduce new network services, or network services with properties that need to be rapidly adapted to new contexts, deployments, and application needs. Likewise, the business landscape may require users of network services to be able to rapidly adapt services to their needs. This will require advances in network programmability. Today's model of vendor-defined (supporting service features via new firmware or hardware-based networking features) or operator-defined (supporting service features via programmable software-defined networking (SDN) controllers,

Virtualized Network Functions (VNF), Service Function Chaining (SFC), even slicing will no longer be sufficient. Instead, networking technologies will need to enable development lifecycles that are much more agile than today and move from "Dev Ops" to "Flow Ops" (i.e., dynamic programmability of networks at the flow level). This will require support of novel network programming models. It also requires development of new programmable networking hardware, which offers the ability to map novel network programming primitives into packet processing pipelines and the execution of custom logic at line rate.

- Manageability: Some emerging networking applications place very high demands on latency and precision that need to be supported at very high scales, coupled with expectations of zero loss and disruption, and much higher availability than today. This requires corresponding manageability capabilities, for example, to be able to rapidly and proactively identify and eliminate any potential sources of service level degradations while managing networks and services at unprecedented scale. However, today's manageability capabilities very much reflect the "best effort" mindset of Internet technology itself, relying on network and flow statistics that are heavily sampled and thus provide limited network visibility. Advances in internetworking technology must be accompanied by corresponding advances in manageability, from the ability to provide telemetry that is both comprehensive in its coverage and "smart" in terms of being actionable, towards better support for operational scale as promised, e.g., by intent-based networking. All of these are hampered by the current state-of-the-art in IP, for example limitations in terms of the amount of in-situ Operations, Administration, Management data (iOAM) (Brockners et al., 2020) that can be piggybacked and transferred using IP packets and limitations in the ability to rapidly adapt which telemetry being collected on a per-packet basis as demanded by the current situation.

- Privacy: There is a growing awareness of lack of privacy in the Internet by the general public. New networking services and applications need to be able to comply with heightened user privacy expectations in order to be viable. However, current Internet technology is notoriously lacking in many regards, not only at the application level. For example, the current architecture and best practices tend to use long-lived address allocations that makes it easy to track a user, and most information in packet headers are in the clear and therefore observable by eavesdroppers.

As relevant as those aspects are, arguably the most important one is security. Security encompasses a whole basket of properties, from encryption to keeping information secure to inherent network properties that make a service or user much harder to attack. Perhaps most important among these is the assurance that communication is indeed trustworthy. This includes assurance that packet content that is received is indeed authentic, i.e., that it has not been altered while in transit and that it is complete (or, if incomplete, any missing data and breaches in authenticity are immediately obvious). It should also not be observable from outside parties, touching also on concerns for privacy.

At the same time, trustworthiness includes ensuring that information about the source or origin of the packet is authentic, i.e., that a sender cannot simply impersonate someone else. It is this aspect in particular where current IP technology is intrinsically lacking. At the root of the problem is that the source address information in IP data packets is not authenticated. This makes it very easy to spoof addresses (i.e., substitute someone else's address as source), which is at the root of a wide range of notorious attack vectors.

For example, spoofing IP addresses facilitates Denial of Service (DoS) attacks by obfuscating the true origin of the attack. Worse, it facilitates reverse amplification attacks, in which the volume of attack traffic is amplified manifold by unsuspecting systems. The fundamental attack pattern has an attacking system that sends a set of short requests to a large set of legitimate systems using the attack victim's IP address as source. Those systems in turn send their responses to the attack victim. When the responses that are generated are significantly larger than the requests themselves, the volume of attack traffic is magnified as a result. Likewise, fraudulent schemes such as phishing or spam are facilitated by the ease with which IP addresses can be spoofed, as it makes it easier for attackers to impersonate a different originator, making it easier to avoid both suspicion and detection.

It should be noted that the requirement to avoid false impersonation is not to be confused with prohibiting networking traffic from being anonymous. To the contrary, it is a perfectly legitimate and in fact important requirement to allow senders to obscure their identity to outside observers, even to service providers, and allow them to remain anonymous if they wish to do so. This might even include the option of not including a source address at all. It is then up to the discretion of the receiver whether or not to process such anonymous traffic. However, when a source address is used, the receiver and the network should be able to rely on it as authentic – the right to be anonymous should not be confused with the ability to impersonate others at will.

Of course, over the years many security capabilities have been added to IP, offering encryption of payload and tunneling of packets, making them very secure from outside observation and tampering. There are even clever schemes that have been devised to deal with the problem of IP address spoofing, from schemes to maintain "safe sender" lists to proposals that require senders of email to submit micropayments with their messages that would be reimbursed only if the receiver deemed it not to be spam. The idea is to discourage sending of spam by making large volumes prohibitively expensive, while making the cost of individual, legitimate emails to be negligible. However, despite all these efforts, security remains a problem, fundamentally caused by that it is not an intrinsic part of IP but an afterthought that requires other components to make it worth. As a result, secure solutions are more complex, harder to operate, and more difficult than they would otherwise have to be, in turn leading to the many security vulnerabilities that are an unfortunate reality of the Internet today.

NEW IP AND ITS NEW FUNDAMENTAL FUNCTIONS

Evolution of Foundational Components

Since the very beginning, the Internet has followed the datagram forwarding model of packet delivery, which is up to the intervening routers to get a packet to the correct destination by using the destination address contained in the packet. IP has evolved from packet switching in early 1960s, to IPv4 in 1981, and to IPv6 in 1995. A general-purpose and fixed-format IP address is used and general-purpose connectivity is provided, despite of some failed efforts to introduce variable-length addresses (Deering (1992), Francis (1994)). As analyzed in the previous sections, emerging applications require what existing IP is not able to support, for example, guarantees of arrival time, packet loss ratio and throughput, and assurances of security and reliability for packet deliveries.

In this section, we describe a new protocol which evolves from statistical multiplexing to computational multiplexing, best-effort forwarding to high-precision communications, from "One Size Fits All" fixed-format addressing to multi-family free-choice addressing, and from transport that is based on fixed loss-retransmission cycle to user-defined qualitative communications as pictured in Figure 2.

Figure 2. Evolution of foundational components

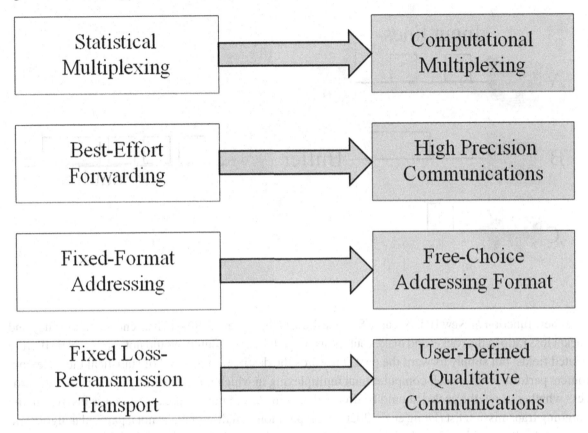

Computational Multiplexing

In packet-switched networks, statistical multiplexing, as shown in Figure 3, is used to multiplex data packets from multiple input lines and forward them to multiple outputs following the first-come first-serve order or other scheduling disciplines. In this way, many data flows can share the network resources on a common forwarding path, in the meantime the scheduling conflicts and resource competition of the simultaneously arriving packets are resolved by following a handful of packet forwarding rules. The aggregation of flows in a multiplexer is governed by statistical relationships such that over a certain period the entire flow usually has a consistent bit rate with smooth variation as compared to single packet in a flow and all flows enjoy the same statistically equal opportunity in using network resources. Although statistical multiplexing can make the most efficient use of network resources and accommodate traffic bursts, routers are not aware of latency requirements and thus treat all packets equally in allocating network resources and offering forwarding services to them so that mission-critical applications would often miss their deadlines. For example in Figure 4, the latency-sensitive packet 3 arrives at the tail of an already built-up queue (behind packet 1 and packet 2) of an output port, but under the statistical multiplexing the packet 3 that needs to depart as soon as possible will only get forwarded after all packets ahead of it are sent out.

Figure 3. Statistical multiplexing

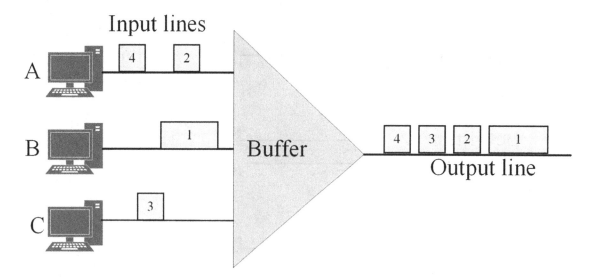

A new function of New IP is to carry Service-Level Objectives (SLO) such as end-to-end latency and packet loss ratio in the packet and make routers aware of it. Legacy routers would not process New IP SLO related fields, but simply forward the packet towards the destination. Instead of statistical multiplexing, routers perform what we call computational multiplexing in which it is decided by a computational process whether or not the packet should be dropped, and in case of not, where the packet is inserted in the outgoing transmission list (Dong et al., 2020). Computational multiplexing is not a particular algorithm. It is a multiplexing principle, which is no longer statistical, but taking packets' SLOs into consideration, e.g. latency guarantee (how much time left before the packet is considered to fail the latency SLO) and adjusting the packets' queueing positions before they are transmitted. Although DiffServ treatment in the network is achieved by marking traffic class or priority of the packet, DiffServ does not adapt to packet level SLO variation and has very raw granularity at class level in terms of QoS guarantee (Shenker et al., 1997). Going back to [REMOVED REF FIELD] Figure 3 again, by running a computational process at packet level, the router will find that Packet 3 should be inserted before Packet 1 and Packet 2 in the outgoing list as pictured in Figure 4. If a packet is too late for its deadline, the packet should be dropped even if there is still room in the packet buffer. That said, the outgoing packet buffer is not a queue any more but a linear list. Different types of SLOs require different algorithms, data structures and scheduling disciplines in the computational process for multiplexing.

High-Precision Communication

As analyzed in previous sections, what the current IP provides is essentially best-effort type services, but new applications such as industrial control and automation often require guaranteed SLOs. In particular, High Precision Communications (HPC) are of interest, which concern the guaranteed latency, packet loss ratio and throughput. The target performances such as latency, reliability, throughput, etc. may be defined at the much finer granularity of a packet, a group of packets, or a flow.

Figure 4. Computational multiplexing

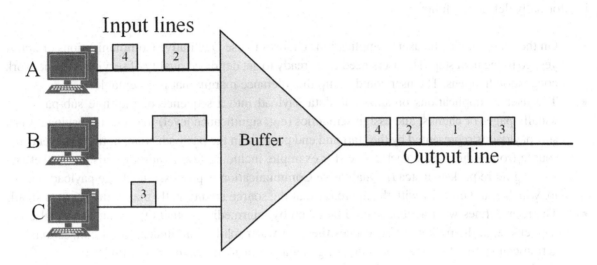

Best-effort service is not predictable and is based on the current network state. There is little or no prior knowledge about available performance, and no control over the network at any time. The best-effort network infrastructure could delay, buffer, or drop packet indiscriminately. Reliability is mainly provided by retransmission with other more advanced mechanisms such as Traffic Engineering (TE). However, retransmission can guarantee neither throughput nor latency. In New IP, we bring new network capabilities that can be used for High Precision Communications. The network should be able to distinguish packets in transit and treat them appropriately to achieve the requested SLOs.

ManyNets and Free-Choice Addressing

As analyzed in previous sections, the existing IP adopts a "one size fits all" approach and defines a general-purpose fixed address format. But in reality, the fixed-format address does not really fit all nicely. Many types of networks (that are called "ManyNets" in this chapter) have been emerging with different types of addresses, with the satellite networks and IoT networks being part of ManyNets.

In order to connect ManyNets – and especially those that are currently unknown but may come out in the future - to the Internet, New IP defines a mechanism to accommodate any type of addressing systems, which is referred to as Free-Choice Addressing.

Qualitative Communications

In the user payload of the current packet, all the bits and bytes are equally significant. When congestion or other network errors arise, the packet may be dropped as a whole. But for some applications in reality, for example, images, video frames, and holographic objects, bits and bytes are not equally significant and what's important is their semantics or entropy. Instead of dropping the entire packet, application may prefer dropping less significant parts of packets and keeping more significant ones if possible. It opens up a new communication method, called Qualitative Communications, which is still under active research (Li et al., 2019) (Dong et al., 2019) (Dong et al., 2020) and one of the possible implementations is informally defined as follows:

- On the sender node, the user or applications chooses to use Qualitative Communications or not. If yes, go to the next step. The users need to be ready to get degraded quality of service if the network congestion happens. The user could set up the tolerance margin that is acceptable.
- The user or applications organize the data payload into a sequence of multiple sub-payloads, usually pages or chunks, and assign semantics (e.g. significance level) to each sub-payload. Each sub-payload is represented by the start and end position in the payload. Note, nothing prevents the source from reducing the packet size (for example, including fewer sub-payloads per packet and sending more packets instead). Qualitative Communication is proposed for large payload scenario, which could co-exist with the approach that the source intentionally makes the payload small.
- The user defines what actions should be taken by intermediate routers when an abnormal event happens, e.g., the packet buffer reaches the high-water mark as an indication of congestion. The action can simply be "drop" or "cut", or generally "wash" that is currently under research (Li et al., 2019). For example, when the buffer reaches the high-water mark, the router drops first sub-payload and the last sub-payload, but keeps the rest of sub-payloads. This allows for partial drop rather than entire drop. If checksum exists, it would be applied to in the chunk level. The user can also define rules for the receiver's use, for example, ignoring checksum, ignoring dropped sub-payloads, repairing methods for lost sub-payloads, etc.
- On the intermediate routers, if no abnormal event happens, no actions are taken. But in case of abnormal event such as network congestion, the router will drop sub-payloads as specified by the sender. Note that the router will not check the content of the payload. It is sufficient to know where the sub-payload starts and ends to process the sub-payloads.
- On the receiver node, the receiver will perform the rule as specified by the sender. If abnormal event has happened on the path, usually the receiver will ignore the checksum.

In Qualitative Communications, we care about their qualitative properties instead of their quantitative bytes. Qualitative communications promise a new direction that would support holographic type communications. Please refer to (Li et al., 2019) (Dong et al., 2019) (Dong et al., 2020) for some research progress.

In New IP, we design a mechanism to support qualitative communications by utilizing in-network signaling and context-based qualitative payload formats. The qualitative payload formats associate a differentiating property or relationship within the packet payload. Potentially the payload is divided into multiple parts with a degree of importance, entropy, contextual information, etc., linked to each part or a group of parts. With such knowledge carried along within the packet and known to the network, actions taken by the network will not necessarily be on the entire packet, but at much finer granularity, i.e., on the part(s) of the packet. This may prevent entire packet dropping as well as re-transmissions in the networks, and yet still be able to deliver partial data to the receiver with a tolerable quality. Applications that are willing to trade-off between entire re-transmissions and a bearable degraded quality of data are most suitable for such qualitative payloads.

Figure 5. Resemblance between classical mail and IP packet

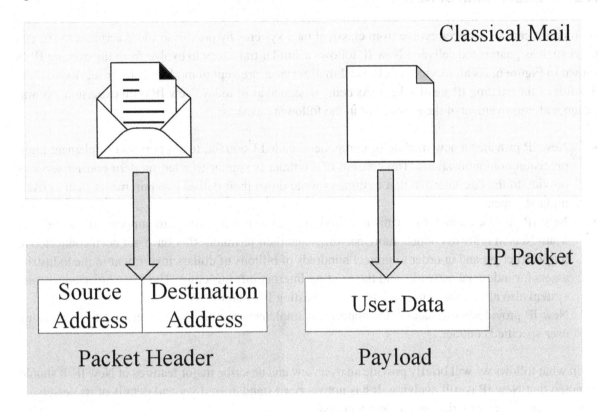

Courier Services Analogy

The data transport in the Internet draws resemblance to the delivery logistics in postal or courier services, which is very well understood. As shown in Figure 5, the packet header is analogous to the sender and receiver address on the envelope, and the packet payload is analogous to the letter enclosed within the envelope. The mail is then dispatched by the postal service while the sender and receiver do not have any knowledge of the route or time taken by the delivery. This is how the best-effort service in the current Internet works.

Over the years, the courier services have evolved to offer value-added services to meet new business and economical requirements by the customers. Also, the sender and receiver addresses may be in different languages and in different formats to accommodate international mails. Now the courier services become customizable, trackable, and assurable. For example, the customers are able to customize the guaranteed delivery time, e.g., overnight delivery (urgent and fast).

While modern courier services have evolved, the data delivery model in the Internet has not changed much. In order to bridge the gaps identified above and to meet requirements of future applications, we will follow the idea in the courier service evolution to design a new Internet protocol.

A Brief Description of New IP

As modern courier services evolve from classical mail systems by providing more services to the end users such as guaranteed delivery, New IP follows a similar trajectory to evolve from the existing IP as shown in Figure 6. As all services of classical mail services are kept in modern courier services, all the features of the existing IP are also kept. As being designed as of today, New IP is an extension, optimization and improvement of the existing IP in the following aspects:

- New IP provides a new module or component, called Contract, to support and implement high-precision communications. The concept of Contract is similar to what modern courier services provide to the customers so that customers write down their delivery requirements such as overnight shipment.
- New IP provides a new mechanism, called Free-Choice Addressing, to support and implement ManyNets in order to connect more networks and their terminals that have not been connected to the Internet yet and in order to protect hundreds of billions of dollars investment in the industrial assets for industrial networks and the existing Internet infrastructure. The free-choice addressing system also allows the continued use of the existing IPv4 and IPv6.
- New IP provides a mechanism to support and implement Qualitative Communications by using user-specified contract.

In what follows we will briefly provide an overview and describe major features of New IP. It should be noted that New IP is still evolving. It has not yet been standardized yet and details of its design are subject to change as experiences are being gained.

Figure 6. Resemblance between modern courier express mail and New IP packet

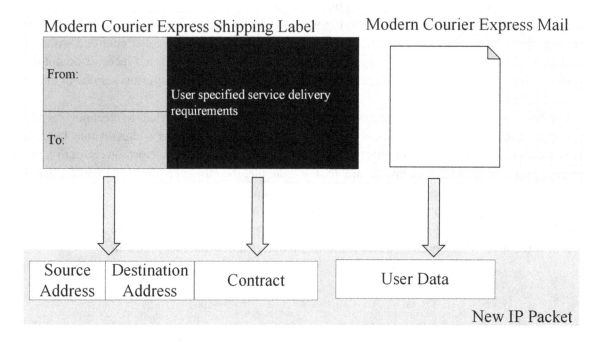

New IP Packet Format

The New IP packet format is designed to include three major elements as shown in Figure 7:

- The *New IP Shipping* element is motivated by the fact that a fixed type of addressing does not fit all the reachability scenarios in different verticals and diversified network infrastructures. New IP allows for hybrid formats of addresses according to the functionality and end devices' access network types. The New IP shipping takes the integrability with the existing address schemes (e.g., IPv4 and IPv6) as the highest priority, while allowing different types of addresses to be integrated and communicated in a flexible way.
- The *New IP Contract* is all about new network capabilities and services such as high-precision communications, as well as the network service customization. It provides a method to enable new types of modern courier-like network services at the finest packet-level granularity. Contracts do not only create avenues for the next level of user-defined networking on the data plane, but also aim to be compatible with network operator's requirements to perform telemetry, operation, administration and management, as well as elastically grow services on-demand and create new business models.
- The *New IP Payload* can be the same as that in the existing IP, but can also be a sequence of sub-payloads, which share the same sources and destinations, but may have different priorities in terms of packet drop when congestions or other abnormal conditions arise. In the existing IP, a sub-payload can be encapsulated in a single but smaller packet by itself. When all such single but smaller packets for sub-payloads arrive at the same router at the same time, if there is not enough free space in the packet buffer, the router will randomly drop them one by one until the buffer holds the remaining ones. New IP qualitative payload will provide a drop-differentiating preference to the intermediate routers so that the routers will drop sub-payloads in the order of sender-defined preference. A major application of this feature is to send qualitative images such as holographic objects over networks using jumbo frames (Borman et al., 1999) or super jumbo frames.

Header Specification

The New IP packet is a sequence of four specifications started with the Header Specification. The Header Specification, also called Manifest Field sometimes, keeps the packet logistics such as Time-To-Live and Total Length, and in particular, contains three pointers to the other three specifications, respectively:

- Shipping Pointer (Addressing Offset) specifies the offset and Shipping Type.
- Contract Pointer (Contract Offset) specifies where the Contract Spec starts.
- Payload Pointer (Payload Offset) specifies the offset and length of the Payload Spec.

Currently, the Header Specification has the following fields as shown in Table 2, with exact formats and lengths still subject to the standardization.

The IPv6 extension header mechanism provides an opportunity to define more features, mostly on routing aspects, e.g., SRv6. If the IETF agrees, it is possible to define a new type of extension headers that would do what the 'Contract' does. But as of this writing, there is no such existing extension header

Figure 7. New IP packet format

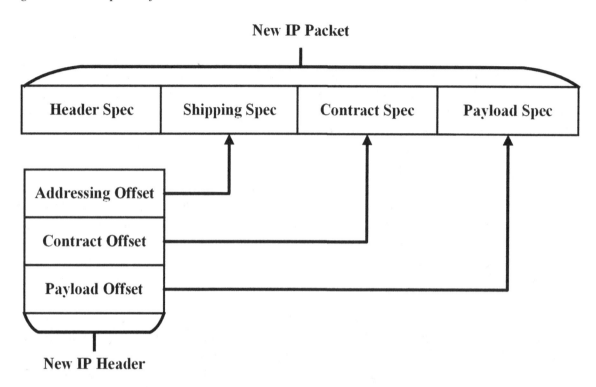

nor discussions on extending such headers to support and implement what the 'Contract' does. On the other hand, even if such extension header be agreed and standardized for IPv6, it would not work with other types of addresses such as IPv4 addresses and others.

Although new IPv6 extension headers might be defined and leveraged to carry the contract portion of New IP with many architectural restrictions set forth in RFC8200; New IP has three major distinctions and benefits that are summarized as follows:

- New IP is hardware and line rate processing friendly. New IP enables parallel processing of contract information. For example, in time guarantee, status collection and accounting can be processed and realized simultaneously. While IPv6 has sequential processing, with chains of header extensions. New IP enables faster loading and processing of contract and metadata as it has clear markers in the header. On the other hand, the Contract processing and the Addressing processing

Table 2. New IP Header Specification

Flags and Logistics			
TTL	User Data Protocol		Total Length
Shipping Type		Shipping Pointer	
Contract Pointer			
Payload Pointer			

- are also independent of each other, and therefore some related features can be processed in parallel as well.
- When a tunneling is introduced, the Contract will always sit on the outermost "header" so that the intermediate routers will honor and fulfil the contract. In contrast, when an IPv6 packet is encapsulated by another tunneling protocol, the extension header will be encapsulated inside by the tunneling protocol so that the routers will only see and process the outermost tunneling protocol without knowledge of any encapsulated protocols.
- New IP is a next generation framework and provides foundation for the future evolution. For example, most of current industrial networks are private, which means the addressing used in those industrial networks could be various. With the cloudification trend, the industrial networks are likely to be connected to the Internet. It is intended to protect the address types used in the industrial networks to continue being used, thus New IP provides a shipping spec to allow any kind of addressing types to be incorporated, and potentially allow hybrid addressing types for source and destination. The 'Contract' is uniform with and oblivious to any addressing systems. It works with IPv4 addresses, IPv6 addresses, and many others.

Shipping Specification

The Shipping Specification is a mandatory section of the New IP packet and specifies the sender and receiver's addresses. Depending on the Shipping Type, the Shipping Specification may have different formats.

In order to be compatible with IPv4, IPv6, and MPLS and in order to re-use IPv4 and IPv6 addresses, New IP defines the following Shipping Types as being reserved at the time of this writing (2021):

1: The Shipping Specification field is an IPv4 packet header.
2: The Shipping Specification field is an IPv6 packet header.
3: The Shipping Specification field is an MPLS packet header.

When Shipping Type is a reserved number above, the Shipping Field is a self-contained packet as defined above, and the Contract pointer and Payload pointer are ignored.

Other new Shipping Types are being defined as follows:

4: The Shipping Specification field contains IPv4 addresses for both the source and the destination (but no other IPv4 header fields).
5: The Shipping Specification field contains IPv6 addresses for both the source and the destination (but no other IPv6 header fields).

Other shipping types are still under research, for example, Flexible addressing system (variable length addresses) (Jia, Chen, & Jiang, 2020), (Jia, Li & Jiang, 2020) (Tang et al., 2020), Geography-based addresses (longitude, latitude), Location + ID, Service ID, and the source and destination addresses are mix-and-match of IPv4 and IPv6 addresses.

How the Shipping Types are defined and their numbers are assigned will depend on a standardization process. For most applications, the sender and the receiver addresses are either IPv4, or IPv6, or their

Table 3. A special case of New IP packet

Header Spec	IPv4 address	IPv4 address	Contract Spec	Payload Spec

mix and match. In particular, Shipping types 4 and 5 are of interest, and in the case of IPv4, a packet is structured as shown in Table 3.

Contract Specification

A Contract describes a formal service specification of a service expected by the sender. If a packet is delivered to the receiver, but its Contract is not fulfilled, the delivery is considered to be unsuccessful. There has been research on Contract in the literature, and the extensions of packets with Contracts (or equivalents) have been called Big Packet Protocol (BPP) (Li et al., 2018) (Dong & Li, 2019). In this sub-section, we describe the basic features of Contracts and give examples.

Declaratively, a contract is a set of "Event-Condition-Action" rules described as follows (Figure 8):

Figure 8. New IP contract

\<Contract\> := \<Contract Clause\> | \<Contract Clause\> AND \<Contract\>

\<Contract Clause\> := \<Contract Item\> | \<Contract Item\> OR \<Contract Clause\>

\<Contract Item\> := \<Event. Condition. Action\> | \<Metadata\> | \<Event. Condition. Action\> \<Metadata\>

\<Event, Condition, Action\> := \<Action\> | \<Condition\> \<Action\> | \<Event\> \<Condition\> \<Action\>

A major use of Contract is to specify the requirements for high-precision communications at the packet level. For example: In-Time latency Guarantee for 10 ms. The contract can be conceptually specified as "\<Action\>\<Metadata\>" with \<Action\> being "in-time-guarantee" and the \<Metadata\> being "10 ms".

Basic contracts can be combined together. For example, in-time latency guarantee for 10 ms and packet loss ratio guarantee for 1/1000000.

There are potentially many uses of Contract, but for our purposes we are particularly interested in the following uses as of now:

- In-Time Latency Guarantee
- On-Time Latency Guarantee
- Packet Loss Ratio Guarantee
- Throughput Guarantee
- Drop ordering of sub-payloads when congestion or other error conditions arise

In the protocol specification, the above conceptual descriptions of actions, conditions, events and metadata are encoded by numbers and subject to its standardization process. More actions, conditions and metadata types can be added when necessary.

High-Precision Communications as discussed in previous sections are specified as a contract by using In-Time Latency Guarantee, On-Time Latency Guarantee, Packet Loss Ratio Guarantee, and/or Throughput Guarantee.

The implementation of contracts in routers involve a large array of techniques including network-wide structural techniques, forwarding-path level techniques, and inter and intra-host techniques, buffer management, scheduling disciplines, etc. For example, (Dong et al., 2020) gives a quantified analysis on the latency requirement that network-based Augmented Reality and Virtual Reality and future holographic applications impose to networking and summarizes how New IP functions support the precise low latency requirement. Latency-Based Forwarding (LBF) (Clemm and Eckert, 2020) proposed to averagely distribute the time budget to the remaining hops when packets require in-time or on-time guarantee, with such requirement and time budget being carried in the contract. Dong and Li (2020) further investigated how to schedule multiple packets in the outgoing queue with in-time guarantee requirement such that the total average dwell time of the packets in the router can be minimized. Han et al. (2020) and Dong et al. (2021) leveraged New IP in order to achieve in-band signaling for flow admission and resource reservation at intermediate routers. The granular flow-level latency guarantee service with scalable control plane and data plane were proposed.

Payload Specification

The New IP payload can be a traditional payload, a sequence of bits/bytes, or it may be a *qualitative payload* that carries *quality, entropy* or *semantics* of the payload. Such payloads are subject to qualitative communication service (Dong et al., 2019) processing when corresponding events happen. New IP Contract can be utilized to carry the context of a qualitative packet. The context could specify how significant a particular piece of data within the payload is. As an example, a media frame can be arranged in such a manner that the initial part of the payload is the most significant frame, the middle and last part enhance the resolution of this frame. The context could specify the encoding relationship among the different pieces of data within the payload. Proposals realizing qualitative communications by applying random linear network coding (Fragouli et al., 2006) are proposed by Dong and Li (2019) and Dong et al. (2020). In those proposals, the payload could be divided into multiple equal-sized pieces and applied with linear network coding, such that the significance of each piece does not differ. When qualitative processing to the packet is needed, the network node could initialize a random drop or drop from the tail as many as permitted and as needed until the packet can be retained in the forwarding buffer.

Brief Discussion on How New IP Addresses The Gaps

The gaps that were pointed out in previous section can be summarized into the following four major categories:

- Service level guarantee at packet level.
- Lossless networking.
- Diversity in addressing schemes.

- Embedded security.

While it is impossible to cover how we address all these aspects in detail, we briefly discuss how the above-described New IP evolutions bridge those gaps. High-precision communication constructs can be realized through the extensible and hardware processing friendly contracts. Computation multiplexing aims to provide at packet level service guarantees, e.g., in-time guarantee and on-time guarantee. Contract carried in the packet is intended for the network to be aware of the SLOs and take the corresponding actions. There is a lot more than protocol level support needed for these to be achieved in the deployments; those include but not limited to granular resource reservations, admission control and a better host network feedback. Similarly, lossless networking that is required by volumetric, real-time, and intelligent data delivery for future immersive media can be realized with the user-defined Qualitative Communication, which intends to largely eliminate the possibilities for packet re-transmissions while trading-off between user's satisfaction for experienced latency and slight media quality degradation within tolerable degree. A flexible addressing mechanism in the header beyond current 32-bit and 128-bit only options address many deployment scenarios (industrial, satellite and spectrum efficient communications) and provide security by obscurity in some industrial deployments. Security and inter-domain aspects are briefly discussed in the following other considerations sub-section, and we also call them out as one of the future work items.

Other Considerations

Beyond the protocol specification itself, there are many additional considerations that need to be addressed to make New IP a complete solution. While a detailed discussion would go beyond the scope of the book, this section would not be complete without at least touching on a number of those. It should also be mentioned that New IP is still on the "bleeding edge" of the technology and we expect further refinements as implementation and deployment experiences are gained. Further refinements can be expected once New IP is subjected to standardizations.

One set of considerations concerns the ability to support New IP in high-performing networking hardware at line rate. Most aspects of New IP, such as the mapping of header and shipping spec, are straightforward to support. A more interesting aspect concerns the contract specifications. Contracts may involve a variable number of rules, each of which can contain multiple conditions and actions. This per se can make mapping to existing packet processing pipelines challenging. However, there are a number of factors to consider to alleviate that concern, several of which have been investigated by Francois et al (2020). For one, contracts can be augmented with indications of any serialization dependencies for each clause (i.e., for each condition or action). This facilitates mapping into pipelines with concurrent stages, allowing for parallelized processing of contract clauses. The length of the pipeline is determined by the maximum number of steps needing to be serialized; support of pipelines of longer lengths will require corresponding silicon support. Also, implementation can be simplified, and performance gained by using contract templates, i.e., constraining contracts to be of a certain structure (such as, a number of conditions that is not to be exceeded, or of contract clauses needing to be serialized). As more powerful hardware processing capabilities emerge, any such usage constraints can be subsequently relaxed.

Another set of considerations concerns security. Both traditional concerns, such as addressing the possibility of source address spoofing, and new concerns, such as the potential for tampering with contracts, need to be addressed. For this reason, New IP needs to support inherent authentication of shipping and of contract specs. This can be accomplished using special security contracts which do allow to carry and refer to security material as part of that contract.

A third set of considerations concerns possibilities for flow-level performance optimization. Including the same contract with every packet can be wasteful in case of applications involving flows with high volumes of packets that are each subjected to the same packet. In those cases, it would be beneficial to allow for the possibility of defining a contract at the level of a flow which is then implicitly referred to by each of the flow's member packets. Indeed, such a facility can be provided through stateful extensions referred to as "statelets". Statelets in effect constitutes glorified pieces of flow cache memory that can be used, among other things, to cache flow contracts at nodes along a path. As part of its processing of a packet, a node will check for presence of a statelet and apply any applicable contract. Various second order considerations and challenges deal with path congruency and management of the statelet cache itself. For further details on this, as well as for another interesting set of New IP applications, interested readers are asked to refer to Clemm and Chunduri (2019).

Deployment

Digitization is happening across the industry verticals from transportation and distribution, financial services, health care, manufacturing, factory automation to mining and agricultural sectors. Not all these industrial sectors need stringent SLAs and better privacy/security from the network connectivity perspective, but a vast number of them do need. New IP is motivated by expanding the limit and scope of the Internet so as to connect the networks and terminals that require stringent KPIs and that have not been connected to the Internet with better privacy and security properties suited beyond ICT. Thus, the deployment of New IP will expand the scope of the Internet from current ICT industry to beyond ICT, and in particular to Operational Technology (OT). New IP is especially suited for industrial machine-type communications that often require high-precision KPIs and whose devices may be assigned other addresses than IPv4/IPv6 addresses. Some typical deployment examples include: (1) Large manufacturing companies that go over a large number of workshops or production floors; (2) Applications for vehicles to the infrastructure; (3) To connect 5G (R)AN (gNB) to the Core Network; (4) To connect 5G gNB to MEC sites; (5) Metropolitan-range networks for smart city applications. From the architectural point of view of the Internet, New IP can be deployed in an Autonomous Systems (AS) within the current Internet architecture. For example, applications that require stringent and high-precision KPIs, as pictured in Figure 9, is one such deployment scenario. In what follows we will take a look at some issues and examples more closely.

Compatibility and Interoperability

This section discusses the interoperability issue when New IP is deployed in a brownfield environment. As discussed earlier, being different from the existing IP, New IP by itself does not define any specific addressing system. Instead, it provides a free choice addressing mechanism to use or reuse whatever addressing systems the users and network operators choose to use for their networks and applications. As IPv4 and IPv6 are the protocols used in the existing Internet, we will discuss the following scenarios:

- New IP host/router sending a packet to a New IP network
- IPv4/IPv6 host/router sending a packet to a New IP network

Figure 9. New IP deployment in the Internet

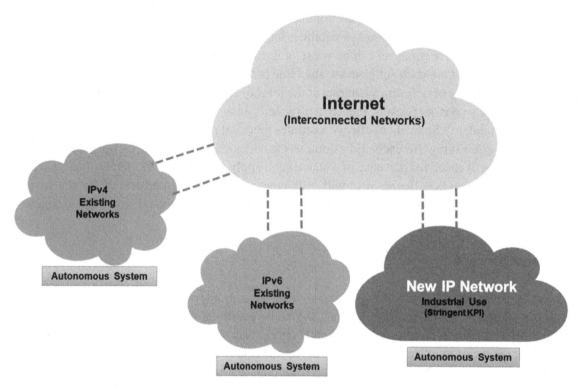

- New IP host/router sending a packet to an IPv4/IPv6 network
- New IP host/router sending a packet to a network where New IP is partially deployed

New IP Host/Router Sending A Packet To A New IP Network

This is the scenario we have perceived for new applications discussed in previous sections. This is mostly for greenfield network deployments, for example, a new OT network which needs beyond best

Figure 10. New IP greenfield deployment

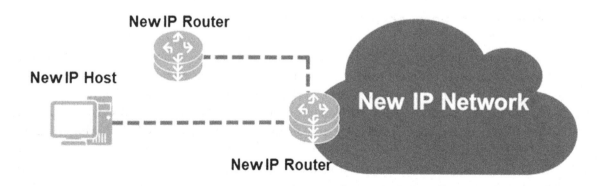

effort transmission. In this scenario, every router supports New IP as shown in Figure 10, and therefore all/full benefits of New IP can be reaped from high precision services, free-choice addressing as well as increased security.

IPv4 and IPv6 are the addressing scheme of the existing Internet. The free-choice addressing mechanism of New IP allows IPv4/IPv6 to continue to be used in New IP networks with the additional features and capabilities provided by the Contract of New IP. The routing protocols for IPv4 and IPv6 can also continue to be used for basic connectivity and can be enhanced for new capabilities as needed.

Any new addressing scheme other than current 32-bit (IPv4) and 128-bit (IPv6) needs enhancements to the routing protocols. However, most of the widely used routing protocols today support multiple address families and addition of new addressing schemes do necessitate routing protocol enhancements to support these. Though this is a change to the existing routing protocol specifications and implementations, it is not a foundational change to the protocols operation/deployment and multiple address families can continue to co-exist.

For other addressing schemes, the free-choice addressing mechanism of New IP allows them to be used seamlessly. For any unknown addressing scheme today but to be developed in the future to meet a particular industry segment, the free-choice addressing mechanism provides the desired extensibility. Any semantic addressing and flexible length addressing schemes could be used inside New IP after they are agreed in the eco-system and standardized through a due standardization process for interoperability.

Another aspect of free-choice addressing concerns with translations needed in certain E2E scenarios. Free-choice routing and addressing does not imply the need for address mappings or translations all the time. In fact, it is the goal to enable flexible addresses without the need for such mapping steps, which add complexity to deployments and introduce the need for state. This topic is further discussed in detail in Song H. et al.

IPv4/IPv6 Host/Router Sending A Packet To A New IP Router

In this scenario as depicted in Figure 11, when the New IP edge router receives a packet from an IPv4/IPv6 interface, the IPv4/IPv6 packet will be put into a New IP packet by simply using the corresponding reserved Shipping Type (1 for IPv4 packet and 2 for IPv6 packet).

This scenario may happen when an existing network management system is used to configure a New IP network through a New IP edge node, thus enabling New IP features in that domain. This allows gradual migration of the end systems and other networks connecting to the New IP island.

Figure 11. Legacy host/routers interaction with New IP island

New IP Host/Router Sending The Packet To An IPv4/IPv6 Network

In this scenario, as depicted in Figure 12, a New IP packet is sent from a New IP router to an edge IPv4/IPv6 router of an IPv4/IPv6 network

- If the New IP packet does not contain a contract and uses IPv4/IPv6 addresses, the edge router will natively reduce the New IP packet to an IPv4/IPv6 packet by truncating the Manifest field;
- If the New IP packet does not contain a contract and does not use IPv4/IPv6 addresses, when the remote next hop (the exit edge router) is known, as usual a tunnel (e.g., GRE, IP-in-IP, or IP-in-UDP) can be used to transport the New IP packet to the remote exit edge router.
- If the New IP packet contains a contract, the full capabilities of the New IP packet would not be supported in the existing IPv4/IPv6 network, and thus the packet is dropped. Note that the addition of the Contract field in New IP packets distinguishes New IP from IPv4/IPv6 for future applications.

Figure 12. New IP host/router interaction via a legacy island

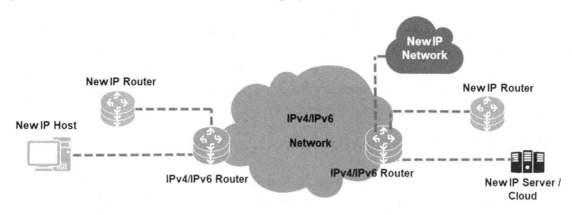

New IP Host/Router Sending A Packet To A Network Where New IP Is Partially Deployed

This scenario, as depicted in Figure 13, represents a partially upgraded IPv4/IPv6 network connected to a New IP network. With the traffic engineering technique (including SR) being used, a New IP packet can be forwarded along a specific path over which all routers support New IP (e.g., R11, R12, R13, and R14 in Figure 13). Though it is depicted in this example that all the nodes in the path have New IP support, concepts like loose path (e.g., R11, R13, and R14) or strict paths can be applicable in this scenario to make incremental deployments possible. In this example of loose path, as R12 does not support New IP, the packet has to be encapsulated and transported to node R13. For this to work, procedures similar to those defined in RFC 8663, in which MPLS-SR is carried over IP nodes, needs to be specified and further details for this scenario beyond is out of scope for this chapter. It is imperative all of the features of New IP can't be realized in those incremental deployments or in the loose path scenarios. The main

Figure 13. Green on brownfield – Partially deployed New IP in a legacy island

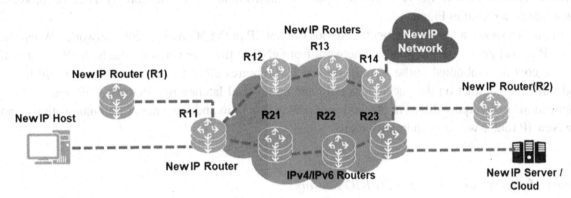

take away here is incremental deployments for new data plane technologies like New IP is possible and can be leveraged effectively even in the partial deployment scenarios.

Mobile Backhaul Transport for 5G Applications

5G systems provide and support three major features: enhanced mobile broadband (eMBB), massive machine-type communications (mMTC), and ultra-reliable low latency communications (uRLLC), and 3GPP defines the system architecture for 5G (3GPP, 2017) to be a radio access network (RAN) and a packet core network. The RAN and the packet core network are connected by a backhaul transport network.

Because of eMBB, mMTC and uRLLC, many applications have been envisioned to be enabled and supported, for example, intelligent transportation, smart factories, new immersive media (AR/VR, holographic), etc. For 5G-enabled uRLLC applications, all RAN, backhaul transport network, and the core network are required to support high reliability and low latency communications. For the purpose of this chapter, we are interested in the backhaul transport networks that connect 5G-RAN and the 5G-CORE segments. In 4G/LTE, IP/MPLS is usually deployed to connect the RAN to the Core, but IP/MPLS may not able to guarantee end-to-end high reliability and low latency (uRLLC). For 5G uRLLC

Figure 14. 3GPP Protocol Stack with New IP at UE/Backhaul

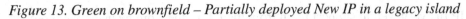

communications, New IP fits very well to support them from the UE to the Core by using the protocol stack that is depicted in Figure 14.

Figure 15 shows a few deployment scenarios of New IP in the 5G mobile core networks. When the New IP packet goes over the backhaul network from gNB to the core network, the New IP router will see the contract embodied in the New IP packet. If it requires uRLLC, the New IP router will honor and fulfil the contract on the packet loss ratio and end-to-end latency requirement. Different uRLLC applications may require different precisions of packet loss ratio and low latency communications, and the New IP router will treat them differently.

Figure 15. New IP deployment in 5G/B5G Networks

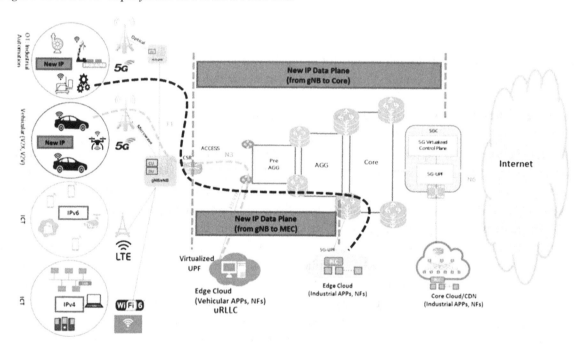

FUTURE WORK AND CONCLUSION

The research that has led to the development of "New IP" is motivated by and aimed at solving problems in Industrial machine-type communications, IP Mobile Backhaul Transport, Emerging Industry Verticals, and convergence of emerging networks. Some of these are discussed within ITU-T Network 2030. New IP has evolved from a small project to a multi-party community project with participation from many organizations throughout the world. Some network operators and industrial-manufacturing-related companies have shown their interest in New IP, some research and experimental results have been published by the ITU, IEEE, and ACM; some meetings and workshops dedicated to New IP have been held.

There are several Proof-of-Concept implementations of New IP. Experiences from those implementations are used to evolve New IP further and to make it ready for eventual commercial deployment. Standardization of New IP has yet to occur and will be one of the next steps as it matures and more experience is gained.

While New IP has come a long way since its beginning, there is still work that remains to be done. Likewise, as problems get solved, new opportunities for research open up. We conclude this chapter by providing a brief overview of some of the challenges that remain, many of which are coming into focus precisely because of the new possibilities that New IP allows for.

For example, New IP's emphasis on high-precision networking brings into focus the need for additional techniques that allow for further reduction of latency and possibility of packet loss. While New IP facilitates meeting of service level objectives, advances in buffer management and in optimization of dynamic resource allocation are still needed to make best use of resources and maximize network utilization. Advances in scheduling algorithms are needed to not only meet service level objectives but to also optimize for other considerations such as fairness. Another topic area concerns dynamic forwarding path selection for various optimization criteria and under constraints extracted from contracts, such as the need to avoid certain geographies or untrusted devices.

One area that we did not describe in greater detail concerns security. To eliminate problems such as the possibility for source address spoofing or the unauthorized tampering with contracts by nodes encountered in transit, New IP needs to be accompanied with mechanisms that allow for inherent authentication of both shipping and contract specs. For this purpose, special security contracts that carry security material as part of a packet's contract specification. Further work is needed to finalize hardware-friendly designs.

Another area in need of further research concerns the impact of New IP on how networks are programmed and interacted with by applications. The unprecedented ability to define contracts or to request dynamic service level guarantees on a per-flow and per-packet basis opens up exciting new possibilities that will enable more powerful network programming models in the future. Harnessing these capabilities will require, for example, new networking APIs to enable users and operators to take full advantage of them.

REFERENCES

Blake, S., Black, D., Carlson, M., Davies, E., Wang, Z., & Weiss, W. (1998). *An Architecture for Differentiated Services*. IETF RFC 2475.

Boman, D., Deering, S., & Hinden, R. (1999). *IPv6 Jumbograms*. IETF RFC 2675.

Brockners, F., Bhandari, S., & Mizrahi, T. (2020). *Data Fields for In-situ OAM*. IETF draft-ietf-ippm-iom-data.

Chunduri, U., Clemm, A., & Li, R. (2018). Preferred path routing – A next-generation routing framework beyond segment routing. IEEE GLOBECOM 2018.

Clemm, A., & Chunduri, U. (2019). Network-programmable operational flow profiling. *IEEE Communications Magazine, 47*(7), 72–77.

Clemm, A., & Eckert, T. (2020). High-Precision Latency Forwarding over Packet- Programmable Networks. *IEEE/IFIP Network Operations and Management Symposium (NOMS 2020)*.

Clemm, A., Torres Vega, M., Ravuri, H. K., Wauters, T., & De Turck, F. (2020). Toward truly immersive holographic-type communication: Challenges and solutions. *IEEE Communications Magazine, 58*(1), 93–99.

Deering, S. (1992). *Simple Internet Protocol (SIP) Specification*. Retrieved February 2021, from https://tools.ietf.org/html/draft-deering-sip-00

Dong, L., & Han, L. (2021). New IP Enabled In-Band Signaling for Accurate Latency Guarantee Service. *IEEE Wireless Communications and Networking Conference (WCNC 2021)*.

Dong, L., Han, L., & Li, R. (2020). Support Precise Latency for Network Based AR/VR Applications with New IP. EAI Mobimedia 2020.

Dong, L., & Li, R. (2019). In-Packet Network Coding for Effective Packet Wash and Packet Enrichment. *IEEE GLOBECOM 2019 Workshop on Future Internet Architecture, Technologies and Services for 2030 and Beyond*.

Dong, L., & Li, R. (2019). Big Packet Protocol: Advances the Internet with In-Network Services and Functions. MMTC Communications – Frontiers, 14(5).

Dong, L., & Li, R. (2020). Packet Level In-Time Guarantee: Algorithm and Theorems. IEEE GLOBECOM 2020.

Dong, L., Makhijani, K., & Li, R. (2020). Qualitative Communication Via Network Coding and New IP. In *IEEE High-Performance Switching and Routing*. HPSR.

Finn, N., Thubert, P., Varga, B., & Farkas, J. (2019). *Deterministic Networking Architecture*. IETF RFC 8655.

Fragouli, C., Boudec, J. Y. L., & Widmer, J. (2006). Network coding: An instant primer. *Computer Communication Review*, *36*(1), 63–68.

Francis, P. (1994). *Pip Header Processing*. IETF RFC 1622.

Francois, J., Clemm, A., Maintenant, V., & Tabor, S. (2020). BPP over P4: Exploring Frontiers and Limits in Programmable Packet Processing. *IEEE Global Communications Conference (GLOBECOM)*.

GAA – 5G Automotive Association. (2017). Toward fully connected vehicles: Edge computing for advanced automotive communications (White Paper).

GACIA – 5G Alliance for Connected Industries and Automation. (2020). Key 5G Use Cases and Requirements (White Paper).

GPP – 3rd Generation Partnership Project. (2017). System Architecture for 5G System, Stage 2, 3GPP TS 23.501 v2.0.1.

GPP – 3rd Generation Partnership Project. (2018). TR 22.804, Technical Specification Group Services and System Aspects, Study on Communication for Automation in Vertical Domains (Release 16).

Han, L., Qu, Y., Dong, L., & Li, R. (2020). A Framework for Bandwidth and Latency Guaranteed Service in New IP Network. *IEEE INFOCOM 2020 Workshop on New IP*.

Industrial Internet Consortium. (2017). *Smart Factory Applications in Discrete Manufacturing*. Retrieved February 2021, from https://www.iiconsortium.org/pdf/Smart_Factory_Applications_in_Discrete_Mfg_white_paper_20170222.pdf

ISO/IEC 23009-1. (2019). Information technology – Dynamic adaptive streaming over HTTP (DASH) – Part 1: Media presentation description and segment formats.

ITU-T. (2010). The international public telecommunication numbering plan (E-164).

ITU-T FG-NET2030 Focus Group on Technologies for Network 2030. (2019). New Services and Capabilities for Network 2030: Description, Technical Gap and Performance Target Analysis.

ITU-T FG-NET2030 Focus Group on Technologies for Network 2030. (2020). Gap Analysis of Network 2030 New Services, Capabilities and Use Cases (NET2030-O-039).

Jia, Y., Chen, Z., & Jiang, S. (2020). *Flexible IP: An Adaptable IP Address Structure*. IETF draft-jia-flex-ip-address-structure.

Jia, Y., Li, G., & Jiang, S. (2020). *Scenarios for Flexible Address Structure*. IETF draft-jia-scenarios-flexible-address-structure.

Li, R., Clemm, A., Chunduri, U., Dong, L., & Makhijani, K. (2018). A New Framework and Protocol for Future Networking Applications. *ACM Sigcomm Workshop on Networking for Emerging Applications and Technologies (NEAT 2018)*, 637–648.

Li, R., Makhijani, K., & Dong, L. (2020). New IP: A Data Packet Framework to Evolve the Internet. *Proceedings of IEEE HPSR 2020*.

Li, R., Makhijani, K., Yousefi, H., Westphal, C., Dong, L., Wauters, T., & De Turck, F. (2019). A Framework for Qualitative Communications Using Big Packet Protocol. *Proceedings of the 2019 ACM Sigcomm Workshop on Networking for Emerging Applications and Technologies (NEAT 2019)*, 22–28.

Schwarz, S., Preda, M., Baroncini, V., Budagavi, M., Cesar, P., Choud, P., Cohen, R., Krivokuca, M., Lasserre, S., Li, Z., Llach, J., Mammou, K., Mekuria, R., Nakagami, O., Siahaan, E., Tabatabai, A., Tourapis, A., & Zahkarchenko, V. (2019). Emerging MPEG Standards for Point Cloud Compression. *IEEE Journal on Emerging and Selected Topics in Circuits and Systems*, 9(1), 133–148.

Shenker, S., Partridge, C., & Guerin, R. (1997). *Specification of Guaranteed Quality of Service*. IETF RFC 2212.

Song, H. (2020). Adaptive Addresses for Next Generation IP Protocol in Hierarchical Networks. *IEEE 28th International Conference on Network Protocols (ICNP)*.

Tang, J., Zhang, W., Gong, X., Li, G., Yu, D., Tia, Y., Liu, B., & Zhao, L. (2020). A Flexible Hierarchical Network Architecture with Variable-Length IP Address. *IEEE Conference on Computer Communications Workshop on New IP: The Next Step*, 267-272.

Time-Sensitive Networking (TSN) Task Group. (2020). Available from https://1.ieee802.org/tsn/

Wikipedia. (2021). *Lindbergh operation*. Available from https://en.wikipedia.org/wiki/Lindbergh_operation

Wroclawski, J. (1997). *Specification of the Controlled-Load Network Element Service*. IETF RFC 2211.

Xu, X., Pan, Y., Lwin, P. P. M. Y., & Liang, X. (2011). 3D holographic display and its data transmission requirement. *2011 International Conference on Information Photonics and Optical Communications*.

ZigBee Alliance. (2015). *ZigBee Specification* (ZigBee Document 05-3474-21). Author.

ADDITIONAL READING

Albalawi, A., Westphal, C., Yousefi, H., Makhijani, K., & Garcia-Luna-Aceves, J. J. (2020). QUCO: Enhancing End-to-End Transport through Packet Trimming. In *IEEE Global Communications Conference (GLOBECOM 2020)*.

Bhat, J., & AlQahtani, S. (2021). 6G Ecosystem: Current Status and Future Perspective. IEEE Access, doi:10.1109/ACCESS.2021.3054833

Bryant, S., Chunduri, U., Eckert, T., Clemm, A. (2021). Forwarding Layer Problem Statement. IETF draft-bryant-arch-fwd-layer.

Calvanese Strinati, E., & Barbarossa, S. (2020). 6G Networks: Beyond Shannon Towards Semantic and Goal-Oriented Communications. arXiv:2011.14844.

Calvanese Strinati, E., Barbarossa, S., Gonzalez-Jimenez, J. L., Ktenas, D., Cassiau, N., Maret, L., & Dehos, C. (2020). 6G: The Next Frontier: From Holographic Messaging to Artificial Intelligence Using Subterahertz and Visible Light Communication. arXiv:2011.14844.

Cao, Y., Dai, B., Mo, Y., & Xu, Y. (2020). IQoR: An Intelligent QoS-aware Routing Mechanism with Deep Reinforcement Learning. In *Proceedings of the 45th Conference on Local Computer Networks (LCN 2020)*. IEEE.

Chen, Z., Wang, C., Li, G., Lou, Z., Jiang, S., & Galis, A. (2020). New IP Framework and Protocol for Future Applications. In *Proceedings of NOMS 2020 Network Operations and Management Symposium*, IEEE and IFIP.

Clemm, A., Zhani, M. F., & Boutaba, R. (2020). Network Management 2030: Operations and Control of Network 2030 Services. *Journal of Network and Systems Management*, 28(4), 721–750.

Dong, L., & Clemm, A. (2021). High-Precision End-to-End Latency Guarantees Using Packet Wash. In *Proceedings of 2021 International Symposium on Integrated Network Management*, IFIP and IEEE.

Dong, L., & Han, L. (2021). New IP Enabled In-Band Signaling for Accurate Latency Guarantee Service. In *IEEE Wireless Communications and Networking Conference (WCNC 2021)*, IEEE.

GAA – 5G Automotive Association. (2017). Toward fully connected vehicles: Edge computing for advanced automotive communications (White Paper).

GPP – 3rd Generation Partnership Project. (2018). TR 22.804, Technical Specification Group Services and System Aspects, Study on Communication for Automation in Vertical Domains (Release 16).

Jiang, S., Li, G., & Carpenter, B. (2020). A New Approach to a Service Oriented Internet Protocol. In *IEEE 2020 INFOCOM Workshop on New IP: The Next Step.*

King, D., Dang, J., Farrel, A. (2021). Challenges for the Internet Routing Infrastructure Introduced by Changes in Address Semantics. IETF draft-king-irtf-challenges-in-routing.

Makhijani, K., Li, R., & ElBakoury, H. (2019). Using Big Packet Protocol Framework to Support Low Latency based Large Scale Networks. In *Proceedings of the 15th International Conference on Networking and Services (ICNS 2019).*

Malcomson, S. (2016). *Splinternet: How geopolitics and commerce are fragmenting the World Wide Web.* OR Books.

Ren, S., Yu, D., Li, G., Hu, S., Tian, Y., Gong, X., & Moskowitz, R. (2019). Routing and Addressing with Length Variable IP Address. In *ACM Sigcomm 2019 Workshop on Networking for Emerging Applications and Technologies (NEAT 2019).*

Selinis, I., Wang, N., Da, B., Yu, D., & Tafazolli, R. (2020). On the Internet-scale Streaming of Holographic-type Content with Assured User Quality of Experiences. In *IFIP 2020 Networking Conference.*

Song, H., Zhang, Z., Qu, Y., & Guichard, J. (2020). Adaptive Addresses for Next Generation IP Protocol in Hierarchical Networks. *Proceedings of ICNP 2020 NIPPA Workshop.*

Torres Vega, M., Mehmli, T., van der Hooft, J., Wauters, T., & De Turck, F. (2018). Enabling Virtual Reality for the Tactile Internet: Hurdles and Opportunities. In *Proceedings of the 14th International Conference on Network and Service Management (CNSM 2018).*

Tulumello, A., Belocchi, G., Bonola, M., Pontarelli, S., & Bianchi, G. (2019). Pushing Services to the Edge Using a Stateful Programmable Dataplane. *Proceedings of the 2019 European Conference on Networks and Communications (EuCNC)*, 389-393.

Zhang, W., Gong, X., Tian, Y., & Tang, J. (2020). High Speed Route Lookup for Variable-Length IP Address. *Proceedings of ICNP 2020 NIPPA Workshop.*

KEY TERMS AND DEFINITIONS

Contract: A construct in a 'New IP' packet header that contains additional guidance for intermediate nodes along a path for how the packet should be processed. For example, a contract might contain a Service Level Objective for end-to-end latency for an in-time guarantee or a conditional directive to advise a forwarding decision depending on dynamic circumstances.

Free-Choice Addressing: A 'New IP' mechanism that allows applications to use any addressing mechanism instead of being constrained to IPv4 or IPv6 addresses as the only option.

High-Precision Communications (HPC): Communication services that are able to deliver on stringent service level guarantees (such as packet loss, end-to-end latency, and throughput) with a very high degree of accuracy, making them suitable for mission-critical applications that have no tolerance for degradations in service levels.

Holographic-Type Communications (HTC): Communication services that are able to transmit and stream holographic data across a network. HTC is characterized by its simultaneous support of very high throughput and very low latency across multiple concurrent and synchronized communications channels.

New IP: A new network layer protocol and framework that is characterized by its built-in support for Free Choice Addressing, Qualitative Communications, and Contracts.

Operational Technology (OT): A technology, including networking technology, that addresses the needs of industrial applications, such as monitoring and control of industrial equipment. Such applications require very tight performance guarantees. OT is seen as a counterpart to IT (Information Technology), used by enterprises as part of their back-end office infrastructure that has less critical performance needs.

Qualitative Communications (QC): A communication mechanism that is meant to structure packet payloads into chunks of different priority, allowing for the selective dropping of chunks instead of packets as a whole when congestion is encountered. This mechanism is useful for the implementation of a form of dynamic compression useful for latency-sensitive applications.

Service-Level Objective (SLO): A target value for a service level of a networking service that must be met. For example, SLO is used to characterize the requirement of a guaranteed service, for example, an in-time service.

Chapter 2
Collaborative Networking Towards Application– Aware Networking

Tirumaleswar Reddy Konda
McAfee, India

ABSTRACT

Application-aware networking (AAN) is a framework in which applications can discover services offered by a network and explicitly signal their flow characteristics and requirements to the network. Such framework provides network nodes with knowledge of the application flow characteristics, which enables them to apply the correct flow treatment (e.g., bind the flow to a network slice, bind the flow to a service function chaining, set appropriate quality of service marking, invoke policing and shaping rules) and provide feedback to applications accordingly. This chapter describes how an application enabled collaborative networking framework contributes to solve the encountered problems. The chapter also describes recent proposals such as the PAN (path-aware networking) framework discussed within the IRTF and the APN (application-aware networking) framework that is meant to convey application identification and its network performance in-band.

INTRODUCTION

Todays' networks, whether public or private, are challenged to support and thus deliver rapidly increasing amounts of traffic having distinct requirement on underlying networks. Also, new channels for originating and consuming rich media are deployed at a rapid pace. Pervasive video and on-demand access are becoming second nature to consumers. Applications make extensive use of rich media, placing unprecedented quality of experience (QoE) demands on the underlying networks. These trends present challenges for network planning (including traffic forecast).

In order to deliver services as expected by users and set by applications themselves, now more so than ever before, identification and differential treatment of flows are critical for the successful deployment and operation of applications, especially in the post-covid era whore more and more

DOI: 10.4018/978-1-7998-7646-5.ch002

sensitive services have to be carried over the Internet. These applications use a wide range of signaling protocols and are deployed by a diverse set of application providers that are not necessarily affiliated with the network providers across which the applications are used (i.e., application flows are forwarded). Network Operators often rely upon identification capabilities to deploy and therefore support a wide range of applications with the adequate quality. Such applications generate flows that may have specific characteristics and requirements such as bandwidth or latency constraints that can be met if made known to the network.

Historically, the identification of application flows has been accomplished using heuristics that infer flow characteristics based on transport port number ranges (e.g., TCP/25), network separation, or inspection of the flow itself. These inspection techniques include, but not limited to:

- Deep packet inspection (DPI), which matches against characteristic signatures (e.g., key string, binary sequence).
- Deep flow inspection (DFI), which analyzes statistical characteristics (e.g., packet length statistics like ratio of small packets, ratio of large packets, small payload standard deviation) and connection behavior of flows.

Each of these techniques suffers from limitations, particularly in the face of the challenges outlined previously.

Heuristic-based approaches may not be efficient and require continuous updates of application signatures. Port-based solutions suffer from port overloading and inconsistent port usage. Network separation techniques like IP sub-netting are error prone and increase network management complexity. DPI and DFI are computationally expensive, prone to error, and become more challenging with greater adoption of encrypted signaling and secured media. An additional drawback of DPI and DFI is that any insights developed at one network node are not available, or need to be recomputed, at nodes further down the application flow path.

The goal of the Application-Aware Networking (AAN) framework is to offer mechanisms that allow applications to request differential network treatment for their flows and to learn what the network can do for them while preserving flow encryption practices. The intent is for the applications to have the ability: (1) to initiate information exchanges in order to provide a more precise allocation of network resources and thus a better user experience, while ensuring security for the flow data, and for application flows to convey metadata that will be by the underlying network to provide a differentiated forwarding and process service.

The underlying logic is that applications that share information to be consumed by the networks while preserving the application-specific data privacy together with networks that are prepared in advance with applications flow treatment requirements will select and thus enable the appropriate means to offer the differentiated forwarding and traffic management behaviors matching those requirements while preserving data encryption practices end-to-end. Applications can be designed to separate the protection of the data that is intended to be consumed by involved networks and the one that is exclusively restricted to the application remote endpoint(s). Typical requirements clauses are described in Boucadair, Jacquenet & Wang (2014).

The technical realization of the proposed architecture as discussed in Section "Solutions and Recommendations" is meant to illustrate sample functional components that may be involved. Other mechanisms may be used to achieve the target architecture. This chapter does not provide implementation recommendations but sketches the ambitions to guide network transformations for the sake of more openness and flexibility to accommodate applications requirements. Doing so avoids making assumptions on the applications requirements, which may lead to "hard" and "frozen" engineering rules. Such rules are not deterministic as they rely upon heuristics that may be broken as a function of the evolution of the applications.

BACKGROUND

Evidently, media bandwidth requirements always depend on the service being used. For example, common services like e-mail require less bandwidth. By contrast, other services such as cloud-hosted virtualized desktops can place heavy per-user demands on an Internet connection, especially in deployments with high resolution desktops or multimedia. Similar reasoning applies for Augmented Reality (AR)/Virtual Reality (VR) services. Also, some tasks can be highly variable. For example, cloud storage services, whether straightforward file sharing such as Box and Dropbox or more complex document management such as SharePoint, end up using a variable amount of bandwidth. Photographs and video files can be huge and uploading these resources could consume a fair amount of the available bandwidth, creating problems such as congestion, that are especially problematic on shared connections.

Latency considerations are also very important. Some applications, such as e-mail, are latency insensitive while real-time applications require small latencies. For example voice over IP (VoIP) applications become unusable in the presence of high end-to-end latency; even short delays of a few tens of milliseconds are enough to make a poor audio experience while hundreds of milliseconds can render them almost unlistenable, with 150 milliseconds generally regarded as the limit for tolerable voice calls.

Determining the bandwidth requirements of an application, or the services that can be used given the available bandwidth might not be trivial. The availability of required bandwidth is not the only important consideration as making good use of the bandwidth is also important. An approach to overcome this is for the networks to be able to identify traffic flows in order to infer and then provide a differentiated treatment to flows based on their requirements. A common approach to identify traffic flows of applications in a network is to rely upon dedicated content-aware devices. These devices not only parse fields on the IP and transport headers but also recognize application-related information carried as application payload.

Content-awareness is mainly realized through DPI functionality, which inspects characteristic signature (e.g., key string, binary sequence), and DFI, which analyzes statistical characteristics and connection behaviors of traffic flows, to identify applications. However, there are limitations when deploying and operating these tools. IP applications, their characteristics and requirements change frequently and it takes time to complete application traffic analysis and update a signature database after a new application or release is available. This results in time windows where these new applications are unusable and identification is not accurate. In addition there are investment costs that cannot be neglected. Sometimes the cost to identify the traffic is no less than that of forwarding the traffic. Operational cost of the additional identifying nodes is also an important issue. More potential failure points and possible optical power split may affect the network quality and therefore the user experience.

Application-Aware Networking (AAN) addresses these problems by allowing networks to disseminate and advertise their capabilities and applications to request differential treatment for their flows from network (with a focus on access networks). Networks may satisfy the explicit requirements that are signaled in dedicated signaling messages or in-band. If so, appropriate actions are undertaken by the network to accommodate the application requests.

APPLICATION-AWARE NETWORKING

Problem Statement

For successful application deployment and operation, networks require some visibility into traffic (preferably without decrypting the user payload) in order to troubleshoot, plan capacity, and perform accounting and billing. This is implemented by exporting observed traffic analysis via dedicated protocols such as Internet Protocol Flow Information Export (IPFIX) and Simple Network Management Protocol (SNMP) as well as other proprietary protocols. In addition, policy-based networking can be enabled using techniques that include traffic classification, policing and shaping, providing admission control, impacting routing, and permitting passage of specific traffic (e.g., firewall functions).

These techniques, require traffic visibility, and differentiated network services, are critical in many networks. However, relying on inspection and observation limits their deployment. Reasons for this include:

- Identification based on IP addresses/prefixes is difficult to manage. The addresses may be numerous and may change; they may be dynamic, private, or otherwise not meant to be exposed and treated for identification purposes. With Content Delivery Network InterConnection (CDNI, Betrand et al., 2012), content could be served from an upstream CDN or any of a number of downstream CDNs, and it would not be possible to manually track the IP addresses of all the CDN surrogates. Even in cases where IP-based identification is possible, more granular identification of individual flows is not possible (e.g., audio vs. video vs. data).
- Classification based on TCP/UDP port numbers often result in incorrect behavior due to port number overloading, i.e. port numbers used by applications other than those claiming the port with IANA (Internet Assigned Numbered Authority). Let alone applications that use on purpose the same port number to bypass filters (e.g., DNS over HTTPS (DoH) that uses the same port number as HTTPS traffic).
- The emergence of protocols that multiplex multiple streams on the same 5-tuple (e.g., HTTP/2.0, QUIC).
- More and more traffic is encrypted, rendering DPI and DFI impossible, inefficient, or much more complex, and sometimes done at the expense of privacy or security (e.g., applications might be required to share encryption keys with an intermediary proxy performing DPI/DFI). An iconic example is the identification of the QUIC control signals.
- Visibility generally requires inspecting applications' signaling traffic. Signaling traffic may flow along a different path than the actual application data traffic. Attempts to apply differentiated network services are not effective in this scenario.
- There is a trend toward multi-pathing, allowing both signaling and data traffic to follow multiple paths, so that the entire flow is visible on any path.

- Extensions to signaling protocols and changes to how an application use them can result in false negatives or false positives during traffic inspection.
- Inspection techniques are completely non-standard, so the ability and accuracy to identify traffic varies across vendors, and different implementations are likely to give different results for the same traffic. Some users consider them as a form of man in the middle attack as they act on the traffic without explicit consent from the user and without revealing to the users what usage is made based on the gleaned data. Exposing interfaces to application to explicitly request a network treated is an important transparency effort.
- Inspection techniques that require parsing the payload of packets impact the performance due to additional processing but also impact memory due to the growing number and size of signatures to identify new protocols. Let alone that DPI devices are usually deployed in strategic nodes that concentrate most of the traffic transiting in a network. Enabling DPI in addition to additional advanced function such as mirroring, which might be required by regulatory, may exacerbate performance degradation.
- Network services leveraging heuristic-based classification have a negative effect on the application behavior by impacting its traffic while not providing explicit feedback to the application. This results in lost opportunity for the application to gain insight and adjust its operation accordingly.

Sample AAN Use Cases

This section covers a number of use cases that are relevant in the context of AAN, including the details and challenges for each use case.

Note that Li et al. (2020) follows another classification of the AAN use cases:

- Application-aware network slicing: This allows an application to be bound to a given network slice (that is, a network partition that will is customized for specific service/customer needs). This use case requires signaling means to be supported so that flows that belong a given applications are unambiguously associated with a network slice.
- Application-aware deterministic networking: A set of use cases are elaborated in (Grossman (2019). As a reminder, deterministic networking refers to the techniques that allows a network to deliver what it committed in terms of performance guarantees.
- Application-aware Service Function Chaining (SFC): This use case is meant to allow applications to control the set and the sequencing of the service functions that will be invoked when forwarding application flows within a network.

These use cases are variants of the ones listed hereafter.

Efficient Capacity Usage

Network traffic is bursty and often follows diurnal usage patterns such that there are times of day where traffic levels are at a peak, and other times of day where they are at a valley. Proper network and capacity planning should be able to cater to traffic at peak. Maintaining a network with consistent demand and usage patterns requires building capacity at a faster rate than the growth of the peak while satisfying requirements for diversity, fault tolerance and performance; this may result in traffic being forwarded, prioritized, or dropped during congestion periods .

There are several problems to consider in this contex

- Simply building enough capacity for peak usage is not always efficient and cost-effective because not all traffic needs to transit the network at the exact moment it is queued. For example, streaming video, real time communication, and head-to-head gaming need immediate access, while data synchronization with the cloud for backups, downloading software updates, or preloading content onto a CDN could be deferred to times when more capacity is available. Today, all of the traffic competes for the same capacity at the same time. Few tools exist to provide applications with the information they need to make more "intelligent" decisions on demand, and thus they mostly default to "as soon as possible".
- Queue management is not a substitute for capacity, and often a network designed for long periods of congested operation provides a poor user experience, since queue management is ultimately a method to identify which traffic should be dropped first.
- A network that is not at peak usage has "idle" capacity. A well-managed network where capacity is added in increments may observe idle capacity, for example if bandwidth is added in increments of 10G or 100G, with only a small fraction of it being used before growth catches up. This inefficiency is magnified when one considers the spare capacity designed into most networks to tolerate failures in the network with minimal traffic impact. In many cases, the "idle" capacity even at peak may be up to 50%, and at off peak, it could be much higher.
- Few networks have consistent demand and usage patterns. While the average usage may follow a rough pattern, this does not always provide for flash demands, where a large number of users are simultaneously downloading an OS update, watching the same event via streaming video, more heavily using the network during weather events like snowstorms. Typical usage patterns also do not take into account the effects of outages like shifting large volumes of traffic around in the network, and so managing these exception events either requires further spare capacity, or acknowledgement that some traffic will be dropped due to congestion, with a noticeable impact to end user experience.

Firewall Traversal and Identification of New Applications

Firewalls use application-layer gateways (ALGs) to perform policy enforcement. For example, firewalls may implement a SIP-aware ALG function that examines the SIP signaling and manages the appropriate (firewall) pinholes for the Real-Time transport Protocol (RTP) media. In particular, a firewall extracts media transport addresses, transport protocol, and port numbers from session description (potentially for each direction "in/out"), and creates dynamic mapping(s) (i.e., pinhole(s)) for audio/video media to flow through. This model does not work in the following cases:

- Session signaling is end-to-end encrypted, e.g., using TLS (Dierks & Rescorla, 2008).
- The firewall does not understand the session signaling protocols or extensions that are used by the endpoints (e.g., WebRTC as defined by Bergkvist et al., 2013 or even new Session Description Protocol (SDP) attributes)).

- Session signaling and media traverse different firewalls (e.g., signaling exits a network via one firewall whereas media exits a network via a different firewall).
- Session signaling and/or media is split across multiple paths (e.g., using Multipath TCP or Concurrent Multipath using Transfer Stream Control Transmission Protocol (CMT-SCTP)) so that a full exchange is not visible to any individual firewall.

Figure 1 illustrates an example of failure to identify new application resulting in media drop.

Figure 1. Failure to identify new application resulting in media drop

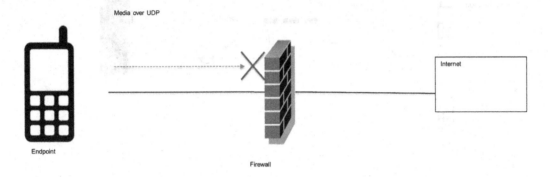

Video Bit Rate Adaptation

HAS, (HTTP Adaptive streaming, n.d) is an umbrella term for various HTTP-based streaming techniques that allow an HTTP client to switch between multiple bitrates, depending on current network conditions.

A HAS client requests and receives a manifest file that contains information about the available streams at different bit rates together with the segments of the streams. After parsing the information encoded in this manifest file, the HAS client sequentially requests the chunks listed in the manifest file, starting from the lowest bitrate stream. If the client determines that the download speed is greater than the bitrate of the segment downloaded, then it requests the next higher bitrate segments. If later it finds that the network throughput has deteriorated by observing lower downstream speed, then it will request a lower bit rate segment.

Figure 2 depicts examples of clients with high, low, and varying bandwidth and playback conditions. The problems with HAS are as listed below

- A HAS client selects the initial bitrate without knowing current network conditions. This could cause start-up delay and frame freezes while a lower bitrate chunk is being retrieved. A HAS client does not have a mechanism to learn current network conditions or to signal the flow characteristics and flow priority to the network.
- A HAS server can mark the packets appropriately but setting a DSCP codepoint has limitations. The DSCP value may not be preserved or honored over the forwarding path (especially, over the Internet) and the hosting Operating System may not allow setting DSCP values.

Figure 2. HTTP adaptive streaming

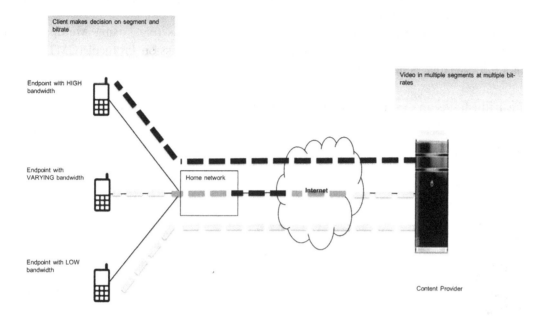

- A network provider can use DPI to prioritize one-way video streaming content but this technique is expensive and fails if the traffic is encrypted.
- An application always knows better than DPI its connectivity requirements. Content providers may need a mechanism to convey the flow characteristics and desired treatment to the network provider. Existing mechanisms and the associated limitations are:
  - A network provider can be informed of the IP addresses used by content providers to identify the traffic originating from its servers. As with any configuration, this is prone to human errors and requires timely updates when changes occur. With CDNI, content could be served either from the upstream CDN or any of a number of downstream CDNs and it is not possible to manually track the IP addresses of all the CDN surrogates. There is also no way to differentiate content that could be available in different bitrates.
  - If a HAS client is behind a NAT and a content provider uses a RESTful API (such as OneAPI, n.d.) to install differentiated QoS, the network provider has to find the pre-NAT information (that is, correlate the external IP address and port number with an internal IP address and port number as handled by the NAT). The content provider also needs to be aware of the network provider to which the client is attached and the IP address(es) of the Policy Decision Point (PDP) in the network provider to which it needs to signal the flow characteristics.

Multi-Interface Selection

Hosts are nowadays operating in multiple-interface environments. For each communication, a host with multiple interfaces needs to choose the best interface(s) to be used. Oftentimes, this decision is based on a static configuration and does not consider the link characteristics of that interface, resulting in negative user experience. The network interfaces may have different link characteristics; however, in the absence of data about the upstream and downstream characteristics of the access link, the host and/or application may select the least fit interface. The application would also benefit from knowing the end-to-end path characteristics.

In Figure 3, a typical example of a mobile device with two network interfaces, WLAN (typically a Wireless LAN (WLAN) interface) and 4G, is shown. Since applications running on the device are not aware of network conditions, they may end up using an interface with lower bandwidth, higher delay, and jitter.

Figure 3. Host in multi-interface environment

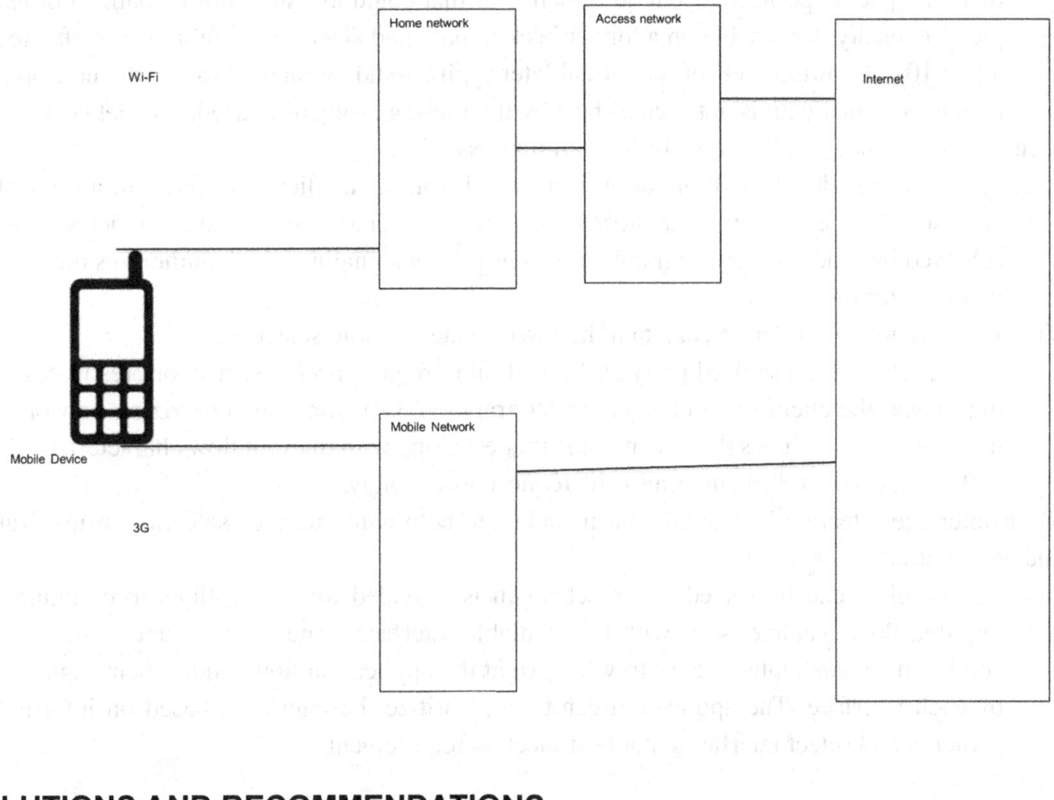

SOLUTIONS AND RECOMMENDATIONS

The goal of AAN is to offer mechanisms that allow applications to request network services for better user experience. The following techniques and solutions are proposed to address the issues described in the previous section.

- Efficient resources usage:
  - AAN is a mechanism for networks to provide applications with information about network resource availability, so that individual applications can manage their demands. Such demand management will help to adequately handle the traffic by redirecting some of the demand to off-peak, and has an analog in the power industry where demand-based pricing or smart grid

technology signals devices that use a large amount of power so that they can be intelligent about their demands and reduce the burden on the available capacity of the electrical grid.

○ Similarly, AAN provides a means for applications to communicate their required performance requirements. This information can be used by the network to determine the best way to deliver the requested service (within its scope).

○ Provide a means for "below best effort" or scavenger class data transmission so that traffic marked as scavenger will be carried in periods of no congestion, but may be discarded during periods of congestion due to either peak usage or outages.

○ The solution can be used in conjunction with techniques like Traffic Engineering (Auduche et al., 2001) and Segment Routing (Filsfils et al., 2018) in order to provide capacity for traffic that has specific performance requirements, or that could use sub-optimal paths. For example, if capacity is available on a longer backup path and since some traffic is not affected by a few 10s of milliseconds of additional latency, it should be marked to use the non-optimal path even if that path is not seen as best by the routing protocol in use in the network.

- Identification of new applications for firewall traversal:

○ The host provides the authorization it received from an application server, to a server that is trusted by the network to authorize flows and associated actions (e.g., policies). This is achieved by sending a cryptographic token as part of signaling which authorizes the firewall mapping for the media.

- Video Adaptation: use client metadata to help with video bit rate selection:

○ A HAS client can use third party authorization to request access to network resources. At a high level, the client first obtains a cryptographic token from the authorizing network element, and then includes that token in the request along with relevant flow characteristics. The ISP validates the token and grants the request accordingly.

- Multi-interface selection by using client metadata to help with interface selection, prioritization and aggregation:

○ The problem can be solved if a mechanism is provided for applications to communicate required flow characteristics with the available interfaces, and to know about the network conditions of each interface, or to what extent the application flow requirements can be met by each interface. The application can then prioritize the interfaces based on information gathered and select interfaces that best meet its requirements.

The remaining of the section covers the details of the AAN approach and describes some of the techniques and protocols that it uses.

High Level AAN Approach

In the previous sections the need of communication between applications and networks was identified. In order to provide an implementable solution, the following requirements have to be considered:

- Identify the protocol(s) that best fit to solve the problem(s) depending on the use case, the application that is going to use it, the connectivity and the network type jointly with the trust level present in a running environment.

- Provide the specification on how the protocol(s) is/are used to solve the problem(s) and describe the required extension(s).

Applications continue to grow in number, type, and diversity. They are running on a multitude of host types and OSes and following different delivery models (native, web, cloud). Many use peer-to-peer (P2P) or client-server models and open standard protocols for establishing connectivity.

Applications run in diverse environments such as enterprises, home networks, home automation environments, factory floors, hospital setting, and utilities. Devices hosting the applications may connect to the network in diverse ways, using different technologies, having multiple interfaces to the same or different network devices, connecting over diverse technologies such as cable, digital subscriber line (DSL), fiber to the home (FTTH), cellular, and wireless,. In order to operate in these environments, some applications already run lightweight client-server network protocols. One example of such protocols is the Session Traversal Utilities for NAT (STUN) to discover public addresses when behind NAT devices or (Rosenberg et al., 2008). Another is the Port Control Protocol (PCP) detailed in the work of Wing et al. (2013) and used to create explicit port forwarding rules.

The AAN solution requires a protocol to be used for signaling the application flow characteristics to the network and getting feedback from the network. At the time of writing this book, few existing protocols with new extensions are being considered:

1. Client-server network protocol: PCP with flow metadata extensions. . Handles both TCP and UDP flows, but also other transport protocols (SCTP).
2. On-path application protocol: STUN with flow metadata extensions between hosts. Handles UDP flows (media streams).
3. On-path network protocol: RSVP (Braden et al., 1997) with flow metadata extensions. Handles all TCP, UDP, and raw IP flows. RSPV is limited to controlled environments.

Note that Li et al. (2020) suggests a framework that falls under AAN and in which application identification and required network performance are carried in the packet itself. A new encapsulation is used for this purpose. Such supplied information is mean to facilitate performing application-level traffic steering and network resource adjustment as a function of the conveyed requirements.

Flow Metadata Processing

In AAN, applications signal the flow characteristics and service required. The network responds back to applications with the result of processing the request.

Depending on its nature and needs, the application may request different services (e.g., bandwidth accounting, report of available bandwidth within service class, notification on certain events). As the application requirements change, the flow characteristics communicated to the network may be revised. When network state changes or when different events occur, if needed, network elements can send updates.

For example, at startup, an application may send bandwidth, delay and jitter requirements. The network performs bandwidth accounting against the matching service class and sends a response to the application. In another example, an application requests the bandwidth available for a class with certain delay and jitter guarantees. The network responds and the application adjusts the rate to the available bandwidth. If the available bandwidth changes, the application is notified and can read just the bit-rate.

Port Control Protocol (PCP)

Port Control Protocol (PCP, Wing et al., 2013a) provides a mechanism to describe a flow to the network. The primary driver for PCP has been creating port mappings on NAT and firewall devices. When doing this, PCP pushes flow information from the host into the network (specifically to the network's NAT or firewall device), and receives information back from the network (from the NAT for firewall device). PCP allows applications to create mappings from an external IP address, protocol, and port to an internal IP address, protocol, and port. These mappings are required for successful inbound communications destined to machines located behind a NAT or a firewall. Figure 4 illustrates the PCP messages exchanged to create a mapping on the PCP controlled device.

Figure 4. PCP Generic client-server interaction

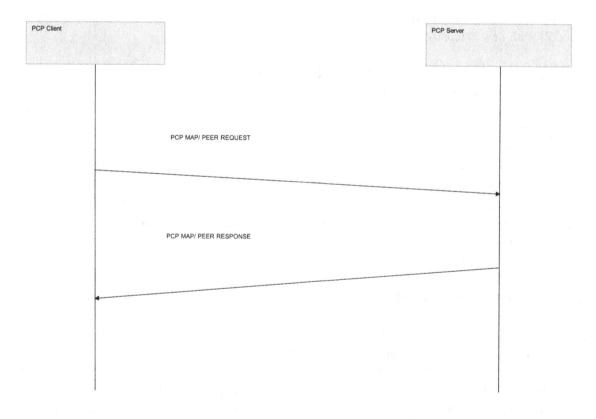

This simple bi-directional communication of flow information using PCP makes PCP a very suitable candidate to signal other interesting flow information, useful for AAN, from a client to a server.

PCP FLOWDATA Option

The FLOWDATA option (Wing et al., 2013b) described in this document allows a host to signal the bi-directional characteristics of a flow to its PCP server. A few examples are minimum and maximum bandwidth, delay and loss tolerance for upstream direction. Downstream direction characteristics can also be signaled.

After signaling, the PCP server determines if it can accommodate that flow, making any configuration changes if necessary to accommodate the flow, and returns information in the FLOWDATA option indicating its ability to accommodate the described flow.

Usage and Processing

A host may want to indicate to the network the priority of a flow after the flow has been established (typical if the host is operating as a client) or before the flow has been established (typical if the host is operating as a server). Both of these are supported and depicted in the following diagrams.

Figure 5. Client initiated connection before flow prioritization

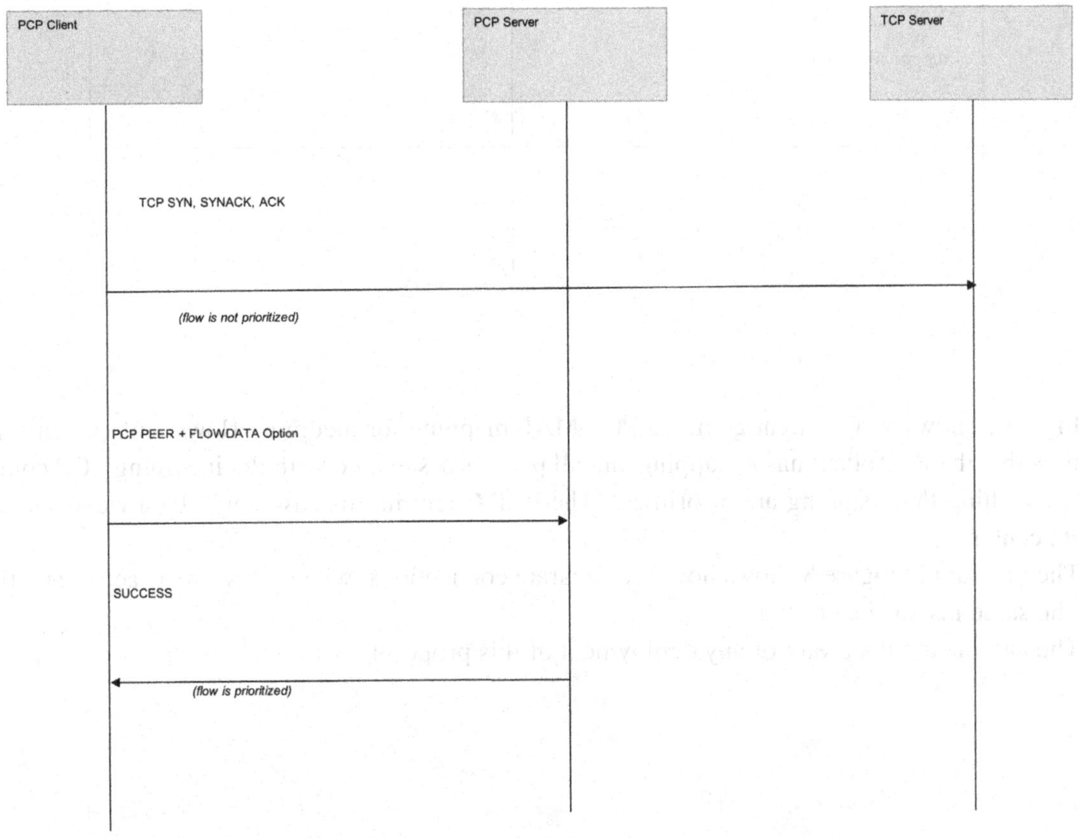

Figure 5 shows a connection being first established and then the flow being prioritized. This allows for the fastest connection setup time with the server.

The diagram in Figure 6 shows first the client asking the network to prioritize a flow, then establishing a flow. This is useful if the priority of the flow is more important than establishing the flow quickly.

Figure 6. Client initiated connection after flow prioritization

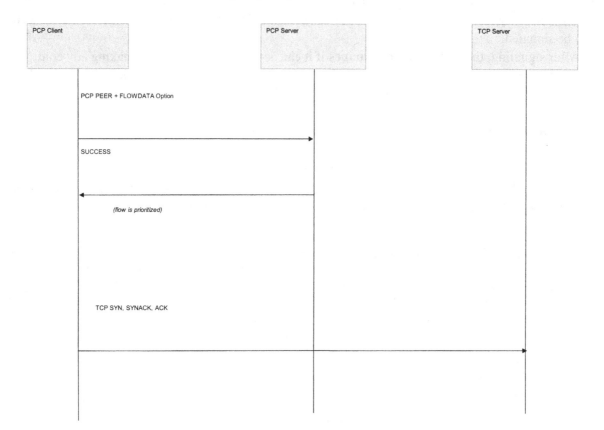

Figure 7 shows a PCP client getting a PCP MAP mapping for incoming flows with priority. This ensures that the PCP client has a mapping and all packets associated with the incoming TCP connections matching that mapping are prioritized. The PCP Client in this case could be a video server in a data center

The diagram in Figure 8 shows how two separate connections, where only one is active at a time, use the same instance identifier.

The authors are not aware of any deployment of this proposal.

Figure 7. Server initiated connection after flow prioritization

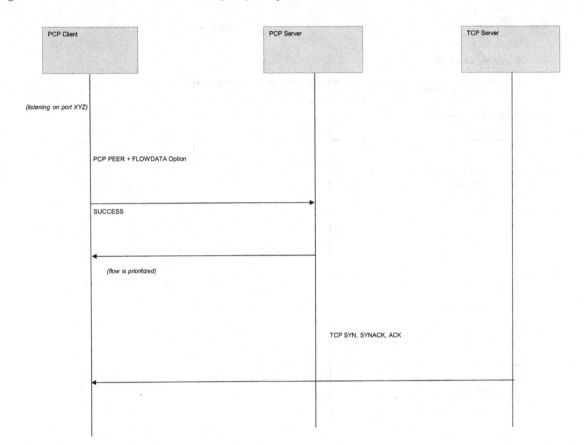

Traversal Using Relay NAT (TURN)

Traversal Using Relay NAT, TURN, (Mahy et al, 2020) is a protocol that is often used to improve the connectivity of P2P applications. By providing a relay service, TURN ensures that a connection can be established even when one or both sides are incapable of a direct P2P connection. A client can choose to signal flow characteristics of a relay channel to the TURN server, so that the TURN server is aware of the flow characteristics of the channel. The TURN server can potentially signal back to the client that it can (fully or partially) accommodate the flow. This sort of signaling will be useful for long-lived flows such as media streams or WebRTC data channels, traversing through the TURN server. The TURN server can further communicate the flow information to a number of on-path devices in its network using a Policy Decision Point (e.g., a SDN controller). Thus, the network hosting the TURN server can accommodate the flow. With this mechanism, a TURN client can request the TURN server to provide certain characteristics for the relayed channel on both legs (client-to-server, server-to-peer).

Figure 9 depicts a TURN client signaling the desired flow characteristics to a TURN server over the TURN ChannelBind request.

Figure 8. Two server connections with same instance ID

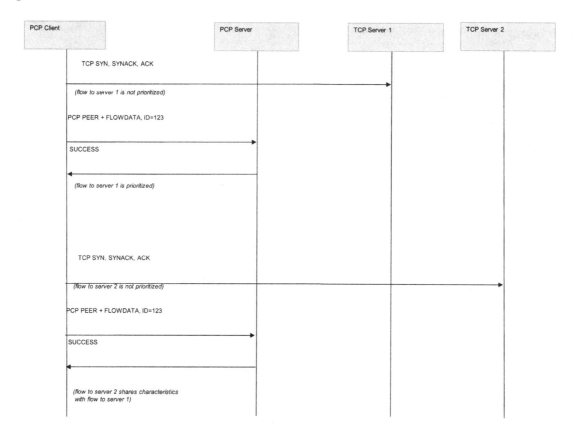

AAN SDN

One of the goals of SDN is to define a set of techniques, existing or new, that allows for easy automation and offer means to interact with network resources dynamically in order to ensure optimized resource usage. A comprehensive overview of the SDN landscape and the functional taxonomy of the techniques used can be found in the work of Boucadair & Jacquenet (2014).

There are several proposals on how the network can be programmed with flow information in order to enable different service policies (e.g., traffic prioritization). Typically this involves a controller that collects flow information by receiving copies of flow data packets or performing DPI if on-path. Many flows today are very dynamic, time-bound (short lived), encrypted and asymmetric, and require different priorities depending on network conditions, direction, time of the day, and other factors. Therefore, this means that controller examination of the flow packets cannot be used successfully to infer flow and metadata information (Penno et al., 2014).

Figure 9. Message diagram, operating a server

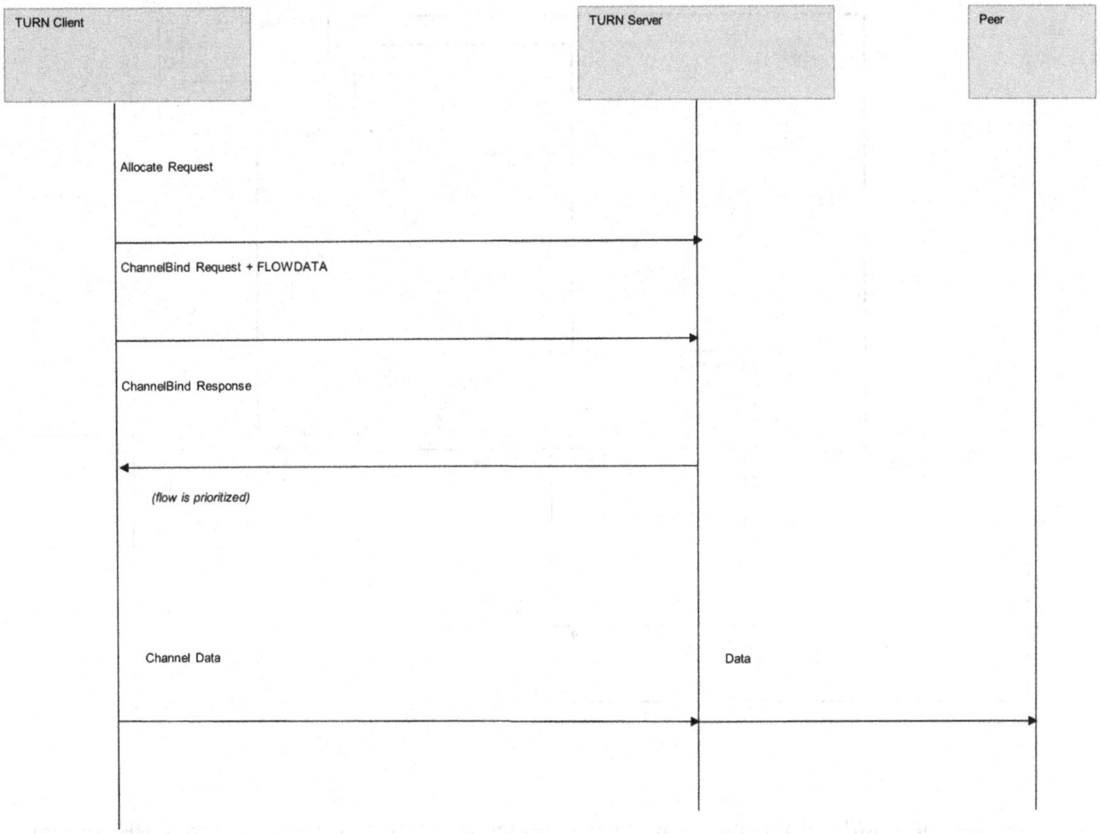

Architecture

In order to automate the resource allocation and usage, AAN proposes the following SDN architecture and message flow as illustrated in Figure 10 (Penno et al., 2014)

- Applications running on the end points (e.g., User Equipment, Data Center Servers, CPE routers) signal associated metadata to Network Elements. This can be achieved by using PCP (Wing et al. 2013a) with the PCP Flow Extension (Wing et al., 2013b) which allows a PCP Client to signal flow characteristics to the network, and the network to signal its ability to accommodate that flow back to the host.
- The Policy Decision Point (PDP, Yavatkar et al., 2000) manages resources and triggers configuration operations based on applicable policies. To achieve this, a protocol that has built-in primitives for reliable real-time messages and that, ideally, shares information about network availability between the network device and the PDP is required. REST, Extensible Messaging and Presence Protocol (XMPP) (Saint-Andre, 2011) or similar protocols are good candidates.
- PDP installs the flows in routers or switches and assigns them a series of actions, modify flow actions, collect statistics, or (more importantly) extend the provisioning of these flows end-to-end. PCP with THIRD_PARTY option, NETCONF (Enns et al., 2011) or any similar protocols.

Figure 10. ACEN signaling flow with SDN

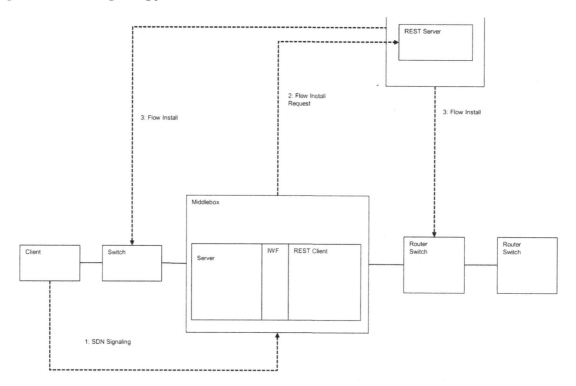

In Figure 10, the middlebox is any flow-aware device (e.g., edge router, switch, CPE router). Some advantages of the AAN architecture are:

- Host driven: The host/ application, which has the information required to make the correct service request is responsible for communicating the flow metadata according to the application needs. The approach works with encrypted and multi-party flows.
- Network Authorization: When network access control is required, the host gets authorization from the Application Server trusted by the network in order to install flows and associated actions (e.g., policies). The Application Server could be deployed in a third party network. This is important for networks that do not trust the host.
- Immediate incremental value for endpoints and applications in an end-to-edge manner: once a AAN CPE router is installed, applications could signal flow characteristics to the network for both directions and benefit from traffic prioritization, firewall pinholes and other services without other changes to the network.

Message Flow

When an end host installs a flow entry in the middlebox through a PCP message, a call is made to the PDP. This message carries the following information:

- Match condition elements, including source/destination IP, source/destination port, Layer 4 Protocol, VLAN Id.
- Metadata conveyed in PCP FLOWDATA option.
- Lifetime in the PCP response which is mapped, for example, to the OpenFlow's idle_timeout (Openflow, 2014). This way, the PCP client is aware when the flow entry is removed.

The PDP uses any relevant protocol, e.g., NETCONF (Enns et al., 2011) or OpenFlow (Openflow, 2014) to add, delete and modify flows and their metadata. For example, an OpenFlow controller could get the information of configured queues and their properties. The OpenFlow controller either associates the flow with appropriate queue or instructs the OpenFlow-enabled network device to rewrite the DiffServ Code Point (DSCP) bits for the flow based on the metadata conveyed in the REST message.

When an application-driven flow times out or is explicitly deleted, if required, a REST API call is generated and the controller is notified. This allows the PDP to delete the flow from other devices in the network.

The PDP could also decide on its own to remove the installed flow. In this case, a PCP unsolicited response is sent to the PCP Client owner of such flow.

Deployment Considerations and Challenges

There are a few challenges with enabling the AAN technique. The selection and extensions of the signaling protocol(s) is one. In many cases, the use of an existing protocol limits the deployment to the use cases that were targeted by the initial protocol specification.

The other challenge with the signaling protocol is path congruency with the associated flow (path-coupled vs. path-decoupled). With client-server signaling protocols (out of band signaling), the application needs to contact the server on a node that is on the forwarding path. In some cases, e.g., dual homing or when a server is not directly connected, this may not always be possible.

Path-coupled (also known as "on-path") protocols try to guarantee that signaling messages follow the same path as the data packets. They typically do this by encapsulating the messages they initiate with the same header as the data packets. Intermediate nodes are enabled to inspect and intercept these packets. In addition they probe routing or forwarding with a locally created dummy data packet and then pre-route the packet accordingly. One example is RSVP. Path congruency with data flow is ensured as long as all devices on path are enabled. But this is rarely the case and the reality is that these types of protocols are only deployed today in small controlled environments, never in the public Internet.

In-band signaling protocols carry the signaling messages in packets that are, for the purpose of routing or switching, identical with the data packets. STUN is one such protocol. There are no congruency issues with these types of protocols. However, as in the case of on-path signaling, they open up security holes.

A network device receives application messages either because they are addressed to the device or the device is configured to intercept them. Most requests need to be processed and some create state. A request message will consume network resources such as CPU, memory, hardware entries required for classification, and bandwidth. To prevent denial of service attacks, it is important that non-authenticated and non-authorized messages are dropped early in the processing chain. Also, network devices should allow operator selection for the type of processing (e.g., process, drop or forward only).

There are cases where a signaling message specifies flow data for either or both directions of the flow and it is possible for network devices to receive conflicting flow data for a given direction of the flow. Appropriate conflict resolution is important in this case and needs to be clearly specified by the standards.

As discussed in Trammel (2020), an important challenge for AAN is the trustworthiness of discovered network information, including path properties (Enghardt & Kraehenbuehl (2020)). Absent reliable mechanisms, information disseminated by networks for use by applications can be intercepted and manipulated by misbehaving nodes. Means to authenticate path property information must be supported.

From a deployment standpoint, and as adequately discussed in Trammel (2020), an open question is "how can the incentives of network operators and end-users be aligned to realize the vision of path aware networking, and how can the transition from current ("path-oblivious") to path-aware networking be managed?".

FUTURE RESEARCH DIRECTIONS

Some of the challenges to deploy AAN are listed below:

- Formalize how practically an application can determine its network requirements and how it decides which parts can be managed at the application layer (e.g., application-specific congestion control) and those require a cooperation from the underlying network.
- Update applications to support AAN.
- Update some network elements to support AAN.
- Support from browsers and OSes to provide appropriate AAN API to applications.
- Provide UIs to tweak the priority of flows on an endpoint.

AAN must consider security and privacy implications to provide protection again false claims, leakage of private information, and unwarranted differentiated treatment of flows. For example, the network may need to validate application provided flow information before using it to provide differential treatment of the application's flows. Similarly, an application may need assurance of confidentiality protection before providing potentially sensitive information.

A basic security requirement of AAN is that there must be a mechanism for mutual authentication between the application signaling flow information and the network entity that uses this flow information to provide differential treatment for flows as well as feedback to applications about such treatment. Without this, the solution is open for attacks with fake applications falsely claiming to be legitimate applications that require special treatment, i.e., the network infrastructure is at risk of being misused. Should the network entity be spoofed, applications could be misled that the network has accommodated the requested flow characteristics.

AAN is being actively pursued within the IETF standardization community and has gathered momentum and interest from service providers, vendors, and application providers.

CONCLUSION

The goal of AAN is to provide a framework for programmable networks that allows applications to seek for collaboration by typically signaling flow characteristics that help network providers to unambiguously identify and therefore tweak the treatment of associated application flows.

This is a very important step in moving towards a model where a host, based on application use, can demand appropriate treatment anywhere and anytime. This will also serve as an important step for network monetization by means of differentiated connectivity offered and guaranteed to applications. This collaborative approach is also important the overall QoE will be enhanced at each layer.

REFERENCES

Awduche, D., Berger, L., Gan, D., Li, T., Srinivasan, V., & Swallow, G. (2001). RSVP-TE: Extensions to RSVP for LSP Tunnels. *IETF*. Retrieved December 09, 2020, from https://tools.ietf.org/html/rfc3209

Bergkvist, A., Burnett, D. C., Jennings, C., & Narayanan, A. (2013). WebRTC 1.0: Real-time Communication Between Browsers. *World Wide Web Consortium*. Retrieved December 09, 2020, from www.w3.org/TR/webrtc/

Bertrand, G., Stephan, E., Burbridge, T., Eardley, P., Ma, K., & Watson, G. (2012). Use Cases for Content Delivery Network Interconnection. *IETF*. Retrieved December 09, 2020, from https://tools.ietf.org/html/rfc6770

Boucadair, M., & Jacquenet, C. (2014). Software-Defined Networking: A Perspective from within a Service Provider Environment. *IETF*. Retrieved December 09, 2020, from https://tools.ietf.org/html/rfc7149

Boucadair, M., Jacquenet, C., & Wang, N. (2014). IP Connectivity Provisioning Profile (CPP*). IETF*. Retrieved December 09, 2020, from https://tools.ietf.org/html/rfc7297

Braden, R., Zhang, L., Herzog, S., Berson, S., & Jamin, S. (1997). Resource ReSerVation Protocol (RSVP). *IETF*. Retrieved December 09, 2020, from https://tools.ietf.org/html/rfc2205

Dierks, T., & Rescorla, E. (2008). The Transport Layer Security (TLS) Protocol Version 1.2. *IETF*. Retrieved December 09, 2020, from https://tools.ietf.org/html/rfc5246

Enghardt, T., & Kraehenbuehl, C. (2020). *IRTF*. Retrieved October 07, 2020, from https://datatracker.ietf.org/doc/draft-irtf-panrg-path-properties/

Enns, R., Bjorklund, M., Schoenwaelder, J., & Bierman, A. (2011). Network Configuration Protocol (NETCONF). *IETF*. Retrieved December 09, 2020, from https://tools.ietf.org/html/rfc6241

Filsfils, C., Previdi, S., Decraene, B., Litkowski, S., Horneffer, H., Milojevic, I., Shakir, R., Ytti, S., Henderickx, W., Tantsura, J., & Crabbe, E. (2018). Segment Routing Architecture. *IETF*. Retrieved December 09, 2020, from https://tools.ietf.org/html/rfc8402

Grossman, E. (2019). Deterministic Networking Use Cases. *IETF*. Retrieved October 07, 2020, from https://www.rfc-editor.org/info/rfc8578

HTTP Adaptive Streaming. (n.d.). *Wikipedia*. Retrieved December 09, 2020, from https://en.wikipedia.org/wiki/Adaptive_bitrate_streaming

Li, Z., Peng, S., Voyer, D., Xie, C., Liu, P., Qin, Z., Ebisawa, K., Previdi, S., & Guichard. J. (n.d.). Application-aware Networking (APN) Framework. *IETF*. Retrieved October 07, 2020, from https://datatracker.ietf.org/doc/draft-li-apn-framework/

Mahy, R., Matthews, P., & Rosenberg, J. (2020). Traversal Using Relays around NAT (TURN): Relay Extensions to Session Traversal Utilities for NAT (STUN). *IETF*. Retrieved December 09, 2020, from https://tools.ietf.org/html/rfc8656

OneAPI. (n.d.). *GSM Association*. Retrieved December 09, 2020, from https://www.gsma.com/identity/api-exchange

OpenFlow. (2014). OpenFlow Switch Specification Version 1.4. *OpenNetworking Foundation*. Retrieved December 09, 2020, from http://opennetworking.wpengine.com/wp-content/uploads/2014/10/openflow-spec-v1.4.0.pdf

Penno, R., Reddy, T., Boucadair, M., & Wing, D. (2013). Application Enabled SDN (A-SDN). *IETF*. Retrieved December 09, 2020, from https://tools.ietf.org/html/draft-penno-pcp-asdn-00

Rosenberg, J., Mahy, R., & Wing, D. (2008). Session Traversal Utilities for NAT (STUN). *IETF*. Retrieved December 09, 2020, from https://tools.ietf.org/html/rfc5389

Saint-Andre, P. (2011). Extensible Messaging and Presence Protocol (XMPP): Core. *IETF*. Retrieved December 09, 2020, from https://tools.ietf.org/html/rfc6120

Trammell, B. (2020). Current Open Questions in Path Aware Networking. *IRTF*. Retrieved October 07, 2020, from https://datatracker.ietf.org/doc/draft-irtf-panrg-questions/

Wing, D., Cheshire, S., Boucadair, M., Penno, R., & Selkirk, P. (2013). Port Control Protocol (PCP). *IETF*. Retrieved December 09, 2020, from https://tools.ietf.org/html/rfc6887

Wing, D., Penno, R., Reddy, T., & Selkirk, P. (2013). PCP Flowdata Option. *IETF*. Retrieved December 09, 2020, from https://tools.ietf.org/html/draft-wing-pcp-flowdata-00

Yavatkar, R., Pendarakis, D., & Guerin, R. (2000). A Framework for Policy-based Admission Control. *IETF*. Retrieved December 09, 2020, from https://tools.ietf.org/html/rfc2753

KEY TERMS AND DEFINITIONS

ALG: Application-level gateway is a security component deployed on firewall or NAT boxes to allow customized traversal filters in order to support address and/ or port translation for certain application layer protocols.

CDN: Content delivery (or distribution) network is a set of servers deployed in multiple data centers across the internet in order to serve content to end users while also offering high performance and high availability.

DFI: Deep flow inspection is a packet filtering technique that analyzes statistical characteristics like packet lengths, ratio of large packets and small payload standard deviation, and connection behavior of flows, to determine the actions to be applied to application flow or session packets (e.g., classify, mark, redirect, block, drop).

DPI: Deep packet inspection is another form of computer network packet filtering that examines the packet content to decide on the actions to be taken on the packets or for the purpose of collecting statistical information.

PAN: Path-aware networking describes an architecture where endpoints can discover the properties of paths they use and how these endpoints react to these properties that affects the transmission of their flows. As such, PAN covers both the discovery of path properties and path selection by an endpoint.

PCP: Port control protocol is a protocol that allows hosts to control how the incoming IP packets are translated and forwarded by an upstream router that performs Network Address Translation (NAT) or packet filtering (firewall, typically).

SDN: Software-defined networking is a network architecture that allows network administrators to manage network services through abstraction of lower-level functionality. This is achieved through mechanisms that allow decoupling of the control and forwarding planes.

Chapter 3
Content Delivery Networks:
On the Path Towards Secure Cloud–Native Platforms at the Edge

Yannick Le Louédec
Orange S.A., France

Frédéric Fieau
Orange S.A., France

Gaëlle Yven
Orange S.A., France

Patrick Fleming
Orange S.A., France

Valéry Bastide
Orange S.A., France

Ivan Froger
Orange S.A., France

Yiping Chen
Orange S.A., France

Lahcene Haddak
Orange S.A., France

Gwenaëlle Delsart
Orange S.A., France

Nathalie Labidurie Omnes
Orange S.A., France

Mateusz Dzida
Orange S.A., France

Vincent Thiebaut
Orange S.A., France

ABSTRACT

This chapter provides an overview on the recent advances and perspectives on content delivery networks (CDNs). After a reminder on the definition and core features of CDNs, the first section highlights their importance with quantitative illustrations. The second section identifies the various types of CDNs which have been deployed to address different markets. The growth of the CDNs has been driven primarily by video streaming. Next to media content, CDNs have evolved to deliver always more demanding social networks and applications. Security solutions are now fully integrated into CDNs and marketed as flagship products. The third, fourth, and fifth sections outline the challenges and technical evolutions of the CDNs to keep up with their customers' hunger for media content, web performance, and security. The sixth section focuses on the convergence of CDNs and clouds. The seventh section reviews the status and perspectives of different approaches for using multiple CDNs. The last section presents the current positioning and future perspectives of the CDNs in the mobile domain.

DOI: 10.4018/978-1-7998-7646-5.ch003

INTRODUCTION

A Content Delivery Network (CDN) is a set of servers specifically designed and deployed over one or several networks for optimizing the storage and delivery of content (e.g., web objects, audiovisual live or on-demand content, large files). From a high-level and functional perspective (Figure 1) the main components of a CDN include: request routing servers that handle and redirect content requests towards cache node servers, cache node servers (a.k.a., CDN delivery servers) that deliver the requested content, content ingestion servers that ingest content in the CDN, analytics and accounting servers, and management servers.

Figure 1. CDN Functional Model

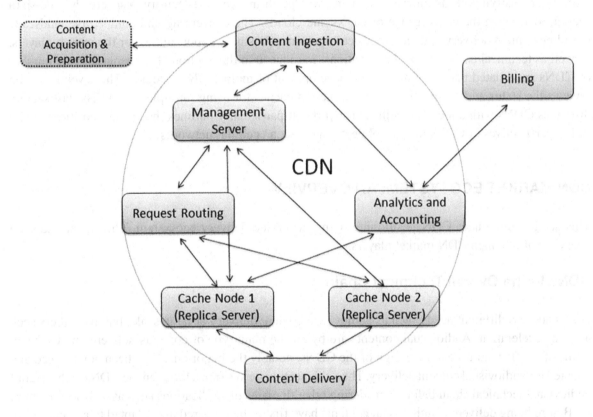

CDNs are expected to handle 72% of the global Internet traffic by 2022 while it handled up to 56% in 2017 (Cisco, 2019a). The outstanding development of CDNs since the late 90s has been driven by their intrinsic strengths: reliability, scalability, improved service latency thereby leading to a better quality of experience for end users, and better network resource utilization leading to a reduction of congestion risks and costs of interconnection links.

From a business perspective, there is an increasing trend for "commoditization" in the CDN industry with strong market competition and price decline. In such challenging context, CDNs must evolve to meet the (new) requirements of the supported applications. CDN players concentrate their technical and business strategies on fast evolving and promising areas such as web acceleration, web security, "serverless" edge computing, convergence with clouds, multi-CDN systems, or IoT and mobile networks.

This chapter aims to provide an overview of these recent advances and perspectives on CDNs.

This chapter is organized as follows. First, the introduction sets the context. After a short reminder of the definition, role and core features of CDNs, this section highlights their importance in today's Internet and provides some quantitative illustrations. The second section identifies the different types of CDNs currently deployed and the market segments targeted. The growth of CDNs has been driven primarily by video streaming in the last decade. Next to media content, CDNs have evolved to deliver content from always more demanding websites, social networks, and web applications. Besides, web security solutions are now fully integrated into CDNs' infrastructures and marketed as flagship products. The third, fourth, and fifth sections outline the challenges and technical evolutions of CDNs to keep up with the intensifying needs for media content, web performance, and security, respectively. The sixth section focuses on the convergence of CDNs and clouds. The converging and competitive landscape of online content delivery and cloud services opens new business opportunities for the market players, as well as technical challenges and innovations, introduced in this section. The increase in the number of CDNs and related players stimulate the development of multi-CDN strategies. The seventh section reviews the status and perspectives of different approaches for using multiple CDNs. The last section discusses CDNs with a focus on cellular networks. It particularly outlines the current positioning and future perspectives of CDNs in the mobile domain (a.k.a., cellular networks).

CDN MARKET ECOSYSTEM: AN OVERVIEW

This section introduces CDN positioning within a service delivery ecosystem. Then, it provides an overview of the main CDN market players.

CDNs In the Overall Technical Chain

CDNs address different needs such as audiovisual content delivery at large scale, but also others such as web acceleration. Audiovisual contents are by far the main type of contents delivered by CDNs in terms of traffic volume. So the design of the CDNs, notably the major ones, has been conditioned and adapted for audiovisual content delivery. Thus, this section makes first a focus on the CDNs in the overall audiovisual technical chain before considering other domains of applications such as web acceleration.

Before being delivered, audiovisual contents have first to be prepared and adapted to accommodate the bandwidth constraints of the underlay networks on which they have to be distributed.

In the technical chains specifically implemented by Telecom operators (a.k.a., Telcos) for their audiovisual service offers, this preparation is achieved by either a Television (TV) head-end or a Content Management System (CMS). The TV head-end component is devoted to live content and, thus, faces strong real-time constraints: video compression must be achieved on-the-fly. Conversely, CMS components are devoted to on-demand content; real-time constraints are released, and video compression may possibly be more efficient.

Audiovisual contents can be destined to a wide variety of devices, ranging from Smartphones to Ultra High Definition TV screens (e.g., 4K, 8K). The screen size, the available storage capacity, but also the supported encoding formats, Digital Rights Management (DRM) and delivery protocols have to be taken into account in the content preparation. As such, each content may have to be translated into several media files.

Last but not least, content preparation must deal with rights management. Some contents, such as royalty-free User-Generated Contents (UGCs), may be free of specific requirements. In contrast "premium" contents may have to be encrypted to be protected from unauthorized viewing. The access to these contents might also be protected, for example by means of URL signing (van Brandenburg, Leung, & Sorber, 2020), and restricted to a specific geographical area (called geo-blocking). In addition, content right-owners may demand requirements on concurrent stream limitations for a given household. These may apply, for example, when the household subscribed to an audiovisual service offer giving access to a catalog of contents on all registered devices and access networks. The CDN plays a major role in fulfilling a part of these requirements.

Once prepared, audiovisual contents are ready to be delivered. Different solutions, hereby designated as "content delivery components", exist to achieve the content delivery, such as CDNs and IP multicast, as well as others that are outside the scope of this chapter, like the Peer-to-Peer (P2P) protocols. Content delivery components can co-exist in the same networks; they can be combined too. IP multicast is the most efficient way to distribute the same content simultaneously to many receivers, be they end-user devices (e.g., for live content delivery) or even CDN delivery servers (e.g., for feeding them with a content catalog). Yet, IP multicast requires specific protocols that are not supported by all end-user devices or activated in all networks. Moreover, it does not suit all types of audiovisual content services and content profiles (e.g., massive catalog of low popularity contents as made available on online social networks). These issues have favored the development of CDNs in the 2000s and 2010s, in parallel to IP multicast. Contents are ingested in the selected or combined set of content delivery components; this means they are made available to these components. In the case where several media files have been prepared for a given content, all these media files must be made available for the end-users, who will pick one of them as a function of various criteria, such as access conditions.

Contents have also to be referenced and exposed, for instance, through an Electronic Program Guide (EPG), web pages or applications that are browsed by end users. In any case, end-users' browsing and content selection is achieved by interacting with a service platform. The service platform satisfies a given end-user's request for a given content item by triggering the delivery by one content delivery component (or by a combination of content delivery components) to this end-user's terminal device of the adequate media file, selected in accordance to the context, which may include the characteristics of the requesting device, user-end's preferences and available bandwidth, among others.

Whatever the content delivery components (or a combination thereof), the media files can be delivered by means of various protocols. The incumbent options consisting in streaming content with the Real Time Streaming Protocol (RTSP) (Stiemerling, Schulzrinne, Rao, Lanphier, & Westerlund, 2016) or in achieving content download or progressive download with the HyperText Transfer Protocol (HTTP) are getting outdated. Instead, ABR (Adaptive Bit Rate) streaming (DASH, 2019) is a disruptive solution, by cutting each content into segments and providing each segment with different qualities or bitrates. Segments are delivered using HTTP. ABR dynamically adapts the format to the available bandwidth and to the terminal device's status (e.g., amount of resources available to decode and display video frames). Now supported by any device, adaptive streaming is an efficient solution letting the device itself select the adequate media file (Bentaleb, Taani, Begen, Timmermer, & Zimmermann, 2018).

The variation of the consumed bandwidth always includes a peak during the busiest hours. Network (including CDN) dimensioning is usually based on these peak hours. It is important to notice that CDN servers - placed close to end users by design - and which have been provisioned before the peak hours may lead to significant improvements.

The CDN Market Players

There are mainly four types of players that are involved in the content delivery chain: CDN vendors, CDN operators, content service providers, and Telcos.

- CDN vendors develop content delivery products and market them to other actors, such as content service providers or telecom operators. Broadpeak©, Varnish Software AB, Qwilt© are positioned on this segment for example (BroadPeak, 2020a);
- CDN operators mainly sell services over their own managed CDNs. CDN operators may also sell a licensed CDN to Telcos. In this case, the Telco has to manage the CDN services provided by a CDN operator solution. Akamai Technologies, Inc. and Limelight Networks, Inc. are examples of CDN operators. Currently (2020), the main CDN operators provide a worldwide coverage for all types of media contents and web resources. They have been negotiating with telecom operators to deploy their CDN servers close to end-users, thereby offering a better Quality of Experience (QoE) and reducing the delivery costs of Telcos.
- Content service providers present a catalog of contents to end-users, ranging from premium content to royalty-free content, representing a large part of the Internet traffic. The largest content service providers, such as Google© with YouTube©, manage their own CDN for their own usage. To reduce costs and improve end-user experience, some of them partner with Internet Service Providers (ISP) to deploy their own CDN delivery servers and deliver their contents from within the ISPs' networks, such as Google with Google caches or Netflix with Open Connect (Netflix 2020).
- Telcos offer network access bundled with audiovisual services. Having the network under their control, they can deploy CDN delivery servers at different hierarchical levels as close to end-users as possible and exploit specific network features like IP multicast, offering the highest quality content with the lowest delay so that the perceived quality of experience is likely enhanced.

Telcos may play different business roles, such as:

- CDN operator role: by deploying a CDN within their networks, either for their own purpose so as to provide "Business-to-Consumer" (B2C) services, or with the objective of reselling CDN services to third companies, which are, thus, called "Business-to-Business-to-Consumer" (B2B2C) services;
- Content service provider role: by deploying a complete content delivery chain to expose, prepare, and deliver its own content. Telcos may further contract with third parties' content service providers to either broaden their content service portfolio or resell a content service.

Finally, it is worth mentioning that this section focuses mainly on the CDN technical chain and market ecosystem for audiovisual content delivery as it represents the majority of the traffic carried by today's CDNs. But, next to audiovisual content services, CDN operators have significantly expanded into CDN-based web acceleration and web security services. This trend is expected to continue to grow and to represent a significant part of the CDN players' revenues in the short to long terms.

CDN AND MEDIA CONTENT DELIVERY SERVICES

This section outlines the challenges and technical evolutions to keep up with the intensifying needs for media content delivery, respectively on the Over-The-Top (OTT) and Internet Protocol Television (IPTV) content delivery markets.

Challenges and Technical Evolutions of OTT Content Delivery

ABR streaming has become a *de facto* standard in the OTT market of live and on-demand audiovisual content streaming applications, mostly supported by CDNs. Yet, this solution faces two major challenges, namely cost and end-to-end live latency:

- The economic burden on CDNs to deliver OTT streaming with ABR technology is destined to increase. The main reasons are: (1) increasing number of terminal devices consuming online audiovisual content, (2) improvements of content resolution, quality, and consequently the increase of the bitrate of the media content streams requested and played by these devices (e.g., 4K, HDR, high frame rates), (3) unicast delivery mode, forcing CDNs to support one delivery stream per user session, and (4) diversity of terminal devices, audiences and network conditions, which mandate to package, store and deliver multiple redundant yet separated combinations of ABR media formats (e.g., MPEG Dynamic Adaptive Streaming over HTTP (DASH), HTTP Live Streaming (HLS)), media components (e.g., audio, video, subtitles), DRM systems, codecs (e.g., AAC (ISO/IEC 14496-3), AVC (ISO/IEC 14496-10), HEVC (ISO/IEC 23008-2)), and ABR representations (resolution and quality levels), jeopardizing CDN delivery efficiency.
- The end-to-end live latency, a.k.a., "glass-to-glass" latency (i.e., from content capture to display) is significantly higher on OTT live streaming with ABR technology - typically 30 to 45 seconds -, than on IPTV or traditional broadcast delivery modes such as Satellite, Cable, and Digital Terrestrial Television (DTT) - commonly 3 to 12 seconds -. This has a direct impact on the bottom line, particularly in OTT live sport streaming market. Limelight's State of Online Video report highlights findings from a series of consumer surveys about online viewing habits and opinions (Limelight, 2019); its latest version (2019) reports that *"57.7 percent [of all respondents] said they would be more likely to watch live sports online if the stream was not delayed from the broadcast"*; and this raises to two thirds among people aged 26-45.

To address these challenges Apple© and Microsoft© launched in 2017 an initiative to standardize a Common Media Application Format (CMAF) at MPEG, backed by other major OTT companies (e.g., Akamai©, Google©, Netflix©). The standard was published in 2018 and revised in 2020 (CMAF, 2020).

The first objective for specifying CMAF was to gain efficiency in content packaging, storage and delivery by having one single media format regardless of the nature and capabilities of the OTT device. The adopted approach has consisted in favoring existing technologies, notably the fragmented MP4 container - derived from ISO's Base Media File format - as container format, the support of the MPEG codec suite AVC, HEVC, and AAC as the baseline for interoperability, and the MPEG Common Encryption (MPEG-CENC, ISO/IEC 23001-7). CMAF is basically a standard container. It does not aim at replacing DASH and HLS, but instead at handling media segments that can be referenced by both DASH manifests and HLS playlists. This allows to manage media files usable by both DASH and HLS, and thus to reduce significantly workflow complexity and costs in content production/packaging. Likewise, for content delivery, using a single CMAF source for several delivery protocols allows to reach higher cache hit ratios, hence a better usage of network and storage resources in the CDNs. Besides, MPEG-CENC allows a given content to be encrypted once and decrypted by multiple playback devices even if they use different DRM systems.

The second objective in specifying CMAF was to ensure low latency in live ABR streaming. The CMAF's low-latency mode (LL-CMAF) relies on the combined exploitation of CMAF chunks, Chunked Transfer Encoding (CTE) data transfer mechanism, and components specifically configured all along the end-to-end live content streaming chain:

- CMAF allows to split the CMAF segments into smaller sub-structures called CMAF chunks. CMAF chunks are addressable entities composed of a header and media samples. So the downstream transfer of the first encoded CMAF chunks of a given CMAF segment can start right away, piece by piece ("on the fly"), before that segment is entirely available.
- The CTE data transfer mechanism of HTTP 1.1 (Fielding, & Reschke, 2014) is used to proceed with this transfer downstream, based upon pieces called HTTP chunks: each HTTP chunk contains a CMAF chunk.
- The components specifically configured all along the end-to-end live content streaming chain include in particular the intermediate CDN servers and the video players used by the terminal devices. They must all support this CTE data transfer mechanism to enable the low-latency mode. In addition the players supporting LL-CMAF must accurately estimate path bandwidth and jitter, and carefully manage their buffering behavior to maintain a smooth low-latency experience.

It is worth mentioning that the legacy ABR players can request and handle CMAF content, but at the granularity of CMAF segments only. So they can exploit CMAF-based media content but with standard (i.e., lower) ABR streaming latency performances.

LL-CMAF allows to deliver ABR streaming content with a live latency from 3 to 9 seconds, and thus lowers the gap with IPTV's live latency, which is typically in the range of 3 to 7 seconds.

Challenges and Technical Evolutions of IPTV Content Delivery

IPTV is confronted to an always increasing competition with OTT streaming. IPTV targets TV sets connected to Telcos' Set-Top Boxes (STBs) mainly, while OTT streaming addresses all screens whatever their connection (e.g., computers, smart TVs, smartphones, tablets, etc.) as well as media streaming boxes and sticks (e.g., Google Chromecast©, Apple TV ©, etc.).

Besides, OTT streaming relies on a single ABR technology regardless of the screen technology. Thus, the developments are more efficient and cost-effective; all the more since they are backed by Internet giants (Apple, Google, etc.). All this favors the growth of an OTT streaming ecosystem, fertile both in terms of innovations and business development.

In contrast, IPTV imposes the co-existence of two separate yet redundant types of operations and technologies: the first one for live services (e.g., IP multicast and MPEG-TS for content delivery, Conditional Access Systems (CAS) for security), and the second one for on-demand applications such as Video on Demand (VoD) (e.g., ABR streaming for content delivery, DRM for security). Moreover, the integration between both types to support advanced features such as (n)PVR (network Personal Video Recorder), trick modes (e.g., pause and fast-forward viewing), as well as innovative monetization models like Dynamic Ad Insertion (DAI), is complex.

The incumbent advantages of IPTV over OTT streaming, namely latency and scalability, tend to shrink, as a consequence of the technical innovations related to OTT streaming, including the aforementioned CMAF, and the financial investments by Internet giants on the OTT streaming markets (Google/Youtube, Netflix, Amazon Prime Video, etc.).

Subsequently, the leading suppliers in the streaming ecosystem tend to converge on OTT technologies and markets. The advanced features they develop for the ABR technology, such as DAI and security, are evolving fast. Meanwhile, MPEG-TS, the IPTV format, is quite frozen, and the number of IPTV STB SoC (System on Chip) and vendors is decreasing. As an illustration, ABI Research forecasts a 5% decline of the STB SoC Market between 2018 and 2023, driven by *"cord-cutters having a wide variety of streaming services and video streaming boxes that don't require a set-top box"* (ABI, 2020).

Initiatives are engaged to design a next-generation IPTV, so as to keep its competitiveness against OTT streaming. These include making IPTV format and technologies converge with OTT, in order to take benefit from the fast evolution and cost-efficiency of the OTT streaming technologies.

Multicast-ABR (mABR) fits into this approach. mABR consists in leveraging the IP multicast technology to distribute content in ABR format over a managed Telco network. As illustrated in Figure 2 a typical mABR architecture involves a "Multicast Server" and a set of "Multicast Gateways". The former ingests content in ABR format and transmits it over the Telco's multicast network. The latter can be deployed either in the Telco's network edge, or more probably in the home gateways, STBs, or terminal devices; they receive the IP multicast packets, extract the ABR-formatted content, to store it temporarily so that it is available to the ABR content playback function(s) located downstream (or within the same device if multicast gateway and playback functions are co-located).

Also, Figure 2 presents the three following functions: content preparation, content hosting, and content playback. Content preparation gathers encoding, encryption, and packaging operations. Content hosting ingests prepared content and makes it available for being distributed over the Telco network. Content playback achieves un-packaging, decryption and decoding operations, so that content can be displayed on the terminal device's screen. All these three functions manipulate content in ABR format only, they are unrelated to the IP multicast-network.

Therefore, mABR allows to exploit on the one hand the efficiency of the IPTV multicast-based distribution scheme, and on the other hand the fast-evolving OTT streaming technologies, with all ABR's advantages, to implement the high-value functions (e.g., codecs, content protection, Ad-Insertion) at the first stages ("headend") and last stages (next to or in the terminal device) of the content delivery chain. In addition to becoming up-to-date and more flexible, this next generation of IPTV is expected to provide cost-efficiency by removing redundancies between the IPTV Live and VoD technologies, and by replacing IPTV security and chipsets in the STBs by cheaper ones from the OTT ecosystem.

In addition, mABR combined with LL-CMAF improves live latency performances up to being comparable with traditional IPTV services in Telcos' managed networks. Traditional IPTV service latency is typically in the order of 3 to 7 seconds. mABR deployed over managed Telco networks with

Figure 2. Adaptive Media Streaming over IP Multicast. Simplified Reference Architecture. (DVB, 2020)

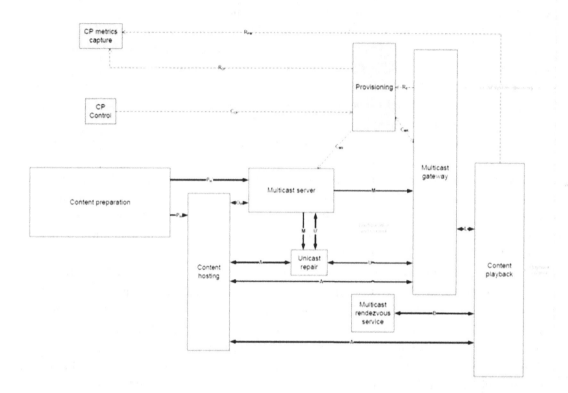

small-buffer players should allow to reach a ~7 second latency on average, down to 3 seconds with LL-CMAF (Tombes, 2019).

The primary business case for mABR is linear content delivery using IP multicast. And the CDN technology shall complement IP multicast in this content delivery architecture. First, the aforementioned content hosting function shall deliver unicast traffic, and the unicast repair function (used to retransmit multicast transport objects that have not been correctly received) as well. So traffic forwarding can be optimized with a CDN to improve scalability and reliability. Second, mABR could be used typically to deliver the most popular linear services, while the less popular ones could be delivered by means of unicast ABR sessions from the CDN. Third, linear services can be enhanced with advanced features, such as DAI, which may require the support of the CDN to pre-position content assets at or close to the terminal devices.

The concept of mABR was developed a few years ago, with Broadpeak's nanoCDN technology. Other companies like Akamai have designed their own solutions since then. It is now attracting a growing interest, notably of IPTV operators, and a standardization work started within DVB, which published successive releases of reference architecture on 2018 and 2020 (DVB, 2018; DVB, 2020; ETSI, 2020).

CDN and WEB ACCELERATION SERVICES

Beyond media delivery, CDN providers are also major players of the web acceleration market. Their distributed platforms support both media and web acceleration services.

Figure 3 presents a reference architecture of the typical core components of a web acceleration platform. It is composed of three segments: acquisition segment, transport segment, and termination segment. This reference basis is exclusively used here as an informational model aimed at spatially decomposing the processing functions executed by the web acceleration systems. In an operational environment, specific systems may comprise only certain segments of this reference architecture. Similarly, functions assigned to certain segments can be merged into common indivisible components (implementations, in particular).

Figure 3. Reference Architecture of Web Acceleration Platform

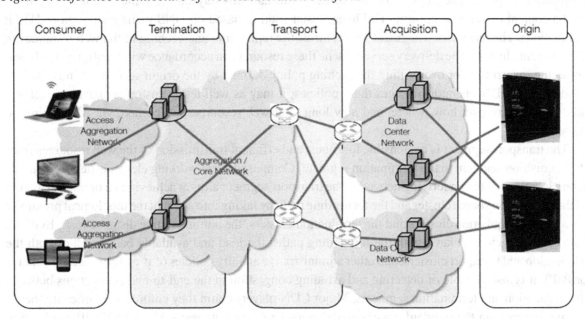

The acquisition segment is responsible for the efficient and secured acquisition of web resources from the originating (authoritative) servers. It protects the origin servers against capacity overload by controlling, limiting, and balancing the number of requests and bandwidth reaching the origin servers (and inferred links). Clusters of acquisition servers can be deployed across various datacenters, possibly close to origin servers. Therefore the acquisition process can be optimized by using a selection of multiple parallel acquisition nodes, taking into account their topological proximity to the origin servers. The acquisition segment can also have the capability to pre-fetch web resources (i.e., to acquire web resources even before they are requested by the end-users) according to predefined policies or on demand, in order to lower the pressure on the origin servers and to improve the latency perceived by the end-users. Besides, it may produce a static version of the dynamic web resources, and deliver this static version when the origin servers are unavailable. It can detect and cache access error messages when origin servers are unavailable, or produce error messages on its own. The acquisition segment secures the origin servers by acting as a reverse proxy for them. Transport protocols with encryption capabilities (e.g., TLS1.3, HTTPS, HTTP/2.0, QUIC/HTTP/3) secure the transmission of the acquired web resources (Bishop, 2020). Specific daemons can also be deployed on the origin servers' infrastructure to create outbound-only connections to the acquisition servers, which avoids the exposure of the IP addresses assigned to origin servers and guarantees all acquisition requests originate from the acquisition segment.

The termination segment is responsible for fast and scalable delivery of the web resources to the end-users. It is composed of termination clusters of delivery servers located at the edge of the operator's network. These servers shall support basic and advanced protocols (e.g., HTTP/1.1, HTTP/2, QUIC/HTTP/3) as well as advanced congestion control mechanisms (at the transport layer, typically). TCP efficiency is optimized either thanks to a selective usage of TCP stacks and parameters, or by using proprietary TCP (optimized) implementations. The same principles apply for UDP-based content delivery with QUIC/HTTP/3, in particular. The termination segment controls and balances the load among the termination clusters. The implementation of these mechanisms rely on the same techniques used for media content delivery (e.g., intra- and inter-cluster routing based on DNS name resolution or HTTP redirection). The termination segment also controls the replication and caching of the web resources in the different clusters. The delivery servers cache these resources in accordance with configured policies: enforcing, overruling, or overwriting the caching policy defined by the origin servers set in the HTTP headers. The CDN operator manages these policies; it may as well let its customers have a direct and advanced control over how, where, and how long their web resources are cached, via APIs acting on these policies.

The transport segment is responsible for robust and efficient transmission of the web resources from the acquisition segment to the termination segment. Composed of networking elements deployed at different locations of the underlying networks, the transport segment aims at achieving an optimal selection of the acquisition source cluster and the forwarding path, by taking into account the topological proximity between the acquisition clusters and the termination clusters, the administrative distance (e.g., BGP AS path) and latency associated with the forwarding paths, the load and available bandwidth of both the acquisition and transport clusters, and other administrative affinity policies (e.g. avoid a specific country or PoP). It is also capable of detecting and avoiding congestion in the end-to-end connections between the acquisition and termination segments. Major CDN players claim they enforce a significantly better routing policy than the standard (BGP-based) Internet routing policies: e.g., Akamai's IP Application Accelerator© (IPA) (Akamai, 2020a) and Cloudflare's Argo Smart Routing© (Cloudflare, 2020a).

Specific features can be set up on any of these three core components of the web acceleration platform, such as web resource compression and adaptation functions. Compression functions can be applied on text and graphical resources depending on the platform's load and the configured policies. Adaptation functions are meant to optimize text resources with various techniques (e.g., HTML injection, text merging, splitting, "minification"), as well as to adapt the size and resolution of the graphical resources in accordance with the capabilities of the end users' terminal devices.

In addition to these three core components, a web acceleration platform generally encompasses two complementary elements, namely a DNS infrastructure and a monitoring/analytics platform:

- The DNS part has a direct contribution to the end-to-end performance of the web acceleration systems. Therefore, the major CDN players manage their own DNS infrastructure with particular care. Cloudflare© claims that it ensures *"DNS lookup speed of 11ms on average and worldwide DNS propagation in less than 5 seconds"* (Cloudflare, 2020b). At the time of writing (October

2020), DNS performance benchmark tools available online like "www.dnsperf.com" (Dnsperf, 2020) report results consistent with this statement, with a typical raw performance of 7.81 ms in Europe and 13.29 ms worldwide.

- CDN operators manage monitoring and analytics platforms to get and share with their customers insights on how the web resources and the aforementioned CDN core components and features behave and impact the end-to-end delivery performances. Customers can visualize Real-User Monitoring metrics, advanced real-time analytics on dashboards, and they can also select and direct log streams towards their own performance management tools to continuously improve configurations, cost savings and end-user experience. They may also possibly emulate or test what-if scenarios to assess performances in case of sudden traffic bursts or in the event of security attacks of a great magnitude, for example.

CDN and Security Services

The primary business of CDN operators consists in deploying and managing servers in hundreds to thousands of locations, and in providing content delivery and web acceleration services for many customers, including critical public administrations, leading e-commerce companies, as well as major media and entertainment corporations. As already mentioned, their traffic accounts for 52 percent of the whole Internet traffic in 2017, and up to 72 percent in 2022 (Cisco, 2019a). Needless to say that this essential role of these infrastructures makes them as privileged targets of security attacks. Cloudflare reports its "*42 Tbps network blocks an average of 72 billion threats per day, including some of the largest DDoS attacks in history*" (Cloudflare, 2020c). Akamai provides on its web portal detailed and regularly updated information on the state of web attacks (Akamai, 2020b; Akamai, 2020c; Akamai, 2020d). For example, for the week of October 19 to October 26, 2020, Akamai reports having observed among the most common web attack types 110+ Millions SQL Injection attacks, 18+ Millions Cross-Site Scripting attacks, 3.89 Millions Remote File Inclusion, 145K PHP Injection attacks (Akamai, 2020e).

Therefore, the CDN operators have continuously developed technical expertise and solutions to counter security threats. By the way, they have inherent advantages for being legitimate players in the domain of web security. First they support a significant proportion of the whole Internet traffic. So they are well positioned to get insights on security attacks, as claimed by Akamai: "*Interacting with 130 terabytes of data, 1 billion devices, and 100+ million IP addresses every day gives us unmatched intelligence and insights to protect your business 24/7/365*" (Akamai, 2020f). Second, their infrastructures, distributed at large scale, are intrinsically well suited to mitigate many common attacks with anti-DDoS (Distributed Denial-of-Service) protection and Web Application Firewall (WAF). Quoting Cloudflare: their "*network is 15x bigger than the largest DDoS attack ever recorded, allowing all internet assets on Cloudflare's network to withstand even massive DDoS attacks*" (Cloudflare, 2020d).

So, given the size and strategic importance of the cyber security market, CDN operators have logically target this market as one of their core business with dedicated service portfolios, gaining noteworthy commercial success. As an illustration, Akamai's revenues for the second quarter ended June 30, 2020 was $795 million, up to 13 percent year-over-year, including $259 million (hence one third) from Cloud Security Solutions, up to 27 percent year-over-year (Akamai, 2020g).

The CDN operators mainly address the web application security. The most common vulnerabilities and attacks in this domain are SQL injection, Cross-Site Scripting, (D)DoS attacks, Cross-Site Request Forgery, memory corruption, buffer overflow, and data breach.

The security solutions proposed by the CDN operators own to five categories:

- Solutions to secure the access to applications.
- Solutions to secure the network infrastructure.
- Application security solutions.
- Security hub.
- Security solutions for specific applications.

The first category encompasses the solutions aimed at securing the access to applications. CDN players provide solutions to simplify and secure the access of users to critical applications, including multi-cloud applications (e.g., for online payment, for remote workforce to access enterprise applications). In this domain, traditional access solutions based on VPNs (Virtual Private Networks) come up against issues as users move to cloud-based applications and to mobile devices. Solutions proposed by CDN players include the replacement of VPNs by alternatives that interwork with Identity Providers, such as Azure Active Directory (AAD) or Amazon AWS Identity and Access Management (IAM). Certain CDN players have even expanded into the market of Identity and Access Management, to provide user authentication as a service (e.g., SSO authentication, two-factor authentication, multi-factor authentication), like Akamai with its Cloud Identity solution (Akamai, 2020h; Akamai, 2020i).

The second category (solutions to secure the network infrastructure) includes notably SSL/TLS, Layer 3/4 DDoS and DNS security solutions. Unsurprisingly, as Internet web sites move onto encrypted traffic sessions, CDNs support SSL/TLS protection with all related features to simplify and speed up SSL/TLS session setup: certificate management operations, TLS configuration, support of advanced cipher suites, client authentication, HTTP Strict Transport Security (HSTS), Encrypted Server Name Indicator, etc. At the network and transport layers, CDNs may provide DDoS protection for any TCP/UDP application by relying, for example, on reverse proxy and/or BGP. Concerning DNS, as mentioned in the previous section, the major CDN players manage their own DNS infrastructure, empowered with DNSSEC, and provide protection against DNS attacks such as DNS cache poisoning, on-path attacks, or DNS spoofing. CDN players have also been actively supporting the development of DNS over HTTPS (DoH), its standardization at the IETF (Hoffman, & McManus, 2018) and its deployment in operational networks. DoH consists in carrying the DNS messages between a client (e.g. a browser) and a DNS resolver in an encrypted fashion, over HTTPS. As an illustration, DoH is now activated by default in the USA on Mozilla Firefox browsers and their DoH queries are sent by default to DNS servers operated by the CDN operator CloudFlare (Mozilla, 2020a).

The third category (application security solutions) comprises WAF, Layer 7 DDoS Protection, bot management, and rate limiting solutions. WAF protects applicative servers and web applications against a wide range of suspicious behaviors and known vulnerabilities, like SQL injection, Cross-Site Scripting, and Cross-Site Request Forgery. A WAF inspects each HTTP request against managed rules, attack signatures, predefined template policies for well-known standard applications, accept-lists/discard-lists of URLs or IPs, as well as other possible inputs or databases, such as IP reputation databases and IP geolocation databases. It allows the legitimate requests to pass through; and it blocks, challenges or logs the suspicious ones. The CDN provider regularly updates the managed rules on the WAF as new security threats emerge, to protect the applications. Layer 7 DDoS protection systems exploit various strategies against DDoS attacks, including for example blocking or limiting the traffic per source IP address, exploiting the anycast routing to absorb the attack, and forwarding the legitimate requests to their destinations, resulting in a CAPTCHA challenge. Bot management solutions aim at detecting bots, distinguishing the good ones (e.g., bots from search engines) and mitigating the malicious ones (e.g., marketing click frauds, content scraping, content spams, credit card stuffing, credential stuffing, application DDoS). Rate limiting solutions allows to protect applications from attacks such as DDoS attacks by controlling, blocking or conditioning the traffic using configurable templates and thresholds.

In practical deployments, WAF, anti-DDoS, bot management, and rate limiting solutions work in concert. For example, the first three ones may rely on the fourth ones to counter some attack vectors. More generally, the CDN operators monitor the traffic in their networks to get insights on the evolution of the web security threats. They deploy specific automated systems for continuously aggregating data about the state of their networks, the traffic and the attacks, for analyzing such state with advanced heuristics, behavioral analytics and machine learning techniques, in order to generate alerts and counter-measures consisting in manual or automated updates of the configuration policies of the above-listed security solutions (e.g., WAF managed rules, rate limiters' thresholds, bot management configuration). These solutions are, so to say, interacting with each other over an always learning network. Our fourth category, the security hub, designates this set of automated data aggregation, analysis and alerting systems which achieves the integration with and between the above-listed security solutions.

The fifth category corresponds to the security solutions that certain CDN operators develop for some specific applications, such as IoT applications or Web APIs. For example, Akamai proposes its IoT Edge Cloud products "IoT Edge Connect©" and "OTA Updates©" to securely connect millions of IoT devices and vehicles, for real-time data collection and messaging, as well as for over-the-air updates (Akamai, 2020j). Akamai also proposes an "API Gateway" product which converts all of its CDN edge servers into API gateways. The customers' APIs and servers benefit from the CDN's scalability and security. Some API related processes such as API authentication, authorization, and quota management are managed at the edge. And APIs can be "supercharged" with the other security and web acceleration products of Akamai portfolio (Akamai, 2020k).

CONVERGENCE BETWEEN CDNS AND CLOUDS

CDN operators have been deploying geographically distributed servers to extend their footprint while locating them closer to the end-users. Other OTT actors like Amazon and Microsoft have been providing cloud-based "X-as–a-Service" (XaaS) offers where "X" includes Infrastructure, Platform, and Software. These offers were usually supported by centralized infrastructures, mainly data centers connected somewhere to the Internet. Today, CDN and Cloud services/infrastructures tend to converge, to address intersecting markets, and to adopt common technical principles, such as cloud-native principles.

The CNCF (Cloud Native Computing Foundation) provides a definition of cloud-native: "*Cloud native technologies empower organizations to build and run scalable applications in modern, dynamic environments such as public, private, and hybrid clouds.*" (CNCF, 2019). CNCF refers directly to technologies like containers, service meshes, micro-services, immutable infrastructures, and declarative APIs. We refer in this section to "cloud-native" as a general software development approach that tends to enhance platform capabilities, manageability, and efficiency by means of continuous integration and deployment processes, as well as elastic cloud resources, which can be instantiated on demand.

A first evolution of the CDN operators towards the cloud-native approach has been to deploy a part of their CDN building blocks over cloud infrastructures. More precisely, this trend has been concerning in priority the control plane of CDNs (e.g., request routing and monitoring operations), functions requiring large storage (e.g., origin servers, log management platforms), and other value-added features (e.g., content preparation/encoding or multi-CDN selection as a service (NS1, 2020a; Akamai, 2020l) rather than the data plane of CDNs (e.g., content caching and delivery). From a business perspective, this trend brings stimulating opportunities to both the cloud service providers and their customers: for the former, the development of Infrastructure-as-a-Service (IaaS) or Platform-as-a-Service (PaaS) designs, thereby addressing the needs of content providers and content delivery service providers, and for the latter, the optimization of their infrastructure and data analytics.

Then, a new generation of CDN operators appeared in the last decade to push back the CDN and Cloud boundaries. These players, like Cloudflare© and Fastly©, have adopted cloud-native principles as ground-up technical foundations, and positioned from the outset their CDN infrastructures as edge computing platforms.

This is exemplified by the development of "serverless" edge computing offerings such as Cloudflare Workers, Fastly Compute@Edge©, and Akamai EdgeWorkers©. "Serverless" does not mean absence of servers. "Serverless" refers to a cloud computing execution model in which the cloud provider dynamically manages the allocation of machine resources to its customers' applications. These CDN operators have observed that they will probably never address exactly every possible use case expected by their customers, even if they keep on extending the features to be supported by their infrastructures. So the idea that lies beneath these offerings is to make the edge network programmable and to provide their customers with the capability to write and run their own micro-services directly on the edge computing platform. The role of the CDN operator thus consists in deploying servers in hundreds or thousands of locations all over the world. It is then up to the customers to decide how to use these resources, just like they do with (centralized) Cloud resources.

An infinity of use cases can then be envisioned, resulting in the reduction of the amount of traffic forwarded to origin servers, a faster end-user experience, and an increased reliability: managing at the edge user redirection logic, load balancing with tailored affinity algorithms, custom logic in HTTP caching rules to improve cache hit ratios, geolocation logics for delivering location-specific content, search autocomplete, URL decoding, tailored WAF rules, authorizations and crypto functions, allow-lists and block-lists, API gateways, A/B testing, dynamic content assembly, promotional campaigns, personalized video experiences via dynamic manifest manipulation and ad insertion, etc.

These edge computing platforms open to the customers must meet strong requirements with regards to security (a micro-service written and run by a given customer must affect neither the platform nor the other customers, in particular), scalability and efficiency (be able to deploy each customer's micro-service in hundreds to thousands of locations), as well as acceptance (the technical framework must be relatively easy to master and manage by the customers' web programmers).

For its Worker solution Cloudflare decided to rely on Javascript, on the Javascript Engine V8 developed for Google Chrome and on the W3C Service Workers API:

- The Javascript Engine on the CDN edge servers runs the multiple programs written by the customers, basically in a similar way as a web browser runs the Javascript programs from multiple web servers. The V8 engine was selected for its security maturity as well as its support of WebAssembly. WebAssembly started as a collaborative initiative from Google and Mozilla among others, and has evolved as a web standard published by the W3C (Webassembly.org, 2020; W3.org, 2020). It is an assembly-like language that enables to run programs with near-native performance, and to complement JavaScript in the most recent web browsers. The language comes with complementary tools: (1) toolchains allow to compile various other languages (e.g., C, C++, Rust) into WebAssembly, so programmers can write their code in the language of their choice, (2) WebAssembly Javascript APIs for loading WebAssembly modules and taking advantage of the performances of WebAssemby in JavaScript applications. Javascript being the default language for the V8 engine addresses the aforementioned acceptance requirement as it is anyway essential to every web programmer. And, at the same time, WebAssembly allows the web programmers to write micro-services in the language of their choice and run them as fast as possible on edge servers.

- The Service Workers API is also a W3C standard (Mozilla, 2020b). It has been designed for web browsers to manipulate the cache and the HTTP requests: to redirect or rewrite them, to modify a response, to generate several HTTP requests and combine the results, etc. Cloudflare Workers being written according to this standard Service Workers API are also named Cloudflare Service Workers.

Fastly made a different choice for its Compute@Edge solution (Leach, 2020). In particular Fastly decided to build its own native WebAssembly compiler and runtime, Lucet (Hickey, 2019), and to make it an open source, for that matter (Lucet, 2020). Fastly claims it could thus create a solution that is both secure and performant, with startup times under 35 microseconds (to compare Chromium's V8 engine taking about 5 milliseconds), leading to a completely clean operating environment for every request, and eliminating the security risks related to data persistence between invocations.

Akamai's EdgeWorkers aim at reaching the same objectives with Javascript bundles, like Cloudflare Workers (Akamai, 2020m). Besides, apart from EdgeWorkers, Akamai proposes also its Cloudlets offering (Akamai, 2020n). Cloudlets are a fixed set of applications installed on Akamai's edge servers, including "Application Load Balancer", "Edge Redirector", "Input Validation", "Forward Rewrite", etc. Like EdgeWorkers, they target customers who wish to bring more functionality at the edge to lower the number of requests sent to origins, to ease web operations and eventually improve end-user experience. But in contrast to EdgeWorkers, they don't require any custom software development work.

These serverless edge computing offerings empower the corporate customers and their web developers with capabilities to create and run applications at a global scale, beyond centralized clouds, with advanced levels of performance and security. Moreover, these edge computing platforms built by developers for developers provide their customers with deep insights and controls thanks to their log streaming interfaces as well as their comprehensive APIs and other configuration tools, e.g., Terraform Fastly Provider (Terraform, 2020). Thus customers can quickly integrate these capabilities into their CI/CD workflows and benefit from similar levels of agility for their DevOps processes as those experienced with more centralized clouds.

Besides, the CDN caching capability has generally been deployed until now on dedicated bare metal servers in order to provide the high and stable performances (in terms of session number, throughput, Time To First Byte) required by the large scale content delivery applications. Yet, CDNs are software systems in essence. This makes them potential candidates for being fully deployed on cloud-native virtual infrastructures, for example in containers. The drivers for such a migration take advantage of cloud-native principles:

- Scalability: content delivery service providers and content providers are traditionally heavy users of large content storage and content delivery capacities, and their needs grow as the evolution of their offerings.
- Auto-scaling: cloud-native infrastructures ensure the possibility to use transport, storage, and computing resources strictly dimensioned to the traffic, data and CPU load and to reallocate additional resources to absorb traffic peaks.
- Agility: Server resources can handle work tied to content delivery at peak hours and be switched-off or reallocated to other tasks (e.g. data analytics) otherwise.
- Manageability: to ease software upgrades and roll-backs.

This trend may become conceivable by the dramatic increase of server performances and the emergence of cloud-native solutions such as Kubernetes which supports features overlapping with CDNs (e.g., Ingress, Healthcheck, Logs management, Clustering, Scaling, Storage management). Nevertheless, CDN applications raise technical requirements that suggest customized designs:

- Controlled performances to ensure the adequate QoE expected by the end-user.
- Reservation of large amounts of resources for special events (e.g., Olympics).
- Specific requirements about cache locations; this looks easy to implement from a global vision where the objective would be to cache content in data centers at the granularity of countries, yet high audience content delivery services may require to cache contents in Telcos' networks much closer to the end-users.

Finally, the convergence between CDNs and Clouds is also boosted by the "CDN-ization" of services and applications that used to be deployed on centralized clouds only. This decentralization of cloud service offerings is based upon the vision that centralized data centers, as historically designed for cloud computing infrastructures, are not necessarily well suited for global scale applications, real-time applications or for high bandwidth consuming applications. For example, the performances of security solutions like anti-DDoS systems benefit from being exploited at a global scale. The massive adoption of cloud offers by both the enterprise and mass market segments fosters the storage of all types of data in the cloud; therefore, it becomes relevant to allow end-users and remote workforce to access more rapidly these data by handling and caching the most important or popular data closer to the end-user location, typically on CDN edge servers. Cloud gaming and immersive applications requiring low latency and high speed connectivity are expected to become strong drivers for edge computing in fixed and 5G networks. Video surveillance solutions in smart cities should rely on Artificial Intelligence technologies deployed at the network edge. The amount of traffic caused by uplink video and data streaming should also decrease in networks.

MULTI-CDN STRATEGIES

The growing number of CDNs (and CDN players) have been stimulating initiatives to enforce multi-CDN strategies. And various reasons have motivated CDN players to collaborate or content providers to use multiple CDNs for footprint extension, features extension, cost optimization, overload management, performance optimization and resilience. Yet, these initiatives have not been all based on the same vision and principles. Two main models emerged, that we name the CDN federation model and the multi-CDN selection model, with different technical and business implications.

CDN Federation Model

A first model consists in interconnecting two (or more) CDNs so as to constitute a content delivery infrastructure offering larger footprint, more capacity and/or features. Cisco© picked the name "CDN federation" to designate such *"multi-footprint, open CDN capabilities built from resources owned and operated by autonomous members"* (Puopolo, Latouche, Le Faucheur, & Defour, 2011).

A CDN federation shall preferably appear as a single delivery platform (a "one stop shop") to its customers (i.e., the content providers), so as to simplify their technical and business experiences, and market it as a competitive asset.

At the technical level it implies that only one CDN, hereby designated as the "Prime CDN", interacts with the customer, in order (1) to ingest its content and content metadata (e.g., content validity period), (2) to provide the customer with reporting information, and (3) to give to the customer some control on its cached content (e.g., capacity to purge instantly some content from the CDN caches if needed). Yet, we may expect that some or all the other members of the CDN federation participate in the delivery of the content of that given customer. Thus, they must all be able (1) to ingest content and content meta-data from the Prime CDN, (2) to generate reporting information that the Prime CDN aggregates for the customer, and (3) to enforce control operations triggered by the customer and relayed by the Prime CDN to the other CDN federation members. In addition, they must coordinate their request routing process with the Prime CDN, so that users' content requests delegated by the Prime CDN to the other federation members are correctly handled by the latter. This illustrates the first major characteristic of the CDN federation model: it imposes the definition of commonly agreed technical interfaces, as well as the associated processes and protocols, inside the CDN federation to ensure a comprehensive set of operations in a coordinated and efficient way.

Besides, the only fact that the CDN federation model adds one or several intermediate cascaded CDNs in a given content delivery chain has a real impact on several content delivery mechanisms involving interactions with the terminal devices. This is the second major characteristic of the CDN federation model: it imposes to review and adapt certain content delivery processes, including (1) the management of the content delivery sessions over TLS, and the related credential management, (2) the management of URI signing and token authentication, (3) the management of Cross-Origin-Resource-Sharing (CORS), and (4) the efficient management of ABR sessions. Let us consider TLS for example. The promise of a CDN federation is to propose to the customer a one-stop-shop model in which it would interact with a Prime CDN only. But the CDN federation must also guarantee the security of the entire architecture. Thus, it must preserve a chain of trust in HTTPs that involves CDN players the customer may not be aware of. This leads to problematic situations. As an illustration, in the Recursive DNS-based Redirection mode (Seedorf, Peterson, Previdi, van Brandenburg, & Ma, 2016), the client establishes a TLS session with a CDN cache server that belongs to one CDN of the federation. And this client shall expect that this CDN cache server possesses the required TLS credentials of the customer. But the customer would never make available its credentials to CDN players it is not aware of. So specific solutions had to be defined to address such problematic situations.

This has motivated the production of specifications by standardization bodies and industry fora:

- the definition of technical standards on CDN interconnection, mainly at IETF (Internet Engineering Task Force) CDNI (Content Delivery Networks Interconnection) working group (IETF, 2020), ETSI (ETSI, 2013), and
- the elaboration of specifications, recommendations and best practices in industry forums, in particular within the Open Caching Working Group of the Streaming Video Alliance (SVA) (SVA, 2020).

The production from the IETF CDNI WG is iconic of the work that has been accomplished so far. These activities have been focusing on defining interfaces between two CDNs, assuming that any more complex configuration (involving more than two CDNs) is the combination of several instances of this basic two CDN patterns. In this point-to-point relationship between CDNs, the CDN that has a contract with the Content Provider is the upstream CDN (uCDN). The uCDN settles an interconnection with another CDN called a downstream CDN (dCDN). The dCDN is the infrastructure that actually delivers the content to the end-users. Note that there can be several cascaded CDNs: in this case, the uCDN is always the one that delegates the request and the dCDN is the one that receives the delegated request from the uCDN.

Figure 4 shows the five interfaces that compose the reference model of the IETF CDNI framework.

Figure 4. IETF CDNI Reference Model

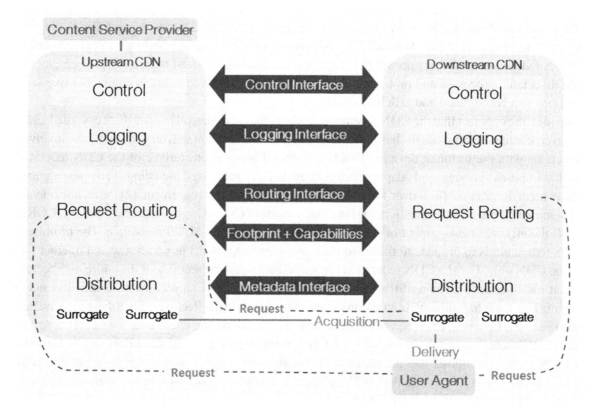

The Control Interface is involved in two types of processes: the first ones concern the bootstrapping and configuration of the other CDNI interfaces, the second ones (also named "trigger" processes) relate to content management operations such as pre-positioning, revalidating and purging content and/or content metadata. The Request Routing interface is split into two distinct sub-interfaces, the Footprint and Capabilities Advertisement interface and the Request Routing Redirection Interface, which are used respectively for exchanging routing information and for redirecting the users' content requests. The Metadata interface governs how the content should be delivered (e.g., exchange of geo-blocking directives, availability windows, access control mechanisms, purge instructions). The Logging interface exchanges logs about the delivery activities, both in real-time used for runtime traffic monitoring and offline information suitable for analytics and billing. All these specifications are freely available online (IETF, 2020).

The IETF CDNI WG has also assessed the impacts of cascaded CDNs on specific content delivery processes, such as HTTPS delegation (Fieau, Stephan, & van Brandenburg, 2020), URI signing (van Brandenburg, Leung, & Sorber, 2020), and ABR streaming (van Brandenburg, van Deventer, Le Faucheur, & Leung, 2013).

The Open Caching Working Group within SVA focuses on interoperability among content providers, commercial CDN operators, technology vendors and Telcos for delegation and delivery of streaming video with the goal of improving latency and QoE. An objective of this WG is to produce technical specifications for an Open Caching architecture enabling CDNs to delegate content requests to "Open Caches" located at the edge of the Telcos' networks on behalf of the CDN's customers (i.e., the content providers) (Finkelman, Devabhaktuni, & Stock, 2017). Given the proximity with IETF CDNI WG's objectives, the SVA Open Caching WG adopts the specifications of CDNI interfaces from the IETF as a reference, or proposes extensions wherever relevant, for example with regards to Relayed Token Authentication (Klein, Gressel, & Biran, 2020). The CDN federation model and Open Caching specifications from the Streaming Video Alliance benefit from the active support of significant market players like Cisco, Qwilt, and Disney.

Multi-CDN Selection Model

We name the second model the multi-CDN selection model. Its main principle, and essential difference with the CDN federation model, resides in that the content provider has a direct view and control on the CDN selection process, i.e., the process of redirecting the user requests among the CDNs involved. This model does not contain intermediate cascaded CDNs, unlike the CDN federation model.

The technical implementation of this model requires at least a CDN selection (or CDN balancing) system. This sole component may suffice if the request redirection process needs to apply static rules only, based on time periods, content types, or user locations for example. Yet, this does not enable the redirection process to take into account the actual CDN status or the quality as experienced by the end-users. Therefore, most implementations rely also on CDN performance data systems. These systems collect experience measurement and monitored data, which are exploited to improve accuracy and responsiveness in the decision process of the CDN selection system. Advanced implementations may even deploy agents in the terminal devices, such as Broadpeak's Diversity system (Broadpeak, 2020b), to support switching between CDNs during a traffic session, or simultaneous utilization of multiple CDNs in a single traffic session (e.g., to request ABR segments from different CDNs during an ABR streaming session).

Thus, a variety of implementations may co-exist, so as to accommodate different categories of content providers and requirements. Besides, the different CDNs participating in such a multi-CDN selection model may not even interact. This illustrates the major characteristic of the multi-CDN selection model: it does not require the achievement of some specific standardization works to be implemented, unlike the CDN federation model. Only some specific implementations may impose a higher level of integration between the players involved. For example, the use of the aforementioned Broadpeak's Diversity system assumes that involved CDNs have the same content source (same origin). Another advantage is that the additional complexity raised by the federation model because of the cascaded CDNs approach doesn't exist in the multi-CDN selection model.

But this model has also some drawbacks. The main disadvantage is that the scarcity of technical standards may force content providers to engage substantial tailored development and integration works so as to implement this model.

To address this issue, content providers may resort to multi-CDN solution providers. They belong to different categories:

- CDN selection (or CDN balancing) solution providers, such as Akamai Global Traffic Management© (GTM) (Akamai, 2020l) and Amazon Route 53© (Amazon, 2020).
- CDN performance data solution providers, like Conviva© (Conviva, 2020), Catchpoint© (Catchpoint, 2020) and Dynatrace© (Dynatrace (2020).
- Providers offering ranges of solutions or integrated solutions for implementing multi-CDN strategies. For example, Broadpeak markets CDN products, as well as a CDN selection product named UmbrellaCDN©, and performance data collection solutions (e.g., Smartlib and Diversity systems) (BroadPeak, 2020a). Akamai also provides CDN services and performance data solutions, in addition to its GTM product. CDNetworks© and CloudFlare© are both CDN and CDN balancing solution providers as well (CDNetworks, 2020). Citrix Intelligent Traffic Management© (which acquired the French company Cedexis© in 2018) and NS1© are both CDN balancing and performance data solution providers (Brooks, 2020; NS1, 2020b), and may thus act as "CDN brokers".

Perspectives

The multi-CDN selection model has been broadly adopted, notably by content providers, while the CDN federation model has not yet truly picked up. Actually these models are not necessarily conflicting or incompatible. Indeed they rely on some common technical mechanisms; for example methods for enforcing request routing decision are generally based on DNS resolution or possibly on HTTP request redirection in both models. In addition, developments achieved for one model should benefit to the other. In particular, the standards and recommendations published by standardization bodies and industry forums for the CDN federation model should contribute to harmonize the practices and APIs of the CDN service providers and multi-CDN solution providers, and thus simplify the implementation of multi-CDN strategies whatever the model.

CDN AND CELLULAR NETWORKS

This last section discusses CDN usage in cellular networks. Particularly, it outlines the current positioning and future perspectives of the CDNs in the mobile domain.

In the current decade, CDNs have been constantly evolving to keep up with continuing trends in the mobile domain. First, they had and have to scale with the mobile traffic growth (seven-fold from 2017 to 2022 globally, two times faster than fixed IP traffic), primarily due to video (79 percent of global mobile data traffic by 2022, compared to 59 percent at the end of 2017) (Cisco, 2019a). Second, a specific trait of the mobile domain is the large diversity of terminals (e.g. feature phones, Smartphones, tablets, tethered PCs), with heterogeneous hardware and software characteristics in terms of screen size, storage, CPU, graphic chipset, mobile generations, operating system and APIs. Each of these characteristics may influence the way content are handled and delivered in general, including by CDN. For instance, different adaptive streaming solutions may have to be used depending on the nature of the terminal device: HLS for Apple devices, DASH or Microsoft Smooth Streaming (MSS) for others. Nevertheless, there is a clear trend towards a broad adoption of high-end devices which generate the majority of mobile traffic and drive the increase of the mobile connection speeds (from 1.38 Mbps in 2013 to 6.8 Mbps in 2016 and 28.5 Mbps by 2022). Third, next to user devices, M2M modules (e.g. cameras, sensor systems) are being deployed massively (four-fold growth between 2017 and 2022, up to 3.9 billion); thus CDN players develop specific offerings for this market segment, such as Akamai IoT Edge Cloud products. Fifth, the considerable number of mobile-connected devices (12.3 billion by 2022, up from 8.6 billion in 2017), their respective vulnerabilities (GSMA, 2020; Imani, 2018; Taleby Ahvanooey, 2017), and the now established practices of users to access cloud-based applications in mobility have led CDN players to pay a special attention to mobile security (Cisco, 2019a; Cisco, 2019b).

Yet, from an architectural viewpoint, CDN and mobile networks have developed separately until now. Historically, CDNs were first deployed to deliver content over fixed networks, and then utilized also for already deployed mobile networks. Besides the user plane of the mobile networks up to and including 4G is composed of three parts basically: (1) the Radio Access Network (RAN) that connects the mobile devices to the Packet Core network and includes the radio interface, (2) the Packet Core Network that performs all functional operations for data forwarding, including traffic forwarding to and from the Internet, mobility handling, charging, and security handling, (3) the sGi-LAN that connects the last gateways of the mobile Packet Core network (e.g., 3G GGSN (Gateway GPRS Support Node) or 4G PGW (Packet Data Network GateWay)) to the Internet and third networks. The sGi-LAN may encompass additional IP-based equipment to provide advanced features (e.g., NAT, firewalls, content caching and compression, Traffic Detection Function (TDF), legal filtering). For a more detailed information about 3G and 4G mobile architectures, the reader may for instance refer to the 3GPP standard documents (3GPP, 2020a) or also to Cox (2012). In these mobile networks all data packets exchanged with the mobile device are encapsulated in GTP tunnels (GPRS Tunneling Protocol) (3GPP, 2020b; 3GPP, 2021) between the (e) NodeB and the last gateways of the mobile Packet Core network, the 3G GGSNs or the 4G PGWs. CDN delivery servers are thus inevitably deployed outside of the RAN and the Packet Core network, so between these last gateways and the origin servers: either in the sGi-LAN, on the Internet, or on any other 3rd party network involved in the delivery chain. By the way, these gateways are quite centralized in mobile networks; and this remains unchanged in 3GPP 5G Non-Standalone Architecture (NSA). Most mobile operators in the race to the first 5G deployments start with 5G NSA leveraging their existing 4G physical core network and do not deploy virtualized core network. Therefore, CDNs did not and will not really contribute to release the traffic pressure on these mobile networks, be they 3G, 4G or 5G NSA.

3GPP has standardized solutions to improve the efficiency of content distribution within the cellular networks, such as (e)MBMS. MBMS stands for Multimedia Broadcast Multicast Services and eMBMS is the LTE version of MBMS. This technology relies upon multicasting content in the mobile network and broadcasting it on the radio interface. It has benefitted from continuous improvement at 3GPP since Release-6 for MBMS and Release-9 for eMBMS. Enhancements in Release-12 included in particular MOOD (Multicast Operation On Demand), which enables to seamlessly and automatically switch terminal devices between multicast and unicast delivery schemes depending on users' demand. Then Release-14 added among others the Standardized xMB interface as a unified framework for managing services and sessions with content providers, as well as longer range and better efficiency at the radio access level (3GPP, 2020c). But eMBMS has never been massively adopted yet by mobile operators even if few commercial services have been launched, by Telstra in Australia for example (Telstra, 2018). Apart from these exceptions unicast remains the only delivery mode in these mobile networks whatever the content delivered to terminal devices (and mostly from CDNs).

This should evolve with 5G SA, opening new perspectives as regards to CDNs and cellular mobile networks.

First, 5G SA should implement the concept of Network Slicing that appeared in 3GPP Release-15. This enables to manage transport, storage, and computing resources as independent end-to-end logical networks, called network slices, over a shared physical infrastructure. It becomes much easier to apply custom caching and processing jobs as well as routing and QoS policies at mobile network edge, deployed deeper with 5G SA than before, so still closer to terminal devices. So CDNs could distribute CDN delivery servers deeper at mobile network edge to improve latency and bandwidth efficiency of content delivery. This organic integration of CDNs and mobile networks could also lead to a stronger functional integration. For example sharing information on the end-user's localization between the cellular network (for mobility management among others) and the CDN (for CDN delivery server selection and request redirection management) would become worthwhile, since CDN delivery servers get closer to the 5G NR interface.

Second, as the boundaries between CDN and Cloud Computing technologies tend to blur, CDNs shall evolve towards the delivery of advanced applications such as AR (Augmented Reality) streaming, by leveraging the unprecedented performances of the 5G NR interface, as well as new distributed processing paradigms between edge nodes and terminal devices (e.g., split rendering of XR viewport).

Third, CDNs are promised to become an essential component in the design of future mobile TV services, possibly combined with the upcoming evolutions of (e)MBMS, ABR, mABR, CMAF, DAHOE (support of hybrid DASH/HLS over MBMS) (3GPP, 2020d), and Dynamic Ad Insertion systems, among others.

CONCLUSION

CDNs play a strategic role today in the networks and the global ecosystem. As the latter evolves, so will the CDNs. The main drivers are to improve scalability, flexibility and cost efficiency of the content delivery infrastructures, as well as end-user Quality of Experience. This chapter focused on a set of major trends, highlighting the main challenges, from both the technical and business perspectives.

First, the convergence between OTT and IPTV media content delivery chains is underway. The audiovisual architectures which used to be dedicated to specific access networks and services evolve towards a single technical chain and aim at addressing the "any content, anytime, anywhere" motto. In this evolution, the management of content metadata and strategic positioning of the different types of market players will be instrumental. The incumbent advantages of IPTV over OTT streaming, namely latency and scalability, tend to shrink, as a consequence of the recent technical innovations on OTT streaming like CMAF and of the financial investments made by the Internet giants into the OTT streaming markets. In return, initiatives have bloomed to design a next-generation of IPTV, so as to keep it competitive against OTT streaming. These include making IPTV format and technologies converge with OTT via solutions like mABR, in order to take advantage of the fast evolution and cost-efficiency of the OTT streaming technologies.

Second, next to audiovisual content services, CDN operators have strongly expanded into web acceleration and web security services. They have inherent advantages for being legitimate players in both domains. Indeed, they generate a significant proportion of the whole Internet traffic. So they are well positioned to get insights on web delivery inefficiencies as well as on security attacks. Moreover, their infrastructures, distributed at large scale, are intrinsically well-suited to optimize web delivery performances, and to mitigate many common attacks. Given the size and strategic importance of both these markets, CDN operators have logically set them among their core business operations with dedicated service portfolios, gaining noteworthy commercial success.

Third, CDN and Cloud services and infrastructures tend to converge, to address intersecting markets and to adopt common technical principles, such as cloud-native principles. CDN players are now positioning their infrastructures as edge computing platforms. This is exemplified by the development of serverless edge computing offerings such as Cloudflare Workers, Fastly Compute@Edge and Akamai EdgeWorkers. These offerings empower their customers with capabilities to create and run applications at a global scale, beyond centralized clouds, with advanced levels of performance and security. They can quickly integrate these capabilities into their CI/CD workflows and benefit from similar levels of agility for their DevOps processes as those experienced with more centralized clouds. Besides, CDNs are software systems in essence. This makes them potential candidates for being fully deployed on cloud-native virtual infrastructures. At last, the convergence between CDNs and Clouds is also boosted by the "CDN-ization" of services and applications that used to be deployed on centralized clouds only.

Fourth, the growing number of CDNs and CDN players have been stimulating to enforce multi-CDN strategies. Various reasons have motivated CDN players to collaborate or content providers to use multiple CDNs, including footprint extension, feature extension, cost optimization, overload management, performance optimization, and resilience. Yet, these initiatives have not been all based on the same vision and principles. Two main models emerged, with different technical and business implications: the CDN federation model and the multi-CDN selection model. They are not necessarily conflicting or incompatible. The developments achieved for one model should benefit to the other one.

Fifth, CDNs have been constantly evolving to keep up with continuing trends in the mobile domain. Yet, from an architectural viewpoint, CDN and mobile networks have developed separately until now. This shall evolve with 5G SA, opening new perspectives for CDNs and cellular mobile networks. Network Slicing and edge computing shall enable the distribution of CDN nodes closer to the end-users. This organic integration of CDNs and mobile networks could also lead to a stronger functional integration. Then, as the boundaries between CDN and Cloud Computing technologies tend to blur, CDNs shall evolve to deliver advanced applications like AR streaming at the edge of mobile networks. And CDNs shall continue to be an essential component in the design of future mobile TV services.

REFERENCES

W3.org. (2020). *W3.org WASM Web Page.* Retrieved October 27, 2020 from https://www.w3.org/wasm/

ABI. (2020). *ABI Research. Cord-cutting driving decline in set-top box soc market from US$2.4 billion in 2019 to US$2 billion in 2023. April 4, 2019.* Retrieved October 30, 2020 from https://www.abiresearch.com/press/cord-cutting-driving-decline-set-top-box-soc-market-us2-billion-2023/

Akamai. (2012). *Press Release. November 20, 2012. Orange and Akamai form Content Delivery Strategic Alliance.* Retrieved October 23, 2020 from https://www.prnewswire.com/news-releases/orange-and-akamai-form-content-delivery-strategic-alliance-180145801.html

Akamai. (2020a). *Akamai IP Application Accelerator Web Page.* Retrieved October 30, 2020 from https://www.akamai.com/us/en/products/performance/ip-application-accelerator.jsp

Akamai. (2020b). *Visualizing Akamai Web Page.* Retrieved October 30, 2020 from https://www.akamai.com/us/en/resources/visualizing-akamai/

Akamai. (2020c). *Visualizing Akamai Web Page, Enterprise Threat Monitor.* Retrieved October 30, 2020 from https://www.akamai.com/us/en/resources/visualizing-akamai/enterprise-threat-monitor.jsp

Akamai. (2020d). *Akamai State of the Internet Report, Security Report Web Page.* Retrieved October 30, 2020 from https://www.akamai.com/us/en/resources/our-thinking/state-of-the-internet-report/global-state-of-the-internet-security-ddos-attack-reports.jsp

Akamai. (2020e). *Akamai Web Attack Visualization Web Page.* Retrieved October 30, 2020 from https://www.akamai.com/us/en/resources/our-thinking/state-of-the-internet-report/web-attack-visualization.jsp

Akamai. (2020f). *Akamai Security Web Page.* Retrieved October 30, 2020 from https://www.akamai.com/us/en/security.jsp

Akamai. (2020g). *Press Release. July 28, 2020. Akamai Reports Second Quarter 2020 Financial Results.* Retrieved October 30, 2020 from https://www.akamai.com/us/en/about/news/press/2020-press/akamai-reports-second-quarter-2020-financial-results.jsp

Akamai. (2020h). *Akamai Customer Identity and Access Management Web Page.* Retrieved October 30, 2020 from https://www.akamai.com/us/en/solutions/security/customer-identity-and-access-management.jsp

Akamai. (2020i). *Akamai Customer Identity Cloud Web Page.* Retrieved October 30, 2020 from https://www.akamai.com/us/en/products/security/identity-cloud.jsp

Akamai. (2020j). *Akamai IoT Edge Cloud Products Web Page.* Retrieved October 30, 2020 from https://www.akamai.com/us/en/solutions/iot-edge-cloud/

Akamai. (2020k). *Akamai API Gateway Web Page*. Retrieved October 30, 2020 from https://developer. akamai.com/akamai-api-gateway/

Akamai. (2020l). *Akamai Global Traffic Management Web Page*. Retrieved October 30, 2020 from https://www.akamai.com/us/en/products/performance/global-traffic-management.jsp

Akamai. (2020m). *Akamai EdgeWorkers Web Page*. Retrieved October 30, 2020 from https://developer. akamai.com/akamai-edgeworkers-overview/

Akamai. (2020n). *Akamai Cloulets Web Page*. Retrieved October 30, 2020 from https://www.akamai. com/us/en/products/performance/cloudlets/

Amazon. (2020). *Amazon Route53 Web Page*. Retrieved October 30, 2020 from https://aws.amazon. com/route53/

Bentaleb, A., Taani, B., Begen, A., Timmermer, C., & Zimmermann, R. (2018). A Survey on Bitrate Adaptation Schemes for Streaming Media over HTTP. IEEE Communications Surveys & Tutorials (IEEE COMST), 1(1).

Bishop, M. (2020). *Hypertext Transfer Protocol Version 3 (HTTP/3). draft-ietf-quic-http-32*. Retrieved October 30, 2020 from https://tools.ietf.org/html/draft-ietf-quic-http-32

BroadPeak. (2020a). *Broadpeak Web Portal Page*. Retrieved October 30, 2020 from http://www.broad-peak.tv/

BroadPeak. (2020b). *Broadpeak Press Release. April 5, 2016. Broadpeak Launches CDN Diversity, Dramatically Improving Live/VOD Content Delivery and QoE*. Retrieved October 30, 2020 from https:// broadpeak.tv/newsroom/broadpeak-launches-cdn-diversity-dramatically-improving-livevod-content-delivery-and-qoe/

Brooks, M. (2020). *Introduction to Citrix Intelligent Traffic Management*. Retrieved October 30, 2020 from https://docs.citrix.com/en-us/tech-zone/learn/tech-briefs/itm.html#intelligent-traffic

Catchpoint. (2020). *Catchpoint Web Portal Page*. Retrieved October 30, 2020 from https://www.catch-point.com/

CDNetworks. (2020). *CDNetworks Web Portal Page*. Retrieved October 30, 2020 from https://www. cdnetworks.com/

Cisco. (2019a). *Cisco Visual Networking Index: Global IP Forecast, 2017–2022*. Retrieved October 30, 2020 from https://www.cisco.com/c/en/us/solutions/collateral/service-provider/visual-networking-index-vni/white-paper-c11-741490.html

Cisco. (2019b). *Cisco Visual Networking Index: Mobile Forecast Highlights, 2017–2022*. Retrieved October 30, 2020 from https://www.cisco.com/c/dam/assets/sol/sp/vni/forecast_highlights_mobile/pdf/ Global_2022_Forecast_Highlights.pdf

Cloudflare. (2020a). *What is the Difference Between Routing and Smart Routing?* Retrieved October 30, 2020 from https://www.cloudflare.com/en-gb/learning/performance/routing-vs-smart-routing/

Cloudflare. (2020b). *Cloudflare DNS Web Page.* Retrieved October 30, 2020 from https://www.cloudflare.com/dns/

Cloudflare. (2020c). *Cloudflare DDoS Web Page.* Retrieved October 30, 2020 from https://www.cloudflare.com/en-gb/ddos/

Cloudflare. (2020d). *Cloudflare Web Page.* Retrieved October 30, 2020 from https://www.cloudflare.com/

CMAF. (2020). *ISO/IEC 23000-19:2020. Information technology - Multimedia application format (MPEG-A) - Part 19: Common media application format (CMAF) for segmented media. Publication date: 2020-03.* Retrieved October 30, 2020 from https://www.iso.org/standard/79106.html

CNCF. (2019). *Cloud Native Computing Foundation Annual Report 2019.* Retrieved October 30, 2020 from https://www.cncf.io/cncf-annual-report-2019/

Conviva. (2020). *Conviva Web Portal Page.* Retrieved October 30, 2020 from https://www.conviva.com/

Cox, C. (2012). *An Introduction to LTE: LTE, LTE-Advanced, SAE and 4G Mobile Communications.* John Wiley & Sons. doi:10.1002/9781119942825

DASH. (2019). *ISO/IEC 23009-1:2019/DAmd.1:2020. Information technology - Dynamic adaptive streaming over HTTP (DASH) — Part 1: Media presentation description and segment. Publication date: 2019-12.*

Dnsperf. (2020). *Dnsperf Web Page.* Retrieved October 27, 2020 from www.dnsperf.com/

DVB. (2018). *Adaptive media streaming over IP Multicast. DVB Document A176. March 2018.* Retrieved October 30, 2020 from https://www.dvb.org/resources/public/standards/a176_adaptive_media_streaming_over_ip_multicast_2018-02-16_draft_bluebook.pdf

DVB. (2020). *Adaptive media streaming over IP Multicast. DVB Document A176 (Second edition). March 2020.* Retrieved October 30, 2020 from https://dvb.org/wp-content/uploads/2020/03/A176_Adaptive-Media-Streaming-over-IP-Multicast_Mar-2020.pdf

Dynatrace. (2020). *Dynatrace Web Portal Page.* Retrieved October 30, 2020 from https://www.dynatrace.fr/

ETSI. (2013). *CDN Interconnection Architecture. ETSI TS 182 032 V1.1.1 (2013-04).* Retrieved October 23, 2020 from http://www.etsi.org/deliver/etsi_ts/182000_182099/182032/01.01.01_60/ts_182032v010101p.pdf

ETSI. (2020). *Digital Video Broadcasting (DVB); Adaptive media streaming over IP Multicast. ETSI TS 103 769 V1.1.1 (2020-11).* Retrieved October 30, 2020 from https://www.etsi.org/deliver/etsi_ts/103700_103799/103769/01.01.01_60/ts_103769v010101p.pdf

Fieau, F., Stephan, E., & Mishra, S. (2020). *CDNI extensions for HTTPS delegation, draft-ietf-cdni-interfaces-https-delegation-04.* Retrieved October 23, 2020 from https://tools.ietf.org/html/draft-ietf-cdni-interfaces-https-delegation-04

Fielding, R., & Reschke, J. (2014). Hypertext Transfer Protocol (HTTP/1.1): Message Syntax and Routing. Internet Engineering Task Force RFC 7230. Retrieved from https://tools.ietf.org/html/rfc7230

Finkelman, O., Devabhaktuni, J., & Stock, M. (2017). *Open Caching Content Management Operations Specification. Version 1.0 (November, 2017).* Retrieved October 21, 2020 from https://www.stream-ingvideoalliance.org/document/open-caching-content-management-operations-specification/

GPP. (2020a). *3GPP Technologies Home.* Retrieved November 28, 2020 from http://www.3gpp.org/technologies/technologies

GPP. (2020b). *Digital cellular telecommunications system (Phase 2+); (GSM);Universal Mobile Tele-communications System (UMTS); General Packet Radio Service (GPRS); GPRS Tunnelling Protocol (GTP) across the Gn and Gp interface (3GPP TS 29.060 version 16.0.0 Release 16).* ETSI TS 129 060 V16.0.0 (2020-11). Retrieved December 28, 2020 from https://www.etsi.org/deliver/etsi_ts/129000_129099/129060/16.00.00_60/ts_129060v160000p.pdf

GPP. (2020c). *LTE; Evolved Universal Terrestrial; Radio Access Network (E-UTRAN); General aspects and principles for interfaces supporting Multimedia Broadcast Multicast Service (MBMS) within E-UTRAN (3GPP TS 36.440 version 16.0.0 Release 16).* ETSI TS 136 440 V16.0.0 (2020-07). Retrieved October 23, 2020 from https://www.etsi.org/deliver/etsi_ts/136400_136499/136440/16.00.00_60/ts_136440v160000p.pdf

GPP. (2021). *Universal Mobile Telecommunications System (UMTS); LTE; 5G; 3GPP Evolved Packet System (EPS); Evolved General Packet Radio Service (GPRS) Tunnelling Protocol for Control plane (GTPv2-C); Stage 3 (3GPP TS 29.274 version 16.6.0 Release 16).* ETSI TS 129 274 V16.6.0 (2021-01). Retrieved February 12, 2021 from https://www.etsi.org/deliver/etsi_ts/129200_129299/129274/16.06.00_60/ts_129274v160600p.pdf

GPP. (2020d). *3rd Generation Partnership Project; Technical Specification Group Services and System Aspects; Multimedia Broadcast/Multicast Service (MBMS); Protocols and codecs (Release 16).* 3GPP TS 26.346 V16.6.1 (2020-10).

GSMA. (2020). *Mobile Telecommunications Security Threat Landscape.* January 2020. Retrieved October 21, 2020 from https://www.gsma.com/security/wp-content/uploads/2020/02/2020-SECURITY-THREAT-LANDSCAPE-REPORT-FINAL.pdf/

Hickey, P. (2019). *Announcing Lucet: Fastly's native WebAssembly compiler and runtime.* Retrieved October 23, 2020 from https://www.fastly.com/blog/announcing-lucet-fastly-native-webassembly-compiler-runtime

Hoffman, P., & McManus, P. (2018). *DNS Queries over HTTPS (DoH).* Internet Engineering Task Force RFC 8484. Retrieved from https://tools.ietf.org/html/rfc8484

IETF. (2020). *Cdni Status Pages.* Retrieved October 23, 2020 from http://tools.ietf.org/wg/cdni/

Imani, A., Keshavarz-Haddad, A., Eslami, M., & Haghighat, J. (2018). Security Challenges and At-tacks in M2M Communications. *9th International Symposium on Telecommunications.* 10.1109/IS-TEL.2018.8661044

Klein, E., Gressel, Y., & Biran, S. (2020). *Open Caching Relayed Token Authentication.* Streaming Video Alliance Technical Publication. Retrieved October 21, 2020 from https://www.streamingvideoalliance.org/document/open-caching-relayed-token-authentication/

Leach, S. (2020). *Performance matters: why Compute@Edge does not yet support JavaScript.* Retrieved October 23, 2020 from https://www.fastly.com/blog/why-edge-compute-does-not-yet-support-javascript

Limelight. (2019). *Limelight Networks Market Research. The State of Online Video 2019.* Retrieved October 30, 2020 from https://fr.limelight.com/resources/white-paper/state-of-online-video-2019/

Lucet. (2020). *GitHub Repository of Lucet Project from Fastly.* Retrieved October 23, 2020 from https://github.com/fastly/lucet/

Mozilla. (2020a). *Firefox DNS over HTTPs Web Page.* Retrieved October 30, 2020 from https://support.mozilla.org/en-US/kb/firefox-dns-over-https/

Mozilla. (2020b). *Mozilla's Service Worker API Web Page.* Retrieved October 30, 2020 from https://developer.mozilla.org/fr/docs/Web/API/Service_Worker_API

NS1. (2020a). *NS1 Multi-CDN Web Page.* Retrieved October 30, 2020 from https://ns1.com/multi-cdn/

NS1. (2020b). *NS1 Web Portal Page.* Retrieved October 30, 2020 from https://ns1.com/

Netflix. (2020). *Netflix Open Connect Program.* Retrieved October 30, 2020 from https://openconnect.netflix.com/

Puopolo, S., Latouche, M., Le Faucheur, F., & Defour, J. (2011). *Cisco white paper. Content Delivery Network (CDN) Federations. How SPs Can Win the Battle for Content-Hungry Consumers.* Retrieved October 30, 2020 from https://www.cisco.com/c/dam/en/us/products/collateral/video/videoscape-distribution-suite-service-broker/cdn_vds_sb_white_paper.pdf

Seedorf, J., Peterson, J., Previdi, S., van Brandenburg, R., & Ma, K. (2016). *Content Delivery Network Interconnection (CDNI) Request Routing: Footprint and Capabilities Semantics.* Internet Engineering Task Force RFC 8008. Retrieved from https://tools.ietf.org/html/rfc8008

Stiemerling, M., Schulzrinne, H., Rao, A., Lanphier, R., & Westerlund, M. (2016). *Real-Time Streaming Protocol Version 2.0.* Internet Engineering Task Force RFC 7826. Retrieved from https://tools.ietf.org/html/rfc7826

SVA. (2020). *Web Portal of the Open Caching Working Group from the Streaming Video Alliance.* Retrieved October 30, 2020 from https://www.streamingvideoalliance.org/working-group/open-caching/

Taleby Ahvanooey, M., Li, Q., Rabbani, M., & Rajput, A. R. (2017). A Survey on Smartphones Security: Software Vulnerabilities, Malware, and Attacks. *International Journal of Advanced Computer Science and Applications., 8*(10), 2017.

Telstra. (2018). *Press Release. Telstra deploys Australia's first LTE-Broadcast technology to support sports streaming. July 11, 2018.* Retrieved October 23, 2020 from https://www.telstra.com.au/aboutus/media/media-releases/Telstra-deploys-Australias-first-LTE-Broadcast-technology-to-support-sports-streaming

Terraform. (2020). *Terraform Registry of Fastly Provider.* Retrieved October 23, 2020 from https://registry.terraform.io/providers/fastly/fastly/latest/

Tombes, J. (2019). *White Paper. Multicast ABR, Low-Latency CMAF, CTE, and Optimized Video Playback. Reducing Latency in Live Online Video.* Retrieved October 30, 2020 from https://www.theoplayer.com/whitepaper-abr-cmaf-low-latency/

van Brandenburg, R., Leung, K., & Sorber, P. (2020). *URI Signing for CDN Interconnection (CDNI), draft-ietf-cdni-uri-signing-19.* Retrieved October 23, 2020 from https://tools.ietf.org/html/draft-ietf-cdni-uri-signing-19

van Brandenburg, R., van Deventer, O., Le Faucheur, F., & Leung, K. (2013). *Models for HTTP-Adaptive-Streaming-Aware Content Distribution Network Interconnection (CDNI).* Internet Engineering Task Force RFC 6983. Retrieved from https://tools.ietf.org/html/rfc6983

Webassembly.org. (2020). *Webassembly.org Web Page.* Retrieved October 27, 2020 from https://webassembly.org/

KEY TERMS AND DEFINITIONS

Adaptive Bit Rate (ABR) Streaming: Content delivery scheme based on segmenting content into small objects called segments encoded at multiple bitrates. The client accesses the content by requesting one after the other the segments that best fit the terminal and network conditions.

Caching: Special form of memory deployed in networks (on specific servers) as well as on computer architectures and web browsers. When the same object is requested several times, caching aims at avoiding this object to be accessed as many times from its origin location so as to minimize resource utilization and latency.

Cloud: Set of servers as well as software and databases that run on them, accessed remotely, possibly via Internet, to manage, collect, manipulate, store, and deliver data.

Content Delivery Network (CDN): Set of servers specifically designed and deployed over one or several networks in order to optimize the storage and delivery of content objects (e.g., web objects, audiovisual live or on-demand content, large files).

Content Delivery Network Interconnection (CDNI): Relationship between CDNs that enables one CDN to provide content delivery services on behalf of other CDNs.

Home Network: The private local network inside the end-user's premise, including all the terminal devices connected to it. The home network is connected to the internet via a home gateway.

Over-the-Top (OTT): Designate an Internet market player, application or service that does not rely upon Telcos or internet service providers, except for just getting connected to the end-users via the internet.

Chapter 4
Green for ICT, Green by ICT, Green by Design

Joël Penhoat
Orange S.A., France

Mikko Samuli Vaija
Orange S.A., France

Dinh-Thuy Phan-Huy
Orange S.A., France

Guillaume Gérard
Orange S.A., France

Zakaria Ournani
Orange S.A., France

Dominique Nussbaum
Orange S.A., France

Gilles Dretsch
Orange S.A., France

Quentin Fousson
Bouygues Telecom, France

Marc Vautier
Orange S.A., France

ABSTRACT

The Intergovernmental Panel on Climate Change claims that global warming can be avoided by "reaching net zero carbon dioxide emissions globally around 2050 and concurrent deep reductions in emissions of non-carbon dioxide forcers, particularly methane." To protect the planet and guarantee prosperity for

DOI: 10.4018/978-1-7998-7646-5.ch004

all, The United Nations has set up a sustainable development program made up of 17 goals. Among them, Goal 12 establishes sustainable consumption and production patterns so that a social and economic growth does not increase the pressure on Earth's resources, and Goal 13 constrains global warming. This chapter explores some actions the telecommunication companies have implemented: assessing the issues of mineral resources on network equipment, improving data centre energy consumption, reducing the average electricity intensity of the transmitting data, contributing to the energy transition.

ENVIRONMENTAL STAKES

Climate Change

In 2018, the Intergovernmental Panel on Climate Change (IPCC) asserts that (Masson-Delmotte et al., 2018) "human activities are estimated to have approximately 1.0°C of global warming above pre-industrial levels, with a likely range of 0.8°C to 1.2°C. Global warming is likely to reach 1.5 °C between 2030 and 2052 if it continues to increase at the current rate." According to the IPCC (Rogelj et al., 2018), reaching the 1.5 °C can be avoided by "reaching net zero carbon dioxide emissions globally around 2050 and concurrent deep reductions in emissions of non-carbon dioxide forcers, particularly methane. Such mitigation pathways are characterized by energy-demand reductions, decarbonization of electricity and other fuels, electrification of energy end use, deep reductions in agricultural emissions, and some form of carbon dioxide removal with carbon storage on land or sequestration in geological reservoirs."

Figure 1. The seventeen United Nations sustainable development goals - Source United Nations

The United Nations Sustainable Development Goals

The United Nations are involved to protect the planet and guarantee prosperity for all through a sustainable development program (United Nations, 2020) made up of seventeen goals (Figure 1[REMOVED REF FIELD]). Among them, the goal number twelve establishes sustainable consumption and production patterns so that a social and economic growth does not increase the pressure on Earth's resources due to the rebound effect, and the goal number thirteen constrains the global warming to 1.5 °C.

The GSM Association (GSMA), an association that represents nearly 800 mobile operators and manufacturers in 220 countries around the world, endorses the seventeen goals and claims that the mobile devices are useful to achieve the sustainable development goals (GSMA, 2019a) and that the mobile industry is playing a role in tackling climate change, developing a decarbonisation pathway aligned with the science-based target initiative (Science-based Targets, 2020) and in line with the Paris Agreement target of achieving net-zero emissions by 2050.

The GSMA first main idea is that electricity being used to power the telecommunication networks, switching from fossil fuels to renewable energies to lower their carbon footprint is a realistic option (GSMA, 2020). This is done through a mix of power purchase agreements, buying green electricity with associated guarantees of origin and additional unbundled guarantees of origin, and green electricity self-generation. The second one is that improvement of energy efficiency and circular economy are not sufficient to reach carbon neutrality. Therefore, for those scope 1 and 2 emissions that cannot be avoided, carbon offsets are the only remaining option. Concerning the scope 3 emissions, it is the responsibility of each player along the value chain to contribute to climate targets.

Mineral Resources Are Scarce and Critical For Network Equipment

The issues related to mineral resource scarcity have been covered for several industries such as the energy industry (Zepf et al., 2014), for industries located in a specific country (Department of the Interior, 2018) or even for an entire supranational union industry (European Commission, 2020). All this research effort highlights that the modern industry uses more and more materials and for very specific purposes (e.g., germanium in optical fiber).

For the telecommunication industry the issue of scarce materials content in network equipment, or the different parameters to be considered when setting up a methodology on material criticality, has been discussed in (Vaija & Philipot, 2020). In these environmental assessments, the "when will it be depleted?" issue is examined for mineral resources. It is handled on one hand with the life cycle assessment methods, such as Abiotic Depletion Potential (Van Oers, De Koning, Guinée & Huppes, 2002) which considers, for a large set of elements (for example gold, silver, copper), a ratio between the world's annual production of a given material divided by the size of its world reserves. On the other hand with methods that allow to classify raw material as "critical"; these ones focus on parameters such as reliance to imports, capabilities to substitute the material by a non-critical one or recyclability rate.

Internet-Induced Global Energy Consumption is A Challenge

Fossil fuels contribute to the global warming: relying on them is not sustainable because their adverse impacts for the subsequent generations are high. Moreover, their availability in the medium term is problematic. In 2018, the International Energy Agency announced that the peak production of conventional oil had been reached around 2010, and even if shale oil production has offset this decrease it will not invalidate the concept of peak oil (Salameh, 2013). And the renewable energies are not yet there to relay fossil fuels: in 2018 only half of the growth in energy demand was provided by new deployments of renewable energies, the other half being produced by coal.

With respect to Internet energy consumption, it consumes 4.2% of the world's primary energy and 5.5% of the world's electricity, while being responsible for 3.5% of the global CO_2 emissions (Bordage, 2019). Even if the fixed and mobile telecommunication networks represent less than 1% of the global CO_2 emissions, the commitment in corporate social responsibility implies a strong involvement in the greenhouse gas emissions and the telecommunication companies should take actions to promote the transition to a carbon-free economy by offering other sectors solutions to reduce their own CO_2 emissions.

HOW TELECOMMUNICATION COMPANIES GRAB THE CLIMATE STAKES

By Assessing The Issues of Mineral Resources On Network Equipment

With the knowledge about the materials contained in the network equipment obtained thanks to life cycle assessments, it is possible to have a better understanding regarding the methodology to undertake in order to reduce the environmental footprint as efficiently as possible. This comes in the form of dismantling the equipment and gathering data at electronic and mechanical component level, for example with Materials Declarations[1], as underlined in (Vaija & Philipot, 2020). However, even with good quality data on the content of the materials, a practitioner must be careful in the methodological choices to be made, whether they are based on the life cycle assessment or the criticality of the materials.

The following paragraphs give some insights on two methods applied to a network equipment, namely Abiotic Depletion Potential and handling critical raw material, allowing to work on the reduction of its environmental footprint.

Abiotic Depletion Potential Method Applied To A Radio Access Network Equipment

Regarding the methodologies related to the mineral resources, it has to be noted that the Abiotic Depletion Potential method considers for instance different types of approaches to evaluate the size of the reserves. Among these approaches, the "Ultimate reserves" approach considers the quantity of resource that is ultimately available in the earth crust (for example up to a depth of 10 km). The "Reserve base" approach considers only the identified resource that meets specified minimum physical and chemical criteria related to current mining practice. On top of these variants the fact that the world annual production of an element varies from one year to another has triggered the publication of updates (Van Oers, Guinée & Heijungs, 2020). When carrying out an assessment at equipment level the choice of the method can affect drastically the results (i.e., which elements of the equipment have the highest contribution to the abiotic depletion issue), as it was described for indium and phosphorus (Pradel, Garcia & Vaija, 2021).

The Abiotic Depletion Potential methodology was carried out on a baseband unit for a second generation (2G), a third generation (3G), and a fourth generation (4G) configuration including chassis, different baseband cards, optical transceivers as well as power units by Orange in 2020.

Figures 2, 3, and 4 describe the contribution of different elements to the Abiotic Depletion Potential for this equipment, considering respectively the 1999 ultimate reserves method, the 2015 ultimate reserves method, and the 1999 reserve base method.

Between Figure 2 and Figure 3, the contribution of Gold to the total Abiotic Depletion Potential increased from 82.32% to 92.69%, which can be explained by the increase of the demand for this metal. Gold world primary production, i.e., mine production, jumped from 2330 tons in 1999 to 3000 tons in 2015 (National Minerals Information Center, 2020). In Figure 4 the main contributor to the Abiotic Depletion Potential is Indium. However, as it was underline in (Pradel, Garcia & Vaija, 2021), the issue with this metal is that the reserve base was estimated for 1999 on a very limited supply of 5700 tons. Since this value has been revised several times with, for example, estimations as large as 125,000 tons if all the zinc and copper ore that could be used as a source for indium was used (Gunn, 2014). Thus, with updated figures on the reserve base for all the different elements used in the base band unit manufacturing the results will undoubtedly be different.

Figure 2. Abiotic Depletion Potential results with the ultimate reserves 1999 method for a baseband unit (2G/3G/4G configuration) - Source life cycle assessment carried out by Orange™

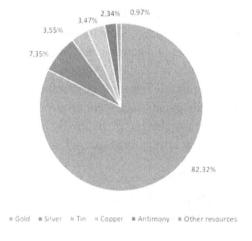

Figure 3. Abiotic Depletion Potential results with the ultimate reserves 2015 method for a baseband unit (2G/3G/4G configuration) - Source life cycle assessment carried out by Orange

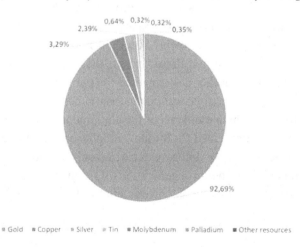

Figure 4. Abiotic Depletion Potential results with the reserve base 1999 method for a baseband unit (2G/3G/4G configuration) - Source life cycle assessment carried out by Orange™

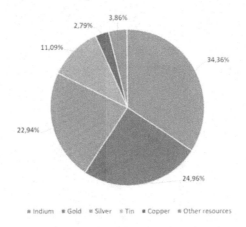

To analyse the limitation of the Abiotic Depletion Potential method, the assessment can be carried out with the reserve base and the world mine production figures from the U.S. Geological Survey publications.

Figure 5 shows how the assessment can be done for Antimony, a metalloid used for example as flame retardant (National Minerals Information Center, 2020). The blue bars show the years of reserve of a given year, simply by dividing the available reserve base by the world mine production For instance, for in 1996 the figures are respectively 4 200 000 metric tons of reserve for a world production of 108 000 metric tons. The red bars show the remaining years of reserves in 2019 if the given year was used as reference. For instance, with 1996 as reference the reserves are estimated to be sufficient for about 39 years thus in 2019 we would still have 16 years of supply.

For Antimony, the average reserves are almost always estimated to be about 10 to 15 years between 1999 and 2019. If the values from 1999, 2000, 2001, 2003 or 2004 had proved to be accurate for forecasts it would mean that in 2019 Antimony would have already been depleted. However, as these values are calculated according to the reserve base it means that the amount of identified resource that meets specified minimum physical and chemical criteria related to current mining practice have been modified from year to year. This makes the assessment of depletion of elements a difficult task. Mining practices improve, the price of the ore fluctuates, new reserves can be discovered, the demand for the material can skyrocket (e.g., indium with the advent of Liquid Crystal Display technologies, touch panels and smartphones) or plummet if a substance is banned or a better one is introduced on the market, etc. All these factors will affect the estimation of the remaining years of reserves.

Method Handling Critical Raw Material Applied To A Radio Access Network Equipment

In addition to these calculations based on life cycle assessment and reserves, the same exercise can be carried out with methodologies on material criticality such as the one developed by the European Union (Blengini et al., 2020) or in (Vaija & Philipot, 2020).

By applying this second methodology to the material content of the baseband unit studied previously, the results shown in Figure 6 can be derived. It has to be noted that these results combine the

Figure 5. Years of reserves of Antimony in the world for a given year (blue bars) and remaining years of stock in 2019 if the given year was used as reference - Source calculations carried out by Orange™

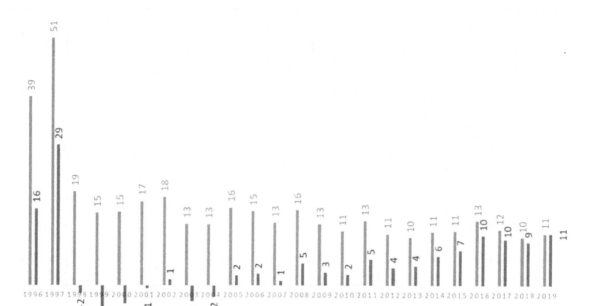

mass of each material (in milligrams) with its criticality index. The latest being calculated by Orange for a selection of materials, on a scale from 0 to 1, according to a combination of years of reserves, global supply risk, substitution economic importance, substitution supply risk and end-of-life recycling rate. As the mass of tin, contained in the alloy used to solder most of the electronic components on the printed circuit boards, is much higher than the mass of bismuth the results are mostly influenced by the material content in the equipment.

Insights About The Eco-Design Process

This work implies to dive deep in the supply-chain and it requires for a telecommunication operator to work in partnership with the equipment provider, the electronic components providers and their raw materials suppliers. Standards as the General method to declare the use of critical raw materials in energy-related products, or the International Electrotechnical Commission (IEC) project PNW 111-604 ED1 (Material declaration – Part 1: General requirements) should also improve the way different companies are able to communicate on the material content of their equipment. Indeed, one of the main objectives of the IEC project is to "*allows organizations to use this information in their environmentally conscious design process and across all product life cycle phases*". But the ability to communicate from one end of the supply chain to the other will not be the only requirement. All the materials used in these equipment have a specific purpose, for instance indium-tin oxide for its combination of properties (optically transparent, electrically conductive, compatible with current mass market manufacturing process for

Figure 6. Criticality index for a selection of material contained in the baseband unit - Source calculations carried out by Orange™

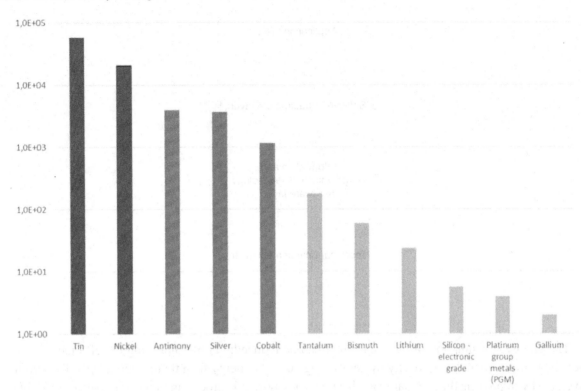

Liquid Crystal Display, Organic Light-Emitting Diode or touch-panels). This is why substituting these materials is and will be challenging.

By Improving The Data Centers Energy Consumption

A data center can be represented as an overlay of layers, sketched in Figure 7, each layer providing a service to the layer immediately above it. From the bottom to the top, the first layer provides to the Information and Communication Technology (ICT) hardware layer tailored energy according to the layer's requirements. The second layer provides to the software infrastructure layer all the resources (e.g., compute, network, storage) it needs to process and store all the information it receives. The third layer provides to the application layer all the resources (e.g., virtual machines, containers, and orchestrators) it needs to process and store all the information it receives.

The data center layer-based model (depicted in Figure 7) can be seen as a system that takes energy coming from a public grid as input, transforms this energy to processing power used by all the software it hosts, and disposes of the resultant heat. Two stages, shown in Figure 8[REMOVED REF FIELD], are involved in the transformation. In the first one, the incoming energy is split between the energy required by the ICT hardware layer and the energy required by the facilities. The second one consists of the transformation of the energy received by the ICT hardware layer into processing power used by both the software infrastructure layer and the service layer.

Figure 7. Data center layer-based model

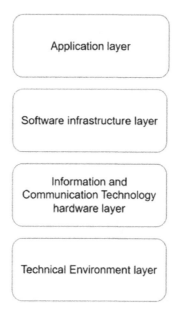

The energy consumption of the data center can be reduced: (1) by improving the efficiency of the technical environment layer, ideally by consuming no more energy than that required by ICT hardware layer, (2) by improving the ICT hardware layer efficiency, that is processing power delivered for a given amount of energy, (3) by improving the software infrastructure layer efficiency, and (4) by reducing the demand by the application layer on processing power.

Figure 8. Data center energy transformation

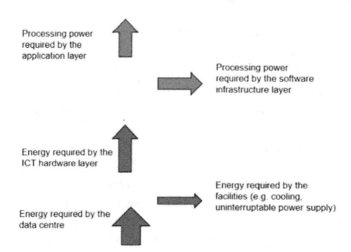

Improving The Technical Environment Layer Efficiency

While several now widespread technologies of cooling, such as hot and cold aisle arrangement, free cooling and passive cold door cooling, reduced the energy spent in cooling so that many state-of-the-art data centers may reach a power usage effectiveness[2] lower or equal to 1.3 (Coles, 2014), promising techniques will in the future keep on going the cooling system energy consumption reduction:

- Direct liquid cooling, where a liquid directly cools most heat-consuming components in a specific ICT equipment using dedicated piping (Douchet, Nortershauser, Le Masson & Glouannec, 2015).
- Submersion cooling, where conditioned off-the-shelf ICT equipment is immersed into a non-conductive liquid.
- Thermosyphon loop based on a micro-channels evaporator and a condenser constituted of finned tubes (Nadjahi, Louahlia-Gualous & Le Masson, 2020) in order to have real passive cooling solution.
- Artificial Intelligence controlling the cooling and humidity control equipment especially for data centers at low load or in a versatile climatic environment.

State-of-the-art data centers may also expect a reduction of their energy consumption by up to 5% when moving their power distribution from the traditional alternative current and the uninterruptible power supply units to the 400 volts direct current and the 400 volts direct current power supply units.

Figure 9. 400 volts direct current (400VDC) architecture versus alternative current (AC) architecture - Source Orange™

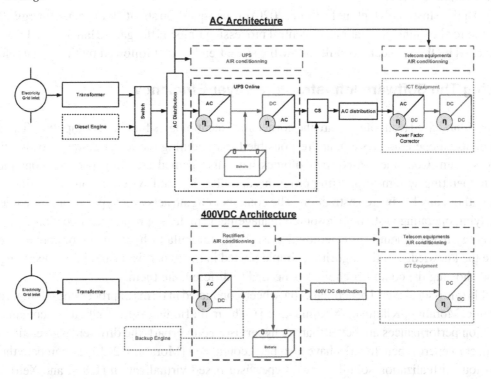

Indeed, as shown in (Pratt, Kumar & Aldridge, 2007), the 400 volts direct current power distributions exhibit a better efficiency compared to the traditional alternative current ones. This better efficiency is obtained by reducing the number of conversion stages in the 400 volts direct current power distributions compared to the alternative current ones, from the grid to the electronic components in the equipment, and by reducing the power losses in the cable distribution.

Beyond energy efficiency, the 400 volts direct current offers the possibility to directly connect renewable energy sources to the direct current bus without inverter to convert direct current to alternative current as is required in the alternative current architecture. It also reduces the volume occupied by the uninterruptible power supply by 10% and the maintenance cost by 20-30% compared to the alternative current uninterruptible power supply.

Improving The Hardware Layer Efficiency

Despite the sustained traffic growth, the increase in the ICT hardware performance per watt has succeeded to thwart the increase of the data centers energy consumption (Jones, 2018). Manufacturers, like Intel®, design their chipsets with hardware controlled energy efficiency features aiming to influence on both the energy they consume and the performance they deliver (Schone et al., 2019). Since the chipset thermal design power[3] affects the cost of the provisioning power, lowering it helps to get more performance without having to redesign the rack power envelop and the entire power distribution in a data center. Improvements in performance per watt should also come from custom application-specific integrated circuit deployed in Google's data centers for the inference phase of neural networks (Jouppi, Young, Patil & Patterson, 2017). In addition to the works undertaken for increasing the performance per watt, ICT hardware is now built to support wider temperatures and relative hygrometry ranges (ASHRAE Technical Committee, 2016).

But the Uptime Institute[4] (UptimeInstitute, 2020) raises a question about the expected energy efficiency gains for the forthcoming generations of central processing units: if the gains flatten out, the amount of energy needed by the data centers will follow the same trend as that followed by the demand for data.

Improving The Software Infrastructure Layer Efficiency

Virtual machine-based technologies are the cornerstone technologies for cloud computing. The hypervisors, acting as an operating system, are responsible for scheduling the resources and hosting the guest operating system. Container-based technologies have also gained attention because containers only require an operating system, supporting programs and libraries, and system resources to run a specific program without any hardware abstraction. The container engine acts as a hypervisor while it leverages the underlying operating system for resource management (including resource allocation).

The energy management is affected by the use of an umbrella of hypervisors or container engines. Therefore the knowledge of the algorithms implemented in the hypervisors and in the operating system of the node hosting the container engines is needed to differentiate them.

To tackle this issue, several benchmarks have been conducted in terms of processing, storage, memory and network (Morabito, Kjällman & Komu, 2015). The main finding is that, albeit the container-based virtualization performances are better than its hypervisor counterpart, the difference is relatively small. With respect to energy, benchmarks have also been conducted (Morabito, 2015) to compare the performance of four virtualization solutions: two hypervisor-based virtualization (KVM and Xen), and two container-based ones (Docker and LXC). The results showed that the power consumption of the four solutions is similar when stressed with heavy CPU and memory workloads. In the case of network performance analysis, Docker and LXC introduce lower power consumption.

To provide insights to the designers of the software infrastructure layer, the energy management has been evaluated by combining different hardware, different workloads and different hypervisors and container engines (Jiang et al., 2019). The study produced the following outcomes:

- The different hypervisors exhibit different power and energy consumptions on the same hardware running the same workload.
- Although the hypervisors have different energy efficiencies aligned with different workload types and workload levels, no hypervisor outperforms the other hypervisors on all platforms in terms of power or energy consumption.
- The container-based technology is not more power-efficient than the conventional virtualization technology.
- Although the ARM64 server has low power consumption, it completes computation tasks with a long execution time and, sometimes, high energy consumption.

Improving The Software Energy Efficiency

Software energy efficiency consists of taking into account the energetic cost of software during its lifecycle from the design to the usage phase. It is important as it impacts a wide range of users' devices and ICT equipment. Both academic and industrial works are being conducted in order to cover software energy efficiency.

The first aspect and probably the most basic one that unlocks other considerations is the measure, where the purpose is to have accurate and fine-grained tools that can be used at multiple steps of the software coding process (code, build, test, etc.). Having accurate measures would help detecting the slightest changes on the software energy consumption and investigating the causes, while fine-grained measures would allow measures at process, thread and even instruction level. As actual hardware measurement tools can be very accurate but not fine grained, many attempts have been made to build and improve software measurement tools to target the two previous requirements such as PowerAPI (Colmant et al., 2018) or Joolmeter (Mittal, Kansal & Chandra, 2012).

Once accurate and fine-grained measures are available, the efforts will go towards taking actions to reduce software energy consumption. Many works that provide insights and guidelines on how to enhance software energy efficiency are available. For example, during the coding phase, it is possible to consider both reducing the produced code energy consumption (Hasan et al., 2016; Pereira et al., 2017) and the energy consumption of the coding phase itself (Kumar, Li & Shi, 2017).

While technical studies are important to advance the current state of knowledge about green software design, conducting quantitative and qualitative studies are as important to investigate developers' considerations on software energy efficiency. Works such as (Manotas et al, 2016; Linares-Vasquez et al., 2014; Li & Halfond, 2014; Jagroep et al., 2017; Ournani et al., 2020) highlight that the performance and security of software products take precedence over their energy efficiency, making harder the production of energy efficient software. In addition, the aforementioned lack of tools to reduce the energy consumption of software, the lack of developers' knowledge on software eco-design, the lack of a documentation, and the lack of good practices, increase the difficulty to provide energy efficient software.

By Reducing The Average Electricity Intensity of Data Transmission

According to (Aslan, Mayers, Koomey & France, 2017) the average electricity intensity of data transmission, measured as kilowatt-hours per gigabyte, has decreased by half approximately every two years since 2000 for core and fixed-line access networks. An approach to identify the telecommunication networks energy efficiency lacks is to see them as separate protocol layers and look at each protocol layer individually. Two main layers can be identified:

- The transmission layer: its role is to transmit information over the physical medium between two nodes of the network with respect to constraints such as error-free, integrity, authentication, ciphering; it thus corresponds to both the PHY and LINK layers of the OSI model.
- The network layer: its role is to choose a path through the networks to transmit a packet with respect to constraints such as latency, bandwidth, or packet header information. Some additional constraints (e.g., delay, capacity) can be taken into account by advanced routing/forwarding schemes. This is usually referred to as traffic engineered paths.

Improvements In The Transmission Layer

Most energy efficiency improvements in the transmission layer focused on the physical layers. With respect to the mobile radio networks, the different 3GPP-specified generations (i.e., second generation, third generation, fourth generation and fifth generation) have gradually implemented mechanisms intended to increase the data speed. Three strategies have been applied and combined together: increasing the spectrum bandwidth, increasing the spectral efficiency and finally increasing the energy efficiency.

In the first strategy, the signal basic waveform is improved to support larger spectrum bandwidths. For instance, in mobile networks, Gaussian Minimum-Shift Keying, Code Division Multiple Access, and Orthogonal Frequency Division Multiplex, were introduced for 2G, 3G and finally 4G/5G, respectively, to support hundreds of kHz, few MHz, and finally dozens to hundreds of MHz, respectively.

In the second strategy, without using more spectrum, the user data rate is adaptively improved when the user's device gets closer to the radio base station or access point (i.e. in a location where the signal-to-noise ratio is better) thanks to recent advances in adaptive modulation and coding and in Multiple Input Multiple Output (MIMO) antenna techniques (Rusek et al., 2013). Indeed, the user's device multiplies its data rate by a factor of 2, 4 and up to 10, simply by upgrading its modulation from Binary Phase-Shift Keying (BPSK), to Quadrature Phase-Shift Keying (QPSK), 16QAM and up to 1024QAM (Quadrature Amplitude Modulation), when it experiences a higher signal-to-noise ratio. Similarly, a user device equipped with several antennas, typically 4 for 5G, gets its data rate multiplied by a factor of 2 to 8 when it gets a higher signal-to-noise ratio. Some radio propagation conditions involving reflections and scattering are also necessary. Fortunately such conditions are frequently met in environments such as indoor or dense urban areas. This second strategy increases the spectral efficiency in bits per second per Hz.

By combining the second strategy with a third and last strategy, the user data rate can be further improved without radiating more power. Indeed, in the third strategy the signal-to-noise ratio is boosted at the user's device location thanks to the MIMO beamforming technique which adaptively focuses the energy in the direction of the device. This strategy increases the energy efficiency, in bits per second per Hz and per radiated power. Note that instead of being used to increase the data speed, the beamforming technique can be used to reduce the radiated power to meet a certain target data rate. In the case where the radiated power is a major part of the energy consumption, reducing the radiated power does reduce the energy consumption. This is typically the case when the network is loaded and actively transmitting data.

These conventional techniques for managing the spectral and energy efficiency of data transmission are now supplemented by specific technologies explicitly designed to optimize energy utilization:

- Power amplifier improvement in efficiency due to new technology based on Gallium Nitride.
- Advanced sleep modes which consist in saving power by deactivating some electronic components during idle periods when no data needs to be transmitted or received and when there are no synchronization signals to be sent.
- Massive MIMO (i.e. scaling up MIMO technology from few antenna-elements to several dozens or even hundreds) and improvements on efficiency of the related chipset, when the network is highly loaded.

The power amplifiers, which are the main consuming part of the radio base stations as radio signals need to be strongly amplified to ensure cell coverage, have seen their efficiency (ratio between emitted power and consumed power) increase from 30% for 3G amplifiers to 50% for 4G power amplifiers. It is slightly different for 5G in 3.5GHz band. 5G active antennas called massive MIMO are not mainly made of amplifiers as the antennas of the previous generations. The amplifiers are only a part of the massive MIMO power consumption as they include a lot of digital components mandatory for beam-forming techniques used with this technology. Consequently, massive MIMO units are quite consuming but significant progress is expected in digital chipset area, leading to an improvement of the 5G average electricity intensity of transmitting data in the coming years. The aforementioned tenfold ratio should be reached in 2025 and could even increase further to twentyfold by 2030 (Orange, 2020). Figure 10 highlights the improvement of the average electricity intensity of transmitting data starting from the second generation to the fifth generation.

Figure 10. Average electricity intensity of transmitting data (in kWh/GB) of successive mobile radio networks generations - Source Orange™

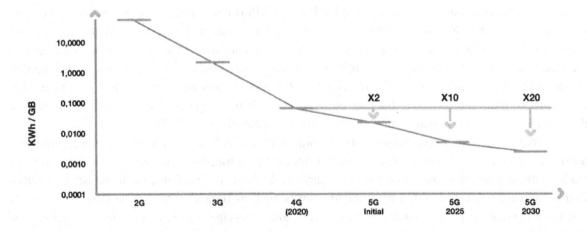

To understand the contribution of the advanced sleep modes in the energy efficiency of the mobile radio networks, it is important to know that they are dimensioned to handle the peak traffic of the busy hours. During low traffic periods, in particular during night-time, several energy saving features, shutting down some radio components (switch-off redundant frequency carriers, shutdown power amplifiers, reduce input voltage etc.), can be activated by the operators to decrease the energy consumption of their mobile radio networks. With all the available features activated on all the cellular generations (2G/3G/4G) of the mobile radio networks generations of a given site, a decrease of 10% of the average electricity intensity of transmitting data can be expected. As some components are disabled when a given feature is active, a trade-off between the average electricity intensity of transmitting data and the quality offered to the users must be found. In 5G, some strategies, implemented with the use of advanced sleep modes (Salem, Gati, Altman & Chahed, 2017), exhibit that high energy gains can be obtained albeit some degradation in the users' throughput and latency.

Innovative solutions have been explored to keep massive MIMO beamforming the most energy efficient possible, even under challenging conditions: typically, when the network has to focus towards very fast moving connected vehicles (Phan-Huy, Wesemann, Bjoersell & Sternad, 2018) or a dumb devices (light in electronics and signal processing) such as a connected object (Phan-Huy, Wesemann & Sehier, 2019).

Even though each new generation of wireless networks is more energy efficient than the previous, due to the fast data traffic growth, wireless networks keep on consuming more energy. The Electro-Magnetic Field exposure due to all technologies is also increasing and getting closer to the thresholds fixed by some countries in Europe where the exposure thresholds are set to lower values (GSMA, 2021) than the ones set by the international regulation (GSMA, 2019). To cope with this challenge, the research community has started to explore ultra-low power solutions to convey more data rate without radiating additional waves. Two strategies are being currently explored:

- Smart radio environments using Reflective Intelligent Surfaces (RIS) (Di Renzo et al., 2019).
- Ambient backscatter communications (Liu et al., 2013; Van Huynh et al., 2018).

In smart radio environments, an alternative to network densification is proposed to improve the coverage and capacity of an existing wireless network. Instead of deploying new access point to cover an area in need of capacity or coverage, one can deploy RISs, A RIS is not radiating any waves and is therefore an ultra-low power technology. A RIS acts as a mirror for waves, and deviates their propagation. An example of RIS implementation is an array of antenna-elements connected to tunable impedances that are electronically controlled to create a reflection from an intended incident direction to an intended output direction. A wireless network connected to RIS (though low rate wireless links or cables) can control RISs to deviate waves so that they converge towards the target coverage area or intended user. RISs can be seen as relays that do not actively radiate (Di Renzo et al., 2020).

In ambient backscatter communications, a promising technical enabler for energy-free communications and self-powered Internet of Things, a radio-frequency tag transmits a message to a radio-frequency reader without generating any radio wave. It simply reflects in all directions, i.e. it backscatters radio-frequency waves already emitted by ambient sources such as broadcast television (Liu et al., 2013). The tag modulates its level of backscattering to transmit a message. The reader detects the message by analysing the variations induced by the tag in the signal it receives from the source. The principle to introduce "energy-free communicating" tags in 5G networks is also proposed (Gati et al., 2019). Such tags would backscatter the waves from 5G base stations and would be read by 5G mobile devices. Conversely they would also backscatter 5G device waves and would be read by 5G base stations. Tags are self-powered devices and first prototypes (Rachedi et al., 2019; Rachedi, Phan-Huy, Ourir & De Rosny, 2019) powered by a small solar-panel show promising results. They also show the limitations in terms of rate (few bps to few kbps) and range (few centimetres to few meters) due to the weakness of the signal that is backscattered by the tag. Innovative solutions based on the improvements at the tag side (Fara et al., 2020a; Fara et al., 2020b; Kokar et al., 2019), for instance by exploiting polarization diversity, and massive MIMO at the source side (Fara, Phan-Huy & Renzo, 2020) or the reader side (Fara et al., 2020c) are being explored.

The energy efficiency improvements may also use some of the features of the network protocols sitting in or above the physical layer. Table 1 highlights some of these features.

Table 1. Network protocol features hosting the energy efficiency improvements

Protocol feature mechanisms	Explanation	Examples
Keep alive	Reduce number of retransmissions; increase the associated timer	TCP, Diameter, GTP
Failure retries	Reduce number of retransmissions; increase the associated timer	Diameter, GTP, DSCP
Periodic transfers	Reduce number of periodic transfers when possible	Applications
Security features	Choose energy efficient cryptographic algorithms	LAKA, RSACRT
Options	Adopt the maximum number of default options if simplifies negotiation, without other negative effect	SIP, TCP
Header compaction	Adopt a compact format of headers when available	SIP
Header compression	Use a compressed and energy-efficient header format (with possible side effects to check)	ROHC (IP, UDP, TCP, ESP), HPACK (HTTP2)
Request prioritization	Use request prioritization tags when available	Diameter
Flow aggregation	Multiplex several flows over the same connection, in order to minimize overhead due to supplementary connections	SCTP or HTTP/2 multiple streams
Application data coding	Use compact user data coding: partial URIs, compact charsets, compression, compact code (e.g., ISO 8859-1 ASCII instead of ISO 10646)	SIP, HTTP, SDP
Maximum Transmission Unit	Be aware of Maximum Transmission Unit constraints, and adapt the payload size to the Maximum Transmission Unit offered by the under layer in order to avoid rejects, fragmentation, overhead	PMTUD
Padding	Avoid padding and blank lines	SIP, HTTP, SDP

The coder-decoder (codec) can also be optimized to reduce the use of the following resources:

- Processor used for compression and decompression;
- Memory used for buffering;
- Network used for transmission;
- Middle boxes to perform transcoding.

Improvements In The Network Layer

The issue of reducing the energy in the networks can be partly addressed by putting their nodes (service cards, network cards, or any other component) and links in low energy states and the European Telecommunications Standards Institute (ETSI) provides an information model for the fixed-networks based on the concept of Energy-Aware State (ETSI ES 203 237, 2014). An Energy-Aware State (EAS) is a property associated to a network component and has the following attributes:

- Power consumption: contains the electrical power (in Watt) of this EAS;
- Network performance: contains the quality of service parameters offered by this EAS;
- State transition: contains the set of the EAS reachable from this EAS and the transition delays (in second) between this EAS and the reachable EAS.

The nth EAS of a network component is modeled by a set of standby ($S^{(k)}$) and power ($P^{(j)}$) capabilities:

n^{th} EAS $= \{S^k(n), P^j(n)\}$ with $0 \leq k \leq K$ and $0 \leq j \leq J$

Where:

- $S^{(k>0)}(n)$ represents the kth standby state during which the network component is sleeping. In the Kth standby state, $S^{(k=K)}(n)$, the component is completely off;
- $S^{(k=0)}(n)$ is the active state in with the network component is working;
- $P^{(j>0)}(n)$ is the jth level in the active state where the network component provides a given performance and consumes a given power;
- $P^{(j=0)}(n)$ is the active state where the network component provides the highest performance and consumes the highest power;
- $P^{(j=J)}(n)$ is the Jth level in the active state where the network component provides the lowest performance and consumes the lowest power.

The interface called "Green Standard Interface" is in charge of providing the commands set necessary to the discovery, the access, the provisioning, the configuration, and the monitoring of the EAS.

Changing the energetic state of a network, by shutting down and waking up network components, means that it is possible to change its topology across the time of the day with respect to the traffic demands. Therefore, its control plane must be aware of the network components states in order to be sure that they will be able to forward the traffic flows. A proof of concept extending the OpenFlow Protocol[5] with the Energy-Aware State concept demonstrated its usefulness to reduce the networks power (Bolla & Bruschi, 2015). The network power reduction is greater than the one obtained in works, such as (Cianfrani, 2012), which only address the network links states in contrast to the ETSI standard which addresses all the network components states.

In contrast with the real networks where the routes are established while the future traffic demands are unknown, the proof of concept knows them beforehand. To be closer to the real networks, an advanced scenario shall compute the routes with a machine learning technique based on the traffic demands history knowledge. Here, the hypothesis it that this knowledge contains information to predict the future demands and compute the routes with respect to an objective such as minimizing the network congestion.

In (Valadarsky, Schapira, Shahaf & Tamar, 2017) two machine learning techniques were analysed: the supervised learning and the reinforcement learning. In the first one, the optimal routes are computed for each traffic demand and the predicted traffic demand triggers the route computation with respect to that demand. In the reinforcement learning, an agent learns a mapping between the traffic demand history and the routing strategies. The more the agent receives rewards, the better the mapping. Since the analysis outcome suggests that the reinforcement learning outperforms the supervised learning, the machine learning technique implemented in the advanced scenario should be the reinforcement. In the scenario, the issue of the quality of service degradation induced by the latencies associated with the transitions between the Energy-Aware States, which are provided by the "state transition" attribute, should be understood.

The Energy-Aware States are hardware component states. In the virtualized networks, which are addressed within the ETSI Network Functions Virtualisation (NFV) architectural framework (ETSI GS NFV 002, 2013), the hardware resources are shared between the virtualized resources. The energy they consume is called virtualized energy, and their Energy-Aware States are called virtualized Energy-Aware States (vEAS). These vEAS are standardized in (ETSI ES 203 682, 2019) for the Network Service (NS) level, the Virtualised Network Function (VNF) level and the Virtualised Network Function Component (VNFC) level. Their usefulness in the NFV context are explained in (Bianchi et al., 2019).

CONCLUSION AND FUTURE RESEARCH DIRECTIONS

According to the Intergovernmental Panel on Climate Change, the global warming can be avoided by "reaching net zero carbon dioxide emissions globally around 2050 and concurrent deep reductions in emissions of non-carbon dioxide forcers, particularly methane. Such mitigation pathways are characterized by energy-demand reductions, decarbonization of electricity and other fuels, electrification of energy end use, deep reductions in agricultural emissions, and some form of carbon dioxide removal with carbon storage on land or sequestration in geological reservoirs".

To protect the planet and guarantee prosperity for all, The United Nations has set up a sustainable development program made up of seventeen goals. Among them, the goal number twelve establishes sustainable consumption and production patterns so that a social and economic growth does not increase the pressure on Earth's resources, and the goal number thirteen constrains the global warming.

This chapter provided an overview of some actions that the telecommunication companies implement to grab the climate stakes:

- **By assessing the issues of mineral resources on network equipment**. Some insights are given on two methods applied to a network equipment, namely Abiotic Depletion Potential and handling critical raw material, allowing to work on the reduction of its environmental footprint;
- **By improving the data centers energy consumption**. The energy consumption of the data center can be reduced: by improving the efficiency of the technical environment layer, ideally by consuming no more energy than that required by the hardware layer; by improving the hardware layer efficiency, that is processing power delivered for a given amount of energy; by improving the software infrastructure layer efficiency; and by reducing the demand by the application layer on processing power;

- **By reducing the average electricity intensity of the transmitting data**. An approach to identify the telecommunication networks energy efficiency lacks is to see them as separate protocol layers and look at each protocol layer individually. Two main layers can be identified: the transmission layer and the network layer. Most energy efficiency improvements in the transmission layers focused on the physical layers. Improvements in the network layer are tackled by putting the network nodes and links in low energy states.

Not all the actions are here examined because of their multitude. For example, collaborative networking is needed so that networks that implement energy-inferred optimisation will advertise such capability to the applications (e.g., discover session timeouts, provide the control over a session). These applications will then use such capabilities to optimize the power consumption by avoiding to overload the network with frequent keepalives (e.g., by adjusting the keepalive interval as a function of the timeout advertised by the network). Also, Because of the rebound effect, the search for energy efficiency will not to be enough to girdle the telecommunication networks energy consumption, and the telecommunications companies should consider sobriety implementation. Beyond only focusing on their networks, the telecommunications companies seek to contribute to the energy transition by enabling the green energy consumption share to increase.

REFERENCES

ASHRAE Technical Committee. (2016). *Data Center Power Equipment Thermal Guidelines and Best Practices*. https://ecoinfo.cnrs.fr/wp-content/uploads/2016/08/ashrae_2011_thermal_guidelines_data_center.pdf

Aslan, J., Mayers, K., Koomey, J. G., & France, C. (2017). Electricity intensity of internet data transmission: Untangling the estimates. *Journal of Industrial Ecology*, 22(4), 785–798. doi:10.1111/jiec.12630

Bianchi, G., Bianco, C., Boldi, M., Bolla, R., Le Grand, O., Meo, M., Penhoat, J. & Renga, D. (2019). Sustainability, a key issue of 5G network ecosystem. *The 5G Italy Book 2019: a Multiperspective View of 5G*.

Blengini, G. A., Latunussa, E. L. C., Eynard, U., de Matos, C. T., Wittmer, D., Georgitzikis, K., Pavel, C., Carrara, S., Mancini, L., Unguru, M., Blagoeva, D., Mathieux, F., & Pennington, D. (2020). *Study on the EU's list of Critical Raw Materials (2020) Final Report*. European Commission Technical Report.

Bolla, R., Bruschi, R., Davoli, F., & Lombardo, C. (2015). Fine-Grained Energy-Efficient Consolidation in SDN Networks and Devices. *IEEE eTransactions on Network and Service Management*, 12(5), 132–145. doi:10.1109/TNSM.2015.2431074

Bordage, F. (2019). *The environmental footprint of the digital world*. https://www.greenit.fr/wp-content/uploads/2019/11/GREENIT_EENM_etude_EN_accessible.pdf

Cianfrani, A., Eramo, V., Listanti, M., Polverini, M., & Vasilakos, A. V. (2012). An OSPF-Integrated Routing Strategy for QoS-Aware Energy Saving in IP Backbone Networks. *IEEE eTransactions on Network and Service Management*, 9(3), 254–267. doi:10.1109/TNSM.2012.031512.110165

Coles, H. C. (2014). *Demonstration of Rack-Mounted Computer Equipment Cooling Solutions, Environmental Energy technologies division*. Ernest Orlando Lawrence Berkeley National Laboratory. https://eta.lbl.gov/sites/default/files/publications/demo_of_rack-mounted_computer_equip_cooling_solutions.pdf

Colmant, M., Rouvoy, R., Kurpicz, M., Sobe, A., Felber, P., & Seinturier, L. (2018). The next 700 CPU power models. *Journal of Systems and Software, 144*, 382–396. doi:10.1016/j.jss.2018.07.001

Department of the Interior. (2018). Final List of Critical Minerals 2018. *Federal Register, 83*(97). https://www.govinfo.gov/content/pkg/FR-2018-05-18/pdf/2018-10667.pdf

Di Renzo, M., Debbah, M., Phan-Huy, D.-T., Zappone, A., Alouini, M.-S., Yuen, C., & Sciancalepore, V. (2019). Smart radio environments empowered by reconfigurable AI meta-surfaces: An idea whose time has come. *EURASIP Journal on Wireless Communications and Networking, 2019*(1), 129. doi:10.118613638-019-1438-9

Di Renzo, M., Ntontin, K. S., Song, J., Danufane, F. H., Qian, X., Lazarakis, F., De Rosny, J., Phan-Huy, D.-T., Simeone, O., Zhang, R., Debbah, M., Lerosey, G., Fink, M., Tretyakov, S., & Shamai, S. (2020). Reconfigurable Intelligent Surfaces vs. Relaying: Differences, Similarities, and Performance Comparison. *IEEE Open Journal of the Communications Society, 1*, 798–807. doi:10.1109/OJCOMS.2020.3002955

Douchet, F., Nortershauser, D., Le Masson, S., & Glouannec, P. (2015). Experimental and numerical study of water-cooled datacom equipment. *Applied Thermal Engineering, 84*, 350–359. doi:10.1016/j.applthermaleng.2015.03.030

ETSI ES 203 237. (2014). *Environmental Engineering (EE); Green Abstraction Layer (GAL); Power management capabilities of the future energy telecommunication fixed network nodes*. ETSI. https://www.etsi.org/deliver/etsi_es/203200_203299/203237/01.01.01_60/es_203237v010101p.pdf

ETSI ES 203 682. (2019). *Environmental Engineering (EE); Green Abstraction Layer (GAL); Power management capabilities of the future energy telecommunication fixed network nodes; Enhanced Interface for power management in Network Function Virtualisation (NFV) environments*. https://www.etsi.org/deliver/etsi_es/203600_203699/203682/01.01.00_50/es_203682v010100m.pdf

ETSI GS NFV 002. (2013). *Network Functions Virtualisation (NFV); Architectural Framework*. https://www.etsi.org/deliver/etsi_gs/NFV/001_099/002/01.01.01_60/gs_NFV002v010101p.pdf

European Commission. (2020). *Communication from the commission to the European parliament, the council, the European economic and social committee and the committee of the regions, Critical Raw Materials Resilience: Charting a Path towards greater Security and Sustainability*. https://eur-lex.europa.eu/legal-content/EN/TXT/?uri=CELEX:52020DC0474

Fara, R., Bel-Haj-Maati, N., Phan-Huy, D.-T., Malhouroux, N., & Di Renzo, M. (2020c). First Experimental Evaluation of Ambient Backscatter Communications with Massive MIMO Reader. *31st International Symposium on Personal, Indoor and Mobile Radio Communications*.

Fara, R., Phan-Huy, D.-T., Ourir, A., Di Renzo, M., & De Rosny, J. (2020b). Robust Ambient Backscatter Communications with Polarization Reconfigurable Tags. *IEEE 31st Annual International Symposium on Personal. Indoor and Mobile Radio Communications*.

Fara, R., Phan-Huy, D.-T., Ourir, A., Prevotet, J.-C., Hélard, M., Di Renzo, M., & De Rosny, J. (2020a). *Polarization-Based Reconfigurable Tags for Robust Ambient Backscatter Communications. IEEE Open Journal of the Communications Society.*

Fara, R., Phan-Huy, D.-T., & Renzo, M. D. (2020). Ambient backscatters-friendly 5G networks: creating hot spots for tags and good spots for readers. *IEEE Wireless Communications and Networking Conference*, 1-7. 10.1109/WCNC45663.2020.9120781

Gati, A., Salem, F. E., Galindo-Serrano, A. M., Marquet, D., Le Masson, S., Rivera, T., Phan-Huy, D.-T., Altman, Z., Landre, J.-B., Simon, O., Le Rouzic, E., Bourgart, F., Gosselin, S., Vautier, M., Gourdin, E., En-Najjary, T., El-Tabach, M., Indre, R.-M., Gerard, G., & Delsart, G. (2019). (Submitted to). Key technologies to accelerate the ict green evolution: An operators point of view. *IEEE Communications Surveys and Tutorials*. https://arxiv.org/abs/1903.09627

GSMA. (2019). *GSMA EMF Policy*. https://www.gsma.com/publicpolicy/consumer-affairs/emf-and-health/emf-policy

GSMA. (2019a). *The Mobile Economy*. https://data.gsmaintelligence.com/api-web/v2/research-file-download?id=39256194&file=2712-250219-ME-Global.pdf

GSMA. (2020). *Position paper on the European Green Deal*. https://www.gsma.com/gsmaeurope/wp-content/uploads/2020/06/GSMA-position-paper-on-Green-Deal-June_2020.pdf

GSMA. (2021). *European EMF and antenna siting policy*. https://www.gsma.com/publicpolicy/european-emf-and-antenna-siting-policy

Gunn, G. (2014). Critical Metals Handbook. John Wiley & Sons, Ltd. doi:10.1002/9781118755341

Hasan, S., King, Z., Hafiz, M., Sayagh, M., Adams, B., & Hindle, A. (2016). Energy Profiles of Java Collections Classes. *38th International Conference on Software Engineering*, 225-236.

Jagroep, E., Procaccianti, G., Werf, J. M. V. D., Brinkkemper, S., Blom, L. & Vliet, R. (2017). Energy efficiency on the product roadmap: An empirical study across releases of a software product. *Journal of Software: Evolution and Process, 29.*

Jiang, C., Wang, Y., Ou, D., Li, Y., Zhang, J., Wan, J., Luo, B., & Shi, W. (2019). Energy efficiency comparison of hypervisors. *Sustainable Computing: Informatics and Systems, 22*, 311–321.

Jones, N. (2018). How to stop data centers from gobbling up the world's electricity. *Nature, 561*(7722), 163–166. doi:10.1038/d41586-018-06610-y PMID:30209383

Jouppi, N. P., Young, C., Patil, N., & Patterson, D. (2017). In-Datacenter Performance Analysis of a Tensor Processing UnitTM. *Proceedings of the 44th International Symposium on Computer Architecture.* 10.1145/3079856.3080246

Kokar, Y., Phan-Huy, D.-T., Fara, R., Rachedi, K., Ourir, A., De Rosny, J., Di Renzo, M., Prévotet, J.-C., & Hélard, M. (2019). First experimental ambient backscatter communication using a compact reconfigurable tag antenna. *IEEE Global Communications Conference.* 10.1109/GCWkshps45667.2019.9024698

Kumar, M., Li, Y., & Shi, W. (2017). Energy consumption in Java: An early experience. *Eighth International Green and Sustainable Computing Conference*, 1-8. 10.1109/IGCC.2017.8323579

Li, D., & Halfond, W. G. J. (2014). An investigation into energy-saving programming practices for Android smartphone app development. *Proceedings of the 3rd International Workshop on Green and Sustainable Software*, 46–53. 10.1145/2593743.2593750

Linares-Vásquez, M., Bavota, G., Bernal-Cárdenas, C., Oliveto, R., Di Penta, M., & Poshyvanyk, D. (2014). Mining energy-greedy API usage patterns in Android apps: an empirical study. *Proceedings of the 11th Working Conference on Mining Software Repositories*, 2–11. 10.1145/2597073.2597085

Liu, V., Parks, A. N., Talla, V., Gollakota, S., Wetherall, D. J., & Smith, J. R. (2013). Ambient backscatter: wireless communication out of thin air. *Proceedings of the ACM SIGCOMM 2013 conference on SIGCOMM*, 39–50. 10.1145/2486001.2486015

Manotas, I., Bird, C., Zhang, R., Shepherd, D., Jaspan, C., Sadowski, C., Pollock, L., & Clause, J. (2016). An empirical study of practitioners' perspectives on green software engineering. *Proceedings of the 38th International Conference on Software Engineering*, 237–248. 10.1145/2884781.2884810

Masson-Delmotte, V., Zhai, P., Pörtner, H.-O., Roberts, D., Skea, J., Shukla, P. R., Pirani, A., Moufouma-Okia, W., Péan, C., Pidcock, R., Connors, S., Matthews, J. B. R., Chen, Y., Zhou, X., Gomis, M. I., Lonnoy, E., Maycock, T., Tignor, M., & Waterfield, T. (2018). *Summary for Policymakers, In: Global Warming of 1.5°C. An IPCC Special Report on the impacts of global warming of 1.5°C above pre-industrial levels and related global greenhouse gas emission pathways, in the context of strengthening the global response to the threat of climate change, sustainable development, and efforts to eradicate poverty.* https://www.ipcc.ch/site/assets/uploads/sites/2/2019/05/SR15_SPM_version_report_LR.pdf

Mittal, R., Kansal, A., & Chandra, R. (2012). Empowering developers to estimate app energy consumption. *Proceedings of the 18th annual international conference on Mobile computing and networking*, 317–328. 10.1145/2348543.2348583

Morabito, R. (2015). Power Consumption of Virtualization Technologies: an Empirical Investigation. *8th IEEE/ACM International Conference on Utility and Cloud Computing*.

Morabito, R., Kjällman, J., & Komu, M. (2015). Hypervisors vs. Lightweight Virtualization: a Performance Comparison. *IEEE International Conference on Cloud Engineering*.

Nadjahi, C., Louahlia-Gualous, H., & Le Masson, S. (2020). Experimental study and analytical modeling of thermosyphon loop for cooling data center racks. *Heat and Mass Transfer*, 56(1), 121–142. doi:10.100700231-019-02695-x

National Minerals Information Center. (2020). *Mineral Commodity Summaries*. https://www.usgs.gov/centers/nmic/mineral-commodity-summaries

Orange. (2020). *5G: energy efficiency by design. Orange.* https://hellofuture.orange.com/en/5g-energy-efficiency-by-design/

Ournani, Z., Rouvoy, R., Rust, P., & Penhoat, J. (2020). On Reducing the Energy Consumption of Software: From Hurdles to Requirements. *Proceedings of the 14th ACM / IEEE International Symposium on Empirical Software Engineering and Measurement*, 1–12.

Pereira, R., Couto, M., Ribeiro, F., Rua, R., Cunha, J., Fernandes, J. P., & Saraiva, J. (2017). Energy efficiency across programming languages: how do energy, time, and memory relate? *Proceedings of the 10th ACM SIGPLAN International Conference on Software Language Engineering*, 256–267. 10.1145/3136014.3136031

Phan-Huy, D.-T., Wesemann, S., Bjoersell, J., & Sternad, M. (2018). Adaptive Massive MIMO for fast moving connected vehicles: It will work with Predictor Antennas! *22nd International ITG Workshop on Smart Antennas*, 1-8.

Phan-Huy, D.-T., Wesemann, S., & Sehier, P. (2019). How Wireless Dumb Devices Could Attain High Data Rates Thanks to Smart Massive MIMO Networks. *23rd International ITG Workshop on Smart Antennas*, 1-8.

Pradel, M., Garcia, J., & Vaija, M. S. (2021). A framework for good practices to assess abiotic mineral resource depletion in Life Cycle Assessment. *Journal of Cleaner Production*, *219*, 123296. doi:10.1016/j.jclepro.2020.123296

Pratt, A., Kumar, P., & Aldridge, T. V. (2007). Evaluation of 400V DC distribution in telco and data centers to improve energy efficiency. *29th International Telecommunications Energy Conference*, 32-39. 10.1109/INTLEC.2007.4448733

Rachedi, K., Phan-Huy, D.-T., Ourir, A., & De Rosny, J. (2019). Spatial characterization of the ambient backscatter communication performance in line-of-sight. *IEEE International Symposium on Antennas and Propagation and USNC-URSI Radio Science Meeting*. 10.1109/APUSNCURSINRSM.2019.8889046

Rachedi, K., Phan-Huy, D.-T., Selmene, N., Ourir, A., Gautier, M., Gati, A., Galindo-Serrano, A. M., Fara, R., & De Rosny, J. (2019). Demo abstract: *Real-Time Ambient Backscatter Demonstration*. *IEEE International Conference on Computer Communications*.

Rogelj, J., Shindell, D., Jiang, K., Fifita, S., Forster, P., Ginzburg, V., Handa, C., Kheshgi, H., Kobayashi, S., Kriegler, E., Mundaca, L., Séférian, R., & Vilariño, M. V. (2018). *Mitigation Pathways Compatible with 1.5°C in the Context of Sustainable Development, In: Global Warming of 1.5°C. An IPCC Special Report on the impacts of global warming of 1.5°C above pre-industrial levels and related global greenhouse gas emission pathways, in the context of strengthening the global response to the threat of climate change, sustainable development, and efforts to eradicate poverty*. https://www.ipcc.ch/site/assets/uploads/sites/2/2019/02/SR15_Chapter2_Low_Res.pdf

Rusek, F., Persson, D., Lau, B. K., Larsson, E. G., Marzetta, T. L., Edfors, O., & Tufvesson, F. (2013). Scaling Up MIMO: Opportunities and Challenges with Very Large Arrays. *IEEE Signal Processing Magazine*, *30*(1), 40–60. doi:10.1109/MSP.2011.2178495

Salameh, M. G. (2013). *The United States' Shale Oil Revolution in Perspective*. USAEE Working Paper No. 13-099. doi:10.2139srn.2201990

Salem, F. E., Gati, A., Altman, Z., & Chahed, T. (2017). Advanced Sleep Modes and Their Impact on Flow-Level Performance of 5G Networks. *IEEE 86th Vehicular Technology Conference (VTC-Fall).*

Science-based Targets. (2020). *Science-based Targets.* https://sciencebasedtargets.org/

United Nations. (2020). *Sustainable Development Goals.* https://www.un.org/sustainabledevelopment/

UptimeInstitute. (2020). *10th annual Data Center Industry Survey Results.* https://uptimeinstitute.com/2020-data-center-industry-survey-results

Vaija, M. S., & Philipot, E. (2020). L'importance des métaux rares pour le secteur des technologies de l'information et de la communication, le cas d'Orange. *Responsabilité & Environnement, 99.* http://annales.org/re/2020/re99/2020-07-4.pdf

Valadarsky, A., Schapira, M., Shahaf, D., & Tamar, A. (2017). A Machine Learning Approach to Routing, Cornell University. https://arxiv.org/abs/1708.03074

Van Huynh, N., Hoang, D. T., Lu, X., Niyato, D., Wang, P., & Kim, D. I. (2018). Ambient Backscatter Communications: A Contemporary Survey. *IEEE Communications Surveys and Tutorials, 20*(4), 2889–2922. doi:10.1109/COMST.2018.2841964

Van Oers, L., De Koning, A., Guinée, J. B., & Huppes, G. (2002). *Abiotic resource depletion in LCA Improving characterisation factors for abiotic resource depletion as recommended in the new Dutch LCA Handbook.* https://www.leidenuniv.nl/cml/ssp/projects/lca2/report_abiotic_depletion_web.pdf

Van Oers, L., Guinée, J. B., & Heijungs, R. (2020). Abiotic resource depletion potentials (ADPs) for elements revisited - updating ultimate reserve estimates and introducing time series for production data. *The International Journal of Life Cycle Assessment, 25*(2), 309–310. doi:10.100711367-019-01709-4

Zepf, V., Simmons, J., Reller, A., Rennie, C., Ashfield, M., & Achzet, B. (2014). *Materials Critical to the Energy Industry: An Introduction* (2nd ed.). BP Plc.

ADDITIONAL READING

Schöne, R., Ilsche, T., Bielert, M., Gocht, A., & Hackenberg, D. (2019). Energy Efficiency Features of the Intel Skylake-SP Processor and Their Impact on Performance. *International Conference on High Performance Computing & Simulation*, 399-406.

Key Terms and Definitions

Circular Economy: Is an economic system of exchange and production which, at all stages of the life cycle of products (goods and services), aims to increase the efficiency of the use of resources and reduce the impact on the environment while developing the well-being of individuals.

Decarbonization: Consists of gradually reducing the consumption of fossil fuels (coal, oil and natural gas) emitting greenhouse gases (mainly carbon dioxide and methane) or to store carbon dioxide underground.

Efficiency: Is the set of techniques that allow a service or product supplier to fulfil the demands with a reduced energy and mineral resources footprint. Efficiency may be split in component-based efficiency and end-to-end efficiency: • Component-based efficiency is the set of techniques that allow the optimization of energy consumption during operation of a hardware or software component of a network; • End-to-end efficiency enables network architects and service designers to optimize the usage of resources which are made used end-to-end on the purpose of delivering the service.

Energy Transition: Is driven by the global carbon emissions that must be brought to zero to keep the global warming below 1.5 °C. It is built upon the increased integration of renewable energy in the realm of daily life.

Green by Design: Analyses the design of digital applications with the goal in mind of reducing their environmental footprint.

Green by ICT: Provides digital tools to reduce the environmental footprint of all the human activities.

Green for ICT: Consists in measurement tools and methods for reducing the environmental footprint of the ICT systems.

Power Purchase Agreement: Is a third-party financing model among the consumer, the renewable energy system owner, and the utility. The utility enters into a long-term contract, referred to as the power purchase agreement, to purchase the electricity generated by the system from the system owner.

Rebound Effect: Is the overall effect of technical, organizational and social progress, which increase the efficiency of the economy and consumption.

Scope: Refers to the classification of a company's greenhouse gases emissions according to the greenhouse gas protocol. Three scopes are defined: • Scope 1 relates to the emissions emanating from fossil fuels that the company burns to produce energy; • Scope 2 covers the emissions generated during the production of the purchased energy by the company; • Scope 3 covers the emissions on the remaining value chain over which the company has some influence. On the upstream direction of the value chain: emissions generated for the production of the customers' equipment (mobile phones, boxes, computers, etc.) and for the networks equipment, for their transportation and distribution, for the business travels, etc. On the downstream direction of the value chain: use of sold products by the customers, end of life management, etc.

Sustainability: Is about changing the way resources are exploited or hazards are managed so that adverse impacts downstream or for subsequent generations are reduced.

ENDNOTES

[1]   International Electrotechnical Commission 62474, Material Declaration for Products of and for the Electrotechnical Industry, https://std.iec.ch/iec62474

[2]   The power usage effectiveness reports the percentage of the energy yearly used by the ICT hardware layer with respect to the amount of energy yearly used by the data center.

[3]   The thermal design power is the maximum amount of heat generated by a computer chip that the cooling system in a computer is designed to dissipate under any workload.

[4]   The Uptime Institute helps owners and operators to quantify their ability to provide a predictable level of performance from their data centers, regardless of the status of external factors.

[5]   https://opennetworking.org/wp-content/uploads/2014/10/openflow-switch-v1.5.1.pdf

Section 2
Latest Developments in Network Automation

Chapter 5
Future SDN–Based Network Architectures

Evangelos Haleplidis
University of Piraeus, Greece

Christos Tranoris
University of Patras, Greece

Spyros Denazis
University of Patras, Greece

Odysseas Koufopavlou
University of Patras, Greece

ABSTRACT

The goal of this chapter is to provide a clear view of SDN, its origin, and its possible future. This chapter starts by taking a step backwards and looks at SDN in a historic perspective by visiting the history of network programmability and identifies how it helped pave the way and shape SDN. This historic journey will provide a general context of SDN and put SDN into perspective. Then the authors show the current view of SDN as defined by standard development organizations (SDOs), provide a sense of SDN's malleability, explore SDN interactions with different networking architectures, and finally, provide a vision of a possible SDN future.

SDN: AN INTRODUCTION AND SOME HISTORICAL BACKGROUND

More than a decade has passed, since the advent of what is called, Software-Defined Networking (SDN). Network research gained a burst of activity and innovation in 2008 when SDN was introduced as a term by Stanford University researchers (McKeown et al., 2008) as an attempt to operate networks in a more programmable fashion and to run experiments (such as new protocols, interfaces, or algorithms) on real production networks.

DOI: 10.4018/978-1-7998-7646-5.ch005

The main premise was that simulations and emulations can only provide insights of whether a proof of concept may be applicable. To actually deploy and test new protocols or architectures on real hardware, the researchers would have to convince hardware manufacturers to adopt their ideas, which they are very understandably reluctant to do so as the design cycle of a new device could take a lot of time and provide limited to no return of investment. The only path left was to develop hardware themselves, using custom-based hardware as described by Lockwood et al. (2007). This custom-based hardware approach was embraced by the networking community.

SDN initially begun with the precept of separating the forwarding plane, the portion of the device that moves packets around, from the control plane, the portion of the device that decides how packets should be moved around, for research purposes. SDN gave the applications to program the forwarding behavior of network devices via a standardized interface. However, based on research and demonstration of SDN-enabled technologies, the industry realized that by utilizing the concepts proposed by the SDN proponents, they could solve real-world problems. For example, in environments such as Data Centers (DCs) where it is important to optimize resources and, thus, the capabilities to customize the forwarding behavior of the network and automating configuration tasks are key factors.

The separation adopted by SDN is achieved by abstracting the forwarding plane and providing an open interface to the control plane. Such a separation incurs many benefits to both planes as it allows research and innovation to occur independently in each plane. Developers could create network applications that directly program the forwarding functionality of network devices irrespective of the device and these applications can be physically located outside of the device itself.

SDN, while at that time a disruptive and empowering technology, was not a new concept. On the contrary, the concept of separating the control plane from the forwarding plane has been present in the networking field for a long time, as documented by Feamster et al. (2013) and Mendonca et al. (2013). As discussed in Feamster et al. (2013) and later in this chapter, the main reasons for SDN adoption was the need for programmability, especially in DCs, where it was more cost-effective to write sophisticated control programs than using proprietary switches that could not support new features without engagement of the equipment vendors. It is important for the sake of historical accuracy and given the context, to take a step back and discuss the precursors to SDN.

The concept of separation to create new services dates even back with ITU's SS7 (ITU, 1993) networks, where the signaling of telephone calls was separated from the actual phone call to setup and tear down phone calls, thus, enabling new services to be formed such as local number portability and number translations. In the networking domain, ITU's ATM recommendations (ITU, 1990) were also based on the concept of separating signaling and data path, with signaling being used to set up virtual circuits prior to sending any packets and TINA (as discussed in Lengdell et al. (1996)) where network resources where modeled using the Network Resource Information Model (NRIM) to provide abstractions to service software.

Next came the era of Active and Programmable Networks (A&PN), as surveyed by Tennenhouse et al. (1997) and Campbell et al. (1999), where network programmability was the focus. A&PN was based upon a richer model than programmability and presented two alternatives: in-band and out-of-band controls.

In-band control was the most representative approach of the active networking school of thought from those years, where the concept was that code would be traversing the network alongside the packets to be executed at specific nodes in the network such as Active Node Transfer System (ANTS) discussed by Wetherall et al. (1998). However, it was the out-of-band control (i.e., the programmable networks approach) that was the privileged topic of research and experimentation. The programmable networks concept was to allow software to control how the devices process packets, a concept that would later be the rationale of SDN development.

There was a couple of interesting research projects that came out of the A&PN era such as the P1520 (Biswas et al, 1998), and Tempest (Rooney et al., 1998) projects. The IEEE P1520 standardization effort addressed the need for a set of standard software interfaces for programming networks in terms of rapid service creation and open signaling by defining a set of levels of abstraction and their respective interfaces similar to SDN concepts. The Tempest project, taking a cue from the advances of network virtualization enabled multiple virtual networks to coexist on the same set of physical switches by allowing software controllers to control how network devices should forward traffic.

Network virtualization and the results of Tempest were also picked up and the experimentation research trend manifested itself in national programs such as the Global Environment for Network Innovations (GENI) in USA, and Future Internet REsearch (FIRE) [REMOVED REF FIELD]in Europe, which involved the majority of research labs and teams of the A&PN era.

Born out of the vision of network programmability and driven by the Network Processing Forum (NPF) in 2001, the Forwarding and Control Element Separation (ForCES) working group was chartered in the IETF. ForCES (RFC 3746), in a few words provides a modelling language (RFC 5812) to describe network resources as blocks, called Logical Functional Blocks (LFBs) which, when interconnected create a graph of resources. A group of LFBs constitute a Forwarding Element (FE) and a group of FEs along with Control Elements (CE) constitute network elements. LFBs inside an FE can represent configurable device functions which when grouped together (even within an NE) can create network services. LFBs also can represent resources pertaining to managing NE resources. In addition, ForCES also specified an open and secure protocol (RFC 5810) that can query and control these LFBs.

Followed by a couple of research projects such as the 4D project (Greenberg et al., 2005) and the Routing Control Platform (RCP) (Caesar et al., 2005), the Ethane project (Casado et al., 2007) led to the specification and the development of the OpenFlow protocol (McKeown et al., 2008).

OpenFlow (McKeown et al., 2008) as a framework was initially developed in 2009 to provide a way for researchers to run experiments and protocols in networks. At that time network equipment were mostly black boxes to researchers who were unable to test new routing algorithms in real networks with real hardware equipment instead of software or simulations. OpenFlow provided a common programmable interface towards the forwarding plane that allowed researchers to dynamically populate the Forwarding Information Based maintained by OpenFlow switches. Although it was initially advanced as part of the Stanford Clean Slate Program as stated in Roberts (2009), later development and specification was taken over by the Open Networking Foundation (ONF) which has continued to extend it. It has undergone several versions and iterations since its inception.

The OpenFlow framework, consists of a controller and a switch. The controller uses the OpenFlow protocol to manage a static model of an OpenFlow switch. Incoming packets are grouped into flows based on specific match fields, e.g., the same source and destination IP address, or the same TCP/UDP port numbers. When a packet enters an OpenFlow switch it goes through one or a series, depending on the version, of Flow Tables. Each Flow Table maintains a set of Flow Entries. If a packet header matches a Flow Entry, then the instructions of the Flow Entry are executed.

One interesting byproduct of OpenFlow was the introduction of more programmable networking slices (Sherwood, 2010). While network virtualization was typically done by Virtual Local Area Network (VLANs), (Sherwood, 2010) demonstrated the use of Flowvisor, an architecture to create custom slices of networks based on specific flow characteristics.

The static nature of OpenFlow led to the latest SDN incarnation, Programming Protocol-independent Packet Processors, commonly known as P4 (Bosshart et al., 2014). P4 was originally defined by Stanford and in 2018 joined the ONF and the Linux Foundation. In a few words, P4 is a programming language that allows a developer to program a P4-enabled hardware on how to parse incoming packets, match them based on custom fields, and create the actions that should be enacted upon matched packets.

With the P4 language a developer defines three distinct structures. The first is the description of possible distinct incoming headers, with fine grained definition, all header fields named and specified at bit-precision level. The second is a parse tree detailing all the possible combination of expected header fields contained in packets and how these should be parsed. The third and final structure is similar to OpenFlow's "match-action" table where packets are matched based on parsed header fields, and, when matched, the exact action to be performed. The notable difference in the last structure between OpenFlow and P4 is that the developer is expected to define in P4 the exact action performed.

Initially P4 did not include a control interface and was configured by a Command Line Interface (CLI). However, during the development of P4 the need for a common control protocol arose, and, as such, the proponents of P4 defined the P4Runtime specification (P4Runtime Specification 2020). The P4Runtime specification is a Remote Procedure Call (RPC) mechanism for controllers to configure the P4 data plane. The P4Runtime specification is based on Google's RPC mechanism (gRPC) (Google RPC, 2020).

It is not coincidental that SDN and the concept of network programmability strongly reemerged with the advent of cloud computing, virtualization, and DC technologies. The lack of network programmability in a clear and uniform approach irrespective of the heterogeneity of devices was still a challenge that was being overcome. SDN's overall motivation, in addition to solving network cloud provisioning is driven by the desire to deploy, control, and manage (virtual) networks, devices and services (e.g., load balancers, firewalls) by introducing a high level of automation in the overall service delivery and operation procedures. Virtualization and DC technologies have steadily increased the number of devices, physical and virtual that a data center IT team needs to manage and maintain, as well as considering Virtual Machine (VM) migration, multi-tenancy, and custom services, all these add up to an ever-increasing operational load on network administrators.

The aforementioned problem was usually addressed with scripts or manual configurations, but SDN provided a clean and deterministic approach. The solution that SDN provided was to provide applications a standardized and centralized approach to control and manage the network, providing a very appealing toolset for network administrators. In addition, as a side benefit, it provided a software-based approach to virtualize the network, as discussed in Sherwood et al. (2009), allowing researchers to take control of a portion of the actual hardware and network for experimentation. SDN had a very fertile ground where there was a specific need to be covered, such as DC resource usage optimization as discussed earlier, the level of technological maturity was right, which made SDN a success whereas earlier attempts on network programmability failed to move ahead.

One of the most notable SDN examples is Google's SDN-based WAN (Jain, 2013) for interconnecting DCs using OpenFlow. Google showcased that using SDN concepts for WAN interconnection can greatly improve performance in link utilization and that centralizing a controller to aggregate link topologies reduces the system load and increases the overall network availability.

SDN has come a long way, but during its course since 2008 and due to the increased interest of the community, it has undergone many changes, e.g., OpenFlow evolved through several iterative versions, from 1.0 to 1.5; P4 has undergone a similar evolution through different versions since its inception, namely the P4-14 and P4-16 (1.0, 1.1, and 1.2 versions). SDN was also embraced in different ways by Standard Development Organizations (SDOs) and many network equipment vendors attempted to brand their product, architecture or research as SDN. This has inadvertently led to a fragmented and disjoint view of what SDN is, what is its architecture, what layers and planes it encompasses, and what are its abstractions and interfaces.

Having visited the history of network programmability and how it helped pave the way and shape SDN, the rest of this chapter attempts to provide a more general context of what SDN is by taking a step back and putting SDN in perspective. We will start with the current view as defined by SDOs, provide a sense of SDN's malleability, explore SDN interactions with different networking architectures, and finally provide a vision of a possible SDN's future.

A Broad and Current View of SDN

RFC7426 provides a detailed description of the SDN layers architecture. By dividing the SDN architecture into distinct planes, abstraction layers, and interfaces, RFC7426 aims to clarify SDN terminology and establish a set of commonly accepted ground across the SDN community. Figure 1 takes SDN into perspective and visualizes the architecture, the layers, and the interfaces that take part in the overall picture.

It must be noted that Figure 1 provides an abstract view, meaning that implementations may vary. For example, many implementations in the past have opted for placing the management plane on top of the control plane. This can be interpreted as having the control plane acting as a service to the management plane. Also, while not shown explicitly in the figure, these planes can be placed in a recursive manner, for example multiple control planes one on top of the other, or services and applications may span multiple layers such as both the control and management.

A network device, as shown in Figure 1, is an entity that receives packets on its ports and performs one or more network functions on them. The sum of network devices, along with their links, in a network is otherwise known as the infrastructure layer. Network devices are composed of resources, such as ports, and they can also be composed of multiple individual resources. The network device can also be considered as a complex resource. Resources are not limited to networking, but also include CPU, memory, and ports, among others. It is important to notice that in this abstract view there is no distinction between physical or virtual devices, or whether such devices are implemented in hardware or software.

There are two distinct planes associated with network devices: the forwarding and the operational planes. The forwarding plane provides switching, and filtering functions, among others. Resources of the forwarding plane include, but are not limited to meters, queues, and classifiers. The operational plane on the other hand is responsible for the operational state of the network device, for instance, with respect to status of network ports and interfaces. Operational plane resources include, but are not limited to, memory, CPU, ports, interfaces, and queues.

The resources of these two planes are abstracted and exposed by the Device and Resource Abstraction Layer (DAL). The DAL may be expressed by multiple abstraction models. For example, ForCES LFBs or the OpenFlow's switch specification are instantiations of a DAL. The ForCES LFB model, YANG (RFC 6020, RFC 7950), or SMI are examples of modeling semantics that can be used to define DAL abstractions (a.k.a., data models). Having a common set of abstractions, or a way to define abstractions in a unified approach is paramount in SDN, as it is important for the upper planes to view all devices in the same manner. Specific SNMP Management Information Bases (MIBs), for example, where such DAL instances are still being used.

Figure 1. High Level View of SDN Architecture

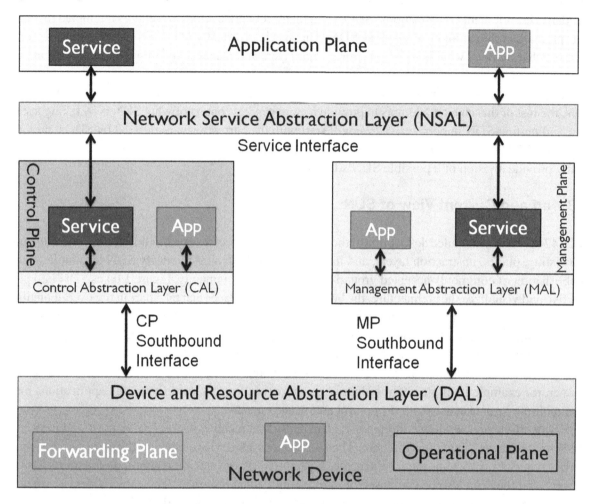

To provide a sense of what DAL is, the only requirement is a formal description of the resources of the device (or a function). OpenFlow did not provide any specification language for the forwarding plane or any way to formally define custom abstractions, but instead described the abstractions in a specification document, with the protocol. Having no formal language to model the resources of an OpenFlow switch, required a new OpenFlow specification to be written whenever any change in the model occurs. For the operational plane, OpenFlow provided the OF-CONFIG (OF-CONFIG, 2013) specification which is based upon NETCONF and YANG data models.

Any language that can adequately describe the resources of any device can be used. For example, google protobufs (Google Protobufs, 2020) and Apache's Thrift Interface Description Language (Apache Thrift IDL, 2020) are two examples of data serialization and deserialization mechanisms for messaging that is extensible enough to be able to describe DAL abstractions. On the other hand, OpenConfig's (OpenConfig data models, 2020) YANG modules are DAL instantiations, with YANG being the DAL.

It is worth discussing the DAL since having the right abstractions is paramount to the success of SDN. A lot of effort is being directed towards defining the DAL. The OpenFlow specification designates a specific abstraction of an OpenFlow's switch which is a DAL instance. To distinguish different features between OpenFlow switches, the ONF has published a white paper for Table Type Patterns (ONF 2014, TTP) as an abstract switch model. Nakao (2012) and Song (2013) follow the example of OpenFlow but are different in that they allow flexible match patterns for classifying packets. Another school of thought consists in applying a common set of abstractions based upon various versions of OpenFlow, as described in Parniewicz et al. (2014).

Above the devices there are two distinct planes: the control and the management planes. SDN controllers, which control and manage the devices, reside on one or both planes. The control plane is responsible for making decisions on how packets should be processed by one or more network devices (or functions) and pushing such decisions down to the forwarding plane of the network devices for execution. Since the control plane's main focus is to instruct the forwarding plane about how it should process packets, it also requires operational plane information to influence the decision-making process. Such information includes the current state of a particular port or its capabilities, for example.

The management plane is responsible for monitoring, configuring and maintaining network devices and its main focus is on the operational plane of the device and less on the forwarding plane. The management plane may also configure the forwarding plane, but it usually does so infrequently and in a batched approach. At the introduction of SDN, the management plane was considered out of scope (ONF, 2012 and ONF, 2013) and indeed the earlier definitions of SDN suggested that SDN is all about the separation of forwarding from control. ONF (ONF, 2014) and ITU (ITU SG13, 2014) have also included the management plane as part of SDN.

The control plane and management plane manage the network device and its resources through respective interfaces: the Control Plane Southbound Interface (CPSI) and the Management Plane Southbound Interfaces (MPSI). These interfaces have their own distinct characteristics depending on the respective planes, namely: timescale, persistency, locality, and Brewer's theorem also known as the CAP theorem.

Timescale specifies how fast a plane responds and needs to respond. For example, the control plane needs to respond in a timely manner as packets may wait for being forwarded while the control plane decides where to forward them. The management plane on the other hand may not necessarily need to react fast to changes.

Persistency refers to how long the state of the device will remain stable. Control plane state may fluctuate and change rapidly in a matter of milliseconds and thus are more ephemeral, whilst management plane state is usually more stable and may remain static for a longer period of time.

Locality is an interesting characteristic as with the concept of SDN to separate the control plane from the forwarding plane and have a logically centralized computation logic, the control plane tends to act more as a management plane. Usually control plane functionalities were collocated with the forwarding and operation planes and distributed, whilst management plane functionalities were more centralized and off the device. It is important, therefore, for SDN controllers to take into account issues that used to be addressed for the management plane, such as availability.

The last characteristic is the CAP theorem. The CAP theorem states that for a distributed system, between three characteristics (Consistency, Availability, and Partitioning tolerance), a designer can only select two at best. For example, if partitioning tolerance is given, then a designer can choose between consistency or availability. In the context of SDN, this means that a centralized management system has a consistent view of the network devices, knows all the states but has reduced availability when, for example, losing connectivity with some devices if links go down. A distributed control plane on the other hand improves availability as it is directly connected to devices but loses consistency as propagation of state takes time. Since SDN proponents initially investigated a design where the SDN computation logic would be logically centralized, CAP provides a good tool to specify the issues that such a design may raise. Panda et al. (2013) discussed approaches on how to address issues raised by CAP when applied to SDN.

Both control and management plane have their respective abstraction layers, the Control Abstraction Layer and the Management Abstraction Layer that abstract their respective southbound interface operations. The control and management planes may support more than one interface and the CAL and MAL abstract the interface functionalities. The OpenDaylight controller also supports a CAL and MAL plugin modular architecture in its architecture designated as the Service Abstraction Layer as discussed in Hemid (2017). Additional examples of CAL and MAL are the Container Network Interface (CNI) and Modular Layer 2 (ml2) where plugins can be added to provide the necessary southbound interfaces for network configuration. CNI is used in Docker and Kubernetes with Xu (2018), for example, using CNI as CAL and Linux existing tools providing the DAL access to create network QoS policies, and ml2 for OpenStack with Shin (2015) as an example of creating an OpenFlow plugin for OpenStack.

The interfaces between the device and control/management planes are also important for SDN and are often designated as "southbound" interfaces. These interfaces formalize the interaction between the controllers/managers and the devices: command operations in the protocol such as 'query', 'config', and 'subscribe' for specific events are handled via such interfaces. Each respective interface has its own characteristics, for example the control plane southbound interface needs to react fast to changes and support multiple events per second, whilst the management plane southbound interface needs to be more user friendly as it is likely to be solicited by network administrators.

Examples of control plane southbound interfaces include interfaces through which ForCES, OpenFlow, and SNMP commands are communicated, while examples of management plane southbound interfaces include NETCONF/RESTCONF, SNMP, OVSDB, and PCEP, amongst others. It is worth noting that all these protocols can be used indifferently to exchange information through the southbound interface for control and management purposes for example. The differences lie in the characteristics of each protocol, i.e. a binary protocol is usually faster than an ASCII protocol and can transfer more data per second and as such, is more suited for a control plane protocol.

While having a protocol with a comprehensive set of functionalities (e.g., security, transaction capabilities) is preferable, other approaches can be considered to exchange information through such interfaces. Any kind of serialization-deserialization protocol can be used so long as it contains a specific set of protocol messages that support SDN needs, such as discovery and configuration. For example, gRPC (Google RPC, 2020) and Apache Thrift (Apache Thrift, 2020) are also protocols that can be used to exchange information through these "southbound" interfaces.

Finally, the application plane is where user applications reside. Applications differ from services as services provide functionality to other services or applications, whereas applications only consume services. The application plane hosts applications/services that are not related to control or management plane activities but only make use of them.

The Network Service Abstraction Layer (NSAL) abstract services, control and management as well as application plane services to other services and applications that consume them. The NSAL is also known as the SDN northbound interface and was not initially standardized. SDN proponents suggest RESTful or RPC APIs for NSAL. RESTful abstractions are designed according to the REpresentational State Transfer (REST) design approach that includes resource identification, self-descriptive messages, and no connection state. RPCs are APIs where a client needs to know the procedure and the associated parameters a priori before using it. The IETF has published a number of solutions, such as the SUPA framework (RFC 8328) that documents a library of generic policies that can be used to construct a service, or RESTCONF (RFC 8040), a REST-like protocol to access a NETCONF server datastore.

RFC8597 took the separation of SDN a little further, by separating the Transport and Service stratums. Each stratum may be controlled by a different SDN controller in order to simplify and provide separate management capabilities. RFC8579 uses the layers defined in RFC7426 as building blocks for its architecture and uses them in a recursive approach, a set of layers for the transport stratum and above them another set of layers for the service stratum.

A simplified description of the SDN architecture that was specified by ONF (ONF, 2014) is depicted in Figure 2. The ONF architecture introduces the data plane, the control plane, the application plane as well as the management plane. Also, the ONF architecture, and especially the definition of control and management, resembles the SDNRG discussion (RFC 7426). Similarly to RFC7426, the ONF architecture provides an abstract view which does not provide any implementation details.

Figure 2. Simplified ONF SDN Architecture

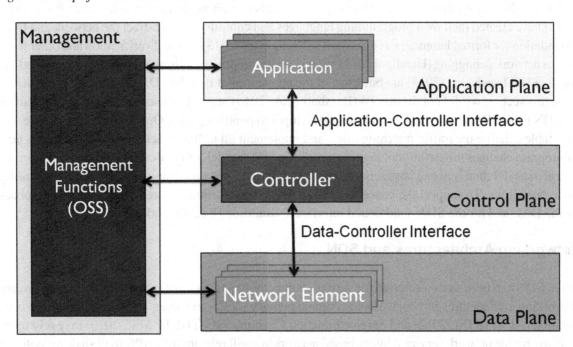

There are some differences between the ONF and SDNRG definitions. (ONF, 2014) provides much more internal view of the control plane and takes into account more interfaces between planes and it also discusses virtualization in greater detail. The ONF architecture provides a view of how multi-technology, multi-trust domains, and multi-tenancy networks operate following an SDN approach.

For the purposes of the ONF, the DAL, as initially defined in RFC 7426, is considered to be the combination of OpenFlow and OF-CONFIG. OF-CONFIG uses in essence YANG data models via the NETCONF protocol to manage OpenFlow switches.

ITU (ITU SG13, 2014) has also defined an architecture which is similar to the one described in Figure 2. (ITU SG13, 2014) includes the resource layer instead of the data plane, the SDN control layer, the application layer, and multi-layer management functions. The SDN control layer in (ITU SG13, 2014) includes resource abstractions such as the DAL defined in RFC 7426, but introduces the concept of orchestration as a means to provide control and management of network resources covering, for example, management of physical and virtual network topologies, network elements, and data traffic.

Having discussed all the necessary layers of an SDN architecture, there is common ground upon which all further discussion can be placed. For example, SDN controllers such as Beacon (Erickson et al., 2013) and NOX (Gude et al., 2008), are control plane services that use OpenFlow to carry information through the control plane southbound interface and provide services to other application and services. Flowvisor (Sherwood et al., 2009) is actually a control plane service that provides service to other control planes, since it is actually a proxy controller that resides between an SDN controller and the device. There are many other open source or commercial surveyed SDN controllers, which are catalogued by Salman et al. (2016) and Zhu et al. (2019), such as OpenDaylight introduced by Medved et al. (2014) and ONOS introduced by Berde et al. (2014) but they are not discussed further in this chapter.

Inspired by software programming languages, researchers such as Monsanto et al. (2012), Foster et al. (2011) have created their own programming languages and compilers that abstract the network and form a foundation for formal languages as discussed by Guha et al. (2013). Formal verification and other tools such as network debugging (Handigol 2012), integrated development environments (IDE) such as NetIDE discussed by Facca et al (2013) are but a few of the recent toolkit that the SDN community is releasing.

In this section we did not discuss P4 (Bosshart et al., 2014) at all. The reason is that P4 is not part of the SDN layers. P4 is a language that allows a developer to populate, in the OpenFlow nomenclature, the flow tables, define the traffic matching rules, and implement all available actions. In SDN terms a new P4 program changes the definition, in other words the DAL model, of the device itself and therefore its abstractions. P4 then is not an abstraction layer or an interface, but a mechanism that outputs forwarding plane operations. To support the concepts of SDN, the P4 consortium has selected Google's protobufs for the DAL and for the SDN southbound interface P4Runtime (P4 API working group, 2020).

Networking Architectures and SDN

While SDN can be seen as a solution for various connectivity and automation problems, there are many networking architectures in which SDN is complementary to. For example, Network Functions Virtualization (NFV) (ETSI, 2012) and Service Function Chaining (SFC) (IETF SFC, 2020) may rely upon SDN to provide network services. Intent-based networking will rely on SDN APIs to push down policies at the network level, once the intent has been translated into policies and also to retrieve telemetry data, to assess how properly the intent is addressed. 5G network specifications include the use of SDN to provide networking services for connectivity and network slicing, by providing topology change events to upper layers such as the management layer where orchestration capabilities may reside. This section will discuss all related technologies which SDN can interoperate with to solve more complex issues and deliver programmable infrastructures and services.

Few years after the emergence of SDN and, owing to the advances of virtualization, some of the major operators got together in Darmstadt (Germany) in on October 2012 and published the first white paper that introduced Network Functions Virtualization (NFV) (ETSI NFV, 2014). The goal was simple yet powerful and is three-fold. Firstly, to reduce the Capital Expenses (CAPEX) costs due to the purchase of physical, dedicated and sometimes expensive network equipment such as firewalls. Such equipment may be sparsely used as the purchase is often based upon projected usage and may turn up underused, thereby increasing the overall CAPEX. Secondly, to allow quick innovation and deployment cycles of new functions to provide new services for users. Finally, to reduce the Operational Expenses (OPEX) costs of managing a large and always evolving number of such devices by automation.

NFV virtualize network functions, such as firewalls and routers, and deploy them as software on virtual platforms, e.g., Virtual Machines (VM), residing in high volume servers on a per-need basis. NFV could be applied to any data plane or control plane function; in practice, some functionalities may not be well suited for virtualization, but this is not the focus of this chapter. Such an approach will allow operators to design, implement, and dynamically deploy and withdraw network functions while optimizing resource usage by provisioning only the necessary amount of infrastructure resources. As such, NFV provides flexibility, elasticity, and adaptability to new user requirements for services.

Furthermore, the IETF's Service Function Chaining (SFC) working group specified "an architecture for service function chaining that includes the necessary protocols or protocol extensions to convey Service Function Chain and Service Function Path (SFP) information to nodes that are involved in the dynamic enforcement of differentiated traffic forwarding policies, as instantiated through the structuring of SFCs composed of an (ordered) set of Service Functions that usually reflect a connectivity service.

SFC resource allocation and deployment require the mapping of an SFC onto the underlying physical infrastructure and the allocation of resources to SFC nodes (e.g., bandwidth, computing, and storage). The SFC control plane is responsible for constructing the (loose of strict) SFPs and propagates that information to underlying nodes.The SFC controller locates all available service functions and uses policies to construct service function chains. An SFC maybe static or it can be dynamic allowing the network to apply some or all of the forwarding decisions made by the Service Function Forwarder (SFF), as a function of traffic load conditions of service functions, for example.

Taking a broader view of network service lifecycles, NFV relates to network resource management which includes allocation, instantiation, and withdrawal, SFC relates to resource chaining and SDN relates to control and management of resources. All the three techniques, SDN, NFV, and SFC may be combined to facilitate the overall service delivery and operation procedures during service lifecycle as illustrated in Figure 3. Haleplidis, Salim et al. (2014) discuss how a common abstraction model for SDN and NFV is applicable using ForCES to achieve the aforementioned concept.

Future network architectures are likely to be completely elastic and on demand as an overlay on top of a base infrastructure. A developer using a VNF app store may be able to select the necessary VNFs, create the connections between them, or define a policy of what such connections should look like Then, the implementation of the service will be done automatically with all the toolset that SDN, NFV, and SFC provide. This is a research direction that is considered in the literature such as John et al. (2013) specifically in a unified cloud and carrier network approach.

SDN is not only applicable to such a future network architecture scenario, but is one of the key enablers. SDN provides the toolkit that can accommodate the rapid changes that NFV introduces in the network. With NFV, new functions can be instantiated into the network and it is up to SDN to interconnect these functions without the need for manual configuration which may jeopardize the time to deliver a service, depending on the number and the complexity of the configuration tasks.

SDN's DAL, the resource abstraction layer, provides a unified approach on how resources are modeled and controlled, and is applicable to the NFV domain as well. The use of formal languages also suggests that in the future, network architectures may as well become software-defined, a developer

Figure 3. SDN, NFV, SFC and the network lifecycle

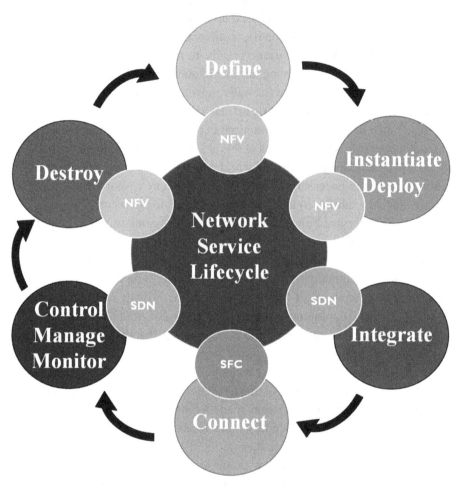

may, thus, provide a more high-level overview of what the required network configuration is. This high-level abstraction is then translated into a set of configuration commands that will be processed by the participating devices to provide the requested connectivity service. SDN operation relies upon an underlying infrastructure that will support overlay networks whose resources are allocated by the SDN computation logic, as depicted in Figure 4.

Such design takes advantage of SDN (e.g., optimization, automation) and network virtualization. Having a logically centralized controller with a global, systemic, view of the network resource and their status allows the SDN controller to facilitate service delivery and operation, optimize resource usage, and also to enforce service-inferred instantiated policies (forwarding, routing, traffic engineering, security, etc.). Applications can drive the SDN-contributed automation of processes such as high availability, and load sharing. In addition, new network virtualization techniques are emerging; these techniques allow multiple users to use the same infrastructure while being guaranteed that their traffic will be isolated from a forwarding standpoint. These techniques existed prior to SDN, however SDN provides a programmatic approach to reshaping their full potential without resorting to custom scripts, command line interfaces and Telnet into multiple devices to monitor, configure and manage.

Figure 4. SDN as key building block for future network architectures

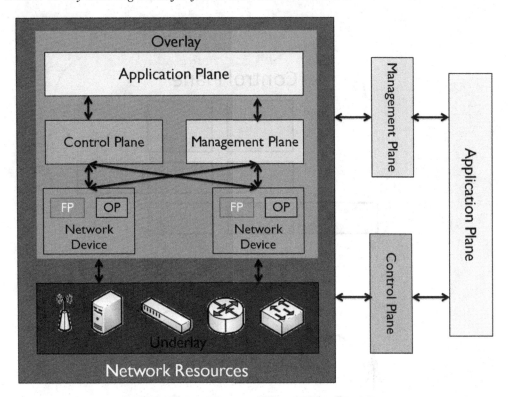

A specific application example scenario for SDN, NFV, and SFC that illustrates some of the previous discussion relates to the 3GPP's Long Term Evolution (LTE) Evolved Packet Core (EPC). The Evolved Packet Core (EPC) as described in Olsson (2009) is the core network architecture of LTE networks. The user equipment (UE) connects to a base station, which directs traffic through a serving gateway (SGW) over a GPRS Tunneling Protocol (GTP) tunnel and through a packet gateway (PGW) and then to the Internet.

The SGW forwards data packets, while also acting as the mobility anchor for the user plane during handovers. The Packet Gateway (PGW) enforces Quality of Service (QoS) policies by signaling with the Policy and Charging Rules Function (PCRF) and monitors traffic to perform billing by signaling to the Online (OCS) and Offline Charging Systems (OFCS). The PGW also filters packets and connects to the Packet Data Network (PDN). PDN includes network services as well as access to the Internet and other cellular data networks and PDNs, and hosts service functions like firewalls and deep packet inspection.

By using SDN, it is possible to separate the PGW's and SGW's control part from the data plane, as described in Li et al. (2012), Basta et al. (2013), and Haleplidis et al. (2015) which was based on a Proof of Concept demonstration for ETSI (ETSI 2015). Separating and virtualizing these functions allows the instantiation and scaling of each part independently. A single SGW or PGW control application can control more than one SGW and PGW data paths. In addition, the control applications (SGW-C, PGW-C) can now be collocated with other signaling entities of the LTE architecture and reduce latency for the signaling portion of the network, thus creating different paths for signaling and data. Figure 5 depicts a concept of separating the control and the data paths in the 3GPP architecture.

Figure 5. Concept of separation in the 3GPP LTE's architecture

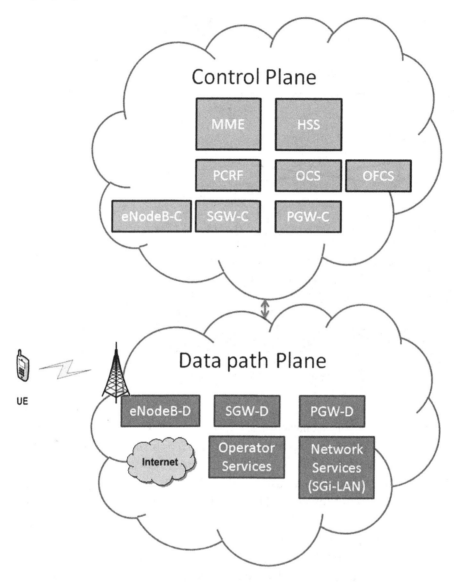

Grey boxes are the control network and purple boxes represent the data path portion of the network. Using SDN concepts, the architecture is transformed, but remains 3GPP compliant by not changing any interface between the SGW, PGW and the other LTE systems. This separation allows each domain to scale as required. Control plane entities can be collocated to reduce latency and improve network experience and data plane entities can be reduced to simply perform forwarding at faster rates.

While this example may be outdated with 5G on the horizon, it provides an example of how SDN research brings innovation and impacts industry specifications. This line of research eventually led to the definition of Control and User Plane Separation (CUPS) by the 3GPP (3GPP 2020) being essential to 5G networks.

Taking this concept one step further with virtualization as discussed in the previous section and in other chapters of this book, new control plane entities can be instantiated to support an increase demand of new customers, or data path plane entities could be instantiated to provide each user with a personalized (to a very extreme scenario) data path using virtualization techniques.

SDN Technological Transformation Trends

The resurgence of SDN with OpenFlow as the main proponent initially begun by providing programmability for wired networks and specifically for parts of the Ethernet, IP and TCP headers in the first version of OpenFlow (ONF, 2009). As discussed in the first section, successive OpenFlow specifications introduced new header fields. Since then, SDN has been applied on multiple network domains. The research reference list discussed in this section is not exhaustive and only covers a small portion of SDN's applicability, but the intended purpose is to provide a sense of SDN's ubiquitous presence in the networking world.

The first attempts at SDN migration from wired networks using OpenFlow begun in 2010 with work related to mobility and network management in Wireless Network such as discussed in OpenRoads (Yap, 2010), routing and forwarding in Wireless Mesh Networks (Dely, 2011), MobiFlow, an OpenFlow Software Based Mobile Networks architecture for 4G networks (Pentikousis, 2013), an SDN reference architecture where data path control, user authentication and mobility management are applications for a wireless access network (Bernardos, 2014).

Another area SDN quickly migrated to, via OpenFlow, was optical networking with work defining (Gringeri, 2013) and extending the initial OpenFlow match fields to support optical flow specification such as subwavelength switching header information and time slots (Channegowda, 2013). OF-CONFIG, using NETCONF has also been used to configure Adaptive Sliceable-Bandwidth Variable Transceivers (Nadal, 2019).

Wireless sensor networks and IoT was another area where SDN techniques could apply. Luo et al (2012) extended OpenFlow's flow-match entries to support sensors networks. Qin et al. (2014) presented an SDN controller for IoT networks on top of a middleware, named MINA, that acts as the DAL and which provides a southbound interface to sensors. De Oliveira et al. (2015) as well as Margi el al. (2018) built an SDN framework specifically for sensor nodes, with De Oliveira et al. (2015) using a controller application on a sensor node utilizing a serial/USB connection for accessing the sensor and Margi et al. (2018) defined IT-SDN, a Software Defined Wireless Sensor Network (SDWSN) tool, with their own flow tables with Contiki network drivers.

SDN controllers allow applications to interact and manage resources for each access network technology. Since 2015, a UK project called Towards Ultimate Convergence of All Networks (TOUCAN) has been chartered with the goal to unify all access network technologies and infrastructure under a single DAL. The project concluded in December 2020. Another approach for unifying SDN approaches is the work provided by OpenConfig. OpenConfig has adopted YANG, a semantics that is used to specify data models published by the IETF in particular. Such models can serve DAL for networking, both for wired, wireless, and optical transports.

It then seems clear that by providing the necessary abstractions to applications irrespective of the underlying network substrate will facilitate a fine-grained application of SDN techs regardless of the underlying infrastructure. Such abstractions will allow applications to request network paths, make use of combined architectures to solve resource, efficiency and high utilization requests on any abstracted network substrate.

Programmability concepts and abstractions provided by SDN already impact new designs and concepts. The focus is now on applications. Specifically, how to define high level policies and how these will be translated into a series of commands towards the devices. SDN networking languages have attempted to describe constructs for high level policies whose information is exchanged through the northbound interfaces, in particular.

A number of high-level languages were created such as: Procera introduced by Voellmy et al. (2012), which is a policy language that introduces the notion of functional reactive programming, or NetCore described by Monsanto et al. (2013), which is a declarative language for expressing dynamic policies for packet forwarding. Frenetic by Foster et al. (2011) define reusable abstractions to generate and install OpenFlow rules and later Pyretic presented by Reich et al. (2013) a Python-based platform that allows users to define packet forwarding policies. Smith et al. (2016) was submitted to the IETF to specify how high level policies can be transmitted to a policy agent using the OpFlex protocol, which in turn will be derived into a series of commands to be executed by the underlying hardware irrespective of the interface, but was discontinued.

Shifting from a decentralized control with each device having a view of the network, to a centralized control application capable of viewing the network as a program, gave way to another interesting approach: the network verification. One of the first papers was edited by Kazemian et al. (2012) introduces packet header space analysis that can take as input packet headers and is used to conduct a reachability analysis and to detect loops and slice isolation issues. A network debugger was introduced by Handigol et al. (2012) that attempted to emulate Linux's gbd for networking to create network 'backtraces' and detect where a packet has been in the network to detect configuration issues and network application bugs. Other tools were created, such as SDN traceroute by Agarwal et al. (2014) a tool for tracing the path of a packet flow for OpenFlow switches. Fang et al. (2020) designed a scheme for dynamic data plane verification in SDN, based upon header space analysis.

Having a single point of view of the network also provides a useful approach to extract analytics and telemetry using SDN. Sokolov et al. (2014) collected statistics using OpenFlow to assess resource availability. Medved et al (2014) introduced OpenDaylight as a controller using multiple DALs that performe network analytics. Yan et al. (2017) proposed a network analytics framework for optical networks based on extended OpenFlow for optical networks and OpenDaylight as the SDN controller.

The concept of in-network telemetry started with the emergence of P4. Van et al. (2017) introduced the concept of in-network telemetry, using P4 and ONOS, by appending a new packet header that is applied to the packet when it enters a P4-enabled network. For every P4 node the packet traverses, the telemetry header is being enriched with new information and finally being removed once the packet leaves the P4-enabled network and the telemetry information is sent to the controller. This increases the bandwidth overhead but improves visibility of the network and of network paths. This concept has been extended to other domains, as presented by Isolani et al. (2020), who enhanced QoS delivery through slice orchestration in Radio Access Networks (RANs) using fine-grained information gathered by implementing several extensions on the Ryu SDN controller as well as the forwarding plane using the Click modular router (Kohler et al. (2000)).

SDN REALIZATION AND IMPLEMENTATION CHALLENGES

SDN has the potential to provide several benefits to implementers, such as automated error recovery, higher link utilization, and customizing network behavior. However, SDN's global and full adoption is still underway, with a few deployments in production networks so far. A recent survey conducted by Verizon (2018) found that a small percentage of organizations had deployed SDN and that number was expecting to increase by 50% within two years. Cisco's (2020) annual report based on an IDC 2018 report, indicated that around 39% of 1202 enterprises have currently deployed SD-WAN with more planning to deploy more.

However, with the rise of 5G and the need for SDN, as will be discussed in the next section, it is expected that SDN will enjoy larger and global adoption. Many large networking vendors already provide SDN solutions. There are several issues that account for this lack of massive adoption. This section discusses these current issues.

At the onset of SDN the main issue was the maturity of the SDN technology, including abstractions, architecture, tools and applications. Earlier in this chapter three SDN architecture definitions were introduced by different SDOs. While these definitions have much in common, other SDOs will have their own SDN definition which will not help to progress a common view of what SDN is and how it can apply to networks.

The maturity of abstractions was yet another issue that proves to be a difficult challenge. SDN, as also depicted in Figure 1, involves at least two abstraction layers.

Concerning DAL, OpenFlow provided some specific abstractions which were enhanced over successive versions of the protocol. The goal was to provide more generic abstractions Bosshart et al. (2013) and Song (2013).

Another issue with OpenFlow and all SDN implementations that take all the control functionality out of the device, is that it requires to reinvent all current network functions, such as discovery using LLDP or ARP handling without the ability to utilize hardware that already support that function. If a hybrid solution is used, both using OpenFlow for configuring the forwarding tables and the usual device configuration for other functions, then the state of the non-OpenFlow switch is unavailable to the OpenFlow Controller.

Another problem was the multiple and quick succession of OpenFlow versions. OpenFlow being now developed by the ONF, with the latest version of publicly available OpenFlow 1.5.1, last published in April 2015. Network operators and big companies needed time to test and develop solutions to consider adopting them or other solutions. As new versions were published in rapid succession that were not backwards compatible, such as OpenFlow 1.0 and 1.1 tended to complicate this trial process.

As discussed earlier, besides OpenFlow there are other solutions that can be utilized for the DAL, such as the ForCES model, YANG, SMI, among others. These provide language constructs with which DAL resources can be abstracted. The issue with this approach is that there can be multiple different abstractions, proprietary or conflicting, that may hinder adoption. The best current practice to avoid this pitfall is the creation of standard data models, such as MIBs, LFB libraries and YANG modules. In addition, controllers that can abstract such different models may be one approach to resolve these issues, as discussed in Medved (2014) which attempts to provide homogeneity between heterogeneous abstractions.

While there has been significant research and implementation for the DAL, there is little progress on the NSAL abstractions. The two leading interfaces as discussed earlier are RESTful or RPC interfaces. However, there is little work done on what abstractions are going to be used and how services that both the control and/or management plane are going to be available to applications. Since most of the added value of SDN is the ability of applications to modify network behavior, the lack thereof hinders the deployment of SDN.

Admittedly, building SDN solutions is not an easy task; there are several SDN challenges that need to be addressed. Sezer et al. (2013) discuss four fundamental issues in building an SDN solution. The first is performance versus flexibility and how SDN networks can achieve high-throughput, security, and performance in a scalable fashion. With the sometimes-necessary packet redirection to the controller, performance becomes an issue. However recent advances in networking hardware and the performance achieved by new processors, better overall performance can be achieved.

The second is scalability and how a controller can maintain a consistent view of the network. This problem can also be viewed with the CAP theorem in mind. Should a controller be centralized or distributed? How would state between controllers be distributed and how fast would the network state converge? These are the questions a designer needs to keep in mind when designing an SDN network.

The third is security. Security is of paramount importance in networks but also in SDN environments where more interfaces are introduced thereby exposing more targets for potential attacks. In addition, since the SDN controller is usually defined as a logically centralized entity, it is easier to focus attacks on the controller as well as to perform DoS and DDoS attacks. When the controller is taken down, the network will either stop working or will not be updated. As a consequence, information maintained by the network becomes inconsistent with the information maintained by the SDN controller. Kreutz et al. (2013) provides also another view of the SDN security aspects and identifies potential points of attack on SDN architectures, for example the interface between the controller and the network devices and between controllers.

The last issue discussed by Sezer et al. (2013) is interoperability and how existing legacy solutions can interact with SDN-enabled network devices. How should legacy, SDN-unaware equipment be treated by a SDN computation logic? As black boxes that "just" forward traffic? Sezer et al. (2013) discuss this issue and proposes Path Computation Element (PCE) and also further development on other solutions that will alleviate this problem and provide backwards compatibility with IP and MPLS technologies.

Additionally, Hakiri et al. (2014) introduced more challenges such as inter-SDN controller communication. How can different SDN domains exchange information? The ONF (ONF, 2014) architecture introduces such an interface. Such a challenge will need to be addressed in order for SDN to be used across multiple networks, e.g., to design, deliver and operate inter-domain VPN/slice services. Ideas likes the Software-defined Internet Exchange discussed by Feamster et al. (2013) may solve such issues.

Jammal et al. (2014) introduced the issues of reliability and (optimized) controller placement. In the case of reliability the controller must be able to configure and validate network topologies and configurations to prevent any configuration error. In addition, if connection with the controller is lost what will happen if problems occur within the network? The other issue is controller placement. Jammal et al. (2014) discusses this issue raised by SDN-WAN deployments, controller placement is crucial as multiple SDN controllers are required to improve reliability and their placement affects many metrics in the network such as latency, fault tolerance and performance. Considering the fact that there are scenarios that every packet the device does not know what to do with is sent to the controller, the placement of controllers is crucial.

A lot of issues were addressed by research and experimentation as the number of pilots have been conducted by some operators, such as Kepes et al. (2014) by implementing SDN in the University of

Pittsburg, or Google's B4 (Jain et al., 2013), Giorgetti et al (2019) implemented ONOS on an optical testbed and Telefonica and Huawei performing a commercial SDN traffic in Peru (Huawei, 2016).

However, Batool (2019) identified five issues raised by the lack of massive SDN adoption. The first is SDN security and monitoring which has been discussed previously, the second was the lack of skilled developers who can take full advantage of SDN techs for automating service delivery procedures. The third is the lack of familiarity of SDN in comparison to knowledge of existing legacy network. The fourth is the lack of standardized certifications of personnel and finally the lack of motivation from enterprises that see the introduction of SDN unnecessary or expensive.

The fifth issue exposes how enterprises and people are affected by this increasing programmability. This transition may require training programs or other Human Resources actions to adjust the skill profile of the workforce. However, the adoption of SDN and programmable infrastructures in general, provides significant opportunities for faster service deployment, and for automating operational processes. This automation may require adjustments to staffing levels (ATIS 2013)

SDN APPLICABILITY ON FUTURE NETWORK ARCHITECTURES

As discussed earlier, SDN provides data plane programmability amongst other capabilities. However, SDN has become a versatile toolkit in any network architecture. This section explores SDN's applicability to current and future network architectures and provides an outlook on SDN's future.

It is no wonder that the advantages provided by SDN, NFV, and SFC have heavily influenced the development of 5G networks. In fact, the architectural document of 3GPP (3GPP 2020) states that SDN and NFV are amongst the techniques to be used. As discussed in the 5G PPP white paper (5GPPP 2020), 5G networks will encompass multiple access technologies, wireless and fixed, as well as edge and cloud resources. All these resources will be sliced and provided "as-a-service" to different tenants. 5G also requires a complete resource and service lifecycle management that SDN and NFV can provide.

Discussion about the use of SDN in 5G networks started as early as 2013 by Demestichas et al. (2013) followed by Yousaf et al. (2017) where SDN is introduced as one of the main emerging and enabling technologies. Cho et al. (2014) investigated the integration of SDN and Software-Defined Radio (SDR). SDR should not be confused with SDN as it refers to the implementation of hardware radio as software on personal computers or embedded systems (Mitola, 1992). Cho et al (2014) introduced a cross-layer control which can act as an administrator of both SDN and SDR layers. Bouras et al. (2017) discussed the 5G requirements and the relevant SDN solutions that can address them. Sun et al (2015) proposed an SDN framework for 5G heterogeneous networks as 5G will encompass different access technologies, including satellites.

Another important issue for 5G is slicing. Foukas et al. (2017) performed a survey on slicing and SDN, alongside NFV, are identified as prominent technologies to create an end-to-end slice orchestration and management. Ordonez-Lucena et al. (2017) examined the issues regarding 5G slicing with the integration of SDN and NFV based on the ONF slicing architecture. Chekired et al. (2019) researched a service slicing model based on a hierarchical SDN architecture for Fog, Edge and Cloud layers with four SDN controllers to reduce network congestion for autonomous driving capabilities. Similar to Cho et al (2014), Barmpounakis et al. (2020) designed a cross-layer control for network slicing-enabled Radio Access Network management for 5G, by utilizing the Open Air Interface (OAI) for the radio control using the RYU SDN controller for the network.

5G designs may use Edge, Fog, and Cloud resources. SDN can be used to manage such resources. Cloud infrastructures are network architectures where SDN is already implemented. Edge and Fog computing are new distributed computing approaches where computation and storage is closer to the edges of the network and therefore to the users, so as to improve latency and save bandwidth. Baktir et al. (2017) investigated the use of SDN in edge computing and identified a number of benefits such as VM mobility, adaptability and service-centric implementations. Huang et al. (2017) implemented a data offloading system inside a Mobile Edge Computing architecture using an SDN controller to provide connectivity between vehicles through the cellular network. Cao et al. (2020) designed a mobile-edge computing model with SDN, using Open vSwitch with a Floodlight controller to accelerate and optimize service requests. Zaballa et al. (2020) introduces SDN for fog computing with P4 switches that implement specific features such as local mobility for the network between the edge devices and infrastructure.

Regarding DC connectivity, one area that has recently attracted a lot of interest is SD-WAN. SD-WAN refers to the management of connectivity between data centers or cloud instances using SDN techniques. As stated in Yang et al. (2019), SD-WAN is meant to simplify networking operations in wide area networks and introduce innovation and flexibility. Andromeda et al. (2020) performed a techno-economic analysis in the implementation of SD-WAN in a 4G/LTE case study and came to the conclusion that it is feasible and profitable with a return of investment around 3.4 years. Troia et al. (2020) implemented an SD-WAN solution using OpenDaylight as the controller and Open vSwitches to control virtual Customer Premises Equipment (CPEs) to achieve connectivity. Tootaghaj et al. (2020) identified the key issues raised by network reconfiguration and routing decisions that are made locally and they proposed a topology and route management in SD-WAN overlays to address such issues.

New research approaches in networking can also benefit from SDN. Intent-Based Networking (IBN), is a form of network administration using Machine Learning (ML) techniques. It is based on intents, which, as discussed in Zeydan et al (2020) are an evolution of the term policy, defining a high level view of the operational and business objectives (Cisco 2018). The goal is to create intents which will in turn be translated eventually into device parameters. IBN is also part of the charter in the IRTF Network Management Research Group (nmrg) Clemm et al. (2020).

SDN is particularly useful to IBN as an SDN controller can offer a single point of control and administration of the network offering the IBN system both resource discovery as well as the ability to derive the intent into service-inferred configuration tasks and policy instantiation. Examples of research towards that direction include Pham et al. (2016) that uses ONOS's northbound interface to create an IBN interface allowing applications to express objectives, policies and requirements and Alalmaei et al. (2020) which proposed a framework focusing on the creation of an SDN northbound API to handle service consumer intents in "cloudified" CDN environments.

Besides IBN, ML techniques are being investigated for networking purposes as they can improve the efficiency of SDN designs to achieve various goals. Machine learning has been used for security purposes, as discussed in Sultana et al. (2019), for intrusion detection, anomaly detection, and Distributed Denial of Service (DDoS) attack detections as well as in Ahmad et al. (2020) that identified various SDN security issues tackled by machine learning such as control plane threats and communication vulnerabilities. However, with the emergence of Graph Neural Networks (GNN) other approaches soon begun taking shape such as RouteNet in Rusek et al. (2020) which uses GNNs to generalize arbitrary topologies and traffic flows to predict packet loss and perform a joint optimization of mean delay, jitter and loss. Zhu et al. (2020) proposed a multi-path routing optimization system combining GNN and SDN, with SDN providing a global view of the whole network and control of MPTCP connections, based on the Floodlight controller (Floodlight).

SDN can be used in any networking scenario where programmability is required. The malleability of SDN to adapt to any underlying network infrastructure makes SDN applicable in any domain. While 5G networks are already deployed in some countries, 6G research already ignited as discussed in Letaief et al. (2019) where SDN plays a key role. Other domains embrace SDN, such as battlefield networking in Nobre et al. (2016) or home networks in Xu et al. (2016).

As for future SDN architectures, Foster et al. (2020) proposed a framework. New SDN architectures will become custom-based end-to-end close looped verifiable systems which run autonomously. Network operators will define the parameters of their network using some intent-based policy language defining what they want to achieve, and address SLAs, latency and bandwidth requirements. Machine learning algorithms will take as input the intent as well as the infrastructure resources and derive the service design accordingly, as discussed in Foster et al. (2020). Other machine learning algorithms will be used for closed-control loop purposes, by monitoring data and assess that what has been delivered complies with what has been requested/negotiated. Towards this direction, ONF has announced a new project called PRONTO which has garnered a 30 million US$ grant from DARPA (Pronto, 2021).

CONCLUSION

This chapter discussed the history of SDN and how it emerged. It also described the current views on SDN architectures, layers and interfaces. This chapter also discussed how SDN relates to other networking technologies, specifically NFV and SFC. With a better understanding of SDN, its adaptability to various environments was highlighted. Finally, the chapter concluded with a few examples of SDN applications to current and future network architectures.

To sum the chapter up, SDN-based network programmability becomes an attractive toolkit for automated network design and operation. With its current incarnation, SDN has several key roles to play on future network architectures.

First by completely separating signaling from the actual data path, it is possible to redefine how a network can be designed. For example, a network designer may choose to create a completely separate network for carrying signaling traffic, for the sake of optimizing resource usage.

Second, by providing a common DAL, it is now possible to unify all the heterogeneous network domains such as wired, wireless and optical under a common controller. Unifying all domains will empower SDN and allow its use in networks that are comprised of various infrastructures.

Finally, by combining SDN, NFV, and SFC, it will be possible to use software resources to manage the network lifecycle and to allow software applications to actually define the network infrastructure and then control and manage it. Followed by the emergence of programming languages, like P4nd research in areas like Intent Based Networking and Machine learning, SDN is moving towards complete autonomous and zero-touch networking.

This chapter closes with an attempt to provide a general definition of what exactly SDN is in a few words: SDN is a network programmability technique, which can be used as an enabler to provide applications with the ability to program the network. Using other techniques such as Machine Learning and Intent-Based networking, SDN can progress into the next stage of completely autonomous networks.

REFERENCES

3rd Generation Partnership Project, Interface between the Control Plane and the User Plane Nodes v16.6.0. (2020). *Stage 3, Release 16*. 3GPP.

3rd Generation Partnership Project, System architecture for the 5G System v16.6.0. (2020). *Stage 2, Release 16*. 3GPP.

P4 API working group. (2020). *P4Runtime Specification*. https://p4.org/p4runtime/spec/master/P4Runtime-Spec.html

Agarwal, K., Rozner, E., Dixon, C., & Carter, J. (2014). SDN traceroute: Tracing SDN forwarding without changing network behavior. In *Proceedings of the third workshop on Hot topics in software defined networking* (pp. 145-150). Academic Press.

Ahmad, A., Harjula, E., Ylianttila, M., & Ahmad, I. (2020). Evaluation of Machine Learning Techniques for Security in SDN. In *IEEE Global Communications Conference, GLOBECOM 2020*. IEEE Institute of Electrical and Electronic Engineers.

Alalmaei, S., Elkhatib, Y., Bezahaf, M., Broadbent, M., & Race, N. (2020). SDN Heading North: Towards a Declarative Intent-based Northbound Interface. In *2020 16th International Conference on Network and Service Management (CNSM)* (pp. 1-5). IEEE.

Andromeda, S., & Gunawan, D. (2020). Techno-economic analysis from implementing sd-wan with 4g/lte, a case study in xyz company. In *2020 International Seminar on Intelligent Technology and Its Applications (ISITIA)* (pp. 345-351). IEEE.

Apache Thrift. (n.d.). https://thrift.apache.org/

Apache ThriftI. D. L. (n.d.). https://thrift.apache.org/docs/idl

ATIS. (2013). *Operational Opportunities and Challenges of SDN/NFV Programmable Infrastructure*. October 2013, Report.

Baktir, A. C., Ozgovde, A., & Ersoy, C. (2017). How can edge computing benefit from software-defined networking: A survey, use cases, and future directions. *IEEE Communications Surveys and Tutorials*, *19*(4), 2359–2391.

Barmpounakis, S., Maroulis, N., Papadakis, M., Tsiatsios, G., Soukaras, D., & Alonistioti, N. (2020). Network slicing-enabled RAN management for 5G: Cross layer control based on SDN and SDR. *Computer Networks*, *166*, 106987.

Basta, A., Kellerer, W., Hoffmann, M., Hoffmann, K., & Schmidt, E. D. (2013). A Virtual SDN-enabled LTE EPC Architecture: a case study for S-/P-Gateways functions. In *Future Networks and Services (SDN4FNS), 2013 IEEE SDN for* (pp. 1–7). IEEE.

Batool, R. (2019). Review, Analysis of SDN and Difficulties in Adoption of SD. *Journal of Information & Communication Technology*, *13*(1).

Berde, P., Gerola, M., Hart, J., Higuchi, Y., Kobayashi, M., Koide, T., Lantz, B., O'Connor, B., Radoslavov, P., Snow, W., & Parulkar, G. (2014). ONOS: towards an open, distributed SDN OS. In *Proceedings of the third workshop on Hot topics in software defined networking* (pp. 1-6). Academic Press.

Bernardos, C. J., de la Oliva, A., Serrano, P., Banchs, A., Contreras, L. M., Jin, H., & Zúñiga, J. C. (2014, June). An Architecture for Software Defined Wireless Networking. IEEE Wireless Communications Magazine.

Bierman, A., Bjorklund, M., & Watsen, K. (2017). *RESTCONF Protocol*. IETF RFC 8040.

Biswas, J., Lazar, A. A., Huard, J. F., Lim, K., Mahjoub, S., Pau, L. F., ... Weinstein, S. (1998). The IEEE P1520 standards initiative for programmable network interfaces. *Communications Magazine, IEEE, 36*(10), 64–70.

Bjorklund, M. (2010). *YANG – A Data Modeling Language for the Network Configuration Protocol (NETCONF)*. IETF RFC 6020.

Bjorklund, M. (2016). *The YANG 1.1 Data Modeling Language*. IETF RFC 7950.

Bosshart, P., Daly, D., Gibb, G., Izzard, M., McKeown, N., Rexford, J., Schlesinger, C., Talayco, D., Vahdat, A., Varghese, G., & Walker, D. (2014, July 28). P4: Programming protocol-independent packet processors. *Computer Communication Review, 44*(3), 87–95.

Bosshart, P., Daly, D., Izzard, M., McKeown, N., Rexford, J., Talayco, D., . . . Walker, D. (2013). *Programming protocol-independent packet processors*. arXiv preprint arXiv:1312.1719.

Bouras, C., Kollia, A., & Papazois, A. (2017), March. SDN & NFV in 5G: Advancements and challenges. In *2017 20th Conference on innovations in clouds, internet and networks (ICIN)* (pp. 107-111). IEEE.

Caesar, M., Caldwell, D., Feamster, N., Rexford, J., Shaikh, A., & van der Merwe, J. (2005). Design and implementation of a routing control platform. In *Proceedings of the 2nd conference on Symposium on Networked Systems Design & Implementation-Volume 2* (pp. 15-28). USENIX Association.

Campbell, A. T., De Meer, H. G., Kounavis, M. E., Miki, K., Vicente, J. B., & Villela, D. (1999). A survey of programmable networks. *Computer Communication Review, 29*(2), 7–23.

Cao, S., Wang, Z., Chen, Y., Jiang, D., Yan, Y., & Chen, H. (2020). Research on Design and Application of Mobile Edge Computing Model Based on SDN. In *2020 29th International Conference on Computer Communications and Networks (ICCCN)* (pp. 1-6). IEEE.

Casado, M., Freedman, M. J., Pettit, J., Luo, J., McKeown, N., & Shenker, S. (2007). Ethane: Taking control of the enterprise. *Computer Communication Review, 37*(4), 1–12.

Channegowda, M., Nejabati, R., & Simeonidou, D. (2013). Software-defined optical networks technology and infrastructure: enabling software-defined optical network operations. *Optical Communications and Networking, IEEE/OSA Journal of, 5*(10), A274-A282.

Chekired, D. A., Togou, M. A., Khoukhi, L., & Ksentini, A. (2019). 5G-slicing-enabled scalable SDN core network: Toward an ultra-low latency of autonomous driving service. *IEEE Journal on Selected Areas in Communications, 37*(8), 1769–1782.

Cisco. (2018). *Intent-Based Networking: Building the bridge between business and IT*. https://www.cisco.com/c/dam/en/us/solutions/collateral/enterprise-networks/digital-network-architecture/nb-09-intent-networking-wp-cte-en.pdf

Cisco. (2020). *Cisco Annual Internet Report (2018–2023)*. https://www.cisco.com/c/en/us/solutions/collateral/executive-perspectives/annual-internet-report/white-paper-c11-741490.html

Clemm, A., Ciavaglia L., Granville L., Tantsure J. (2020). *Intent-Based Networking – Concepts and Definitions*. IRTF draft, draft-irtf-nmrg-ibn-concepts-definitions.

Contreras, LM., Bernardos, CJ., Lopez, D., Boucadair, M., & Iovanna, P. (2019). *Cooperating Layered Architecture for Software-Defined Networking (CLAS)*. IETF RFC 8579.

De Oliveira, B. T., Gabriel, L. B., & Margi, C. B. (2015). TinySDN: Enabling multiple controllers for software-defined wireless sensor networks. *IEEE Latin America Transactions, 13*(11), 3690–3696.

Dely, P., Kassler, A., & Bayer, N. (2011). Openflow for wireless mesh networks. In *Computer Communications and Networks (ICCCN), 2011 Proceedings of 20th International Conference on* (pp. 1-6). IEEE.

Demestichas, P., Georgakopoulos, A., Karvounas, D., Tsagkaris, K., Stavroulaki, V., Lu, J., Xiong, C., & Yao, J. (2013). 5G on the horizon: Key challenges for the radio-access network. *IEEE Vehicular Technology Magazine, 8*(3), 47–53.

Erickson, D. (2013). The beacon openflow controller. In *Proceedings of the second ACM SIGCOMM workshop on Hot topics in software defined networking* (pp. 13-18). ACM.

European Telecommunications Standards Institute. (2012). *Network Functions Virtualisation, white paper*. Retrieved February 09, 2021, from https://portal.etsi.org/NFV/NFV_White_Paper.pdf

European Telecommunications Standards Institute. (2015). *Report on SDN Usage in NFV Architectural Framework, white paper*. Retrieved February 09, 2021, from https://www.etsi.org/deliver/etsi_gs/NFV-EVE/001_099/005/01.01.01_60/gs_NFV-EVE005v010101p.pdf

Facca, F. M., Salvadori, E., Karl, H., López, D. R., Gutiérrez, P. A. A., Kostic, D., & Riggio, R. (2013). NetIDE: First steps towards an integrated development environment for portable network apps. In *Software Defined Networks (EWSDN), 2013 Second European Workshop on* (pp. 105-110). IEEE.

Fang, Y., & Lu, Y. (2020). Real-Time Verification of Network Properties Based on Header Space. *IEEE Access: Practical Innovations, Open Solutions, 8*, 36789–36806.

Feamster, N., Rexford, J., Shenker, S., Clark, R., Hutchins, R., Levin, D., & Bailey, J. (2013). *SDX: A software-defined internet exchange*. Open Networking Summit.

Feamster, N., Rexford, J., & Zegura, E. (2013). The road to SDN. *Queue, 11*(12), 20.

Floodlight, S. D. N. (n.d.). *OpenFlow Controller*. Retrieved February 09, 2021, from https://github.com/floodlight/floodlight

Foster, N., Harrison, R., Freedman, M. J., Monsanto, C., Rexford, J., Story, A., & Walker, D. (2011). Frenetic: A network programming language. *ACM SIGPLAN Notices, 46*(9), 279–291.

Foster, N., McKeown, N., Rexford, J., Parulkar, G., Peterson, L., & Sunay, O. (2020). Using deep programmability to put network owners in control. *Computer Communication Review, 50*(4), 82–88.

Foukas, X., Patounas, G., Elmokashfi, A., & Marina, M. K. (2017). Network slicing in 5G: Survey and challenges. *IEEE Communications Magazine, 55*(5), 94–100.

Future Internet REsearch (FIRE). (n.d.). Retrieved February 09, 2021, from https://ec.europa.eu/digital-single-market/en/future-internet-research-and-experimentation-fire

Giorgetti, A., Sgambelluri, A., Casellas, R., Morro, R., Campanella, A., & Castoldi, P. (2019). Control of open and disaggregated transport networks using the Open Network Operating System (ONOS). *Journal of Optical Communications and Networking, 12*(2), A171–A181.

Global Environment for Network Innovations (GENI). (n.d.). Retrieved February 09, 2021, from https://www.geni.net/

GoogleR. P. C. (n.d.). https://grpc.io/

Google Protobufs. (n.d.). https://developers.google.com/protocol-buffers

Greenberg, A., Hjalmtysson, G., Maltz, D. A., Myers, A., Rexford, J., Xie, G., ... Zhang, H. (2005). A clean slate 4D approach to network control and management. *Computer Communication Review, 35*(5), 41–54.

Gringeri, S., Bitar, N., & Xia, T. J. (2013). Extending software defined network principles to include optical transport. *Communications Magazine, IEEE, 51*(3), 32–40.

Gude, N., Koponen, T., Pettit, J., Pfaff, B., Casado, M., McKeown, N., & Shenker, S. (2008). NOX: Towards an operating system for networks. *Computer Communication Review, 38*(3), 105–110.

Guha, A., Reitblatt, M., & Foster, N. (2013). *Formal Foundations For Software Defined Networks*. Open Net Summit.

Hakiri, A., Gokhale, A., Berthou, P., Schmidt, D. C., & Thierry, G. (2014). Software-defined Networking: Challenges and Research Opportunities for Future Internet. *Computer Networks*.

Haleplidis, E., Joachimpillai, D., Salim, J. H., Lopez, D., Martin, J., Pentikousis, K., Denazis, S., & Koufopavlou, O. (2014). ForCES applicability to SDN-enhanced NFV. In *2014 Third European Workshop on Software Defined Networks* (pp. 43-48). IEEE.

Haleplidis, E., Pentikousis, K., Denazis, S., Salim, J. H., Meyer, D., & Koufopavlou, O. (2014). *RFC 7426 Software Defined Networking: Layers and Architecture Terminology*. IRTF SDNRG.

Haleplidis, E., Salim, J. H., Denazis, S., & Koufopavlou, O. (2014). Towards a Network Abstraction Model for SDN. *Journal of Network and Systems Management*, 1–19.

Handigol, N., Heller, B., Jeyakumar, V., Mazières, D., & McKeown, N. (2012). Where is the debugger for my software-defined network? In *Proceedings of the first workshop on Hot topics in software defined networks*(pp. 55-60). ACM.

Handigol, N., Heller, B., Jeyakumar, V., Maziéres, D., & McKeown, N. (2012). Where is the debugger for my software-defined network? In *Proceedings of the first workshop on Hot topics in software defined networks* (pp. 55-60). Academic Press.

Hemid, A. (2017). Facilitation of The OpenDaylight Architecture. *The 4th Computer Science Conference for University of Bonn Students.*

Huang, C. M., Chiang, M. S., Dao, D. T., Su, W. L., Xu, S., & Zhou, H. (2018). V2V data offloading for cellular network based on the software defined network (SDN) inside mobile edge computing (MEC) architecture. *IEEE Access: Practical Innovations, Open Solutions, 6,* 17741–17755.

Huawei. (2016). *News report: Telefonica and Huawei Announce Industry's First SDN IP+Optical Field Trial with Commercial Traffic in Peru.* Accessed 13/01/2021 from https://www.huawei.com/en/news/2016/2/industry-first-sdn-ip

IETF SFC working group. (n.d.). Retrieved September 01, 2020, from https://datatracker.ietf.org/wg/sfc/charter/

Isolani, P. H., Haxhibeqiri, J., Moerman, I., Hoebeke, J., Marquez-Barja, J. M., Granville, L. Z., & Latré, S. (2020). An SDN-based framework for slice orchestration using in-band network telemetry in IEEE 802.11. In *2020 6th IEEE Conference on Network Softwarization (NetSoft)* (pp. 344-346). IEEE.

ITU-T Study Group 13. (2014). *Y.3300, Framework of software-defined networking.* Retrieved February 09, 2021, from https://www.itu.int/ITU-T/recommendations/rec.aspx?rec=12168

Jain, S., Kumar, A., Mandal, S., Ong, J., Poutievski, L., Singh, A., ... Vahdat, A. (2013). B4: Experience with a globally-deployed software defined WAN. In *Proceedings of the ACM SIGCOMM 2013 conference on SIGCOMM* (pp. 3-14). ACM.

Jammal, M., Singh, T., Shami, A., Asal, R., & Li, Y. (2014). *Software-Defined Networking: State of the Art and Research Challenges.* arXiv preprint arXiv:1406.0124.

John, W., Pentikousis, K., Agapiou, G., Jacob, E., Kind, M., Manzalini, A., & Meirosu, C. (2013, November). Research directions in network service chaining. In *Future Networks and Services (SDN4FNS), 2013 IEEE SDN for* (pp. 1–7). IEEE.

Kazemian, P., Varghese, G., & McKeown, N. (2012). Header space analysis: Static checking for networks. In *9th USENIX Symposium on Networked Systems Design and Implementation (NSDI 12)* (pp. 113-126). USENIX.

Kepes, B. (2014). *SDN meets the real-world: Implementation benefits and challenges.* GIGAOM RESEARCH, Giga Omni Media, Inc.

Kohler, E., Morris, R., Chen, B., Jannotti, J., & Kaashoek, M. F. (2000). The Click modular router. *ACM Transactions on Computer Systems, 18*(3), 263–297.

Kreutz, D., Ramos, F., & Verissimo, P. (2013). Towards secure and dependable software-defined networks. In *Proceedings of the second ACM SIGCOMM workshop on Hot topics in software defined networking* (pp. 55-60). ACM.

Lengdell, M., Pavon, J., Wakano, M., Chapman, M., & Kawanishi, M. (1996). The TINA network resource model. *IEEE Communications Magazine*, *34*(3), 74–79.

Letaief, K. B., Chen, W., Shi, Y., Zhang, J., & Zhang, Y. J. A. (2019). The roadmap to 6G: AI empowered wireless networks. *IEEE Communications Magazine*, *57*(8), 84–90.

Li, L. E., Mao, Z. M., & Rexford, J. (2012). Toward software-defined cellular networks. In *2012 European workshop on software defined networking* (pp. 7-12). IEEE.

Liu, W., Xie, C., Strassner, J., Karagiannis, G., Klyus, M., Bi., J, Cheng, Y., & Zhang, D. (2018). *Policy-Based Management Framework for the Simplified Use of Policy Abstractions (SUPA)*. IETF RFC 8328.

Lockwood, J. W., McKeown, N., Watson, G., Gibb, G., Hartke, P., Naous, J., . . . Luo, J. (2007). NetFPGA--An Open Platform for Gigabit-Rate Network Switching and Routing. In *Microelectronic Systems Education, 2007. MSE'07. IEEE International Conference on* (pp. 160-161). IEEE.

Luo, T., Tan, H. P., & Quek, T. Q. (2012). Sensor OpenFlow: Enabling software-defined wireless sensor networks. *IEEE Communications Letters*, *16*(11), 1896–1899.

Margi, C. B., Alves, R. C., Segura, G. A. N., & Oliveira, D. A. (2018). Software-defined wireless sensor networks approach: Southbound protocol and its performance evaluation. *Open Journal of Internet Of Things*, *4*(1), 99–108.

McKeown, N., Anderson, T., Balakrishnan, H., Parulkar, G., Peterson, L., Rexford, J., & Turner, J. (2008). OpenFlow: Enabling innovation in campus networks. *Computer Communication Review*, *38*(2), 69–74. doi:10.1145/1355734.1355746

Medved, J., Varga, R., Tkacik, A., & Gray, K. (2014). OpenDaylight: Towards a Model-Driven SDN Controller architecture. In *A World of Wireless, Mobile and Multimedia Networks (WoWMoM), 2014 IEEE 15th International Symposium on* (pp. 1-6). IEEE.

Medved, J., Varga, R., Tkacik, A., & Gray, K. (2014). Opendaylight: Towards a model-driven sdn controller architecture. In *Proceeding of IEEE International Symposium on a World of Wireless, Mobile and Multimedia Networks 2014* (pp. 1-6). IEEE.

Mendonca, M., Nunes, B. A. A., Nguyen, X. N., Obraczka, K., & Turletti, T. (2013). *A Survey of software-defined networking: past, present, and future of programmable networks*. hal-00825087.

Mitola, J. (1993). Software radios: Survey, critical evaluation and future directions. *IEEE Aerospace and Electronic Systems Magazine*, *8*(4), 25–36.

Monsanto, C., Foster, N., Harrison, R., & Walker, D. (2012). A compiler and run-time system for network programming languages. *ACM SIGPLAN Notices*, *47*(1), 217–230.

Monsanto, C., Reich, J., Foster, N., Rexford, J., & Walker, D. (2013). Composing Software Defined Networks. In NSDI (pp. 1-13). Academic Press.

Nadal, L., Fabrega, J. M., Moreolo, M. S., Casellas, R., Muñoz, R., Rodríguez, L., Vilalta, R., Vílchez, F. J., & Martínez, R. (2019). SDN-enabled sliceable transceivers in disaggregated optical networks. *Journal of Lightwave Technology*, *37*(24), 6054–6062.

Nakao, A. (2012). *Flare: Open deeply programmable network node architecture.* Academic Press.

Nobre, J., Rosario, D., Both, C., Cerqueira, E., & Gerla, M. (2016). Toward software-defined battlefield networking. *IEEE Communications Magazine, 54*(10), 152–157.

OF-CONFIG. (2013). *OpenFlow Configuration and Management Protocol.* ONF. https://www.open-networking.org/standards/of-config

Olsson, M., Rommer, S., Mulligan, C., Sultana, S., & Frid, L. (2009). *SAE and the Evolved Packet Core: Driving the mobile broadband revolution.* Academic Press.

ONF TR-526. (2016). *Applying SDN Architecture to 5G Slicing.* Academic Press.

Open Networking Foundation. (2009). *OpenFlow Switch Specification v1.0.0.* Retrieved August 20, 2020, from https://opennetworking.org/wp-content/uploads/2013/04/openflow-spec-v1.0.0.pdf

Open Networking Foundation. (2012). *Software-Defined Networking: The New Norm for Networks.* ONF White Paper.

Open Networking Foundation. (2013). *SDN Architecture Overview.* Retrieved February, 2021, from https://opennetworking.org/wp-content/uploads/2014/11/TR_SDN-ARCH-1.0-Overview-12012016.04.pdf

Open Networking Foundation. (2014). *SDN Architecture, Issue 1.* Retrieved February 2021 from https://opennetworking.org/wp-content/uploads/2014/10/TR-521_SDN_Architecture_issue_1.1.pdf

Open Networking Foundation. (2014). *OpenFlow Table Type Patterns Version 1.0.* Retrieved February 09, 2021, from https://opennetworking.org/wp-content/uploads/2013/04/OpenFlow%20Table%20Type%20Patterns%20v1.0.pdf

OpenConfig. (n.d.). www.openconfig.net

OpenConfig data models. (n.d.). https://www.openconfig.net/projects/models/

Ordonez-Lucena, J., Ameigeiras, P., Lopez, D., Ramos-Munoz, J. J., Lorca, J., & Folgueira, J. (2017). Network slicing for 5G with SDN/NFV: Concepts, architectures, and challenges. *IEEE Communications Magazine, 55*(5), 80–87.

Panda, A., Scott, C., Ghodsi, A., Koponen, T., & Shenker, S. (2013). CAP for Networks. In *Proceedings of the second ACM SIGCOMM workshop on Hot topics in software defined networking* (pp. 91-96). ACM.

Parniewicz, D., Doriguzzi Corin, R., Ogrodowczyk, L., Rashidi Fard, M., Matias, J., Gerola, M., ... Pentikousis, K. (2014). Design and implementation of an OpenFlow hardware abstraction layer. In *Proceedings of the 2014 ACM SIGCOMM workshop on Distributed cloud computing* (pp. 71-76). ACM.

Pentikousis, K., Wang, Y., & Hu, W. (2013). Mobileflow: Toward software-defined mobile networks. Communications Magazine, IEEE, 51(7).

Pham, M., & Hoang, D. B. (2016). *SDN applications-The intent-based Northbound Interface realisation for extended applications. In 2016 IEEE NetSoft Conference and Workshops (NetSoft).* IEEE.

PPP Architecture Working Group. View on 5G Architecture. (2020). *Version 3.0.* https://5g-ppp.eu/wp-content/uploads/2020/02/5G-PPP-5G-Architecture-White-Paper_final.pdf

Pronto. (2021). Retrieved 13 January 2021, from https://prontoproject.org/

Qin, Z., Denker, G., Giannelli, C., Bellavista, P., & Venkatasubramanian, N. (2014) A Software Defined Networking Architecture for the Internet-of-Things. In *Network Operations and Management Symposium (NOMS)*. IEEE.

Reich, J., Monsanto, C., Foster, N., Rexford, J., & Walker, D. (2013). Modular SDN Programming with Pyretic. *USENIX, 38*(5), 128-134.

Roberts, J., (2009). The clean-slate approach to future Internet design: a survey of research initiatives. *Annals of Telecommunications-Annales des Télécommunications, 64*(5-6), 271-276.

Rooney, S., van der Merwe, J. E., Crosby, S. A., & Leslie, I. M. (1998). The Tempest: A framework for safe, resource assured, programmable networks. *Communications Magazine, IEEE, 36*(10), 42–53.

Rusek, K., Suárez-Varela, J., Almasan, P., Barlet-Ros, P., & Cabellos-Aparicio, A. (2020). RouteNet: Leveraging Graph Neural Networks for network modeling and optimization in SDN. *IEEE Journal on Selected Areas in Communications, 38*(10), 2260–2270.

Salman, O., Elhajj, I. H., Kayssi, A., & Chehab, A. (2016), April. SDN controllers: A comparative study. In *2016 18th Mediterranean Electrotechnical Conference (MELECON)* (pp. 1-6). IEEE.

Sezer, S., Scott-Hayward, S., Chouhan, P. K., Fraser, B., Lake, D., Finnegan, J., . . . Rao, N. (2013). Are we ready for SDN? Implementation challenges for software-defined networks. Communications Magazine, IEEE, 51(7).

Sherwood, R., Chan, M., Covington, A., Gibb, G., Flajslik, M., Handigol, N., Huang, T. Y., Kazemian, P., Kobayashi, M., Naous, J., & Seetharaman, S. (2010, January 7). Carving research slices out of your production networks with OpenFlow. *Computer Communication Review, 40*(1), 129–130.

Sherwood, R., Gibb, G., Yap, K. K., Appenzeller, G., Casado, M., McKeown, N., & Parulkar, G. (2009). *Flowvisor: A network virtualization layer.* OpenFlow Switch Consortium, Tech. Rep.

Shin, Y. Y., Kang, S. H., Kwak, J. Y., & Yang, S. H. (2015). iNaaS: OpenStack and SDN/OpenFlow based network virtualization with OpenlRIS. In *2015 17th International Conference on Advanced Communication Technology (ICACT)* (pp. 517-520). IEEE.

Smith, M., Dvorkin, M., Laribi, Y., Pandey, V., Garg, P. & Weidenbacher, N. (2016). *OpFlex Control Protocol.* IETF individual draft, draft-smith-opflex-03.

Sokolov, V., Alekseev, I., Mazilov, D., & Nikitinskiy, M. (2014). A network analytics system in the SDN. In *2014 International Science and Technology Conference (Modern Networking Technologies) (MoNeTeC)* (pp. 1-3). IEEE.

Song, H. (2013). Protocol-oblivious forwarding: Unleash the power of SDN through a future-proof forwarding plane. In *Proceedings of the second ACM SIGCOMM workshop on Hot topics in software defined networking* (pp. 127-132). ACM.

Sultana, N., Chilamkurti, N., Peng, W., & Alhadad, R. (2019). Survey on SDN based network intrusion detection system using machine learning approaches. *Peer-to-Peer Networking and Applications*, *12*(2), 493–501.

Sun, S., Gong, L., Rong, B., & Lu, K. (2015). An intelligent SDN framework for 5G heterogeneous networks. *IEEE Communications Magazine*, *53*(11), 142–147.

Telecommunication Standardization sector of ITU. (1990). *CCITT Recommendation 1.361, B-ISDN ATM Layer Specification*. Geneva, Switzerland: ITU.

Telecommunication Standardization sector of ITU. (1993). *ITU, Q.700: Introduction to CCITT Signalling System No. 7*. Geneva, Switzerland: ITU.

Tennenhouse, D. L., Smith, J. M., Sincoskie, W. D., Wetherall, D. J., & Minden, G. J. (1997). A survey of active network research. *Communications Magazine, IEEE*, *35*(1), 80–86.

Tootaghaj, D. Z., Ahmed, F., Sharma, P., & Yannakakis, M. (2020). Homa: An Efficient Topology and Route Management Approach in SD-WAN Overlays. In *IEEE INFOCOM 2020-IEEE Conference on Computer Communications* (pp. 2351-2360). IEEE.

Troia, S., Zorello, L. M. M., Maralit, A. J., & Maier, G. (2020). SD-WAN: An Open-Source Implementation for Enterprise Networking Services. In *2020 22nd International Conference on Transparent Optical Networks (ICTON)* (pp. 1-4). IEEE.

Van Tu, N., Hyun, J., & Hong, J. W. K. (2017). Towards onos-based sdn monitoring using in-band network telemetry. In *2017 19th Asia-Pacific Network Operations and Management Symposium (APNOMS)* (pp. 76-81). IEEE.

Verizon. (2018). *Embracing the disruptive power of software-defined networking*. Report.

Voellmy, A., Kim, H., & Feamster, N. (2012). Procera: a language for high-level reactive network control. In *Proceedings of the first workshop on Hot topics in software defined networks* (pp. 43-48). ACM.

Wetherall, D. J., Guttag, J. V., & Tennenhouse, D. L. (1998). ANTS: A toolkit for building and dynamically deploying network protocols. In Open Architectures and Network Programming, 1998 IEEE (pp. 117-129). IEEE.

Xu, C., Rajamani, K., & Felter, W. (2018). Nbwguard: Realizing network qoS for kubernetes. In *Proceedings of the 19th International Middleware Conference Industry* (pp. 32-38). Academic Press.

Xu, K., Wang, X., Wei, W., Song, H., & Mao, B. (2016). Toward software defined smart home. *IEEE Communications Magazine*, *54*(5), 116–122.

Yan, S., Aguado, A., Ou, Y., Wang, R., Nejabati, R., & Simeonidou, D. (2017). Multilayer network analytics with SDN-based monitoring framework. *Journal of Optical Communications and Networking*, *9*(2), A271–A279.

Yang, Z., Cui, Y., Li, B., Liu, Y., & Xu, Y. (2019). Software-defined wide area network (SD-WAN): Architecture, advances and opportunities. In *2019 28th International Conference on Computer Communication and Networks (ICCCN)* (pp. 1-9). IEEE.

Yap, K. K., Kobayashi, M., Sherwood, R., Huang, T. Y., Chan, M., Handigol, N., & McKeown, N. (2010). OpenRoads: Empowering research in mobile networks. *Computer Communication Review*, *40*(1), 125–126.

Yousaf, F. Z., Bredel, M., Schaller, S., & Schneider, F. (2017). NFV and SDN—Key technology enablers for 5G networks. *IEEE Journal on Selected Areas in Communications*, *35*(11), 2468–2478.

Zaballa, E. O., Franco, D., Aguado, M., & Berger, M. S. (2020). Next-generation SDN and fog computing: A new paradigm for SDN-based edge computing. In *2nd Workshop on Fog Computing and the IoT* (pp. 9-1). Schloss Dagstuhl-Leibniz-Zentrum fur Informatik GmbH, Dagstuhl Publishing.

Zeydan, E., & Turk, Y. (2020). Recent advances in intent-based networking: A survey. In *2020 IEEE 91st Vehicular Technology Conference (VTC2020-Spring)* (pp. 1-5). IEEE.

Zhu, L., Karim, M. M., Sharif, K., Li, F., Du, X., & Guizani, M. (2019). *SDN controllers: Benchmarking & performance evaluation*. arXiv preprint arXiv:1902.04491.

Zhu, T., Chen, X., Chen, L., Wang, W., & Wei, G. (2020). GCLR: GNN-Based Cross Layer Optimization for Multipath TCP by Routing. *IEEE Access: Practical Innovations, Open Solutions*, *8*, 17060–17070.

ADDITIONAL READING

Boucadair, M., & Jacquenet, C. (2014). Software-Defined Networking: A Perspective from within a Service Provider Environment. RFC 7149.

Google. (2012). Inter-Datacenter WAN with centralized TE using SDN and OpenFlow. Retrieved February 09, 2021, from https://opennetworking.org/wp-content/uploads/2013/02/cs-googlesdn.pdf

Goransson, P., Black, C., & Culver, T. (2016). *Software defined networks: a comprehensive approach*. Morgan Kaufmann.

Kreutz, D., Ramos, F., Verissimo, P., Rothenberg, C. E., Azodolmolky, S., & Uhlig, S. (2014). Software-Defined Networking: A Comprehensive Survey. arXiv preprint arXiv:1406.0440.

Liu, Z., & Zhou, J. (2020). Introduction to Graph Neural Networks. *Synthesis Lectures on Artificial Intelligence and Machine Learning*, *14*(2), 1–127.

Nadeau, T. D., & Gray, K. (2013). *SDN: Software Defined Networks*. O'Reilly Media, Inc.

KEY TERMS AND DEFINITIONS

Abstraction Layer: A layer that abstracts one or more layers below to a layer above.

Control Plane: Network functionality that assigns one or more network devices on how to treat packets.

Forwarding Plane: Resources of network devices that relate to the data path.

Management Plane: Network functionality responsible for maintaining and managing the network.

Network Device: A device that performs one or more network operations.

Network Functions Virtualization: An architecture where functions are virtualized and instantiated as needed on an off-the-shelf high-end infrastructure.

Resource: A component available within a system.

Service Function Chaining: A technique to sequentially invoke a set service functions.

Software-Defined Networks: A software-based approach to program networks.

Chapter 6
Network Functions Virtualization (NFV):
Challenges and Deployment Update

Diego R. Lopez
Telefónica I+D, Spain

Pedro A. Aranda
Universidad Carlos III de Madrid, Spain

ABSTRACT

Network functions virtualization (NFV) is consolidating as one of the base technologies for the design, deployment, and operation of network services. NFV can be seen as a natural evolution of the trend to cloud technologies in IT, and hence perceived as bringing them to the network provider environments. While this can be true for the simplest cases, focused on the IT services network providers rely on, the nature of network services raises unique requirements on the overall virtualization process. NFV aims to provide at the same time an opportunity to network providers, not only in reducing operational costs but also in bringing the promise of easing the development and activation of new services, thereby reducing their time-to-market and opening new approaches for service provisioning and operation, in general. In this chapter, the authors analyse these requirements and opportunities, reviewing the state of the art in this new way of dealing with network services. Also, the chapter presents some NFV deployments endorsed by some network operators and identifies some remaining challenges.

ENTER THE SOFTWARE-DEFINED ERA

The integration of Information Technologies and Communications, commonly referred as ICT, has been more a long-term goal than a reality for a long time. Roughly speaking, networking and computing knew an evolution at comparable pace till the global availability of the Internet and the almost pervasive application of its protocols and the architecture supported by them to any networking problem. Not surprisingly, the very success of the Internet basic technologies made the evolution of the technologies

DOI: 10.4018/978-1-7998-7646-5.ch006

applied for providing end-to-end connectivity more and more difficult, precisely because these network technologies were the base for the radical changes that were taking place in the IT arena, around the ideas of Internet-based services and, most of all, the cloud.

IT evolution and, in particular, the evolution of Internet-based services, have been rooted on successive revolutions in software development practices, and in more and more powerful abstractions easing their conception, creation, and operation. This software-based nature has allowed business actors in the IT services arena to become agile in terms of satisfying new requirements and deploying new solutions, best exemplified by the DevOps approach in Loukides (2012), a set of best practices gaining strong momentum in the IT industry and focused on the tight communication (and even integration) of the activities related to development, operations, and quality assurance.

Network infrastructures, on the other side, became tied to their topologies and the requirements on using open, standard interfaces among the different nodes in these topologies. While the development of network nodes became certainly software intensive, the evolution of network services was tied to longer innovation cycles, requiring the agreement on standards among node vendors for interoperability purposes. What is more, the generalization of the network node as the basic functional unit implied an enormous degree of heterogeneity in network elements and their management procedures, which translated into additional problems for any attempt to make network infrastructure evolution agile or able to easily satisfy evolving user requirements.

On the Internet arena we had on the one hand network service providers, dealing with highly-heterogeneous and difficult to evolve infrastructures, and unable to address in a timely manner specific user requirements or to cover long-tail demand at a reasonable cost, while on the other hand there were the IT service providers, much more agile, relying on an almost uniform infrastructure, and able to adapt and evolve their software at a much faster pace, therefore being able to increase their value while network infrastructures were becoming increasingly ossified.

The advent of cloud computing was not only a forward step in IT service virtualization, as they did not need to be hosted at a physical infrastructure operated by the IT service provider anymore, but at the same time it implied some additional requirements on the network infrastructure that could not be solved by legacy (networking) techniques so far. These additional requirements on flexibility (i.e., the network had to adapt to the ever-changing cloud configuration) and abstraction (as applications needed to interact with the network as a resource among others) brought the need for a different conceptual framework for networks, beyond the usual approaches based on physical devices hosting a fixed, limited set of functionalities. Furthermore, the idea of running IT services on virtualized infrastructures made some researchers think about the possibility of doing the same for the functions performed in the network nodes, resulting in what will be referred to in the following as network functions. These two orthogonal directions constituted the basis for the current trends in network *softwarisation*.

Network softwarisation is a general term referring to all techniques oriented towards the application of two main and related principles:

- Providing a general interface for the provisioning, management, control and invocation of network resources, by means of software abstractions that hide complexity and deployment details of actual network infrastructures.
- Decoupling the different planes composing the network (data, control and management), and using open interfaces between them, in order to make the supporting infrastructure as much regu-

lar and homogeneous as possible and relying on software mechanisms to support specialized functionalities.

With this approach, network services are provided by a layered structure, grounded on general-purpose, homogenous hardware, with one or several software layers running on top of it and defining network behaviour and functionalities in general. Everything running on the network, from basic functionalities to user applications, and including management and operation elements, becomes software modules that use the open interfaces exposed by each layer.

The evolution of virtualisation mechanisms towards the so-called "cloud-native" goal, that in despite of lacking a well-structured definition (the best ones are sort of circular, of the style of *"an approach that applies cloud computing to build and run scalable applications in dynamic environments such as public, private, and hybrid clouds"*, as the Wikipedia defines it) is associated with technologies such as lightweight virtualization containers or development patterns related to the micro-service approach. This cloud-native goal translates into building loosely-coupled, resilient systems that can be managed by means of highly automated procedures.

There are two key directions for network softwarisation that can be applied independently, though they greatly benefit from being followed simultaneously, to the degree of being suitable to be considered essentially intertwined. Software-Defined Networking (SDN) goes for the decoupling of the control and data planes in a network to gain programmability and simplify data plane elements, while Network Functions Virtualization (NFV) follows an orthogonal approach, advocating for the general separation of functionality (on software) and capacity (on one or more general virtualization layers running upon commodity hardware), hence increasing network elasticity, in terms of its capacity to adapt to different usage scenarios and traffic patterns, and drastically reducing the burden of vendor lock-ins because of the heterogeneity of the supporting infrastructure. SDN and NFV are not competing technologies, but complementary. NFV goals can be achieved using non-SDN mechanisms, relying on the techniques currently in use in many datacentres, but approaches relying on the separation of the control and data forwarding planes as proposed by SDN can enhance performance, simplify compatibility with existing deployments, and facilitate operation and maintenance procedures. Given a network environment based on virtualized functions, the provision of the different virtual appliances and, particularly, the logical connectivity among them would need to be as flexible as possible. It would be hard to understand that a flexible environment where virtual network nodes could be created and expanded on demand were possible but setting up the connectivity among these virtual appliances required semi-manual provision. Furthermore, NFV is able to support SDN by providing the infrastructure upon which the SDN software can be run.

This chapter is dedicated to the description and analysis of NFV and its main features. The NFV essential concepts and its expected benefits will be discussed in the following section, followed by a brief history of the idea and its main milestones. We will follow with a description of the main drivers and use cases for NFV, plus a definition of the different fundamental elements that constitute the NFV architecture framework: the virtualized infrastructure, the functional components and their design patterns, and the management of the orchestration required to put infrastructure and components to work so they can build the intended network infrastructure services. A reference example of the application of NFV technologies will be discussed as well, with special emphasis on the orchestration aspects. Finally, since a technology evolution like this cannot be free of (important) challenges, we will conclude the chapter with a description of the most salient ones.

The NFV Concept, Benefits, and Risks

NFV is a set of technologies aimed at building network infrastructure services the same way IT services are constructed relying on current cloud infrastructures. NFV advocates for a supporting infrastructure that provides computing, storage, and connectivity mechanisms, and that can be accessed through a set of well-defined interfaces. This infrastructure is expected to be accessed through a common virtualization interface by involved software elements that implement the actual network functions. It is important to note the double role of network facilities. There is a layer that provides a homogeneous interface to virtualized network mechanisms used to support the interconnection of the elements (hardware and software) required by the software modules. These modules are hosted in the second layer, and which is the upper layer of network functions as shown in Figure 1.

Figure 1. The general NFV model

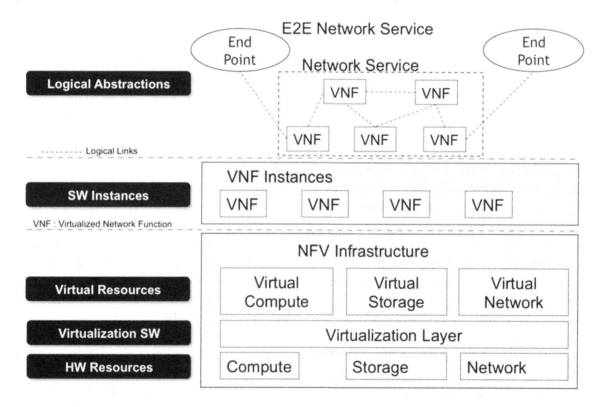

The diagram depicted in Figure 1 illustrates the general model for NFV showing its different layers. The NFV model relies upon the following functional blocks:

- The NFV Infrastructure (NFVI) is able to provide a set of virtual resources for computing, storage and networking through a virtualization layer that abstracts actual hardware resources that provide the required support to the computing, storage and networking mechanisms.

- The set of software instances implementing the Virtualized Network Functions (VNFs, think of virtualized intrusion detection systems, virtualized Evolved Packet Core elements, virtualized home gateways, etc.). Each of these software (SW) instances are deployed on top of the NFVI and, as such, are suitable for relocation, replication, deletion, and any other kind of operation required to maintain the appropriate performance (including reliability) of the functions they provide.
- The network services (NSes) are created by composing several of the VNFs, and physical functions as required, in a Forwarding Graph (FG) and attaching them to network endpoints. It is worth noting the most complete realization of such FGs is contemplated in IETF SFC, as defined in RCF 7665.

As a common practice, we can consider the NFVI as composed by a cloud-like infrastructure of physical computing and storage servers running hypervisors or lightweight virtualisation solutions, interconnected by means of a regular switching fabric that supports common network virtualization mechanisms such as overlays or VLANs, possibly with detached data and control planes by using OpenFlow defined by McKeown et al. (2008) or any other relevant protocol like NETCONF, for example. The NFVI can be distributed, i.e., located at different points of presence and this implies that, in most cases, WAN (Wide Area Network) links and their control are to be considered within the NFVI.

The execution of a VNF can be seen as the result of the concomitant execution of functions hosted in one or more Virtual Machines (VMs) or containers, executing the software performing the VNF functionality on the NFVI hypervisors and lightweight virtualisation environments. These VMs are usually termed VNF Components (VNFC) and are interconnected by means of NFVI network mechanisms to guarantee the functional (equivalent to their non-virtualized counterparts) and non-functional requirements (in terms of performance, security, reliability, etc.) of the associated network function. In the case of lightweight VNFCs, two new terms have emerged: the more generalised Container Network Function or CNF and the more specific Kubernetes Network Function (KNF). This terminology mainly highlights the underlying technology, since there are no fundamental architectural differences between the different VNF variants.

The VNFs built this way become part of network services constructed by composing them in a service forwarding graph. It is worth noting that this architecture is essentially recursive: the network services built this way can constitute the underlying network layer supporting a VNF in an upper layer.

More Than Carrier Clouds

We used the term "cloud-like infrastructures" in previous sections to refer to the NFVI and implicitly made a reference to usual cloud characteristics (e.g., resilience, elasticity by replication). Actually, it would seem natural to consider that NFV could be achieved by a direct application of cloud technologies to substitute the physical network elements by virtual implementations running on the current cloud infrastructures, probably enhanced to support additional requests on resiliency and reliability according to what has come to be called "carrier cloud" or "telco cloud".

While this was probably an initial guess in many cases, there are three essential aspects that distinguish NFV from the direct application of cloud technologies to provide network infrastructure services and which therefore require going beyond carrier clouds to implement NFV.

First, the kind of workloads of NFV may include components that are completely different from the kind of workloads considered by the current cloud practice. These VNFCs are extremely dependent on direct I/O and memory operations, and much less on direct computing or storage access. And this does impact the performance of the VNF as a whole when deployed directly following "classical cloud" mechanisms, but also (and even most significantly) on the portability of VNF instances across the cloud infrastructure. Available experimental evidence shows high performance deviations among workload distributions that were considered completely equal by classical cloud VM placement mechanisms in ETSI-NFV-ISG (2014a). To properly achieve performance and portability goals, it is necessary to improve cloud orchestrators, hypervisors, kernels, and even hardware drivers to support finer-grained placement policies, provide better control of direct memory communication among software instances, and override the virtualization layer for direct I/O to network interfaces for these components. Many of the required techniques are inspired by those currently applied in high-performance computing, like NUMA in Cong & Wen (2013).

Secondly, network services need to adapt to network shape. While the classical cloud applications are endpoints in a communication (the archetypal web server in many cases), most network infrastructure services are middle-points (for example, a router or a firewall) and many of them are subject to stringent requirements such as delay constraints. That implies that infrastructures and VM placement strategies must adapt to the network shape and support both highly centralized and consolidated datacentres in the cases they can be used and their economies of scale applied, and much more decentralized schemas, where the cloud becomes close to the fog concept presented in Bonomi et al. (2012). The important point here is not only to support both kinds of deployments but also to be able to seamlessly integrate them.

Finally, when it comes to the orchestration and management of the resources, it is worth noting again that we are dealing with networks at two layers: the supporting infrastructure already present in the current clouds and the upper network service layer provided by VNFs and their composition into services. To guarantee the overall service performance, upper network services may need to directly manipulate the underlying network infrastructure well beyond the limits of usual control interfaces exposed by the SDN controllers that are being deployed within current cloud datacentres. When dealing with VNFs based on hypervisors, these requirements have motivated different approaches to optimize mechanisms for virtual switching and/or routing, as provided by hypervisors and infrastructure orchestrators. In the case of VNFs implemented by lightweight containers, there is an active exploration of enhancements to current container network models suitable to properly support NFV needs, as it is the case of the Network Service Mesh project (https://networkservicemesh.io/).

Actors in NFV and the Interfaces Between Them

The diagram depicted in Figure 2 illustrates the different actors that can intervene in a fully virtualized network infrastructure, according to the layered model we discussed above for NFV.

1. NFVI Providers offer access to the rest of the actors: they provide access to datacentre and communication links that constitute the NFVI, mostly using the access models already described for cloud, like IaaS and PaaS, but additional ones as well, as it is the case of NaaS (Network-as-a-Service).
2. VNF Tenants run their VNFs on top of the NFVI; they can provide VNFs to potential users on an individual basis (VNFaaS), or together with additional tooling kits supporting higher-level integration and management (VNPaaS).
3. Admins of different enterprises integrate the VNFs into their network services, either for internal use or for actively providing them to third parties.

Figure 2. Actors in the NFV ecosystem

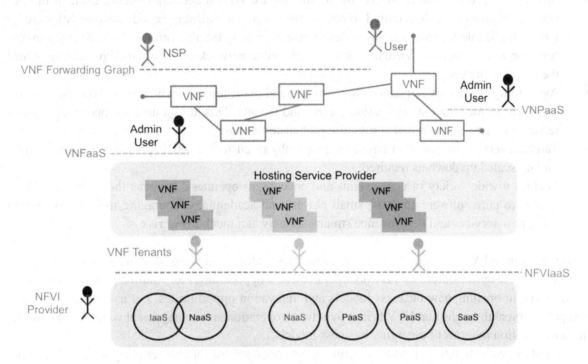

4. Network Service Providers assemble VNFs and attach them to a public network according to a VNF Forwarding Graph, creating a virtualized network service. These services will imply in many cases the integration of virtualized and non-virtualized elements.

5. Finally, Users consume the services offered by NSPs or their Admins.

It is obvious that any two or more of the roles described in points 1 to 4 above can be merged, and that the most likely scenario for the initial phases will consist of a full integration of all roles by the network service provider, with a coming stage where independent NFVI providers will emerge and their NFVI offer will be utilized by network operators to run (part of) their VNFs and services. Mixed scenarios, where high integration is applied for certain kinds of functions, while other specialized ones are provided by specific tenants are foreseeable as well.

Another important point is that any of the four degrees of freedom described above can be split into additional layers according to the state of the network infrastructure market and even because of regulatory reasons requiring to guarantee or enhance open competition in that market.

The Expected Benefits of NFV

The original whitepaper in Chiosi et al. (2012) that we can consider as the founding manifesto of NFV, states an initial list of potential direct benefits from applying virtualization to network functions:

- Reduced equipment costs and reduced power consumption through consolidating equipment and exploiting the economies of scale of the IT industry.

- Increased speed of Time to Market by minimizing the typical network operator cycle of innovation. Economies of scale required to cover investments in hardware-based functionalities are no longer applicable for software-based development, making feasible other modes of feature evolution. Network Functions Virtualization should enable network operators to significantly reduce the maturation cycle.
- Availability of network appliance multi-version and multi-tenancy, which allows the use of a single platform for different applications, users and tenants. This allows network operators to share resources across services and across different customer bases.
- Targeted service introduction based on geography or customer sets is possible. Services can be rapidly scaled up/down as required.
- Enables a wide variety of eco-systems and encourages openness. It opens the virtual appliance market to pure software entrants, small players and academia, encouraging more innovation to bring new services and new revenue streams quickly at a much lower risk.

Beyond this, NFV proponents foresee a great business value in applying NFV in terms of cost savings and additional revenue sources for network operators, new opportunities for solution providers and, most importantly, in opening new business models and innovation opportunities. Let us consider the most compelling breakthroughs that NFV brings to network operation and management while we identify its main implication in terms of emerging business models.

First of all, when building the infrastructure, a network operator (or another party willing to become an infrastructure provider) can invest in a pool of general resources that are configured on-demand for specific purposes when needed, rather than investing in multiple pools of specific network devices with tailored functions. These pools can be:

- Shared by different business units within an operator, bringing new internal business organization and planning.
- Shared by different operators, paving the way for much deeper and more flexible mechanisms for infrastructure sharing.
- Provided by third parties, which implies new business opportunities for infrastructure providers and new potential models for network service providers to operate.

To provide network functionality, a virtual function can be instantiated on-demand whenever it is needed in the network, rather than only when capacity is available at those points where the dedicated device is located. This decoupling of function and location brings possibilities for:

- Independent providers to offer network functions as a service to network service providers, following similar technology and charging patterns to those currently in use in cloud infrastructures.
- Network operators to provide long-tail services that are practically impossible to address with current infrastructures, covering new market niches, expanding their service and charging options, and enabling a new breed of application services relying on them.
- Entrepreneurs of the Over-the-Top (OTT) family to become able to compete in quality-of-experience with established providers at reasonable costs by means of agreements with network service providers for specialized services.

Taking advantage of the virtualization layer, the pool of servers can be updated in a much easier way. Therefore, network service providers can benefit more quickly from advances in hardware and translate them into gains for all their network functions and services. This enhanced update capability allows for:

- Shorter innovation cycles in hardware infrastructures, enabling innovative agents to gain market momentum at a much faster pace, and reducing the entry barrier for new players.
- A more open competition among infrastructure vendors, infrastructure providers, and network service providers themselves.

Furthermore, new functions can be added or improved by updating a software image applying CI/CD techniques, rather than waiting for a vendor to develop and manufacture a dedicated appliance. This is probably the most revolutionary aspect of NFV, and it implies:

- Breaking the current vertical integration silos that link network hardware, network software, and network management elements.
- Bringing open-source development and business models to network design, operation and management.
- Simplifying the evaluation and adoption of new solutions, enhancing the market applicability of research and innovation results.
- Opening the field for new service models, integrating network and application services.
- Allowing the application of well-known software development principles and tools to network planning, design, development, and operation.

Finally, management and operation can be performed by means of software image configuration and activation, reducing the complexity of managing a myriad of dedicated, heterogeneous devices. This characteristic is very much connected with the one just discussed above, and related to CI/CD procedures as well. However, the management and operation aspects have interesting implications to current network business models, as they:

- Allow a much easier support for network multi-tenancy and slicing, supporting new mechanisms for managed services in both directions: either managed by the operators for customers, or managed by third parties for the operators, and any combination thereof.
- Enable the application of DevOps principles in network management, aligning them with the practices that have made IT service providers so agile in addressing user requests and incorporating innovation results.
- Facilitate the application of strong automation procedures, supporting the current trends towards zero-touch management, simplifying both the data collection from the running network functions and the execution of control actions.

And the Risks

As any significant change in the base network technologies, the evolution towards NFV implies risks that can translate into higher costs and performance degradation. The major risk factors are related to potential gaps derived from technology consolidation and the required changes in operational models currently in use.

NFV defines a new set of standards that imply a deep reshaping of the concepts that have guided the creation of network infrastructures, and the development of the hardware and software implementing network functionality, bringing new principles for essential properties like redundancy, resiliency and security. Furthermore, the changes in operational models will not only deeply affect the structure of network provider operations at all levels (e.g., business process, support systems, staffing) but also bring a new definition of the relationships between operators and vendors.

From a general risk management perspective, NFV deployments shall consider maintaining a high level of pre-integration where possible and to closely follow, evaluate, and test the available technology solutions and applicable standards. Furthermore, it also makes sense to start by migrating selected services in early phases, starting for well-controlled scenarios focused on specific geographical areas, end user profiles or target application environments. This approach may limit the complexity of troubleshooting and also serve as an isolated system where technologies, tools and methodologies for troubleshooting can be refined and evaluated in parallel to building competence.

A practical example of the combination of the risks mentioned above is the lack of the appropriate combination of sufficiently powerful tools and the years-long expertise currently available in network operations, from testing and validation procedures to fault diagnosis and troubleshooting. This could imply much higher costs in terms of fault management and performance degradation assessment. Lack of tooling support could translate mostly into higher rates of escalation to second-line management, while lack of a widespread expertise could result in errors in root cause detection and longer response time. This can have a great impact on OPEX and even translate into poor end-user performance if the number and severity of second-line incident reports increase beyond the capacity of the second-line management. Any realistic NFV deployment plan will require both the infrastructure technology and the virtualized network functions to be equipped with good tracing capabilities and whatever other troubleshooting tools ready from day one. Similarly, the technology transformation has to be matched with a sufficient level of staff competence – either provided in-house through hands-on training or brought in from external sources.

In a second stage, NFV faces the risk of heterogeneity. As mentioned before, one aim is to adapt to the network shape. Recent developments allow the integration of edge/fog computing-based services into the NFV world. While it is obviously an attractive source for growth for Network Operators aiming to cover IoT and Industry 4.0 in their service portfolio, *fog services* (i.e., network services deployed over a fog computing infrastructure) add an additional dimension to the existing problem in the sense that the footprint and resource restrictions in these environments are diametrically opposed to those of services deployed at the network core.

A SHORT HISTORY OF NFV

Network operators and some network equipment manufacturers had been working on technologies related to network virtualization for some years, and in particular on the ideas around running network functions on general-purpose servers and cloud infrastructures, mostly inspired by the impact of cloud technologies in all fields of IT. By the beginning of the 2010 decade, encouraging results on the performance of these solutions for real-world network workloads were attained. Some informal discussions began to take place, mainly among operators, and there was a general will of seeking a common understanding and facilitating industry progress in this area.

A meeting of several of the world largest network operators in Paris in June 2012 not only coined the term "Network Functions Virtualization" to label the technology, but also was the starting point for convening a wider industry forum and starting the preparation of a joint whitepaper intended to define the vision and goals of NFV, and to galvanize the community about what the group was sure was a radical paradigm shift in the networking industry. The whitepaper, with the contribution of 13 network operators worldwide, was made public on October 2012, as a "call to action".

One of the first decisions to foster the development of the just named NFV was to make the industry forum supporting it as open as possible, so the decision was to follow the principles of open standards. A second decision, to root the forum at an existing standards organization, was taken in order to shorten the time necessary to formally establish it. After the consideration of several choices, an Industry Specification Group (ISG) under ETSI was created, as it appeared as the right combination of flexibility and formal guarantees for this goal, and experience has confirmed this impression.

The first plenary of the NFV ISG took place in January 2013, with an initial mandate of two years that has been renewed until now, as new goals and specific work items were identified. To facilitate its work, the ISG is structured in six working groups, coordinated by a Technical Steering Committee (TSC):

- EVE, analysing opportunities for future evolution of the NFV technology.
- IFA, in charge of defining architectural aspects.
- REL, aimed at satisfying the stringent reliability requirements of network services.
- SEC, dedicated to the analysis of the potential security issues related to the NFV approach.
- SOL, with the goal of defining specific solutions: APIs, descriptors, protocols, etc.
- TST, focused on implementation (open source) and testing aspects.

Since its creation, the ISG has gone through three document releases, and it is currently involved in a fourth one. Each of these releases has a specific objective, structuring the contents of the specifications and reports associated to it. The successive NFV documentation releases and their objectives are:

- Release 1 was focused on demonstrating the feasibility of NFV, delivered the baseline studies and specifications, and set the NFV architectural framework.
- Release 2 main goal was to ensure the interoperability of NFV solutions, detailing requirements and specification of interfaces and descriptors based on the NFV architecture.
- Release 3 defined features enriching the NFV architectural framework, readying NFV for deployment and operation, and addressing enhancements such as policy framework and "cloud-nativeness".
- Release 4 is working on the cloudification and simplification of network deployment and operations, defining interfaces and models to support, among others, container-based deployments, 5G requirements and service-based architecture concepts.

The group has also established a framework to define and run Proof-of-Concept (PoC) experiments and perform early interoperability events, hosted under ETSI Plugtests rules. While PoC experiments are intended to both explore technology options in the NFV space and to contribute to demonstrate the feasibility of the NFV approach and create awareness on it, interoperability events are focused on

Figure 3. The NFV Reference Architecture Framework as in ETSI-NFV-ISG (2014)

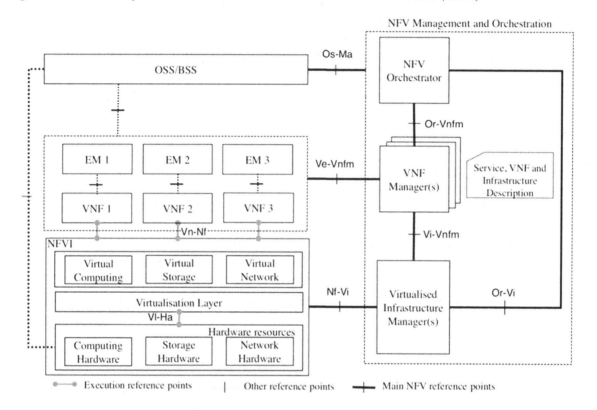

facilitating the development of open solutions aligned with NFV specifications and validating their applicability to real developments addressing concrete use cases.

The activities around NFV have not been limited to the ETSI ISG, but have spawned into other Standards Defining Organizations (SDOs). To just name a few, these other bodies include the IETF/IRTF (with initiatives like VNFPOOL and the recently closed NFVRG), TMForum and its ZOOM and LeanNFV projects, BBF, DMTF, and the ONF.

From an implementation point of view, NFV is embracing different virtualisation-related technologies which have emerged in the past years. It started by adopting full virtualisation and virtual machines and has lately included lightweight virtualisation techniques such as containers in their different impersonations like Linux Containers, Docker and Kubernetes. The obvious connection between NFV and cloud technologies has translated into direct contributions to open-source projects, starting with OpenStack and continuing with Kubernetes as main focus, as well as infrastructure-focused projects such as OPNFV and CMTF. The importance of the MANO stack in the operation of NFV-based deployments has been the foundation of projects addressing network orchestration platforms such as ONAP and OSM.

Drivers and use Cases

Both SDN and NFV have been made possible by the growth in computing power and the extension of virtualization-specific support functions in mainstream processors we have experienced in the last years. Current commercial-off-the-shelf (COTS) servers have enough computing power to implement network functions with high throughput requirements. In addition, cloud computing has delivered tools to automate and control high-volume deployments in datacentres. In contrast, network equipment has been based on extremely specialized hardware and software platforms. From the point of view of a network operator, this has resulted in vendor lock-in, practically no possibility of reusing equipment as their service portfolio evolves and very long time-to-market and innovation cycles. With strong competitive pressures, due to the emergence of OTT service providers with radically different cost structures and the increase in competition, and the advent of new requirements associated with the evolution of networks towards 5G and beyond, network providers regard NFV as an opportunity to reduce vendor lock-in, improve reusability, foster infrastructure reusability and, in general, reshape their cost structure in order to address future demand and improve their profit margins.

NFV capitalizes on the *softwarisation* of the network: network functions are implemented as programs that run on standard software and, when a certain service is not required anymore, the resources (i.e., the servers) where it was implemented can be easily repurposed for new services.

Use cases were originally analysed by the ETSI NFV ISG, and which has kept analysing these use cases, motivating different application environments for the NFV architectures and highlighting the benefits of the introduction of NFV for the network architecture and for the services running on it. The architectural use cases are rooted in the concept of *everything as a Service* (XaaS) introduced in the cloud computing world. These use cases include:

- Network Functions Virtualization Infrastructure (NFVI) as a Service
- VNF Forwarding Graphs and composable services
- Support for network slicing
- The application of software development patterns: DevOps, quick service deployment, CI/CD and A/B testing
- Other provisioning models, such as VNF as a Service, or Platform as a Service

And a series of service-related use cases that highlight different challenges:

- Mobile core network and IMS
- Mobile base stations
- Home environment
- Content Delivery Networks (CDNs)
- Fixed access network
- Virtualizing IoT
- Enhanced security: Crypto-as-a-Service, Security-as-a-Service

Extending and building on the concepts and lessons learnt from the *Infrastructure as a Service* (IaaS) concept in the Cloud world, NFV has introduced the notion of Network Functions Virtualization as a Service (NFVIaaS). If IaaS allowed datacentre providers to offer their infrastructure to clients who are not in a position to implement their own full-fledged datacentres in the form of virtual datacentres, NFVIaaS foresees the emergence of big NFV Infrastructure providers that resell their resources to clients who want to implement their services based on NFV but are not able to implement their own infrastructure.

In addition to translating the lessons learned in cloud environments, the ETSI NFV ISG also shows how VNF graphs can be used to compose services end-to-end. It is based on a catalogue of VNFs that have a set of published, standard interfaces at different layers. The VNFs implement the same functionalities as equivalent physical network functions that are readily available in the market. It then compares both solutions and shows the benefits introduced by the VNF solution. This comparison, shown in Table 1, holds for VNFs in general and not only for a specific use case.

Table 1. Comparison of physical and virtualized network functions

	Physical Appliance	**Virtual Appliance**
Efficiency	Dedicated (rigid) and sized for peak load (underutilized)	Function and size depending on current load
Resilience	Backup on specific hardware and dedicated resources. In most cases, it requires additional network capacity	Backup may share resources and network capacity.
Flexibility	Lengthy deployment cycles, upgrade sometimes not possible	Shorter cycles and easier deployment, since functions are SW based
Complexity	Graph depends/can only be deployed on a given physical network layer	Virtualized networking layer can be adapted easily to forwarding graphs
Deployability	Requires physical boxes when deployed on another provider's premises/infrastructure	Virtualization eases the deployment of a given function on another provider's infrastructure

The promise of network slicing does not only entail the use of a single infrastructure to provide virtual networks that users see as totally isolated from similar instances running on the same infrastructure, which is achieved by Virtual Private Network (VPN) technologies for more than three decades. Network slicing implies full end-to-end capabilities, policy-based control, on-demand deployment of functions, and independent management and orchestration. Given its ability to dynamically deploy and control the lifecycle of specific functions on cloud-like infrastructures, NFV is acknowledged as one of the key enablers of network slicing, and the basis for future provision of network slices according to the as-a-service paradigm.

Also based on prior experience in the cloud work, NFV is enabling the application of the procedures to facilitate continuous integration and automated testing used in the so-called agile software development. Furthermore, NFV can address the requirements of emerging services by trends like *Bring Your Own Device* (BYOD), etc. Instead of furnishing the (business) end user with additional elements for a complex device that need frequent updates, etc., the network operator implements the required functions on one or several VNFs it provides to the user. This concept is equivalent to the *Software as a Service* (SaaS) concept in the cloud world. The next step in the cloud world was to allow a client to mix and match offerings from several providers in what is known as the *Platform as a Service* (PaaS) paradigm. In the NFV use cases, it translates into the *Virtual Network Platform as a Service* (VNPaaS). This use case illustrates the sharing of an infrastructure by several clients and the need for authorization as well as resource control in order to guarantee the correct functioning of the infrastructure. It shows how multi-tenancy can be implemented at the VNF level.

The service-oriented use cases present the case of virtualizing different components of the network and the positive aspects in doing so. The mobile core virtualization is a realistic target: a network infrastructure with a significant number of functions which mainly reside in the control plane of the network and which are currently distributed in different boxes and, in fact, the 5G standards for the mobile core assume NFV as a fundamental enabler. Likewise, access technologies are evolving towards incorporating NFV principles and reporting progress of their application. Given the high pervasiveness of access networks, the cost savings and automation supported by NFV will have the highest impact.

One of the emerging trends in telecommunications is the so-called '*fog computing*' which extends Cloud Computing to Internet of the Things (IoT) and other environments. An implementation of a connector between OSM Release 8 (2020) and the fog infrastructure manager was implemented by the fog05 project (de la Oliva et. al., 2019) This connector provides OSM with an IoT-enabled VIM, allowing the creation of Network Services specifically tailored at IoT deployments, where initiatives like Industry 4.0 come to mind. This field has been in the viewpoint of network operators.

Infrastructure

The objective of NFV is essentially to separate the software that defines the network functionality (VNF) from the hardware and generic software providing its capacity to function (NFVI). It is therefore a requirement that the VNFs and the NFVI be separately specified.

The NFV architecture framework defines the term NFVI as the totality of the hardware and software components constituting the environment in which VNFs are deployed and run. The NFVI is deployed as one or more nodes that collectively implement the required functionality to support the execution environment for VNFs. A location where a NFVI node is deployed is an NFVI Point of Presence (PoP). A PoP may contain one or more nodes as well as other network elements. The NFVI PoPs form a distributed infrastructure that can support the locality (in terms of network topology) and latency requirements of the particular functions and their flexible deployment and operation. NFVI nodes and PoPs build the dynamically reconfigurable platform for the execution of the VNFs, according to the requirement of the different actors in the NFV ecosystem we described in a previous section.

Cloud Computing and the NFVI

Cloud computing is clearly an essential enabler for NFV, and it is at the root of the NFV concept itself. NFV has to leverage technologies that are currently applied to cloud computing. At the core of these technologies are hardware virtualization mechanisms by means of hypervisors, and the usage of virtual Ethernet switches for forwarding traffic between virtual machines and physical interfaces (though other possible virtualization mechanisms could be applicable, the current focus of the NFV community is on these techniques). Furthermore, current cloud approaches provide methods to enhance resource availability and usage by means of orchestration and management mechanisms, applicable to the automatic instantiation of VNFs, resource management, re-initialization of failed VNFCs, creation of VNFC state snapshots, migration of VNFCs, etc.

According to the NIST definition of cloud computing in Mell & Grance (2011), NFV can be seen as a type of Private Cloud IaaS where VNFs are executed in support of the services that a network operator provides. The execution environment for VNFs is provided by the distributed NFVI, which implies a challenge to the common understanding about management centralization as a relevant benefit of cloud computing, as we noted above when talking about adapting NFV to the network shape.

The NIST definition of cloud computing identifies five essential characteristics of cloud services. Since NFV encompasses these five characteristics, it could be considered as an application of cloud technology and it is clear that a NFVI should provide equivalent support of these essential characteristics:

- **On-demand self-service**. The consumer of the NFVI expects to be able to unilaterally provision and allocate existing deployed NFVI resource capacity (server time, storage capacity, etc.). In many cases, this resource allocation will be made directly by the VNFs or, more properly, by the management and orchestration functions coordinating them. Allocation shall follow the patterns required to provide a sustainable and predictable VNF performance.
- **Broad network access**. NIST describes broad network access in cloud computing as providing capabilities that are available over the network and can be accessed through standard mechanisms that promote use by heterogeneous client platforms. The NFVI PoPs are to be accessed remotely, and VNFs will handle the network traffic of a variety of existing network elements and terminal types. The network access capacity required at a particular PoP will depend on the fields of application of the VNFs instantiated at that PoP, which is also related to the requirement to adapt the NFVI to the *shape* of the network.
- **Resource pooling**. While a single VNF might be deployed at a single PoP, in general, the NFVI is expected to support multiple VNFs from different service providers in a multi-tenant model. Resource demands on the NFVI are expected to change dynamically with the service load processed by the VNFs. Location independence is an objective in that specific VNFs should not be constrained to only run on dedicated NFVI hardware resources, beyond requirements related to their semantics, such as latency or resiliency.
- **Rapid elasticity**. VNF operation will request rapid elasticity along with automated provisioning and release of the computing, storage and communication resources of the NFVI. In most cases these requests should be triggered in response to events related to the service load processed by the VNF, to the rearrangement of resources for the optimization of NFVI usage by the management and orchestration mechanisms, as well as to failover and recovery procedures.
- **Measured service**. The management and orchestration of VNFs will normally require the automatic control and optimization of NFVI resource usage by the VNFs. This optimization implies that the use of those resources by individual VNFs is metered in some fashion appropriate to each particular resource.

In the light of the service models applicable to cloud, the advent of NFV provides different opportunities, not only for network operators but also to other potential new actors in the network service arena. VNFs are software applications running on cloud-like infrastructures, offering functions that can process data and control plane traffic for a network operator rather than just web services:

- In IaaS, the capability provided is the provisioning of compute, storage and communication resources so that applications can be run on them. Here, the VNFs are the applications intended to be run and the virtualization infrastructure in which they are executed provides an IaaS for the network operator. The NFVI should provide the appropriate security mechanisms to ensure that only authorized entities have access to NFVI resources.

- NFV provides an opportunity to significantly improve the speed with which new services and applications are developed and deployed. The PaaS model provides a service model consistent with deployment of services constructed by the composition of multiple VNF instances.
- While many VNFs are expected to be typically executed according to a private cloud model by the network operator, some categories may be amenable to be executed in a third-party cloud infrastructure and utilized in a SaaS model.

Finally, let us consider the different deployment models for cloud infrastructures and their applicability to the NFV case. In a first stage, most (if not all) of the NFVI and VNF instances will be deployed and operated by the same network operator using them. Hence, this initial deployment will be essentially aligned with the private cloud model. A possible next step could be the constitution of collaboration models among operators, or even among operators and software or service vendors. These models could lead to the deployment of community clouds, though the scope and extension of such community clouds remain to be seen. While it seems rather unlikely that VNFs and the services using them will integrally be hosted in current public clouds, a model based on an evolution of this public cloud approach could see the light as NFV matures and a clearer understanding of Service Level Agreements (SLAs) and security requirements becomes available. Finally, operators may be interested from the initial stages in a hybrid cloud deployment model where they maintain an IaaS private cloud for their own services. However, this infrastructure is offered on a wholesale basis to host VNFs from other service providers and extended to provide VNFs-as-a-Service for enterprises, or other operators.

Container-Based Solutions

In an effort to increase utilisation, lightweight isolation tools provided by modern Operating Systems (OSes) have established themselves in the cloud computing landscape. With Linux Containers as the paradigmatic example, different technologies like Docker and Kubernetes provide the next level in softwarisation and integration of software production techniques in NFV. The lightweight nature of these solutions allows a more effective deployment for NSes or VNFCs therein that do not have real-time constraints.

Container-based solutions feature a higher granularity than virtual machines in that they allow different predefined layers to be packaged at launch-time to provide specific functionalities, bringing the development cycle close to current software development cycle models. In addition, these solutions include scaling features equivalent to those offered in VM-based cloud computing environments, which ease the implementation of scalable NSes.

The NFVI Domains

In order to deal with the complexity of the infrastructure, the ETSI NFV ISG has identified three domains within the NFVI, which are clearly differentiated at a functional and a practical level: the compute domain (including both computing and storage resources), the hypervisor domain and the infrastructure network domain. Each of these domains deals with specific problems that can be treated independently. So, for example, the selection of the computing infrastructure is largely unaffected by the selection of the underlying infrastructure network. This separation of concerns allows for largely autonomous supply and evolution of each one.

The role of the compute domain is to provide the computational and storage resources, supported by COTS hardware, needed to host individual components of VNFs. The use of industry standard high-volume servers is a key element in the economic case for NFV. An industry standard high-volume server is a server built using standard IT components (for example x86 or ARM architectures) and sold at a massive scale. A common feature of industry standard high-volume servers is that there is competitive supply of the subcomponents that are interchangeable inside the server. The computing domain considers a functional 'unit of compute' basically integrated with the computational hardware device. This unit of compute is functionally defined as:

- An entity capable of executing a generic computational instruction set (the CPU)
- An entity able to hold state (the storage)
- An element in charge of reading and writing data to the network (the NIC)
- Other "acceleration" hardware, such as elements for encryption and decryption or "enhanced" packet forwarding. However, the value of this acceleration hardware needs to be carefully assessed, because it reduces the portability of the VNFs based on it and implies a cost of prior provision.

The hypervisor domain mediates the resources of the computer domain to the virtual machines implementing the VNFs. In essence, the hypervisor can emulate every piece of the hardware platform, even to the point, in some cases, of completely emulating a CPU instruction set. Even when not emulating a complete CPU architecture, there can still be aspects of emulation which cause a significant performance hit.

In addition, as there may be many virtual machines all running on the same host machine, they are likely to be connected one to the other. The hypervisor provides emulated virtual NICs for the VMs. However, there is also the need for a virtual Ethernet switch to provide connectivity between the VMs and between the VMs and the physical NICs. This is handled by the hypervisor virtual switch (vSwitch). The vSwitch may also be a significant performance bottleneck.

There is a number of features available in current and forthcoming server hardware greatly improving the performance of VMs, including multicore processors, system-on-chip processors that integrate multiple cores and interfaces, specific CPU enhancements/instructions to control memory allocation and direct access on I/O, and PCI-e bus enhancements. These allow high performance VMs to run effectively as if they were running natively on the hardware, while under the full control of the hypervisor.

The resulting hypervisor architecture is one of the primary foundations of the NFV infrastructure, providing the full performance of 'bare metal' while supporting the full orchestration and management provided by the hypervisor. The NFV community is actively developing the necessary enhancements for the realization of this architecture and contributing them to the relevant open-source projects in this area.

The infrastructure network domain performs a number of essential roles, supporting the communication channels required for:

- The VNFCs in a distributed VNF
- The different VNFs building a service
- Any VNF and its orchestration and management
- Orchestration and management to interact with the NFVI components
- Remote deployment of VNFs

- The interconnection with the existing network where the network service is to be attached

The role of the infrastructure network is to provide a large number of discrete connectivity service instances. In general, it is a fundamental requirement that these services are separate from each other and not accessible to each other. This is the antithesis of the universal networking in the wider Internet. These essential roles imply that the infrastructure network availability must predate any VNF deployment, and must provide sufficient network connectivity to address the VNF goals. In order to achieve this, the infrastructure network must have all the essential elements needed for providing connectivity already self-contained within the infrastructure management domain, including an addressing scheme, routing and bandwidth allocation processes, and the necessary operational mechanisms to assess the reliability, availability, and integrity of the connectivity services. Many active players within the NFV community believe that SDN constitutes the basic technology for providing these elements.

In addition, Kubernetes environments for the deployment of lightweight VNFCs have been added to the picture. These environments are not fully functional NFVIs, but are rather external components that *add* container-based VNFCs to the picture and allow NFV developers to take advantage of the myriad of components that are available for Kubernetes. Typical examples of components that may be better served in a Kubernetes cluster are databases and Web service support.

Recently, platforms to deploy fog computing services have been integrated to NFV. Fog computing aims at being deployed in Internet of Things (IoT) environments in particular, with network devices with stringent footprint constraints. This field is extremely appealing to network operators looking to expand their service portfolio to Industry 4.0 scenarios. The current fog computing platform supports both virtual machines and container-based virtualisation.

VNFs, Components, and Design Patterns

A VNF is a network function that is capable of running in a NFV Infrastructure (NFVI), being orchestrated by an NFV Orchestrator and a VNF manager as shown in Figure 3. Each VNF may be controlled by an Element Management System (EMS). In addition to interfacing to the VNF Manager and the EMS, the VNF provides well-defined interfaces to other VNFs.

In the same way a Network Service might be a composition of several VNFs, the VNF provider may choose to use one VNF Component (VNFC) or use VNFC composition to implement a VNF. In this context, the work of the Service Function Chaining (SFC) working group (IETF (2020)) in the IETF is also significant. The creation of services from VNFs by composition can be generalized as the creation of services as service function chains (SFCs). The SFC working group has defined the mechanisms to create and operate service function chains. The need to monitor the operational state of the VNFs composing a service and to be able to pinpoint points of failure is being discussed and different Operations and Management (OAM) frameworks are being considered.

VNFs may or may not need to store state during their lifetime. Examples of these cases are a stateful firewall, and a stateless tunnel termination function, respectively. The VNF architecture specification document ETSI-NFV-ISG (2014) describes alternatives for how VNF state is stored and handled depending on the VNF type. In addition, it identifies other design patterns that include patterns to deal with traffic evolution. Thus, for example, VNFs may or may not be instantiated in parallel within a VNF to scale in and out as a response to changes in traffic, resource allocation, etc. When VNFs are instantiated in parallel, the VNF provider will have to specify how many instances may be instantiated in parallel

Figure 4. VNF Functional architecture

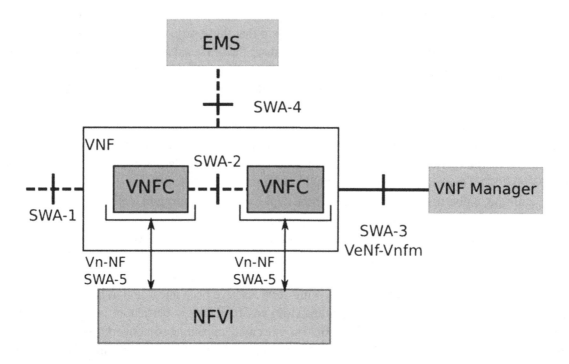

within a VNFC, what kind of scaling models may be used and what are the alternatives to implement load balancing within a VNF and between VNFs.

VNFs are software components that have specific life-cycle management requirements in order to implement network functions. The lifecycle of a VNF is inspired both by current best practices in network management and in the datacentre worlds. One of the main opportunities of NFV is the fact that some types of network functions implemented in software can, in specific cases, be scaled in and out, i.e., the network function can be instantiated with different resource requirements depending on the throughput it is expected to provide. Scaling can be implemented with well-known techniques applied to virtual machines in the data-centre world. However, these techniques cannot be generally applied, since there are VNFs that require a careful consideration before deployment within the NFVI in order to guarantee adequate levels of performance. Factors like underlying hardware (i.e., CPU type, Network Interface Cards (NICs), memory, internal buses, etc.), virtualization layer (i.e., hypervisor, virtualization mode, etc.) and operating system can have a severe impact on the performance that can be achieved for a given VNF. The ETSI NFV ISG has issued a document on "Performance Considerations and Best Practices" in ETSI-NFV-ISG (2014a) analysing the different factors and providing guidelines and specific descriptors to capture the requirements for both the NFVI and the VNFs.

NFV deployment should be transparent to the end-user and, therefore, similar levels of service availability to those provided by traditional, discrete networks are to be expected. In other words, the NFV system has to be designed to be as resilient as traditional networks. However, the paradigm shift from hardware- to software-based systems implies that instead of a design that is meant to guarantee a given uptime, NFV suppliers design their technology to minimize the impact of failures on the service. An NFV system will be provided with automated recovery from failures. The main challenge in an NFV environment is threefold:

- An underlying architecture needs to be provided that does not exhibit a single point of failure.
- All designs have to be applicable to a multi-vendor environment.
- The infrastructure will be hybrid, with components that are implemented in portable software and components that come from the discrete network and that will be gradually phased out.

The ETSI NFV ISG has issued a resiliency requirements document in ETSI-NFV-ISG (2015) that analyses the resiliency problem in NFV environments. Resilience is tightly coupled with security. VNFs are network functions running on a virtual machine, a network built of VNFs is exposed to the same threats as the physical network functions plus the threats that apply to virtualization. In addition, new threats arise from the mere fact of combining virtualization and networking. ETSI-NFV-ISG (2014b) analyses such threats with the objective of documenting the problem statement as well as further insight to be incorporated into security accreditation processes for NFV-based products. Despite the additional threats, virtualization also furnishes some interesting tools like secure boot and/or trusted boot that allow operators to check the validity of VNF images before they are executed on an NFV platform and avoid the introduction of forged VNFs.

Container-Based Network Services

Besides VM-based VNFCs, one of the emerging trends in virtualisation in general and in network service creation in particular is the use of lightweight isolation techniques like containers. The main benefits of containers are lower resource usage and quicker boot times than full virtualisation. Although network services based on containers may not meet real-time constraints needed in some cases, they are a fitting solution for many backplane components that are more relaxed in that aspect. The proliferation of components to build Cloud Network Services can be seen in the growth of component repositories from the very beginning (Arijs, 2016). Currently, solutions like Docker or Kubernetes feature several repositories to download components that reach from database backends or Web servers, to domain name (DNS) or directory (Lightweight Directory Access Protocol (LDAP)) services. In fact, any network service that has a software implementation has already been or can be implemented in a container.

Container-based solutions further close the gap between the network service development cycle and the *traditional* software design cycle, allowing developers to either reuse existent solutions or cherry-pick components from proven sources (i.e., container repositories) to compose the network service to their requirements.

Management and Orchestration: MANO

In the environment of telecommunications networks, network functions must be able to support remote configuration and management. For this purpose, network functions provide an interface to the management and orchestration (MANO) mechanisms used by the operators. This interface is often denoted as their "Northbound interface". Given the objective of NFV of separating capacity (NFVI) from functionality (VNFs) it is natural that this separation includes their management and orchestration. On the one hand, VNFs are not any longer required to deal with the management of the infrastructural aspects, while on the other hand, efficient VNF lifecycle management has to be provided to support the new features brought by virtualization (fast delivery and recovery, auto-scaling, etc.) The goal of NFV management and orchestration is to provide a high level of common MANO functionality with a common interface for it to be utilized by the network provider's business and operational support systems.

MANO functions are structured by means of three layers that group the management and orchestration functions at the infrastructure, VNF and service levels. At each layer, a functional entity is defined by the NFV MANO architecture, ensuring the exposure of services that provide access to these functions in an open, well-known abstracted manner. These services can be consumed by other authenticated and properly authorized NFV MANO functions, and by the business and operation support systems applied by the network operator.

The management of any element in the network is associated to mechanisms defined according to FCAPS. Beyond these Specific Management Functional Areas (SMFAs), specific aspects introduced by virtualization must be considered for NFV MANO. Fault and performance management are functionalities required by any networking framework, and especially sensitive in the case of NFV, as it requires a radically new approach to any kind of fault processing, from notification to root-cause analysis, as well as new mechanisms for performance metrics collection, metrics calculation and aggregation. In addition, policy definition and enforcement mechanisms have to incorporate support for the specific issues associated to virtualization and the new operations permitted by it.

ICT resource allocation is a complex task in general, given the number of (even conflicting) requirements and constraints that need to be satisfied at the same time. For the NFVI, the specific requirements for network allocation and performance add new complexity compared to the resource allocation strategies applied so far in current cloud environments. While the management and orchestration functions at the NFVI level must be necessarily oblivious to the VNFs it hosts, resource allocation and release will be likely requested throughout these VNF lifetimes if we want to take advantage of the NFV ability to dynamically adapt VNF capabilities to load fluctuations. The NFV MANO functions that coordinate virtualized resources are grouped under the name of the Virtual Infrastructure Manager (VIM).

At the VNF level, MANO aspects must contemplate the newer aspects introduced by the virtual nature of the supporting infrastructure, which require a set of management functions focused on the creation and lifecycle management of the resources used by the VNF. In the NFV architecture, this lifecycle management corresponds to the functional entity known as the VNF Manager (VNFM), responsible for operations such as instantiation, scaling, updating, upgrading and terminating a VNF. The VNFM must rely on a VNF deployment template describing the attributes and requirements necessary to realize such a VNF and to manage its lifecycle. Though most of the VNFM functions can be considered generic common functions applicable to any type of VNF, the NFV MANO architecture considers the case where certain VNFs may need specific functionality for their lifecycle management. The architecture does not assume any predefined mapping among a given VNFM and the number and classes of VNFs it can manage: A VNFM may be in charge of a single VNF instance, or the management of multiple VNF instances of the same class or of different classes. What is more: VNFs can be classified according to their particular purpose, the type of service they participate in, or their provider just to name a few possibilities. During the lifecycle of a VNF, the VNFM can monitor the performance of the VNFs under its control, according to their deployment template, and use this information for triggering management operations, most typically scaling ones.

The MANO function in charge of network service lifecycle uses the service deployment templates describing them and performs tasks related to:

- On-boarding the services by registering their templates in the service catalogue, including those required by the composing VNFs.
- Instantiating the services by means of the artefacts provided in their deployment templates.
- Scaling the services, growing or reducing their whole capacity.
- Updating the services by supporting configuration changes, such as inter-VNF connectivity or the particular instances of the composing VNFs.
- Creating and updating the inter-VNF connectivity and their attachment to the general network infrastructure through the service's VNF Forwarding Graph (VNFFG).
- Terminating the services, including the de-provisioning of their VNFFG, the termination of the composing VNFs, and the release of the NFVI resources in use.

A network service deployment template typically includes the description for managing the associations between different network functions (either virtualized or not: a service can have heterogeneous components), and the VNFFGs associated with the Network Service. These tasks are performed by a functional block named NFVO (NFV Orchestrator), which is also in charge of the orchestration of NFVI resources across multiple VIMs.

This dual nature of the current NFVO role is related to the foreseeable situation of separated administrative domains. As discussed before, reasonably mature scenarios for NFV will not have a single organization controlling and maintaining the whole NFV system. Administrative domains can be mapped to different organizations and therefore can exist within a single service provider or distributed among several service providers. At least two basic domains can be initially foreseen: the infrastructure domain and the tenant domain. An infrastructure domain can be generally defined by the NFVI resources under a single administration and may provide infrastructure to a single or multiple tenant domains. Infrastructure domains are oblivious to the VNFs and services its tenants deploy on it, and in charge of the necessary VIM(s) and the NFVO resource orchestration functions. A tenant domain can use the NFVI in a single or multiple infrastructure domains and it will be concerned with general service and VNF management, including FCAPS aspects, VNFM(s) and the service orchestration functions of the NFVO.

When considering containerized VNFC implementations, a new set of MANO functionality has to be considered, related to the Container Infrastructure Service Management (CISM), responsible for the management of containerized workloads. The CISM is responsible for the deployment, monitoring, and lifecycle management of containerized workloads running in OS containers. It exposes corresponding APIs to its consumers and translates incoming requests into operations which are enforced towards the CISM. The CISM is further responsible to parse and interpret descriptors and configuration files of the containerized workloads. Several options are considered to incorporate the CISM functionality into the MANO stack, ranging from embedding it within the VIM to associate this functionality with a stand-alone MANO block, and including a more radical approach in which the CISM subsumes the VIM and VNFM, what would translate into a simplification of the MANO stack in container-based deployments.

DEPLOYMENT EXPERIENCES

Since the technology foundations were established back in 2012, network service providers have worked in the deployment of NFV-based network infrastructures, attempting to take advantage of the new support to network services, spreading the use of more agile procedures and the support of highly automated solutions. Let's analyze three paradigmatic examples of this endeavor.

Telefónica's UNICA[1] is a several-year program to transform a legacy network infrastructure into an NFV-enabled one, with the additional constraint of making it simultaneously in a number of operations with disparate environments, in Europe and Latin America. The project has defined a common technology substrate (whose second generation is underway), developed and validated in collaboration with a reduced set of technology providers and supported by a strong commitment to an open-source MANO stack steered by Telefonica. From this common substrate, local *competence centers* were established to address the particular use cases and conditions at each operation, as well as to validate VNFs by properly onboarding them and exercising their composition to build network services. Most of the operations focused on mobile core network functions, making good progress on virtualizing IMS and EPC components, and demonstrating their ability to cope with additional capacity demands. Within the UNICA strategy, physical functions will eventually be phased out by their virtual counterparts when they come up for renewal.

Starting from a completely different situation, Rakuten[2] has defined a clean-slate mobile network, fully based on NFV and SDN, partnering with some big technology providers. The design, already operative and intended to serve millions of subscribers based on 5G technology, was initially launched using 4G LTE cell sites and WLAN (Wireless Local Area Network), with a transition into 5G taking place. The softwarised infrastructure is committed to support mobile edge computing, addressing low-latency services such as immersive services based upon the use of Augmented Reality techniques.

The 5GinFIRE project[3] was an initiative to establish an open and extensible 5G NFV-based ecosystem of experimental facilities for third parties, used by more than 25 successful experiments[4], focused on a wide set of heterogeneous topics. The users of the 5GinFIRE platform, in their role as experimenters, had originally access to more than 50 public VNFs and 30 public NSDs, with a total number of VNFs and NSDs that triples the number of function and service descriptors available at the public repository. A number of mechanisms to support onboarding and initial validation were put in place, to address the needs of function developers and service (experiment) builders, taking advantage of the portability of virtualized functions and services from development to production environments. Beyond this, an important lesson learned by defining and executing experiments on the 5GinFIRE platform is how NFV enhances experiment repeatability and reproducibility, one of the biggest challenges not only for networking science, but also for sound engineering practice in this field.

THE CHALLENGES AHEAD

We believe that the paradigm shift that NFV brings to network design and operation has become clear along the previous sections. Such a paradigm shift implies great challenges, not only in what relates to the technical aspects but to organizational and even cultural aspects. Given the scope of this book, we will not elaborate on the latter, though we think it would be interesting to make a few reflections on them as well. In parallel to addressing these organizational challenges, and in many cases before organizations deal with them, there is a number of technology aspects to be considered. Most of them have already been characterized by the NFV community and are subject to active research.

Many of the challenges presented below can be mitigated by limiting initial NFV deployments to a single NFV Infrastructure in a single administration domain and by limiting its offerings to only network services (VNF Forwarding Graphs) sold to end-users. As pending challenges are addressed, NFV deployments can become more sophisticated and offer a richer range of services across different NFV infrastructures and administrations. This strategy will allow network operators, customers and VNF vendors, to gain immediate benefits.

Functional and Service-Level Considerations

NFV induces new design patterns at all network levels, from the elements themselves to service inception. Ultimately breaking the "box boundaries" opens new ways for element componentization, as well as infrastructure and service abstractions that should allow translating the infrastructure virtualization into more powerful network virtualization. To support these virtualization patterns, new mechanisms for infrastructure and service function description are required, especially declarative languages and tools for supporting the design flows. Finally, these design patterns require the application of system-wide optimizations at all levels, from the physical infrastructure up to the composite services.

Orchestration is the key element for achieving the goals of operation automation and elasticity that constitute the core of the NFV benefits. We have insisted throughout this chapter on the need for going beyond current cloud practice to cover the requirements of NFV, and this is especially relevant when it comes to orchestration (including short provision cycles). This implies the availability of network-aware orchestration methods that can support features like the automation of service function chaining and autonomous service behaviour such as tracing, self-configuration, self-diagnostic, and self-healing. Another relevant aspect is related to the possibility of applying analytics methods to enhance orchestration, so that NFV can benefit of the great amount of data that the simpler deployment of software probes can feed into cloud-based analytics engines. Thus, analytics (or big data, if you allow us to use another hyped word) could be put in the management loop allowing a much more flexible and efficient network operation. Probably the most important consequence of the availability of these advanced orchestration mechanisms will be the simplification of operational procedures, allowing for a tighter integration of business process and network management that will bring the expected service development agility to the levels envisaged by the NFV concept. Note that many of the concepts we have identified here are not new and are being explored in the broader world of SDN. In fact, SDN and NFV enjoy a symbiotic relationship where each of them benefits from the advances in the State-of-the-Art of the other.

Heterogeneity

As mentioned above, the current picture includes traditional cloud-computing environments able to cope with hardware constraints in order to provide acceleration features needed by certain network components, novel container-based clouds for services or components without strict real-time constraints, legacy components and fog computing clouds. This implies a very high level of heterogeneity which may actually hinder the consolidation of the technology, at least partially, if models to encompass the differences are not found. The current implementation of OSM distinguishes between Kubernetes-based Network Functions (KNFs) and Virtual Network Functions and has not put the Kubernetes Cluster as the deployment place for KNFs at the same level as the VIM yet. This situation reveals some inconsistencies, because the fog05 controllers, which can currently be used as VIMs, already cope with KVM Virtual Machines, Linux Containers (LXD) and native applications (Linux and Windows), with Docker containers being part of the pipeline.

Security Considerations

Security issues constitute one of the most important challenges for the success of NFV. We must bear in mind that a great part of current network security is based on the physical security that prevents insider attacks, but this will no longer hold when virtualization becomes commonplace, and network functions will become essentially executed on off-the-shelf hardware and software, which implies more reported and unreported (zero-day) vulnerabilities, more attack tools (such as virus and rootkits), and an increased motivation for attackers, as they could exploit NFV-based networks to cause larger scale disruption.

It is therefore required to reduce the combined attack surface, and with that goal a first set of measures can be derived from the current security practice in IT virtualization, taking advantage of enlarged mitigation mechanisms provided by hypervisors via techniques like introspection, as analyzed in Wang et al. (2015), and containment, as described in Huang et al. (2012). Beyond that, there are specific aspects that must be addressed to guarantee a secure development of NFV, mostly connected to the fact that NFV faces the combination of the network as an infrastructure and the network as an application. A first item among these aspects is related with image and infrastructure attestation: there must be ways to guarantee the installed software corresponds to the intended function and is provided by a trusted origin and, conversely, a given function must be assured it is running on the appropriate environment. While models like TPM have been proposed for these procedures, it is necessary to test their ability to scale up to the requirements of dynamic network service provisioning.

A second front is related to topology validation and enforcement, so that VNFs can be assured of being connected according to the appropriate functions in the service chain and not going through any potential data leakage or man-in-the-middle. There are incipient techniques applied in SDN deployments for that purpose, but apart from them and their required maturity, procedures are required above the infrastructure network.

The introduction of NFV raises new security issues when it comes to Authentication Authorisation and Accounting (AAA) as discussed in Vollbrecht et al. (2000), as it implies using identity and accounting facilities at two or more layers: the network and virtualization infrastructure (e.g., identifying the tenant or guest service providers) and the network function (e.g., identifying the end-users). A generalized AAA schema for identifying users utilizing a particular tenant infrastructure and/or a tenant acting on behalf of a user is required to support these patterns and the new operational and business models they will bring. Current AAA mechanisms assume there will be a single identity, single policy decision and enforcement points, a single level of policy, and a single accounting infrastructure. Even if a strict separation by functional encapsulation and containment (as current practice seems to suggest) would be feasible without breaking some of the promised NFV enhancements in what relates to scalability, agility and resilience, there exist risks related to each one the three components in AAA. Authentication procedures can imply privacy breaches associated to the disclosure of user information at layers that are not intended to consume certain identity attributes. Authorization risks are mostly related to privilege escalation produced by wrapping unrelated identities that cannot be verified at a given layer. Finally, accounting needs to be performed at all the underlying infrastructure layer(s), and they will not only require accounting at the granularity of virtualized applications that use the infrastructures, but also at the coarser granularity of the tenants running virtualized network functions.

Deployment Considerations

As described in Sato et.al. (2013), it is the combination of both technologies, SDN and NFV that will deliver the tools for a more flexible and cost-effective network, based on a unified end-to-end model for the network comprising the end user. A crucial aspect of NFV is the infrastructure onto which NFV will be deployed. A general misconception is that state-of-the-art datacentres will suffice. The networking layer and the virtual machine placement algorithms need to be redesigned from scratch. Current datacentres are designed with north-south and east-west traffic profiles in mind, which correspond to a virtualization paradigm that does not take into account where the virtual machines are placed and how they interact. The NFV datacentre, in contrast, needs to have a precise knowledge of where the different VNFs are placed and how the network traffic between them is flowing. Additionally, the placement of the NFV datacentres themselves has to be considered. Basta et.al. evaluate the influence of the network topology on the network load overhead introduced by the fact of decomposing the LTE network stack into different functions and placing them on a reduced number of datacentres in a disperse geography like the USA, while having to cope with service limitations like the delay budget (Basta et al. (2014)).

A real hurdle is associated to the incumbent equipment vendors that see open, pervasive NFV as a threat to their current business model. Incumbents have used Fear, Uncertainty and Doubt (FUD) tactics to slow down the pace of NFV evolution and adoption, or played the card of operational complexity. Acquiring successful start-up companies in order to control the evolution of the SDN/NFV landscape is another tactic used by some big equipment providers. Another threat comes from the claim of using "Open and Standard" interfaces. In many cases, this claim just translates into the use of standard protocols or basic coding (e.g., XML, YANG, NETCONF) and hides the fact that proprietary extensions are needed to perform any sensible control function.

And A Few Organizational Considerations

For several decades, the networking industry (operators, manufacturers, integrators, etc.) has been largely organized around the idea of physically distinguishable nodes providing well-identified services, and almost physically distinguishable links connecting them. To put it in plain words, boxes and cables connecting them. These boxes have been extremely intensive in software for quite a long time, but this software could not go beyond the limits of the box it was intended to run on. NFV opens a completely new set of possibilities, where software is not only confined to a particular "box" and can even be used to implement the "cables" connecting it to other elements.

These changes will require all kinds of actors. To begin with, working methodologies must get closer to the current DevOps practices and shorter times to market. Second, organizational structures will have to contemplate shorter paths between business management and engineering (or development, that is). We cannot forget that commercial relationships between these actors shall change as well, as virtualized infrastructures allow for much more fluid business models. And, above all, organizations and the individuals that compose them will have to adapt their experience and culture to a new way of thinking of their jobs and products (whatever they are: services, network nodes, technologies, etc.), let alone their skills.

REFERENCES

Arijs, P. (n.d.). *Docker Usage Stats: Adoption Up in the Enterprise and Production.* https://dzone.com/articles/docker-usage-statistics-increased-adoption-by-ente

Basta, A., Kellerer, W., Hoffmann, M., Morper, H. J., & Hoffmann, K. (2014). Applying NFV and SDN to LTE Mobile Core Gateways, the Functions Placement Problem. In *Proceedings of the 4th workshop on all things cellular: Operations, applications, & challenges* (pp. 33–38). New York, NY: ACM. 10.1145/2627585.2627592

Bonomi, F., Milito, R., Zhu, J., & Addepalli, S. (2012). Fog computing and its role in the internet of things. In *Proceedings of the first edition of the mcc workshop on mobile cloud computing* (pp. 13–16). New York, NY: ACM. 10.1145/2342509.2342513

Chiosi, M., Clarke, D., Willis, P., Reid, A., López, D., ... A. M. (2012, October). *Network Functions Virtualisation. An Introduction, Benefits, Enablers, Challenges and Call for Action.* https://portal.etsi.org/NFV/NFV_White_Paper.pdf

Clemm, A. (2007). Network Management Fundamentals. Cisco Press.

Cong, G., & Wen, H. (2013). (2013). Mapping Applications for High Performance on Multithreaded, NUMA Systems. In *Proceedings of the ACM international conference on computing frontiers* (pp. 7:1–7:4). New York, NY: ACM.

De la Oliva. (n.d.). *5G Coral: a 5G Convergent Virtualized RAN living at the edge.* http://5g-coral.eu

ETSI-NFV-ISG. (2014a). *Network Functions Virtualisation (NFV); NFV Performance & Portability Best Practises* (Tech. Rep.). ETSI. https://www.etsi.org/deliver/etsi_gs/NFV-PER/001_099/001/01.01.01_60/gs_NFV-PER001v010101p.pdf

ETSI-NFV-ISG. (2014). *Network Functions Virtualisation (NFV); Architectural Framework* (Tech. Rep.). ETSI. https://www.etsi.org/deliver/etsi_gs/NFV/001_099/002/01.02.01_60/gs_NFV002v010201p.pdf

ETSI-NFV-ISG. (2014b). *Network Functions Virtualisation (NFV); NFV Security; Problem Statement* (Tech. Rep.). ETSI. https://www.etsi.org/deliver/etsi_gs/NFV-SEC/001_099/001/01.01.01_60/gs_NFV-SEC001v010101p.pdf

ETSI-NFV-ISG. (2015). *Network Function Virtualisation (NFV); Resiliency Requirements* (Tech. Rep.). ETSI. https://www.etsi.org/deliver/etsi_gs/NFV-REL/001_099/001/01.01.01_60/gs_NFV-REL001v010101p.pdf

ETSI-NFV-ISG. (2017). *Network Functions Virtualisation (NFV); Use Cases* (Tech. Rep.). ETSI. https://www.etsi.org/deliver/etsi_gr/NFV/001_099/001/01.02.01_60/gr_NFV001v010201p.pdf

Huang, Y., Chen, B., Shih, M., & Lai, C. (2012). Security Impacts of Virtualization on a Network Testbed. *2012 IEEE Sixth International Conference on Software Security and Reliability*, 71-77. 10.1109/SERE.2012.17

IETF. (2020, Nov). *Service Function Chaining Charter* (Tech. Rep.). IETF. https://datatracker.ietf.org/wg/sfc/charter

Loukides, M. (2012). *What is DevOps? Infrastructure as Code*. O'Reilly Media.

McKeown, N., Anderson, T., Balakrishnan, H., Parulkar, G., Peterson, L., Rexford, J., & Turner, J. (2008, March). OpenFlow: Enabling innovation in campus networks. *Computer Communication Review*, *38*(2), 69–74. doi:10.1145/1355734.1355746

Mell, P., & Grance, T. (2011). *The NIST Definition of Cloud Computing* (Special Publication No. 800-145). Computer Security Division, Information Technology Laboratory, National Institute of Standards and Technology. https://csrc.nist.gov/publications/nistpubs/800-145/SP800-145.pdf

Sato, Y., Fukuda, I., & Tomonori, F. (2013, December). Deployment of OpenFlow/SDN Technologies to Carrier Services. *IEICE Transactions*, *96-B*(12), 2946–2952. doi:10.1587/transcom.E96.B.2946

TPM Main Specification. (2011, March). https://www.trustedcomputinggroup.org/resources/tpm_main_specification

Vollbrecht, J., Calhoun, P., Farrell, S., Gommans, L., Gross, G., de Bruijn, B., & Spence, D. (2000, August). *AAA Authorization Framework* (Tech. Rep. No. 2904). IETF. RFC 2904.

Wang, G., Estrada, Z., Pham, C., Kalbarczyk, Z., & Iyer, R. (2015).Hypervisor Introspection: A Technique for Evading Passive Virtual Machine Monitoring. *9th USENIX Workshop on Offensive Technologies (WOOT15)*.

ADDITIONAL READING

Feamster, N., Rexford, J., & Zegura, E. (2013). The road to SDN. *Queue*, *11*(12), 20–40. doi:10.1145/2559899.2560327

Jammal, M., Singh, T., Shami, A., Asal, R., & Li, Y. (2014). *Software-Defined Networking: State of the Art and Research Challenges*. arXiv preprint arXiv:1406.0124.

KEY TERMS AND DEFINITIONS

Carrier Cloud: A term that refers to cloud infrastructures suitable to provide telco carrier services that are able to bring the advantages of cloud computing to the telco environment by fulfilling the reliability requirements for critical infrastructures.

Composition: Is a technique for building complex elements by the (dynamic) composition of simpler ones. It requires components with well-known interfaces and verifiable service level agreements (SLA)

NFV (Network Functions Virtualization): Refers to a technology framework for the development and provisioning of network services, based on the separation of the functionality, implemented as software, and the capacity, provided by a homogeneous hardware infrastructure inspired on current cloud computing.

Orchestration: Is the process that governs the creation, instantiation, and composition of the different elements that a service consists of. It includes a coordinated set actions at several supporting infrastructures (e.g., computing, storage, and connectivity) and layers (local and WAN network).

Virtualization: Is a technique that consists in the creation of virtual (rather than actual) instance of any element, so it can be managed and used independently. Virtualization has been one of the key tools for resource sharing and software development, and now it is beginning to be applied to the network disciplines.

ENDNOTES

[1]   https://www.telefonica.com/documents/737979/140082548/Telefonica_Virtualisation_gCTO_FINAL.PDF/426a4b9d-6357-741f-9678-0f16dccf0e16?version=1.0

[2]   https://rakuten.today/tech-innovation/rakutens-upcoming-end-to-end-cloud-native-mobile-network.html

[3]   https://5ginfire.eu/

[4]   https://5ginfire.eu/experiments/

Chapter 7
Automation of Network Services for the Future Internet

Samier Said Barguil
Universidad Autonoma de Madrid, Spain

Oscar Gonzalez de Dios
Telefonica I+D, Spain

Victor Lopez
Telefonica I+D, Spain

Kellow Pardini
Vivo (Telefonica Brasil), Brazil

Ricard Vilalta
Centre Tecnològic de Telecomunicacions de Catalunya (CTTC/CERCA), Spain

ABSTRACT

Internet service providers are shifting to an open, modern, software-based architecture that enables both new operating and business models. The target architecture is loosely coupled, cloud-native, data and artificial intelligence-driven, and relies on traffic engineering-related protocols to get the full potential of the network capabilities. The components need to use standard interfaces to be easily procured and deployed without the need for customization. Achieving these goals will require a significant change in how the network resources are architected, built, procured, licensed, and maintained. Some levers to drive this transformation rely on adopting open protocols such as NETCONF/RESTCONF or gNMI to operate the network and use standard data models to interact with the network more programmatically. This chapter presents such architecture, including service provider experiences.

DOI: 10.4018/978-1-7998-7646-5.ch007

INTRODUCTION

According to the Internet world stats described in (Hootsuite & We Are Social, 2021), the number of Internet accesses has reached almost 5 billion during the last decades. This massive growth of accesses and Internet applications has brought an increasing unstoppable demand for bandwidth among consumers, fostered even more by the irruption of new technologies such as Internet of Things (IoT), enhanced mobile broadband, or 5G, which ambitions to augment even more the number of industrial applications to make use of the available infrastructure with more stringent requirements.

Many Service Providers (SPs) had to explore different alternatives to satisfy the (fast-changing) customer expectations and create new business opportunities beyond the "traditional" connectivity. At the same time, they need to offer competitive prices and maintain the robustness required to withstand possible Network failures. All this while the Average Revenue Per User (ARPU) remains "quasi" stable (if not decreasing) since the customer base has remained constant in most of the market segments and the new income has been derived to the over-the-top applications. Thus, to remain viable in a highly competitive market, the deployment of convergent IP networks with programmable interfaces for the automation of day-to-day tasks in the network and the ability to develop new network services in a short time has been considered an essential target for Service Providers.

In order to trigger the 'network of the future' and move the whole industry to a new era, the emerging technologies that are considered as the building blocks by SPs are Software-defined networking (SDN) in combination with Network Function Virtualization (NFV) and Machine Learning technologies. The "promise" of these technologies is to allow SPs to program their networks with the agility of the IT industry instead of the old-school slow pace of the telecom industry. However, nowadays, no SP has entirely changed how the transport network (the infrastructure that moves the bulk of the traffic) is operated. Nevertheless, according to Research and Markets (2020), SDN has been one of the fastest-growing markets in the Communications industry, reaching 13.7 million in 2020.

SDN, as described by ONF in (ONF TR-502, 2014) and IRTF in RFC 7426 (Haleplidis et al., 2015), relies upon a modular architecture, focused on the capabilities offered by a computation logic (a.k.a., SDN controller) to separate the control plane from the data plane. The SDN controller is the key element to interact with equipment and systems (Operational Support Systems (OSS) and Business Support Systems (BSS)) through data-driven programmatic Network Application Programming Interfaces (APIs). The definition/usage of these network APIs is the base of the whole network automation approach mainly for the following reasons:

- The less human intervention for the day-to-day tasks and the reduction of management touchpoints due to single network control points.
- The controller can run offline tasks to make network resources optimization continuously; this can derive in faster and on-demand provisioning.
- The standardized interfaces usage reduces the vendor dependency, without completely removing it, and thus allows to customize features as applications.
- The controller can make advanced traffic steering policies and sophisticated service-aware management.
- Each API can be considered as an application; these applications can share network information to make advanced decisions.

Table 1. Levers to enable Network Automation

Business Benefits
Close to real time service creation and rapid provisioning
Improved customer satisfaction
Time-to-market improvements.
On demand service modification
Elastic, scalable, network-wide capabilities
IoT and 5G Slicing easy adoption
Policy Definitions and Enforcement: Standard interfaces and centralized control

To facilitate the automation of service delivery procedures in multi-vendor networking environments and make these network APIs reusable, Standard Definition Organizations (SDOs) like the IETF and industry for a such as OpenConfig have defined a set of protocols (NETCONF, gNMI, BGP-LS, etc.) and vendor-agnostic data models. In combination, they can be used to cover the planning and operation needs of a carrier. However, there is a continuous need to standardize new service types or cover new functionalities, which has led to the publication of several standards and specifications by SDOs and Industry fora, such as ONF, IETF, OpenConfig, or the Metro Ethernet Forum (MEF). Thus, some initiatives are based on a gradual adoption of standards and/or the evolution of legacy network architectures to take advantage of more agile and automatic deployments.

The network automation brings not only technical advantages, all the aforementioned SDOs and fora agree upon the commercial levers and the technical requirements that motivate to migrate current networks to more automated schemes as depicted in Table 1 and Table 2.

Table 2. Levers to enable Network Automation

Technology and Operation Benefits	
Virtualization of network functions	
Programmatic control of network	
Deep network resources optimization based on the usage of traffic engineering (TE) policies as described in RFC 3272	
Standards-based protocols for resource allocation and configuration purposes and companion data models	Standard Northbound interfaces (NBI) leveraging RESTCONF/YANG
	Standard Southbound interfaces (SBI) leveraging NETCONF/YANG.
	YANG data models based on the latest work of standards development organizations (SDOs), Open Networking Foundation (ONF), and OPENCONFIG.
Reduce device management touchpoints	

Some Proofs of Concept (PoCs) have been carried out involving all the elements that make up the supply chain of a connectivity service, also taking into account the evolution of IP/MPLS brownfield architectures towards multipurpose networks controlled by software. All these initiatives have led to the adoption of disaggregation at the optical transponders' level and the possibility of integrating white boxes in IP networks as access equipment as described by *Campanella et al. (2019)*. However, despite all these advances, there are still large operational gaps that prevent some SPs from putting this set of emerging technologies into production.

This chapter provides an overview of the proposed service providers' network automation frameworks and the industry initiatives from the most relevant fora. The programmability of network services is explained, with a focus on the data modeling aspects. Finally, a set of trials and experiences led by Service Providers is presented.

STATE OF THE ART OF NETWORK AUTOMATION FRAMEWORKS

As discussed earlier, sdn brings the promise of adding network programmability and accelerating network innovation. The industry has proposed several frameworks to implement the concepts and share key architectural components between them. In this section, we discuss some of the relevant frameworks that have influenced the industry and present some initiatives samples presented and publicized by several sps to deploy them.

Among first so-called SDN architecture was proposed by Casado et al. (2012). In this approach, the control plane functionality is completely stripped off the device as depicted in Figure 1, which runs an agent to implement the forwarding instructions dictated by the Controller.

Figure 1. Decoupling of control & data plane proposed by Casado et al. (2012).

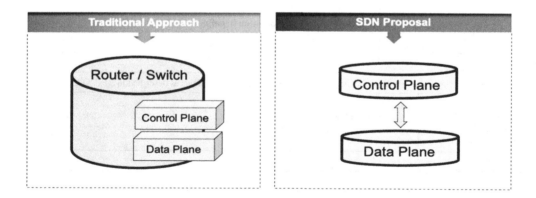

The ONF proposed in ONF TR-502 an architecture that introduces the concept of SDN Controllers. It provides a first definition of the whole set of functionalities and interactions between the controller and the network. The ONF architecture does not advocate for a full decoupling of functionalities as described initially by Casado et al. (2012), but allows the network elements to run some control functions governed by the controller.

One of the architectures that can be considered as precursors of SDN is the Path Computation Element (PCE) architecture defined in the IETF RFC 4655. In a PCE architecture, a central element, called the PCE is in charge of computing and providing the best paths to carry the network traffic. However, the PCE is highly focused on a specialized function, and it is not intended at becoming a wider scope.

An IETF-hosted initiative focused on providing a clear definition of what SDN can mean in the Service Provider environment, clarifying the perspective of the requirements, issues, and possible implementations gaps to make the technology ready for production in (*Boucadair & Jacquenet, 2014).*

Other IETF initiatives aim at covering the standardization gaps to foster the deployment of standard SDN solutions are presented in (*Bemby et al., 2015).* The ETSI has defined the functional blocks required to promote the combination of "pure" SDN controllers with well-defined APIs to support both legacy and SDN ready-devices (*Virtualisation, 2015).* The architectures that have this kind of support was named hybrid-SDN. Hybrid SDN flavors has been categorized in (*Vissicchio et al., 2014)* depending on certain variables like the topological distribution, he services supported, or the classes managed between each kind of devices.

Also, the IETF Operations and Management Area Working Group (OPSAWG) defined a reference automation framework in (*Wu el at., 2021)* to describe the architecture for service and network management automation taking advantage of YANG modeling technologies. This framework uses a layered architecture to allow the reusability of the components and increase the abstraction provided by each of the components and has become the main reference for implementation in the networking industry. In fact, the whole industry has embraced the use of YANG as the basis of programmability. The IETF automation framework considers all the lifecycle of the network services, considering not only the provisioning, but also the service assurance and decomposition.

The architecture considered in this chapter, proposed by *Telecom Infra Project (2021),* allows a bottom-up or top-down implementation. It provides clear segmentations between the layers/models/ protocols and the interfaces used in each case can be shown in terms of components and relationships in Figure 2. The main architectural pillars and concepts are as follows:

- **Transport SDN:** The entire transport network of an SP, including the backhaul, IP/MPLS backbone, and the underlying optical infrastructure. The transport network is logically divided into several domains as a function of scalability, technology, or administrative considerations. It can include the packet (IP/MPLS), Optical, or Micro-Wave technological domains with SDN capabilities.
- **SDN Domain Controller:** It oversees a set of network elements of the same technology. It has standard network-facing interfaces, supported on well-known technology independent protocols, to communicate with the network elements for management, control and telemetry. The telemetry provides a continuous feedback from the network elements. The control intelligence is shared between the network elements, which do run a control plane that can survive autonomously, and the controller, which enhances the control plane function with the whole network view (e.g., providing a better path computation and a full domain view of a network service). The SDN Domain Controller pivots around the "data model" concepts. In that sense, it is synchronized with the devices to maintain a device-level view. The programming at the controller level is based on the

manipulation of data structures representing the devices, the network, and the "network services. The SDN controller has two primary interfaces:

- **Network Operator Interface (a.k.a., North Bound Interface):** It fits with the **SDN Hierarchical Controller SBI** interface (see below). It is often based on RESTCONF. It has a network resource-facing module and describes various aspects of a network infrastructure, including devices and their subsystems, and relevant protocols operating at the link and network layers across multiple devices (e.g., network topology and traffic engineering modules). The controller can also have the function of aggregating the telemetry information towards big data systems which can perform closed loop automations at whole network level.

- **Device Oriented Interface (a.k.a., South Bound Interface):** This interface is primarily based on NETCONF with function-specific (e.g., a routing engine) YANG modules used to provide a service (e.g., BGP, NAT). Through this interface, the controller can maintain a complete view of a network device. The interface is complemented with a telemetry protocol to extract, either periodically or near real time, information from the device.

- **SDN Hierarchical Controller:** In an ideal world, an SDN controller would have the full detailed end-to-end network view. However, for scalability reasons, the detailed domain views are limited to a single technology and a subset of the network nodes' total. Hence, the next step in complementing the control plane is providing a multi-layer and multi-domain view within a hierarchical controller. The SDN Hierarchical Controller (H-SDNc) can provide orchestration functions across domains and maintains the interconnection of them, but not having the detailed internal view of each domain. The H-SDN controller has to cooperate with the domain controllers in order to provide and maintain the end-to-end service requirements. This implies that a multi-layer topological view is maintained, facilitating the knowledge on the resources used by a given service through the whole network. A continuous feedback is required between the controllers, so ensure the end-to-end multi-layer view is consistent with the updates happening in a domain (e.g., an optical path changes, incurring in a new delay which may impact an IP path, impacting a delay constraint service). The H-SDNc interfaces with the BSS/OSS Systems to provide the enhanced network view, as it is the sole element that glues different technologies. The primary interfaces are:

  - **BSS/OSS Systems Interface:** Is based mostly upon customer-facing modules that are designed to provide a common model construct. For example, the service level can be used to characterize the network service as an abstract entity to be delivered with guarantees between service nodes (ingress/egress) as defined in corresponding Service Level Agreements (SLAs).

  - **SDN Hierarchical Controller SBI:** Typically, it is a RESTCONF interface that is meant to allow the integration between the H-SDNc and the domain controllers. It is used to coordinate the information between the **SDN Transport** and the SDN domain controllers.

- **Data model:** A data model describes how data is represented and accessed. The SDN architecture manipulates data models with different level of abstractions. A data model contains:

  - **Configuration data:** that is, the consumer of the data model can manipulate it.

  - **State data:** which is read-only and produced to capture state information (e.g., interface counters).

It is essential to highlight that a data model can automatically derive into a programmatic API. Today's the facto standard for producing network data models is YANG. Some SDOs uses UML and then YANG.

A brief summary of the work that has been accomplished by some SDOs is depicted in Table 3.

Figure 2. SDN architecture proposed for end-to-end network programmability and abstraction levers

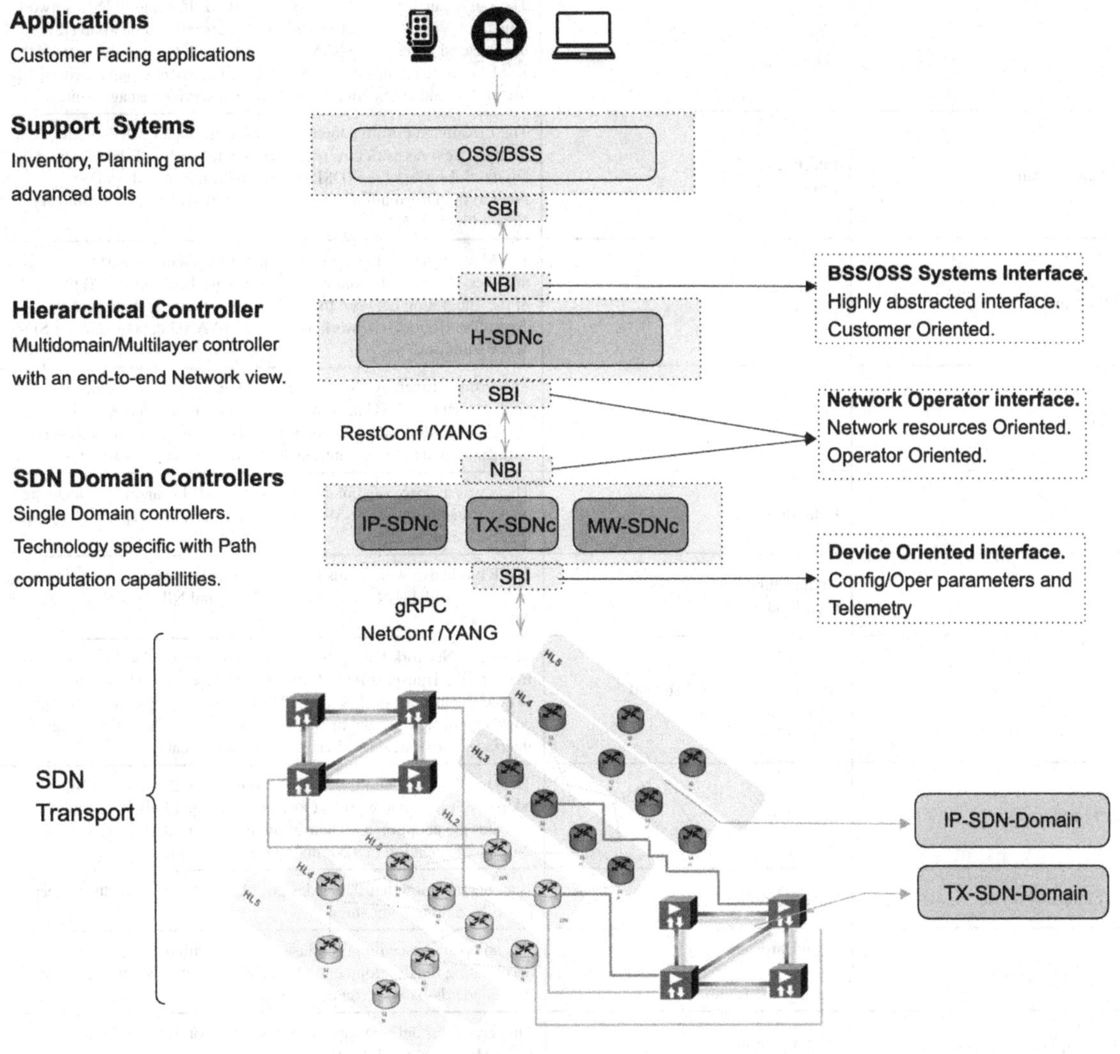

Network Services Programmability and Manageability

The network management has lagged behind other technologies quite drastically. In more than 20 years, there has not been a radical improvement of the device management area. One of the significant advances was related to the usage of SSH instead of TELNET to secure configuration tasks. However, scripts based on the EXPECT library defined by Libes (1995) are the most programmatic way to access the

Table 3. SDN Adoption in SDOs

SDO	Category	Main Contributions
IETF	Architecture and Data Models	Has led the standardization of protocols such as NETCONF and RESTCONF. It has promoted the YANG adoption in all the technological domains as one key driver for network automation.
ETSI	Architecture and Data Models	The European Telecommunication Standards Institute (ETSI) Network Functions Virtualization (NFV) Industry Specification Group (ISG) has released cornerstone NFV specifications. ETSI has also created the ZSM - Zero touch network & Service Management group to work in the full end-to-end automation of network and service management.
Broadband Forum	Interfaces and Data Models	The Broadband Forum adopted YANG as the data modelling language for the access network covering technologies such as Ethernet, fiber, Digital Subscriber Line (DSL), Very-high-bit-rate DSL (VDSL), Fiber to the Distribution Point (FTTdP), PPPoE, or Passive Optical Networking (PON).
MEF Forum	Interfaces and Data Models	The Metro Ethernet Forum has recently focused on the service's YANG modules. A series of standard interfaces have been defined as part of the integration between the service orchestrator and the network controller. Besides, the work has included YANG data models for SD-WAN solutions.
OpenConfig	Data Models	This group, driven by Google and Telco operators, has defined a common set of YANG data models to configure IP and Optical devices. The Repository includes models to configure hardware (cards, pluggable) and software (interfaces, network instance) attributes.
IEEE	Data Models	There was a close collaboration between the IEEE and IETF, focusing on the transition from SNMP MIBs to YANG models specified by both the IEEE and the IETF.
3GPP	Architecture and Data Models	3GPP has active work items to define YANG models for the Network Resource Model (NRM), Network Slicing, and NR RAN (Radio Access Network).
ONF	Architecture, Controllers and Data Models	The Open Network Foundation has been the home of several projects like ONOS, Transport API (TAPI), Core Model (TR-512), or the Wireless transport models (532). Those projects ranged from the open controller design and deployment to the delivery of technology-agnostic interfaces for Optical or Micro-Wave management.
Linux Foundation	Controllers	The OpenDaylight controller project was one of the early YANG adopters. It is a source project formed under the Linux Foundation to foster the adoption and innovation of software-defined networking through the creation of a common vendor-supported framework.
Open Compute Project	Open Hardware	Is an organization that shares designs of data center products and best practices among companies.
Telecom Infra Project	Open Hardware and Use cases definition	It is an open consortium of industry players with the goal of accelerating the development and deployment of open, disaggregated, and standards-based technology solutions.
OpenROADM	Open Hardware	This group has defined specifications for Reconfigurable Optical Add/Drop Multiplexers (ROADM).
TM Forum	Architecture and Data Models	From the OSS/BSS perspective, TM Forum has been leading the architectural definitions and the integration models. Has projects related to Autonomous network deployment. Those projects incorporate a "simplified" network architecture, autonomous domains, and automated (intelligent) business/network operations.

service providers' devices worldwide. A good reference of the main network automation techniques can be found in (*Edelman et al., 2018*).

There are several toolkits for network management (e.g., SNMP-MIBs, PIBs, or TR-069), however compared with other technologies, it seems there is a lack of end-to-end network/service programmability. For example, cloud providers have been offering on-demand growth services since years, including hypervisor managers, wireless controllers, or DevOps tools as part of their Continuous Integration/ Continuous Development (CI/CD) solutions. Some of these tools are tightly coupled with a particular vendor. However, others are more loosely aligned to allow multi-platform management, operations, and agility as described in (*Demchenko et al., 2016; Mittal et al., 2017; Edelman et al., 2018).*

To allow network programmability in the service provider's networks, it is essential to use SDN as the reference for introducing the concept of network APIs. These network APIs are not just related to the automation of service delivery procedures (service delivery often assumes a set of repetitive tasks), but also to automate and offer much more than pushing configuration parameters. Network APIs can be used to create closed loop actions and cover all the FCAPS (Fault, Configuration, Accounting, Performance, and Security) ISO-defined specific management functional areas (and network planning tasks:

- Network planning tasks if we include APIs to export distributed information such as the entries of Routing Information Bases (RIBs), Forwarding Information Bases (FIBs), and TE databases maintained by the routers of the network.
- It is used to deploy close-loop decision systems to take actions based on events reported by the devices.
- Automatically visualize the network relationships between the IP/MPLS and the Optical packet transport domains, thereby creating a multi-layer network view.

Due to the network programmability considerations, protocols described in Section "STANDARD PROTOCOLS TO ENABLE NETWORK AUTOMATION IN SERVICE PROVIDER ENVIRONMENTS" and data models described in Section "SERVICE MODELS FOR OPERATIONAL SDN NETWORK DEPLOYMENT" must be supported to allow the interaction between the network controllers and devices. There has been a great interest in using YANG to define these data models. Such YANG-based set of definitions may include two groups of models. One set is used strictly to control the devices and the second set is related to describe services in a customer-oriented manner (independently of which network operator uses the model).

This differentiation between Service and Device Models introduced early 2018 leads to the creation of a data repository that resides in the control plane and whose contents are maintained and updated by the SDN controller. In a typical Policy-Based Management context, such data repository is called the Policy Information Base, where (service-inferred) policies (forwarding and routing, Quality of Service, traffic engineering, security, etc.) are instantiated according to the service parameters that may have been dynamically negotiated between the customer and the service provider. The service models may be used as part of the SDN architecture, and they describe the data exchanged between the network controllers, OSS systems, and the control plane (*Wu et al., 2018).* In contrast, the device models describe the various functions supported by the network elements. From the aforementioned instantiation of policies as per the service that needs to be delivered, the SDN controller forwards policy-provisioning information to the selected components and other service function instances so that their invocation contributes to the delivery of the service.

Standard Protocols to Enable Network Automation In Service Provider Environments

Over the past decade, computer networks have been changing to end-to-end programmable platforms. Early work on SDN mainly focused on the control plane and data plane separation. Hence, for the first time, network owners had (full) control over the devices' software. Most of the first SDN implementations used OpenFlow switches controlled by a central entity. However, the OpenFlow protocol has known functional limitations (it was originally designed to dynamically populate the FIBs maintained by the switches to enforce specific traffic forwarding policies whereas no other resource (NAT, firewall, TCP optimizer, etc.) could be configured by OpenFlow), especially in brownfield scenarios. One of the reasons that explain the low (if no) adoption of OpenFlow in WAN environments is because these scenarios include a significant number of nodes and have high reliability and stability requirements. Maintaining the full detailed forwarding information base of thousands of devices, distributed geographically, from a central controller has significant scalability challenges. Hence, the use of the very low-level programmability is feasible for more controlled environment such as data centers. For the wide area network, an hybrid approach has gained more traction.

Specific protocols can be used for programmability purposes, but assuming there is a control plane running, so there is a level of abstraction in between. Hence, these protocols will interface with the routing system of the device and allows to change the behavior of the control plane protocols in a programmatic way. The protocol to program the network should be independent of the data model so that it can be used to configure any data model supported by a device, a service function, etc.

NETCONF

Network operators and protocol developers discussed a minimum set of requirements to define how to improve the execution of configuration tasks in a workshop held back early 2000s. RFC 3535 (Schoenwaelder, 2003) reports the main outcome of the discussions in that workshop, for example:

- SNMP has failed in Configuration Task. There is too little deployment of writable MIB modules, although some deployments were reported.
- Command line interfaces (CLI) often lack proper version control for the syntax and the semantics.
- The industry needs a language to configure the network as a whole and minimize the impact of configuration changes.

Then, the NETwork CONFiguration protocol (NETCONF) was specified by the IETF in RFC6241 (Enns et al., 2011). It represents a mechanism through which a network device can be fully managed (e.g., configured, upgraded, rebooted). NETCONF uses a simple Remote Procedure Call (RPC)-based mechanism to establish communications using a client-server structure:

- The client can be a script, an application running as part of a network domain controller.
- Some open NETCONF servers like "ncclient" or "yang-suite" are available for testing and application development purposes.
- The server is typically a network device or a function.

NETCONF defines several datastores to maintain the data (Start-Up, Running, or Candidate) and allows Create, Read, Update, and Delete (CRUD) operations on them. The available NETCONF RPCs are detailed in Table 3.

Datastore Management

Figure 3. Original NETCONF Datastores vs NMDA datastores

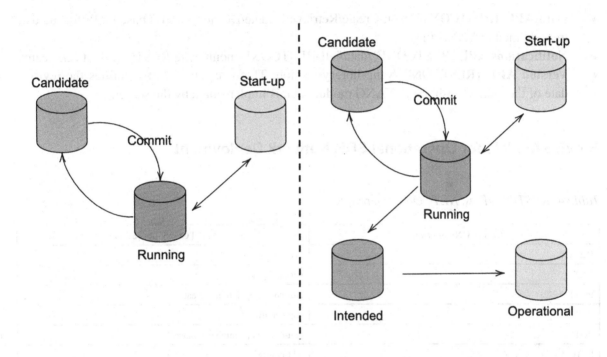

Figure 3 depicts the NETCONF datastore management. According to the latest IETF specifications, two approaches are considered:

- **The original model (RFC 6241)**: Defines three states; the running datastore contains the complete configuration operating on the device. Its initial default state is the start-up datastore. The candidate data store includes the desired changes to update the current device status and place it into a new desired operational position.
- **Network Management Datastore Architecture (NMDA)**: NMDA published by *Bjorklund et al. (2018),* defines two additional datastores: Intended configuration and Operational. The intended configuration datastore is read-only. It represents the configuration after all configuration transformations to running are completed. The operational state datastore is a read-only datastore consisting of all "config true" and "config false" nodes defined in the datastore's schema.

RESTCONF

It is defined in RFC8040 (Bierman et al., 2017) as an HTTP-based protocol that provides a programmatic interface for accessing data defined in YANG. RESTCONF re-uses the datastore concepts defined by NETCONF but relies upon HTTP methods to provide equivalent Create, Read, Update, and Delete operations to the NETCONF RPCs. Table 3 shows how the RESTCONF operations can be mapped to NETCONF protocol operations.

The RESTCONF specification consists of a set of resources available from:

- **Data API:** {RESTCONF}/data: Create/Retrieve/Update/Delete (CRUD) based API for the data trees defined in YANG files.
- **Notifications API**: {RESTCONF}/data/ietf-RESTCONF-monitoring:RESTCONF-state/streams.
- **Version API**: {RESTCONF}/yang-library-version: This mandatory leaf identifies the revision date of the "ietf-yang-library" YANG module that is implemented by the server.

Service Models for Operational SDN Network Deployment

Table 4. RESTCONF vs. NETCONF operations

RESTCONF operation	NETCONF operation
HEAD	get-config, get
GET	get-config, get
POST	edit-config operation="create"
PUT	copy-config
PUT	edit-config operation="replace"
PATCH	edit-config
DELETE	edit-config operation="delete"

Service models are used to describe network services in a portable way (i.e., independent of which network operator uses the model and the device vendor). As "service" is an overloaded term, in this context, we define a "network service model" as "a set of device configurations that enables packets from a customer entering at selected locations in the network to reach other locations following the desired behaviors". Note that, the "service" in the OSS/BSS layer includes the lifecycle and resource management. The responsibilities are shared among the SDN control layer and the OSS layer. This split requires APIs to be defined for the interface between them.

Network services, for example, Layer 3 VPNs or Layer 2 VPNs, enable customers to exchange traffic between locations through a service provider network. There are two types of service models to consider.

The model usage depends on the consumer of the data model. On the one hand, the **customer service models** aim to be implemented by the service orchestration layer and can be used by customers to express their needs, negotiate the SLAs, etc. Such models do not contain internal information of the service provider. On the other hand, the **Network Service Models,** usually denoted as "network models", are used to interact with the network controllers, as depicted in Figure 4. Such models are used to instantiate the service in the network. Network models are used to provide an intermediate level of abstraction between what the customer requires and the configuration that actually implemented in the underlying network nodes. It provides the notion of a network service, which really it is a set of configurations in the devices that happen to realize the customer needs. It is important to highlight that the services of the network models only exist in the controller. In the network nodes, protocols, routing instances, tunnels, routing profiles, access control lists, etc., for example, are configured to implement such service. Also, note that due the separation of roles, the assignment of resources, for example, selecting the right interface for a customer or choosing an address or taking the decision of giving or not certain bandwidth is a role of the service orchestration layer. The network models are a good base to define the Resource-Facing services used by OSS applications.

Figure 4. YANG data-models used in each control level

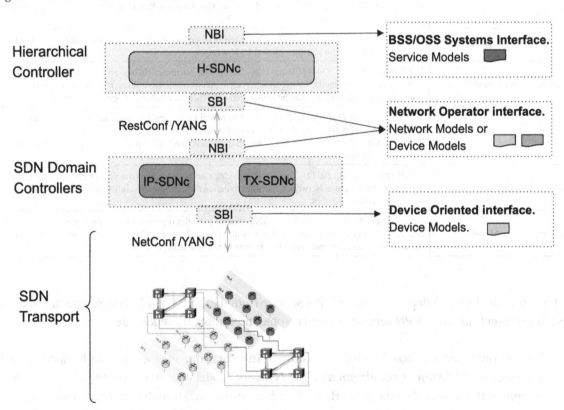

- **Customer Service Model:** Is defined in RFC 8921. Such models capture the characteristics and requirements of the service solely from the customer point of view. For example, the requirements in terms of latency and bandwidth between customer locations are part of the service definition. The customer service model describes the location of the customer sites and a reference to its entry point in the service provider network. However, as the customer service models are exposed to customers, all internal network details are hidden.

- **Network Service Model:** Describes the service from the point of view of the service provider network. The network service models capture the nodes that are involved in the delivery for of the service, without requiring intermediate translations and the interfaces through which the customer traffic is received. Programmatically, new (service) endpoints can be added and removed. The underlay transport preferences, that is how packets are sent between the edge packet devices, can also be defined.

Examples of each model category are described in Table 5.

Table 5. Service and Network YANG Models examples

Category	Model Name
Customer Service Model	L2SM (RFC 8466) Wen et al. (2018), released in 2018 defines a YANG data model that can be used to configure a Layer 2 provider-provisioned VPN service.
Customer Service Model	L3SM (RFC 8299) Qin et al. (2017), released in 2017 defines a YANG data model that can be used to configure a Layer 3 provider-provisioned VPN service.
Customer Service Model	IETF Topology (RFC 8345) (Clemm et al., 2018). This document defines an abstract (generic, or base) YANG data model for network/service topologies and inventories. It serves as a generic topology of the network that can be augmented with specific topology or operative parameters.
Service Model	TE (Saad et al., 2021) since 2015 a YANG data model for the configuration and management of Traffic Engineering (TE) tunnels, Label Switched Paths (LSPs), and interfaces have been part of the TEAS working group in the IETF. The model is divided into YANG modules that classify data into generic, device-specific, technology agnostic, and technology-specific elements.
Network Service Model	L3NM (Barguil et al., 2021a). The model provides a network-centric view of L3VPN services. L3NM is meant to be used by a Network Controller to derive the configuration information that will be sent to relevant network devices.
Network Service Model	L2NM (Barguil et al., 2021b). This YANG module provides representation of the Layer 2 VPN Service from a network standpoint. The module is meant to be used by a Network Controller to derive the configuration information that will be sent to relevant network devices.

For example, Figure 5 depicts the same VPN service from the L3SM and L3NM perspectives. Both models represent the same VPN service; however, some important differences are:

- The customer service model includes **Customer Information,** such as the site location, postal addresses, and **Customer requirements.** The Network Model does not cover the customer information, as it is centered on the network needs, which are derived from the customer requirements.
- The customer service model does not cover the Provider Edge (PE)-to-PE connectivity, which is how the internal operator's network devices communicate with each other. The Network models include the ability to select, and even program, the underlay transport technology. The ability to set a preference on which underlay to use is instrumental in networks with multiple domains and NNI types. Examples of the supported options are Border Gateway Protocol (BGP), Label Distribution Protocol (LDP), Segment Routing, Segment Routing-Traffic Engineering (SR-TE),

and Resource Reservation Protocol-TE (RSVP-TE). An underlay based on traffic engineering is the basis for the transport network slicing with stringent Quality of Service (QoS) requirements.

- The network model includes routing and connectivity details such as the Route Distinguisher (RDs) and the Route-Targets (RTs). Those parameters are fundamental for the service deployment on the network (Clemm et al., 2018). They describe the customer information in terms of reachability information (e.g., IP addresses) that can be reached, MAC addresses, etc., to feed the Virtual Routing and Forwarding (VRF) instances that will be maintained by the PE routers in the case of a BGP/MPLS VPN design. Three possible behaviors are needed to address the following use cases:
- The network controller auto-assigns logical resources (RTs, RDs) whenever a new VPN service needs to be delivered.
- The Network Operator/Service orchestrator assigns the RTs and RDs explicitly. This case will fit with a brownfield scenario where some existing services need to be updated by the network operators. In addition, there are multi-domain cases were the RTs and RDs need to be coordinated with other domain, so the network controller no longer has the freedom to auto-assign.
- The Network Operator/Service orchestrator explicitly wants no RT/RD to be assigned. This case will fit in VRF-Lite scenarios, CE testing inside the Network or just for troubleshooting purposes.
- Corporate VPNs usually require specific BGP configuration. The service model covers generic connectivity between CEs and PEs. In the network model, alternative options are available.

Figure 5. Comparison between a VPN service that is defined by using a Service Model and a Network Model

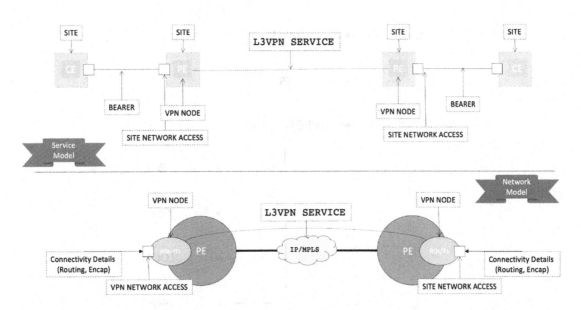

Device Models to Enable Network Automation In Service Provider Environments

Device-specific data models are used to manipulate the device configuration and retrieve its counters to evaluate the network status, as viewed from the device. These data models must cover all the information pushed/collected by the network operators. Several YANG data models are available, each trying to cover the service provider's specific needs. This is the case of OpenConfig, which started as a collaborative work between Google and some vendors and Service Providers, and now it is an industrial reference for device-specific configuration purposes. The philosophy behind OpenConfig is to add functionality to the device models based on the operator's needs, to avoid complex models which are not implemented in the real life.

The IETF is the SDO that is responsible for the formal standardization of the YANG models in general. Several models that are developed in the IETF have their starting point in OpenConfig and

Figure 6. Example of device models valid for an IP/MPLS router

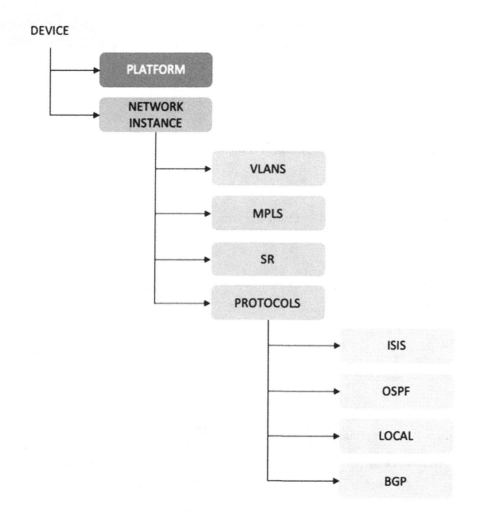

vice versa. There are minor differences in the philosophy of implementing the YANG models in both organizations. While the IETF models assume NMDA compatibility, the OpenConfig models don't have that assumption and explicitly indicate configuration and state data nodes.

Device YANG models describe a device and its essential networking features, all the way ranging from interfaces, VPNs (Network Instances), or routing protocols like the Border Gateway Protocol (BGP) or the Open Shortest Path First (OSPF). Figure 6 shows the set of models which represent an IP/MPLS router. The OpenConfig platform model of a device ("ietf-harwdare" in the equivalent model in IETF) represents a system component inventory, which can include hardware or software elements arranged in an arbitrary structure. The primary relationship supported by the model is containment, e.g., components containing subcomponents. The interfaces associated to the ports of the cards present in the platform model are present in the rest of the model. This way, it is possible to make complex associations and troubleshooting.

The network instance model (defined in both the IETF and OpenConfig) represents a private routing instance in a device. Protocols, interfaces, routing policies, etc. are attached to this routing instance. The network services require detailed knowledge of the network instance. The type of the network instance can be changed, which then triggers how the forwarding entries are installed on the device. Signaling protocols also use the network instance type to infer the type of service they advertise. For example, MPLS signaling for an L2VSI network instance would infer a Virtual Private LAN Services (VPLS) service whereas a type of L2PTP would infer a Virtual Private Wire Service (pseudo-wire) service. The Network instance supported in OpenConfig model are as follows:

- Default instance: Refers to the main routing table on the device. It allows the configuration of the protocol stack and main forwarding attributes to interconnect the router with the other network devices (e.g., IGP, LDP/RSVP, MPLS, MP-BGP).
- L2PTP: Virtual private wire service (VPWS) Layer 2 VPNs employ Layer 2 services over MPLS to build a topology composed of point-to-point connections between customer sites. From the customer perspective, these Layer 2 VPNs provide a virtual leased line to interconnect the sites.
- L2VSI: Refers to a virtual switching instance in each of the nodes involved in service deployment. This switching instance allows the Ethernet information propagation between the sites involved in the service.
- L3VRF: The VPN service defined in RFC 4364 provides a multipoint, routed service to the customer over an IP/MPLS core. The L3VPNs are widely used to deploy 3G/4G, fixed, and enterprise services mainly because several traffic discrimination policies can be applied in the network to deliver services with specific SLAs to the mobile customers.

Identifying the correct version of each data model and track the changes that are introduced by each SDO is a challenge for network deployments and even worse when each organization adopts a different approach. For example,

OpenConfig is maintained in a Git repository with various CI/CD scripts to validate the structure and the compatibility between the models. This approach facilitates the improvement of data models, by means of agility. However, SPs experienced a lack of control on the backward compatibility between releases during initial OpenConfig implementations.

The work accomplished by the OpenConfig consortium until now is focused on solving one of the main problems in implementing and integrating multi-vendor scenarios: the need for per-vendor per-operating system customization of the communication the network device and the entity in charge of its management. Nowadays, it's common to require new developments for a new device or feature integration in the whole service delivery chain. This customization usually increases the integration costs and complicates the migration between vendors, device families, or solutions. Common YANG specifications would reduce the number of deviations required and, in essence, mean that the SDN controllers forward configuration information to the participating components regardless of their technology.

IETF models can be found and extracted from different RFCs and compiled in the YANG catalogue (YANG Catalog, 2021).

NETWORK AUTOMATION FRAMEWORKS TRIALS AND EXPERIENCES IN SERVICE PROVIDERS

A service provider's transport network usually involves many devices, running a stack of protocols, and supports several applications. Many day-to-day tasks have been automated by operation teams with smart scripts. Also, the service provisioning has been automated from the OSS with complex business logics and templates. Hence, the degree of automation reached by every operator depended on the resources spent in understanding every vendor technology and the capabilities of such vendor devices or network management systems. Thus, there is no evidence that any service provider has fully implemented a programmable network. However, there is a conceptual agreement about the requirements and the components that should be part of it since years ago. Many service providers released their plan to implement their 'Future Network'. Those plans have a variety of unusual names but were built on top of the same set of fundamental principles:

- **AT&T Domain 2.0** (*Birk et al., 2016*): All the media agencies announced this project with a notable sentence: "AT&T on target to virtualizing 75% of its Network by 2020". However, to support such ambitious plan, the Domain 2.0 project was built on top of three main goals: Openness,

Figure 7. SDN architecture proposed by AT&T in the Domain 2.0 Program

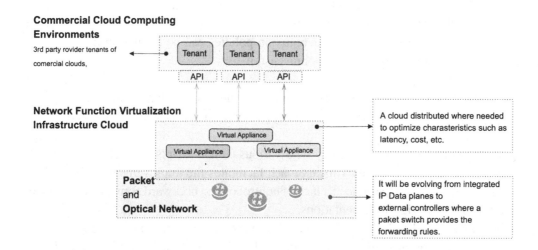

Simplification, and Scalability. This proposal's main goal was to increase the number of suppliers and partners reducing the vendor lock-in and opening the market to new competitors. AT&T want to dynamically scale based on customer requirements (on demand growth). To do so, a set of APIs and dynamic policy control options should be exposed by a cloud distributed Network Function. The whole domain 2.0 architecture sample is depicted in Figure 7.

- **Google,** (*Jain et al., 2013; Kok-Kiong Yap et al., 2017*): Google has announced they put in production its SDN backbone named B4. This backbone is used for data center interconnection exclusively and does not connect end-users nor peer networks. However, its architecture relies on open network interfaces and open hardware. According to their reports, Google can move traffic through its network based on customer experience metrics.
- **Verizon** (*Planning, 2016*): Verizon released its network transformation plan in 2016. That plan relies upon the deployment of NFV and SDN techniques. The plan defines on a centralized network control to find significant benefits for its customers including elastic and scalable network-wide service creation and near real-time service delivery; The central control element introduce agility to its operative areas via dynamic resource allocation as well as automation of network provision. The solution has a multilayer coverage and proposes an End-to-End orchestrator on top of an SD-WAN controller interacting with the physical and virtual network functions.
- **Telefonica iFusion** (*Contreras et al., 2019*): The iFusion architectural design beholds the legacy and SDN-Ready devices' coexistence. Each major technology is treated as a domain and managed by its controller. These set of controllers directly interact with the network devices. On top of the domain controllers, there is a Software-Defined Transport Network Controller (SDTN), which is the main entry point to the network and the element that has the complete multi-technology/multi-domain view of the network. The full iFusion architecture is depicted in Figure 8.

Figure 8. SDN architecture proposed by Telefonica in the iFusion Program

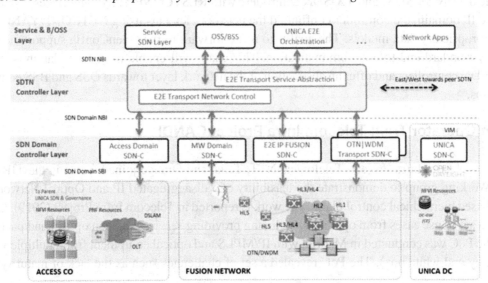

- **MUST** (Telecom Intra Project, 2020): In the Telecom Infra Project, several operators have joined their forces to create an Open Optical and Packet Transport SDN initiative. This initiative has promises like the open reference designs, programmability, and convergent networks to support the 5G networks' sustainable deployment.

Operator Trials: Telefonica iFusion Trials

Telefonica is carrying out the iFusion initiative, as explained in Contreras et al. (2019). In this initiative, a set of Operator's trials have been carried out in the past years. A field trial was carried out in Telefonica Colombia including multiple network controllers (two for IP/MPLS and two for DWDM) and a real-commercial-multi-vendor-operational network in order to demonstrate the viability of the implementations of programmable network interfaces that rely upon standard data models and protocols.

The work reported by Barguil et al. (2020) shows a Cisco implementation of an SDN controller using the iFusion interfaces and demonstrates that automation is possible, as documented in several IETF drafts. The experience acquired by this trial validates its implementation, compares the time consumed by the controller to implement a service using a data model with different workflows. That is, the same network data model can be used in several ways to produce similar results.

In Brazil, within the Vivo laboratory (Telefonica Brasil), a PoC was performed with the participation of the leading SDN solution providers, aiming at the development of a model of Northbound interface (NBI) and Southbound Interface (SBI) based on open standards definitions, to integrate the IP and optical domains. The methodology defined by Vivo to tackle the most significant number of limitations present in its day-to-day network operation and considering the short development time was through the usage of an agile methodology to rapidly release new functionalities based on the use cases definition and prioritization. The planning and operating teams divided the use cases into different groups based on their priority: Service Provisioning, Traffic Engineering, Inventory Support, Topology Discovery, Performance Management Support, Fault Management Support, and Network Creation. The final users exhaustively test each sprint/functionality and always validated, expecting the same result.

Following the interfaces' evolution and standardization, the manufacturers offered support for their Hierarchical SDN, IP-SDN, and TX-SDN controllers with RESTCONF/YANG interfaces support.

For the IP domain, the controller configured the network elements using NETCONF/YANG adapters using proprietary data models. The goal is to move forward to the OpenConfig support, achieving an entirely standard end-to-end communication. This chain will enable the consolidation of entirely agnostic SDN controllers and offer an abstraction of the network layer towards OSS and BSS equipment and systems.

Multiple Operator Trail: Telecom Infra Project CANDI

Within the Telecom Infra Project, Telefonica, NTT, Telia, and Orange joined forces in the TIP OOPT CANDI Working group to demonstrate the feasibility of a disaggregated IP and Optical Network with an SDN-based hierarchical control plane. The work is reported in Telecom Infra Project (2019). CANDI collected a set of use cases from operators, including providing services in open optical and packet networks. The PoC was conducted in Madrid, with IP/MPLS and optical equipment from multiple vendors (both legacy and white box). The PoC revealed a set of challenges such as the lack of maturity of the open interfaces supported by both Optical and IP/MPLS devices. In this PoC, OpenConfig was selected as the data model to use.

Research Trials: The Metro Haul Trials

Several operators joined together with research centers and SMEs to form the Metro Haul project. The project demonstrated the use of a hierarchical SDN architecture with a multi-layer network to support 5G Verticals. The SDN architecture of the demonstration is based on the concept of hierarchical orchestration, serving data connectivity to an OSM-based NVF-O. The parent controller acts as the single-entry point for support systems (OSS/BSS) to request network resources and plays the role of the hierarchical controller as defined earlier in the chapter.

One of the demonstrations, presented by *Muqaddas et al. (2020),* includes the deployment and testing of a crowdsourced live video streaming (CLVS) Network Service (NS). A CLVS is an example of an NS, in which thousands of users who attend an event (sports, concert, etc.) stream video footage from their smartphones to a CLVS platform. The content from all the users is edited in real time, producing an aggregated video, which can be broadcast to many viewers. The CLVS use case took advantage of the Metro-Haul infrastructure, since its Control and Management SDN-based system can rapidly provision a slice on top of the end-to-end compute/network resources and support the high capacity and low latency requirements. The multi-layer end-to-end network slices include Virtual Network Functions (VNFs) in multiple datacenters (with multiple Virtual Infrastructure Managers) and simultaneously dedicates packet and optical network resources, including Layer 2 VPNs and photonic media channels.

FUTURE PERSPECTIVES

As described in the chapter, SDN have been in the market for more than ten years with great technological success, allowing network "softwarization" and becoming a part of new network deployments. Since the introduction of the OpenFlow protocol in 2008, new and more advanced generations of SDN protocols have emerged and introduced into transport networks, cross-haul networks, Data Centers (DCs), and campus networks. Despite this optimistic market posture, the crude reality is that network operators are only slowly adopting bare SDN deployments. As described before, several SDOs are leading and continually introducing new technological features to the current SDN architecture; thus, some operators can claim no clear path to introduce SDN in their networks. Several barriers are currently blocking the adoption of this technology. However, the first SDN adoption barrier is related to network operator culture. Network engineers' workforce typically consists of hardware-focused technicians who deal with dedicated physical boxes. SDN will make software developers the primary workforce: they write code in development environments and configure networks using software configuration tools.

To fully enable network automation, it is critical to define viable use cases and workflows with standard interfaces that can operate in Greenfield and Brownfield deployments as suggested by "Hybrid SDN".

We have observed the confluence of Artificial Intelligence/Machine Learning (AI/ML) and 5G networks during the last few years. Similar to SDN, the AI/ML adoption is slowly evolving and does not have a clear adoption path yet. Automation and ML are two flips of the same coin and the applicability of automated decisions in this context is uncertain when dealing with challenges in network management, security, optimization, and scalability.

As service providers deploy 5G technology, 3GPP has released 17 and upcoming Beyond 5G (B5G) specification that will require massive flow management. Automation is essential in these scenarios, in which humans will not be able to manage and operate these networks. SDN has to provide the capabilities to fulfil these requirements. For example, flow aggregation at the network core is not efficient enough. Current SDN controller solutions, such as ONOS or OpenDayLight, cannot handle many flows realized as network intents. Current controller solutions consist of a monolithic software core that can synchronize with other deployed SDN controllers through specific protocols. Some limitations to this current software architecture have been raised lately by network operators. Organizations dealing with such controllers are slowly looking at possible solutions by completely redesigning SDN controllers. For example, μONOS promises to provide a cloud-native SDN controller. Cloud-native architectures consist of stateless microservice which interact with each other to fulfil network management tasks. However, only considering a microservice-based software architecture (even at the edge) is not enough to achieve this goal, as there is also a clear need for hardware-specific offloading in support for B5G scenarios. This can be achieved with the introduction of P4-based programmable switches as well as (FPGA-based) Smart NICs, GPUs, 5G gNodeB BS, and more physical network functions. Apart from hardware offloading and acceleration techniques, another significant challenge is to address both computational and network resources in a unified way. Network and computation resources represent a continuum within the network topology, where edge resources tend to be constrained as they geographically spread, while a centralized DC contains the cloud resources. There is a trade-off in resource efficiency between obtaining cheap computation resources in a centralized DC while needing network resources to reach the centralized DC. This also leads to the need to integrate SDN controllers in NFV and Mobile Edge Computing (MEC) orchestration approaches to be applied to B5G networks.

CONCLUSION

This chapter discussed the evolution from the "original" SDN approach defined by the separation of the control from the data plane, towards a "hybrid" SDN approach where control functions are spread over network elements and controllers. The "hybrid" SDN is an approach followed by operators to introduce automation and programmability at different levels, making it suitable for the optimization of resource usage while accommodating the most greedy applications. This chapter also highlights the work conducted by several SDOs.

Finally, the chapter presents how network providers are currently implementing SDO-documented frameworks and how such frameworks help them achieve the desired automation. In particular, hybrid SDN implementations from Brazil and Spain are presented, along with their challenges.

There is still a long path forward before achieving a data-driven network, mainly because SDOs are continuously producing models to cover new technologies. Available controllers need to evolve to a production-ready level to handle thousands of devices and precise abstractions between network and systems need to be provided by the controller to facilitate resource programming.

The network models are still in their infancy and are primarily influenced by how the SPs design network services.

Glossary

The Table 5 contains the abbreviations and glossary of the present chapter.

Table 6. Abbreviations and Glossary

Abbreviation	Definition
API	Application programming interface
BGP	Border Gateway Protocol
BSS	Business Support Systems
CE	Customer Edge
CRUD	Create, Read, Update and Delete
DWDM	Dense Wavelength Division Multiplexing
IETF	Internet Engineering Task Force
IGP	Interior Gateway Protocol
L2SM	L2VPN Service Model
L3NM	L3VPN Network Model
LDP	Label Distribution Protocol
LSP	Label Switch Path
MEF	Metro Ethernet Forum
MPLS	Multiprotocol Label Switching
NBI	Northbound interface
NMDA	Network Management Datastore Architecture
ONF	Open Networking Foundation
OSS	Operation Support Systems
PCE	Path Computation Element
PCEP	Path Computation Element Communication Protocol
PE	Provider Edge
QoS	Quality of service
RD	Route Distinguisher
RPC	Remote Procedure Call
RSVP	Resource Reservation Protocol
RT	Route Target
SBI	South Bound Interface
SDN	Software Defined Network
TAPI	Transport API
TE	Traffic engineering
TTL	Time to live
VLAN	Virtual local area network
VPN	Virtual Private Network
VRF	Virtual Routing and Forwarding

ACKNOWLEDGMENT

The work carried out to prepare the chapter includes outcomes of multiple IETF discussions, research carried out in the Metro Haul H2020 project and the iFUSION project in Telefonica.

REFERENCES

Awduche, D., Chiu, A., Elwalid, A., Widjaja, I., & Xiao, X. (2002). *Overview and principles of internet traffic engineering.* IETF RFC 3272.

Barguil, S., Gonzalez de Dios, O., Lopez, V. Gagliano, R., & Carretero, I. (2020). *Experimental validation of L3 VPN Network Model for improving VPN Service design and Provisioning.* CNSM 2020.

Barguil, S., O, G. d. D., Boucadair, M., Munoz, L., & Aguado, A. (2021b*). A Layer 3 VPN Network YANG Model.* IETF draft-ietf-opsawg-l3sm-l3nm.

Barguil, S., de Dios, O. G., Boucadair, M., Munoz, L., Jalil, L., & Ma, J. (2021a). *A Layer 2 VPN Network YANG Model.* IETF draft-ietf-opsawg-l2nm.

Bemby, S., Lu, H., Zadeh, K. H., Bannazadeh, H., & Leon-Garcia, A. (2015). Vino: SDN overlay to allow seamless migration across heterogeneous infrastructure. In *2015 IFIP/IEEE International Symposium on Integrated Network Management (IM)*, (pp. 782–785). IEEE. 10.1109/INM.2015.7140375

Bierman, A., Bjorklund, M., & Watsen, K. (2017). *RESTCONF protocol.* IETF RFC 8040.

Birk, M., Choudhury, G., Cortez, B., Goddard, A., Padi, N., Raghuram, A., Tse, K., Tse, S., Wallace, A., & Xi, K. (2016). Evolving to an SDN-enabled ISP Backbone: Key Technologies and Applications. *IEEE Communications Magazine, 54*(10), 129–135. doi:10.1109/MCOM.2016.7588281

Bjorklund, M. (2010). *YANG-a data modeling language for the network configuration protocol (NETCONF).* IETF RFC6020.

Bjorklund, M. (2016). *The YANG 1.1 Data Modeling Language.* IETF RFC 7950.

Bjorklund, M., Schoenwaelder, J., Shafer, P., Watsen, K., & Wilton, R. (2018). *Network Management Datastore Architecture (nmda).* IETF RFC, RFC 8342.

Boucadair, M. & Jacquenet, C. (2014). *Software-defined Networking: A Perspective from within a Service Provider Environment.* IETF RFC 7149.

Campanella, A., Okui, H., Mayoral, A., Kashiwa, D., de Dios, O. G., Verchere, D., Van, Q. P., Giorgetti, A., Casellas, R., & Morro, R. (2019). ODTN: Open disaggregated transport network. Discovery and control of a disaggregated optical network through open source software and open APIs. In 2019 OpticalFiber Communications Conference and Exhibition (OFC), (pp. 1–3). IEEE.

Casado, M., Koponen, T., Shenker, S., & Tootoonchian, A. (2012, August). Fabric: a retrospective on evolving SDN. In *Proceedings of the first workshop on Hot topics in software defined networks* (pp. 85-90). 10.1145/2342441.2342459

Clemm, A., Medved, J., Varga, R., Bahadur, N., Ananthakrishnan, H., & Liu, X. (2018). *A yang data model for network topologies.* IETF RFC 8345.

Contreras, L., Gonzalez de Dios, O., Lopez, V., Fernandez-Palacios, J., & Folgueira, J. (2019). iFUSION: Standards-based SDN Architecture for Carrier Transport Network. In *2019 IEEE Conference on Standards for Communications and Networking (CSCN)*, (pp. 1–7). IEEE. 10.1109/CSCN.2019.8931386

Demchenko, Y., Filiposka, S., de Vos, M., Regvart, D., Karaliotas, T., Grosso, P., & de Laat, C. (2016). Zerotouch provisioning (ZTP) model and infrastructure components for multi-provider cloud services provisioning. In *2016 IEEE International Conference on Cloud Engineering Workshop (IC2EW)*, (pp. 184–189). IEEE.

Edelman, J., Lowe, S. S., & Oswalt, M. (2018). *Network Programmability and Automation: Skills for the Next-Generation Network Engineer.* O'Reilly Media, Inc.

Enns, R., Bjorklund, M., Schoenwaelder, J., & Bierman, A. (2011). *Network Configuration Protocol.* IETF RFC 6020.

Farrel, A., Vasseur, J. P., & Ash, J. (2006). *A Path Computation Element (PCE)-based Architecture.* IETF RFC 4655

Haleplidis, E., Pentikousis, K., Denazis, S., Salim, J. H., Meyer, D., & Koufopavlou, O. (2015). *Software-defined networking (SDN): Layers and architecture terminology.* IETF RFC 7426.

Hootsuite & We Are Social. (2021). *Digital 2021 Global Digital Overview.* Retrieved 11 March 2020 from, https://datareportal.com/reports/digital-2021-global-digital-overview

Jain, S., Kumar, A., Mandal, S., Ong, J., Poutievski, L., Singh, A., Venkata, S., Wanderer, J., Zhou, J., Zhu, M., Zolla, J., Hölzle, U., Stuart, S., & Vahdat, A. (2013). B4: Experience with a globally-deployed software defined wan. *Computer Communication Review*, *43*(4), 3–14. doi:10.1145/2534169.2486019

Libes, D. (1995). *Exploring Expect: a Tcl-based toolkit for automating interactive programs.* O'Reilly Media, Inc.

Lopez, V., Vilalta, R., Uceda, V., Mayoral, A., Casellas, R., Martinez, R., Munoz, R., & Palacios, J. P. F. (2016). Transport API: A solution for SDN in Carriers Networks. In *ECOC 2016; 42nd European Conference on Optical Communication*, (pp. 1–3). VDE.

Mittal, V., Nautiyal, L., & Mittal, M. (2017). *Cloud testing-the future of contemporary software testing.* In *2017 International Conference on Next Generation Computing and Information Systems (ICNGCIS)*, (pp. 131–136). IEEE. 10.1109/ICNGCIS.2017.11

Muqaddas. (2020). *Field Trial of Multi-Layer Slicing Over Disaggregated Optical Networks Enabling End-to-End Crowdsourced Video Streaming.* ECOC 2020.

ONF TR-502. (2014). *The SDN architecture, issue 1.0.* Available online at https:www.opennetworking.orgimagesstoriesdownloadssdn-resourcestechnical-reportsTR_SDN_ARCH_1.0_06062014.pdf

Planning, V. N. I. (2016). SDN-NFV reference architecture. *Version*, *1*, 8–34.

Research and Markets. (2020). *$32+ Billion Worldwide Software-Defined Networking Market to 2025 - Featuring Cisco, Huawei & VMware Among Others.* Retrieved 10 March 2021 from, https://www.globenewswire.com/news-release/2020/08/18/2079769/0/en/32-Billion-Worldwide-Software-Defined-Networking-Market-to-2025-Featuring-Cisco-Huawei-VMware-Among-Others.html

Saad, T., Gandhi, R., Liu, X., Beeram, V., & Bryskin, I. (2021). *A YANG Data Model for Traffic Engineering Tunnels, Label Switched Paths and Interfaces.* IETF Draft, draft-ietf-teas-yang-te-25.

Schoenwaelder, J. (2003). *Overview of the 2002 IAB Network Management Workshop.* IETF RFC 3535.

Telecom Infra Project. (2019). *CANDI First Experimental Demonstration.* Available online at https://www.ntt.co.jp/topics_e/tip2019/pdf/TIP_CANDI_1st_Experimental_Demonstration.pdf

Telecom Intra Project. (2020). *Open Transport SDN Whitepaper.* Available online at https://cdn.brandfolder.io/D8DI15S7/at/jh6nnbb6bjvn7w7t5jbgm5n/OpenTransportArchitecture-Whitepaper_TIP_Final.pdf

Virtualisation, E. N. F. (2015). Ecosystem; report on SDN usage in NFV architectural framework. *ETSI Netw. Funct. Virtualisat. Ind. Specif. Group GS NFV-EVE, 5,* V1.

Vissicchio, S., Vanbever, L., & Bonaventure, O. (2014). Opportunities and research challenges of hybrid software defined networks. *Computer Communication Review, 44*(2), 70–75. doi:10.1145/2602204.2602216

Wen, B., Fioccola, G., Xie, C., & Jalil, L. (2018). *A YNAG Data Model for Layer 2 Virtual Private Network (l2vpn) Service Delivery.* IETF RFC 8466.

Wu, Q., Boucadair, M., Lopez, D., Xie, C., & Geng, L. (2021). *A Framework for Automating Service and Network Management with YANG.* IETF RFC 8969.

Wu, Q., Litkowski, S., Tomotaki, L., & Ogaki, K. (2018). *YANG Data Model for L3VPN Service Delivery.* IETF RFC 8299.

Wu, Q., Liu, W., & Farrel, A. (2018). *Service Models Explained.* IETF RFC 8309.

YANG Catalog. (2021). Available at https://yangcatalog.org/

Yap, K. K., Motiwala, M., Rahe, J., Padgett, S., Holliman, M., Baldus, G., ... Vahdat, A. (2017, August). Taking the edge off with espresso: Scale, reliability and programmability for global internet peering. In *Proceedings of the Conference of the ACM Special Interest Group on Data Communication* (pp. 432-445). 10.1145/3098822.3098854

KEY TERMS AND DEFINITIONS

NETCONF: Network Configuration Protocol (NETCONF) is a network management protocol developed in the IETF. It provides mechanisms to install, manipulate, and delete the configuration of network devices. Its operations are realized on top of a simple Remote Procedure Call (RPC). The NETCONF protocol uses an Extensible Markup Language (XML) based data encoding for the configuration data as well as the protocol messages. The protocol messages are exchanged on top of a secure transport protocol.

RESTCONF: Uses HTTP methods to provide Create, Read, Update, and Delete operations on a server that implements NETCONF datastores.

SDN: Software-defined networking (SDN) is an architecture that decouples the network control and forwarding functions enabling the network control to become directly programmable and the underlying infrastructure to be abstracted for applications and network services.

SDN Controller: Is a key component of the SDN architecture. It is in charge of a set of network elements. It has standard South Bound Interfaces to communicate with network elements. It also has a North Bound Interface to communicate with the SDN orchestrator and the OSS.

YANG Data Model: A data model describes how data is represented and accessed using the YANG language.

Chapter 8
ONAP:
An Open Source Toolkit for Zero Touch Automation

Eric Debeau
Orange S.A., France

Veronica Quintuna-Rodriguez
Orange S.A., France

ABSTRACT

The ever-increasing complexity of networks and services advocates for the introduction of automation techniques to facilitate the design, the delivery, and the operation of such networks and services. The emergence of both network function virtualization (NFV) and software-defined networks (SDN) enable network flexibility and adaptability which open the door to on-demand services requiring automation. In aim of holding the increasing number of customized services and the evolved capabilities of public networks, the open network automation platform (ONAP), which is in open source, particularly addresses automation techniques while enabling dynamic orchestration, optimal resource allocation capabilities, and end-to-end service lifecycle management. This chapter addresses the key ONAP features that can be used by industrials and operators to automatically manage and orchestrate a wide set of services ranging from elementary network functions (e.g., firewalls) to more complex services (e.g., 5G network slices).

INTRODUCTION

The evolution of telecommunication networks towards on-demand services has raised the need for automation to facilitate the massive deployment of tailored services. The emergence of virtualization technology has clearly played a crucial role in this groundbreaking evolution. The introduction of cloud native principles when implementing network functions promises flexible and accurate management of both resources and services. Network operators can then instantiate virtual functions on the fly at various network locations as needed to meet customers' requirements.

DOI: 10.4018/978-1-7998-7646-5.ch008

Today, End-to-End (E2E) network services can be conceived as a chain of Cloud-native Network Functions (CNFs), Virtual Network Functions (VNFs), Physical Network Functions (PNFs), or a combination thereof. The intrinsic principles of cloud native networks implemented as a bundle of microservices particularly enable network scalability, reliability, and agility. Microservices may be instantiated on Commercial Off-the-Shelf (COTS) servers, while these servers are distributed at different levels of the network.

To manage hundreds of servers, the widely adopted NFV architecture (ETSI-NFV, 2013) considers the so-called Virtualized Infrastructure Management (VIM). It particularly performs the allocation of computing, storage, and network resources. The VIM is also responsible for collecting and monitoring data. The VIM is part of the Management and Orchestration (MANO) framework proposed by the European Telecommunications Standards Institute (ETSI) (ETSI-NFV-MAN, 2014) where resides the Network Service Orchestrator functional block.

Beyond resource allocation, various challenges come with network virtualization and particularly with the required automation, e.g., VNF placement, multi-vendor solutions, VNF lifecycle management, monitoring automation, E2E orchestration, multi-domain and multi-cloud management, close loop automation, etc.

To address these challenges, ONAP was created in 2017 (ONAP, 2021b) as a result of a merger of OpenECOMP and Open Orchestrator (Open-O) solutions. ONAP is an open source project hosted by the Linux Foundation with contributions from major network operators (e.g., AT&T, China Mobile, Orange, Bell Canada, Deutsche Telekom, Vodafone, SwissCom, Telecom Italia, Telstra), main network vendors (e.g., Ericsson, Huawei, Nokia, Cisco, and ZTE), and IT integrators (e.g., Amdocs, IBM, Tech Mahindra). The full list of members can be found at (Members, 2021). The main goal set for ONAP is to develop a policy-driven orchestration and automation platform while considering a full lifecycle management of network services and their components, i.e., VNFs, CNFs, and PNFs. ONAP works in strong relation with standardization bodies as 3GPP, ETSI, IETF, and TMF in order to align the ONAP features to the available standards. Other orchestration platforms are under development such as Open Source MANO (OSM) which is particularly based on ETSI-NFV MANO (OSM, 2020) or Open Baton.

For network operators, ONAP enables orchestration, control, and automated operation of end-to-end network services. ONAP aims to simplify integration of multi-vendor equipment and products while reducing Capital Expenditure (CAPEX) and Operational Expenditure OPEX costs. ONAP additionally promises advanced monitoring and analytics in order to guarantee negotiated Service Level Agreements (SLAs). The dynamic negotiation can be performed between a customer and a service provider (namely, network operators) whose outcomes give rise to a customized service model and feed the orchestration logic to be addressed during the whole service lifecycle, i.e., ONAP enables to dynamically design and structure the service that best accommodates to the customer's needs.

Supporting performance monitoring, control-loop automation, and service optimization is especially important when considering the virtualization of critical network functions that have to fulfill very stringent requirements in terms of latency and/or throughput. That is notably the case of mobile networks, especially when considering the Radio Access Network (RAN).

This chapter addresses the main features offered by ONAP (as per 2021) and introduces a set of illustrative use cases that evidence the strengths of this platform to manage end-to-end network services. The chapter is organized as follows:

- Section "Zero Touch Automation Principles" introduces the approach of deploying and maintaining networks without human intervention.
- Section "The ONAP Ecosystem" describes the main interaction between ONAP, standardization bodies, and other open source initiatives.
- Section "ONAP architecture, components and assets" describes the main ONAP components as well the required workflow to design and deploy network services.
- Section "ONAP, a catalyst for network efficiency" presents the ONAP features that open the door towards efficient networks by means of optimization techniques, closed control loops, AI-based analytics, etc. CNFs and PNFs management are also described by means of two use cases.
- Section "Key ONAP use cases around 5G" particularly addresses the E2E Network Slicing use case, the service deployment automation from the customer order, and ORAN-based access networks.
- Section "Conclusions and Perspectives" concludes the chapter with some future perspectives.

This chapter does not provide neither guidelines to use ONAP nor detailed modeling concepts. The authors invite the readers to refer to (ONAP Wiki, 2021), the official ONAP documentation (ONAP, 2021b), and existing courses (ONAP Courses, 2021) to start their ONAP journey.

ZERO TOUCH AUTOMATION PRINCIPLES

The increasing number of network services is pushing service providers and notably network operators to fully automate the lifecycle of communication services. Zero-touch is about minimizing human intervention from the activation up to deactivation of service chains. It includes instantiation, monitoring, and Service Level Agreement (SLA) enforcement. The diversity and complexity of services together with the incessant traffic growth are making automation an imperative and not an option.

The key enablers of zero-touch automation are network function virtualization, artificial intelligence and CI/CD (continuous integration and continuous deployment) features. Software-based networks must fit modularity, extensibility, and scalability principles, while management and orchestration procedures need to implement efficient closed control loops to automatically monitor the network behavior and to execute actions when needed. Automated orchestration platforms that include CI/CD procedures enable deploying new software-based network releases without manual intervention to upgrade the network.

Zero-touch automation is becoming a priority for future networks; the ETSI has particularly created in 2017 a new industry standard group to address fully automation, namely Zero-Touch Network and Service Management (ZSM) (ETSI-GS-ZSM, 2019). The ZSM group was chartered to drive the design of reference architecture, identify requirements, and propose management solutions for zero-touch automation. The baseline ZSM architecture enables end-to-end service automation while including processes involved in delivery, deployment, configuration, assurance, and optimization.

Full automation brings new business opportunities, since it does not only simplify and optimize operations allowing time-to-market acceleration of products, but boosts new network behaviors, e.g., latency reduction, data rate improvements while using AI RAN controllers or AI-based Cooperative Multi-Point (CoMP) solutions.

Main benefits of zero-touch automation are in relation with optimization. Beyond cost reduction, automation introduces agility and reliability when deploying and operating services. Automation enables resource efficiency utilization when instantiating VNFs or CNFs across several network domains (e.g., RAN, Core, Transport). VNF placement algorithms can be implemented in specialized modules that are in charge of allocating cloud resources (computing capacity, storage) to virtual network functions. Other examples of network optimization that might be better accommodated with automation are energy saving, the correct allocation of network resources, and the usage of optimized schedulers for processing critical tasks (e.g., those of radio signal processing in mobile networks) avoid wasting resources and energy.

The ability to automatically manage and operate end-to-end service chains enables the customization of services which can be offered from a template-based catalog. Such service catalog exposes to the business layers the available network services that can be customized and automatically deployed by the production entities such as ONAP. Management automation is also a key enabler for 5G use cases, notably for the massive deployment of network slices and private networks for vertical markets.

THE ONAP ECOSYSTEM

ONAP as an orchestrator has a central position for consolidating and making possible the implementation of new architectures (as those that are proposed by standardization bodies ETSI-NFV, 3GPP, TMF, or IETF) proposed in the framework of future networks over the past few years.

From its outset, the ONAP community has worked in tight relation with Standards Developing Organizations (SDOs), introducing as much as possible standardized interfaces between the various ONAP components, and exposing the required boundary interfaces to interact with external components.

In order to improve this collaboration, the ETSI ZSM group is particularly adding efforts to help the coordination between SDOs and open source solutions. The goal is to align approaches coming from various SDOs and implement them into a single software solution. In addition, ONAP works in collaboration with other communities or alliances (e.g., O-RAN) based on the openness approach in order to assure the overall consistency of solutions. Figure 1 shows the current interactions between ONAP, SDOs, and other communities.

ONAP as a global orchestration platform can be considered by various initiatives that addresses the digital transformation of telecoms. For instance, the Open Core Network (OCN) (OCN, 2021) of Telecom Infra Project (TIP) (TIP, 2020), which particularly considers the development of cloud-native core functions, may use ONAP as a multi-domain (RAN, Core, Transport) orchestration platform. It is worth noting that OCN already addresses the design and development of an orchestration framework for managing OCN microservices; an upper orchestration layer can be then considered for dealing with E2E services.

IETF

ONAP works in strong relation with IETF models. ONAP has particularly adopted the IETF Framework for Automating Service and Network Management with YANG (IETF, 2021) in the Cross Domain and Cross Layer VPN (CCVPN) use cases. ONAP uses IETF-based transport YANG models as the southbound interface of ONAP in order to ensure interoperability.

Figure 1. ONAP relationships

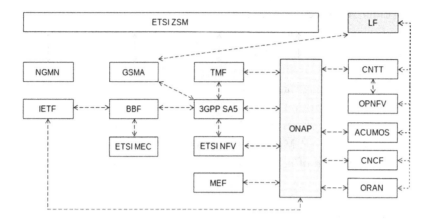

MEF

Since 2017, ONAP and Metro Ethernet Forum (MEF) - an industry forum (MEF, 2021) - work together to accelerate the rollout of agile services across automated and software based networks. ONAP and MEF are leveraging resources from a global federation of more than 250 network, cloud and technology providers.

ETSI NFV

ONAP and ETSI's NFV ISG are evolving at a different pace. However, their strong relationship facilitates the convergence towards the definition of packages for various network functions. ETSI's NFV (ETSI-NFV, 2013) ISG, chartered in 2012, specifies the Network Functions Virtualization (NFV) architecture and the main building blocks like Virtual Infrastructure Manager (VIM) or MANO as well as a set of REST APIs. ONAP's Service Design and Creation (SDC) embeds some descriptors that are compatible with those defined by ETSI's NFV ISG. Furthermore, the Service Orchestrator offers a set of APIs that comply with ETSI's NFV specifications. In addition, the Service Orchestrator provides an interface with the Virtualized Network Function Management (VNFM).

3GPP

The 3rd Generation Partnership Project (3GPP) gathers various telecommunications standard development organizations to produce specifications for telecommunication services mainly based on cellular networks. ONAP and 3GPP have particularly established a strong partnership to align the specifications for the network management and orchestration areas. Management, Orchestration and Charging for 3GPP Systems is addressed by the 3GPP SA5 group. An example of this collaboration is the implementation of the Virtual Event Streaming (VES) (3GPP-VES, 2020) specially used for monitoring VNFs. The VES was specified by 3GPP, implemented and extended by ONAP.

TMF

TM Forum is an association gathering the main actors in the telecommunications area with a strong focus on the Information System. ONAP has leveraged various concepts and interfaces from TMF. This is particularly the case of the Northbound Interface (NBI) module. The NBI plays a crucial role to support the concept of open architectures, decoupled management, and digital business as specified by the TMF Open Digital Architecture (ODA). ODA aims to transform business models by introducing deployment agility and interoperability, by simplifying solutions to be easily integrated and upgraded, and furthermore by digitizing the management of services and commercial relations. ODA aims to replace the traditional Operation Support System (OSS) and Business Support System (BSS).

CNTT

The Cloud iNfrastructure Telco Taskforce (CNTT) was born in 2019 (LFN, 2021) through a partnership between Global System for Mobile Communications Association (GSMA) and the Linux Foundation involving service providers, VNF suppliers, and infrastructure companies. The goal of CNTT is to provide standardized infrastructures for both VNF-based and CNF-based network functions. CNTT works in close collaboration with Linux Foundation Networking (LFN) and OPNFV (OPNFV, 2021) which implements, tests and deploys tools to optimize the integration and deployment of NFV infrastructures and the onboarding of VNFs/CNFs.

ACUMOS

Acumos is an open source project hosted by the Linux Foundation Artificial Intelligence (LF AI) group (LFAI, 2020). Acumos provides tools to share AI models and to convert them to ready-to-use Docker containers with REST APIs. ONAP and Acumos collaboration opens the door to use applications produced by Acumos as ONAP services within the Data Collection Analytics and Events (DCAE) module. Events received by ONAP feed a data lake to help data scientists to build their models relative to the networks. Acumos transforms this model into a set of microservices that are compatible with ONAP and which can be used in a control loop to complement the current set of analytic tools. ONAP and Acumos communities are working together to improve the integration of AI models on top of events managed by ONAP.

CNCF

The Cloud Native Computing Foundation (CNCF) was created in 2015 under the Linux Foundation umbrella (CNCF, 2021). It hosts a large number of open source projects (Kubernetes, Helm, Prometheus, Jaeger) to manage applications based on containers. ONAP is closely collaborating with the CNCF to leverage the cloud native approach for ONAP components. Within ONAP, installation is based on Helm and the various components run on top of a Kubernetes cluster. To manage CNFs (i.e., network functions deployed as Docker containers in Kubernetes clusters), ONAP fully relies on Kubernetes and is currently evaluating how to include telemetry solutions from CNCF.

ORAN

The O-RAN Alliance was founded by operators to define open interfaces and to accelerate the delivery of products, notably those involved in the New Radio (NR) for 5G networks. The O-RAN architecture particularly involves the Radio Access Network (RAN) units and introduces RAN Intelligent Controllers (RICs). ONAP is adapting various components in order to meet the requirements of the O-RAN architecture (O-RAN, 2020). RAN unities and the RICs directly interfaces with a Service Management and Orchestration (SMO) platform that can be supported by ONAP. ONAP particularly embeds the Non Real Time RIC which is in charge of RAN optimization as well as of performing Fault, Configuration, Accounting, Performance, and Security management (FCAPS) procedures.

On The ONAP Community

A Technical Steering Committee (TSC) drives the main technical directions of the ONAP community. The TSC prioritizes the features to include in the incoming releases and defines the road-map. The ONAP community involves also various sub-committees which are dedicated to cover transverse topics. They are: Architecture subcommittee, Control Loop Subcommittee, Modeling subcommittee, ONAP Security coordination, Open Lab Subcommittee, and Requirements subcommittee. Two main task forces are also set up to deal with ONAP for Enterprise Business and Cloud Native aspects.

Around thirty projects are responsible for implementing ONAP functions and delivering source code. Most of them are dedicated to the provisioning of ONAP components while few others cover integration, installation (namely, ONAP Operation Manager (OOM)) and documentation. In 2020, more than 600 developers coming from 40 organizations committed code in ONAP (LFN Analytics, 2020).

Each ONAP project is responsible for developing new features according to the rules defined by the TSC (code quality, tests, documentation, etc.). Every code modification is associated within a Continuous Integration chain that executes the various Jenkins (Jenkins, 2020) jobs to validate the code. Orange has particularly introduced a 'Gating' mechanism that enables the deployment of a full ONAP solution and performs a large number of tests for every code modification in the OOM project (Richomme & Desbureaux, 2020). Tests include security and health checks on every component and on end-to-end procedures.

On the ONAP Adoption by Network Operators

Various operators joined ONAP as founding members in 2017, in the aim of developing an ecosystem to help the uptake of NFV-based solutions. ONAP promises to keep software independence and openness.

In 2018, Orange and AT&T led a multi-tenant ONAP demonstration while building on-demand end-to-end layer-two services in a multi-site environment, i.e., a site managed by AT&T and another by Orange (MEF, 2018). From first releases, network operators have been leading the implementation of various modules, use cases and contributing to test and document. For instance, Orange led the deployment of a full SD-WAN service in 2019 (Debeau & Al-Hakim, 2019), China Mobile is leading the E2E network Slicing use case from Frankfurt release, AT&T is leading the development of the control loop framework, etc.

To accelerate ONAP adoption, network operators set up lab trials to test ONAP enhancements and to contribute to the identification and development of new features. For example, Orange made available an OpenLab platform to boost the ONAP adoption. The final goal is to let start using and testing ONAP (OpenLab, 2018) to community members but also to external people as academics, individuals, and developers. Furthermore, Orange in collaboration with Deutsche Telekom have built a Phyton-based SDK to automate the onboarding and instantiation procedures with restricted features (Desbureaux & Richomme, 2020). This SDK also enables improving the integration chain, mainly the code validation proposed by the various contributors.

ONAP has been widely adopted in research, for instance to evaluate the management and orchestration of 5G networks. ONAP enables on-boarding open-source based network functions. The deployment of an end-to-end 4G mobile network (involving Core and RAN functions) on the basis of open source solutions as OAI, where commercial devices can be connected, is presented in (Quintuna, Guillemin, & Boubendir, 2019), lifecycle management and control loops for network slicing is addressed in (Quintuna, Guillemin, & Boubendir, 2020a). The Cloud-RAN factory use case which supports the deployment of remote, distributed and centralized RAN units is demonstrated in (Quintuna et al., 2020b).

To facilitate the VNF and CNF onboarding while using ONAP, network operators are including ONAP compliancy requests in their RFPs. Such requirements relate to VNF/CNF descriptors, availably of open APIs to fully configure VNFs/CNFs, and the capability of monitoring network services while using ONAP DCAE collectors.

ONAP ARCHITECTURE AND COMPONENTS

ONAP provides a unified framework to design, deploy, and maintain network services. ONAP aims to be both vendor- and infrastructure- agnostic (ONAP, 2021b). For network operators or more generally, Communication Service Providers (CSPs), ONAP enables the orchestration of physical, virtual, and cloud-native network functions. These network functions (PNFs/VNFs/CNFs) can be deployed, for example, on dedicated, VM-based, or container-based infrastructures.

The ONAP platform adopts a modular and layered architecture which facilitates integration and enables supporting heterogeneous environments. It particularly provides two key frameworks, design- and run-time environments, whose components are maintained by ONAP Operations Manager (OOM). Both frameworks fulfill operators and network/cloud provider requirements.

The design-time enables network service designers to model a service. It provides tools to define resources, services, and products including policies (rules), packaging, and testing.

The run-time performs actions that have been defined during the design time, i.e., executing policies and managing the various network components and artifacts that belong to a network service.

To deal with the full life-cycle of network services within either design- or run-time, ONAP (ONAP, 2021b) is composed of several components. ONAP architecture is shown in Figure 2.

Main ONAP Components

ONAP is composed of a large number of elements including various interfaces towards external systems, modeling tools, controllers, etc. Each ONAP component involves various modules and offers REST APIs that are deployed as Docker (Docker, 2020) containers on top of a Kubernetes cluster.

Figure 2. ONAP Components

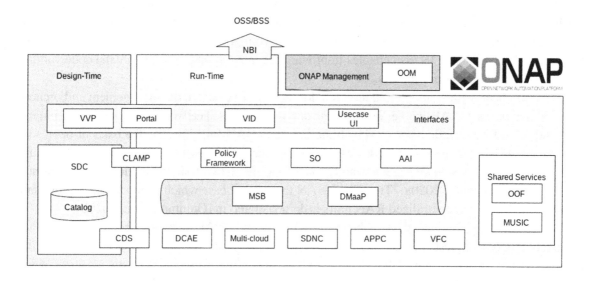

Design-Time Components

- **Service Design and Creation (SDC)** is a modeling and design tool that manages both resources and services. SDC produces and maintains metadata describing these elements (resources and services) and their operations. The assets at the resource and service levels are stored in a repository (namely, the Catalog) and used by all ONAP components during both design- and run-time.
- **Controller Design Studio (CDS)** used to define various rules to be executed during pre- and post-instantiation of network services. It is then possible to apply rules (e.g., naming conventions for virtual machines) or require external systems to acquire parameters during the deployment phase of network services (e.g., an IP address from an IP Address Management (IPAM) system). These rules are stored in a Controller Blueprint Archive (CBA) and are then associated to the network function by the SDC.
- **VNF Validation Program (VVP)** is used in order to validate the network service models, i.e., the heat files that describe the network and cloud components of a given network service.

Run-Time, Interfaces & Components

- **North-Bound Interface (NBI)** defines a set of TMF-based Application Programming Interfaces (APIs) through which external environments can interact with ONAP, e.g., Business Support System (BSS) (ONAP, 2021a). NBI APIs mainly concern service orders, service inventory, and service specifications.
- **Portal** provides a web-based dashboard to access both design- and run-time functionalities, based on user roles: designer, tester, governor, operator, and super-user.
- **Use case User Interface (UUI)** aims to provide a Graphical User Interface (GUI) for end-users (mainly operators) to access specific ONAP use cases, e.g., the 5G slicing GUI developed to man-

age services, slices, and sub-networks belonging to the E2E network slicing use case. Other GUIs are proposed to support E2E lifecycle management, VNF package management, etc.

- **Virtual Infrastructure Deployment (VID)** component enables the instantiation of network functions or components as well as scaling and upgrading existing VNF instances.

Run-Time, Workflow Engine and Controllers

- **Service Orchestrator (SO)** provides a workflow engine based on open-soure Camunda (Camunda, 2020) and uses the Business Process Model and Notation (BPMN) (OMG, 2021). The ONAP SO aims at providing an ETSI-aligned hierarchical orchestration platform for dealing with E2E services, network services, VNFs/CNFs/PNFs, infrastructure services and resources. The ONAP SO particularly automates the creation, modification and removal of these assets.
- **Multi-VIM/Cloud** enables the deployment and the operation of network services on multiple infrastructure environments either VM- or container-based platforms (e.g., OpenStack, Kubernetes).
- **Software Defined Network Controller (SDNC)** is a global controller provided by ONAP which manages the network configuration of cloud computing resources. SDNC is based on open-source OpenDayLight and can be interconnected with third-party SDN controllers. Commonly, a single SDN controller shall be deployed by each orchestration environment; however, dedicated or local SDN controllers can be invoked if needed.
- **Application Controller (APPC)** manages the application configuration of Network Functions (NFs).
- **Virtual Function Component (VFC)** provides both an ETSI NFV-compliant Network Function Virtualization Orchestrator (NFVO) and a Virtual Network Function Management (VNFM), which manage virtual services and the associated infrastructure.

Run-Time, Control-Loop Components

- **Data Collection Analytics and Events (DCAE)** provides a set of modules to collect events coming from the various network elements. DCAE can also provide analytics based on collected data. The collected data is mainly consumed by the analytic services, but can be also used by other components such as Policy Framework.
- **Control Loop Automation Management Platform (CLAMP)** enables the design and the management of control loops for a given network service at both design- and run-time. CLAMP is particularly interesting for operators since it aims to automate the lifecycle of services and their individual components, e.g., VNFs/CNFs, enabling OPEX reduction. CLAMP interacts with various ONAP components mainly DCAE, SDC, Data Movement-as-a-Platform (DMaaP), and Policy Framework.
- **Policy Framework** enables the definition, the deployment, and the execution of operation rules or policies which are specific to the network services and/or to their elements (e.g., VNFs, CNFs, VNF Components (VNFCs)). The goal of this component is to automate the policy enforcement of virtual network services (or other applications) in order to meet the performance requirements of a given service (e.g., reducing latency while dynamically migrating microservices as close as possible to end users). The ONAP policies are structured according to Topology and Orchestration Specification for Cloud Applications (TOSCA) data models (ONAP, 2021b, ONAP, 2021d).

Run-Time, Shared Services

ONAP makes available various shared services enabling added value capabilities like policy-driven workload optimization, resource allocation, multi-side coordination, and security. The most relevant shared services are listed below:

- **Active and Available Inventory (A&AI)** is a data structure designed to storage design- and run-time information of services, resources, and products in order to provide a real-time view of each of them and their relationships with each other.
- **Data Movement-as-a-Platform (DMaaP)** is a topic-based message bus that allows effective communication between ONAP components and processes. DMaaP relies on Kafka Message Queuing (MQ) services (Kafka, 2020), and enables data transport from any source (producer) to any target (consumer).
- **ONAP Optimization Framework (OOF)** provides a framework to build optimization services such as NF placement across various sites and/or clouds on the basis of optimization strategies or customized algorithms relying on service constraints, platform capabilities, etc. Optimization algorithms can then be implemented and associated to network services.
- **Multi-Site Coordination (MUSIC)** supports global scale infrastructure requirements, e.g., it enables to register and manage service states across multi-site deployments.
- **MicroService Bus (MSB)** provides fundamental operation features and particularly microservices registration and discovery for ONAP components.
- **ONAP Operations Manager (OOM)** is a key component which maintains the life-cycle of all ONAP components. OOM uses Kubernetes capabilities to provide scalability, resiliency, and efficiency to ONAP components.

ONAP Assets For Managing Network Services

ONAP deals with two levels of assets: resources and services.

Resources

A resource is composed of a single or several network components, together with the required information to manage the resource from its instantiation until its removal. ONAP particularly considers three kinds of resources:

- Application resources, which enable defining over-the-top software applications, e.g., virtual reality, gaming software, etc.
- Network resources, which refer to all network functions, i.e., VNFs/CNFs/PNFs, for instance the Access and Mobility Management Function (AMF) of 5G core. ONAP enables defining by means of heat templates or helm charts, the virtual network functions and their associated resources (ports, networks, VMs/containers).
- Infrastructure resources that enable the definition and configuration of computing, RAM and storage capacity.

Services

Services are composed of a bundle of resources (Figure 3). This hierarchical model enables the definition of network services based on service function chaining principles where E2E network services can be formed by a chain of VNFs, CNFs, and PNFs.

Figure 3. ONAP assets

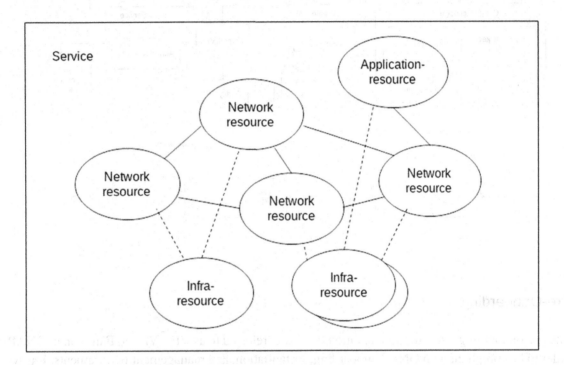

The service definition (as well as resource definition) involves both information and deployment artifacts. Information artifacts include the service features which are provided by the vendor. On the other hand, the deployment of artifacts includes the required ONAP information in order to manage the lifecycle of the underlying services (or resources).

Service Deployment Workflow

The process for readying a service for distribution involves various roles and stages which are based on a specific workflow. Before instantiating a network service various actions need to be performed, they include onboarding, approving (i.e., validating the software components of a service) and deploying procedures.

As shown in Figure 4, the workflow involves five main stages: pre-onboarding, onboarding, service conception, testing and approvals, and instantiation. These various stages are part of the design-time and are explained below (Quintuna & Guillemin, 2019).

Figure 4. Service Deployment Workflow

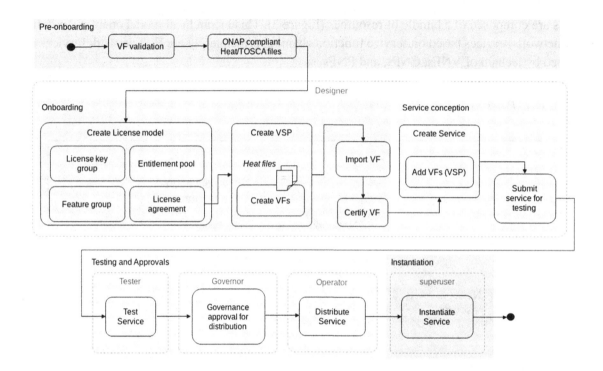

Pre-Onboarding

The pre-onboarding refers to the adaptation of VNFs (referred to as VF – Virtual Function in ONAP) in order to be compliant with ONAP onboarding, instantiation, and management requirements. It is worth noting that VFs can be provided by various vendors where each of them can use their own notation and modeling approaches. The 'VF validation' is particularly required for VM-based VFs, since Heat templates must comply with specific naming conventions and address best practice requirements defined by ONAP. In addition, ONAP requires mandatory metadata when defining resources. For instance for a given VNF, metadata must include the following parameters: 'vnf_name', 'vnf_id', and 'vf_module_id'.

On the other hand, Helm charts (for container-based VNFs) do not need to fulfill specific ONAP requirements. At the end of the validation and adjustment procedures, ONAP-compliant Heat files are available.

Onboarding

The goal of the onboarding phase is to add VNF models and other artifacts required to create, configure, instantiate, and manage VNFs. This stage is carried out by the designer by means of the SDC. The onboarding includes:

- License model creation

- Vendor Software Product (VSP) creation
- VF creation: VFs instances are the building blocks of a service.
- Importing VFs
- Certifying VFs

Service Conception

The service conception is performed by the designer, who builds a service by chaining available (already on-boarded in ONAP) VFs, infrastructure resources, and/or applications. The service conception involves three sub-stages:

- Service Creation.
- Service composition from available VFs and/or other resources.
- Submit service for testing.

Testing and Approvals

This step is carried out by the 'tester' who validates the service and submits it for approval. Once the 'governor' approves the service, it is thus ready for distribution. The 'operator' role distributes the service, leaving it available for instantiation.

Instantiation

The service instantiation is the last stage of the deployment workflow. At this stage, ONAP interacts with the hosting infrastructure (e.g., OpenStack, Kubernetes) and creates an instance of all VMs and/or containers (hosting VNFs and CNFs) composing a given service. This action is performed by the 'superuser'.

ONAP, A CATALYST FOR NETWORK EFFICIENCY

ONAP is a catalyst for network efficiency since it enables cost reduction, resource savings, and faults recovery by automatically managing the lifecycle of network services. ONAP also enables implementing specialized optimization algorithms, for instance to optimize VNF placement.

This section addresses main ONAP features to improve network efficiency as the optimization framework, control loop framework, data collection and analytic modules and the flexibility to manage both cloud native and physical network functions.

Other use cases using real-time and policy-driven ONAP features to orchestrate and automate network services can be found in (ONAP, 2021b). For instance, providing high-speed, flexible and intelligent services using ONAP is addressed by the Cross Domain and Cross Layer VPN (CCVPN) use case. It particularly considers high-speed Optical Transport Networks (OTN) across multiple carrier networks. CCVPN takes advantage of the ONAP capabilities to perform unified management and scheduling of resources and services. CCVPN enables physical network discovery and modeling, cross operator end-to-end service provisioning, and intelligent optimization. While CCVP is focused on layers 2 and 3, the

Multi-domain Optical Network Service (MDONS) use case supports cross operator layer 1 orchestration from the service order.

Various other use cases that illustrate the advanced ONAP functionality to manage networks were identified (e.g., Voice over LTE (VoLTE), virtual CPE (vCPE), 5G Blueprint which follows 3GPP, TMF, ETSI and ORAN specifications, virtual Firewall, virtual DNS).

Optimization Framework

The ONAP Optimization Framework (OOF) is policy-driven and includes various features to address placement and other infrastructure optimization problems. OOF is agnostic towards service, application and optimization technology or language. It enables both developing new optimization applications and reusing existent optimization engines (e.g., linking CPLEX-based optimization algorithms). OOF particularly includes a generic solver based on the open source MiniZinc (MiniZinc, 2020) which interfaces with third-party optimizers.

The Optimization Service Design Framework (OSDF) makes available a set of common libraries to facilitate the connection between ONAP components (A&AI, DCAE, Multicloud, Policy) involved in network efficiency. Figure 5 shows the main OOF modules and the interactions with other ONAP components.

Figure 5. Main modules of ONAP Optimization Framework

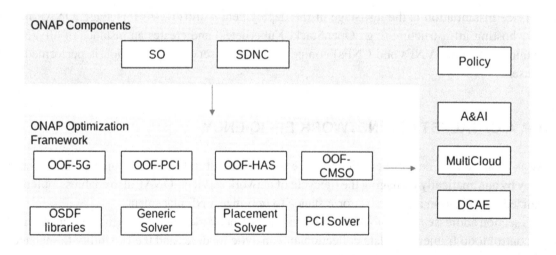

- OOF Homing Allocation Service (HAS) is a policy-driven placement optimizer on heterogeneous platforms. It enables to automatically deploy services across multiple cloud-sites while considering resource capacity, latency, load balancing, etc. OOF HAS enables optimizing the VNF placement on the basis of policies managed by the Policy Framework and A&AI information (e.g., server capacity). When the Service Orchestrator receives a new service request, it first decomposes the service into the various VNFs to be deployed and then requests the OOF-HAS to find the best cloud locations to deploy VNFs. The OOF-HAS computes this data and sends back a list of VNF locations. Implementation examples for vCPE Homming use case and Homming 5G RAN VNFs are available in (ONAP Wiki, 2018a; ONAP Wiki, 2018b).

- OOF Change Management Schedule Optimization (CSMO) is an optimization component that enables scheduling VNF changes by means of SO workflows. It includes a scheduling optimizer that can detect the best time window to execute the required workflow.
- OOF Physical Cell ID (PCI) is a solution developed for Self-Organizing Networks (SONs) particularly for the access segment. It provides an algorithm for PCI optimization based on a dedicated heuristic solver. In addition, the OOF-PCI makes an API available with the information to reconfigure radio access network cells. The OOF-PCI relies on a dedicated data-base to fetch configuration cell information. OOF 5G is an evolution of OOF PCI and particularly involves alignments with the O-RAN architecture.

In the 5G slice management use case, OOF provides an application to select the best NSI (Network Slice Instance) and NSSI (Network Slice Subnet Instance).

The OOF framework is also evolving to include Machine-Learning models in VNF placement and Hamming algorithms.

Building an Optimization Service

To define a new optimization service, three main steps are necessary:

- **Step 1:** Create an optimization model and policies if not already available.
- **Step 2:** Get relevant data from various sources (e.g., A&AI, MultiCloud) and adapt them if required.
- **Step 3:** Develop or use an existing solver.

Control Loop Framework

The control loop framework contributes to the management of the lifecycle automation of network services which can be composed of different network functions that are located in different sites. The closed loop concept in ONAP enables automatic recovery of faults and allows defining policies to automatically manage the performance of services without human intervention. The final goal of closed control loops is to validate and to enforce the negotiated SLAs between customers and providers. Closed loops in ONAP involve (i) event detection, (ii) policy validation, and (iii) actions execution.

A dedicated platform has been built in ONAP to deal with control loops, namely the Control Loop Automation Management Platform (CLAMP). The goal of CLAMP is to avoid user interaction with other components for managing the lifecycle of network services. As shown in Figure 6, CLAMP involves various ONAP components:

- SDC to define control loops
- DCAE to collect data and to perform analytics. It uses TOSCA blueprints for launching the loops.

- Policy Framework, which is fully TOSCA compliant, to describe the policy-based actions to be executed when an event occurs. The policy framework shall direct a request to the Service Orchestrator, controllers, or 3rd party systems based on the scope of the action.
- DMaaP bus is used to exchange messages between the various microservices composing the closed loop framework. DMaaP is based on Kafka (Confluent, 2021, Kafka, 2021) which is a "publish-subscribe" messaging system. Messages in Kafka are categorized into topics, where producers create new messages while consumers read messages.

Control Loop Design-Time

The control loop design involves the following steps:

- **Step 1:** Select the DCAE Analytics service to be executed during the control loops (e.g., TCA when using measurement events or Holmes for fault events).
- **Step 2:** Select an existing policy or develop a new one based on the Policy framework.
- **Step 3:** Create the Control-Loop Template as DCAE Blueprint that includes the information on the control loop: name, DCAE microservice to be used, Policy to be executed
- **Step 4:** Onboard the DCAE Blueprint in the SDC with the previously modeled network service.
- **Step 5:** Configure the parameters using CLAMP (e.g., a threshold value).

Control Loop Run-Time

As shown in Figure 6, the control loop execution includes the following steps:

- **Step 1:** A network element sends an event notification to ONAP via a DCAE collector.
- **Step 2:** The DCAE collector interprets the event and sends it to DmaaP on the topic that is associated with a given closed loop.
- **Step 3:** The DCAE Analytics captures all the events on dedicated topics (categories), analyses the data and emits an event on the 'Control-Loop' topic if some criteria are met (e.g., threshold crossed).
- **Step 4:** The Policy component is listening to the 'Control-Loop' topic and applies the rules according to the defined loop model during the control-loop design-time via CLAMP.
- **Step 5:** The Policy selects the "executor" component that will execute the action according to the nature of the required task (e.g., APPC enables scaling up/down a VNF) Components that may execute actions are Service Orchestrator, SDNC, CDS, or APPC.
- **Step 6:** The "executor" sends the request to the element that need to be reconfigured (e.g., a VNF) or starts/stops it.

Automating The Lifecycle of A Network Service

The lifecycle automation of a network service involves four stages: modeling, deployment, monitoring, and policy enforcement.

Figure 6. CLAMP components and main runtime closed loop steps

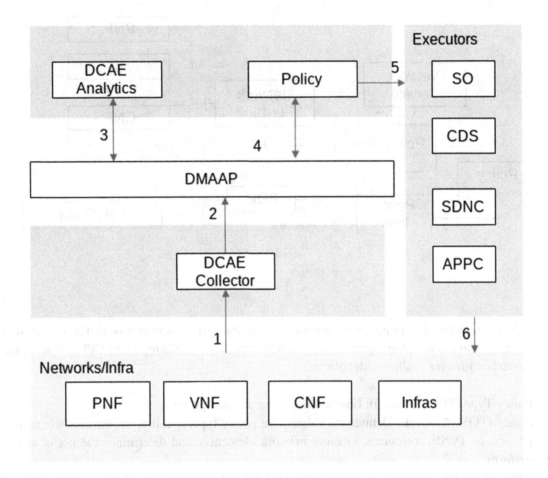

Modeling. A network service can be built in ONAP by means of virtual, physical network functions, or a combination thereof. A detailed ONAP-compliant model for a standalone 5G network hosted by an enterprise is given in (Quintuna, Guillemin, & Boubendir, 2019). In order to automatically manage a network service, a control loop needs to be associated. Policies shall trigger specific actions when conditions are met during the runtime. A simplified data model involving network services and policies in ONAP is shown in Figure 7.

Deployment. The various VNFs/CNFs/PNFs composing the network service give rise to VNF/CNF instances running on multi-cloud and/or multi-site infrastructures. The policies attached to the network service are also launched in this phase.

Monitoring. In ONAP, the monitoring is assured by various components notably DCAE and Virtual Event Streaming (VES) (see Figure 9). After event collection, policies are called for enforcing actions. VES agents can be attached to each and every one of the network service components that require to be controlled (e.g., VNFs, servers, network links).

Figure 7. Simplified Data Model to define Control Loops

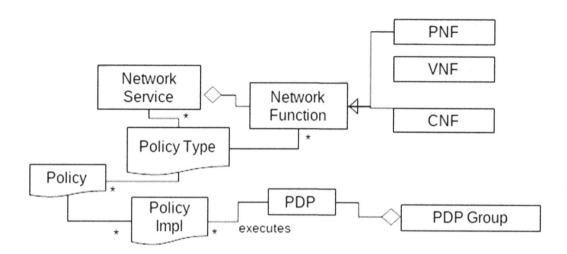

Policy enforcement. The policy enforcement involves the various actions that can be executed in the case of degradation of the global performance of a service, e.g., allocating more CPU capacity. ONAP uses various entities for dealing with policies:

- Policy Type (TOSCA-based): Enables designing abstract policies.
- Policy (TOSCA-based): Defines the values of a policy type, specifies the entities where the policy acts on (VNFs, resources, or other network elements), and determines the list of actions to perform.
- Policy Type Implementation: Defines the implementation of a Policy Type by means of APEX, XACML, Drools or other.
- Policy Implementation: Is the runnable version of a Policy, which is built from both Policy and Policy Type Implementation.
- Policy Decision Point (PDP): Executes the policies (more precisely, Policy Implementation). PDP returns the decision either to the requester (synchronous mode) or to another entity (asynchronous mode). During asynchronous invocations the requester is not waiting for the policy execution result.
- The policy framework allows the allocation of PDPs to a PDP Groups and Subgroups so that they can be managed as microservices.

The Case of Closed Loop Automation For Scaling 5G Functions

To illustrate the use of control loops in ONAP, the scale up and scale in of cloud resources can be considered, e.g., the scale up of RAM resources of the Access and Mobility Management Function (AMF) entity when the number of existing User Equipment (UE) contexts is greater than a given threshold, or the scale out of the User Plane Function (UPF) entity for enabling differentiated traffic (best-effort and dedicated channels), i.e., to provide a specific service. It is worth nothing that ONAP offers complementary features to native healing and scaling functions embedded in containers or VMs.

ONAP enables both 'Closed Loop' and 'Open Loop' behaviors to respectively support fully automated control loops and loops that require manual intervention to execute actions. It is shown in Figure 8.

Figure 8. Control Loop, 5G case

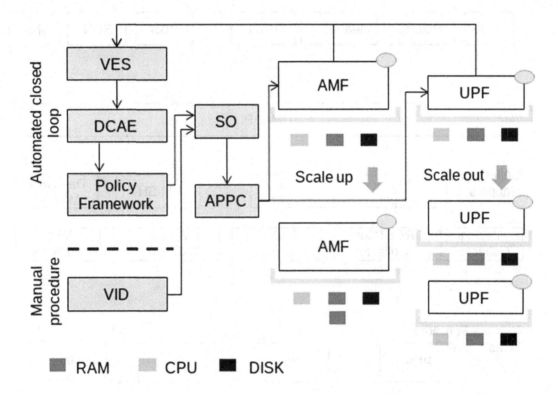

On Data Collection and Analytics

The specialized module for data collection and analytics, DCAE, includes a large number of modules as depicted in Figure 9. ONAP introduces a new format for events based on JSON carried over HTTP(S): the Virtual Event Streaming (VES). It harmonizes the data structure for the different events that are notified by the network functions. A VES event includes various mandatory fields such as:

- The domain associated with the event.
- Event ID, name, and type to uniquely represent the event.
- Priority, which can be set to "High, Medium, "Normal or Low"
- Timestamps

- Source information of the event

DCAE modules can be classified into five groups:

Figure 9. Data Collection Analytics and Events modules

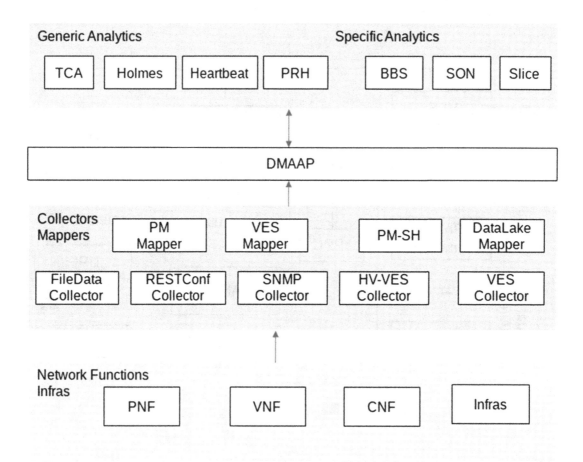

- **Shared modules** that interact with other ONAP components (DMaaP, Policy, CLAMP, internal database).
- **Collectors** to manage various event types: Virtual Event Streaming (VES), High-Volume VES based on Google Buffer Protocol GBP), Simple Network Management Protocol (SNMP) events, DataFile and RESTCONF.
- **Event processors** that perform data transformation and write events on:
  - DataLake Handlers, which store the various events sent to DMaaP into a database.
  - VES Mapper to convert RESTCONF events to VES events.
  - Performance Management (PM) Mapper to transform 3GPP XML files to VES events.

- ○ PM Subscription Handler (PM-SH) to configure the activation of Performance Management events.
- **Generic analytics** that analyzes data and triggers control loops. For instance:
  - ○ Docker based Threshold Crossing Analytics (TCA) which manages 'measurement events' and generates control loop events when a given metric reaches a threshold.
  - ○ Heartbeat Services that manages VNF heartbeat events and triggers control loop events when an action is missed in a predefined window time.
  - ○ Holmes that correlates 'fault' events and determines the cause relying on the network topology stored in the A&AI.
- Specific analytics developed for use cases
  - ○ BBS-EventProcessor (BBS-EP) that manages the various events coming from the Optical Network Terminals (ONTs) and typically detects when an ONT has moved.
  - ○ PNF Registration Handler (PRH) to populate the A&AI when a registration event is emitted by a new PNF.
  - ○ Slice Analysis collects performance measurements and correlates them with the configuration storing the cell informations. It triggers a control loop message on DmaaP when the number of connections reaches a predefined threshold.
  - ○ SON-Handler Service is used for SON-based use-cases.

Flexibility To Manage Cloud Native Functions

ONAP enables the deployment of CNFs. Such capabilities have been introduced in the Dublin Release with workarounds (e.g., dummy Heat files) to fit with the ONAP modeling schemes. In Guilin Release (Kumar et al., 2020) required features to manage CNF deployment have been added.

Helm charts are used to define the network services and resources to be deployed on a Kubernetes cluster, i.e., services, pods, volumes, secrets, etc. The K8S ONAP plugin uses Resource Bundle templates to deploy a CNF. Figure 10 depicts the main ONAP components that are involved in the onboarding and deployment of CNFs.

Onboarding Process

The onboarding process of CNFs involves:

- **Step 1:** Declare in the A&AI the Kubernetes cluster that can host the CNF and configure the K8S Plugin with kube configuration files.
- **Step 2:** On-board on the SDC a CNF with a Helm package.
- **Step 3:** Define a service that embeds the CNF.
- **Step 4:** Define additional rules to be managed at the pre- or post-instantiation phase (e.g., CBA to be executed by the CDS component).
- **Step 5:** Distribution of the various artifacts from the SDC to the ONAP components.

Deployment Process

The instantiation process of CNFs happens as follows:

Figure 10. Onboarding and deploying CNFs in ONAP

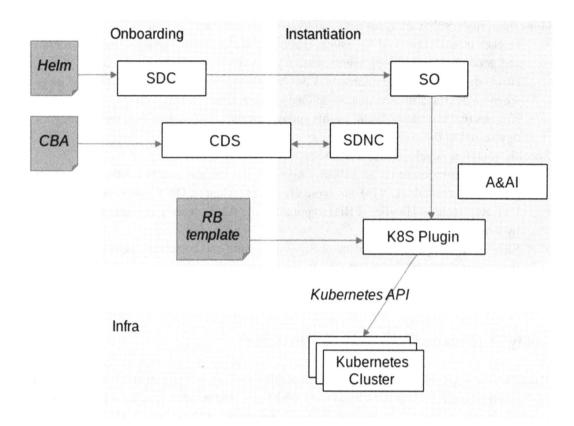

- **Step 1:** The service order towards the Service Orchestrator gets input parameters that are used to configure the CNF.
- **Step 2:** The Service Orchestrator analyses the service model, decomposes it by using the package received during the distribution phase.
- **Step 3:** The Service Orchestrator sends a request to the CDS and the K8S plugin enriches the Resource Bundle Template associated to the CNF with values coming from the input request and via the CDS resolution mechanism.
- **Step 4:** By using the 'CNF Adapter' module, the Service Orchestrator requests the K8S plugin to deploy the CNF on the cluster provided as input in the request. The K8S Plugin exposes the Configuration API that can also be included in a CBA.
- **Step 5:** Based on the feedback from the K8S Plugin, the Service Orchestrator updates the A&AI.

Note that a validation tool for verifying best-practices when defining CNF is not available (e.g., to avoid hard-coded values).

Managing PNFs, The Case of Broadband Services For Residential Connectivity

The BroandBad Service (BBS) use case illustrates how ONAP can manage and orchestrate services across different locations and domains (access, core), as well the ONAP capabilities to manage PNFs. The use case addresses the automation of a residential Internet connectivity based on fiber access using a Passive Optical Network (PON). It particularly considers the mobility of Optical Network Terminals (ONTs), and enables designing, deploying, and monitoring broadband services.

The broadband service is modeled by means of a Customer Facing Service (CFS) based on two Resource Facing Services (RFS) for access and Internet network services. A PNF is used to define Optical Line Termination (OLT) equipment (Pérez Caparrós, Al-Hakim, & Carey, 2019). Figure 11 presents the ONAP components required for the use case. The broadband blueprint particularly includes dedicated microservices into the DCAE which enables mobility detection. They are:

- PNF Registration Handler (PRH): detects when an ONT is connected to the network.
- BBS Event Processor (BBS-ep): manages the PNF re-registration internal events and the ONT authentication.

In addition, specific policy rules have been included into a control loop to automatically manage the mobility. Thus, when a subscriber moves an optical terminal to another location, the closed loop automatically triggers the required actions to reconfigure the OLT.

KEY ONAP USECASES AROUND 5G

ONAP has particularly introduced a 5G blueprint which is a multi-release effort and addresses network slicing, PNF/VNF lifecycle management and network optimization. The 5G blueprint is carried out in strong collaboration with standardization bodies. The Guilin release particularly evaluates 5G OOF SON, E2E Slicing and 5G PNF Plug and Play use cases (ONAP, 2021b). This section focuses on the baseline principles to deploy and manage a fully virtualized end-to-end 5G network which can be deployed as a Private 5G Network (OCN, 2021), i.e., a Stand Alone Non-public Network according to the 3GPP TS 23.251. ONAP progress on network slicing is presented by means of the E2E Network Slicing use case. Finally, this section presents the service deployment automation from the customer order coming from the Core Commerce layer according to TMF which can be used to offer on-demand Private Networks or network slices.

Network Service Modeling, The Case of A Mobile Network Deployment

This subsection illustrates the baseline principles to model and onboard a service. It particularly considers the deployment of an end-to-end mobile network on the basis of the Wireless Edge Factory (WEF) (Bcom, 2020), a fully virtualized core network, and the open source RAN network, namely Open Air Interface (OAI) (OAI, 2020).

As shown in Figure 12 the virtualized core network is based on a complete separation of the user plane from the control plane as recommended by 3GPP for 5G networks and referred to as Control User Plane Separation (CUPS). When an UE (User Equipment) attaches to the network, the Authentication,

Figure 11. ONAP components used for BroadBand Service

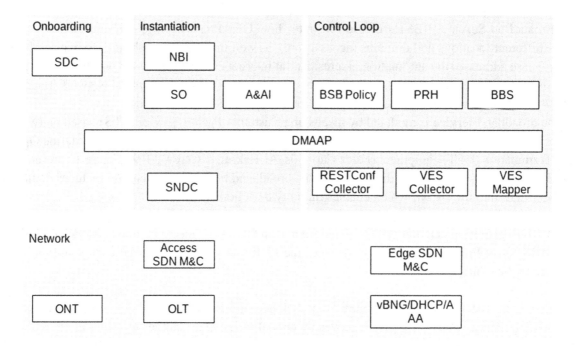

Authorization, and Accounting (AAA) procedure is triggered by the Mobility Management Entity (MME). User profiles are validated by the Home Subscriber Server (HSS) database which stores various parameters such as Access Point Name (APN), International Mobile Equipment Identity (IMEI), Subscriber Identification Module (SIM) card information OP, key, Mobile Network Code (MNC), Mobile Country Code (MCC), among others. When access is granted to the UE, the DHCP component assigns an IP address to the UE. Such IP address is taken out of the address-pool established in the AAA component. The end-to-end connection is established over the GTP-U and GTP-C tunnels. The Network Address Translation (NAT) component to handle privately-addressed IPv4 traffic is deployed on the (S)Gi interface.

From an ONAP standpoint, the aforementioned components need to be defined as network resources, VFs, and services in order to be managed and orchestrated by ONAP. Furthermore, in ONAP, a network service is formed by one or more VFs interacting with each other. The ONAP E2E service model used to onboard and to instantiate the E2E mobile network is shown in Figure 13. The model particularly considers three network services, Core Connection Point (CP), Core Data Plane (DP), and RAN (Radio Access Network). Each service is formed by a single VF, i.e., WEF-CP-VF, WEF-DP-VF and OAI-RAN-VF. Each VF is in turn formed by various components. VFs are defined and on-boarded in ONAP by means of Heat Templates (one for each of them). VF components correspond to Openstack resources for instance: OS::Nova::Server, OS::Neutron::Net, OS::Neutron::Subnet, OS::Neutron::Port, etc. After onboarding, creation, testing and approvals, the resulting services and their respective composition can be observed by using the SDC dashboard. Figure 14 shows the SDC view of on-boarded components of the core control plane.

Figure 12. Elements of E2E mobile network use-case

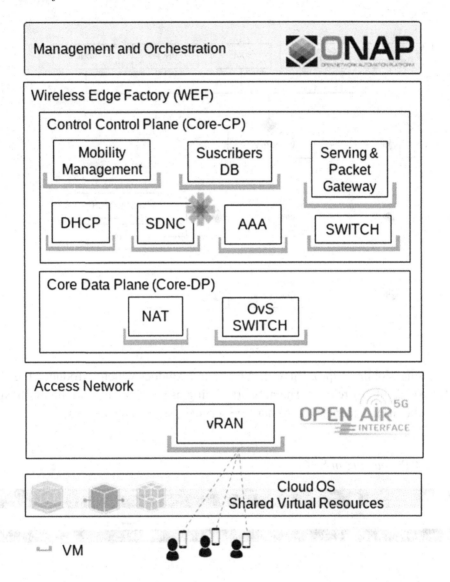

E2E Network Slicing Using ONAP

Network slicing is a key feature of 5G networks. It enables the sharing of the underlying 5G infrastructure while dedicating resources to address requirements raised by customers. Network slices can be, for example, used to define logical network segments dedicated to vertical industries (e-health, automotive, manufacture automation). A network slice is considered as a bundle of sub-networks (core, access, transport) which are interconnected to deliver a given service according to a negotiated SLA between the customer and the service provider. First steps of ONAP-based network slice E2E management were taken by Orange (Quintuna, Guillemin, & Boubendir, 2019). ONAP has devoted special attention to network slicing and has defined the E2E network slicing use case framework. This use case is especially

Figure 13. Service Model of an E2E Mobile Network deployed by ONAP

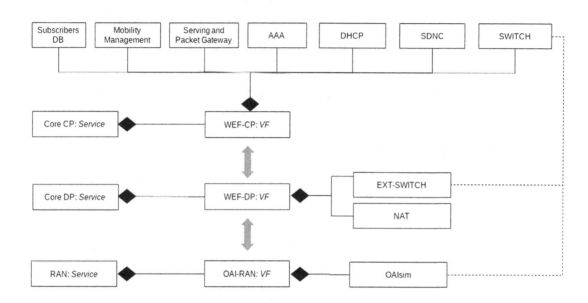

sponsored by China Mobile, Wipro, Huawei, AT&T, and Amdocs which introduced the slicing framework since ONAP Frankfurt release. The network slicing use case adheres to the 3GPP specifications and considers three management levels to manage services, slices, and subnets:

Figure 14. Core CP modeling in SDC

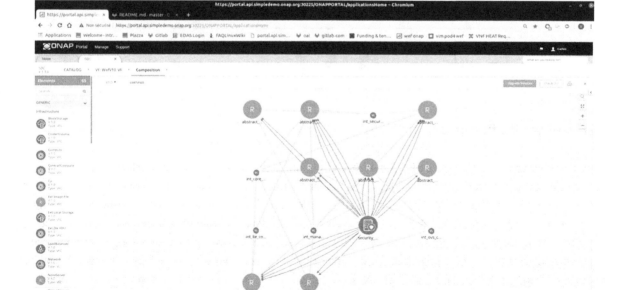

- Communication Service Management Function (CSMF): Responsible for translating the customer based service requirements into a technical solution (namely, a network slice instance).
- Network Slice Management Function (NSMF): Responsible for the management and orchestration of the Network Slice Instance (NSI) as well as deriving the requirements related to the subnet (core, access, transport).
- Network Slice Subnet Management Function (NSSMF): Responsible for the management and orchestration of the Network Slice Subnet Instance (NSSI) and the communication with the NSMF.

Operators can then provide Communication Service Instances (CSIs) on the basis of one or more Network Slice Instances (NSIs). Network Slice Subnet Instances (NSSIs) are then associated to slices and hold deployment information.

Besides 3GPP, other SDOs are currently addressing network slicing. ONAP considers the slicing implementation the definitions proposed by GSMA, TMF, IETF, and MEF. For instance, the E2E slicing use case perfectly fits concepts as the Generic Slice Template (GST) and Network Slice Type (NEST) introduced by the GSMA Network Slicing Taskforce working group (GSMA, 2021) to define the customer requirements. The NEST structure is a GST with values. The TMF Open Digital Architecture (ODA) principles which address the intent-based approach to define services are also considered. ODA notably defines Customer Facing Services (CFS) structures to specify the slice requirements from customer point of view. The E2E slicing use case enables the slicing definition while using a simplified abstraction of the resource layer by means of a Portal. CFSs are then converted to Resource Facing Services (RFSs) which enable the selection and instantiation of slices.

Slicing Information Model

Regarding the Information Model, ONAP defines various data structures to support service, slice and subnet concepts. The ONAP data model is particularly based on the Network Resource Model defined in the 3GPP TS 28.541 specification, as well as on data structures proposed in 3GPP TR 28.805 which addresses order-care, customer and service aspects, and introduces Customer Facing Service Specification (CFCS) and Resource Facing Service Specification (RFCS) concepts (ODA compliant). ONAP considers both 3GPP and TMF customer and resource facing approaches. It is worth nothing that 3GPP has a bottom-up focus while TMF is top-down oriented.

As shown in Figure 15, ONAP enables defining slices by means of four templates which are used in the design time. The Communication Service Template (CST) is used to collect SLA requirements from the Portal. This template can be used to directly map the CFS parameters required in the ODA architecture. The Service Descriptor (SD) is used to translate the customer facing requirements into network facing requirements. The Network Slice Template (NST) and the Network Slice Subnet Template (NSST) are used during the deployment, both contain infrastructure and network information required to respectively instantiate slices and subnets.

During the runtime a service profile data structure is used to specify the slice features while the slice profile is devoted to the subnet parameters. The Network Slice Instance (NSI) parameters and the Network Slice Subnet Instance (NSSI) are respectively associated to the Service profile and to the Slice Profile. Communication Service and Communication Service Profile (CSP) structures are used to describe parameters defining end-to-end services that can be performed by one or more slices (Figure 15).

Figure 15. Slicing Data Structures in ONAP

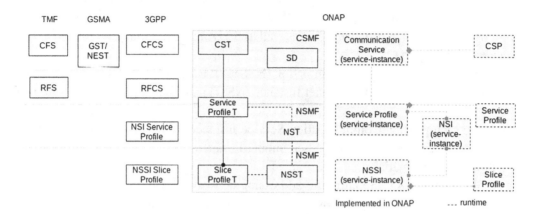

Slicing Implementation

To implement the three management layers, ONAP has evaluated five scenarios which are illustrated by Figure 16. These scenarios consider the inclusion or exclusion of CSMF, NSMF, and NSSMF management functions within ONAP's SO. The scenario number four was held back for Frankfurt. It considers the implementation of the CSMF and NSMF in ONAP and the NSSMF as a third party. Scenario number one is implemented in the Guilin release. It considers the implementation of the three management functions in SO, i.e., CSMF, NSMF, and NSSMF for transport, core and RAN networks. Enhancements of both scenarios (1 and 4) shall be developed in the Honolulu release (expected in 2021).

The CSMF is implemented throughout the Service Orchestrator, A&AI and UUI modules. It implements the slice lifecycle management workflow and the customer interface to define slices. The CSMF workflow (defined in the Service Orchestrator) collects the user requirements in a Communication Service Template (CST) and generates a Single-Network Slice Selection Assistance Information (S-NSSAI). The S-NSSAI is used to uniquely identify a network slice; it is notably formed by the Slice Service Type (SST) and a differentiator. The CSMF translates the customer facing information (stored in the CST) to network facing requirements which are stored in a Service Profile Template.

The NSMF is implemented in the Service Orchestrator, the A&AI, the OOF and the UUI modules. The ONAP NSMF defines the slice instance lifecycle management workflow, as well as the optimization of the slice instance selection. A portal is available to manually modify slice instances that are automatically recommended by the system to carry out the service needs coming from customers. The NSMF workflow deploys the service instance defined in the Service Descriptor and associates the S-NSSAI to the NSI.

Slicing Lifecycle

ONAP follows the lifecycle management described in the 3GPP TS 28.530 specification for both Frankfurt and Guilin releases. As shown in Figure 17, the lifecycle management involves the preparation, commissioning, and decommissioning phases. During the preparation phase, the slice instance does not exist. This phase includes the network slice design, onboarding and the evaluation and preparation

Figure 16. Slicing deployment scenarios in ONAP (ONAP, 2021b; ONAP Wiki, 2021)

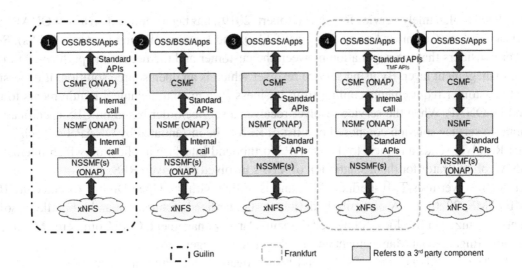

of the functions for the creation of the NSI. The commissioning, allows the creation of the NSI, which triggers the allocation of all the required resources. The operation phase includes slice activation, supervision, monitoring, performance reporting, modification and de-activation. When a slice is activated, it is ready to support service communication. Decommissioning includes the termination of all disabled slice components that are not shared.

The Frankfurt release, considers the steps framed in red, so the design and onboarding of the preparation phase, the creation of the commissioning and activation and deactivation in the operation phase and termination during the decommissioning. The Guilin release particularly introduces the monitoring and reporting functions which are implemented in cooperation with CLAMP for the automation of closed loops. The first steps to automatically manage slicing modification are implemented in Guilin as well; however real time updating of a slice is still an open issue.

Figure 17. Lifecycle of Network Slices using ONAP (ONAP, 2021b; ONAP Wiki, 2021)

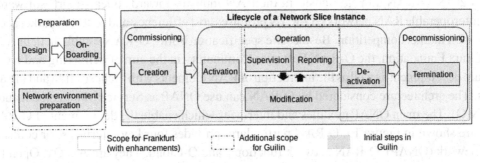

Service Deployment Automation From The Customer Order

A specialized tool, namely Service Resolver (Robert, 2019), has been deployed on top of ONAP to manage service orders, Customer Facing Services (CFSs), and Resource Facing Services (RFSs). Service Resolver considers that the negotiation between the customer and the network is performed through a service management layer. By using service resolver which is an open source solution, it is possible to translate customer requirements coming from business systems into technical requirements to be addressed by ONAP. When the service resolver receives a service order based on CFS specifications, it elaborates a service solution composed of a list of RFS to be instantiated by ONAP. For each RFS, the Service Resolver sends a request to the ONAP Northbound Interface application which interacts with the ONAP orchestrator for the instantiation of VNFs involved in a given RFS.

Service resolver uses TMF-defined APIs and is in line with the Open Digital Architecture (ODA) of TMF (TMF, 2020). ODA particularly defines a standardized architecture and a bundle of software elements organized in five loosely coupled domains Party Management, Core Commerce Management, Production, Engagement Management and Intelligence Management.

While the Party Management (Who? and Why?) deals with entities and actors involved in a given business process (e.g., customers, employees, providers, etc.), the core commerce management (What?) focuses on activities enabling buying and selling. The Production domain is then dedicated to the lifecycle management of services. Thus, ONAP can be placed within the scope of the production domain defined by TMF. The CFSs coming from Core Commerce are consumed by the upper Production entity in charge of converting CFSs in RFS to be deployed by ONAP.

In a down-top approach, the Production block exposes the service capabilities to the upper ODA layers by means of northbound interfaces going from production towards the Core Commerce Management entity. ONAP makes available the NBI module which implements various TMF interfaces, namely Service Catalog APIs (TMF 633), Service Order APIs (TMF 641), Service Inventory APIs (TMF 638), in order to interact with the external systems, e.g., Core commerce or legacy BSS.

This group of APIs enables the BSS to execute service orders to deploy new network services or to find the existent ones in the aim of getting Key Performance Indicators (KPIs) or other features. Figure 18 shows the architecture layers from the customer order to the service deployment while using ONAP.

O-RAN Based Access Networks

The O-RAN Alliance was founded by AT&T, China Mobile, Deutsche Telekom, NTT DOCOMO and Orange, in 2018. O-RAN aims to transform the RAN industry towards open, smart, software-defined and fully interoperable RAN networks. O-RAN promises cost efficiency and time-to-market acceleration within an open market competition. Besides the specification effort, O-RAN established, in cooperation with the Linux Foundation, the O-RAN Software Community in the aim of delivering and coordinating the software development as well as the interaction of RAN elements with orchestration and infrastructure platforms. The architecture considered by O-RAN can use ONAP as Service Management and Orchestration (SMO). The main ONAP modules and interfaces which enable the deployment of O-RAN-based networks are shown in Figure 19. O-RAN particularly provides four key interfaces for connecting: the SMO framework (ONAP), O-RAN network functions, and O-Cloud. They are A1, O1, Open Fronthaul M-plane (Optional) and O2.

Figure 18. Service deployment from the customer order using ONAP

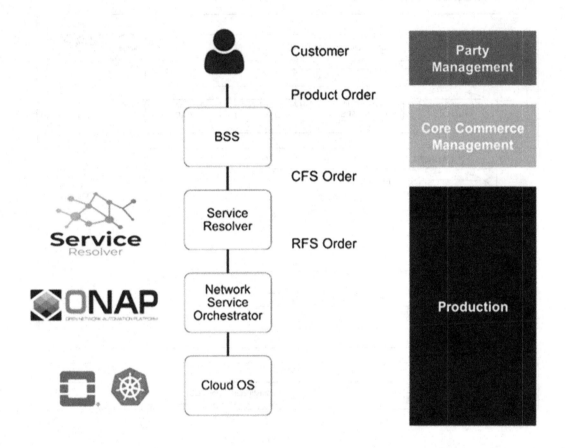

Service Management and Orchestration (SMO) Using ONAP

The SMO provides network management functionalities beyond RAN, i.e., Core Management, Transport Management, E2E Slice Management, etc. O-RAN requires the following capabilities of the SMO. They are supported by ONAP:

- **Fault Configuration Accounting Performance and Security management (FCAPS):** FCAPS of RAN functions can be accessed through the O1 interface which is compliant with the 3GPP specifications for RAN element management purposes. ONAP enhancements are required to fully comply with O-RAN specifications. O1 support has been moved to ONAP Guilin-Release. The main impacted systems to implement O1 are
  - DCAE: Impact for adopting new VES domain. A VES domain refers to event categories, e.g., faults, heartbeat, measurements (ONAP, 2021c). First enhancements added Change

Figure 19. ONAP interfaces to interconnect O-RAN elements

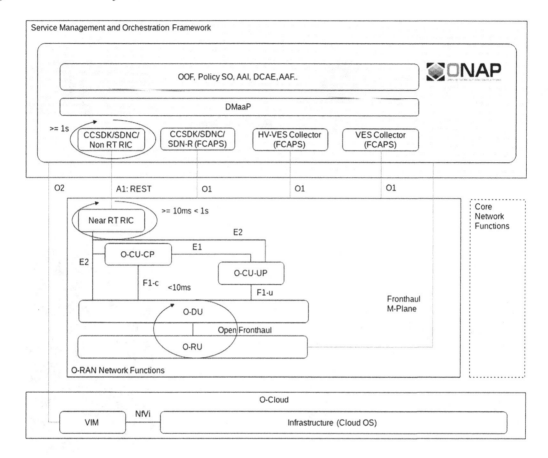

Management notify domain to the VES collector, updated common effect format, and updated routing configuration in VES to point to "DMaaP CM_Notify".

○ DMaaP: adds static unauthenticated CM Notification (VES CM notification events).

- **Non-Real Time RIC (Non-RT RIC)** for RAN optimization: The main goal of Non RT RIC is to support intelligent RAN optimization by providing policy-based guidance, e.g., radio resource management in non-real time scenarios. The Non-RT-RIC is connected to the Near-RT-RIC through the A1 interface. In ONAP, the A1 adapter listens to DMaaP events and interacts with the A1 Mediator (Near-RT RIC) via REST APIs. A1 mediator is a RIC component which behaves as a single entry peer of A1 to RIC. The A1 adapter gets A1 policy via DMaaP and converts it to A1-compliant message. The A1 adapter also gets the response from RIC and posts a relevant message to DmaaP. ONAP impacted systems to achieve A1 fundamentally are:

  ○ SDNC: Implement southbound adaptation layer to communicate with Near-Real Time RIC using an A1-specified protocol (most likely REST).

  ○ CDS: Expand CDS to design intent-based policy configuration to send to Near-Real Time RIC using the A1 interface.

- **O-Cloud management**: O-RAN architecture considers a dedicated interface (namely, O2) for dealing with the cloud infrastructure. It shall provide FCAPS of O-Cloud platforms, scale-in/out for O-Cloud, discovery and management of O-Cloud resources, software management of Cloud platform and deployments.

O-RAN Network Functions

ONAP implements the O1 interface between the orchestrator and the various O-RAN functions.

O-CU implements the upper layers of the E-UTRAN protocol stack (mainly, PDCP), O-DU implements the RLC, MAC and high-PHY (channel coding and modulation) and terminates the E2, F1 and the Open Fronthaul Interface. O-RU implements low-PHY (signal generation) functions and terminates the Open Fronthaul Interface (as well as the Open Fronthaul M-plane when considered).

Beyond RU, DU, CU, O-RAN considers intelligent controllers, namely RIC which performs control loops in at least three levels: RT RIC, Near-RT RIC and Non-RT RIC, where this later is considered as part of the SMO (i.e., ONAP).

O-Cloud

ONAP implements the O2 interface between the SMO and the O-Cloud which contains a collection of physical infrastructure nodes to host the relevant O-RAN functions as Near-RT RIC, O-CU, ODU, etc., the supporting Cloud-OS and the management and orchestration functions (ONAP). The main functionalities of O-Cloud are:

- Exporting the O-RAN O2 interface for cloud and workload management to provide discovery, registration, software life-cycle management, fault management, performance management, and configuration management.
- Exporting the O-RAN AAL for hardware acceleration purposes.

CONCLUSION AND PERSPECTIVES

ONAP is an open source solution to fully automate the network operations covering the different types of network functions that co-exist in a service chain, i.e., PNFs, VNF, and CNFs. ONAP offers a set of powerful mechanisms to design, deploy, and manage network services on heterogeneous infrastructures and multi-cloud environments.

The ONAP community aligns the developments to the main standards particularly considering 3GPP, TMF, ETSI, and IETF specifications. ONAP is also interconnected with other open source initiatives, e.g., Acumos. Furthermore, ONAP follows a pragmatic approach to leverage emerging technologies developed by the Cloud Native Computing Foundation.

The promise of a zero touch automation platform that enables automatically managing the entire lifecycle of network services, still requires reliability, security hardening, simplifying and optimizing procedures and more cloud readiness. Created by service providers to service providers, ONAP shall start demonstrating its capabilities on 5G use cases.

It is worth noting that ONAP is well positioned with regards to 5G networks relying on O-RAN specifications, ETSI NVF principles and 3GPP concepts. The strong alignment between ONAP and the main standardization bodies as well as between ONAP and other open source initiatives shall facilitate the ONAP adoption. The ONAP implementation in operational environments shall support its evolution and guarantee its survival. Feedback from deployments should feed the community to assess the level of flexibility offered by the platform and identify further concrete enhancements to be endorsed in order to better satisfy operations.

ACKNOWLEDGMENT

Morgan Richomme, Orange
   Sylvain Desbureaux, Orange
   Lukasz Rajewski, Orange

REFERENCES

Bcom. (2020). *Wireless Edge Factory*. https://b-com.com/fr/bcom-wireless-edge-factory

Camunda. (2020). *Reinventing Process Automation for the Digital Enterprise*. https://camunda.com/

Cncf. (2021). *Building sustainable ecosystems for cloud native software*. https://www.cncf.io/

Confluent. (2021). *Cloud-native reliability for Apache Kafka*. https://www.confluent.io/

Debeau, E., & Al-Hakim, C. (2019). Retrieved 02 March 2021 from, https://events19.linuxfoundation.org/wp-content/uploads/2018/07/ONS2019-SDWAN-POC-Orange-Huawei-Final-LFN.pdf

Desbureaux, S., & Richomme, M. (2020). *Introduction to ONAP python SDK*. Academic Press.

Docker. (2020). *Developing with Docker*. https://www.docker.com/why-docker

ETSI-GS-ZSM. (2019). *Zero-touch network and Service Management (ZSM); Reference Architecture*. ETSI GS ZSM 002 V1.1.1

ETSI-NFV. (2013). *Network Functions Virtualization (NFV) Architectural Framework*. ETSI GS NFV 002 V1.1.1.

ETSI-NFV-MAN. (2014). *Network Functions Virtualization (NFV) Management and Orchestration*. ETSI GS NFV-MAN 001 V1.1.1.

GPP-VES. (2020). 5G; Management and orchestration; Generic management services. *ETSI TS*, *128*, 532.

GSMA. (2021). *5G Network Slicing*. https://www.gsma.com/futurenetworks/ip_services/understanding-5g/network-slicing/

Helm. (2020). *The package manager for Kubernetes*. https://helm.sh/

IETF. (2021). *A framework for Automating Service and Network Management with YANG*. IETF RFC 8969.

Jenkins. (2020). *Jenkins, an open source automation server*. http://www.jenkins.io

Kafka. (2021). *Introduction to Kafka*. https://docs.confluent.io/home/kafka-intro.html

Kumar, M., Rajewski, L., & Banka, K. (2020). *NFO – Guilin CNF Improvement Overview*. Retrieved 02 March 2021 from, https://wiki.lfnetworking.org/spaces/flyingpdf/pdfpageexport.action?pageId=46105100

LFAI. (2020). *Linux Foundation Artificial Intelligence*. https://lfaidata.foundation/

LFN. (2021). *CNTT*. https://www.lfnetworking.org/about/cntt/

LFN Analytics. (2020). https://insights.lfx.linuxfoundation.org/projects/lfn/onap/dashboard

MEF. (2018). *Orange is designing standardized APIs to facilitate the interoperability of Ethernet services from operators to businesses*. Retrieved 02 March 2021 from, https://hellofuture.orange.com/en/orange-designing-standardised-apis-facilitate-interoperability-ethernet-services-operators-businesses/

MEF. (2021). *Empowering Digital Transformation*. https://www.mef.net/

Members. (2021). Available at https://www.lfnetworking.org/membership/members/

MiniZinc. (2020). *A free and open-source constraint modeling language*. https://www.minizinc.org/

O-RAN. (2020). *Operator Defined Open and Intelligent Radio Access networks*. https://www.o-ran.org/

OAI. (2020). *Open Air Interface*. https://www.openairinterface.org/

OCN. (2021). *Open Core Network*. https://telecominfraproject.com/open-core-network/

OMG. (2021). https://www.omg.org/spec/BPMN/

ONAP. (2021a). *Offered APIs*. https://docs.onap.org/projects/onap-externalapi-nbi/en/latest/offeredapis/offeredapis.html#offeredapis

ONAP. (2021b). *ONAP documentation*. https://docs.onap.org/en/latest/

ONAP. (2021c). *Service: VES Event Listener 7.1.1*. https://docs.onap.org/projects/onap-vnfrqts-requirements/en/latest/Chapter8/ves7_1spec.html#datatype-commoneventheader

ONAP. (2021d). *TOSCA Policy Primer*. Retrieved 02 March 2021 from, https://docs.onap.org/en/elalto/submodules/policy/parent.git/docs/architecture/tosca-policy-primer.html

ONAP Courses. (2021). *Introduction to ONAP: Complete Network Automation*. https://training.linuxfoundation.org/training/introduction-to-onap-complete-network-automation/

ONAP Wiki. (2018a). *Homing 5G RAN VNFs*. https://wiki.onap.org/display/DW/Homing+5G+RAN+VNFs

ONAP Wiki. (2018b). *vCPE Homing Use Case*. https://wiki.onap.org/display/DW/vCPE+Homing+Use+Case

ONAP Wiki. (2021). https://wiki.onap.org/

OpenLab. (2018). *The 1st Orange ONAP OpenLab platform*. Retrieved 02 March 2021 from, https://www.lfnetworking.org/wp-content/uploads/sites/55/2018/09/Orange-OpenLab_ONS-EU-vf-.pdf

OPNFV. (2021). *OPNFV*. https://www.opnfv.org/

OSM. (2020). *Open Source Mano*. https://osm.etsi.org/

Pérez-Caparrós, D., Al-Hakim, C., & Carey, T. (2019). *BBS: Broadband Services Orchestration with ONAP*. Retrieved 02 March 2021 from, https://events19.linuxfoundation.org/wp-content/uploads/2018/07/ ONS2019_BBS_Broadband_Services_Orchestration_with_ONAP.pdf

Quintuna, V., Corbel, R., Guillemin, F., & Ferrieux, A. (2020b). Cloud-RAN Factory: Instantiating virtualized mobile networks with ONAP. *2020 11th International Conference on Network of the Future (NoF)*.

Quintuna, V., & Guillemin, F. (2019). *End-to-end virtual mobile network deployment on ONAP Onboarding. Distributing and instantiating the Wireless Edge Factory (WEF)*. NASA Deliverable.

Quintuna, V., Guillemin, F., & Boubendir, A. (2019). Automating the deployment of 5G Network Slices using ONAP. *10th International Conference on Networks of the Future (NoF)*.

Quintuna, V., Guillemin, F., & Boubendir, A. (2020a). 5G E2E Network Slicing Management with ONAP. 2020 23rd Conference on Innovation in Clouds. *Internet and Networks and Workshops (ICIN)*.

Richomme, M., & Desbureaux, S. (2020). *Gating retrospective*. Retrieved 02 March 2021 from, https:// wiki.lfnetworking.org/download/attachments/25364127/gating_retrospective_final.pptx?version=1&m odificationDate=1579086074000&api=v2

Robert, R. (2019). *Service Resolver*. https://gitlab.com/Orange-OpenSource/lfn/onap/service-resolver

TIP. (2020). *Telecom Infra Project*. https://telecominfraproject.com/

TMF. (2020). *Open Digital Architecture. A blueprint for success in the digital markets of tomorrow*. https://www.tmforum.org/oda/

ADDITIONAL READING

Deng, L., Deng, H., & Terrill, S. (2019). Harmonizing Open Source and Open Standards: The Progress of ONAP. https://www.onap.org/wp-content/uploads/sites/20/2019/04/ONAP_HarmonizingOpen-SourceStandards_032719.pdf

LFN-EUAG. (2020). ONAP Consumption Models. A Service Provider's Perspective. LFN End User Advisory Group (EUAG). https://www.onap.org/wp-content/uploads/sites/20/2020/06/ONAP_EUAG_ Whitepaper_061720.pdf

ONAP. (2020). ONAP E2E Network Slicing. Technical Overview. https://www.onap.org/wp-content/ uploads/sites/20/2020/06/ONAP_E2E_Slicing_Technical-Overview_061820.pdf

ONAP. (2021). Guilin 5G Use Cases & Requirements. https://www.onap.org/architecture/use-cases-blue-prints

KEY TERMS AND DEFINITIONS

Automation Framework: A set of tools enabling to design models, policies or rules to be executed without manual intervention. An automation framework can focus on: policy framework, CI/CD, control-loop, workflow engine, tests.

Cloud Native Network Functions: Represents network functions designed and developed to be run on cloud infrastructures. CNFs follows the cloud native approaches defined in the Cloud Manifesto. CNFs are designed as microservices and executed in Docker containers. CNFs are also deeply integrated with automation tools to facilitate their lifecycle.

Control Loop: Is a term coming from the industrial control systems and refers to an automation pattern where a system is able to react based on events received from network functions in a full automation way. In telecoms, a control loop is based on a set of predefined rules that are executed by an orchestrator to launch the required actions to fulfill service requirements. In general, a control loop starts with an event emitted by a network element and then a policy framework identifies the rules to be executed by controllers to correct the detected issue.

Model-Driven: Is an approach to fully separate what is expected from the execution. For the orchestrator, model-driven approaches avoid defining the set and sequences of actions to be executed via a workflow. The orchestrator analyzes the model, decompose it into a set of predefined tasks, and then run the different actions.

Network Function Placement: Is an optimization problem to select the hosting service to instantiate VNFs or CNFs. Placement strategy depends on various technical factors such as locations, capacity, affinity or anti-affinity rules, or other constraints (e.g., regulation ones). NF placement may be statically defined during the engineering phase or via policies that are dynamically executed during the handling of a service request.

Orchestrator: An orchestrator is usually based on a set of predefined models, policies, rules, or workflows and executes the required set of actions to deploy on-demand services. The goal of an orchestrator is also to guarantee that services run as expected. Different types of orchestrators are involved in the operation of network services. Some orchestrators focus on virtual resource layer such as OpenStack/Heat or Kubernetes, on network layer such as controllers like OpenDayLight while others like ONAP have a broader scope to cover end-to-end services while interacting with the vertical orchestration layer stack.

Policy: Is a set of rules defining actions to be executed. Typical policies include placement policies, scaling policies, or QoS-related policies.

Chapter 9

Granular VNF–Based Microservices:
Advanced Service Decomposition and the Role of Machine Learning Techniques

Zhaohui Huang
King's College London, UK

Vasilis Friderikos
King's College London, UK

Mischa Dohler
King's College London, UK

Hamid Aghvami
King's College London, UK

ABSTRACT

The dawn of the 5G commercialization era brings the proliferation of advanced capabilities within the triptych of radio access network, end user devices, and edge cloud computing which hopefully propel the introduction of novel, complex multimodal services such as those that enlarge the physical world around us like mobile augmented reality. Managing such advanced services in a granular manner through the emerging architectures of microservices within a network functions virtualization (NFV) framework allows for several benefits but also raises some challenges. The aim of this chapter is to shed light into the architectural aspects of the above-envisioned virtualized mobile network ecosystem. More specifically, and as an example of advanced services, the authors discuss how augmented reality applications can be decomposed into several service components that can be located either at the end-user terminal or at the edge cloud.

DOI: 10.4018/978-1-7998-7646-5.ch009

INTRODUCTION

One of the emerging network challenges for the provision of advanced network services within a Network Function Virtualization (NFV) ecosystem of 5G and beyond mobile communication systems is to manage dynamically and efficiently the virtual and physical network elements (the so-called virtual network functions (VNFs) and physical network functions (PNFs)) belonging to 5G networks especially for provisioning granular support in the form of microservices. In a nutshell, NFV techniques allow deploying network functions (such as load balancers, firewalls, image and video compression/optimization to name just a few) as software instances, called VNFs, running on generic hardware through software virtualization techniques such as virtual machines (VMs), containers[1] or a combination of these two[2]. The aim hereafter is to delve into service decomposition with emphasis on augmented reality and how this decomposition can be considered under the realms of VNF-based microservices. To this end, different microservices architectures are discussed and analyzed with special focus on the benefits as well as the challenges in terms of network management. Finally, in order to overcome these challenges, we review data-driven machine learning techniques that will allow taming the underlined complexity of granularized network support for advanced services.

The chapter provides an immersion into key technologies related to microservices and how advanced services can be decomposed in order to acquire the full benefits of such architectures. The key aspect however is efficient management of the underlying network (including cloud resources). A high degree of granularity brings scalability aspects that are discussed in detail as well. The data driven machine learning that can assist in performing informed decision management are then highlighted together with open-ended aspects that deserve further research attention. The chapter revolves around the case of mobile augmented reality as an example of a rich service offering where the above-mentioned aspects need to be amalgamated in order to provide efficient service delivery; however, the overarching aspects are equally applicable to other rich service offerings beyond augmented reality.

(MOBILE) AUGMENTED REALITY (AR)

Emerging advanced services in mobile communication networks including AR can be categorized into several types based on their running platforms. Those that can be deemed as hardware-specific services usually require a specially designed device (e.g., Pokémon Plus, Bluetooth wearable device) and as a result suffer from a rather excessive cost with insufficient flexibility (Qiao et al., 2019; Frank, 2016). Although some app-based services like Pokémon Go and IKEA Place have been successful, downloading and installing apps on platforms like smartphones and iPads are still inconvenient for users and lack of cross-platform ability (Qiao et al. 2019). As pointed out by Li et al. (2020), rendering high quality images with AR techniques consumes much storage space and computational resources especially in a 3-dimensional (3D) scenario. As a result, web-based applications have been proposed and are regarded as having a considerable potential to solve these problems. It is worth point out that these applications can be decomposed into a set of atomic functions and apply a web-scale deployment to achieve better efficiency (Cziva and Pezaros, 2017; Akhtar et al., 2018). Through 5G or Beyond 5G (B5G) networks, the transmission latency is also envisioned to be significantly reduced which leads to further accelerating the use of such an application with low latency response to the requesting user (Qiao et al., 2019; Gero et al., 2017). According to Li et al. (2020), Liu et al. (2018) and Guo et al. (2020), resource allocation and request assignment in a network can be translated into different types of optimization problems. Supported by techniques like "branch and bound", it is possible to find optimal solutions for such NP-hard problem suffer from the so-called curse of dimensionality meaning that can be used for low to medium network instances; for large network instances heuristic techniques that can provide non optimal but competitive performance will have to be deployed. Likewise, machine learning techniques will play a significant role as discussed in the following sections. Other research efforts have focused on a certain stage (e.g., caching, data detection) within the AR chain which can further propel to elevate the performance of Mobile Augmented Reality (MAR) apps (Wu et al., 2014; Liu et al., 2019). However, there are still lots of challenges in this area such as the better addressing of user mobility, the standardization of mobile web browsers and the design of low-cost architectures (Qiao et al., 2019; Li et al., 2020; Cziva and Pezaros, 2017).

Mobile edge cloud (MEC) allows the deployment of services at the edge of the network and hence is easier to meet the requirements of latency, computational offloading and responsiveness (Satyanarayanan, 2017). The service placement of MEC becomes a challenge because the adjacent cloud node might change in a mobility event (Satyanarayanan, 2017). Service migration is considered as a typical way to handle the mobility effect. A solution provided by Wang et al. (2016) tries to minimize the latency and deals with dynamic changes in micro mobile clouds (MMC). Wang et al. (2016) introduce predicted values to find and compare each configuration's future costs. After defining a look-ahead window to find a suitable time slot for prediction, the proposed scheme aims to minimize the average latency during this specific period. Both simulations and real-world traces reveal that their proposed algorithms are close to the optimal solution and the gap to the optimum increases with more arrived requests in the network.

However, according to Weyns et al. (2010), functional aspects of different components of the architecture like locations (single/distributed) and coordination type (centralized or not) should be considered in a more meticulous manner for allowing better flexibility, scalability and ability of approaching global optima by different proposed algorithms. Thus, a regional planning architecture, that makes use of functions like monitoring and analysis of components at each mobile device while a centralized plan component makes the final decision, is proposed and compared with a fully decentralized one (each node has all the underlying components) by Persone and Grassi (2019). Simulation experiments reveal that the proposed regional planning has a better overall performance since it is meant to achieve much lower system cost with only a small increase on the cost of the mobile terminal due to the duplicate deployment.

The combination of MEC and MAR can further reduce the transmission latency and provide a better solution for this NP-hard resource allocation problem. The FACT (fast and accurate object analysis) algorithm (Liu et al., 2018) and the UAP (user allocation-aware placement) algorithm (Guo et al., 2020) are presented and compared as examples. After given a similar mobile edge scenario (as shown in Figure 1), both algorithms consider the service latency as the main driving factor and then propose a trade-off model to solve the problem. It is worth noting that both algorithms bring together wireless delay, wired link delay and computational delay to express the overall service delay. The FACT scheme also considers the frame accuracy that reflects the image quality into consideration while the UAP scheme selects the difference of edge computing (EC) workload to ensure a similar level of performance for all requests. Both algorithms finally introduce a parameter to adjust the weight of two factors in their formulation. According to the results provided by Liu et al. (2018), FACT can achieve a low latency with an acceptable frame accuracy. However, as they point out, diverse workloads with heterogeneous servers lead to the problem that the minimization of latency may not happen for network latency and computational latency simultaneously. In that sense, not all available EC can be made a full use in that scheme. Guo et

Figure 1. MEC scenario (Liu et al., 2018)

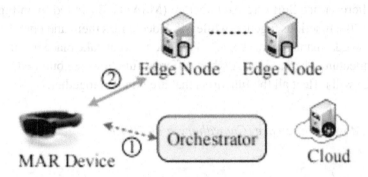

al. (2020) further point out the risk of overloading, underloading or even idle and hence accept the assumption that all EC share the same capacity. Thus, the UAP technique manages to achieve low latency with a generally balanced workload. From the above discussed examples, it is evident that for enabling efficient MEC support, multiple factors should be considered in the network with the corresponding limits of operation. This can be deemed as another level of complexity that comes into play, an issue that will be discussed in the sequel.

MICROSERVICES AND NETWORK FUNCTION VIRTUALIZATION

As already eluded above, NFV is one technique that contributes to the so called "softwarization" of the network. In essence, NFV decouples processing and controlling software from specialized hardware (e.g., load balancer, firewalls, TCP optimizer) (Chowdhury et al., 2019; Mijumbi et al., 2015), thereby leading to the replacement of physical network functions (PNFs) by monolithic software ones (Chowdhury et al., 2019; Selmadji et al., 2020). In addition to that, NFV allows that each service can be represented as an ordered set of different distinct VNF functions (which might be co-located or not), called network service function (NSF) (Laghrissiand et al., 2019). Based on the characteristics of a service request (for example deploying a MAR service or any other application), network operators can flexibly deploy a set of VNFs in the appropriate edge or core servers and chain them. In this case, the data flow is steered to go through all the VNFs in a pre-defined order. When deploying such chains of virtualized network function to create a service an important issue relates to the Quality of Service (QoS) and there have been various research works focusing on optimal chaining to reduce latency (Qu et al., 2016), on practical heuristic techniques for latency minimization (Gouareb et al., 2018) and on end-to-end view on delay (Ye et al., 2019).

Although such monolithic architecture (MA) has been widely applied by different solutions or service providers (e.g., Amazon and eBay) and proved its convenience in development and deployment, it still suffers from the inefficient usage of resources and the excessive cost in maintenance (Chowdhury et al., 2019; Selmadji et al., 2020; Gos and Zabierowski, 2020). According to Chowdhury et al. (2019) and De Lauretis (2019), monolithic VNFs allow lots of repeated functionalities and the corresponding structure grows, which eventually becomes a heavy burden for developing, managing, enabling efficient resource allocation and causes extra processing latencies, especially when networks operators need to steer traffic in the sequences of chained VNFs in the so-called Service Function Chains (SFC). The main difference between MA and Microservice Software Architecture (MSA) is illustrated by in Figure 2 (Chowdhury et al., 2019). MA ties the functions together while MSA decouples them and enables a more flexible arrangement. In other words, managing of the different functions can take place in a more granular manner using the MSA architecture whereas in MA when different functions are bundled together any decision about resource usage will reflect all the functions that are bundled together.

Figure 2. MA (a) & MSA (b) difference (Chowdhury et al., 2019)

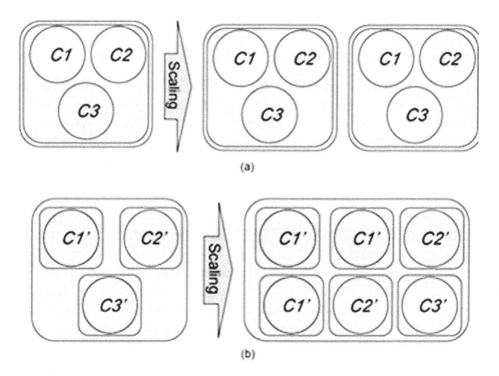

As a result, researchers like Chowdhury et al. (2019) and Karmel et al. (2016) adopt MSA as a better modular design with a more flexible service composition. Recently, microservices are witnessed to be a new trend and an efficient Service Oriented Architecture (SOA) style (shown in Figure 3) (Munaf et al., 2019), where small independent services consist of an application (Selmadji et al., 2020). Microservices are responsible for managing their own data and communicate with others through light weight mechanisms (Selmadji et al., 2020; De Lauretis, 2019). Thus, they are self-contained, loosely coupled and share a common standard communication protocol (API) (Chowdhury et al., 2019). Figure 4 shows the evolution from MA to MSA (Munaf et al., 2019)

A typical architectural design called Flurries can reveal MSA's benefits (Zhang et al., 2016). Flurries, an NFV platform, takes per-flow customization at the data plane into consideration and applies a hybrid polling-interrupt processing to support a large number of Network Functions (NF) (Zhang et al., 2016). In their design shown by Figure 5, an **NF manager** monitors the network and decide whether to forward the flow to its **flow director** (wake/sleep, wakeup order controlled by **Priority Scheduler**). The info is recorded in the **flow table** if the director explores and finds an ideal match for a flow and

Figure 3. Microservices (a) & Basic Service Oriented Architecture (b) (Munaf et al., 2019)

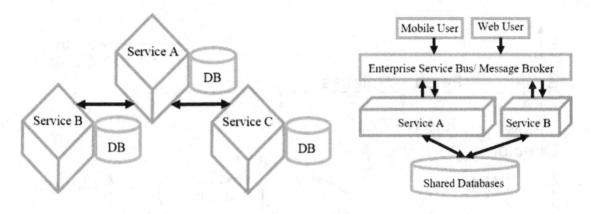

Figure 4. Evolution from MA to MSA [30]

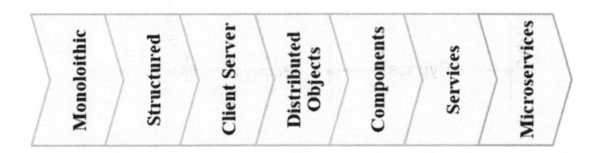

an NF. **RX thread** inside checks and determines if a flow is old with records while **TX thread** reads transmission info and search the flow table to decide whether to send the current flow to another NF. Therefore, Flurries can optimize lots of different NFs per server through its flexible assignment of each flow. This satement is supported by their experiments which show obvious gains in latency, throughput and CPU usage.

Before moving to re-architecting VNFs, it is necessary to consider a suitable decomposition approach. In general, granularity and independence of microservices should be focused during this stage (Selmadji et al., 2020; De Lauretis, 2019). It is extended into 16 coupling criteria (e.g., Latency, Storage Similarity and Consistency Constraint) through a further discussion in literature and industry experience (Gysel et al., 2016). All functionalities that can be decoupled are extracted with a well-defined granularity level and then new functional entities are created based on them (Chowdhury et al., 2019; Boubendir et al., 2017). The service logic should be separated so that microservices will not have a predefined sequence and each of them should be a stateless service, processing each request without being affected by the previous ones (Kablan et al., 2015; Boubendir et al., 2017). Although a decomposition with a fine granularity owns advantages in maintainability, re-usability and scalability, it requires more delay in communication and packet processing (Chowdhury et al., 2019; Selmadji et al., 2020). Thus, during the identification of functionalities and the determination of granularity, domain related knowledge and

Figure 5. Flurries design (Zhang et al., 2016)

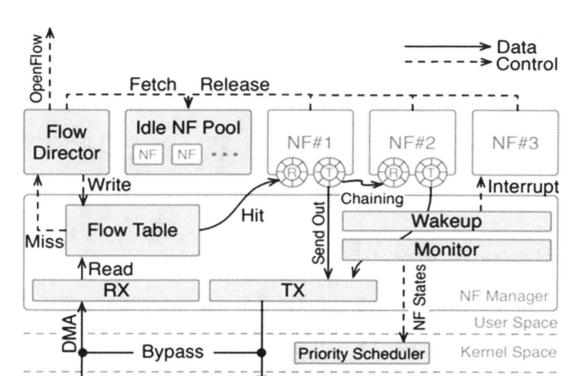

other existing open resource VNFs might help eliminate the monolithic nature and create an efficient decomposition (Boubendir et al., 2017; Chowdhury et al., 2019).

BUILDING BLOCKS (FUNCTIONS) OF NOMINAL MAR SERVICES

The MAR service can be decomposed and identified as a list of functions working in a pre-defined sequence. Broadly speaking, it can be split into four basic functions: Object Detection, Feature Extraction, Object Recognition and Object Matching (Zhang et al., 2018; Qiao et al., 2019). Firstly, frames recorded by camera are detected and those with target objects are selected and uploaded. Then, feature points are extracted and provided for recognizing the original image. Finally, it goes to the database to search and find an appropriate match for presentation on screen. These functions can be extended or further decomposed to satisfy the different requirements and constraints of the MAR system.

The mobile AR system designed for socialization extends the "Feature Extraction" with an offline probabilistic model that encodes feature descriptors to better compress them (Zhang et al., 2018). It also splits "Object Matching" into three minor steps: Template Matching, Object Tracking and Annotation Rendering. Specially focused on 3D objects, Zhang et al. not only find a match for recognized objects but also calculate the position of the target in Template Matching. Object Tracking marks the position and avoids recalculation for other frames. Virtual content is finally determined for displaying or sharing to achieve a better user performance.

The work by Liu and Han (2018), proposes an optimization engine for increased precision on Object Detection with functions of model selection and resource mapping are deployed at an edge cloud. In addition, AR quality monitoring and AR adapting are executed on user device for better presentation on screen. In a slightly different approach from Zhang et al. (2018) and Liu and Han (2018), some research effort focuses on tailoring computationally intensive functions apart and regroup them on mobile devices (Huynh et al., 2017; Zeng et al., 2017) or edge/cloud servers (Liu et al., 2018; Shea et al., 2017). From the above discussion it becomes apparent that advanced services such as mobile AR can be decomposed since the service per se builds by several different complex functions. Therefore, the use of microservices, as explained in the sequel, is a natural fit to explore that inherent decomposition of emerging complex services and applications that embed multi-modal information and require various complex image/vision processing algorithms to run efficiently.

MAR UNDER THE LENSES OF MICROSERVICES

As mentioned above, advanced services including different flavors of augmented reality can be decomposed into multiple elementary functions ordered as a service chain (Cziva and Pezaros, 2017; Akhtar et al., 2018). This can be revealed by the framework proposed by Zhang et al. (2018) and the protocol proposed by Liu and Han (2018). Considering the service function chaining (**SFC**) scenario, Guo et al. (2016), Gharbaoui et al. (2018) and Liu et al. (2019) further discuss the routing optimization issues. These typical designs and algorithms are presented below to show their state of art when treating emerging mobile AR services as microservices.

Figure 6 (Zhang et al., 2018) shows the architecture of a framework based on decomposed functions mentioned in section 3: Building Blocks of Nominal MAR Services. In the application layer, the Recognition Proxy serves as a bridge that links both layers. With the support of the Visual Tracker and the Annotation Renderer, the application can track the object's position in continuous camera frames and augments objects based on virtual content sent from the Recognition Proxy. In the Base Layer, a list of microservices handles frames uploaded from the application layer. The Scene Matcher ensures a suitable match between AR objects and local resources with the support from a Cloud Manager. The Motion Detector monitors the status of recognized objects to determine whether they satisfy the current camera frames. The Peer Manager together with the Annotation Synchronizer enable the simultaneous sharing and interactions between different devices. As shown by arrows in Figure 5 (Zhang et al., 2018), the flow has a pre-defined order among main microservices while some other modules provide functionalities to satisfy extra requirements like detecting required poses and enabling socializing.

From the overview of protocols shown by Figure 7, Model Selection, Resource Allocation, Frame Rate and Frame Size can be optimized with the support from three components: Quality of Augmentation (QoA) Monitor, AR adaptation and Optimization Engine (Liu and Han, 2018). The flow follows the marked order in SFC to execute each function provided by different microservices. MAR clients first send requests with measurements of network conditions to the edge server. Then the optimization engine determines the suitable size of frames with computation models for Object Detection. Requests are mapped for better computational resource allocation. Such optimized configuration data are sent back to clients so that the AR Adaption module will adapt rate and size of frames accordingly. Afterwards,

Figure 6. Collaborative Augmented Reality for Socialization (CARS) Framework architecture (Zhang et al., 2018)

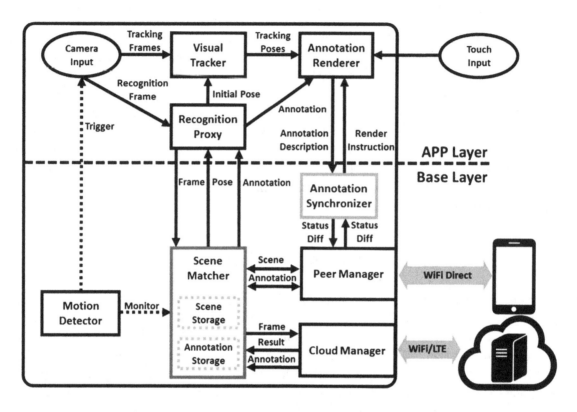

Figure 7. Dynamic Adaptive Augmented Reality (DARE) protocol overview (Liu and Han, 2018)

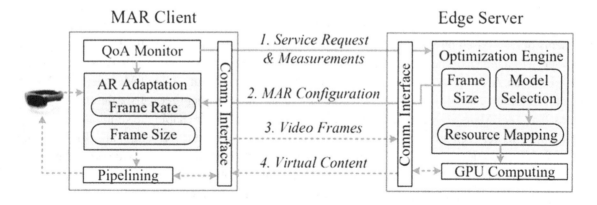

suitable frames containing AR Objects are selected and transmitted for computing purposes. Finally, virtual content will be sent back to augments the target objects on screen.

Given a configured network environment, it is possible to identify the execution status of microservices through logs. Thus, the cost of forwarding packets can be minimized in their multistage graph constructed based on the max-flow min-cut theory (Liu et al., 2019). In Figure 8 (LB: Load balancer, FW: Firewall,

Figure 8. Possible Paths in 5G network (Liu et al., 2019)

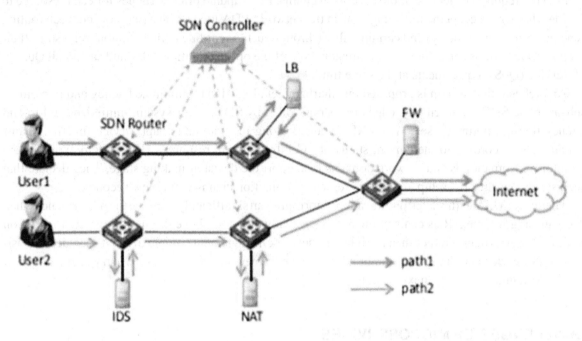

IDS: Intrusion detection Systems, NAT: Network Address Translation), the forwarding of packets between the user and the Internet can go through different paths supported by different VNFs (Liu et al., 2019). Three polynomial time algorithms are designed separately for constructing multistage graphs, deriving minimum cuts for Service Function Chaining (**SFC**) and scaling with minimized transmission cost. According to their experiment results, their scaling algorithm of Service Function Path (**SFP**) is clearly better than deriving a path randomly (RS) or scaling with maximum processing ability (MC).

In the research of Baldoni et al. (2018), NFV-oriented edge computing enhancements are provided to better integrate edge computing orchestration and manage the NFV-based ecosystem. In that context, the authors investigated the additions of three main extensions to the architecture to support the edge computing network for 5G services. First the proposed multi-layer orchestration provides a uniform API for 5G services. Further orchestration functionalities are extracted from original services and decoupled for re-architecting purposes to interoperate with the MEC orchestrator. Finally, a series of components including a system partitioner compose the base of the edge cloud and companion software architecture to enforce edge virtualization security and enable multi-tenancy. Thus, the proposed so-called 5GCity architecture is declared to be NFV-compatible and can support 5G hosts. This is an example of the combination of 5G micro-services, NFV and MEC.

In the research of Guo et al. (2016), Traffic Merging Algorithm (TMA) and Primal Dual update Algorithm (PDA) are designed for offline and online optimization of traffic routing in Software-Defined Networks (SDN). They consider the network flow composed of various network devices that support network functions (firewall, content cache, WAN load balancer, etc.), known as middleboxes. They consider multiple factors that affect the routing performance, which are throughput, edge congestion, weighted aggregate delay and middlebox load ratio. Both TMA and PDA focus on actual chaining and satisfy a series of physical constraints. TMA merges decomposed initial **SFC**s by tree structures and connect them in the required order to explore optimized chains. PDA update price variables for each resource to decide whether to accept the incoming flow in the network. PDA focuses on a trade-off between routing scheme performance (delay) and certain utility (throughput). According to their simulation results, their proposed algorithms can achieve approximately 90% of the optimal routing delay and satisfy all Quality of Service (QoS) requirements at the same time.

An orchestration system is proposed by Gharbaoui et al. (2018) to minimize latency and implement self-adaptive **SFC** on distributed edge clouds controlled by SDN. Their system minimizes end-to-end latency through optimally selecting VNF instances along the path and adapt service function chains dynamically according to the current status of 5G infrastructure resources. The system exploits data monitoring from clouds and network domains to support the decision-making stage. They declare that such system ensures the setup and update for service function chains within few seconds.

Therefore, **MSA** with related optimization algorithms can significantly improve the performance when decomposing mobile AR as chained microservices. However, the above discussion mostly focused on achievable performance rather than the inherent network management complexity that such decomposition of the service and the application of microservice frameworks might entail. We try to shed light on that important aspect in the next Section.

CHALLENGES OF MICROSERVICES

Undeniably, several key challenges arise when deploying granular microservices and the most significant ones are listed and briefly explained below following discussions (Chowdhury et al., 2019; Munaf et al., 2019):

- Interactions: it does not only mean the communication among microservices but also includes clients. As illustrated by Figure 9, too many requests from users may lead to a serious congestion in the network. Thus, a balance should be achieved between the simplicity of client-side software and extensive implementation of microservices at edge nodes. An adapted traffic forwarding strategy should be proposed based on the amount of data, the frequency of exchanges (e.g., based upon duty cycle management procedures in IoT environments) and latency constraints. In addition, the entry module and the workload of microservices should be carefully considered to avoid potential risks of overloading.
- Deployment and resource allocation: It is about placing VNFs and allocating sufficient resources to meet QoS requirements. Even for a static scenario of this problem (without user mobility), the complexity grows in a rather (high degree) polynomial manner. The underlying complexity of this problem is illustrated by Figure 10; this toy example illustrates the number of possible configurations (in this case 24) in the case of 4 CPU cores, 3 possible utilization levels and 2 memory allocations (4x3x2). It is evident that as the level of granularity increases the complexity increases substantially (cubic degree of polynomial) and therefore suitable mechanisms should be in place to allow for an autonomous operation that can allow efficient decision policies to be implemented. On that frontier, data-driven based Machine Learning (ML) -based algorithms are regarded as solutions with significant potential that will allow managing such complex interactions in both near-optimal manner as well as providing decision making in real time which is amenable for real time implementation.

Figure 9. Direct interactions from Users to Microservices (Munaf et al., 2019)

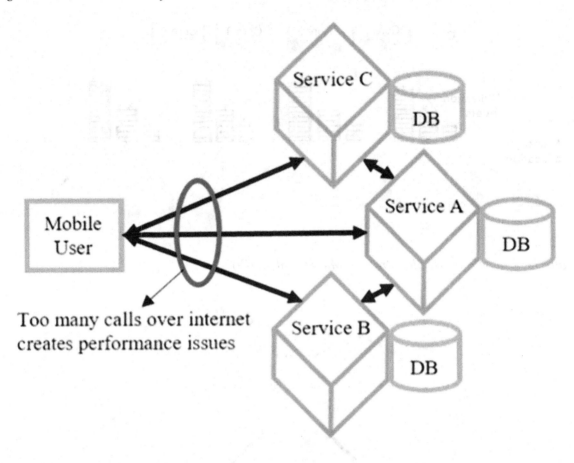

- Transactions and security: Data ownership should be clarified and data exchange among microservices and distributed databases should be carefully managed to ensure ACID (Atomicity, Consistency, Isolation, Durability). An example transaction process with security requirements is shown below in Figure 11. The service is first ordered by microservice module "B". Then module "A" manages the booking of related items and sends data to module "C" for final payment. If any errors (or exceptions) are spotted during this process, mechanisms like rollback are triggered. Thus, the usage and transmission of data should be recorded and monitored by specialized modules. Such feature can be naturally applied in ML-based designs which requires empirical records to provide reliable predictions and suggestions.

- Service discovery: It is necessary to find the appropriate microservice instance for a certain request, especially in a large and complex infrastructure. The suitable path and availability of a certain functional entity should be recorded and updated. Similarly, path-planning problem is closely related to service deployment and resource allocation. ML-based designs seem to have advantages in finding good-quality paths approaching to optimal ones within the service latency limit. A standard component (and communication protocol) is recommended to register all microservices with their location and status in a dynamic fashion.

Figure 10. Complexity of Microservices Problem via a toy example

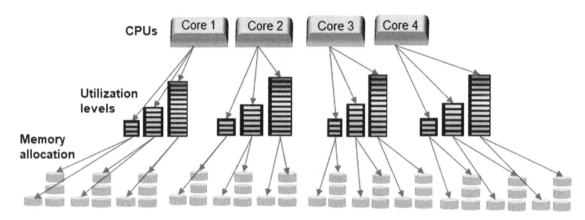

Figure 11. Example Transaction Process (Munaf et al., 2019)

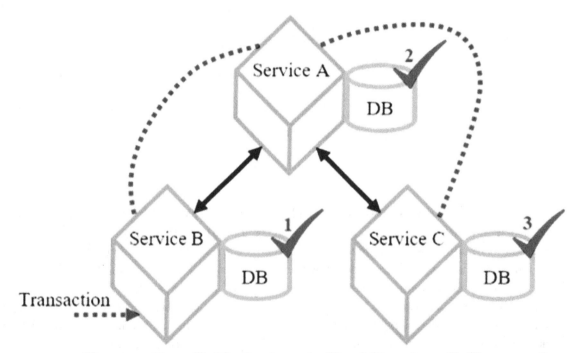

- Operations, Administration and Maintenance (OAM) framework: Overall OAM requirements and especially solutions for monitoring, tracking and checking the performance of an ordered chain of different virtualized functions is another open-ended area. Within IETF an OAM framework for service function chaining has been defined and several key gaps are identified (Aldrin et al.,

2020). In terms of monitoring packets can be placed on different paths and potential lag, or attain slow response resulting in the degradation of the entire system. Active monitoring modules (e.g., Circiut Breaker) are recommended, which are also useful to address transaction and security issues.

· Fault tolerance: The MSA should keep consistency of transactions during the recovery from failures within milliseconds. A proper mechanism including appropriate warning messages and redirection is required to handle partial failures to avoid the ripple effect (disabling the whole system).

TAMING COMPLEXITY VIA MACHINE LEARNING (ML)

As already eluded in the previous section, tackling network complexity issues for provisioning granular advanced services under microservices architectures raises several challenges. Leveraging ML techniques on MSA, such as neural networks or reinforcement learning, are considered to have the potential to solve problems in this area. Till now, several ML-based solutions are proposed with improved prediction capabilities, flow path management and resource allocation features (Bianchini et al., 2020). However, the best way to use ML to address these issues remains unclear. Several typical examples applying ML are described and discussed in the following to identify techniques and related designs with promising potential.

Predicting different network states has been one of the key applications of utilizing data collected from logs and traces. According to Zuo et al. (2019) and their figure (Figure 12), network paths are treated as sequential data to construct a **sequence-to-sequence model**, in which **source input** and **target paths** are treated as a sequence of nodes. An attention mechanism oversees the data collection to compute a relevant path from input sequence to target sequence based on empirical records (summarized as **context vector**). The proposed **beam search** can avoid the sinking in a local optimal solution and further explore global optimal solutions. With the support of deep learning techniques for traffic engineering purposes (neural networks and Natural Language Processing sentences analysis), the proposed technique manages to achieve an efficient network-level path. Furthermore, numerical simulations reveal that such data-driven path planning techniques shows advantages in delay and throughput in both congested and non-congested conditions. Thus, predictions can be generally accurate and useful for network operation with reliable empirical data.

As pointed out by Jalodia et al. (2019), a model applying Deep Reinforcement Learning (Deep Neural Network, DNN) can also provide resource predictions in dynamic NFV environments. Multiple agents spread over the network and provide their asynchronous observations of the network to reinforce their learned policy and hence can achieve optimized prediction output. According to the design shown in Figure 13, DNN algorithms in the Deep Reinforcement Learning (DRL) agent work as a non-linear approximators that provides an automated dynamic scaling solution for resource allocation purposes and has advantages in dealing with large numbers of outcomes and impacts over time (Jalodia et al., 2019). Based on these predictions, their model then moves to an optimum learned stage that optimizes provisioned resources and takes scaling action on the actual 5G infrastructure.

Among the above two solutions, ML algorithms are integrated as isolated modules (Encoder/Decoder by Zuo et al., 2019; DRL Agent by Jalodia et al., 2019) to provide predictions and suggestions for the decision-making stage. Such modules do not directly interfere with the deployment, allocation and configuration of NFVs, which is computationally friendly and enhances the overall independency and flexibility. However, because these algorithms generate solutions based on records and work separately

Figure 12. Schematic structural view of the sequence-to-sequence model (Zuo et al., 2019)

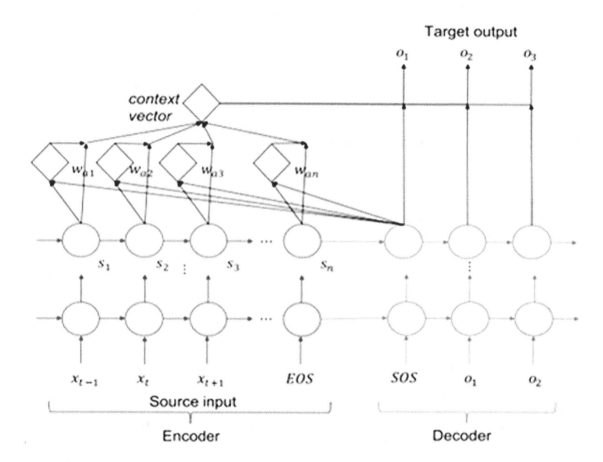

from the SFC, they are not able to validate their solutions immediately; in addition to that, this might cause potential risks like path non-connectivity and low generalization accuracy (Zuo et al., 2019; Jalodia et al., 2019). Extra prevention or re-computation mechanism are applied to increase stability and fault tolerance. This indicates that the ML module can enhance the performance and provide a data-driven decision framework. However, note that several functionalities need to be supported, at the cost of aggravating the overall complexity of the system.

As a result, some recent research efforts tried to combine the ML mechanism directly with containers or SDN controllers. An orchestration framework Pick-Test-Choose (PTC) is proposed by Nath et al. (2019) with an iterative reinforcement learning algorithm (Bayesian Optimization). Different from previous ones, this research directly deploys the algorithm on the edge cloud controller (IoT controller, control devices using fog computing) to solve the micro-service allocation problem. Thus, by monitoring and predicting resource availability and workload characteristics, the framework picks a suitable fog device and gives it a try to see if the actual result satisfies the expectation. This process validates the solution before using it and makes their learning algorithm more adaptive to the environment. As shown in Figure 14, the edge cloud controller manages the offloading and edge cloud devices manage computation and storage related to the service (Nath et al., 2019). Inside the controller, the Application

Figure 13. Architecture of DRL agent's interaction with NFV Service Function Chain (Jalodia et al., 2019)

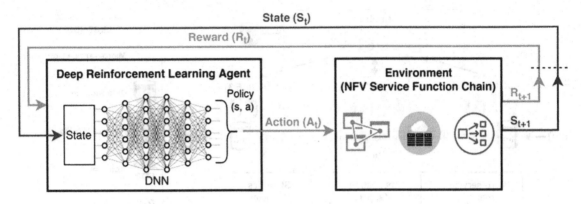

Mapper maps requests to its target application and the application is decomposed into microservices by the Microservice Organizer. The Microservice dispatcher together with the Statistics Collector identifies a suitable placement for microservices. When the controller finds out an improved solution through the adaptive learning algorithm, the Microservice Migration Engine will rearrange microservices on the so-called fog devices. The Sensor and Actuator enables interactions between microservices in containers. Therefore, their orchestration framework can make full use of prior observations and posterior distributions from iterative experiments. This is also supported by their simulation results which shows significant gains in average memory and CPU usage. In addition, the performance of their design in average bandwidth and response time is also slightly better than other baseline schemes. This advantage is more obvious in larger and/or more congested network settings.

Direct integration of ML on container or controller does simplify the overall structure and hence decreases the cost of communication and deployment. However, this also indicates that each different application should come with a set of modules to be hosted in the controller, which leaves the controller a heavy burden of interaction, computation and storage. As argued by Nath et al. (2019), although the number of applications deployed in such centralized framework has an upper limit, this can be enlarged through techniques like paralleling. Thus, as mentioned earlier, the most efficient way of applying ML techniques on microservices still remains a significant challenge and an open-ended research problem.

FINAL REMARKS AND CONCLUSION

The provisioning of advanced services such as multi-modal augmented reality via a granular VNF-based microservices approach with edge cloud support provides significant benefits but those gains come with several challenges that need to be considered and further investigated.

The aim of this chapter is to shed further light and to provide a holistic view on the aspects of advanced service decomposition, the applicability of granular microservices frameworks and on promising ways to curb the underlying network complexity by utilizing emerging machine learning techniques. More specifically, it has been argued that even though microservices architectures have proved to be an efficient network structure for advanced 5G applications like mobile augmented reality, however, issues

Figure 14. Architecture of PTC framework (Nath et al., 2019)

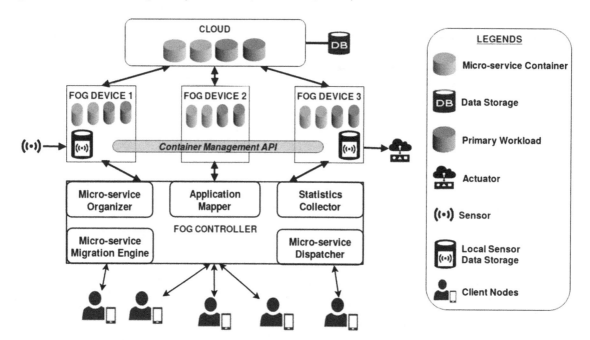

related to service decomposition, path-planning and resource allocation still require further research. To this end, machine learning techniques have the ability of adapting to an evolving network environment and to provide dynamic predictions and suggestions. Therefore, efficient integration of ML with MSA should be further explored not only to master network complexity but also to boost the efficient realization of advanced services and applications such as mobile augmented reality.

REFERENCES

Akhtar, N., Matta, I., Raza, A., Goratti, L., Braun, T., & Esposito, F. (2018, June). Virtual function placement and traffic steering over 5g multi-technology networks. In *2018 4th IEEE Conference on Network Softwarization and Workshops (NetSoft)* (pp. 114-122). IEEE.

Aldrin, A., Pignataro, C., Kumar, N., Krishnan, R., & Ghanwani, A. (2020). *Service Function Chaining (SFC) Operations, Administration, and Maintenance (OAM) Framework*. RFC 8924. Available: https://tools.ietf.org/html/rfc8924

Baldoni, G., Cruschelli, P., Paolino, M., Meixner, C. C., Albanese, A., Papageorgiou, A., & Simeonidou, D. (2018, November). Edge Computing Enhancements in an NFV-based Ecosystem for 5G Neutral Hosts. In *2018 IEEE Conference on Network Function Virtualization and Software Defined Networks (NFV-SDN)* (pp. 1-5). IEEE.

Bianchini, R., Fontoura, M., Cortez, E., Bonde, A., Muzio, A., Constantin, A. M., ... Russinovich, M. (2020). Toward ML-centric cloud platforms. *Communications of the ACM*, *63*(2), 50–59.

Boubendir, A., Bertin, E., & Simoni, N. (2017, March). A VNF-as-a-service design through microservices disassembling the IMS. In *2017 20th Conference on Innovations in Clouds, Internet and Networks (ICIN)* (pp. 203-210). IEEE.

Chowdhury, S. R., Salahuddin, M. A., Limam, N., & Boutaba, R. (2019). Re-architecting NFV ecosystem with microservices: State of the art and research challenges. *IEEE Network*, *33*(3), 168–176.

Cziva, R., & Pezaros, D. P. (2017, May). On the latency benefits of edge NFV. In *2017 ACM/IEEE Symposium on Architectures for Networking and Communications Systems (ANCS)* (pp. 105-106). ACM.

De Lauretis, L. (2019, October). From Monolithic Architecture to Microservices Architecture. In *2019 IEEE International Symposium on Software Reliability Engineering Workshops (ISSREW)* (pp. 93-96). IEEE.

Frank, A. (2016). *Pokémon Go Plus: Everything you need to know*. Polygon. Vox Media.

Gerő, B., Jocha, D., Szabó, R., Czentye, J., Haja, D., Németh, B., & Murillo, L. M. C. (2017). The orchestration in 5G exchange—A multi-provider NFV framework for 5G services. In *2017 IEEE Conference on Network Function Virtualization and Software Defined Networks (NFV-SDN)* (pp. 1-2). IEEE.

Gharbaoui, M., Contoli, C., Davoli, G., Cuffaro, G., Martini, B., Paganelli, F., ... Castoldi, P. (2018, November). Demonstration of Latency-Aware and Self-Adaptive Service Chaining in 5G/SDN/NFV infrastructures. In *2018 IEEE Conference on Network Function Virtualization and Software Defined Networks (NFV-SDN)* (pp. 1-2). IEEE.

Gos, K., & Zabierowski, W. (2020, April). The Comparison of Microservice and Monolithic Architecture. In *2020 IEEE XVIth International Conference on the Perspective Technologies and Methods in MEMS Design (MEMSTECH)* (pp. 150-153). IEEE.

Gouareb, R., Friderikos, V., & Aghvami, A.-H. (2018). Virtual network functions routing and placement for edge cloud latency minimization. *IEEE Journal on Selected Areas in Communications*, *36*(10), 2346–2357.

Guo, L., Pang, J., & Walid, A. (2016, November). Dynamic service function chaining in SDN-enabled networks with middleboxes. In *2016 IEEE 24th International Conference on Network Protocols (ICNP)* (pp. 1-10). IEEE.

Guo, Y., Wang, S., Zhou, A., Xu, J., Yuan, J., & Hsu, C. H. (2020). User allocation-aware edge cloud placement in mobile edge computing. *Software, Practice & Experience*, *50*(5), 489–502.

Gysel, M., Kölbener, L., Giersche, W., & Zimmermann, O. (2016, September). Service cutter: A systematic approach to service decomposition. In *European Conference on Service-Oriented and Cloud Computing* (pp. 185-200). Springer.

Huynh, L. N., Lee, Y., & Balan, R. K. (2017, June). Deepmon: Mobile gpu-based deep learning framework for continuous vision applications. In *Proceedings of the 15th Annual International Conference on Mobile Systems, Applications, and Services* (pp. 82-95). Academic Press.

Jalodia, N., Henna, S., & Davy, A. (2019, November). Deep Reinforcement Learning for Topology-Aware VNF Resource Prediction in NFV Environments. In *2019 IEEE Conference on Network Function Virtualization and Software Defined Networks (NFV-SDN)* (pp. 1-5). IEEE.

Kablan, M., Alsudais, A., Keller, E., & Le, F. (2017). Stateless network functions: Breaking the tight coupling of state and processing. In *14th {USENIX} Symposium on Networked Systems Design and Implementation ({NSDI} 17)* (pp. 97-112). USENIX.

Karmel, A., Chandramouli, R., & Iorga, M. (2016). Nist definition of microservices, application containers and system virtual machines (No. NIST Special Publication (SP) 800-180 (Draft)). National Institute of Standards and Technology.

Laghrissiand, A., & Taleb, T. (2019). A survey on the placement of virtual resources and virtual network functions. *IEEE Commun. Surveys Tuts.*, *21*(2), 1409–1434.

Li, L., Qiao, X., Lu, Q., Ren, P., & Lin, R. (2020). Rendering Optimization for Mobile Web 3D Based on Animation Data Separation and On-Demand Loading. *IEEE Access: Practical Innovations, Open Solutions*, *8*, 88474–88486.

Liu, F., Li, P., Gao, S., Wan, X., & An, W. (2019, December). Optimized Service Function Path Scaling in SDN/NFV Networks. In *Proceedings of the 2019 5th International Conference on Systems, Control and Communications* (pp. 27-32). Academic Press.

Liu, L., Li, H., & Gruteser, M. (2019, August). Edge assisted real-time object detection for mobile augmented reality. In *The 25th Annual International Conference on Mobile Computing and Networking* (pp. 1-16). Academic Press.

Liu, Q., & Han, T. (2018, September). Dare: Dynamic adaptive mobile augmented reality with edge computing. In *2018 IEEE 26th International Conference on Network Protocols (ICNP)* (pp. 1-11). IEEE.

Liu, Q., Huang, S., Opadere, J., & Han, T. (2018, April). An edge network orchestrator for mobile augmented reality. In *IEEE INFOCOM 2018-IEEE Conference on Computer Communications* (pp. 756-764). IEEE.

Mijumbi, R., Serrat, J., Gorricho, J. L., Bouten, N., De Turck, F., & Boutaba, R. (2015). Network function virtualization: State-of-the-art and research challenges. *IEEE Communications Surveys and Tutorials*, *18*(1), 236–262.

Munaf, R. M., Ahmed, J., Khakwani, F., & Rana, T. (2019, March). Microservices Architecture: Challenges and Proposed Conceptual Design. In *2019 International Conference on Communication Technologies (ComTech)* (pp. 82-87). IEEE.

Nath, S. B., Chattopadhyay, S., Karmakar, R., Addya, S. K., Chakraborty, S., & Ghosh, S. K. (2019, December). PTC: Pick-Test-Choose to Place Containerized Micro-Services in IoT. In *2019 IEEE Global Communications Conference (GLOBECOM)* (pp. 1-6). IEEE.

Personè, V. D. N., & Grassi, V. (2019, July). Architectural Issues for Self-Adaptive Service Migration Management in Mobile Edge Computing Scenarios. In *2019 IEEE International Conference on Edge Computing (EDGE)* (pp. 27-29). IEEE.

Qiao, X., Ren, P., Dustdar, S., Liu, L., Ma, H., & Chen, J. (2019). Web AR: A promising future for mobile augmented reality—State of the art, challenges, and insights. *Proceedings of the IEEE, 107*(4), 651–666. doi:10.1109/JPROC.2019.2895105

Qiao, X., Ren, P., Nan, G., Liu, L., Dustdar, S., & Chen, J. (2019). Mobile web augmented reality in 5G and beyond: Challenges, opportunities, and future directions. *China Communications, 16*(9), 141–154. doi:10.23919/JCC.2019.09.010

Qu, L., Assi, C., & Shaban, K. (2016). Delay-aware scheduling and resource optimization with network function virtualization. *IEEE Transactions on Communications, 64*(9), 3746–3758.

Satyanarayanan, M. (2017). The emergence of edge computing. *IEEE Computer, 50*(1), 30–39.

Selmadji, A., Seriai, A. D., Bouziane, H. L., Mahamane, R. O., Zaragoza, P., & Dony, C. (2020, March). From Monolithic Architecture Style to Microservice one Based on a Semi-Automatic Approach. In *2020 IEEE International Conference on Software Architecture (ICSA)* (pp. 157-168). IEEE.

Shea, R., Sun, A., Fu, S., & Liu, J. (2017, June). Towards fully offloaded cloud-based AR: Design, implementation and experience. In *Proceedings of the 8th ACM on Multimedia Systems Conference* (pp. 321-330). ACM.

Wang, S., Urgaonkar, R., He, T., Chan, K., Zafer, M., & Leung, K. K. (2016). Dynamic service placement for mobile micro-clouds with predicted future costs. *IEEE Transactions on Parallel and Distributed Systems, 28*(4), 1002–1016.

Weyns, D., Schmerl, B., Grassi, V., Malek, S., Mirandola, R., Prehofer, C., & Göschka, K. M. (2013). On patterns for decentralized control in self-adaptive systems. In *Software Engineering for Self-Adaptive Systems II* (pp. 76–107). Springer.

Wu, C. C., Tung, L. P., Lin, C. Y., Lin, B. S. P., & Tseng, Y. C. (2014, June). On local cache management strategies for Mobile Augmented Reality. In *Proceeding of IEEE International Symposium on a World of Wireless, Mobile and Multimedia Networks 2014* (pp. 1-3). IEEE.

Ye, Q., Zhuang, W., Li, X., & Rao, J. (2019). End-to-end delay modeling for embedded VNF chains in 5G core networks. *IEEE Internet Things J., 6*(1), 692–704.

Zeng, X., Cao, K., & Zhang, M. (2017, June). MobileDeepPill: A small-footprint mobile deep learning system for recognizing unconstrained pill images. In *Proceedings of the 15th Annual International Conference on Mobile Systems, Applications, and Services* (pp. 56-67). Academic Press.

Zhang, W., Han, B., Hui, P., Gopalakrishnan, V., Zavesky, E., & Qian, F. (2018, February). CARS: Collaborative augmented reality for socialization. In *Proceedings of the 19th International Workshop on Mobile Computing Systems & Applications* (pp. 25-30). Academic Press.

Zhang, W., Hwang, J., Rajagopalan, S., Ramakrishnan, K. K., & Wood, T. (2016, December). Flurries: Countless fine-grained nfs for flexible per-flow customization. In *Proceedings of the 12th International on Conference on emerging Networking Experiments and Technologies* (pp. 3-17). Academic Press.

Zuo, Y., Wu, Y., Min, G., & Cui, L. (2019). Learning-based network path planning for traffic engineering. *Future Generation Computer Systems*, *92*, 59–67.

ADDITIONAL READING

Azuma, R. T. (1997). A survey of augmented reality. *Presence (Cambridge, Mass.)*, *6*(4), 355–385. doi:10.1162/pres.1997.6.4.355

Campbell, A., Coulson, G., & Hutchison, D. (1994). A quality of service architecture. *Computer Communication Review*, *24*(2), 6–27. doi:10.1145/185595.185648

Dragoni, M., Giallorenzo, S., Lafuente, A. L., Mazzara, M., Montesi, F., Mustafin, R., & Safina, L. (2017). Microservices: Yesterday, Today, and Tomorrow. *Present and Ulterior Software Engineering, Springer*, *2017*, 195–216. doi:10.1007/978-3-319-67425-4_12

ETSI NFV ISG. (2014). *Network Functions Virtualisation (NFV)*. Architectural Framework. Group Specification.

Fazio, M., Celesti, A., Ranjan, R., Liu, C., Chen, L., & Villari, M. (2016). Open issues in scheduling microservices in the cloud. *IEEE Cloud Comput.*, *3*(5), 81–88. doi:10.1109/MCC.2016.112

Han, B., Gopalakrishnan, V., Ji, L., & Lee, S. (2015). Network function virtualization: Challenges and opportunities for innovations. *Communications Magazine, IEEE*, *53*(2), 90–97. doi:10.1109/MCOM.2015.7045396

Hawilo, H., Shami, A., Mirahmadi, M., & Asal, R. (2014). NFV: State of the art, challenges, and implementation in next generation mobile networks (vEPC). *IEEE Network*, *28*(6), 18–26. doi:10.1109/MNET.2014.6963800

Roseboro, R. (2016). Cloud-Native NFV Architecture for Agile Service Creation & Scaling. White paper, Retrieved 22 February 2021, from https://www.mellanox.com/related-docs/whitepapers/wp-heavyreading-nfv-architecture-for-agile-service.pdf

Wu, H. K., Lee, S. W. Y., Chang, H. Y., & Liang, J. C. (2013). Current status, opportunities and challenges of augmented reality in education. *Computers & Education*, *62*, 41–49. doi:10.1016/j.compedu.2012.10.024

KEY TERMS AND DEFINITIONS

Augmented Reality (AR): It integrates virtual objects into 3D real world based on computer perceptual information.

Microservices Architecture (MSA): It is an SOA structure that decouples, arranges, and manages service functions in a fine-grained manner with lightweight protocols.

Mobile Edge Cloud (MEC): It constructs a distributed service environment and enables cloud computing capabilities at the edge of a network, which is closer to the user.

Monolithic Architecture (MA): A software structural design that builds the system as a single unit.

Quality of Service (QoS): A measurement of the overall performance of a system or a service. In networking, it also includes traffic prioritization and resource reservation control mechanisms.

Service Function Chaining (SFC): An ordered set of abstract service functions (SFs) and ordering constraints that must be applied to packets, frames, and/or flows selected as a result of classification.

Service Oriented Architecture (SOA): An independent and self-contained software structural design where application components provide services to other ones through pre-defined communication protocols.

Virtual Network Functions (VNF): Network functions are virtualized into building blocks (chain together) to provide services and consist of several Virtual Machines or other containers.

ENDNOTES

[1] VNF hosting on containers are available – at the moment – only in Windows, Linux and Solaris OS.

[2] Using for example OpenStack for VMs and Kubernetes for containers; even though this hybrid approach might entail difficulties in the overall network resource management.

Chapter 10
Revisiting the Concept of Virtualized Residential Gateways

Jorge Proença
CISUC, DEI, University of Coimbra, Portugal

Tiago Cruz
ⓘ https://orcid.org/0000-0001-9278-6503
CISUC, DEI, University of Coimbra, Portugal

Paulo Simões
ⓘ https://orcid.org/0000-0002-5079-8327
CISUC, DEI, University of Coimbra, Portugal

Edmundo Monteiro
CISUC, DEI, University of Coimbra, Portugal

ABSTRACT

A diversity of technical advances in the field of network and systems virtualization have made it possible to consolidate and manage resources in an unprecedented scale. These advances have started to come out of the data centers, spreading towards the network service provider (NSP) and telecommunications operator infrastructure foundations, from the core to the edge networks, the access network, and the customer premises LAN (local area network). In this context, the residential gateway (RGW) constitutes an ideal candidate for virtualization, as it stands between the home LAN and the access network, imposing a considerable cost for the NSP while constituting a single point of failure for all the services offered to residential customers. This chapter presents the rationale for the virtual RGW (vRGW) concept, providing an overview of past and current implementation proposals and discussing how recent technological developments in key areas such as networking and virtualization have given a competitive edge to a RGW virtualization scenario, when compared with traditional deployments.

DOI: 10.4018/978-1-7998-7646-5.ch010

INTRODUCTION

As access networks evolve towards Fiber-To-The-Premises (FTTx) network topologies but also cable (considering the increase of up and downward speeds brought by DOCSIS 3.1 (CableLabs, 2014) deployments, and the considerable upstream increase with the current DOCSIS 4.0 specification (currently finished as 2020), to be deployed in the near future (Cablelabs, 2020)). Digital Subscriber Line (DSL) has been progressively phased out, with some providers discontinuing the service for new customers in 2020, while maintaining the service only for existing ones (Brodkin, 2020). This trend spells the end of an era, where the decline of the old copper-based last mile approach with separated vertical service infrastructures gave room to a converged service delivery model, with operators rethinking their service offerings in order to reduce costs and improve manageability, going well beyond the obvious performance benefits of upgrading the physical transport infrastructure.

Despite the evolution of access networks in terms of its role and underlying physical transport technologies, some components of the legacy access network model still persist, maintaining or even increasing their critical role in modern infrastructures. The Residential Gateway (RGW) is one of those components. Considering the present technology developments, the RGW starts to look like an anachronism, as it is a device that mostly embodies the legacy access network model, which remained almost unchanged until today. As such, there is an opportunity to ponder alternative approaches. It is obviously impossible to completely remove the RGW physical device from the customer premises, since it will always be necessary to connect the terminal devices (computers, set-top-boxes, telephones, smartphones, etc.) to the access network. Yet, there is a whole array of RGW features that can be removed from the physical RGW and that can be hosted within the operator's infrastructure, thanks to advances in virtualization, traffic steering, and access network technologies.

Virtualization technologies have become one of the main driving forces behind the evolution of the Network Service Provider (NSP) infrastructures, also proving instrumental for the introduction of hopefully cost-effective services to end-users, thereby leveraging the return on investment in the infrastructure. This evolution is progressively outgrowing the scope of the data center or the core network, as virtualization reaches towards the edge of the infrastructure and into the access network (Xia, Wu & King, 2013). From this perspective, outsourcing some RGW functionality may appear as a possible application of virtualization techniques potentially contributing to the consolidation and scaling of resources. From this perspective, the vRGW (Virtual RGW) is presented as a logical next step for the evolution of RGW.

Developments in terms of Network Functions Virtualization (NFV) and Software-Defined Networking (SDN) have prompted the industry to start developing standards, specification and companion solutions to incorporate their benefits within NSP infrastructures. Examples such as ETSI's Open Source MANO (OSM) software stack (which is aligned with ETSI's NFV standardization effort), have pushed the industry to adopt standard software pieces to implement virtualized RGW functions.

This chapter was originally published in (Cruz et al., 2015), focused on our own proposal for implementing the vRGW. Now, we revise and update it in order to reflect the considerable evolution of the vRGW concept – based upon the development of new standards and virtualization technologies – over the past few years. The chapter is organized as follows: we start by analyzing the rationale for virtualizing some RGW features, the key technologies used for their implementation in particular, such as the infrastructure requirements and coexistence with the legacy RGWs. Next, we present the evolution of vRGW proposals, by detailing current proposals from the academic field, standardization initiatives, and industry. We also identify and discuss the technological enhancements that strengthen the feasibility of the vRGW. Finally, we conclude the chapter by discussing the forthcoming developments of the vRGW.

The Case For Virtualizing The RGW

The expansion of high-speed broadband access networks, with an increasing growth in the number of connected households was one of the key factors that enabled a new breed of services, such as converged *"n-play"* offers or cloud-based services that are contributing to displace traditional split-medium communication and service delivery models in favour of an *everything-over-IP* approach (Royon, 2007)(Smedt et al., 2006). In line with those developments, the residential Local Area Network (LAN) ecosystem has evolved to become an environment where devices as diverse as PCs, set-top-boxes, VoIP (Voice over IP) telephones, smartphones, media players, smart TVs, and storage devices cohabitate, providing access to a wide range of services to broadband customers. In fact, evolution has moved the role of the NSP towards a service-centric model where the RGW plays a crucial role, since it is placed at the intersection of three domains: connectivity delivery, services, and the customer environment (Figure 1).

Standing on the customer premises, RGWs are standalone devices based on embedded system platforms that interface between the home network and the access network. The main role of these platforms hasn't significantly changed over time. RGWs typically support capabilities such as DNS (Domain Name Service), DHCP (Dynamic Host Configuration Protocol), NAT (Network Address Translation), routing, firewalling, and wireless connectivity. RGWs also provide direct support for added-value services such as IPTV – IGMP/MLD (Internet Group Management Protocol/Multicast Listener Discovery) proxying (Cain et al., 2002) and Virtual Channel Identifier/Virtual Local Area Network (VCI/VLAN) management – and SIP (Session Initiation Protocol) proxies (Rosenberg et al., 2002), and/or analog terminal adapters.

While the current RGW deployment model is still successful, it is heavily influenced by the nature of current service distribution models and, until recently, by the limited IPv4 address space – meanwhile, most operators have triggered migration plans, leading to the provisioning of IPv6 connectivity services that partly rely upon the assignment of an IPv6 prefix to the RGW. Besides, it may represent a significant burden for the operator in some contexts, due to several reasons.

To begin with, the RGW device is relatively expensive, representing an important share of the initial deployment costs. But initial acquisition costs are only part of the equation, as RGWs are a single point of failure, deployed right at the perimeter of the customer premises network. Malfunctioning or misconfigured RGWs may amount to a significant financial penalty for NSPs, both in terms of management, logistics (including on-site maintenance, in extreme cases) and customer loyalty. This situation is aggravated with consolidated service scenarios such as triple-play or quad-play, as the failure of a single RGW may lead to a complete media blackout in the household.

Additionally, the RGW can be an obstacle for remote diagnostic and troubleshooting of home LAN devices (e.g., SIP phones or set-top-boxes) in order to solve problems within the customer LAN. For instance, the management/diagnostics interfaces for certain devices within the home LAN may not be directly accessible without configuring port mappings on the RGW because of the presence of NAT for IPv4 or firewall pinholes for IPv6. The RGW might be an obstruction even for service introduction, as the time to market is often dependent on the device manufacturer to introduce new services which may depend on RGW capabilities (such as CPU or memory size) – this is often aggravated by the subsequent need to remotely upgrade thousands or millions of devices. In extreme cases, operators might be forced to consider mass replacement of RGWs to support new services, as they have reached the end of their

Figure 1. The RGW role across different NSP service models

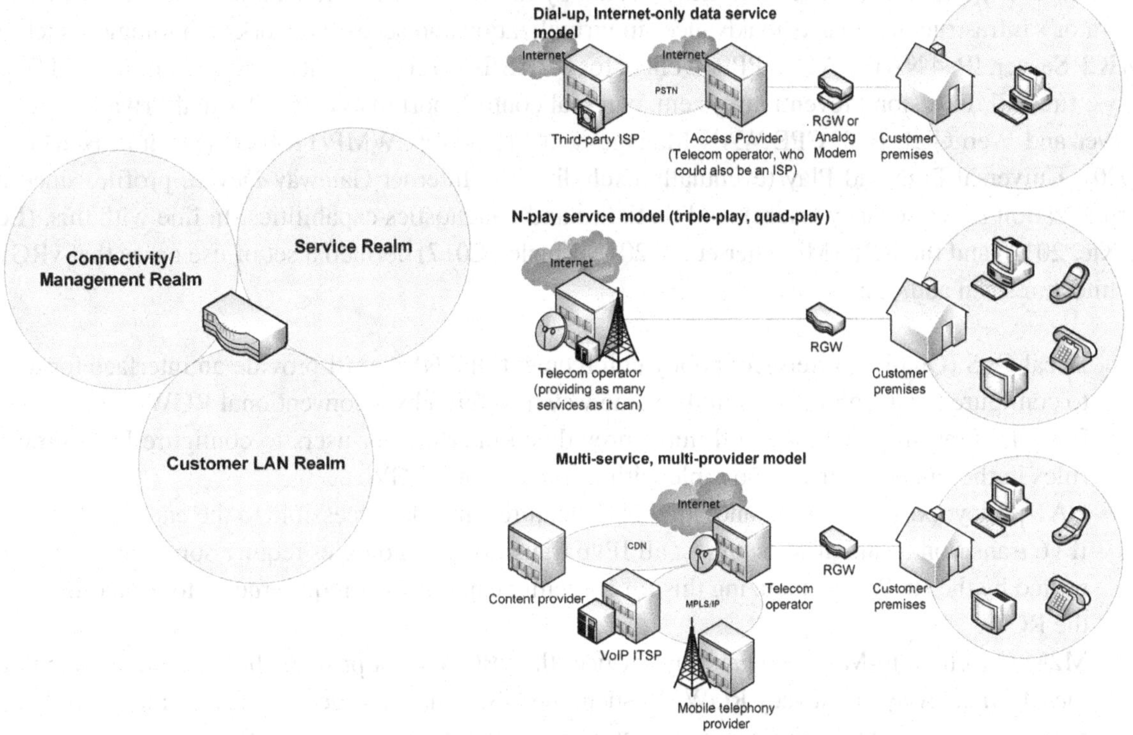

lifecycle and cannot be further upgraded or simply because they have become too limited in terms of their embedded platform capabilities. Furthermore, there is no uniform service set that an RGW vendor can integrate within some sort of "universal" device for all NSPs. Moreover, it is difficult for an operator to keep a homogeneous set of RGWs as even a single model from a single vendor may have minor firmware and hardware revisions. These might gradually compromise uniformity and hamper troubleshooting and management operations. For example, even small hardware differences between revisions of the same RGW model, such as smaller flash memory, may impose limitations from one model to another. Other factors that can contribute to a heterogeneous set of RGWs are incompatibilities between firmware and hardware versions, the existence of heterogeneous feature sets between different models the risk of firmware upgrades (troublesome for a single RGW and even more dangerous for a mass roll-out) that depend on vendor-specific procedures or the management of different device data models.

Finally, there is IPv6 migration. IPv6 provides network transparency as a side benefit: unlike the classic IPv4 NAT scenario, where it is difficult to properly identify a device within the customer premises, IPv6 devices can be assigned Global Unicast Addresses, enabling network and content providers to deliver services to specific devices. The introduction of the vRGW, may eventually contribute to streamline and optimize scenarios where dual-stack coexistence is a reality, by changing the traditional role (and even placement) of the RGW that was inherited from the IPv4 era.Considering this situation, it is attractive to investigate alternative approaches in order to overcome or at least soften these problems. It is obviously impossible to completely remove the RGW device from the customer premises: it will always be necessary to connect terminals (e.g., computers, set-top-boxes, telephones) to the access network. Yet, according to ETSI's Network Functions Virtualization Industry Specification Group (NFV ISG) (Lee & Ghai, 2014), several functions currently hosted by the RGW can be moved to be hosted within the operator's infrastructure, thanks to advances in virtualization and access network technologies, such as: DHCP Server, IPv4 NAT, NAT64, PPPoE client for BRAS/BNG connectivity or Application Level Gateways; firewall, Intrusion Prevention System, parental control, port mapping or Virtual Private Network Server and Web GUI, BBF CPE WAN Management Protocol (CWMP/TR-069) (Wich & Blackford, 2020), Universal Plug and Play (eventually excluding the Internet Gateway Device profile, since its virtualization raises security issues), and Statistics and Diagnostics capabilities. In line with this, (Lee & Xie, 2014) and the BBF (Minodier et al., 2016) (Insler, 2017) defined a set of use cases that vRGW architectures can address:

- Local QoS (Quality of Service) policy enforcement: the NSP must provide an interface for users to configure local QoS policies in the same way as offered by a conventional RGW.
- Personal firewall policy: the NSP must provide an interface for users to configure local firewall rules in the same way that is possible with a conventional RGW.
- NAT policy: port forwarding and other NAT features must be accessible to the end-user.
- IPv6 transition techniques: as almost all IPv6 transition technologies require some functions supported by the RGW – virtualizing this functionality can relax the requirements to be addressed by the RGW.
- M2M (Machine-to-Machine) gateway service: the vRGW must provide the same functionality as the M2M gateway of a legacy RGW. As such, the NSP must provide an interface for M2M device provisioning and application management, to provide services to the users.
- Local storage: RGWs often support local mass storage functionality for personal contents. The NSP might offer a similar functionality to the end-users (the BBF CWMP TR-140 (Kirksey, 2017)).
- VPN (Virtual Private Network) service: RGWs provide a VPN service for remote access (IPsec, Point-to-Point Tunneling Protocol (PPTP), Layer 2 Tunneling Protocol (L2TP), etc.). The NSP must be able to provision and manage a VPN service for users.
- The extension of the customer premises LAN (implied by the vRGW concept) to the operator domain can be instrumental for providing a new experience of browsing private and public sites, possibly using DLNA-like (DLNA, 2016) protocols for that purpose.
- Event notification: as virtualization moves some functions of the RGW outside the customer premises, it becomes tightly coupled with the NSP infrastructure. The RGW must be able to generate notifications. The CWMP protocol has the potential to play an important role (as it supports notifications.

Also, both (Xia, Wu & King, 2013) and (ETSI NFV002, 2014) document a set of requirements that must be satisfied to virtualize RGWs, as they raise several challenges regarding aspects such as bandwidth or computing resources:

- Scalability: functional migration from home devices (such as the vRGW) to the NSP infrastructure implies a considerable number of virtualized instances to be supported. This might raise scalability issues related with aspects such as: resource management, network bandwidth, fault detection and troubleshooting, among others. With estimations for the number of virtualized instances going up to hundreds of thousands (ETSI NFV002, 2014) (Dustzadeh, 2013), an implementation of a VM-based vRGW is therefore likely to consume significant resources. As such, in order to manage cost and scale, an effort must be made towards the maximization of the number of virtualized instances and devices supported on a limited number of CPUs – this also calls for service consolidation to network-located functions, horizontally scaled with server pools (such as DHCP servers) instead of using full virtual instances, but this also raises the problem of coordination as customer resources become scattered over different places – a question addressed by the next item.

- Service dynamics and elasticity: it must cope with the dynamics of the end user's applications and services, driving the virtual service node to be able to accommodate (through an alteration of topologies or functions). Also, the need for orchestration of scattered customer services means that the required per-user functionalities must be adequately instantiated, on-demand. Elasticity is also a key feature, as the ability for meeting demands depends on the capability to scale hardware resources as needed;

- Management and orchestration: regarding management, there are two perspectives to be considered – users and operators. Users do not want to relinquish a certain amount of control over their CPE devices, even if they are virtualized – this calls for some sort of "shared management" approach in which the CPE can be jointly shared by the end-user and the NSP that could eventually evolve towards some form of multi-tenancy, involving third-party content and service providers. As for operators, there are service coordination challenges when some functions are embedded in the vRGW while others are in the network (e.g., ACLs, security filtering rules): an example is documented in the BBF NERG proposal as well as in the split-box documents (Lee & Xie, 2014). These approaches do not account for the scalability, availability or security issues yet. Such issues arise with the decoupling of the data plane and the control plane with the use of an SDN protocol to carry policy-provisioning information in-band. This also calls for the integration of existing management and OSS technologies in the new management approach, in order the cope with the lifecycle management and orchestration of software and virtualized functions as well as the infrastructure resources needed to support them – in this perspective, automation is also a vital feature to enable flexible and cost-effective, on-demand, operations;

- Stability, resiliency and continuity: service continuity and reliability during network or access link failures will remain a critical requisite. This means that the impact of service disruption must be limited, by avoiding single points of failure in the vRGW design (and also in the supporting infrastructure).

- Component portability: enabling the capability to load, execute and move software functions across different data centers. This is key for vRGW component migration (for instance, allowing components to move to a PoP closer to the customer geographic area) or recovery, but also to ease the introduction of VNFs or virtual components from third-party providers.

- Security: the evolution towards a vRGW model must not compromise the home environment security. Also, the evolution towards a virtualized environment might expose the operator and/or customer to external attacks not foreseen or unlikely in legacy infrastructures;

- Energy efficiency: large scale virtualized infrastructures must be designed according to energy efficiency requirements. This transcends the data center energy efficiency issues (that are also important for the vRGW), also including the network infrastructure. For instance, in a vRGW embedded within an OLT or a BNG, there is a need for supplying power to new service cards, as opposed to the classic RGW model, where the customer supports the costs. While such costs might depend on several factors such as the specific characteristics of the deployment, the design of the support hardware and the specific characteristics of each site (power supply availability, reachability, etc.), the consolidation benefits should account for a significant part of the additional expense. As an example, properly implemented power management and balancing within the same device (such as an OLT) can ensure that the vRGW cards sharing the same backplane can consume less energy than the corresponding standalone RGW devices, and even if the energy costs are to be spread among costumers, it may amount to a negligible monetary overhead;

- Coexistence between virtualized and legacy infrastructure components must be ensured. This will be discussed in more detail in the next section.
- Improved Quality of Experience (QoE): the end-user QoE must be significantly improved, as it is a driving factor for the acceptance and introduction of virtualized technologies, even if the end-user might be unaware of the existence of the vCPE. This can be achieved by improving existing services (such as with cloud gaming which benefits from improved latencies) and through the introduction of new, value-added services, discussed in the next point.
- Optimize the delivery of Value-Added Services (VAS): one of the key points for the vRGW proposal is the ability to deliver VAS in a flexible manner. The vRGW must improve the ability to deliver VAS per customer and/or per device in the home, providing enough flexibility to add new VAS from a self-care portal, for instance. The vRGW must ease the introduction of shared services such as parental control, advanced firewall, intrusion detection systems or antivirus, which can be shared among customers. This may also reduce the overhead for VAS operation and maintenance, with an impact on OPEX.

Future developments of the vRGW use case must seriously address these requirements in order to succeed, by leveraging a wealth of potential benefits in terms of CAPEX, OPEX and flexibility. One of the use cases benefits from the extension of the customer premises LAN up to the operator domain, something that may raise concerns about the possibility of eavesdropping, identity spoofing and DDoS attacks coming from malicious individuals or entities.. Nevertheless, this risk already exists with current setups, where the operator remotely manages the physical RGW (which might be used for illegitimate probing). Either with vRGWs or physical RGWs, security concerned users might opt to hide the home network behind an additional level of NAT/firewall – still, this is only true for network traffic that is restricted to the LAN boundaries, because every other network flow must traverse the NSP boundaries, where it can be monitored. For the latter case, end-to-end encryption may be the only available choice for privacy-concerned users.

There are several proposals describing how the vRGW might be actually implemented, differing on several aspects related to implementation, supported use cases and deployment. The next section discusses and analyses several proposals for vRGW implementation, as well as the work that is being developed within standardization bodies such as the BBF, ETSI, Eurescom, or the IETF.

VRGW: One Concept, Several Perspectives

The evolution towards the virtualization of some of the RGW functions started with the first attempts to virtualize generic network router devices (Egi et al., 2007) and (Egi et al., 2010) proposed a solution for RGW virtualization using the Xen Hypervisor (Barham et al., 2003), together with the click modular router and XORP extensible router platforms. An approach for virtual router migration scenarios on Xen hosts was studied in (Pisa et al., 2010). The possibility of network performance penalties with virtualization network appliances was discussed in (Bazzi & Onozato, 2011) and (Zeng & Hao, 2009). And a solution for implementing distributed firewalls using virtualized security appliances was proposed in (Basak et al., 2010)

Later on, and specifically for mass RGW virtualization, the Eurescom Project P2055 (Abgrall et al., 2011) documented (and probably one of the first coordinated approaches to the problem from an operator standpoint) three alternative scenarios to remove the physical RGW from the customer's premises. These scenarios claim to optimize operator's Capital Expenditure (CAPEX) and Operational Expenditure (OPEX):

1. Pushing most of the RGW functionalities to the access nodes such as the BNG. This approach places packet processing capabilities close to the customers and distributes traffic load across several geographically disperse nodes. However, it requires massive hardware upgrades of access nodes and it also fragments computing resources across the operator network, thereby increasing complexity and costs.
2. Integrating RGW functionalities in the BNG, keeping the network design unchanged (unlike the first scenario). However, as BNGs are not expected to support massive RGW virtualization, hardware upgrades, the distribution of computing resources across BNGs would be needed.
3. As a standalone network element (NE) located somewhere in the operator's metro network. This scenario has the advantage of not interfering with already-deployed network elements but it introduces a new hardware component in the NPS's network with inherent costs and maintenance requirements.

(Da Silva et al., 2011) discusses several alternatives to physical RGW replacement, embedding capabilities on the access node (OLT) and decoupling Authentication, Authorization and Accounting (AAA), DHCP and NAT functionality. Some approaches, as those suggested by some Tier-1 equipment providers (Dustzadeh, 2013) favor the introduction of vRGW line cards in the OLT, like Huawei's MA5600T OLT (Huawei, 2010) (which also integrates the aggregation switch and edge router functionality) – this technology was evaluated by *Telefonica* in 2013 (Figure 2).

Figure 2. vRGW integrated within the OLT (simplified diagram)

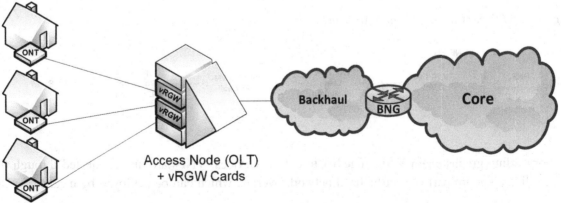

Telefonica was also involved in another development of the vCPE concept, together with NEC (Matsumoto, 2013) which provides virtualization of RGW capabilities, using SDN and NFV technologies, moving RGW features to the edge and core data centers, which led to the organization of trials in Brazil in 2014 and 2015 (Palancar et al., 2015) .

While those proposals paved the way for the first discussions on the vRGW concept, the introduction of new technologies, discussed in the next subsection, have sparked the interest in the concept as they bridge the missing gaps with existing operator infrastructures, providing much needed flexibility.

Introducing NFV and SDN

Nevertheless, as network applications and services scale and evolve (not only in terms of capacity requirements, but also in complexity), they impose an added burden to the supporting NSP infrastructure. From this perspective, NFV (Chiosi et al., 2012) (Chiosi et al., 2014) (Mijumbi et al., 2016) is a significant development that facilitates the creation of on-demand network services – acting standalone or be set up in a Service Function Chain (SFC) (Halpern & Pignataro, 2015)– that is composed of VNF (Virtualized Network Functions, such as NAT, DHCP, BNGs, Firewalls, among many others) functions, hosted in Virtual Machines (VM).

The use of NFV to deploy network functions ambitions to lower both CAPEX and OPEX. Additionally, NFV can change the service design approach. Some services may currently take some time to be delivered (from weeks to months). With NFV that time can significantly be reduced to a few days (Lemke, 2015). In addition to quick deployment, NFV flexibility (to the extent allowed by specific implementations) also allows for targeted and tailor-made services (Han et al., 2015).

The NFV vision attempts to decouple network resources from the network function by conceiving an end-to-end service as an entity that can rely upon the deployment of what ETSI calls Forwarding Graphs (FG, which is a concept that is equivalent to the Service Function Chaining concept documented by the IETF. The major difference between FGs and SFCs is that the latter can combine VNFs and PNFs unlike the former.). FGs are thus service function chains composed of several VNF instances. Service Function Chaining is a technique that facilitates the enforcement of (service-inferred) differentiated traffic forwarding policies within a domain. Figure 3 shows an example of an FG with the virtualized function that packets will go through. In this example, the packets will go through an Intrusion Prevention System (IPS), Load Balancing, Firewall and finally Policy and Licensing.

Figure 3. NFV Forwarding Graph example

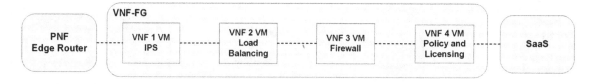

Forwarding graphs chain VNFs together to define services. VNFs are interconnected through the logical links that are part of a virtualized network overlay, which can be deployed by means of SDN

Figure 4. NFV end-to-end service with VNFs (adapted from (ETSI NFV 002, 2014))

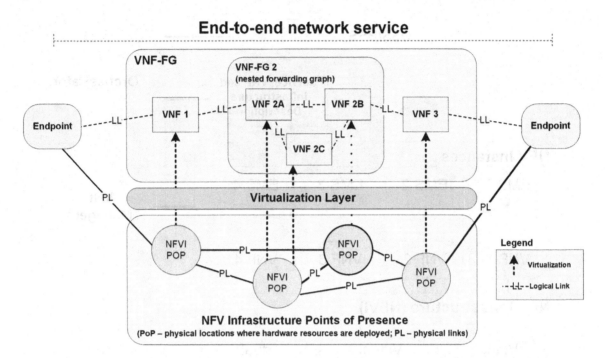

techniques (next discussed) or technologies such as VLANs (IEEE 802.1Q, 2011) or MPLS Pseudowires (Bryant & Pate, 2005), as depicted in Figure 4).

The Physical Network Functions (PNFs) that are embedded in network devices (can also be involved in an SFC. A virtualization layer abstracts the physical resources (computing, storage, and networking) on top of which the VNFs are deployed and implemented – the support infrastructure for such resources is the NFV Infrastructure (NFVI), which may be spread across different physical locations, called Points of Presence (NFVI PoPs).

ETSI's NFV architectural reference framework is depicted in Figure 5. It is composed of several functional modules: the **Network Function Virtualization Infrastructure** (NFVI), providing the virtual resources (using COTS hardware, accelerators and a software-based virtualization layer) which support the VNFs; the **Virtual Network Function** domain, where the software implementation of VNFs reside (VNFs can be hosted in Virtual Machines, for instance) which run on top of the NFVI, also including the corresponding **Element Management Systems** (EMS) to ease its integration with existing Operations Support Systems and Business Support Systems (OSS/BSS), whenever applicable; the **NFV Management and Orchestration** (MANO or M&O) domain deals with the orchestration and the lifecycle management of physical and/or software resources that support the virtualization infrastructure and the lifecycle management of VNFs, as well as the service that relies upon the VNFs.

The MANO domain focuses on the virtualization-specific tasks for the NFV framework, being composed of the following components: The NFV Orchestrator, which is responsible for the lifecycle management of network services across the operator's domain (data centers included); the VNF Manager(s) deals with the lifecycle management for the VNF instances and the Virtualized Infrastructure Manager (VIMs), which are responsible for NFVI computing, storage and networking resource management.

Figure 5. ETSI NFV reference architecture framework, based on (ETSI NFV 002, 2014)

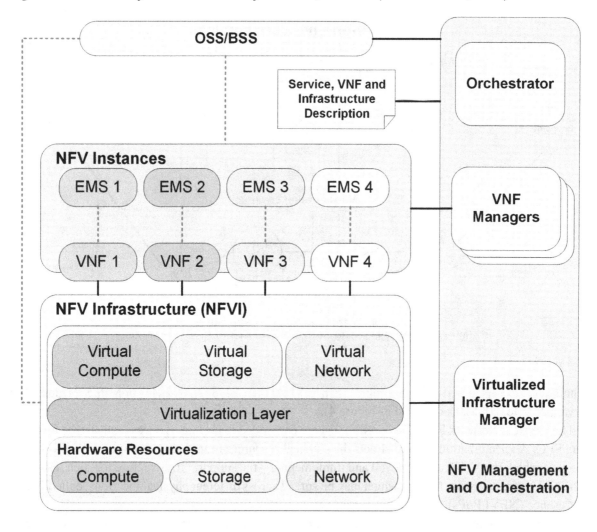

The entire NFV framework is driven by a set of metadata describing services, VNFs and Infrastructure requirements, feeding the MANO with the needed information about the resources it has to manage. This means that different resource providers (e.g., a VNF provider or an Infrastructure component provider, such as an hypervisor) can provide components for specific frameworks, provided they implement the APIs and comply with established data models. This architecture also considers the relationship with the existing OSS/BSS, by defining their interfaces with the corresponding NFV domains.

The standardization efforts conducted by ETSI results in the NFV reference architecture framework, and also led to the chartering of ETSI's OSM (Open Source Mano) project (ETSI OSM, 2016). This project involves several industry players and as aims at specifying an end-to-end network service orchestrator (E2E NSO) within an open-source management and orchestration (MANO) framework and the use of ETSI NFV information models. BBF has also worked on the use of NFV in Multi-Service Broadband Networks (MSBN) through the architectural framework to facilitate the incremental deployment of NFV in MSBN, documented in TR-359 (Carey, Thorne & Allan, 2016).

Figure 6. ETSI OSM context in a service platform (OSM, 2020)

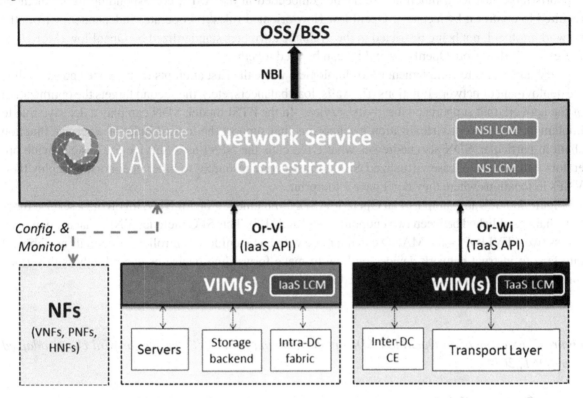

As part of the Linux Foundation, ONAP (Open Network Automation Platform) is an open-source project that released its first version in the end of 2017. Its main objective is to provide an automation platform to manage and orchestrate resources and services.

SDN is an architecture that decouples the data plane from the control plane, with the aim of introducing network programmability. The Open Network Operating System (ONOS) is an example of a SDN controller (Berde, 2014). In an SDN infrastructure, the SDN computation logic (a.k.a. the SDN controller)) controls and programs the network and its resources. This means that, for instance, the forwarding plane of network device (switch, router) can be dynamically reconfigured to address the service and application requirements. The decoupling of the data plane from the control plane is meant to facilitate the programmability of networks.

Several protocols can be used to forward decisions made by a SDN controller (e.g., resource allocation) to the components that will participate to the delivery and the operation of a service: IETF FORCES (Forwarding and Control Element Separation) (FORCES, 2014), which provides a reference architecture for programmable networks, OpenFlow (ONF, 2015), which is the result of a GENI project (Kaljic et al., 2019), NETCONF, BGP-LS, COPS-PR. OpenFlow is a protocol that can be used in switched environments to populate the FIBs maintained by the switches (Latif et al., 2020). The P4 protocol (from Programming Protocol-independent Packet Processors) has algo gained considerable popularity as a SDN-oriented data plane programming language (P4, 2019). OpenFlow and P4 are different approaches, with one key difference being that P4 operates at a lower level, by programming the data plane – application-specific integrated circuit (ASIC) – of the networking devices. By comparison, OpenFlow assumes the switch supports more restricted functional semantics embedded in the ASIC, corresponding to the methods required to control it by means of OpenFlow flow-oriented rules. P4 operates independently from the network protocol, not being restricted to the available attributes standardized by OpenFlow (McKeown & Rexford 2016). Both OpenFlow and P4 can be used together.

NFV and SDN are complementary technologies: while the first attempts to optimize and streamline the deployment of network functions (firewalls, load balancers, etc.), the second targets the optimization of the network that supports connectivity services. In the ETSI model, SDN can play a decisive role to implement the network virtualization mechanisms that support the logical links of a service function chain in particular. SDN also addresses what ETSI calls the NFVI-as-a-Service use case: provide operators with means to lease virtualized NFV Infrastructure resources to other operators, to deploy their VNFs in locations where they don't have a footprint

Figure 7 shows an example of an OpenFlow SDN implementation for NFV, involving a service function chain established between two endpoints ("A" and "B"). This SFC includes VNFs that are deployed across two NFVI PoPs – the MANO can interface with an OpenFlow controller, through its northbound interface to instruct network devices on how to make forwarding decisions accordingly with service function chain-specific information carried in packets.

Figure 7. Example of an OpenFlow SDN implementation for a VNF service forward chain (adapted from (ONF, 2014)

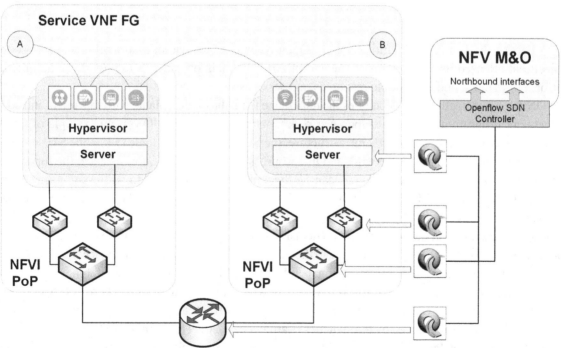

Figure 8. ETSI NFV Virtualization of Home Environment use case (adapted from (ETSI NFV002, 2014))

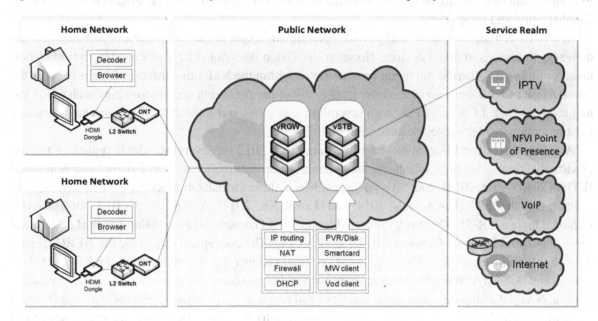

Edge Computing

When functions hosted in a physical RGW are virtualized, some of them raise specific requirements (such as latency). However, when deployed in core datacenters, some of those functions might not be able to fulfill those requirements. A possible option is to move these functions to a close-proximity datacenter located in the network edge, closer to the customer premises (in fact, other key components, such as DNS may have to be moved closer to the customer in order to meet more strict delays). This can reduce the latency between the function processing and the (home) device that uses this function. Edge computing has been a target of recent research as it can be used to address various markets, such as Internet of Things (IoT), services, immersive services based upon augmented reality (AR), etc. (Hernando et al., 2017). In some cases, these applications may experience severe service degradation when latency exceeds several tens of milliseconds. In a residential gateway scenario, the requirements for the virtualized functions will depend on the customer's behavior in terms of service usage. For example, if a customer spends most of his/her time to browse the web, the requirements will be significantly different from those resulting from online gaming or live streaming. The latter expose a higher sensitivity to latency performance. To tackle this issue, frameworks capable of monitoring the resource requirements needed to satisfy customers' requirements have been proposed, such as (Meneses et al., 2019b). These frameworks are capable of moving the functions from one datacenter to another to avoid service degradation due to performance values that do not comply with the contractual SLA, such as latency or processing capabilities.

Unsurprisingly, SDN, NFV, and other developments of network and system virtualization (such as commodity hypervisors and service function chaining techniques) are important for the vRGW concept to become a reality. As such, ETSI's NFV ISG has proposed a Virtualization of Home Environment use case (Figure 8) (ETSI NFV002, 2014) that describes how a RGW (and even a Set-Top Box) might be virtualized and migrated to the service platform located in the network, with benefits in terms of service simplification and integration.

In ETSI's vision, the vRGW still provides private addresses to the home devices and mediates the delivery of services to home devices. However, its vision does not offer a precise description of how nodal or functional distribution might be undertaken within the NSP infrastructure. This is because the introduction of NFV into carrier environments is still under definition (except for cases such as the virtual Evolved Packet Core – vEPC), with several organizations and standard bodies working to evaluate existing options and propose adequate solutions.

Also, the Broadband Forum has been working since 2012 on several standards regarding the use of virtualization technologies for home and business gateway architectures. A liaison letter sent to the IETF in 2014 (Alter, 2014) reported work in progress in these virtualization scenarios, that were already of interest to the IETF (Lee & Ghai, 2014) and (Lee & Xie, 2014). As a result, the BBF published two technical reports TR-317 (Network Enhanced Residential Gateway, NERG) (Minodier et al., 2016) and TR-328 (Virtual Business Gateway) (Insler et al., 2017). The conceptual model for the NERG (Figure 9) explicitly follows an approach where the vG (virtual Gateway) is decoupled from the BRG (Bridged Residential Gateway). While the vG is in charge of service and network functions such as IP forwarding, routing, NAT, IP addressing, data plane functions still reside in the customer premises, e.g., in an Optical Network Terminal (ONT) that embeds an OpenFlow switch). Moreover, the NERG can make use of SDN (possibly based upon the use of OpenFlow) to make it control the BRG from the vG or another network controller. The fact that SDN protocol messages are carried in-band means that protection schemes may have to be implemented to ensure security, due to the increased exposure of the messaging flows.

Figure 9. The Broadband Forum NERG (adapted from (Minodier et al., 2016))

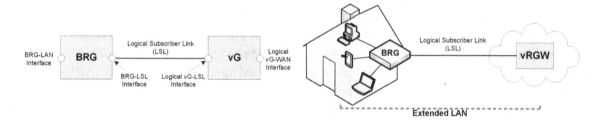

With TR-317, BBF documents an analysis of several approaches to shift some of the functionalities of an RGW to the operator's network, through the use of NFV and SDN technologies. The main goal is to ease the deployment, maintenance and evolution of both existing and new capabilities while simplifying the RGW. TR-317 contemplates a series of nodal distribution scenarios (Figure 10), some of them reflect the Eurescom proposals, contemplating the deployment of the vRGW within the access node, in the BNG or in a data center/.

The BBF also introduces a new distribution model, called *Hybrid boxing* that splits the vRGW into two separate entities: the Service-vRG (which deals with services and SDN control) and the Network-vRG (that deals with the forwarding plane). This approach leverages the power of SDN to implement policy-based forwarding of subscriber traffic.

Figure 10. NFV end-to-end service with VNFs (adapted from (Insler et al., 2017))

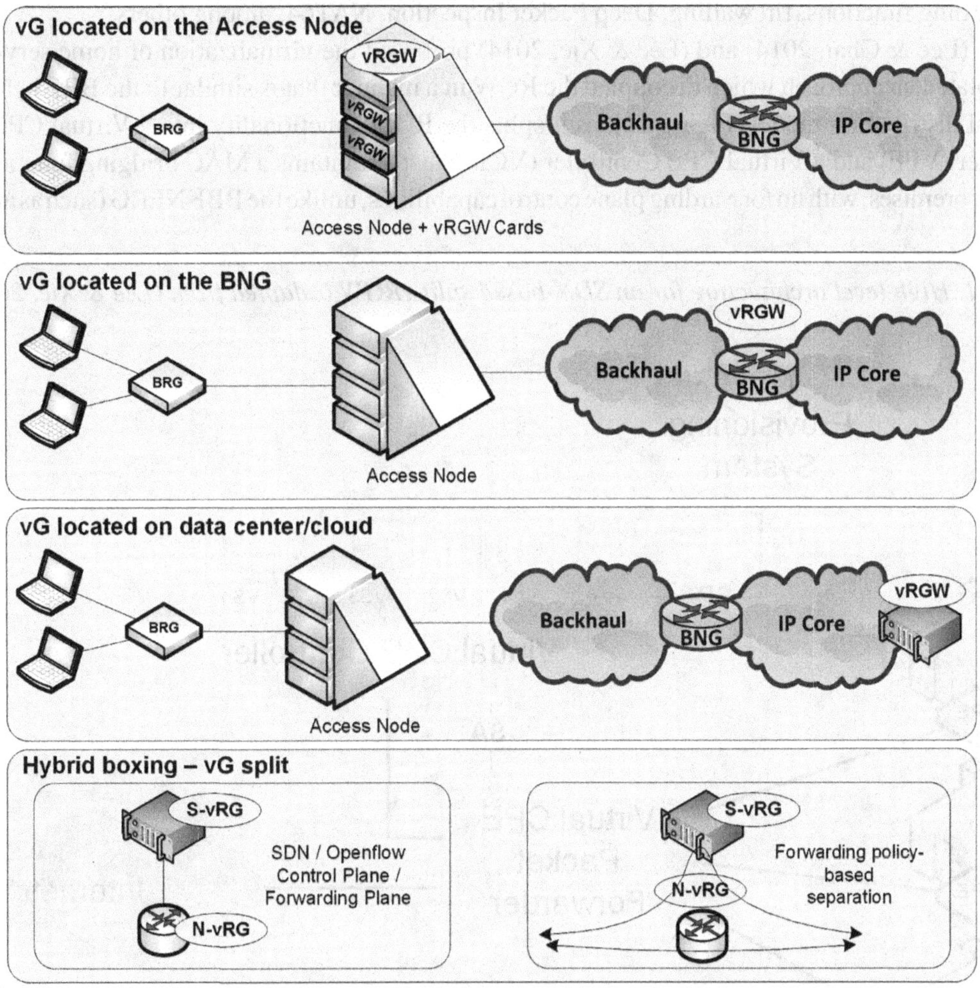

Apart from the generic vRGW use cases already discussed, the BBF planned the NERG as a platform for leveraging the potential of commodity x86-based virtualization progress for redundancy, elasticity and availability, supporting a wide range of applications and services. In fact, the BBF sees this as an opportunity to push an application store model for vRGW – this component-based model is not entirely new, as the BBF already envisions such a business model in TR-157 (Carey et al., 2015), based upon the management of components for RGW-embedded execution environments, such as OSGi (OSGi, 2018).

Also, in 2013 the BBF started to work on SDN-based use cases and their mapping to the BBF network architectures TR-101 and TR-145 (Cui & Hertoghs, 2012), with the publication of WT-302 (Architecture and Connectivity of Cloud Services for Broadband Networks) and SD-313 (Business Requirements and Framework for SDN in Telecommunication Broadband Networks) documents. The BBF also looked into the concept of flexible service function chaining (also applicable to VNFs), as the study document SD-326 suggested (Alter & Daowood, 2014). Proposals from (Niu et al., 2014), (Quinn & Nadeau, 2014), (Boucadair, Jacquenet, Jiang et. al., 2014), (Boucadair, Jacquenet, Parker et al., 2014) and (Jiang & Li, 2014) also support this idea, pointing towards the usage of complex service composition for the creation of value-added service propositions by the chaining of advanced functions besides basic routing or forwarding functions, firewalling, Deep Packet Inspection, NAT64, among others.

Also, (Lee & Ghai, 2014) and (Lee & Xie, 2014) proposed the virtualization of home services that contemplated an approach which decoupled the RGW in a manner that is similar to the BBF hybrid boxing nodal distribution model (Figure 11), as it splits the RGW functionality into a Virtual CPE Packet Forwarder (VPF) and a Virtual CPE Controller (VC). It also maintains a MAC bridging function in the customer premises, with no forwarding plane control capabilities, unlike the BBF NERG (such as an ONT).

Figure 11. High level architecture for an SDN-based split vRGW (adapted from (Lee & Xie, 2014))

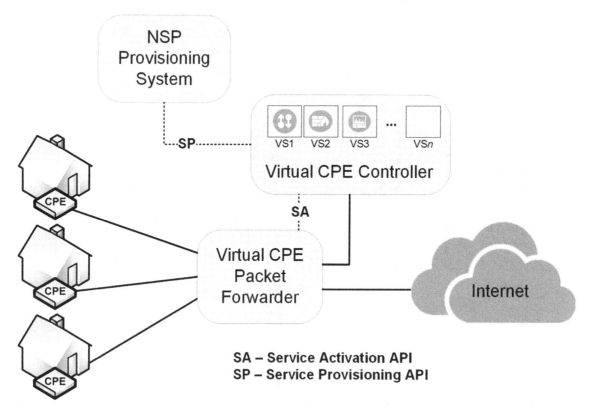

The VPF is a network device that is optimized for packet processing, also including a northbound API for VC communications, to exchange information (ACL rules and QoS parameters, for example). The Virtual CPE Controller embeds the controller for the VPF, together with the Virtual Services (VS) available for the subscribers, and also stores user service subscription rules used to provide the VSs for subscribers. Each VS contains the service definitions and the corresponding service logic: for instance, an IPS, a parental control service or a firewall. It is supposed for an NSP to be able to scale VS resources horizontally, also being able to allocate VS instances on a per-subscriber basis. The NSP provisioning system provides the information the VC needs about customer service activation and service-specific parameters.

Coexistence With The Existing Operator Infrastructure

As per (ETSI NFV002, 2014), coexistence between virtualized and non-virtualized functions is considered mandatory for the NSP infrastructure, mainly because the transition is expected to be gradual and smooth, implying that there will be a period during which legacy infrastructures will coexist with NFV infrastructures, and also because not all functions are eligible for virtualization (and will thus remain PNFs).

Specifically, the ETSI NFV *Virtualization of the Home Environment* use case addresses the virtualization of the RGW and Set-Top Box (the latter being outside the scope of this chapter), also accounting for coexistence issues – Figure 12 and Figure 13depict a scenario where conventional RGWs coexist with vRGWs. It must be noted that equipment such as optical splitters are not depicted, in order to remove unnecessary complexity from the figures.

Conventional RGWs (Figure 12) are connected to the BNG using a PPPoE tunnel or IPoE, which provides connectivity to the Internet and other resources, such as data centers or private cloud infrastructures (which might host parts of the NFVI). Both IPTV and VoIP traffic bypass the BNG, supported via BBF TR-101 and TR-156 aggregation scenarios. These provide support for N:1 transport of service VLANs into the customer network for multicast IPTV and/or VoIP.

Figure 12. Operation of a conventional RGW within a vRGW-enabled scenario (adapted from (ETSI NFV002, 2014))

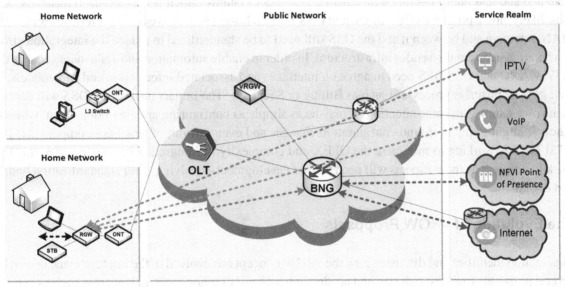

The same scenario can support vRGWs (Figure 13), which are deployed in the NFV network (or NFV front cloud), with the customer private LAN domain being extended to the data center. The vRGW still provides private IPv4 addresses to home devices and might communicate with a virtualized STB (not shown) by using a public or a private address. The vRGW is assigned an an IPv6 prefix by means of

Figure 13. vRGW operation, as per the ETSI NFV vision (adapted from (ETSI NFV002, 2014))

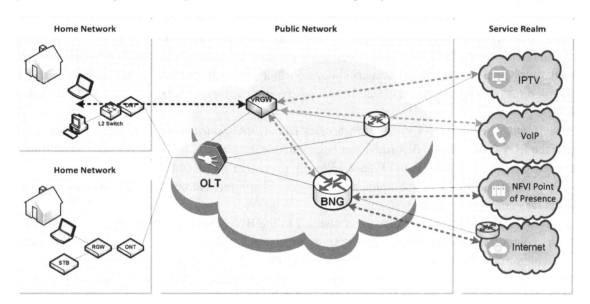

IPv6 prefix delegation (Troan & Droms, 2003). IPv6 addresses that are assigned to the terminal devices are derived from the prefix assigned to the vRGW.

As for the impact on OSS/BSS systems, the MANO components for the ETSI NVFI have been designed and laid out to interact with existing OSS/BSS systems (albeit it is recognized that NFV will most likely have a profound effect on current OSS/BSS architectures). However, the interfaces within the MANO domain and between it and the OSS still need to be standardized to reduce the integration effort in a heterogeneous multi-vendor infrastructure. In order to enable automation and agile management, the NFV MANO and OSS/BSS need to agree on interfaces and associated information and data models, as well as their business processes (such as Billing or Security). The impact on existing OSS will depend on its own nature – in some situations it may be as simple as configuring an integration agent, while in others it might imply profound configuration changes and even roll-out of new OSS components. The ETSI NFV is working to minimize the OPEX and complexity of integration but, once again, this is a work in progress as these aspects will need further development, involving other standardization bodies and organisms.

The Evolution of vRGW Proposals

This section identifies and discusses how the vRGW concept has evolved in the last few years, driven by several proposals from the industry and academia which entail innovations in key areas such as service and network virtualization.

Lower OPEX and CAPEX, for instance, rank among the most relevant requirements to evolve to a vRGW model. At the customer premises, the CAPEX is lowered by having a simpler device, with lower performance requirements despite requiring a set of complex physical features such as CPU, RAM, wireless and wired connectivity. With the functions decoupled from the physical device, long term CAPEX is also lowered as the same device can be in operation for a longer time without the need for an upgrade as it is not deprecated with the introduction of newer, more complex and resource-demanding services. A technically simpler device also provides lower OPEX due to overall tech call reduction and the reduced risk of misconfiguration which may sometimes lead to on-site maintenance intervention. Hosting the functions at the datacenter is also expected to lower CAPEX and OPEX due to resource consolidation with the use of commodity H/W. This increases the overall efficiency.

Computing nodes supporting the services can be easily scaled in or out depending on the number of customers connected at any given time, and the number and type of functionalities they are using. This greatly contrasts with the traditional RGW scenario where all the physical devices (and corresponding computing resources) are scattered through the customers' premises, regardless of whether they are in use or not..

The location of the virtualized functions should not be fixed, and these functions should be able to migrate between datacenters for resilience, efficiency or latency improvement purposes. An edge data-center close to the customer premises should improve customer's QoE, because of a likely improved latency. The live migration of functions can also be required if the current location does not have enough resources, so they can be moved to different computing nodes or datacenters with enough resources available. Mobility of network functions can also come into play in certain scenarios, when a customer moves to a different location and needs access to his/her service from a mobile phone for example.

The reliability of the service can be maintained or improved in a virtualization scenario. As the home device can have reduced service configuration and software within itself, it will have less failure points, which can result in a lower failure rate. As the functions are virtualized into a VM or a container, management actions are simpler, and the network functions can be re-instantiated on demand at the datacenter.

User acceptance of the vRGW model is important. Allowing a user to have control over the service he/she subscribed to should be preserved, by means of web portals. This is current practice in the traditional RGW approach and it should be kept when the CPE's capabilities get virtualized.

Proposals From The Standardization Bodies

Standardization bodies have been working on the vRGW concept. ETSI's NFV ISG defined some use cases around. In (NFV002, 2014), the *Virtualization of Home Environment* use case details how this virtualization can be achieved, with CPE capabilities outsourced in the operator's network. The possibility of virtualizing other customer premises equipment, such as the STB (Set-Top Box), is also considered.

BBF launched two main initiatives about the virtualization of the RGW itself, which were mentioned earlier in this chapter. The architecture for the Network Enhanced Residential Gateway (NERG), published in the TR-317 specification (Minodier et al., 2016), and the virtual Business Gateway (vBG), published in TR-328 (Insler et.al, 2017). The already introduced ONAP Orchestrator also includes the vRGW as one of its use cases (ONAP 2018a), based upon BBF's NERG approach and stating that the main problem is how to dynamically deploy, orchestrate, manage and monitor network services. Furthermore, this use case also provides a blueprint on how the ONAP orchestrator can be used to deploy and manage the services used in a vRGW scenario (ONAP 2018b).

BBF has also been working on the *cloudification* of the central office, which is likely to impact how the RGW is managed. From this perspective, BBF has documented a reference architecture for the CloudCO (Cloud Central Office) in TR-384 (Karagiannis et al., 2018a), along with a set of use cases and scenarios documented in TR-416 (Karagiannis et al., 2018b). More recently, BBF's TR-408 (Hai et al., 2020) proposes strategies for smoothly migrating to a CloudCO while coexisting with the legacy infrastructure during the migration period.

Proposals From The Academic Community

There are several research proposals from the academic community that address the virtualization of the RGW. NFV and SDN technologies are considered these proposals, as they provide a solid and flexible foundation for the functions used by the RGW and the network fabric used for their interconnection.

For M2M environments, (Dillon & Winters, 2014) presented a vRGW proof of concept based on a set of open-source software components. Another proposal, following a containerized approach to implement a vRGW and assess its effects in resource usage reduction, was presented in (Modig & Ding, 2016). The RGW instances were individually virtualized, and the reduction in resource usage derived mainly from having multiple instances sharing the same OS.

Customer's portal usability was studied in (Flores Moyano et al., 2017), with a focus on customers with low technological background. The proposed virtualized management and networking domain (vMANDO) provides service configuration options in an easy-to-understand manner, so that the customer may manage the basic aspects of his/her service. The objective is to reduce operator costs by decreasing the number of support calls and on-premises maintenance. At the same time customer satisfaction is likely to improve because of the improved service quality.

The flexibility of SDN was studied in (Huang et al., 2017), using a multiple flow table strategy that used a simple SDN-enabled network switch as a physical RGW, with most functions hosted in the operator's network edge. This flexibility was also explored in (Proença et al. 2017), with a focus on the enhancement of service design and its contribution to develop and deploy new services.

Zhu and Huang proposed resource sharing between RGW instances for IoT scenarios that can be applied to vRGW scenarios as well (Zhu & Huang, 2018). They deploy VNFs among neighboring (physical) RGWs within the network edge. This approach would become much simpler in a vRGW scenario, where there would be no need to use physical resources of neighbor customers.

A method for migrating from physical RGW instances to a virtualized environment was presented in (Herbaut et al., 2015), with the integration of NFV into the RGW device in the customer premises, using modular gateways. The initial proposals, although functional, often had problems related to the scalability in real production deployments. An operator can have more than a million subscribers and a virtualized environment is feasible only if it is capable of scaling to those values. Tackling this issue, the framework architecture presented in (Meneses et al., 2019a) monitors the computing resources workload and scales the number of cluster nodes up or down, depending on whether they reach certain thresholds (e.g., CPU, RAM, input/output load). Whenever a threshold is reached, the framework checks which vCPE instances have the highest priority requirements and moves them by creating new VNFs and changes the Open vSwitch (OVS) links in a *make-before-break* manner (removing the previous links and VNF instances after the migration). The researchers improved this scenario in (Meneses at al., 2019b), by allowing the vCPE instances to be migrated between core and edge datacenters. The migration also considers the usage requirements of the customer. As an example, a vCPE initially planned for web browsing can be deployed in a core datacenter. However, if the usage shifts to more demanding applications such as online gaming and live streaming, the instance can be migrated to an edge datacenter. This likely reduces end-to-end latency. Authors claim this is achieved with near-zero downtime and without affecting customer's QoE.

Proposals From The Industry

Several operators are promoting the vRGW concept. A number of them actively participate in and contribute to the vRGW-related standardization efforts already discussed (e.g., ONAP, BBF, ETSI). Those efforts will not be mentioned here, and this subsection will instead focus on self-published efforts and proposals such as (Ericsson, 2014) and (NEC, 2016). One of the first publicly known pilots of vRGW were performed in Brazil by Telefonica/Vivo. This concept involved a streamlined gateway providing basic connectivity between the operator's network and the customer premises, with an access point to connect terminal devices (Canto Palancar et al., 2015). It followed an NFV-based approach, moving the RGW functions to the operator's infrastructure.

The CORD (Central Office Re-architected as a Datacenter) (Peterson et al., 2016) is an ONF project that is currently working on the evolution of legacy COs (Central Office) towards a datacenter-based approach. It contains several sub-projects, including the Residential CORD (R-CORD), which is aligned with these proposals as it considers the virtual subscriber gateway (vSG) as one use case. Several service providers have been working within the R-CORD framework and have been announcing in-lab or field trials, including Comcast, DT (Deutsche Telekom), AT&T (OpenCord, 2017a), NTT (Nippon Telegraph and Telephone) (OpenCord, 2017b), and Telefonica (OpenCord, 2020) – although not all of them are working directly with the vRGW concept. Regarding R-CORD, Telefonica has announced a pilot with real customers in 2017. This pilot uses the OnLife Network platform, which has been developed by Telefonica based on CORD principles (Bushaus, 2017).

Taxonomies of vRGW Proposals

A taxonomy for vRGW proposals has been proposed in (Proença et al., 2019), grouping different vRGW-related proposals using four criteria: integration with the operator's ecosystem, function distribution, scope, and compliance with standards. Figure 14 illustrates the classification structure.

The criteria *Integration with the operator's ecosystem* relates to the level of integration with the operators' production environment, a mandatory requirement for successful adoption of vRGW proposals. There are two main points within this criterion: the *integration with OSS and BSS*, and *coexistence with legacy architectures*. The first points out the need for the vRGW to support appropriate connectors to seamlessly integrate with existing OSS and BSS systems. As these are complex and matured systems, a production-ready vRGW must be able to connect to them. *Coexistence* relates to the support of simultaneous operation of traditional and virtualized RGW instances. This point is quite important, as it is not feasible for a large operator to replace all physical RGWs at the same time. The migration needs to be smooth and gradual.

The *Function distribution* criteria focuses on where the RGW functions are located, and can be sub-divided into *functional placement* and *coupling*. Placement relates to the physical location of the function, with three main options: network equipment; operator cloud; and hybrid. It is worth noting that the operator's cloud can locate functions in edge or core datacenters, or a combination thereof. Network equipment deployments can be made for example at the BNG. And the hybrid approach is a combination of PNFs and VNFs hosted in cloud infrastructures. Function coupling can be (i) vertical, when the vRGW functions are isolated and each instance is deployed individually; (ii) co-located (when some functionality is locally shared, such as in DHCP or NAT functions); or (iii) distributed, when functions are massively distributed and geographically spread.

The *Scope* criteria is organized into three self-explanatory categories: *research work* from the academic community; *industry*-initiated proposals; and *initiatives from standardization bodies*.

The *Standards Compliance* criteria focuses on guidelines and standardization compliance, with most of the proposals being (or planning to be) compliant with ETSI's NFV specifications.

Figure 14. vRGW proposals taxonomy. Adapted and updated from (Proença et al., 2019)

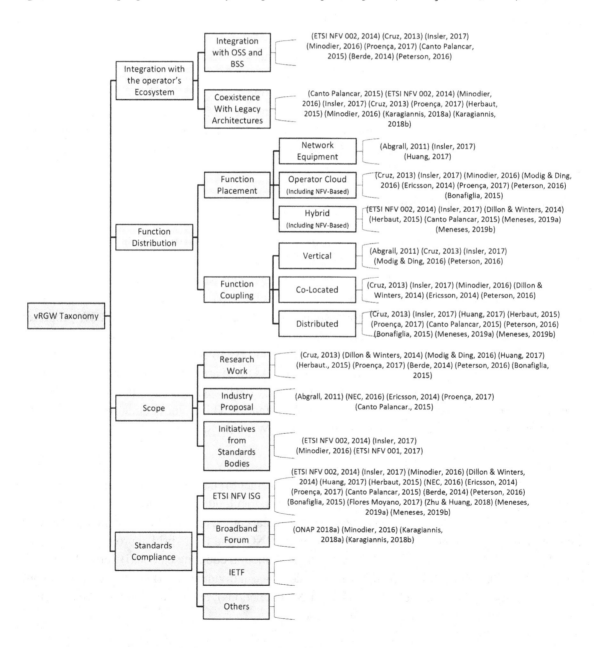

Performance Enhancing Developments

The practical feasibility of the vRGW concept should take advantage of the advances in virtualization techniques that have increased system performance in several aspects. This is especially important because, in order to be a viable option, RGW virtualization must not affect the service performance. Traditionally, the network functions run on specialized hardware, and moving them to COTS (commercial-off-the-shelf) commodity hardware might not be as efficient if not properly configured and planned.

In recent years, significant optimization of the networking performance has been reached, based upon techs like Intel's DPDK (Data Plane Development Kit). DPDK targets the libraries used by high network throughput applications to interact with the server's NIC (Network Interface Card). With DPDK, the CPU is continuously pooling the NIC for new packets to process, rather than using the traditional interrupt method, thus reducing the number of CPU cycles to complete the processing steps and greatly reducing the OS overhead in packet processing (Cerrato et al., 2016). As an example, in (Kourtis, 2015), a DPI (Deep Packet Inspection) application only achieved approximately 1Gbit/s of throughput using a 10Gbit/s NIC and traditional interrupt methods, while with DPDK the application operated at near line rate (i.e., almost 10Gbit/s).

Other techniques such as SR-IOV (Single Root I/O Virtualization) can improve the performance of NFV. Designed by the PCI-SIG (Peripheral Component Interconnect Special Interest Group) (PCISIG, 2010), it can divide a hardware component into several virtual pieces and deliver unique PCI Express Requester IDs and allocate them to individual VMs. The VM gains direct access to the hardware, removing hypervisor overhead in the interaction between the VM and hardware. In (Kourtis et al., 2015), a 19% improvement is observed in a 10Gbit/s link when using SR-IOV compared to a default configuration. There are, however, scenarios when SR-IOV might not be the best option to use, as it can significantly increase RTT (Round Trip Time), such as when using Docker containers (Anderson et al., 2016).

Increasing the network performance may also be done using more hardware-specific methods. The research community has been proposing Field-Programmable Gate Array (FPGA) to boost NFV performance in several ways. However, using FPGA to implement a network function is not viable as boards are expensive, and logic blocks are limited as their reprogramming can take a long time. Li (Li et al., 2018) proposed a dynamic hardware library (DHL) as a framework to abstract FPGA modules as a hardware function library and a set of APIs to be used by VNFs, thus reducing programming to use the FPGA. To accelerate network operations, FPGA boards embark network interfaces (such as NetFPGA) as mentioned in (Zazo et al., 2015): they thus replace conventional NICs. An FPGA would allow for some network operations to be executed directly by the hardware instead of the CPU. A single FPGA board can also be shared among several virtual software appliances. SR-IOV and PCI Passthrough technologies were key to provide 40+ Gbit/s data transmission speeds. In a study from (Sharma et al., 2019), specific VNF tasks such as encryption/decryption and hashing are offloaded to FPGAs, resulting in up to a reduction of the number of nodes required to perform the same number of requests by 20-25%.

Architecturally, containers have enabled the rapid expansion of micro-services, as they enable them to be easily deployed while reducing overheads when compared to VM-based solutions. Modig (Modig & Ding, 2016) achieved interesting performance improvements using a vRGW based on containerized functions with OpenVZ. Less OS overhead was observed, which leads to better resource usage. Memory usage is reduced due to kernel sharing. For the same reason, CPU load was significantly decreased when using a container-based approach instead of using a dedicated VM per customer. The efficiency increase was also noticeable regarding network throughput, although the difference was less than the difference observed in memory usage and CPU load. Besides throughput, the OS overhead reduction of container-based scenarios using Docker has a positive effect on latency and jitter, providing better performance when compared with XEN-based approaches in several studies (Anderson et al., 2016)(Evens, 2015). A comparison of latency in VNF environments using Docker- and KVM-based scenarios is presented in (Bonafiglia et al., 2015).

When using containers as a virtualization base for a large scale virtualized RGW deployment, orchestration plays an important role as the number of customers can be pretty big (several millions). Although somewhat recent, if compared with VM management solutions (which are well-established and mature), container technology attracts a growing interest of the research community, like the corresponding management and orchestration tools. Docker Swarm (Docker, 2020) and Kubernetes (Kubernetes, 2020) are two commonly-used container management platforms. Their security and isolation must be guaranteed to protect customers' privacy and security (Rotter et al., 2016). Sultan (Sultan et al., 2019), for instance, presents a set of use cases at the host and container level to show container security issues and the available methods to improve their security.

WRAP-UP AND CONCLUSIONS

Starting with a discussion on the rationale and motivation for the virtualization, this chapter presented an overview of the current status of the various efforts conducted to promote, specifiy, develop and evaluate the vRGW concept. This approach allows for the decoupling of functionalities currently supported by physical RGWs, keeping a reduced set of features at the customer's premises (based upon a MAC bridge) and moving most network functions (e.g., DHCP, DNS, NAT, firewall, content filtering) to the operator's data center.

The virtualization of the RGW has come a long way since the initial proposals, evolving from the validation of the concept to the development of a complete framework supported by vendors and operators. Technological advances improved the hardware efficiency, enhancing its performance while, at the same time, allowing operators to consolidate hardware, which reduces the resources needed to support the vRGW service instances. Currently, some operators have been conducting test pilots with some of their customers, although there are still no (publicly available) results from operator-led deployments, for the time being.

Standardization efforts have also been instrumental in this approach. Standards that document frameworks like ONAP, CORD, and OSM have been published thanks to a collaboration between vendors and operators in various bodies and forums. Such specifications help achieving the objectives of managing the functions through their lifecycle and also provide the connectors to integrate them within OSS and BSS systems. These frameworks also come with the tools to interface with virtualized infrastructures based upon OpenStack for example, which allows operators to dynamically scale the resources according to the circumstances.

Customer adoption is key for successfully deploying the vRGW at large scale. Although some customers might feel some loss of control because some functions are outsourced, this feeling can be moderated by as the perspective of improving service quality, of the emergence of new services, and of eventual energy savings. Bringing functions closer to the customer is a key condition to improve the quality of service and experience, and although some research has already been published (Meneses et al., 2019a) and (Meneses et al., 2019b), this remains an understudied aspect of the vRGW approach for the time being.

ACKNOWLEDGMENT

This work was partially funded by the Mobilizador 5G (POCI-01-0247- FEDER-024539) P2020 project.

REFERENCES

P4. (2019). *P4 Language Specification v1.2.0*. Retrieved June 2020 from https://p4.org/p4-spec/docs/P4-16-v1.2.0.html

Abgrall, D. (2011). *Virtual Home Gateway: How can Home Gateway virtualization be achieved?* EURESCOM Study Report P2055 D1.

Alter, C. (2014). *Broadband Forum Work on "Network Enhanced Residential Gateway" (WT-317) and "Virtual Business Gateway" (WT-328)*. Broadband Forum's liaison letter to the IETF.

Alter, C., & Daowood, S. (2014). *Broadband Forum Work on Flexible Service Chaining (SD-326)*. Broadband Forum's liaison letter to the IETF.

Anderson, J., Hu, H., Agarwal, U., Lowery, C., Li, H., & Apon, A. (2016). Performance considerations of network functions virtualization using containers. In *2016 International Conference on Computing, Networking and Communications (ICNC)* (pp. 1–7). 10.1109/ICCNC.2016.7440668

Barham, P., Dragovic, B., Fraser, K., Hand, S., Harris, T., Ho, A., Neugebauer, R., Pratt, I., & Warfield, A. (2003). Xen and the art of virtualization. *SIGOPS Oper. Syst. Rev., 37*(5), 164-177. doi:10.1145/1165389.945462

Basak, D., Toshniwal, R., Maskalik, S., & Sequeira, A. (2010). Virtualizing networking and security in the cloud. *SIGOPS Oper. Syst. Rev., 44*(4), 86-94. https://doi.acm.org/10.1145/1899928.1899939 doi:10.1145/1899928.1899939

Bazzi, A., & Onozato, Y. (2011). Feasibility Study of Security Virtual Appliances for Personal Computing. *IPSJ Journal of Information Processing, 19*.

BBF MR-430. (2018). *Broadband Forum MR-430: Cloud Central Office (CloudCO)*. Retrieved September 2020 https://www.broadband-forum.org/marketing/download/MR-430.pdf

Berde, P., Gerola, M., Hart, J., Higuchi, Y., Kobayashi, M., Koide, T., ... Parulkar, G. (2014). ONOS: Towards an Open, Distributed SDN OS. In *Proceedings of the Third Workshop on Hot Topics in Software Defined Networking* (pp. 1–6). New York, NY: ACM. 10.1145/2620728.2620744

Blackford, J., & Digdon, M. (2013). *Broadband Forum, "TR-069 – CPE WAN Management Protocol", Issue 1, Amendment 5, November 2013*.

Bonafiglia, R., Cerrato, I., Ciaccia, F., Nemirovsky, M., & Risso, F. (2015). Assessing the Performance of Virtualization Technologies for NFV: A Preliminary Benchmarking. In *Software Defined Networks (EWSDN), 2015 Fourth European Workshop on* (pp. 67–72). 10.1109/EWSDN.2015.63

Boucadair, M., Jacquenet, C., Jiang, Y., Parker, R., Pignataro, C., & Naito, K. (2014). *Requirements for Service Function Chaining (SFC) (draft-boucadair-sfc-requirements-05).* IETF Internet Draft.

Boucadair, M., Jacquenet, C., Parker, R., & Dunbar, L. (2014). *Service Function Chaining: Design Considerations, Analysis & Recommendations* (draft-boucadair-sfc-design-analysis-02). IETF Internet Draft.

Brodkin, J. (2020). AT&T kills DSL, leaves tens of millions of homes without fiber Internet. *ARS Technica.* Available at: https://arstechnica.com/tech-policy/2020/10/life-in-atts-slow-lane-millions-left-without-fiber-as-company-kills-dsl/

Bryant, S., & Pate, P. (2005). *Pseudo Wire Emulation Edge-to-Edge (PWE3) Architecture.* IETF RFC 3985.

Bushaus, D. (2017). *Telefónica 'gets its hands dirty' with new OnLife Network.* Retrieved September 2020 from https://inform.tmforum.org/news/2017/05/telefonica-gets-hands-dirty-new-platform-architecture/

CableLabs, Inc. (2014). *DOCSIS 3.1 Physical Specification.* CableLabs.

CableLabs, Inc. (2020). *DOCSIS 4.0 Physical Specification.* CableLabs. Available at: https://www.cablelabs.com/technologies/docsis-4-0-technology

Cain, B., Deering, S., Kouvelas, I., Fenner, B., & Thyagarajan, A. (2002). *Internet Group Management Protocol, Version 3.* IETF Standard RFC 3376.

Cantó Palancar, R., López da Silva, R. A., Folgueira Chavarría, J. L., López, D. R., Elizondo Armengol, A. J., Gamero Tinoco, R., … Gamero Tinoco, R. (2015). Virtualization of residential customer premise equipment. Lessons learned in Brazil vCPE trial. *IT - Information Technology, 57*(5), 285–294. . doi:10.1515/itit-2015-0028

Carey, J(2015). *Component Objects for CWMP, TR-157 Issue 1 Amendment 10.* Broadband Forum Tech. Report. Retrieved August 2020 from https://www.broadband-forum.org/download/TR-157.pdf

Carey, T., Thorne, D., & Allan, D. (2016). *Broadband Forum TR-359: A Framework for Virtualization, Issue 1.* Broadband Forum. Retrieved September 2020 from https://www.broadband-forum.org/download/TR-359.pdf

Cerrato, I., Annarumma, M., & Risso, F. (2014). Supporting Fine-Grained Network Functions through Intel DPDK. In *Software Defined Networks (EWSDN), 2014 Third European Workshop on* (pp. 1–6). 10.1109/EWSDN.2014.33

Chiosi, M. (2012). *Network Functions Virtualization – An Introduction, Benefits, Enablers, Challenges & Call for Action. Issue 1.* ETSI White Paper. Retrieved September 2020 from https://portal.etsi.org/NFV/NFV_White_Paper.pdf

Chiosi, M. (2014). *Network Functions Virtualization – Network Operator Perspectives on Industry Progress. Issue 1.* ETSI White Paper. Retrieved September 2020 from https://portal.etsi.org/Portals/0/TBpages/NFV/Docs/NFV_White_Paper3.pdf

Cruz, T., Simões, P., & Monteiro, E. (2015). Optimizing the Delivery of Services Supported by Residential Gateways: Virtualized Residential Gateways. Handbook of Research on Redesigning the Future of Internet Architectures, 432–473.

Cruz, T., Simões, P., Reis, N., Monteiro, E., Bastos, F., & Laranjeira, A. (2013). An architecture for virtualized home gateways. In *Integrated Network Management (IM 2013), 2013 IFIP/IEEE International Symposium on* (pp. 520–526). IEEE.

Cui, A., Hertoghs, Y. (2012). *TR-145: Multi-service Broadband Network Functional Modules and Architecture, Issue 1*. Broadband Forum Technical Report.

Da Silva, R., Fernandez, M., Gamir, L., & Perez, M. (2011). Home routing gateway virtualization: An overview on the architecture alternatives. Future Network & Mobile Summit (FutureNetw), 1-9.

Dillon, M., & Winters, T. (2014). Virtualization of Home Network Gateways. *Computer, 47*(11), 62–65. doi:10.1109/MC.2014.338

DLNA. (2016). *DLNA Networked Device Interoperability Guidelines*. DLNA Consortium Guidelines. Retrieved September 2020 from: https://spirespark.com/dlna/guidelines

Docker. (2020). *Docker Homepage*. Retrieved September 2020 from https://www.docker.com/

Dustzadeh, J. (2013). *SDN: Time to Accelerate the Pace*. Keynote presentation at the Open Networking Summit 2013, Santa Clara, CA. Retrieved July 2020 from https://www.slideshare.net/opennetsummit/ons2013-justin-joubine-dustzadehhuawei

Egi, N., Greenhalgh, A., Handley, M., Hoerdt, M., Huici, F., Mathy, L., & Papadimitriou, P. (2010). A platform for high performance and flexible virtual routers on commodity hardware. *SIGCOMM Computer Communications Review, 40*(1), 127-128. https://doi.acm.org/10.1145/1672308.1672332 doi:10.1145/1672308.1672332

Egi, N., Greenhalgh, A., Handley, M., Hoerdt, M., Mathy, L., & Schooley, T. (2007). Evaluating Xen for Router Virtualization. *Computer Communications and Networks, 2007. ICCCN 2007. Proceedings of 16th International Conference on*, 1256-1261. 10.1109/ICCCN.2007.4317993

Ericsson. (2014). *Virtual CPE and Software Defined Networking*. Whitepaper. Retrieved September 2020 from https://www.ericsson.com/res/docs/2014/virtual-cpe-and-software-defined-networking.pdf

ETSI NFV 001. (2017). *Network Functions Virtualization (NFV); Use Cases, version 1.2.1*. ETSI. Retrieved September 2020 from https://www.etsi.org/deliver/etsi_gr/nfv/001_099/001/01.02.01_60/gr_nfv001v010201p.pdf

ETSI NFV 002. (2014). *Network Functions Virtualization (NFV); Architectural Framework, version 1.2.1*. ETSI.

ETSI NFV ISG. (n.d.). https://www.etsi.org/about/how-we-work/industry-specification-groups

ETSI OSM. (2016). *ONF OSM Open Source Mano*. Retrieved September 2020 from https://osm.etsi.org/

Evens, J. (2015). *A comparison of containers and virtual machines for use with NFV* (M.Sc. Thesis). Retrieved September 2020 from http://hdl.handle.net/1942/19367

Flores Moyano, R., Fernández, D., Bellido, L., & González, C. (2017). A software-defined networking approach to improve service provision in residential networks. *International Journal of Network Management, 27*(6), 1–19. doi:10.1002/nem.1984

FORCES. (n.d.). *IETF Forwarding and Control Element Separation (forces) Working Group Website.* Retrieved November 2020 from: https://datatracker.ietf.org/wg/forces/charter/

Hai, D., Dobrowski, G., Cornaglia, B., Hertoghs, Y., & Zong, N. (2020). *Broadband Forum TR-408: Cloud CO Migration and Coexistence, Issue 1.* Broadband Forum. Retrieved October 2020 from https://www.broadband-forum.org/technical/download/TR-408.pdf

Halpern, J., & Pignataro, C. (2015). *Service Function Chaining (SFC) Architecture.* IETF. Retrieved from https://www.ietf.org/rfc/rfc7665.txt

Han, B., Gopalakrishnan, V., Ji, L., & Lee, S. (2015). Network function virtualization: Challenges and opportunities for innovations. *Communications Magazine, IEEE, 53*(2), 90–97. doi:10.1109/MCOM.2015.7045396

Herbaut, N., Negru, D., Xilouris, G., & Chen, Y. (2015). Migrating to a NFV-based Home Gateway: Introducing a Surrogate vNF approach. In *Network of the Future (NOF), 2015 6th International Conference on the* (pp. 1–7). 10.1109/NOF.2015.7333284

Hernando, G., A. B., Da Silva Farina, A., Bellido Triana, L., Ruiz Pinar, F. J., & Fernandez Cambronero, D. (2017). Virtualization of residential IoT functionality by using NFV and SDN. *2017 IEEE International Conference on Consumer Electronics, ICCE 2017,* 86–87. 10.1109/ICCE.2017.7889240

Huang, N.-F., Li, C.-H., Chen, C.-C., Hsu, I.-H., Li, C.-C., & Chen, C.-H. (2017). A Novel vCPE Framework for Enabling Virtual Network Functions with Multiple Flow Tables Architecture in SDN Switches. In *2017 19th Asia-Pacific Network Operations and Management Symposium (APNOMS)* (pp. 64–69). 10.1109/APNOMS.2017.8094180

Huawei Technologies Co. Ltd. (2010). *SmartAX MA5600T Series Product Website.* Retrieved October 2014 from: http://enterprise.huawei.com/en/products/network/access-network/olt/en_ma5600t.htm

IEEE 802.1Q. (2011). *IEEE Standard 802.1Q-2011, Media Access Control Bridges and Virtual Bridged Local Area Networks.* IEEE 802.1 Working Group.

IETF SFC WG. (n.d.). https://datatracker.ietf.org/wg/sfc/documents

Insler, R. (2017). *Broadband Forum TR-328: Virtual Business Gateway, Issue 1.* Broadband Forum. Retrieved August 2020 from https://www.broadband-forum.org/download/TR-328.pdf

Jiang, Y., & Li, H. (2014). *An Architecture of Service Function Chaining* (draft-jiang-sfc-arch-01.txt). IETF Internet Draft.

Kaljic, E., Maric, A., Njemcevic, P., & Hadzialic, M. (2019). A Survey on Data Plane Flexibility and Programmability in Software-Defined Networking. *IEEE Access: Practical Innovations, Open Solutions, 7,* 47804–47840. doi:10.1109/ACCESS.2019.2910140

Karagiannis, G., Hai, D., Dobrowski, G., Croot, C., Hertoghs, Y., & Zong, N. (2018a). *Broadband Forum TR-384: Cloud Central Office Reference Architectural Framework, Issue 1.* Broadband Forum. Retrieved September 2020 from https://www.broadband-forum.org/download/TR-384.pdf

Karagiannis, G., Hai, D., Dobrowski, G., Croot, C., Hertoghs, Y., & Zong, N. (2018b). *Broadband Forum TR-416: CloudCO Use Cases and Scenarios, Issue 1. Broadband Forum*. Retrieved September 2020 from https://www.broadband-forum.org/download/TR-384.pdf

Kirksey, H. (2017). *TR-140 – TR-069 Data Model for Storage Service Enabled Devices, Issue: 1 Amendment 3, April 2017*. Academic Press.

Kourtis, M.-A., Xilouris, G., Riccobene, V., McGrath, M. J., Petralia, G., Koumaras, H., . . . Liberal, F. (2015). Enhancing VNF performance by exploiting SR-IOV and DPDK packet processing acceleration. In *Network Function Virtualization and Software Defined Network (NFV-SDN), 2015 IEEE Conference on* (pp. 74–78). 10.1109/NFV-SDN.2015.7387409

Kubernetes. (2020). *Kubernetes - Production-Grade Container Orchestration Homepage - v1.19.1*. Retrieved September 2020 from https://kubernetes.io/

Latif, Z., Sharif, K., Li, F., Karim, M. M., Biswas, S., & Wang, Y. (2020). A comprehensive survey of interface protocols for software defined networks. *Journal of Network and Computer Applications*, *156*(January), 102563. doi:10.1016/j.jnca.2020.102563

Lee, Y., & Ghai, R. (2014). *Problem Statements of Virtualizing Home Services* (draft-lee-vhs-ps-00). IETF Internet Draft.

Lee, Y., & Xie, C. (2014). *Virtualizing Home Services Use Cases* (draft-lee-vhs-usecases-00). IETF Internet Draft.

Lemke, A. (2015). *Alcatel Lucent - Why service providers need an NFV platform: Strategic White Paper*. Academic Press.

Li, X., Wang, X., Liu, F., & Xu, H. (2018). DHL: Enabling flexible software network functions with FPGA acceleration. *Proceedings - International Conference on Distributed Computing Systems*, 1–11. 10.1109/ICDCS.2018.00011

McKeown, N., & Rexford, J. (2016). *Clarifying the differences between P4 and OpenFlow*. Retrieved September 2020 from https://p4.org/p4/clarifying-the-differences-between-p4-and-openflow.html

Meneses, F., Fernandes, M., Vieira, T., Corujo, D., Figueiredo, S., Neto, A., & Aguiar, R. L. (2019b). Traffic-aware Live Migration in Virtualized CPE Scenarios. In *IEEE Conference on Network Function Virtualization and Software Defined Networks, NFV-SDN 2019 - Proceedings*. Institute of Electrical and Electronics Engineers Inc. 10.1109/NFV-SDN47374.2019.9039975

Meneses, F., Fernandes, M., Vieira, T., Corujo, D., Neto, A., & Aguiar, R. L. (2019a). Dynamic Modular vCPE Orchestration in Platform as a Service Architectures. In *Proceeding of the 2019 IEEE 8th International Conference on Cloud Networking, CloudNet 2019*. Institute of Electrical and Electronics Engineers Inc. 10.1109/CloudNet47604.2019.9064147

Mijumbi, R., Serrat, J., Gorricho, J., Latré, S., Charalambides, M., & Lopez, D. (2016). *Management and orchestration challenges in network functions virtualization*. Academic Press.

Minodier, D. (2016). *Broadband Forum TR-317: Network Enhanced Residential Gateway, Issue 1*. Broadband Forum. Retrieved August 2020 from https://www.broadband-forum.org/download/TR-317.pdf

Modig, D., & Ding, J. (2016). Performance impacts on container based virtualization in virtualized residential gateways. In *2016 39th International Conference on Telecommunications and Signal Processing (TSP)* (pp. 27–32). 10.1109/TSP.2016.7760823

NEC. (2016). *NEC Advances World's First Virtual Customer Premises Equipment Trial In Brazil*. Retrieved September 2020 from https://www.nec.com/en/press/201606/global_20160622_01.html

Niu, L., Li, H., Jiang, Y., Yong, L. (2014). *A Service Function Chaining Header and Forwarding Mechanism* (draft-niu-sfc-mechanism-01.txt). IETF Internet Draft.

ONAP. (2018a). *ONAP vCPE Use Case*. Retrieved September 2020 from https://docs.onap.org/en/casablanca/submodules/integration.git/docs/docs_vCPE.html

ONAP. (2018b). *ONAP vCPE Blueprint Overview*. Retrieved September 2020 from https://www.onap.org/wp-content/uploads/sites/20/2018/11/ONAP_CaseSolution_vCPE_112918FNL.pdf

ONAP. (2019). *Harmonizing Open Source and Standards: Progress of ONAP*. Retrieved September 2020 from https://www.onap.org/wp-content/uploads/sites/20/2019/04/ONAP_HarmonizingOpenSourceStandards_032719.pdf

ONF. (2014). *Openflow-enabled SDN and Network Functions Virtualization*. ONF Solution Brief, Open Networking Foundation.

ONF. (2015). *OpenFlow Switch Specification, version 1.5.1* (Wire Protocol 0x06). Open Networking Foundation. Retrieved July 2020 from https://opennetworking.org/wp-content/uploads/2014/10/openflow-switch-v1.5.1.pdf

OpenCord. (2017a). *AT&T and R-CORD*. Retrieved September 2020 from https://wiki.opencord.org/pages/viewpage.action?pageId=1966449

OpenCord. (2017b). *NTT and R-CORD*. Retrieved September 2020 from https://wiki.opencord.org/display/CORD/NTT+and+R-CORD

OpenCord. (2020). *Telefónica and R-CORD*. Retrieved September 2020 from https://wiki.opencord.org/pages/viewpage.action?pageId=1967521

OSGi. (2018). *OSGI Service Compendium, Release 7*. OSGi Alliance Specification. Retrieved July 2020 from: http://www.osgi.org /Specifications/HomePage

OSM. (2020). *OSM Scope and Functionality*. Retrieved September 2020 from https://osm.etsi.org/wikipub/index.php/OSM_Scope_and_Functionality

PCI-SIG. (2010). *Peripheral Component Interconnect Special Interest - Special Interest Group Homepage*. Retrieved from https://pcisig.com/

Peterson, L., Al-Shabibi, A., Anshutz, T., Baker, S., Bavier, A., Das, S., Hart, J., Palukar, G., & Snow, W. (2016). Central office re-architected as a data center. *IEEE Communications Magazine, 54*(10), 96–101. doi:10.1109/MCOM.2016.7588276

Pisa, P., Moreira, M., Carvalho, H., Ferraz, L., & Duarte, O. (2010). Migrating Xen Virtual Routers with No Packet Loss. *Proceedings of the First Workshop on Network Virtualization and Intelligence For Future Internet (WNetVirt'10).*

Proença, J., Cruz, T., Simões, P., Gaspar, G., Parreira, B., Laranjeira, A., & Bastos, F. (2017). Building an NFV-Based vRGW: lessons learned. *14th IEEE Consumer Communications and Networking Conference (CCNC 2017).*

Proença, J., Cruz, T., Simões, P., & Monteiro, E. (2019). Virtualization of Residential Gateways: A Comprehensive Survey. *IEEE Communications Surveys and Tutorials, 21*(2), 1462–1482. doi:10.1109/COMST.2018.2874827

Quinn, P., & Nadeau, T. (2014). *Service Function Chaining Problem Statement* (draft-ietf-sfc-problem-statement-07.txt). IETF Internet Draft.

R-CORD. (n.d.). *Residential CORD*. Retrieved September 2020 from https://wiki.opencord.org/display/CORD/Residential+CORD

Rosemberg, J. (2002). *SIP: Session Initiation Protocol*. IETF Internet Standard. RFC 3261.

Rotter, C., Farkas, L., Nyiri, G., Csatári, G., Jánosi, L., & Springer, R. (2016). *Using Linux Containers in Telecom Applications. Innovations in Clouds, Internet and Networks*. ICIN.

Royon, Y. (2007). *Environments d'exécution pour paserelles domestiques* (PhD thesis). Institut National des Sciences Apliquées (INSA/INRIA).

Sharma, G. P., Tavernier, W., Colle, D., & Pickavet, M. (2019). VNF-AAP: Accelerator-aware Virtual Network Function Placement. *IEEE Conference on Network Function Virtualization and Software Defined Networks, NFV-SDN 2019 - Proceedings*, 25–28. 10.1109/NFV-SDN47374.2019.9040061

Smedt, A., Balemans, H., Onnegren, J., & Haeseleer, S. (2006). The multi-play service enabled Residential Gateway. Proc. of Broadband Europe 2006.

Sultan, S., Ahmad, I., & Dimitriou, T. (2019). Container security: Issues, challenges, and the road ahead. *IEEE Access: Practical Innovations, Open Solutions, 7*, 52976–52996. doi:10.1109/ACCESS.2019.2911732

Troan, O., & Droms, R. (2003). *IPv6 Prefix Options for Dynamic Host Configuration Protocol (DHCP) version 6*. IETF Internet Standard RFC3633.

Xia, L., Wu, Q., & King, D. (2013). *Use cases and Requirements for Virtual Service Node Pool Management* (draft-xia-vsnpool-management-use-case-01). IEFT Internet Draft.

Zazo, J. F., Lopez-Buedo, S., Audzevich, Y., & Moore, A. W. (2015). A PCIe DMA engine to support the virtualization of 40 Gbps FPGA-accelerated network appliances. In *ReConFigurable Computing and FPGAs (ReConFig), 2015 International Conference on* (pp. 1–6). 10.1109/ReConFig.2015.7393334

Zeng, S., & Hao, Q. (2009). Network I/O Path Analysis in the Kernel-based Virtual Machine Environment through Tracing. *Proceedings of the 1st Int. Conf. on Information Science and Engineering (ICISE) 2009.*

Zhu, H., & Huang, C. (2018). VNF-B&B: Enabling Edge-based NFV with CPE resource sharing. In *IEEE International Symposium on Personal, Indoor and Mobile Radio Communications, PIMRC* (pp. 1–5). Institute of Electrical and Electronics Engineers Inc. 10.1109/PIMRC.2017.8292421

KEY TERMS AND DEFINITIONS

Broadband Access Networks: Access networks that provide high-speed network connectivity between customers and network service providers.

Network Function Virtualization: In NFV, network node functions, previously carried by dedicated hardware, are virtualized into blocks (Virtual Network Functions or VNFs) that can be chained together to create service abstractions.

Network Service Provider Infrastructures: It corresponds to the infrastructure elements, such as the networking structure or data centers, that support the operations of organizations that provide network access or converged services.

Service Delivery: This encompasses the delivery of converged services over IP networks, whether from the operator itself (as it is the case for Triple-Play offers) or from third parties.

Software-Defined Networking: This is a network architecture that decouples the network control and forwarding plane functions, making it possible to introduce flexible and dynamic, flow-oriented network control programmability.

Virtualized Residential Gateways (vRGWs): An alternative to conventional, physical gateway appliances, where the physical device is replaced by a simple bridge, with all functionality and services being moved to the operator infrastructure, as a virtualized entity.

Chapter 11
Software–Defined Vehicular Networks (SDVN) for Intelligent Transportation Systems (ITS)

Rinki Sharma

Ramaiah University of Applied Sciences, Bangalore, India

ABSTRACT

Vehicular communication is going to play a significant role in the future intelligent transportation systems (ITS). Due to the highly dynamic nature of vehicular networks (VNs) and need for efficient real-time communication, the traditional networking paradigm is not suitable for VNs. Incorporating the SDN technology in VNs provides benefits in network programmability, heterogeneity, connectivity, resource utility, safety and security, routing, and traffic management. However, there are still several challenges and open research issues due to network dynamicity, scalability, heterogeneity, interference, latency, and security that need to be addressed. This chapter presents the importance of vehicular communication in future ITS, the significance of incorporating the SDN paradigm in VNs, taxonomy for the role of SDVN, the software-defined vehicular network (SDVN) architecture, and open research issues in SDVN.

INTRODUCTION

Over the years there has been tremendous advancement in vehicular technology. While network and communication technology made its way into the vehicles for applications such as comfort, driver assist, and fleet management, gradually vehicle communication is advancing towards vehicle-to-everything (V2X) scenarios. Under V2X communication, a vehicle is capable of Vehicle-to-Vehicle (V2V), Vehicle-to-Infrastructure (V2I), Vehicle-to-Cloud (V2C), Vehicle-to-Pedestrian (V2P), Vehicle-to-Device (V2D), and Vehicle-to-Grid (V2G), to name a few. There are standards (including protocols) such as Cellular Vehicle-to-Everything (C-V2X) IEEE 802.11p, Wireless Access for Vehicular Environments (WAVE) and Dedicated Short Range Communication (DSRC), (Wang, Mao & Gong, 2017; Abboud, Omar & Zhuang, 2016; Storck & Duarte-Figueiredo, 2020; Jiang & Delgrossi, 2008; Morgan, 2010; Li, 2010),

DOI: 10.4018/978-1-7998-7646-5.ch011

defined to enable such communications. Enabling vehicles to communicate between each other and with their surroundings paves way for Intelligent Transportation Systems (ITS).

Tremendous rise in communication and computing devices in vehicular networks has led to a surge of the need for bandwidth, storage, and computing power in these networks (Chahal et al., 2017) and (Jaballah, Conti & Lal, 2019). Maintenance and management of contemporary networks using traditional networking techniques is complex and expensive. Hence, traditional networking is being enhanced with Software-Defined Networking (SDN) as it eliminates manual configuration of networking hardware and helps in attaining programmability and flexibility of networks where control and data planes are decoupled (Kirkpatrick, 2013). The SDN techniques facilitate service design, delivery and operational procedures by means of dynamic resource allocation and policy enforcement schemes, data models and automated configuration tasks.

Vehicular communication is an enabler for autonomous vehicles of the future. It involves exchanging messages related to safety, navigation, traffic condition and congestion control, as well as multimedia, general purpose Internet access, location-based services (such as nearby hospitals, service stations, gas stations, parking places or restaurants), traffic conditions, and congestion control. These applications have different delay, and bandwidth requirements. The packet loss and propagation requirements (in terms of communication scheme for example unicast or multicast, symmetric or asymmetric, and bidirectional and unidirectional transmission). While applications such as vehicular safety, navigation, multimedia, traffic conditions, and congestion control require real-time performance, reliability, high bandwidth, and low-latency operation; other applications such as general-purpose Internet access and location-based services may be able to withstand nominal delays. Integration of SDN technology with vehicular networks (VNs) will facilitate the programmability of networks by means of dynamic network resource allocation schemes based on the application requirements and network constraints (among others) (Jaballah, Conti & Lal, 2019; Chahal et al., 2017). SDN-based VNs are termed as Software Defined Vehicular Networks (SDVN).

The remainder of this chapter is organized as follows. Section 2 presents the role of vehicular communication in ITS and the characteristics of vehicular networks. Section 3 discusses the importance of incorporating SDN architectures in vehicular network communication. The taxonomy for the role of SDVN in VN programmability, heterogeneity, connectivity, resource utilization, safety and security, routing and traffic management is provided. Section 4 presents the simplified view of the SDVN architecture comprising the three planes/layers and corresponding interfaces. The operations carried out by the three planes and their respective components are presented. Section 5 discusses the key challenges and open research issues in the area of SDVN. Section 6 concludes the chapter.

ITS and Vehicular Communication

One of the goals of ITS is to achieve high traffic efficiency while reducing the commuting times (e.g., home-to-office travel and back) and provide enhanced traffic safety and comfort. The ITS focuses on traffic management and safety, real-time traffic information and status, emergency and warning systems, infotainment and comfort, and autonomous driving. Vehicular communication plays a crucial role in the implementation and the operation of ITS. Vehicular communication involves real-time communication of vehicles with other vehicles (V2V), roadside infrastructure (V2I), cloud (V2C), other devices (V2D) and pedestrians (V2P). With such variety of communication, vehicular networks are deemed heterogeneous and dynamic. VNs comprising vehicles and other communication entities mentioned earlier exchange information in real time. In these networks, vehicles play the role of source, sink as well as routers. The vehicular networks operate based on peer-to-peer and client-server paradigms depending on the applications and communicating entities. Vehicular ad-hoc networks (VANETs) are the self-organizing V2V communication networks established between moving vehicles (Hartenstein & Laberteaux, 2008), (Hamdi et al., 2020) and (Amjid, Khan & Shah, 2020). In V2V communications all the vehicles are considered as peers, while in V2I and V2C communications a vehicle acts as a client who accesses servers possibly hosted in cloud infrastructures. The highly dynamic nature of VNs leads to constant change in the network topology and status of the communication links resulting in variation of network performance resulting in variation of network performance. Some of the important characteristics of VNs are presented in Figure 1.

Figure 1. Characteristics of VANETs

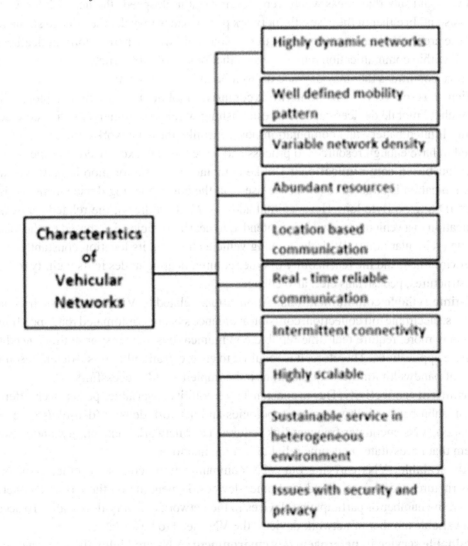

In the following some of the VN characteristics are further detailed:

1. **Highly dynamic networks:** Vehicular ad-hoc networks (VANETs) comprise vehicles that are highly mobile when compared to the mobile devices in a mobile ad-hoc network (MANET). High mobility of VANETs leads to constant change in the topology of these networks, which further leads to breakage of communication links leading to adverse effects on the network performance.

2. **Well-defined mobility pattern:** Unlike mobile ad-hoc networks (MANETs) wherein the mobile nodes move randomly, vehicular nodes usually move in a well-defined pattern such as on a road while following rules on traffic lanes and junctions. This well-defined mobility pattern provides certain predictability to the network topology and connectivity.

3. **Variable network density:** Due to high node mobility and changing node density due to varying terrain (e.g., from narrow city lanes leading to slow moving traffic and traffic jams, to broad highways and suburban areas where vehicles move at high speed) the network topology is highly inconsistent. In either of the cases, the network performance may degrade due to signal interference in dense areas or connection breakages due to sparse network wherein communicating nodes may not fall within communication range of each other or that of infrastructure leading to poor network coverage conditions that may degrade or even break communication.

4. **Sufficient resources:** A mobile network comprises mobile nodes such as laptops, smartphones or handheld mobile devices capable of establishing wireless communication. These devices have usually limited battery and computation power. Unlike these networks, the nodes in VNs are assumed to have enough resources to process and store the data exchanged over the network.

5. **Location-based communications:** Unlike computer networks or mobile networks wherein the communication is targeted to a specific user and the corresponding device using its device ID or group ID (e.g., 6 Byte long Hexadecimal address, MAC address); the related services and communication in a vehicular network are intended to nearby vehicles, i.e., based on the location of the vehicle (vehicular node). With the moving vehicle changing its location constantly, its surrounding environment and the reachability of other communicating nodes in its vicinity (other vehicles, infrastructures, pedestrians etc.) also change.

6. **Real-time reliable communications:** Applications related to VNs and ITS such as autonomous vehicles, electronic toll collection, collision avoidance systems, automated road speed enforcement, and many more, require real-time reliable communications. The response times need to be short for these applications. Therefore, it is required to ensure availability of sufficient resources, e.g. in terms of bandwidth for these applications to be implemented successfully.

7. **Intermittent connectivity:** Due to constant node mobility at variable speeds, over different terrains (urban, suburban, or hilly), varying topologies and network density (densely/sparsely populated networks), VNs encounter frequent link failures, poor network connectivity, and packet loss in a system that necessitates real-time reliable communications.

8. **Highly scalable:** VNs carrying out V2X communications consist of other vehicles, roadside infrastructure, pedestrians, cloud, and other devices. Depending on the terrain and network node density, the number of participating devices in the network can vary drastically. To accommodate these variable number of network devices, the VNs need to be scalable.

9. **Sustainable service in heterogeneous environment:** VNs are highly dynamic and scalable networks, comprising a large variety of participating nodes. These networks operate in heterogeneous environments. While operating in these environments, these networks need to support real-time

applications that require high reliability. Therefore, it is a challenge to achieve service continuity in heterogeneous environments.

10. **Enhanced security and privacy:** Reliability is crucial for VN communication. Vehicular data integrity must not be altered. Security (including the preservation of data privacy) is therefore essential for VN communications like in any other communication technology. While the security mechanisms are expected to be robust, the underlying mechanisms should raise neither computational complexity nor processing delay to unduly high figures.

Software-Defined Vehicular Networks (SDVN)

The constant increase in the demand for remaining connected while on the move, coupled with the essential requirement of traffic safety and efficiency, calls for robust and reliable VN communications. However, VNs encounter numerous challenges owing to their characteristics discussed in Section 2. To achieve robust and reliable VNs that can adapt to the varying network conditions due to the constant movement of the involved entities, Software-Defined Networking (SDN) is being considered as with a technique that can be useful for VN programmability (Zhu et al., 2015) and (He, Cao & Liu, 2016). This section examines the role of SDN in overcoming the challenges faced by the VNs through the SDVN use cases.

Role of SDN In VNs

As discussed in Section 2, the VNs are characterized by a highly dynamic and heterogeneous network environments that require real-time and reliable communication. The varying range of applications and communication protocols supported by these networks raise various QoS requirements. Technologies/methods used for vehicular communication comprise IEEE 802.11p WAVE, DSRC, Wi-Fi, C-V2X, wireless sensor networks, ad-hoc networks and infrared communication. These involve complex algorithms that deal with the issues in routing, connectivity, heterogeneity, scalability, reliability, and security. Also, proprietary and tightly coupled solutions (solutions developed by one manufacturer are unable to work with devices/solutions developed by other manufacturers) make the implementation of VNs complex and inefficient (Yaqoob et al., 2017) and (Ku et al., 2014).

SDN is being considered as the most appropriate technology to deal with such requirements as Integration of SDN techniques facilitate VN programmability, which cannot be achieved by legacy networking techniques alone. The SDN computation logic (a.k.a. SDN controller) resides in the control plane and constantly monitors the network to assess its status and performance. To achieve efficient network communication and address various QoS requirements raised by a VN, an SDN controller helps optimizing the usage of network resources. The SDN controller maintains a global view of the network topology and facilitates efficient network management (Liyanage, 2018).

Since its inception, SDN has been primarily used for wired networks. However, over the years, researchers have developed solutions to deploy SDN architectures for wireless networks. Researchers have implemented the SDN architectures for ad-hoc networks combined with high speed wireless and mobile communication (Benalia, Bitam & Mellouk, 2020) and (Din et al., 2018). Considering the highly dynamic topology and heterogeneity of VNs, SDVN is considered to be the promising solution for VNs and future ITS solutions. SDVNs are composed of vehicles and user-based nodes, Road Side Units (RSUs), Road Side Unit Centers (RSUCs), Software-Defined Network Controllers (SDNC), and Base Stations (BSs) (Chahal et al., 2017; He, Cao & Liu, 2016; Alioua et al., 2017).

The role of SDVNs is presented in Figure 2. The important aspects of VNs wherein SDN plays a significant role are presented in the following subsections.

Figure 2. Taxonomy of the role of SDVN

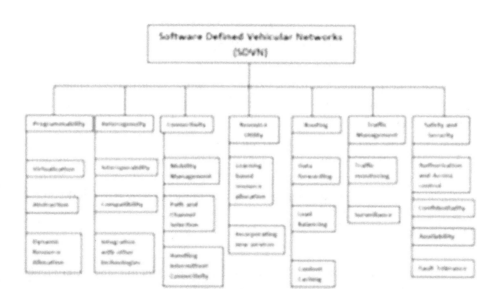

Programmability

With the help of protocols such as OpenFlow, an SDN controller constantly communicates with the network devices such as RSUs, BSs, cloud computing clusters, and fog computing clusters (Zhang et al., 2018; Truong, Lee & Ghamri-Doudane, 2015). The dynamic nature of a VN may require constant programming and reprogramming of the network and its resources to keep up with the user demands. Using SDN in VN environments facilitates virtualization, abstraction and dynamic resource allocation. Vehicular cloud computing (VCC) is used by the vehicles for data and resource sharing. It helps with enhancing the scalability of VN services (Boukerche & Robson, 2018). Network function virtualization (NFV) and network abstraction are essential to programmable networks. SDN techniques can help mastering network virtualization, network abstraction and dynamic resource allocation based on network evolution and user/application demand (Ananth & Sharma, 2017) and (Ananth & Sharma, 2016).

Heterogeneity

A VN is composed of a variety of mobile and infrastructure nodes that enable VN communications. The V2X communication services involve other vehicles, RSUs, cloud, pedestrians, other devices as well as grid. For all these devices to properly interoperate, a standardization effort is required. The C-V2X system from the 3rd Generation Partnership Project (3GPP), the DSRC, and WAVE protocols from IEEE are such standard protocols that are designed to support Cooperative - Intelligent Transportation

Systems (C-ITS) (Zheng et al., 2015). The most important requirements to support heterogeneity in VNs are related to device interoperability. For these devices, protocol converters (e.g., Gateway devices/protocol translators to deal with network heterogeneity) and efficient handoff/handover techniques are implemented. SDN helps in programming heterogeneous VN networks through standard interfaces by virtue of SDN-based network abstraction and virtualization, the heterogeneity of participating network devices can be concealed. The SDVN controller provides abstraction for the VN applications and infrastructure (He, Cao & Liu, 2016; Alioua et al., 2017).

Connectivity

Seamless connectivity is essential to the VNs to operate successfully and reliably. The ITS applications require real-time and robust network connectivity. Due to high mobility, these networks face issues of intermittent connectivity and frequent connection breakages. In a mobile network, high node density and mobility are the causes of network interference and connection breakage, respectively (Thriveni, Kumar & Sharma, 2013). Connectivity and vehicle mobility still remain a challenge for VNs. An SDN controller can maintain the vehicle movement history or anticipate its future trajectory based on GPS or cellular data and maps-based destination information. Authors in (Tang et al., 2019) have proposed a mobility prediction-based routing scheme. Through this scheme, the probability of successful transmission and the achieved average latency can be computed based on node mobility changes with respect to node topology which is estimated through the RSUs and BSs. A buffer-aware streaming approach to maintain an adequate level of QoS is proposed in (Lai et al., 2017) for infotainment multimedia applications over vehicular 5G networks. Based on QoS information, appropriate handoff/handover mechanisms are used by the eNodeBs to select the appropriate paths and communication channels to maintain network connectivity with minimum latency and required QoS.

Resource Utilization

As discussed earlier, VNs need to support real-time, reliable, and robust communications. To that aim, SDVN can be used to program dynamic resource allocation based on node mobility, node density, mobility patterns, and application-specific data rate requirements. Context-aware resource allocation is performed by the SDVN controller to make sure VN traffic is forwarded with the adequate levels of QoS and security, in particular. Machine learning (ML) and Deep Learning (DL) as techniques of Artificial Intelligence (AI) can be incorporated to detect overloaded paths/channels and to take corrective actions as appropriate (Tang et al., 2019) and (Jindal et al., 2018). These corrective actions may include traffic redirection or the allocation of extra bandwidth.

New services such as cloud, fog and edge computing are used for real-time data processing and data sharing (Meng et al., 2015). These services play a significant role in providing resources, in terms of sharing, storage, and processing of VN data. The combination of Multi-access Edge Computing (MEC) and NFV can optimize traffic forwarding and resource management (Peng, Ye & Shen, 2019). Authors of (Huang et al., 2017) have proposed Off-loading with handover decisions made by Software-Defined computation logics: load prediction control scheme wherein the SDN controller decides about data offloading based on vehicle's position, direction of movement, speed and neighboring RSUs/BSs. Future Internet technologies such as Content Centric Networking (CCN), Information Centric Networking (ICN), and Named Data Networking (NDN) which ambition to facilitate Content-based forwarding, supporting real-time, reliable, and robust transmission and processing of data in VN environments (Soua et al., 2017; Khelifi et al., 2019).

Routing

Efficient routing/forwarding within VNs is essential for their robust and reliable operation. In a VANET, the intermediate vehicles act as routers, while the RSUs, BSs, cloud computing and fog computing clusters also support traffic routing, switching, and forwarding capabilities. As the VN topology changes continuously due to node mobility, the VNs experience route changes quite often.

The flexibility, abstraction and programmability features of the SDN may play an important role in efficient traffic forwarding. The SDVN controller maintains the status of different routes. A route computation scheme based on link dynamics and stability in SDVN is proposed in (Sudheer, Ma & Chong, 2017; Sudheer, Ma & Chong, 2019). ML, mobility management along with the resource allocation techniques are used for path computation, selection, establishment and maintenance purposes (Xie et al., 2018; Sun, AlJeri & Boukerche, 2020). Some of the SDN-based routing protocols such as GeoSpray (a geographic routing protocol for vehicular networks), Cognitive Radio - Software Defined Vehicular Networks (CR-SDVN), Software Defined - Internet of Vehicles (SD-IoV) used in VNs are presented in (Sun, AlJeri & Boukerche, 2020; Abbas, Muhammad & Song, 2020; Zhu et al., 2015; Ghafoor & Koo, 2017; Ji, Yu, Fan & Fu, 2016; Venkatramana, Srikantaiah & Moodabidri, 2017). In case congestion path becomes congested, traffic is redirected towards other appropriate paths by virtue of multi-path routing. Traffic redirection accommodates overloaded path conditions, thereby reducing the risk of propagation delays, or packet loss. Load balancing is used to avoid overloading particular network devices and controllers, and to support efficient processing of data. However, it must be noted that a load balancer itself introduces processing delays as mentioned in (Sharma & Reddy, 2019), for example.

Technologies such as CCN, ICN, and NDN along with edge and fog computing clusters carry out content caching and processing at the intermediate nodes/devices for faster responses as required in real-time environments such as those VNs are typically operating in (Kadhim & Seno, 2019).

Traffic Management

Traffic management, including traffic monitoring is essential for appropriate VN and ITS operation, at least to make sure that the design of the VN can accommodate ITS service requirements. As the VNs are composed of highly mobile nodes leading to dynamic network topologies, traffic patterns vary frequently. To maintain network connectivity and allocate network resources, it is essential to constantly monitor network traffic. To avoid bandwidth scarcity, appropriate network planning and traffic engineering methods may be useful (Abugabah et al., 2020) and (Shu et al., 2020). Solutions such as Decentralized Congestion Control (DCC) (Campolo, Molinaro & Scopigno, 2015) enhance the computation of path load estimation, based upon input parameters taken from different vehicles and RSUs.

Safety and Security

VNs can undergo numerous attacks such as malicious applications, compromising server behavior, unauthorized access to the network, modification of flow rules (i.e., data traffic flow rules as defined for a routing mechanism), traffic hijacking, Man-In-The-Middle (MITM) attacks, fake service advertisement, fake devices and topology advertisements, to name a few (Arif et al., 2020)

and (Boualouache, Soua & Engel, 2020). SDVN controllers can constantly monitor the network flows and identify network intrusion by malicious traffic. SDN allows the network administrators to separate malicious traffic from legitimate traffic thereby preventing the network from getting compromised, eventually. However, it needs to be noted that SDVN controllers act as the single point of control and are themselves subject to attacks. Such attacks include (Distributed) Denial of Service (DDoS), the alteration of controller messages, the poisoning of the controller's network view, conflicting controller configuration tasks, etc. (Reynaud et al., 2016).

The SDVN Architecture

A simplified view of the SDVN architecture is presented in Figure 2. The SDVN architecture relies upon three planes and interfaces between the planes. The operations carried out by the three planes and their respective components are also presented in Figure 2. The upper plane is the "application plane" that is designed to provide certain applications and services to the VNs. The applications and services provided by the application plane of the SDVN architecture are presented in the application plane of the simplified view of the SDVN architecture. The "control plane" can be configured and re-programmed based on network requirements, in particular. The services provided by the control plane are presented in Figure 3. The "data plane" is responsible for network connectivity and communication. The technologies used and the required network devices/components are listed under the data plane in the SDVN architecture shown in Figure 3.

This section discusses the SDVN architecture and the roles of the application, control, and data planes of the SDVN architecture.

Application Plane

VNs support several ITS applications. Many non-safety and safety critical applications are handled by the VNs. The future VN technologies aim to make Autonomous Vehicle (AV) a reality. Some of the safety critical applications include traffic services, accident avoidance, driver assist, platooning, autonomous driving, alarm and warning messages (emergency brake/intersection collision/stationary warning systems). The non-safety critical applications include media streaming, infotainment, Internet access by commuters, and electronic toll payments. To support real-time processing of application flows, technologies such as cloud, edge and fog computing can be part of the VN network. A communication or diagnostic history can be stored in the cloud for future use. Information processing requests can be handled by the cloud, edge or fog computing resources. Traffic forwarding and content caching techniques also need to evolve to support VNs. Another important aspect that needs to be handled by the application plane is related to the safety and security of the network and the applications running over these networks. As VNs are highly dynamic and ad-hoc by nature, these networks are prone to attacks such as DDoS attacks, jamming attack, malicious participants, masquerading attack, illusion attack, altered / injected messages, sybil attack, GPS position alteration attack, timing attack, blackhole, and grayhole attacks. Secure vehicular communication requires authenticity, confidentiality, integrity, non-repudiation, privacy and availability. To mitigate these attacks, the VN networks must support message encryption and authentication capabilities, intrusion detection and prevention features, as well as firewalls and secure gateways.

Figure 3. The SDVN Architecture

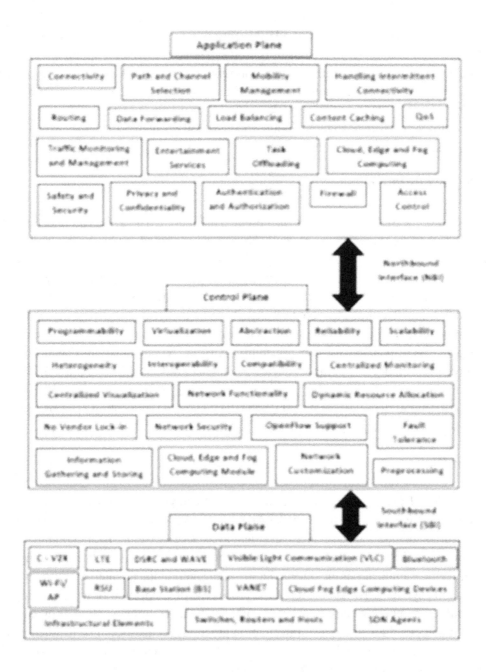

Control Plane

The SDVN controller facilitates the implementation of new applications and allows testing of new services and protocols. The SDVN controller makes decisions about policy enforcement and resource allocation, as a function of various parameters that include (but are not limited to) the status of the network (load conditions, in particular), the nature of the ITS service, network-originated notifications, etc. The controller uses protocols such as open source based OpenFlow to communicate with the network devices. It controls the behavior of the network devices such as switches, routers, RSUs and BSs through the Southbound Interface (SBI). The SDVN controller makes decisions that may be inferred by application requirements, among other inputs.

As the SDVN supports applications ranging from traffic management and monitoring to infotainment services, the important characteristics of VNs such as multi-tenancy, scalability and flexibility are crucial for their performance. VN virtualization facilitates the flexibility in VNs in terms of the types of services offered by the network. To support multi-tenancy and ensure service availability, the virtualization of VN resources is required. One such framework is proposed in (Bhatia, Haribabu, Gupta & Sahu, 2018). The framework proposes the virtualization of the SDVN controller, resource manager, On Board Units (OBUs) and RSUs. The virtualization of network resources is meant to optimize the management of vehicle movement to avoid any service disruption when vehicles are not managed by a physical RSU (due to node mobility or absence of RSU deployment). The virtual OBUs (vOBUs) allows for slicing of the resources available at OBUs to be used by multiple tenants simultaneously. The availability of virtual RSUs (vRSUs) would provide the mobile nodes with seamless connectivity even when they move out of the communication range of the physical RSU. However, to enable this functionality, virtualization of BSs and (Access Points) APs is required. Virtual Resource Managers (vRM) allow the slicing of resources to better address QoS requirements through effective management of resources. The vRM in a VN enables multiple SDN controllers to share the physical resources. The virtual SDVN Controllers (vSDVNC) are used by the tenants to control their infrastructure (Li, Ota & Dong, 2016).

The SDVN scalability can be measured, for example, by the number of switches that a controller can support and the ability to deploy SDVNs over multiple domains. The SDVN controller facilitates network scalability by adapting the physical network capacity according to a scale-out model while managing the network as a single entity (as opposed to multiple network slices managed by different tenants). To maintain network performance and QoS the SDVN controller maintains flow tables that comprise rules for controlling and directing traffic flows in the network.

With route computation and route status management capabilities supported by the SDN controller traffic can be forwarded along different routes to optimize network resources. Also, the QoS parameters can be defined on a flow-by-flow basis, depending on the application requirements. Network reliability can be ensured by means of network redundancy schemes, among other designs. As the SDVN controller has the knowledge of the network configuration, it facilitates programming of network resources to maintain the required network performance and efficiency. VN security is of prime importance particularly because the vehicular nodes are involved in real-time communications and security gaps can be life threatening. SDVN controllers can support authentication and authorization capabilities to grant access to the network and its resources.

Data Plane

The data plane hosts forwarding capabilities. The RSUs, BSs, and APs are used for forwarding traffic from a vehicular node to the core networks and vice versa. These are controlled by an ITS service provider and are interconnected through a wired/wireless link. In case of VANETs, vehicles act as routers. The cloud, fog, and edge computing infrastructures provide storage and processing resources to address the need for efficiency, reliability and real-time processing. The data plane focusses on data collection and forwarding of data to the control plane using the forwarding resources such as routers/switches.

The cellular communication technologies can be adapted by the VNs as they provide very high network capacity capable of support applications requiring high throughput (e.g., autonomous driving, driver-assistance systems). The BSs and RSUs offer broader coverage for vehicles. The vehicles first access the RSUs, and then access the BSs if the RSUs are not able to provide enough resource for wireless access.

The cloud, fog and edge computing infrastructures make an important part of the data plane of SDN based VNs. The cloud computing infrastructure provides remote storage and computational facilities. However, there are concerns about delays involved in transferring the data from vehicles to cloud for storage / processing and retrieving the stored / processed data from the cloud. Due to these concerns, there arises the need to look for solutions that ensure reduced latency and uninterrupted service. To overcome these concerns, the fog and edge computing solutions are used.

The SDVN controller can control the operation of these infrastructure node and ad-hoc forwarding units through the SBI. The behavior of these devices can be programmed on a flow-by-flow basis depending on the application requirements. The transmission capacity in terms of communication channel bandwidth, as well as storage, and computing resources can be configured by the SDVN controller through the SBI.

In hybrid networks as presented in (Ku et al., 2014) and (Salahuddin, Al-Fuqaha & Guizani, 2014), the SDN controller offloads certain tasks to the RSUs and BSs and enforces certain policy rules such as traffic monitoring (traffic statistics and service access billing) and path load balancing (routing data based on application requirements for bandwidth and delay) associated with the forwarding of traffic over the network. The OpenFlow example described in the aforementioned reference, relies upon switches (e.g., OpenFlow-based) that are programmed by the controller to use per-hop criteria for flow control and resource allocation for forwarding and processing of data.

The SDN control is also extended to the vehicular nodes through the OBUs wherein, the OBUs can be programmed by the controller and prompted by the controller to perform certain actions. The SDN controller programs the forwarding devices for appropriate path to avoid interference and to control flows. The forwarding devices can be programmed by the controller with dynamic power transmission based on the vehicle density to avoid/minimize network interference.

The wireless communication technologies used for communication over the VNs are presented in Figure 2. These technologies vary in their data rates, communication range and operating frequency. In the heterogeneous VNs the participating nodes need to switch over between these network technologies or use them simultaneously for different purposes. The VN communication standards and protocols are defined by both 3GPP and IEEE. While 3GPP has defined Cellular - Vehicle to Everything (C-V2X) standards comprising of 4G/5G radio access such as LTE and LTE-A and New Radio (NR) technologies (both as cellular and as direct, side link variant), IEEE has defined the DSRC and WAVE standards. For short range Personal Area Network (PAN) communication technologies such as Bluetooth and VLC are used. Use of Radio Detection And Ranging (RADAR), Light Detection And Ranging (LIDAR) as well as sensors facilitates intra-vehicle and inter-vehicle communication for applications such as pla-tooning, parking assistance, lane management, driver assist and obstacle detection. The channel access mechanisms such as Time Division Multiple Access (TDMA) or Carrier Sense Multiple Access / Collision Avoidance (CSMA/CA) can be programmed by the SDVN controller. As noted by the authors in (Fontes et al., 2017), TDMA is considered to be the better network access technology for low-latency, high-reliability applications in the autonomous vehicle approach.

The rules for traffic forwarding can be determined as a function of the location of the vehicle, as well as the density of vehicles. The geographical locations of the communicating node can be tracked by the

SDN controller through the RSUs or BSs, and the network infrastructure devices can be programmed for processing and traffic forwarding purposes.

KEY CHALLENGES AND RESEARCH ISSUES

As discussed in the previous sections, robust, reliable and efficient VN communication is crucial for the future ITS. The research community is working towards making VN communications and autonomous vehicles a reality. However, issues such as high node mobility, dynamic topology, intermittent connectivity, efficient network resource utilization, interference avoidance, load balancing, and network security still remain major challenges. As legacy networking techniques are not considered to be suitable for VNs, researchers are considering the development of SDVN architectures and related solutions to overcome these challenges. The programmability, scalability, and flexibility offered by SDN can help improve QoS, network's efficiency and reliability. Combining the SDN with cloud/edge/fog computing and NDN/CCN/ICN technology aims to enhance the VN functionality and performance further. The NDN/CCN/ICN are related technologies that carry out data-centric forwarding. Since the users are interested in the content rather than the source of the information, the information distribution is based on the named 'content' rather than numerically addressed hosts. For this, the intermediate nodes cache the information for respective content queries. When a mobile node requests for any information, the nearest host can answer for that query instead of sending the request packet all the way to the server and getting the information. While reducing the delays in fetching the required information, this mechanism also reduces the load on the server.

This section first presents the key pending challenges and open research issues in the field of SDVN. After discussing the challenges and open research issues, the ongoing research and solutions under development in this field are presented.

Key challenges in SDVN are as follows:

1. **Dynamic network topology and node mobility:** Vehicle mobility leads to constantly changing network topology and intermittent connectivity. This constant change in network topology and connectivity makes it difficult for the SDVN controller to manage network resources and maintain an accurate view of the topology. The SDVN controller needs to track node association and disassociation, gather information about network topology, maintain routes/routing tables, and compute appropriate routes for traffic forwarding purposes.

   To deal with this issue, researchers proposed routing principles in SDVN (Zhao et al., 2020). For example, a mobile vehicle sends an association request to the RSU/BS to access the controller, by using suitable a selection mechanism as proposed in (Correia, Boukerche & Meneguette, 2017; Zhu et al., 2015). The controller maintains the changes in network topology. A centralized or hybrid mode of route selection can be used. In the centralized route selection beacons are sent to the central controller while in hybrid mode, the SDVN controller instructs the RSUs that in turn instruct the vehicles about the routing policies to enforce. Based on the network topology, the routing and forwarding mechanisms can be classified into three categories namely centralized and hybrid, single-path and multi-path, beacon based and prediction based (Bozkaya & Canberk, 2015). While researchers have proposed numerous approaches to deal with the issues of dynamic network topology and routing in VNs, these solutions vary in terms of complexity, communication overhead, scalability, and achieved quality of calculated routes such as available bandwidth, Signal-to-Noise Ratio (SNR) and Signal-to-Interference-Noise Ratio (SINR).

Some of the open research issues in this field are:

○ Development of dedicated trajectory prediction algorithms.
○ Reduction of communication overhead.
○ Development of a framework for route selection and management.
○ Development of routing algorithms to be run by the SDN controller.
○ Application of AI to route computation by the SDN controller.
○ Development of mechanisms to overcome failed routing instructions (e.g., broken routes considering node mobility).
○ Development of multicast transmission schemes to be deployed in VNs.
○ Security of routing protocols.

2. **Heterogeneous network:** VNs and V2X involve communications between devices of different characteristics. The participating entities may have been developed by different manufacturers and may support different features. The difference between the communicating nodes, because of their different characteristics, features, protocols, leads to numerous constraints that need to be addressed for seamless communication purposes (thereby avoiding service disruption). For short distance communications, nodes in VNs use Bluetooth, VLC, LIDAR, or sensor networking. For medium distance communications, the IEEE 802.11 based WAVE and DSRC protocols, low-power wide area network (LPWAN), or 3GPP-based C-V2X sidelink technology for V2V connectivity is used. Long distance communication is achieved using cellular 3GPP technology such as LTE or 5G-NR (5th Generation New Radio). Fog, edge, and cloud computing supports remote data access and processing. The 5G-PPP (5th Generation Public Private Partnership Group) is investigating 5G Automotive Vision to attain high data rates, better connectivity and frequent handoffs. All these technologies and protocols involved in successful and efficient communication in VNs vary in their characteristics and features. The heterogeneous radio interfaces on VN nodes find it difficult to interoperate. The future ITS communication platform will be a combination of diverse wireless communication technologies. While the incorporation of SDN relieves the network from the issue of vendor lock-in to some extent, the end nodes may still face challenges. Therefore, it is essential to standardize the communication technologies and protocols in VNs. Many researchers, manufacturers and organizations are working towards the development of standardized solutions for VNs (Mahmood, Zhang & Sheng, 2019). Researchers are working towards of the use of a centralized intelligence in coordination with local computation logics to overcome the single point of failure due to potential outage of centralized SDN controller (Zhu et al., 2016; Dey et al., 2016).

Open research issues to overcome the challenge of heterogeneous networks are as follows:

○ Attain ubiquitous and seamless network connectivity.
○ Handover target selection, necessity and triggering condition estimation (that is, when should the handover take place or should be initiated).
○ Multi-hop routing over heterogeneous network technologies.
○ Node location maintenance and travel trajectory anticipation for handover purposes.

3. **Network Scalability:** The number of nodes/vehicles that will be part of the network at any given time is highly unpredictable due to the dynamicity of the network. The SDVN controller needs to constantly monitor the network and allocate network resources accordingly. Therefore, network resource management and data processing are the main challenges in scalable VNs. Researchers

who aim to address this challenge have developed AI/ML-based solutions to predict the node mobility and network density, so that network resources can be managed efficiently (Correia & Boukerche, 2017). In case the network infrastructure does not function properly due to overload or malfunctioning conditions, the SDVN controller needs to monitor such conditions, either allocate new resources or redirect traffic in order to maintain the adequate level of service quality (Smida et al., 2019).

Some of the open research challenges in this field are:

- Maintenance of network agility and responsiveness with scalability.
- Data offloading and load sharing when the amount of traffic increases.
- Network resource management based on prediction of node mobility and network density.
- Node position sensing and resource allocation.
- Interface sensing and radio resource management.

4. **Network interference and latency control:** VNs use wireless communication media that are prone to signal attenuation and interference. Wireless signals undergo multipath propagation leading to Inter Symbol Interference (ISI), Doppler effect, reflections, scattering, and diffraction. The vehicular communication quality is also challenged due to dense network deployment and heterogeneity, but also because of the difference between uplink/downlink transmission powers of vehicular nodes and RSUs, as well as possible restrictions on public/private network access leading to some interference.

Although current technologies such as Multi Input Multi Output Orthogonal Frequency Division Multiplexing (MIMO-OFDM) are efficient enough to overcome these effects in wireless networks, the node mobility raises additional challenges in VNs. Efficient path and channel selection algorithms are developed to avoid interference. Dual Polarized Directional Antenna (DPDA) is proposed to reduce channel interference while enhancing network efficiency (Rinki, 2014). While Dual Polarization (DP) supports simultaneous transmission over vertical and horizontal polarizations, Directional Antenna (DA) thanks to its broader communication range compared to omnidirectional antenna (OA) reduces latency by reducing the number of intermediate hops in multi-hop communication (Sharma et al., 2016). The Dual Polarized Directional Antenna based Medium Access Control (DPDA-MAC) (Sharma et al, 2015a) and Dual Polarized Directional Antenna based Multipath Routing Protocol (DPDA-MRP) (Sharma et al., 2015b) describe protocols which have been proved to enhance network performance in MANETs thanks to increased throughput, Packet Delivery Ratio (PDR) and reduced latency; and these protocols can be implemented in VANETs as well. Some of the path and channel selection algorithms for VANETs are proposed in (Jang & Lee, 2010; Fazio, De Rango & Sottile, 2015).

Some of the open research issues in this field are:

- Intermittent connectivity and unstable bandwidth usage due to node mobility.
- Channel state estimation in highly dynamic vehicular networks.
- Directional beam steering with rapidly changing node location.
- Enhancement of standardized cellular network architecture to support high mobility VNs.
- Application of deep learning for channel state estimation and optimization.

5. **Network Security:** Network security still remains a significant problem in SDN-based architectures. As an SDN controller is a logically centralized entity, in case the controller is attacked, the whole network operation can be jeopardized. If the SDVN controller is compromised, the whole network can be affected. This issue can be carefully taken into account when exposing Application

Programming Interfaces (APIs). However, there is a lack of standard SDVN APIs, which makes controllers vulnerable to network security attacks (Akhunzada & Khan, 2017).

To overcome the failure of SDVN controllers, some research activities propose the use of primary and secondary network controllers. However, resiliency of SDN controllers still remains an open research challenge. While current research investigates how SDN-based networks can be more secure, in case of SDVN this remains a concern as a compromised controller can endanger human life. Apart from the SDN controller, vehicular nodes are vulnerable too. Electronic Control Units (ECUs) in an intelligent vehicle are exposed to attacks and tampering. Interfaces subject to attacks can be accessed through direct access, short- and long-range wireless communication. The On-Board Diagnostics (OBD) port and compact disc player give direct and largely unrestricted access to the in-vehicle communication network. Short-range wireless attack surfaces include remote keyless breach, Tire Pressure Monitoring System (TPMS), Bluetooth and Wi-Fi. The long-range wireless attacks often use satellite or AM/FM radio interfaces, as well as the cellular communication interfaces. Over The Air (OTA) updates are another major cause of attack in intelligent vehicles. Some of the prominent threats in VNs are MITM, DoS, DDoS, replay attack, bluejacking/bluebugging (sending unsolicited messages over Bluetooth), unauthorized control of vehicle parameters, collection of vehicle's private information, concealing location information, false alerts and tampering of ECU data blue. Some of the solutions proposed to mitigate these attacks are message encryption and authentication, firewalls, use of intrusion detection and prevention capabilities, domain isolation through gateways, secure boot runtime integrity, secure Machine-to-Machine (M2M) integration and secure key storage. Blockchain-based framework for VN security is presented in (Yahiatene et al., 2019). Usage of ML to detect security vulnerabilities and attacks is presented in (Tang et al., 2019).

Some of open research challenges in this area are:

- ◦ Standard northbound/southbound/eastbound/westbound APIs to address security vulnerabilities and attacks.
- ◦ Authentication codes (secure boot), run-time integrity protection and resource control (resource virtualization).
- ◦ Secure messaging and OTA updates.
- ◦ Solutions for firewalls, context-aware message filtering and Intrusion Detection System (IDS).
- ◦ Isolation of vulnerable interfaces such as Transmission Control Units (TCU) and OBD.
- ◦ D2D/M2M authentication solutions.

CONCLUSION

This chapter presents the role of SDN in VNs and the importance of SDVN. The SDVN use cases and related research present the vehicular application areas where SDN can be instrumental for proper VN design, delivery and operation. The chapter also discusses the ongoing research in this field.

The SDVN architecture is presented and roles of the SDVN application, control and data planes are discussed. The chapter outlines and discusses the research challenges and opportunities in the area of SDVN with the aim of investigating and presenting recent research advances in SDVN.

REFERENCES

Abbas, M. T., Muhammad, A., & Song, W. C. (2020). SD-IoV: SDN enabled routing for internet of vehicles in road-aware approach. *Journal of Ambient Intelligence and Humanized Computing, 11*(3), 1265–1280. doi:10.100712652-019-01319-w

Abboud, K., Omar, H. A., & Zhuang, W. (2016). Interworking of DSRC and cellular network technologies for V2X communications: A survey. *IEEE Transactions on Vehicular Technology, 65*(12), 9457–9470. doi:10.1109/TVT.2016.2591558

Abugabah, A., Alzubi, A. A., Alfarraj, O., Al-Maitah, M., & Alnumay, W. S. (2020). Intelligent Traffic Engineering in Software-Defined Vehicular Networking Based on Multi-Path Routing. *IEEE Access: Practical Innovations, Open Solutions, 8,* 62334–62342. doi:10.1109/ACCESS.2020.2983204

Akhunzada, A., & Khan, M. K. (2017). Toward secure software defined vehicular networks: Taxonomy, requirements, and open issues. *IEEE Communications Magazine, 55*(7), 110–118. doi:10.1109/MCOM.2017.1601158

Alioua, A., Senouci, S. M., Moussaoui, S., Sedjelmaci, H., & Boualouache, A. (2017, October). Software-Defined heterogeneous vehicular networks: Taxonomy and architecture. In *2017 Global Information Infrastructure and Networking Symposium (GIIS)* (pp. 50-55). IEEE. 10.1109/GIIS.2017.8169805

Amjid, A., Khan, A., & Shah, M. A. (2020). VANET-Based Volunteer Computing (VBVC): A Computational Paradigm for Future Autonomous Vehicles. *IEEE Access: Practical Innovations, Open Solutions, 8,* 71763–71774. doi:10.1109/ACCESS.2020.2974500

Ananth, M. D., & Sharma, R. (2016, December). Cloud management using network function virtualization to reduce capex and opex. In *2016 8th International Conference on Computational Intelligence and Communication Networks (CICN)* (pp. 43-47). IEEE. 10.1109/CICN.2016.17

Ananth, M. D., & Sharma, R. (2017, January). Cost and performance analysis of network function virtualization based cloud systems. In *2017 IEEE 7th International Advance Computing Conference (IACC)* (pp. 70-74). IEEE. 10.1109/IACC.2017.0029

Arif, M., Wang, G., Geman, O., Balas, V. E., Tao, P., Brezulianu, A., & Chen, J. (2020). SDN-based VANETs, Security Attacks, Applications, and Challenges. *Applied Sciences (Basel, Switzerland), 10*(9), 3217. doi:10.3390/app10093217

Benalia, E., Bitam, S., & Mellouk, A. (2020). Data dissemination for Internet of vehicle based on 5G communications: A survey. *Transactions on Emerging Telecommunications Technologies, 31*(5), e3881. doi:10.1002/ett.3881

Bhatia, A., Haribabu, K., Gupta, K., & Sahu, A. (2018, January). Realization of flexible and scalable VANETs through SDN and virtualization. In *2018 International Conference on Information Networking (ICOIN)* (pp. 280-282). IEEE. 10.1109/ICOIN.2018.8343125

Boualouache, A., Soua, R., & Engel, T. (2020, May). SDN-based Misbehavior Detection System for Vehicular Networks. In *2020 IEEE 91st Vehicular Technology Conference (VTC2020-Spring)* (pp. 1-5). IEEE. 10.1109/VTC2020-Spring48590.2020.9128604

Boukerche, A., & Robson, E. (2018). Vehicular cloud computing: Architectures, applications, and mobility. *Computer Networks*, *135*, 171–189. doi:10.1016/j.comnet.2018.01.004

Bozkaya, E., & Canberk, B. (2015, December). QoE-based flow management in software defined vehicular networks. In *2015 IEEE Globecom Workshops (GC Wkshps)* (pp. 1-6). IEEE.

Campolo, C., Molinaro, A., & Scopigno, R. (2015). From today's VANETs to tomorrow's planning and the bets for the day after. *Vehicular Communications*, *2*(3), 158–171. doi:10.1016/j.vehcom.2015.06.002

Chahal, M., Harit, S., Mishra, K. K., Sangaiah, A. K., & Zheng, Z. (2017). A survey on software-defined networking in vehicular ad hoc networks: Challenges, applications and use cases. *Sustainable Cities and Society*, *35*, 830–840. doi:10.1016/j.scs.2017.07.007

Chahal, M., Harit, S., Mishra, K. K., Sangaiah, A. K., & Zheng, Z. (2017). A survey on software-defined networking in vehicular ad hoc networks: Challenges, applications and use cases. *Sustainable Cities and Society*, *35*, 830–840. doi:10.1016/j.scs.2017.07.007

Correia, S., & Boukerche, A. (2017, December). Toward a scalable software-defined vehicular network. In *GLOBECOM 2017-2017 IEEE Global Communications Conference* (pp. 1-6). IEEE. 10.1109/GLOCOM.2017.8254519

Correia, S., Boukerche, A., & Meneguette, R. I. (2017). An architecture for hierarchical software-defined vehicular networks. *IEEE Communications Magazine*, *55*(7), 80–86. doi:10.1109/MCOM.2017.1601105

Dey, K. C., Rayamajhi, A., Chowdhury, M., Bhavsar, P., & Martin, J. (2016). Vehicle-to-vehicle (V2V) and vehicle-to-infrastructure (V2I) communication in a heterogeneous wireless network–Performance evaluation. *Transportation Research Part C, Emerging Technologies*, *68*, 168–184. doi:10.1016/j.trc.2016.03.008

Din, S., Paul, A., Ahmad, A., Ahmed, S. H., Jeon, G., & Rawat, D. B. (2018, April). Hierarchical architecture for 5g based software-defined intelligent transportation system. In *IEEE INFOCOM 2018-IEEE Conference on Computer Communications Workshops (INFOCOM WKSHPS)* (pp. 462-467). IEEE.

Fazio, P., De Rango, F., & Sottile, C. (2015). A predictive cross-layered interference management in a multichannel MAC with reactive routing in VANET. *IEEE Transactions on Mobile Computing*, *15*(8), 1850–1862. doi:10.1109/TMC.2015.2465384

Fontes, R. D. R., Campolo, C., Rothenberg, C. E., & Molinaro, A. (2017). From theory to experimental evaluation: Resource management in software-defined vehicular networks. *IEEE Access: Practical Innovations, Open Solutions*, *5*, 3069–3076. doi:10.1109/ACCESS.2017.2671030

Ghafoor, H., & Koo, I. (2017). CR-SDVN: A cognitive routing protocol for software-defined vehicular networks. *IEEE Sensors Journal*, *18*(4), 1761–1772. doi:10.1109/JSEN.2017.2788014

Hamdi, M. M., Audah, L., Rashid, S. A., Mohammed, A. H., Alani, S., & Mustafa, A. S. (2020, June). A review of applications, characteristics and challenges in vehicular ad hoc networks (VANETs). In *2020 International Congress on Human-Computer Interaction, Optimization and Robotic Applications (HORA)* (pp. 1-7). IEEE.

Hartenstein, H., & Laberteaux, L. P. (2008). A tutorial survey on vehicular ad hoc networks. *IEEE Communications Magazine, 46*(6), 164–171. doi:10.1109/MCOM.2008.4539481

He, Z., Cao, J., & Liu, X. (2016). SDVN: Enabling rapid network innovation for heterogeneous vehicular communication. *IEEE Network, 30*(4), 10–15. doi:10.1109/MNET.2016.7513858

He, Z., Cao, J., & Liu, X. (2016). SDVN: Enabling rapid network innovation for heterogeneous vehicular communication. *IEEE Network, 30*(4), 10–15. doi:10.1109/MNET.2016.7513858

Huang, C. M., Chiang, M. S., Dao, D. T., Pai, H. M., Xu, S., & Zhou, H. (2017). Vehicle-to-Infrastructure (V2I) offloading from cellular network to 802.11 p Wi-Fi network based on the Software-Defined Network (SDN) architecture. *Vehicular Communications, 9*, 288–300. doi:10.1016/j.vehcom.2017.03.003

Jaballah, W. B., Conti, M., & Lal, C. (2019). *A survey on software-defined VANETs: benefits, challenges, and future directions.* arXiv preprint arXiv:1904.04577.

Jang, C., & Lee, J. H. (2010, September). *Path selection algorithms for multi-hop VANETs. In 2010 IEEE 72nd Vehicular Technology Conference-Fall.* IEEE.

Ji, X., Yu, H., Fan, G., & Fu, W. (2016, December). SDGR: An SDN-based geographic routing protocol for VANET. In *2016 IEEE International Conference on Internet of Things (iThings) and IEEE Green Computing and Communications (GreenCom) and IEEE Cyber, Physical and Social Computing (CPSCom) and IEEE Smart Data (SmartData)* (pp. 276-281). IEEE. 10.1109/iThings-GreenCom-CPSCom-SmartData.2016.70

Ji, X., Yu, H., Fan, G., & Fu, W. (2016, December). SDGR: An SDN-based geographic routing protocol for VANET. In *2016 IEEE International Conference on Internet of Things (iThings) and IEEE Green Computing and Communications (GreenCom) and IEEE Cyber, Physical and Social Computing (CPSCom) and IEEE Smart Data (SmartData)* (pp. 276-281). IEEE. 10.1109/iThings-GreenCom-CPSCom-SmartData.2016.70

Jiang, D., & Delgrossi, L. (2008, May). IEEE 802.11 p: Towards an international standard for wireless access in vehicular environments. In VTC Spring 2008-IEEE Vehicular Technology Conference (pp. 2036-2040). IEEE.

Jindal, A., Aujla, G. S., Kumar, N., Chaudhary, R., Obaidat, M. S., & You, I. (2018). SeDaTiVe: SDN-enabled deep learning architecture for network traffic control in vehicular cyber-physical systems. *IEEE Network, 32*(6), 66–73. doi:10.1109/MNET.2018.1800101

Kadhim, A. J., & Seno, S. A. H. (2019). Energy-efficient multicast routing protocol based on SDN and fog computing for vehicular networks. *Ad Hoc Networks, 84*, 68–81. doi:10.1016/j.adhoc.2018.09.018

Khelifi, H., Luo, S., Nour, B., Moungla, H., Faheem, Y., Hussain, R., & Ksentini, A. (2019). Named data networking in vehicular ad hoc networks: State-of-the-art and challenges. *IEEE Communications Surveys and Tutorials, 22*(1), 320–351. doi:10.1109/COMST.2019.2894816

Kirkpatrick, K. (2013). Software-defined networking. *Communications of the ACM, 56*(9), 16–19. doi:10.1145/2500468.2500473

Ku, I., Lu, Y., Gerla, M., Gomes, R. L., Ongaro, F., & Cerqueira, E. (2014, June). Towards software-defined VANET: Architecture and services. In *2014 13th annual Mediterranean ad hoc networking workshop (MED-HOC-NET)* (pp. 103-110). IEEE.

Ku, I., Lu, Y., Gerla, M., Gomes, R. L., Ongaro, F., & Cerqueira, E. (2014, June). Towards software-defined VANET: Architecture and services. In *2014 13th annual Mediterranean ad hoc networking workshop (MED-HOC-NET)* (pp. 103-110). IEEE.

Lai, C. F., Chang, Y. C., Chao, H. C., Hossain, M. S., & Ghoneim, A. (2017). A buffer-aware QoS streaming approach for SDN-enabled 5G vehicular networks. *IEEE Communications Magazine, 55*(8), 68–73. doi:10.1109/MCOM.2017.1601142

Li, H., Ota, K., & Dong, M. (2016, September). Network virtualization optimization in software defined vehicular ad-hoc networks. In *2016 IEEE 84th Vehicular Technology Conference (VTC-Fall)* (pp. 1-5). IEEE. 10.1109/VTCFall.2016.7881106

Li, Y. J. (2010, November). An overview of the DSRC/WAVE technology. In *International Conference on Heterogeneous Networking for Quality, Reliability, Security and Robustness* (pp. 544-558). Springer.

Liyanage, K. S. K., Ma, M., & Chong, P. H. J. (2018). Controller placement optimization in hierarchical distributed software defined vehicular networks. *Computer Networks, 135*, 226–239. doi:10.1016/j.comnet.2018.02.022

Mahmood, A., Zhang, W. E., & Sheng, Q. Z. (2019). Software-defined heterogeneous vehicular networking: The architectural design and open challenges. *Future Internet, 11*(3), 70. doi:10.3390/fi11030070

Meng, H., Zheng, K., Chatzimisios, P., Zhao, H., & Ma, L. (2015, June). A utility-based resource allocation scheme in cloud-assisted vehicular network architecture. In *2015 IEEE International Conference on Communication Workshop (ICCW)* (pp. 1833-1838). IEEE. 10.1109/ICCW.2015.7247447

Morgan, Y. L. (2010). Notes on DSRC & WAVE standards suite: Its architecture, design, and characteristics. *IEEE Communications Surveys and Tutorials, 12*(4), 504–518. doi:10.1109/SURV.2010.033010.00024

Peng, H., Ye, Q., & Shen, X. S. (2019). SDN-based resource management for autonomous vehicular networks: A multi-access edge computing approach. *IEEE Wireless Communications, 26*(4), 156–162. doi:10.1109/MWC.2019.1800371

Reynaud, F., Aguessy, F. X., Bettan, O., Bouet, M., & Conan, V. (2016, June). Attacks against network functions virtualization and software-defined networking: State-of-the-art. In 2016 IEEE NetSoft Conference and Workshops (NetSoft) (pp. 471-476). IEEE.

Rinki, S. (2014). *Simulation studies on effects of dual polarisation and directivity of antennas on the performance of MANETs* (Doctoral dissertation). Coventry University.

Salahuddin, M. A., Al-Fuqaha, A., & Guizani, M. (2014). Software-defined networking for rsu clouds in support of the internet of vehicles. *IEEE Internet of Things Journal, 2*(2), 133–144. doi:10.1109/JIOT.2014.2368356

Sharma, R., Kadambi, G., Vershinin, Y. A., & Mukundan, K. N. (2016). A survey of MAC layer protocols to avoid deafness in wireless networks using directional antenna. In Mobile Computing and Wireless Networks: Concepts, Methodologies, Tools, and Applications (pp. 1758-1797). IGI Global.

Sharma, R., Kadambi, G. R., Vershinin, Y. A., & Mukundan, K. N. (2015, April). Dual Polarised Directional Communication based Medium Access Control Protocol for Performance Enhancement of MANETs. In *2015 Fifth International Conference on Communication Systems and Network Technologies* (pp. 185-189). IEEE. 10.1109/CSNT.2015.104

Sharma, R., Kadambi, G. R., Vershinin, Y. A., & Mukundan, K. N. (2015, April). Multipath Routing Protocol to Support Dual Polarised Directional Communication for Performance Enhancement of MANETs. In *2015 Fifth International Conference on Communication Systems and Network Technologies* (pp. 258-262). IEEE. 10.1109/CSNT.2015.105

Sharma, R., & Reddy, H. (2019, December). Effect of Load Balancer on Software-Defined Networking (SDN) based Cloud. In *2019 IEEE 16th India Council International Conference (INDICON)* (pp. 1-4). IEEE.

Shu, Z., Wan, J., Lin, J., Wang, S., Li, D., Rho, S., & Yang, C. (2016). Traffic engineering in software-defined networking: Measurement and management. *IEEE Access: Practical Innovations, Open Solutions, 4*, 3246–3256. doi:10.1109/ACCESS.2016.2582748

Smida, K., Tounsi, H., Frikha, M., & Song, Y. Q. (2019, June). Software defined Internet of Vehicles: A survey from QoS and scalability perspectives. In 2019 15th International Wireless Communications & Mobile Computing Conference (IWCMC) (pp. 1349-1354). IEEE. doi:10.1109/IWCMC.2019.8766647

Soua, R., Kalogeiton, E., Manzo, G., Duarte, J. M., Palattella, M. R., Di Maio, A., & Rizzo, G. A. (2017). SDN coordination for CCN and FC content dissemination in VANETs. In *Ad Hoc Networks* (pp. 221–233). Springer. doi:10.1007/978-3-319-51204-4_18

Storck, C. R., & Duarte-Figueiredo, F. (2020). A Survey of 5G Technology Evolution, Standards, and Infrastructure Associated With Vehicle-to-Everything Communications by Internet of Vehicles. *IEEE Access: Practical Innovations, Open Solutions, 8*, 117593–117614. doi:10.1109/ACCESS.2020.3004779

Sudheer, K. K., Ma, M., & Chong, P. H. J. (2017, December). Link dynamics based packet routing framework for software defined vehicular networks. In *GLOBECOM 2017-2017 IEEE Global Communications Conference* (pp. 1-6). IEEE. 10.1109/GLOCOM.2017.8254597

Sudheera, K. L. K., Ma, M., & Chong, P. H. J. (2019). Link stability based optimized routing framework for software defined vehicular networks. *IEEE Transactions on Vehicular Technology, 68*(3), 2934–2945. doi:10.1109/TVT.2019.2895274

Sun, P., AlJeri, N., & Boukerche, A. (2020). *DACON: A Novel Traffic Prediction and Data-Highway-Assisted Content Delivery Protocol for Intelligent Vehicular Networks. IEEE Transactions on Sustainable Computing.*

Tang, F., Kawamoto, Y., Kato, N., & Liu, J. (2019). Future intelligent and secure vehicular network toward 6G: Machine-learning approaches. *Proceedings of the IEEE, 108*(2), 292–307. doi:10.1109/JPROC.2019.2954595

Tang, Y., Cheng, N., Wu, W., Wang, M., Dai, Y., & Shen, X. (2019). Delay-minimization routing for heterogeneous VANETs with machine learning based mobility prediction. *IEEE Transactions on Vehicular Technology, 68*(4), 3967–3979. doi:10.1109/TVT.2019.2899627

Thriveni, H. B., Kumar, G. M., & Sharma, R. (2013, April). Performance evaluation of routing protocols in mobile ad-hoc networks with varying node density and node mobility. In *2013 International Conference on Communication Systems and Network Technologies* (pp. 252-256). IEEE. 10.1109/CSNT.2013.60

Truong, N. B., Lee, G. M., & Ghamri-Doudane, Y. (2015, May). Software defined networking-based vehicular adhoc network with fog computing. In *2015 IFIP/IEEE International Symposium on Integrated Network Management (IM)* (pp. 1202-1207). IEEE. 10.1109/INM.2015.7140467

Venkatramana, D. K. N., Srikantaiah, S. B., & Moodabidri, J. (2017). SCGRP: SDN-enabled connectivity-aware geographical routing protocol of VANETs for urban environment. *IET Networks, 6*(5), 102–111. doi:10.1049/iet-net.2016.0117

Wang, X., Mao, S., & Gong, M. X. (2017). An overview of 3GPP cellular vehicle-to-everything standards. *GetMobile: Mobile Computing and Communications, 21*(3), 19–25. doi:10.1145/3161587.3161593

Xie, J., Yu, F. R., Huang, T., Xie, R., Liu, J., Wang, C., & Liu, Y. (2018). A survey of machine learning techniques applied to software defined networking (SDN): Research issues and challenges. *IEEE Communications Surveys and Tutorials, 21*(1), 393–430. doi:10.1109/COMST.2018.2866942

Yahiatene, Y., Rachedi, A., Riahla, M. A., Menacer, D. E., & Nait-Abdesselam, F. (2019). A blockchain-based framework to secure vehicular social networks. *Transactions on Emerging Telecommunications Technologies, 30*(8), e3650. doi:10.1002/ett.3650

Yaqoob, I., Ahmad, I., Ahmed, E., Gani, A., Imran, M., & Guizani, N. (2017). Overcoming the key challenges to establishing vehicular communication: Is SDN the answer? *IEEE Communications Magazine, 55*(7), 128–134. doi:10.1109/MCOM.2017.1601183

Zhang, Y., Zhang, H., Long, K., Zheng, Q., & Xie, X. (2018). Software-defined and fog-computing-based next generation vehicular networks. *IEEE Communications Magazine, 56*(9), 34–41. doi:10.1109/MCOM.2018.1701320

Zhao, L., Al-Dubai, A., Zomaya, A. Y., Min, G., Hawbani, A., & Li, J. (2020). Routing schemes in software-defined vehicular networks: Design open issues and challenges. *IEEE Intell. Transp. Syst. Mag.*

Zheng, K., Zheng, Q., Chatzimisios, P., Xiang, W., & Zhou, Y. (2015). Heterogeneous vehicular networking: A survey on architecture, challenges, and solutions. *IEEE Communications Surveys and Tutorials, 17*(4), 2377–2396. doi:10.1109/COMST.2015.2440103

Zhu, M., Cai, Z. P., Xu, M., & Cao, J. N. (2015). Software-defined vehicular networks: Opportunities and challenges. In Energy Science and Applied Technology. CRC Press.

Zhu, M., Cao, J., Cai, Z., He, Z., & Xu, M. (2016). Providing flexible services for heterogeneous vehicles: An NFV-based approach. *IEEE Network, 30*(3), 64–71. doi:10.1109/MNET.2016.7474346

Zhu, M., Cao, J., Pang, D., He, Z., & Xu, M. (2015, August). SDN-based routing for efficient message propagation in VANET. In *International Conference on Wireless Algorithms, Systems, and Applications* (pp. 788-797). Springer. 10.1007/978-3-319-21837-3_77

ADDITIONAL READING

Kumar, S., Trivedi, M. C., Ranjan, P., & Punhani, A. (2021). *Evolution of Software-Defined Networking Foundations for IoT and 5G Mobile Networks*. IGI Global. doi:10.4018/978-1-7998-4685-7

KEY TERMS AND DEFINITIONS

Intelligent Transportation Systems (ITS): A amalgamation of contemporary information and communication technologies used for transportations and traffic management systems to efficiently monitor and manage transportation system and enhance their efficiency, safety, and sustainability.

Mobile Ad-hoc Networks (MANETs): A temporary and infrastructure-less network of mobile nodes, wherein the mobile nodes communicate when they are within communication range of each other. The nodes in a MANET can act as source, sink, or router.

Software-Defined Networking (SDN): A networking architecture that decouples network control and forwarding functions and enables the network control to become directly programmable.

Software-Defined Vehicular Networks (SDVN): A Software Defined Networking (SDN) based vehicular network that facilitates programmability of vehicular networks to deal with issues in routing, connectivity, heterogeneity, scalability, reliability, and security.

Vehicle-to-Everything (V2X): Communication between a vehicle and other parts of the traffic system such as other vehicles, infrastructure, Internetwork, cloud, pedestrians, grid, and devices.

Vehicular Ad-hoc Networks (VANETs): A temporary and infrastructure-less network of vehicles that communicate when they come within communication range of each other. Like in MANETs, the vehicles in VANETs can act as source, sink, or router.

Vehicular Communication: Comprises of a communication system and technologies that enable communication between vehicles, roadside units, and other components of a vehicular network.

Vehicular Networks: A network of vehicles, roadside infrastructure, internetwork, cloud, pedestrians, grid, and devices that communicate using wireless communication technologies.

Section 3
Towards "Attack–Proof" Network Security Frameworks

Chapter 12

From Protected Networks to Protective and Collaborative Networking:
An Approach to a Globally Anticipative Attack Mitigation Framework for the Future Internet

Mohamed Boucadair

Orange S.A., France

Christian Jacquenet

Orange S.A., France

ABSTRACT

Security has always been a major concern of network operators. Despite a pretty rich security toolbox that never ceased to improve over the years (filters, traffic wells, encryption techniques, and intrusion detection systems to name a few), attacks keep on increasing from both a numerical and amplitude standpoints. Such protean attacks demand an adapted security toolkit that should include techniques capable of not only detecting these attacks but also anticipating them even before they reach their target. Strengthening future networking infrastructures so that they become protective, instead of being "just" protected must thus become one of the key strategic objectives of network operators and service providers who ambition to rely upon robust, dynamic, security policy enforcement schemes to develop their business while retaining their existing customers. This chapter discusses the various security challenges that may be further exacerbated by future networking infrastructures. It also presents some of the techniques that are very likely to become cornerstones of protective networking.

DOI: 10.4018/978-1-7998-7646-5.ch012

INTRODUCTION

Security has always been a major concern of network operators. Networking infrastructures have been protected for decades with a level of efficiency that proved to be sub-optimal, depending on the nature and the scope of attacks. Despite a pretty rich security toolbox that never ceased to improve over the years (filters, traffic wells, encryption techniques and intrusion detection systems to name a few), attacks keep on increasing from both a numerical and amplitude standpoints. For example, attacks that consist in bringing organizations offline by flooding their websites with bogus traffic have dramatically increased over the past two years. Ransomware or data theft (a group of Russian attackers claimed they have stolen 30 Terabytes of data from companies like Symantec and McAfee) are also increasing (Check Point, 2020).

Such protean attacks demand an adapted security toolkit that should include techniques capable of not only detecting attacks but also anticipating them way before they reach their target. Strengthening future networking infrastructures so that they become *protective*, not just protected: protective networking is likely to become one of the key strategic objectives of operators and service providers who ambition to develop their security business with advanced, highly anticipative, dynamic security policy enforcement schemes.

MAIN FOCUS OF THE CHAPTER

This chapter focuses on an advanced security framework called "Protective Networking". Protective networking aims at providing means to proactively and dynamically detect and mitigate any kind of attack (regardless of its origin, scope, surface, etc.) preferably way before such attacks reach their targets.

Basically, protective networking is seen as a major leap forward in the area of advanced and dynamic security policy enforcement schemes: from three decades of security policy frameworks that namely consisted in protecting the network infrastructures and mitigating attacks to limit the damage done as much as possible to an era where the network becomes actively protective let alone collaborative. Suspicious traffic can be dynamically detected and signaled to computation logics, which dynamically elaborate adapted mitigation plans to counter attacks as close to their source as possible and to exchange attack mitigation practices on a global scale. Partnering networks can thus limit the propagation of the attack, thereby significantly reducing the attack surface, if not eliminating the threat itself.

As detailed in the next sections, protective networking relies upon three pillars: detection, signaling, and mitigation. Protective networking thus provides the means to move from a typical reactive mode that endures for more than 30 years in networks towards a proactive mode that will make the future Internet a safer place. It indeed aims at dramatically limiting the effects of massive attacks while preserving as much as possible the continuity of services accessed by Internet users.

BACKGROUND

Security Demands Global Thinking

Security is a global thing. It not only relates to the protection of infrastructures, customer premises, and end-user applications. It also includes the preservation of privacy data, the ability to provide hard guarantees about the identity of an end-user before he/she can access the service he/she has subscribed to, let alone the ability to provide hard guarantees about the nature of information exchanged between networks, e.g., for route computation purposes as well as the identity of the peer that announces such information. Means to ensure the integrity of this information must be provided. Future networking infrastructures are no exception and the aforementioned security challenges also apply to these infra-structures, hence the need for means to:

1. Access services with proper credentials (and their management).
2. Securely exchange information between operators to deliver multi-domain/multi-tenant services (including the ability to provide guarantees about the identity of such partners before exchanging information with them).
3. Secure the transport of (policy-provisioning/configuration) information between logically cen-tralized computation logics responsible for designing, delivering and operating services and the participating components of the service.
4. Authenticate tenants who may be granted access to service parameters and who may trigger resource negotiation cycles.
5. Make sure decisions made by various computation logics operated by different parties are consistent within the context of dynamically provisioning services that span multiple networks operated by different parties.
6. Dynamically define and enforce appropriate mitigation plans to prevent attacks preferably way before they reach their target(s).

Security Becomes A Major Clause of Service Negotiation

Procedures for the design and operation of connectivity services have become increasingly diverse but also complex. The time it takes to negotiate service parameters and then proceed with the allocation of the corresponding resources can thus be measured in days, weeks, and even months depending on the complexity of the service to deliver. A target for the design of future Internet services is that these parameters would be dynamically negotiated with the service provider, as a function of the available resources, the customer's expectations, the provider's network planning policy, etc.

The definition of a clear interface between the service (including third-party applications) and the network layers would therefore facilitate the dynamic negotiation, thereby improving the overall service delivery procedure by optimizing the service parameter negotiation procedure. From this standpoint, (Boucadair, Jacquenet, & Wang, 2014) introduce a generic and flexible Connectivity Provisioning Profile (CPP) which is a service model that aims at facilitating the exposure of service parameters in a technology-agnostic manner.

As such, the corresponding service requirements (classified into various clauses, such as a security clause) can be addressed by means of a dynamic service parameter negotiation framework that relies upon the aforementioned CPP template and the use of a dedicated, typically client/server protocol that carries the exchanges between a customer and the service provider during the whole service negotiation cycle until it reaches a positive (i.e., a deal is done) or a negative (both parties couldn't agree on the terms of the negotiation) conclusion.

The result of such negotiation would then feed the computation logic hosted by an orchestrator to dynamically design the corresponding service (e.g., by identifying the elementary components of a service – forwarding, and routing, traffic classification and marking capabilities, traffic filters, etc.). Results of such computation would in turn be derived into instructions to be processed by another computation logic that typically resides in a control plane (namely a SDN controller) to proceed with the dynamic allocation of the required resources (instantiation and configuration of the aforementioned service functions) and enforcement of the set of service-inferred, slice-specific policies that include (but are not necessarily limited to) forwarding and routing policies, QoS policies, and security policies.

Security requirements can consist of identifying the various traffic flows that may be forwarded within the network, thereby leading to the definition and the activation of required traffic filters at various locations, the design of tunnel facilities, the need to encrypt traffic (or a part thereof) that will be forwarded within the slice and the corresponding encryption means, etc.

FROM PROTECTED NETWORKS TO PROTECTIVE NETWORKING

Detect, Signal, and Mitigate With The Help of Artificial Intelligence

From the initial traffic monitoring, model library installment and policy enforcement schemes to the resulting (yet presumably distorted) invocation of a set of network security functions and related updates, the network becomes a primary asset to win against villains.

Protective networking relies upon three major components:

- Anticipative detection of suspicious traffic
- Automated signaling of suspicious traffic
- Dynamic mitigation of suspicious traffic, including automatic mitigation upon detection of the signal loss.

Detection may rely upon a library of traffic patterns that reflect the different kinds of legitimate traffic that may be forwarded by the network, and which may also include information about network access conditions, and link capacity (Boucadair, Reddy, Doron, Meiling, & Shallow, 2020). Also, these patterns can include the traffic identification information that was disclosed during a service parameter negotiation cycle. The detection component is a piece of software that may be hosted in physical network devices (possibly including terminals and Customer Premises Equipment (CPE)), as well as in Virtual Network Function (VNF) (hosted by virtual machines or containers) that are typical of a telco cloud networking environment.

Such an agent is therefore activated to monitor part or all traffic going through the device or the VNF, and compares what it observes with the traffic patterns stored in its library. Whenever a flow (defined as a set of packets that share at least one common characteristic such as the same destination address or the same couple of source and destination ports) doesn't match the traffic patterns, the agent may consider the said flow as suspicious. Experience of agents is further improved by means of predictive traffic analysis techniques that help minimize the risk of false positives (e.g., a potentially suspicious flow happens to be the result of a management operation). Of course, the more agents, the better the ability to detect and anticipate attacks way before they reach their target.

Signaling is what agents do whenever they detect suspicious traffic. Such detection dynamically triggers the sending of an attack mitigation request towards a server that is responsible for making the appropriate decision such as defining and instantiating the relevant mitigation plan, which may consist in redirecting suspicious traffic to a scrubbing center. This signaling procedure thus assumes an exchange of information between the agent and the mitigation server besides acknowledging the reception of the mitigation request: this request indeed elaborates on what has been observed. Based on such information, the mitigation server will then construct a mitigation plan which it will communicate to the agent accordingly.

Mitigation is the set of actions that result from the decisions made by the mitigation servers that are responsible for preventing attack propagation. As such, mitigation servers can be seen as an avatar of a logically centralized computation logic that is responsible for dynamically defining and instantiating service-inferred, security policies. The actual enforcement of such security policies is in turn the result of the application of the set of instructions by the Network Security Functions (NSF) involved in the mitigation of the attack – firewalls, filters, traffic encryption, traffic redirection, etc.

Automation Is Instrumental For Protective Networking

Within the context of networks, automation can be defined as a set of techniques that facilitate the delivery and the operation of network services supported by network infrastructures while minimizing declarative and manual interventions.

Network automation is often seen as a major asset by operators who want to dramatically improve the time it takes to build and deliver network services, regardless of their scope, complexity, and the nature of the elementary functions upon which these services rely.

Rationale

Claimed network automation is currently mostly restricted to the elaboration and the execution of configuration scripts, which reflect the application of decision-making procedures that remain manually declarative: the data used to drive the execution of configuration tasks are statically declared. In addition, this rather embryonic automation mostly deals with tasks that remain local to a device to the detriment of a global, network-wise, systemic view that would be able to guarantee the global consistency of the set of actions taken to deliver a service.

Automation is actually far more protean.

From the dynamic exposure and negotiation of service parameters to feedback mechanisms that are meant to assess that what has been allocated complies with what has been negotiated, the automation of service delivery procedures relies upon a set of functional meta-blocks (dynamic discovery of the network, its topology, its components, dynamic negotiation techniques, dynamic resource allocation and policy enforcement schemes, autonomous back-up mechanisms, etc.) coupled with control loops that interact in a deterministic and sometimes autonomic fashion.

Framework and Challenges

Automation is primarily meant to significantly improve the time it takes to deliver a service but also to provide guarantees about the expected, possibly negotiated, quality and robustness of such services (Figure 1).

Figure 1. AI-fueled service delivery procedure

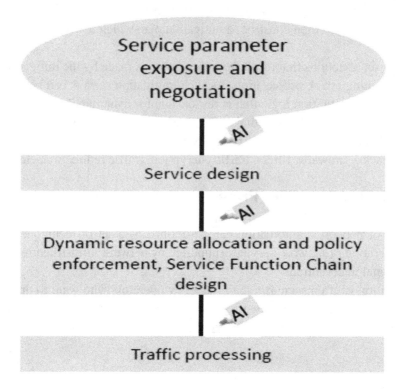

The completion of the service parameter negotiation phase provides an input to the (SDN-based) computation logic of the network automation system. Thus, the corresponding service will then be structured accordingly, i.e., according to the service-specific policy provisioning information that will be derived from the outcome of the said negotiation.

This policy-provisioning information will then be translated into device-specific configuration information. Such policy provisioning information can either be service- or Customer-specific, depending on the nature and the number of services that can be subscribed by a Customer, for example. Upon completion of these configuration tasks, the service is delivered to the Customer in a completely deterministic fashion.

Automated network production and operation must be deterministic.

Indeed, the behavior of systems deployed into operational networks should be predictable and always remain under control. Outputs and states of those systems should be deterministic, and no unexpected behavior should be experienced, at the risk of provoking chaotic situations.

From a deterministic standpoint, a high degree of automation can be introduced inside a system only if such automation relies upon well-known, carefully-designed procedures. The latter can be decomposed into state machines, policies, etc., which will reflect the different behaviors of the system under various conditions. This means that how the service/network will behave within certain circumstances, with particular entries, is known in advance, and the expected result of such behavior is therefore predictable.

Service operation then assumes techniques that are used for Service Fulfillment and Assurance purposes. In particular, monitoring techniques are meant to verify that policies are properly enforced and to ensure that the service delivered complies with what has been negotiated with a Customer.

Artificial Intelligence Is A Cornerstone of Network Automation

Artificial Intelligence (AI) can be defined as a set of cognitive capabilities that contribute to decision-making. AI techniques have many applications in networking environments.

From the dynamic service parameter exposure and negotiation to service fulfillment and assurance, AI-based computation can be seen as the necessary glue to:

- Proceed with the dynamic design of the requested service, based upon the outcomes of a successful service parameter negotiation (Boucadair, Jacquenet, & Wang, 2014; Boucadair, Reddy, Doron, Meiling, & Shallow, 2020) between a customer and a service provider. Such design consists in the identification of the elementary capabilities or Service Functions (SFs) that will compose the service (traffic forwarding and routing capabilities, QoS capabilities like traffic classification and marking, traffic conditioning and scheduling, traffic engineering capabilities, security capabilities, etc.) and their subsequent orchestration to best accommodate the customer's requirements reflected in the contracted Service Level Agreement (SLA).
- Dynamically allocate resources and instantiate (service-inferred) policies (see for example, Liu et al. (2018)) that reflect the aforementioned service design resulting from an AI-fueled computation run by a smart logic typically hosted in a service orchestrator. Such dynamic resource allocation and policy enforcement schemes consist in providing participating SFs with the relevant configuration and policy-provisioning information.
- Design the Service Function Chains (SFC) (Halpern & Pignataro, 2015) that will be supported by the network infrastructure, to dynamically enforce differentiated traffic forwarding policies as a function of the service portfolio (access to the Internet, IPTV services, voice services, etc.) proposed by the service provider. Dynamically structuring an SFC consists in (1) identifying the required SFs that will compose the SFC, (2) identifying the instances of these SFs as a function of various parameters that include (but are not necessarily limited to) the user's location, whether this user is in motion or not, the nature of the service, etc., (3) identifying and applying corresponding traffic classification rules and (4) establishing the Service Function Path (SFP) accordingly, possibly a la traffic engineering (i.e., the SFP is established a priori to best accommodate the service requirements). In that context, AI-based computation can identify the SF instances that best fit the SFC requirements according to various criteria such as traffic load, traffic balancing opportunities, traffic redirection, etc.
- Enforce appropriate feedback mechanisms (e.g., Rawlins et al. (2003)) to (1) assess the efficiency of the said enforced policies and (2) verify that what has been delivered complies with what has been requested and potentially negotiated. These feedback mechanisms usually rely upon the deployment of traffic monitoring systems (including probes and smart agents), which can take advantage of some AI techniques (Machine Learning, for one) to proceed with the aforementioned assessment and possibly affect relevant decision-making processes accordingly (e.g., a Software-Defined Networking (SDN) computation logic may re-instantiate a traffic forwarding policy and allocate extra capacity to address a latency requirement).

- Run control loops at every step of the service delivery procedure (e.g., (Jiang, Strufe, & Schotten, 2017)) to make sure that everything remains in control at any given time. In that case, AI techniques can be used to minimize the risk of the "mad robot" syndrome so that network operators can be informed in real time about the progress of any resource provisioning stage.

The Use of Artificial Intelligence In Protective Networking

Network automation applies to protective networking. It typically consists in the combination of Artificial Intelligence techniques (such as Machine Learning to dynamically acquire data that will be further organized to derive traffic patterns, computation algorithms based upon tools like Reinforcement Learning or Auto-Encoder that will forge neural networks which assist agents in the detection process (i.e., whether the observed traffic that does not match with any of the aforementioned traffic patterns is deemed suspicious or not), and dynamic security policy enforcement and security resource (traffic filter, traffic well, firewall, encryption tools, etc.) allocation schemes used by computation logics such as an SDN controller to elaborate attack mitigation plans that will be further enforced by the relevant components (network device, traffic monitoring agents, etc.).

Protective networking thus assumes the deployment of agents responsible for monitoring the traffic that goes through a network. Several agents can be deployed in various regions and components of the network, including the CPEs and the cloud infrastructures. Data acquired through monitoring thus feed AI computation algorithms whose configuration relies upon a set of traffic parameters that include Source Address/Destination Address pairs, protocol identifiers, source and destination port numbers, etc. (including any combination thereof).

Yang et al. (2020) illustrates the use of AutoEncoder that is trained by a set of traffic patterns that define the library of legitimate traffic samples maintained by an agent. An AutoEncoder relies upon a neural network that learns data encodings in an unsupervised fashion. It then uses the acquired knowledge to generate a representation of the original data input, and which is meant to be as faithful to the original as possible (Figure 2).

Upon completion of the training, the Auto-Encoder is used to detect anomalies observed by an agent. To do so, the agent extracts data from the packets in the form of samples that then feed Auto-Encoder computation logic. The actual detection of an anomaly relies upon the computation of the "difference" between what Auto-Encoder has acquired as part of its training and the samples provided by the agent. Such difference is usually expressed as an error that exceeds a predefined threshold derived from the training phase: since the Auto-Encoder reconstructs input values from legitimate traffic patterns with a reconstruction error Δ, an anomaly is detected whenever the reconstruction of the input value from the sample traffic patterns provided by the agent yields a "Δ" error that is greater than the average of the Δ reconstruction error computed for each legitimate traffic pattern.

Connecting The DOTS For Effective Attack Signaling

According to Jonker et al. (2017), the DDoS ecosystem can be summarized by this sole figure: one third of the ~6 million of /24 IPv4 prefixes that are announced on the Internet have been the target of at least one DDoS attack over the past couple of years. This situation encouraged the development of a new business, called Attack Mitigation Services (AMSes).

Figure 2. Auto-Encoder principle

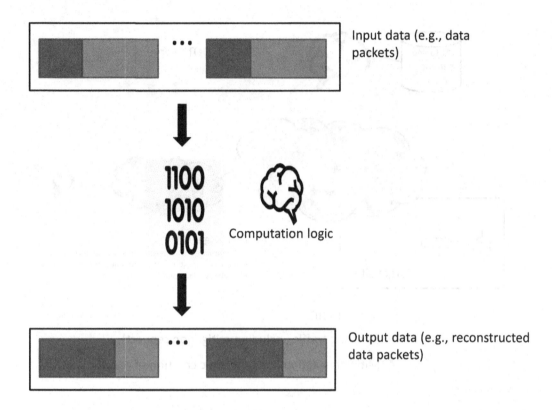

These services are often hosted in cloud infrastructures and prove sub-efficient since they are not usually located on the path to reach the victim's network and proceed with mitigation actions accordingly. Tunnel-based designs where all the incoming traffic forwarded to a given site is inspected by the AMS server have emerged at the cost of degrading the quality of experience perceived by the end-users. In addition, tunnels are known to be attack vectors by design. Even if AMS servers were located on the path that reaches victim networks, further complications would arise as a function of the nature of the traffic.

For example, the QUIC protocol that relies upon UDP and designed to increase web browsing performances compared to the (still) hegemonic HTTP/TCP pair is characterized by encryption capabilities that inevitably complicate the detection of malicious traffic. The inability to access the contents of QUIC control messages because they are encrypted challenges the capacity of an AMS server to distinguish between the traffic consented by the end-user from the traffic that is not.

The DDoS Open Threat Signaling (DOTS) working group was chartered a couple of years ago by the Internet Engineering Task Force (IETF). DOTS standardizes a client/server architecture (Figure 4) to dynamically signal DDoS attack telemetry in real time, so that proper mitigation plans can be derived accordingly. Note that the DOTS framework as defined by Reddy et al. (2020) can be applied to any kind of attacks, including DDoS attacks: it can be effective for Man-in-the Middle (MITM) and identity spoofing attacks.

Figure 3. A simplified DOTS architecture

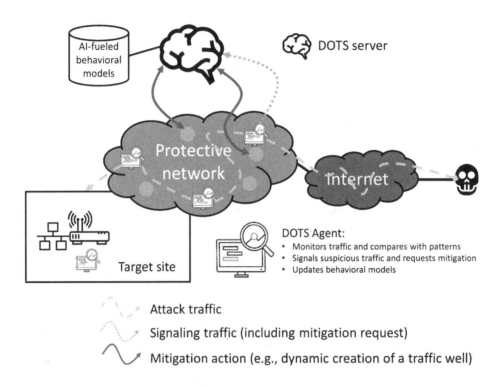

DOTS clients are the agents mentioned in the previous sections. They are responsible for inspecting part or all the traffic they can access from where they are. They compare their observation with the traffic patterns they maintain in a library that is updated by new behavioral models computed by AI tools such as predictive traffic analysis techniques. They can be located close to the attack target or the source of the attack. They can be embedded in various network components including (but not necessarily limited to) border, access and aggregation routers, CPEs or 5G packet gateways. DOTS servers are responsible for handling attack mitigation requests dynamically signaled by DOTS clients, but also for maintaining any useful information about the DOTS clients they manage, such as reachability information and status. DOTS servers can be located in the same domain as the DOTS clients or in a different domain (e.g., when the AMS is provided to multiple customers located in different domains where DOTS clients are implemented).

DOTS clients and servers use two channels to communicate: the data channel and the signal channel. The data channel defined by Boucadair & Reddy (2020) is only used when no attack is in progress. The DOTS data channel is typically used to install rules, such as filtering rules that can rely upon criteria like the source or the destination address or prefix. Conversely, the DOTS signal channel is only used when an attack is detected and in progress. Typically, a DOTS client uses the signal channel to solicit assistance from the DOTS server with an attack mitigation request. The attack mitigation request provides all the relevant information of the attack, including the network prefix under attack. Upon receipt of an attack mitigation request sent by a DOTS client, a DOTS server will take appropriate measures that may solicit one or more mitigation resources (e.g., firewalls). The DOTS server also checks if the request does not conflict with other mitigation requests or traffic filtering rules that are already in effect, for example.

DOTS clients and servers are smart or should be. It's one thing to detect and report an attack in progress in real time so that proper mitigation actions can be taken as soon as possible. It's another thing to make sure that the corresponding mitigation plans will be enforced before the attack reaches its targets, i.e., in a proactive manner.

The required intelligence to make a network truly protective is likely to take advantage of network automation and artificial intelligence techniques. When traffic inspection is in progress, DOTS clients can thus become smart by comparing what they observe with the library of models they maintain. Whenever passing traffic does not fit into one of these models, the DOTS client suspects malice. It will then solicit a DOTS server for assistance. Assuming the said suspicion turns out to be true, the DOTS server derives the appropriate mitigation plan. In other words, it defines a new security policy (or adapts an existing one, e.g., modify the currently enforced filters) that will have to be enforced by the relevant mitigation resources.

Dynamically Enforcing Security Policies

Which brings us to another piece of the protective networking puzzle: *network automation techniques*. Typically, a DOTS server would likely collocate with an SDN (Software-Defined Networking) controller (or an orchestrator, considering the AMS can be dynamically adapted and restructured on the fly) or, put simply, be part of the SDN computation logic.

Whenever a DOTS client solicits a DOTS server, assuming the client's suspicion proves to be true, the DOTS server's decision-making process is triggered accordingly to decide what to do about the attack in progress. Figure 5 illustrates the dynamic security policy enforcement framework that relies upon the mitigation server as part of the AI-fed computation logic of the networking infrastructure and the network security functions involved in the actual enforcement of the said security policies. An NSF is an attack mitigation resource that will be solicited as part of a mitigation plan to ensure integrity, confidentiality, and availability of network communications, and to mitigate the effects of unwanted activity (Figure 4).

Therefore, a future network security framework will rely upon a set of interfaces and data models for controlling and monitoring aspects of physical and virtualized NSFs, so that a DOTS server can enable various security rulesets accordingly. Of course, such rule sets can reflect the dynamic enforcement of security policies based upon the Event/Condition/Action (ECA) triptych. Simplistically, the "event" can be a request for assistance sent by a DOTS client. Upon receipt of this request, the "condition" to derive a mitigation plan is that the suspicion proves to be true, and the "action" becomes the enforcement of the mitigation plan.

From Protective Networking to Collaborative Networking

Customers enable more and more objects that are granted access to the Internet. Future networks will undoubtedly contribute to the deployment of such connected objects on a large scale. Yet, experience has shown that these objects are very likely to be exposed to security breaches that can be exploited by attackers, so that connected objects behave as attack relays. Such attacks jeopardize the *reputation of the*

Figure 4. Policy-based network management to dynamically enforce appropriate mitigation plans

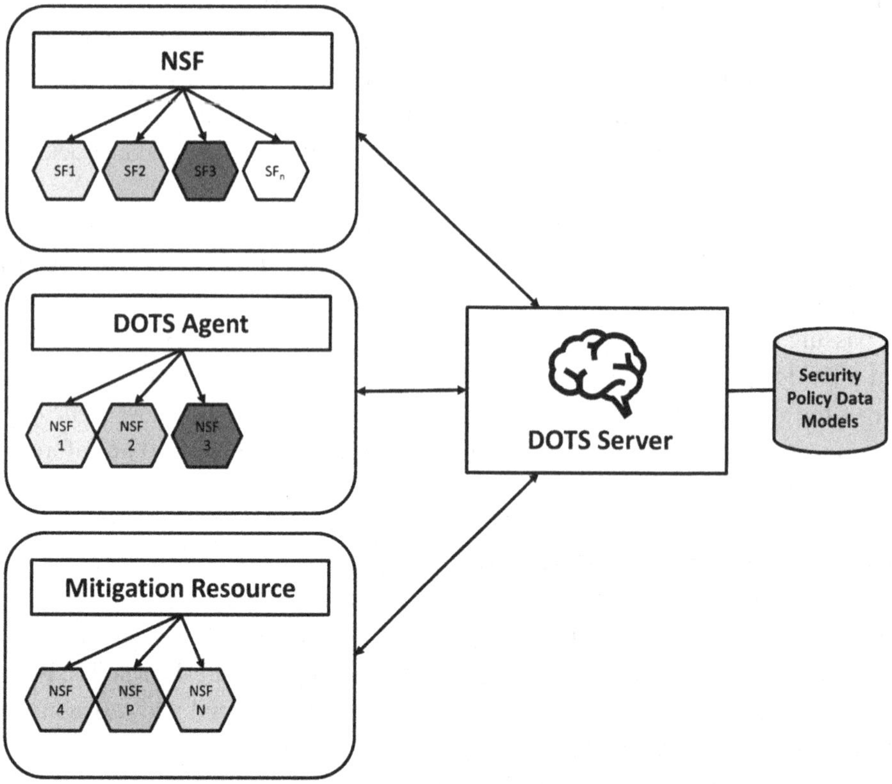

network providers, and also question the stability of the network provider's infrastructure. *Collaborative means to filter attack traffic close to its sources* are critical to avoid overloading the network. It is even more critical as most end-users are not prepared to handle security attacks.

Therefore, it makes sense to conceive a model where Mitigation Service Providers (MSPs) collaborate for the benefit of their respective customers. The objectives of such collaborative networking are manifold:

- Exchange about best security practices and share mitigation experience (Figure 5).
- Assist partnering MSPs, especially within the context of "zero-day" attacks whose a priori unknown nature may complicate the elaboration of adequate mitigation plans.
- Dynamically signal the detection of an attack across DOTS domains (where a DOTS domain would typically correspond to a network) to facilitate the enforcement of the corresponding mitigation plan(s) at a larger scale and let partnering MSPs to anticipate the attack even before any of its traffic enters their domain.

Such collaborative networking encourages AMS partnerships that can rely upon bilateral peer-to-peer agreements or a brokering model. The collaborative networking framework still assumes the combination of AI tools with dynamic signaling and the automated enforcement of mitigation plans. With col-

Figure 5. Collaborative networking environment

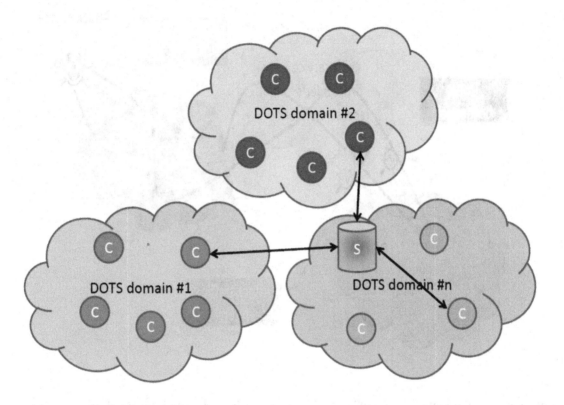

laborative networking, the efficiency of such mitigation plans can only improve, just like the ability of MSPs to limit the propagation of an attack. Let us first start with a typical example where local attack mitigation proves to be insufficient.

A Basic Example: An Enterprise Network Is The Target of A DDoS Attack

Figure 6 illustrates the case of an enterprise network subjected to a DDoS attack whose source is connected somewhere on the Internet. Local mitigation plans are being enforced by the DOTS server operated by the enterprise, but, unfortunately, the attack is still ongoing. The mitigation consisting in blocking the attack traffic at the edge of the enterprise's network is not good enough. The attack traffic will indeed keep on saturating the access and significantly degrading the quality of the services subscribed by the enterprise (e.g., a VPN service), let alone forbidding the access to such services.

Benefits of Collaborative Networking

In the example illustrated by Figure 6, let us now assume the VPN service provider is also an MSP. In that case, the enterprise customer could have solicited the MSP for assistance. Typically, the DOTS

Figure 6. Local DOTS-based mitigation may be insufficient

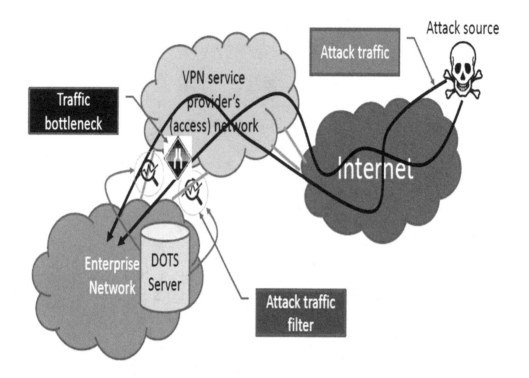

agents hosted in the routers operated by the MSPs would have detected the attack traffic and then proceeded with the enforcement of the adequate mitigation plan (e.g., dynamic creation of a traffic well). Predictive traffic analysis outcomes and subsequent detection results would have been shared between the enterprise customer and its VPN provider/MSP, so that the characterization of the attack would have fostered the execution of the mitigation actions. Such exchange relies upon the DOTS signaling mechanisms whereas a DOTS client hosted in the enterprise's network first solicits the DOTS server operated by its VPN provider/MSP and then informs the DOTS server about the nature of the attack (Figure 7).

The nature of the information that describes the attack is illustrated in the example of Figure 8.

By design, the DOTS signaling mechanism assumes a relationship between a client and its MSP. Depending on the nature of the attack (including its origin that may be located several networks away from where the DOTS architecture is deployed, its scope, its magnitude, etc.), this sole relationship is likely insufficient. There is a need for a more global framework where DOTS-enabled networks can collaborate to mitigate any kind of attack as close to its source as possible.

Collaborative Networking Framework

Collaborative networking assumes the availability of AMSes that have been subscribed by various network operators. Figure 9 illustrates the collaborative networking environment where networks #1 to #n embed one or more several AMS agents that are responsible for:

Figure 7. DOTS client of the enterprise network solicits the DOTS server of the VPN/AMS provider

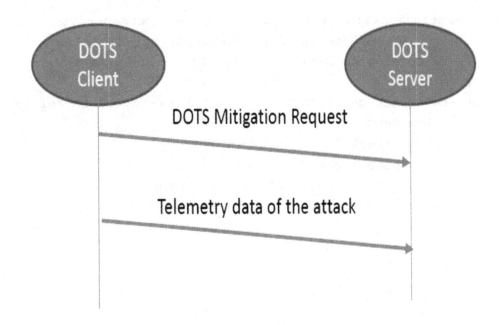

- Monitoring traffic and comparing it against a library of traffic patterns fed by AI tools such as Reinforcement Learning or Auto-Encoder algorithms.
- Dynamically signaling any traffic deemed suspicious and requesting assistance (namely a mitigation plan) as appropriate.

AMS agents interact with other AMS agents operated by the other partnering networks through DOTS. Communications between AMS agents are established using DTLS (Rescorla & Modadugu, 2012) or TLS1.3 (Rescorla, 2018). Communication is established upon completion of a mutual authentication scheme, so that any risk of AMS agent identity spoofing can be minimized. Likewise, AMS agents must subscribe to the AMS Collaborative Networking (ACN) service before any request they may send can be processed by one or several partnering AMS agents.

Communications between AMS agents of an ACN service can either be bilateral (Figure 10) or subject to some kind of brokering scheme (Figure 11). In the latter case, an AMS broker is responsible for dispatching requests originated by AMS agents to other AMS agents, e.g., depending on the nature of the request, the location of the attack source, etc.

To subscribe to the ACN service, an AMS agent sends a SUBSCRIBE message to an AMS agent of another domain or an AMS broker. The SUBSCRIBE message may provide elaboration on the nature of the collaborative mitigation service, e.g., as a function of a mitigation service portfolio and according to set of value codes like:

Figure 8. Example of the description of an attack by means of DOTS signaling

```
augment /ietf-signal:dots-signal/ietf-signal:message-type
          /ietf-signal:mitigation-scope/ietf-signal:scope:
     +--rw total-attack-traffic* [unit] {dots-telemetry}?
     |  ...
     +--rw attack-detail* [vendor-id attack-id] {dots-telemetry}?
          +--rw vendor-id          uint32
          +--rw attack-id          uint32
          +--rw attack-name?       string
          +--rw attack-severity?   attack-severity
          +--rw start-time?        uint64
          +--rw end-time?          uint64
          +--rw source-count
          |  ...
          +--rw top-talker
             ...
```

- "0" means that the AMS agent wants to subscribe to all the mitigation services provided.
- "1" means that the AMS agent wants to subscribe to the DDoS attack mitigation service.
- "2" means that the AMS agent wants to subscribe to the virus-detection service.

Upon receipt of the SUBSCRIBE message, the AMS agent (or the AMS broker) checks whether the requesting agent is entitled to subscribe to the ACN service. If clearance is granted, the receiving agent (AMS agent or broker) extracts the identity of the requesting AMS agent, the AMS domain it belongs to, the nature of the ACN service requested by the subscription request, the subscription period, etc. Such information is stored in a database maintained by the receiving AMS agent or broker. The requesting AMS agent receives an ACK message that confirms its subscription to the ACN service.

Whenever an AMS agent detects suspicious traffic that is already the subject of filters enforced by a partnering AMS agent, the DOTS server informs the latter about the attack mitigation request sent by the agent that detected the suspicious traffic. The latter AMS agent then sends a notification message that informs the initial AMS agent that a mitigation plan is already in progress. The notification message typically includes the description of the mitigation plan, so that the AMS agent that receives the notification can proceed accordingly, possibly assuming an adaptation of the mitigation plan described

Figure 9. AMS Collaborative Networking (ACN) environment

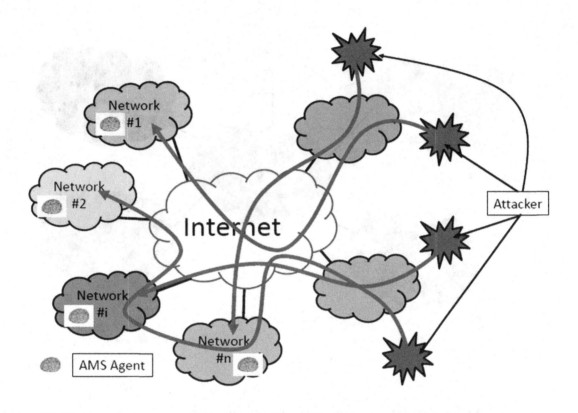

in the notification message. Such an agent can thus anticipate the corresponding attack and make sure that the corresponding traffic will never reach the resources this AMS agent protects.

Typically, the notification message carries the following information:

- The subscription identifier that unambiguously confirms the requesting agent is entitled to access the ACN service.
- An identifier of the attack that is generated by the AMS agent (or broker) that sends the notification message. This identifier is used during the lifetime of the attack.
- A descriptor of the attack: the corresponding field of the notification message can for example include a protocol number, one or several port numbers, the components (hosts, routers, switches, servers, etc.) involved in the attack, the directionality of the attack traffic (inbound or outbound), etc. It's worth mentioning that such a description can evolve during the lifetime of the attack possibly because additional attack sources or protocols are involved. In that case, additional notification messages are sent to reflect the evolution of the attack. The AMS agent that receives subsequent notification messages may then update the mitigation plan, e.g., by updating the traffic filters.
- A "Status" field that indicates the status of the attack, whether it is still in progress or has been successfully mitigated.

Figure 10. ACN messages are exchanged directly between AMS agents (point-to-point communication)

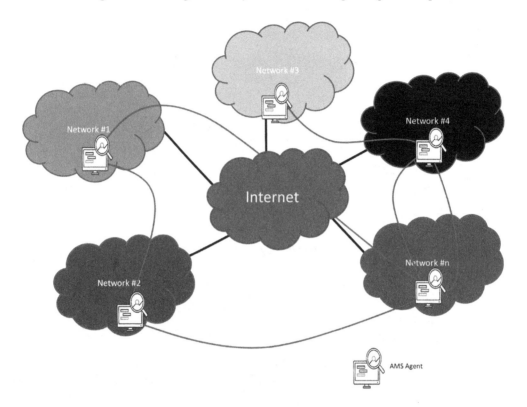

- A "Local Mitigation" field that is meant to describe the mitigation plan defined and enforced by the AMS agent that sent the notification message. The corresponding information is purely informal: it's up to the receiving agent to decide whether it can be useful to elaborate its own mitigation plan or not.
- An "SOS" field that is used to request assistance to another AMS agent so that the attack in progress can be mitigated as soon as possible. This field is valued to "true" by an AMS agent that has no clue about the suspicious traffic it has detected. This could be the case of a "zero-day" attack that is unknown to the said agent, but which has already been experienced elsewhere within the protective networking domain that comprises several AMS domains and agents.

In addition, information about attacks can be correlated for the sake of optimized mitigation. Figure 12 illustrates the case of an AMS agent that associates two notification messages received from two other AMS agents to the very same attack, thanks to the information carried in the "Attack Descriptor" field of the notification messages.

A mitigation plan can rely upon the activation of traffic filters by various network resources, the creation of a traffic well, the allocation of resources that will redirect legitimate or attack traffic along other forwarding paths, etc.

Collaborative networking is key to globally coordinated attack mitigation plans enforced at the scale of the Internet. It should become a cornerstone of globally resilient, attack-proof networking infrastructures that would then be able to anticipate any kind of attack way before they can propagate. Best miti-

Figure 11. ACN messages are dispatched by a kind of AMS broker, e.g., depending on the nature of the mitigation request

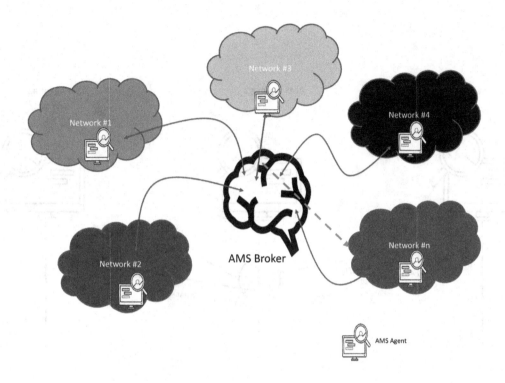

gation practices can be exchanged between MSPs by means of collaborative networking. Collaborative networking is a privileged framework to provide mutual assistance between partnering MSPs, so that attacks can be mitigated as close to their sources as possible.

CONCLUSION

Security of the future Internet is global and protean. With the foreseeable multiplication of services and usages sometimes distorted by exceptional events like the recent COVID-19 pandemic, the attack surface will be dramatically extended. Yet, the security toolkit never ceased to improve over decades. The advent of AI techniques will undoubtedly facilitate the automated design and dynamic enforcement of adapted, anticipative security policy enforcement schemes. Future networks will thus become protective, not "just" protected: besides a dramatically improved protection of the end-users and their privacy, future services and network slices will inevitably gain robustness and resilience.

Protective networking also paves the way to advanced collaborative networking that provides mutual assistance and strengthens attack mitigation experience, whereas quantum physics will make eavesdropping history, from long haul communication to user terminal's authentication. Some of the techniques that will be instrumental for deploying protective networking at a large scale are already there. Others are still nurturing, but progress over the past couple of years is significant in the areas of AI tooling, neural network design, and dynamic security policy enforcement schemes.

Figure 12. Correlation of attack information based upon the contents of ATTACK DESCRIPTOR fields of notification messages

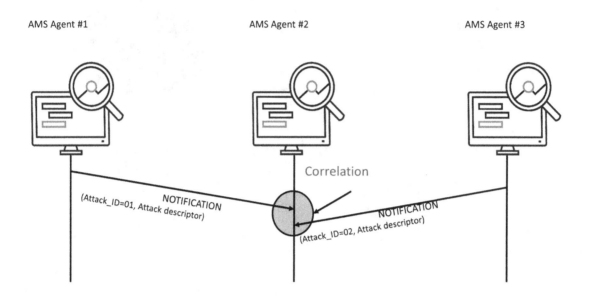

Protective and collaborative networking is, therefore, a promising business opportunity too.

REFERENCES

Bjorklund, M. (Ed.). (2016). *The YANG 1.1 Data Modeling Language*. IETF. RFC 7950. Retrieved October 09, 2020, from https://tools.ietf.org/html/rfc7950

Boucadair, M. (Ed.). (2020). *Distributed Denial-of-Service Open Threat Signaling (DOTS) Telemetry*. IETF. Retrieved October 09, 2020, from https://datatracker.ietf.org/doc/draft-ietf-dots-telemetry/

Boucadair, M. (Ed.). (2020). *Distributed Denial-of-Service Open Threat Signaling (DOTS) Data Channel Specification*. IETF. RFC 8783. Retrieved October 09, 2020, from https://www.rfc-editor.org/rfc/rfc8783.pdf

Boucadair, M., & Jacquenet, C. (2014). *Software-Defined Networking: A Perspective from within a Service Provider Environment*. IETF. RFC 7149. Retrieved October 09, 2020, from https://tools.ietf.org/html/rfc7149

Boucadair, M., Jacquenet, C., & Wang, N. (2014). *IP Connectivity Provisioning Profile (CPP)*. IETF. RFC 7297. Retrieved October 09, 2020, from https://tools.ietf.org/html/rfc7297

Boucadair, M., Jacquenet, C., Zhang, D., & Georgatsos, P. (2020a). *Dynamic Service Negotiation*. IETF. RFC 8921. Retrieved October 09, 2020, from https://tools.ietf.org/html/rfc8921

Cao, Y., Zhao, Y., Wang, J., Yu, X., Ma, Z., & Zhang, J. (2019, March). SDQaaS: Software-defined networking for quantum key distribution as a service. *Optics Express*, 27(5), 6892. Advance online publication. doi:10.1364/OE.27.006892 PMID:30876265

Check Point 2020 Cyber Security Report. (2020). Retrieved February 01, 2021, from https://www.ntsc.org/assets/pdfs/cyber-security-report-2020.pdf

Halpern, J., & Pignataro, C. (2015). *Service Function Chaining (SFC) Architecture*. IETF. RFC 7665. Retrieved October 09, 2020, from https://tools.ietf.org/html/rfc7665

Jiang, W., Strufe, M., & Schotten, H. (2017). Experimental Results for Artificial Intelligence-based Self-Organized 5G Networks. *2017 IEEE 28th Annual International Symposium on Personal, Indoor and Mobile Radio Communications (PIMRC)*. 10.1109/PIMRC.2017.8292532

Jonker, M., King, A., Krupp, J., Rossow, C., Sperotto, A., & Dainotti, A. (2017). Millions of Targets under Attack: a Macroscopic Characterization of the DoS Ecosystem. *Proceedings of IMC'17*. Retrieved February 01, 2021, from https://dl.acm.org/doi/10.1145/3131365.3131383

Liu, W., Xie, C., Strassner, J., Karagiannis, G., Klyus, M., Bi, J., Cheng, Y., & Zhang, D. (2018). *Policy-Based Management Framework for the Simplified Use of Policy Abstractions (SUPA)*. IETF. RFC 8328. Retrieved October 09, 2020, from https://tools.ietf.org/html/rfc8328

Rawlins, D., Kulkarni, A., Chan, K., Bokaemper, M., & Dutt, C. (2003). *Framework Policy Information Base for Usage Feedback*. IETF. RFC 3571. Retrieved October 09, 2020, from https://tools.ietf.org/html/rfc3571

Reddy, T. (Ed.). (2020). *Distributed Denial-of-Service Open Threat Signaling (DOTS) Signal Channel Specification*. IETF. RFC 8782. Retrieved October 09, 2020, from https://www.rfc-editor.org/rfc/rfc8782.pdf

Rescoria, E., & Modadugu, N. (2012). *Datagram transport Layer Security Version 1.2*. IETF RFC 6347. Retrieved October 09, 2020, from https://tools.ietf.org/html/rfc6347

Rescorla, E. (2018). *The Transport Layer Security (TLS) Protocol Version 1.3*. IETF RFC 8446. Retrieved October 09, 2020, from https://tools.ietf.org/html/rfc8446

Yang, K., Zhang, J., Xu, Y., & Chao, J. (2020).DDoS Attacks Detection with AutoEncoder. *2020 IEEE/IFIP Network Operations and Management Symposium*. 10.1109/NOMS47738.2020.9110372

ADDITIONAL READING

Boucadair, M., Reddy, K. T., & Pan, W. (2020). Multi-homing Deployment Considerations for Distributed-Denial-of-Service Open Threat Signaling (DOTS). IETF. Retrieved 01/02/2021, from https://datatracker.ietf.org/doc/draft-ietf-dots-multihoming/

Boucadair, M., & Reddy, T. (2020). Distributed-Denial-of-Service Open Threat Signaling (DOTS) Agent Discovery. IETFRFC8793, Retrieved 01/02/2021, from https://datatracker.ietf.org/doc/rfc8973/

Dobbins, R., Migault, D., Moskowitz, R., Teague, N., Xia, L., & Nishizuka, K. (2020). Use cases for DDoS Open Threat Signaling. IETF. Retrieved 01/02/2021, from https://datatracker.ietf.org/doc/draft-ietf-dots-use-cases/

Mortensen, A., Reddy, T., & Moskowitz, R. (2020). DDoS Open Threat Signaling (DOTS) Requirements. *RFC, 8612*. Advance online publication. doi:10.17487/RFC8612

Nishizuka, K., Boucadair, M., Reddy, K. T., & Nagata, T. (2020). Controlling Filtering Rules Using Distributed Denial-of-Service Open Threat Signaling (DOTS) Signal Channel. Retrieved 01/02/2021 from, https://datatracker.ietf.org/doc/draft-ietf-dots-signal-filter-control/

Reddy, K. T., Boucadair, M., & Shallow, J. (2020). Distributed Denial-of-Service Open Threat Signaling (DOTS) Signal Channel Call Home. IETF, Retrieved 01/02/2021, from https://datatracker.ietf.org/doc/ draft-ietf-dots-signal-call-home/

KEY TERMS AND DEFINITIONS

Attack Mitigation Plan: An instantiation of a security policy that is designed to respond to an attack by any means appropriate (e.g., redirection of the attack traffic, creation of traffic wells, activation of traffic filters), as a function of its nature (e.g., a spoofing attack, a DDoS attack), its origin, its scope, etc.

Attack Mitigation Service (AMS): The service provided by a Mitigation Service Provider, particularly by means of protective networking. An AMS relies upon one or several mitigators and scrubbing centers that are responsible for processing attack mitigation requests signaled by one or more several agents deployed in the protective networking infrastructure. Agents are responsible for monitoring and detecting any suspicious traffic that may correspond to an attack and to report such suspicious traffic to one of the mitigators they communicate with.

Collaborative Networking: A framework that extends the concept of protective networking at a global scale. Collaborative networking includes (but is not limited to) the ability to dynamically exchange best attack mitigation practices between partnering networks, the ability to provide an assistance service where a protective network can help a partnering network to elaborate an attack mitigation plan (AMS) and the ability to instruct partnering networks to proceed with attack mitigation actions that will limit the propagation of an attack.

Network Automation: A set of techniques meant to facilitate the design, the delivery, and the operation of services (e.g., VPN services) supported by a network infrastructure. Within the context of collaborative networking, network automation tools include dynamic security policy enforcement and resource allocation schemes, dynamic signaling mechanisms to report and exchange about a potentially suspicious traffic, as well as a set of Artificial Intelligence (AI) tools such as Machine Learning, computation algorithms like Reinforcement Learning and neural networks that assist attack traffic identification procedures, as well as the elaboration of attack mitigation plans.

· **Predictive Traffic Analysis:** A technique that consists in developing traffic patterns deduced from the observation of the traffic that goes through a network or a network component. The library of normal traffic baseline can be elaborated and maintained by means of Machine Learning techniques. Such traffic patterns are used by agents that monitor the traffic (or a part thereof, according to traffic selection criteria such as the Source Address (SA)/Destination Address (DA) pair, the protocol number, etc.) that goes through a network device or is forwarded along a network segment, so that they can compare what they observe against the normal traffic baseline. By means of AI algorithms, they can detect potentially suspicious traffic that doesn't match with any of the said traffic patterns or update the library of traffic patterns.

Protective Networking: A set of detection, signaling, and attack mitigation means that provide a network with the ability to dynamically anticipate and mitigate attacks (hopefully of any kind), regardless of their origin, scope, and amplitude, way before they reach their targets.

Security Policy: A set of measures (e.g., traffic encryption, traffic filtering, traffic redirection) defined by a security Policy Decision Point (e.g., an SDN controller) and enforced by a set of components (e.g., routers, firewalls) to protect a networking infrastructure and the devices (e.g., Customer Premises Equipment, mobile terminal) connected to it against attacks.

Chapter 13
Drone Security:
Threats and Challenges

Marc Lacoste
Orange S.A., France

David Armand
Orange S.A., France

Fanny Parzysz
Orange S.A., France

Loïc Ferreira
Orange S.A., France

Ghada Arfaoui

Orange S.A., France

Yvan Rafflé
Orange S.A., France

Yvon Gourhant
Orange S.A., France

Nicolas Bihannic
 https://orcid.org/0000-0001-7003-1767
Orange S.A., France

Sébastien Roché
Orange S.A., France

ABSTRACT

This chapter explores the security challenges of the drone ecosystem. Drones raise significant security and safety concerns, both design-time and run-time (e.g., supply-chain, technical design, standardization). Two broad classes of threats are considered, on drones and using drones (e.g., to attack critical infrastructures or vehicles). They involve both professional and non-professional drones and lead to various types of attacks (e.g., IoT-type vulnerabilities, GPS spoofing, spying, kinetic attacks). Trade-offs involving hardware and software solutions to meet efficiency, resource limitations, and real-time constraints are notably hard to find. So far, protection solutions remain elementary compared to the impact of attacks. Advances in technologies, new use cases (e.g., enhancing network connectivity), and a regulatory framework to overcome existing barriers are decisive factors for sustainable drone security market growth.

DOI: 10.4018/978-1-7998-7646-5.ch013

INTRODUCTION

The usage of *Drones*, also known as *Unmanned Aerial Vehicles (UAVs)*, or increasingly as *Unmanned Aircraft Systems (UAS)*, is dramatically expanding (Fotouhi et al., 2019). This is due to technological advances, and to the development of numerous use cases. Drone networking is also seen by service providers and network operators as a business opportunity (Ericsson, 2018; Vodafone, 2018). Drone use cases include disaster management, search and rescue, surveillance, or ad-hoc network connectivity. Drones may also lower adoption barriers, as for autonomous vehicles, or enhance ubiquitous connectivity, e.g., by allowing instant network extensions to absorb temporal traffic load or to deliver connectivity in areas with low or no coverage. In addition, drone momentum has become significant with the ongoing deployment of 5G networks, leading to an impressive number of publications from both industry and academia, field-trialed proof-of-concepts, and real-world scenarios (Joo, 2019).

Drones raise significant security and safety concerns, as witnessed by the expanding number of attacks conducted by means of drones or against drones (Raja, 2020). Some security challenges are drone-specific, while others are common to vertical domains such as the Internet of Things (IoT) or connected and autonomous vehicles. Regulatory barriers are significant and moving fast in this complex ecosystem. Drones may also open novel security service opportunities for Telcos for the benefit of their customers.

This chapter provides a deep dive on drone security to better understand the challenges raised by the drone ecosystem. It also assesses the security implications of drones in terms of threats and countermeasures.

First, the chapter provides some background on drones by presenting the key concepts and the inferred requirements. Then, a review of the main threats related to UAVs is provided, on drones, and using drones. A set of security challenges for UAVs are discussed. Finally, some future perspectives are highlighted.

BACKGROUND

This section presents some general definitions on drones. It then gives an overview of some key requirements. It also reviews the drone regulatory landscape and its impact on drone networking architectures.

Definitions

Unmanned Aerial Vehicles (UAV) or *drones*, are airborne devices that have a huge potential in a wide range of applications in both civilian and military domains[1]. Drones come in different sizes. Early systems were dedicated to single tasks, and formed of a single, usually large aerial node, and of a number of ground nodes. UAVs such as High Altitude Platform Stations (HAPS) may even fly continuously in the stratosphere for extended periods of time above air traffic, providing services such as data gathering or connectivity. Similar to any connected object, UAVs face many threats related to confidentiality, integrity, and availability (Javaid et al., 2012).

The concept of "drone" can be extended to other forms (e.g., climbing drones, maritime drones), collectively referred to as UxV for Unmanned Ground Vehicles (UGV), Unmanned Underwater Vehicles (UUV), etc.

Networks of UAVs, also known as multi-UAV systems or *swarms/fleets of drones*, are composed of multiple drones flying and coordinating together to complete the same mission. Drones of a fleet may communicate with each other, for instance using wireless communications. Drones may form an ad-hoc network called *Flying Ad hoc Network (FANET)*. Figure 1 shows how UAVs work cooperatively, notably with ground and satellite nodes to achieve their mission(s) more efficiently and reliably (Javaid et al., 2012). Whether drones hover or move across a large area is application-specific (Gupta et al., 2016).

An UAV with its pilot or controller and all the on-board and off-board sub-systems required to safely control the UAV is commonly referred to as an *Unmanned Aircraft System (UAS)*. A simple UAS includes a Ground Control Station (GCS), or dedicated static or portable control center, such as a smart device with applications installed on a mobile phone or on a tablet.

Figure 1. UAS overview

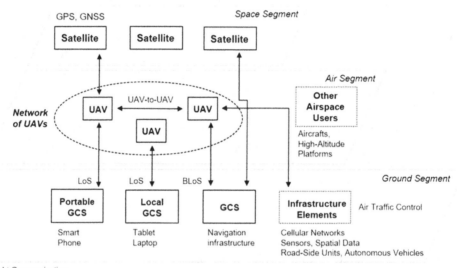

Two types of drone fleets can be considered: *static* or *dynamic* (Akram et al., 2017).

- **Static drone fleets:** members are pre-selected before the mission. During flight, no new drones can enroll into the swarm. Secure communications are set up by the owner of the drones.
- **Dynamic drone fleets:** fleets are open to enrollment of new drones. They can be *closed dynamic fleets*, allowing only enrollment of new drones from the same organization; or *open dynamic fleets* allowing enrollment of drones from third-party organizations, which may raise isolation issues.

Requirements

Depending on deployment scenarios, drones may suffer from different attack types. Smaller aircrafts require significantly less infrastructure and are much easier to deploy. They generally have less battery autonomy, and less processing capabilities. However, they can fly where conventional aircrafts cannot, e.g., indoors, underground, or within industry pipelines.

Rescue, reconnaissance, or relief drone operations may require flying in severe weather conditions, in geographically challenging areas or with limited network coverage. They may operate over particular network infrastructures, like tactical bubbles. Such platforms create or extend network coverage, providing unified services for performance-critical operations, with resilience, safety, and secure communications. They may notably be deployed on-site for military tactical operations, public safety, and during emergency and disaster situations.

Surveillance drones may come with a wide range of sensors and cameras, and fly above critical sites, such as nuclear plants, pipelines and powerlines, borders, or crowded places during a protest. They may have significant processing capabilities and be connected to sensitive infrastructures, which makes security and privacy preservation particularly challenging for this class of drones (Russon, 2016).

Regulatory and Architecture Considerations

In the early 2010s, the "drone explosion" shed light on the necessity to organize the safety of airspaces, to limit incidents, careless and criminal uses, airspace regulation infringements and violations of privacy law. It quickly became clear that drones were not just another vehicle nor IoT device. The aircraft and the person legally responsible for it are not physically located in the same place, which makes accountability more complex. As soon as drones are above ground level (AGL), they fall under national airspace regulation, but fly below Air Traffic Management (ATM) radar coverage. Current conventional ATM for manned aircraft is still hand-operated and relies upon voice communications between air traffic controllers and pilots. This is inappropriate for drone scenarios, given the billions of units expected to fly by 2025 and their variety of uses, recreational or professional, potentially out of predefined aerial corridors or totally automated.

A whole set of new digital services was thus needed for drones. Examples include aircraft/pilot registration, flight planning and approval, airspace dynamic information and geofencing. This function provides the drone pilot with information on the current drone position, but may also limit flying access to some areas. Further examples include real-time drone identification and tracking, and automated "detect and avoid" functionalities, in particular for dense aerial traffic areas. Many players – public or private, from both the aerospace and telecom industries, or from large companies such as Amazon or Google – developed their own solutions for these services. This led to critical challenges regarding data exchange security, legal obligations, and privacy regulations. A framework was thus required to support collaboration between the involved stakeholders and to ensure safe airspace sharing.

To that aim, the concept of *UTM*, for *UAS Traffic Management* (and in Europe, the current more inclusive notion of *U-Space*) has been developed by the various national ministries and armies, as well as by national and supra-national standardization and airspace agencies, including: ASTM International, the International Civil Aviation Organization (ICAO), the Federal Aviation Administration (FAA) and the National Aeronautics and Space Administration (NASA) in the US; the European Aviation Safety Agency (EASA) and the European Organization for the Safety of Air Navigation (EUROCONTROL) in Europe; or the Direction Générale de l'Aviation Civile (DGAC) in France.

As illustrated in Figure 2, the UTM framework can be considered as a "system of systems", in which the *UAS Service Supplier (USS)* plays a pivotal role. For further details on the NASA UTM concepts and architecture, the reader is referred to (Kopardekar et al., 2016). Developed and deployed by private

Figure 2. UTM functional architecture

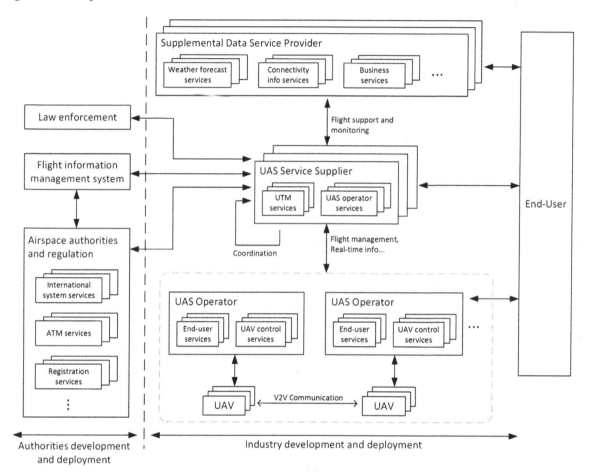

industries, the UTM was at first a tool for pilots and UAS operators to schedule and monitor flights in real-time. Its role rapidly gained importance. The USS should now be provided with interfaces with airspace agencies, law enforcement and other Supplemental Data Service Providers (SDSP) for increased safety, including, for example, weather information, conformance monitoring (checking that UAS are effectively flying according to their declared flight plan) or malicious drone detection.

Such interfaces increase the attack surface of systems external to the UTM, and facilitate cyber-attacks that are neither "on" nor "using" drones, but which leverage systems built to support drone operations. New communication channels are created within the multi-stakeholder drone environment, and open new vulnerabilities and attack vectors for the UTM framework components and the networks. Some threats on UTM for UAS systems are discussed in (Best et al., 2020), with also some counter-measures such as a blockchain-based solution for reliable, secured, and robust data exchange between UTM components. Malicious drone detection in mobile networks may typically be performed using machine-learning based on radio interference measurements (Rydén et al., 2018).

UAV THREATS

Many incidents have been reported which are related to drones (DeDrone, 2020). Cybersecurity risks raised by drones are being well identified (Department of Homeland Security, 2018). Threats and attacks related to UAVs may be classified in two broad families: (1) attacks *on a drone system*; and (2) attacks performed *using a drone system*. The remainder of this section explores in more details each family of threats.

Attacks on Drones

Attacks on drones may be performed through several attack vectors (Nassi et al., 2019), e.g.:

- Protocol-based attacks.
- Sensor-based attacks.
- Compromised hardware components.
- Jammers.
- Physical attacks.

Such attacks are similar to those on IoT systems in general and, for drones with advanced navigation features, to those against autonomous vehicles.

Traditional IoT Vulnerabilities Applied to Drones

Low-cost drones are often designed with naïve security protection rather than strong security.
Some common security issues are:

1. **Weak WLAN configuration:** WLAN (Wireless Local Area Network)-enabled drones activate a WLAN hotspot when they are powered on so that a controller (application on a smartphone or dedicated hardware) may connect to them. On some models, no security is enforced at the WLAN layer to limit access to the hotspot. Several WLAN clients may be allowed to connect at the same time. This means an attacker could connect to the network, wait for the controller of the legitimate user to connect, and then try to exploit vulnerabilities in the network services running on it. The attacker could also passively monitor traffic to get information on the victim. Even if a robust WPA2 (Wi-Fi Protected Access) key has been set, the controller may be forcefully disconnected from the drone unless both the drone and the controller implement Protected Management Frames (802.11w standard), which currently remains the exception, not the rule. For example, such attacks on a Parrot AR Drone 2.0 are reported in (Khan, 2016).
2. **No application-layer authentication:** Very often, authentication mechanisms, when they are implemented, are limited to the radio layer. Once connected to the WLAN hotspot of the drone, an attacker can freely access the services – typically to get the live video stream from the drone without using the legitimate controller, or to get pictures stored previously in the internal flash memory (e.g., from an ftp server or a web interface). Similarly an attacker may be able to send engine control commands or kill processes running on the drone.

3. **Unsecure Radio Frequency (RF) protocols**: As an alternative to WLAN, some drones are controlled using proprietary RF protocols. If such protocols are not secure by design, an attacker may record legitimate commands and replay them at a later time. An attacker may also craft commands from scratch (without having to record them previously). To perform the attack, Software-Defined Radio (SDR) equipment is required.

Professional drones cost around 30K$ and are not exempt from vulnerabilities either: after reverse engineering the controllers (mobile application, RF remote control), illegitimate control of the drone engines may be performed with 40$ hardware by exploiting insecure radio protocols (Rodday, 2016).

Unfortunately, apart from military-level drones, investment in terms of security remains low compared to the cost of the product. While a lot of money goes into having a very high-quality camera or drone autonomy, security still often relies on proprietary RF mechanisms with a security level that has not been assessed by the security research community.

Drones are juicy targets for hackers as the cost of attacks are much lower than the value of a professional drone. For instance exploiting weaknesses in the WLAN configuration costs "nothing": only a standard laptop and open source tools are needed. An SDR tool with transmission capabilities can be acquired starting from 100$, while costs for professional drones greater than 1000$ are fairly common.

Moreover, the radio protocols used by drones often transmit a unique identifier which does not change over time in unencrypted radio frames and could lead to *privacy risks* if correlated with personal information from the pilot. For this reason, standards such as the Drone Remote Identification Protocol (DRIP) from IETF make a distinction between data that must be public, such as a non-spoofable identifier, and data that must only be accessible to authorized parties such as law enforcement personnel (Card et al., 2020 - Privacy requirements and Privacy considerations sections).

Attacks on Autonomous Navigation Features

High-end drones have various sensors to automatically avoid obstacles or navigate autonomously by following a flight plan. While it is not always easy to put in place in practice, it was demonstrated that all those sensors can be remotely attacked in some way.

Radio: Location Spoofing

Similar to the connected car case (Murray, 2019), drones that rely on the Global Positioning System (GPS) or the Global Navigation Satellite System (GNSS) for long distance guidance are vulnerable to attacks. The GNSS protocol does not include any means of proving that a message comes from a satellite rather than from an illegitimate source. Indeed, messages are neither authenticated nor encrypted, except in military implementations, and can therefore be spoofed. In particular, altered GPS L1 band data streams can be generated using open source software such as GPS-SDR-SIM (Version 1.0, 2018) and then converted to RF waves with a SDR tool. Hopefully, GNSS signals will become more trustworthy with the arrival of new GNSS satellites. For instance, the Galileo satellite system in Europe will offer authentication of location data for civilians.

Radio: Control Jamming

Like any product using radio signals, drones are vulnerable to jamming. A strong radio signal emitted at the right frequency will prevent the drone from sending (and/or receiving) messages to/from its controller. In such a case, drones may adopt a predefined behavior such as landing (which may facilitate theft of the drone) or going back to a given location (typically, the base). Some commercial "jamming rifles" are available and may send a directional jamming signal at a distance of several kilometers.

Acoustic: Acceleration Spoofing

Gyroscopes and accelerometers are sensitive to ultrasound at their resonant frequency. Emitting sound by a powerful speaker located not far from the drone can therefore alter its trajectory. It is notably possible to force a drone to land by spoofing its gyroscope's output to maximum values (Son et al., 2015).

Optical: Obstacle Simulation

Some drones rely on data acquired through their camera(s) to stabilize themselves or avoid obstacles. By projecting an image on the ground floor using a laser, some drone models may be induced to drift in order to avoid a non-existent obstacle (Davidson et al., 2016).

Saturating the optical receiver by pointing a laser directly at it might be another threat, although pointing the laser at the right spot may be tricky if the drone is moving.

Summary of Threats

Threats commonly reported for IoT and autonomous vehicles also apply to drones. They put essential security properties at risk as shown in Table 1.

Table 1. Summary of threats

Confidentiality and Privacy	Theft of multimedia data (video, photo) acquired by the drone and stored locally or sent over the air. Tracking of a drone's location based on its unique identifier.
Integrity	Spoofing of radio commands sent to a drone. Spoofing of data processed by sensors involved in autonomous navigation (GNSS, accelerometer, and camera). Modification of software running on the drone or its controller.
Availability	Disconnection of end user from the drone, completely or partially (e.g., disconnect video but not engine control). Sending the drone back to base or destroying it.
Safety	Causing an accident by crashing the drone.

Attacks Using Drones

Using Drone Built-in Features for Attacks

Spying is one of the first obvious attacks leveraging drones. Concretely, the ability of the drone to maneuver in three dimensions allows it to bypass many restrictions protecting against illegitimate access for pedestrians and vehicles located at ground level (e.g., fence, access control at the entrance of a building). The built-in camera found in a very large percentage of drones allows acquiring video footage impacting confidentiality and privacy.

More insidious are *psychological attacks*, as a drone simply hovering near someone can cause them distraction and anxiety.

Kinetic attacks also allow using the drone itself as a projectile and crashing it in a target. This could lead to destruction of property or human harm, e.g., if the drone is intentionally flown in the middle of cars on a highway or collides with an airplane. While commercial drones often come with no-fly zones, those may be bypassed (e.g., by modifying a mobile application used to control the drone). Some expensive drones are also designed specifically as weapons, notably for warfare (Lasconjarias & Maged, 2019).

Using Drones With Transport Features For Criminal Purposes

Some professional drones are designed to carry a payload that can weigh several kilograms (proportional to the weight of the drone itself). This class of drones can be used to provide services, e.g., to deliver packages, after regulatory approval (Amazon Prime Air).

Over the years, such drones have been used for various crimes such as smuggling cocaine, dropping nails, transporting radioactive sand (Associated Press, 2015), or carrying bombs (Herrero & Casey, 2018). Critical infrastructures like datacenters or telecommunication antennas do not have effective counter measures against such airborne attacks, and could become targets. Greenpeace demonstrated lack of protections against drones by crashing an UAV into a nuclear power plant (De Clercq, 2018).

Customizing or Building A Drone For Cyber Attacks

Drones can be used to perform cyber-attacks using some low-cost hardware. For instance, the Kali Drone is a drone on which a cheap Raspberry Pi unit with Kali Linux is installed (Long, 2017). This operating system, popular among security pentesters, is preloaded with tools to exploit vulnerabilities in IT systems by connecting to poorly secured radio links.

The lack of security for radio protocols may be based on the assumption that there is no risk because the attacker cannot get within radio range since access to the premises is controlled. This assumption is often false if there are no anti-drone mechanisms in place. This may lead to intrusions on some systems with dramatic impact, from theft of intellectual property to denial of service or installation of spyware.

Overall, many types of wireless attacks could be carried by a drone equipped with multiple transmitters/receivers optimized for different wireless protocols or a multi-purpose SDR tool more customizable for attacks, especially on proprietary protocols, but less cost-efficient. The drone could be steered until it found a vulnerable target. For instance:

- Join unsecure networks, e.g., open WLAN hotspots.
- Sniff unencrypted traffic, e.g., Bluetooth Low Energy (BLE) traffic, and extract information.
- Connect to devices that enter in pairing mode without authentication, e.g., WPS push, Digital Enhanced Cordless Telecommunications - Ultra Low Energy (DECT-ULE), easy pairing, BLE Just Works.
- Use a laser to trigger remote commands on a vocal assistant (Brewster, 2019).
- Record and replay commands used by unsecure proprietary RF protocols, e.g., remotes that control shutters in a building.

- Exploit vulnerabilities in radio protocols, e.g., KRACK and Kr00k attacks on WLAN (Čermák et al., 2020; *Key Reinstallation Attacks,* 2017); or KNOB attack on BLE (*KNOB Attack*, 2019).
- Jam radio signals.

Thus, attacks using UAS extend well beyond the aircraft itself, to Internet and digital infrastructures, and to the physical world, including: use by cybercriminals, such as filming cash points (Yeung, 2016), infiltration of prisons (BBC News, 2015), chemical attacks (Crawford, 2016), etc. For a survey of best practices to protect against UAS threats, the reader is referred to (Department of Homeland Security, 2020).

SECURITY CHALLENGES AND MITIGATION TECHNIQUES

Security protection must be guaranteed throughout the UAV life-cycle. This section explores some key security challenges, both at design time and at run time. Counter-measures are also discussed.

Design-Time Challenges: Supply Chain Security

Threats

Compromising a drone software or hardware can be achieved through a *supply chain attack*. Hackers, competitors, and nation-state attackers target the supply chain as suppliers are often less protected against cyber-attacks than device vendors. Attackers are indeed still very heavily focused on the supply chain (Checkpoint Research, 2019).

Some companies considered to be "vital operators" by their governments are subject to special cyber security regulations that do not necessarily extend to their vendors. Unfortunately, the process of obtaining contracts in many countries often forces companies to select the vendor bidders proposing the lowest price.

Securing the software supply chain is very complex. For drones, an original and novel cyber-attack targets the fatigue life of quadcopter propellers that can be produced by using 3D printers (Azhar, 2019). The principle relies on manipulating the propeller design file of a 3D printer by compromising the controller terminal. This attack allows the drone to fly at high altitudes before the printed propeller breaks apart.

Counter-Measures

NIST recommends the following mitigation actions (Boyens, 2015; National Institute of Standards and Technology, 2018):

- Identify, establish, and assess cyber supply chain risk management processes and gain stakeholder agreement.
- Identify, prioritize, and assess suppliers and third-party supplier partners.
- Develop contracts with suppliers and third-party partners to address the organization's supply chain risk management goals.
- Routinely assess suppliers and third-party partners using audits, test results, and other forms of evaluation.

- Perform complete testing to ensure suppliers and third-party providers are able to respond to and recover from service disruption.

The NIST framework also encourages organizations to address untrustworthy partnerships in the supply chain, which may be detected through poor manufacturing, counterfeits, tampering, or malicious code. NIST describes in another report (2016) other recommended best practices.

Run-Time Challenges: Overview

To mitigate threats, a number of core security challenges must be addressed. Root causes include unsecure connectivity impacting data protection, or the unmanned nature of UAVs with safety impacts in case of UAV crash (Fotouhi et al., 2019).

Since most UAV systems heavily rely on radio communications, a major challenge is how a drone can continue to function safely, without any crashes or deviations from its mission, in case of a bad radio reception due to a jamming attack. Several techniques have been developed such as:

- Redundancy, by acquiring data from multiple sources (e.g., multiple satellites emitting on different frequencies).
- Frequency hopping, by using multiple channels for communication of command/data, coupled with detection of jammed channels.
- Odometry, to estimate the current location of a drone in the absence of a valid GNSS signal based on the data from the accelerometers.

(Tedeschi et al., 2020) also proposes an interesting approach to locate the source of a jamming and use it as a beacon for a backup position system that will allow the drone to reach its intended destination.

Different counter-measures have also been proposed for more sophisticated attacks than a simple jamming, including drone registration, data protection on the drone, secure connectivity notably in terms of confidentiality, integrity (e.g., for reliable drone tracking), traceability, or protection of the flight controller (Thales, 2018).

The next sections review some challenges such as communication security, including security between end-points and protection against GNSS threats, drone identification, and attestation. For safety, the reader may refer to (Ansys, 2019).

Communication Security

Key Agreement and Secure Tunnel Establishment

Types of UAVs

UAV models can broadly be divided in two types: *professional* devices and *commercial* off-the-shelf devices. The former type features enhanced functionalities and capabilities in terms of power supply, computation, communication range, and incorporates additional equipment (e.g., cameras, sensors) compared to the latter type. This difference is also reflected in their respective cost (see Table 2).

Table 2. Types of UAVs

	Professional UAV	**Commercial off-the-shelf UAV**
Endurance	30-120 min	10-30 min
Communication range	Up to 50 Km	From 250 m to 8 Km
Payload	3-20 Kg	≈ 0
Equipment	Multiple cameras, sensors	1-2 cameras
Price	25,000-30,000 €	40-3000 €

Security Properties

In a FANET, different links may need to be protected:

- Communication between two (or more) UAVs.
- Communication between a GCS (or a relay such as a ground radio gateway) and one (or more) UAVs.
- Communication between ground equipment (e.g., control station, radio gateway).

Depending on the FANET goals, several security properties may be required or desirable. Some required security properties are:

- **Mutual authentication:** This property guarantees the identity of the parties involved in a communication, and prevents illegitimate parties to impersonate legitimate ones.
- **Data authenticity**: This property guarantees that a message received by some party has indeed been issued by the legitimate sender – in particular that the message has not been altered during its transmission (data integrity), and is fresh (i.e., an adversary has not replayed a legitimate message).

Other security properties may be desirable, such as:

- **Data confidentiality:** This property prevents any illegitimate party to get access to the clear content of a message.
- **Resistance to Denial of Service (DoS):** This property avoids a legitimate party wasting resources (e.g., energy, time, and bandwidth) due to the action of an adversary.
- **Forward secrecy:** This property guarantees that past session keys are not compromised even if some long-term keys are disclosed.
- **Anonymity:** This property guarantees that an adversary cannot infer the identity of a legitimate party based on data sent or received by that party.

Pitfalls

A security protocol aims at providing one or several such properties. The ability to implement and execute the protocol depends on the capabilities of a party (GCS, radio relay, UAV) in terms of memory (storage of static or ephemeral parameters), computation (ability to process complex cryptographic operations), and power (to perform (heavy) computations or to transmit (long) messages on the radio link).

These technical constraints may be hard to overcome for communications established with UAVs. The UAV may lack sufficient resources to implement and execute strong cryptographic algorithms to guarantee the aforementioned security properties. However, such properties are more easily achievable by GCS or even radio gateways which benefit from heavier, traditional, computation capabilities, continuous power supply, and wireline transmission – hence, well-known security protocols such as IKEv2/IPsec (Kaufman et al., 2014; Kent & Seo, 2005), TLS 1.3 (Rescorla, 2018) or DTLS (Scheffer et al., 2015) may be applied in this case.

Regarding these constraints, FANETs are similar to other classes of IoT networks, e.g., smart home, wireless sensor network (WSN).

- A FANET aims at providing a (secure) communication link between devices (UAVs) which are self-powered, and only capable of limited computations, with the usage of a restricted memory.
- Compared to a static low-resource object, an UAV must provide enough power to execute the security scheme and ensure other functionalities (such as the radio communication), but also to deal with its own locomotion in a three-dimensional space – in contrast to a (locally) two-dimensional space in VANETs (Vehicular Ad hoc Networks).
- When security mechanisms are required (e.g., to authenticate or encrypt communications between the GCS and an UAV, or within a swarm of UAVs), they must not add a temporal delay detrimental to real-time communications. Otherwise, UAV driving could endanger the UAV and its neighbours. This timing issue is close to what can also be encountered in VANETs.

Two main strategies are usually applied to devise a security protocol intended to low-resource devices:

- One can try to enhance computational aspects of the asymmetric algorithms (e.g., storage of precomputed data) or to improve the efficiency of their implementation. What is gained on the one hand (computation cost) may be lost on the other hand (memory cost). Too much optimisation may also induce vulnerabilities allowing side channel attacks.
- One can also use symmetric-key algorithms which are notably lighter than asymmetric functions. However symmetric-key cryptography does not provide the same functionalities, hence the same security level, as public-key cryptography. Building a security protocol solely with symmetric-key functions implies that a static master secret key is used by a set of parties (UAVs, GCS). The security of the whole system then depends on that master key whose disclosure compromises the whole FANET.

Another possibility is to use additional hardware components powerful enough to execute complex cryptographic operations, which makes (heavy) asymmetric schemes functional on the device. However, the corresponding circuitry must be implemented (in software or in hardware), and additional power delivered. For UAVs, this extra weight must be carried, which reduces the UAV endurance.

Overall, the dilemma is finding a trade-off between security and efficiency. Very often, the latter is chosen at the cost of the former.

Solutions

Several schemes have been proposed to protect a FANET. Most of them aim at securing the communication between UAVs or between a GCS and UAVs, and consider commercial off-the-shelf UAVs.

The proposals aim at providing different security properties and functionalities. The focus is put on two main properties: key agreement (Frymann & Manulis, 2019; Ozmen et al., 2018; Podhradsky et al., 2017; Semal et al., 2018) and secure tunnelling (i.e., exchange of confidential and authenticated messages) (Frymann & Manulis, 2019; He et al., 2017; Ozmen et al., 2018; Podhradsky et al., 2017).

Additional properties are also considered: anonymity (with pseudonyms) (He et al., 2017; Semal et al., 2018), revocation (with a timestamp associated to the private key) (Semal et al., 2018), forward secrecy (using ephemeral secret parameters in the session key computation) (Semal et al., 2018), resistance to DoS (with additional secret keys or puzzles to solve prior to continuing the protocol) (Frymann & Manulis, 2019; He et al., 2017).

The protocol designers consider different kinds of UAV with respect to their cryptographic capabilities. Asymmetric algorithms are conceivable if one deems that an UAV is powerful enough to execute them (Semal et al., 2018), or if the UAV is able to carry a hardware module with sufficient computation capability to perform complex operations (He et al., 2017). Depending on the latter, the authors suggest different strategies to compensate for the lack of the UAV capabilities.

Memory Storage: If memory storage is an issue, and when public key cryptography is deemed efficient enough, a *certificate-less* public key can be preferred (Semal et al., 2018) which dispenses from transmitting, storing, and using certificates. The corresponding private key "embeds" a secret parameter (related to a central authority). The central authority's public key is involved in message encryption. This implicitly guarantees the authenticity of the key during the decryption procedure. Likewise, an *identity-based scheme* can be executed (He et al., 2017). The identity of each party is then used as its public key. The drawback of both schemes is that the private keys (and, in the first case, the public keys) of all UAVs are computed by a central authority.

Computations: To reduce the amount (and the complexity) of computations, *precomputed data* are stored in memory (Ozmen et al., 2018). This allows replacing elliptic curve point multiplications with point additions when encrypting and signing data. Alternatively, a *sign-cryption* scheme can be executed (He et al., 2017). This allows encrypting and signing data at the same time, at a reduced cost compared to "classical", distinct encryption and signature (public key) algorithms.

If the heavy computations implied by public key schemes are deemed as unbearable, one can leverage the "lightweightness" of symmetric-key algorithms (compared to asymmetric cryptography), and build security schemes solely on such functions (Frymann & Manulis, 2019; Podhradsky et al., 2017). The drawback is that a central authority is needed at least during the initialization of the system (e.g., secret key distribution), and optionally during the online phase (establishment of a secure tunnel between UAVs). Moreover, the security schemes based on symmetric-key functions usually suffer from the intrinsic differences that separate symmetric-key from public key cryptography: they do not provide the same security level (and functionalities). In particular they do not guarantee forward secrecy.

Bandwidth: One way to reduce the amount of application messages sent by an UAV is to send one message only to several receivers. This can be done when the different parties share the same group session key (Semal et al., 2018), or by applying a *broadcast encryption scheme* (in such case, each party can decrypt the same encrypted message using its own private key) (He et al., 2017).

Different security protocols are compared in Table 3. The following notations are used:

Table 3. Comparison between several security protocols for FANETs

	(Podhradsky et al., 2017)	*(He et al., 2017)*	*(Semal et al., 2018)*	*(Ozmen et al., 2018)*	*(Frymann & Manulis, 2019)*
Mutual authentication	○	◖	○	○	○
Mutual key agreement	○	●	○		○
Key freshness	○	●	○	○	○
Entity revocation	●	●	◖	●	●
Anonymity	○	◖	○	●	●
Forward secrecy	●	●	○	●	●
Secure tunnel	○	◖	●	◖	○
Message confidentiality	○	○	●	○	○
Message authenticity	◖	◖	●	◖	○
Resistance to DoS	◖	◖	●	●	◖
Symmetric-key functions only	○	●	●	●	○
Security arguments	●	○	○	○	○
No additional hardware	○	◖	◖	◖	○
Evaluation of the protocol	●	●	●	●	○
Central authority	●	○	○	○	●
Type of communication	P2P	P2P, swarm	Swarm	P2P	P2P
Dynamic group	●	●	●	●	●

● The property is guaranteed.

○ The property is partial, may be broken or is at least questionable.

● The property is not guaranteed.

"P2P" indicates a communication between two entities (e.g., two drones, a drone and the GCS). "Swarm" indicates a one-to-many communication. Depending on the kind of cryptographic functions, the impact of the security protocol is different.

Based on symmetric-key cryptography, the protocol described by Frymann and Manulis (2019) allows two UAVs to share a fresh session key in roughly 7 ms. Overall (key agreement and messages sent through the subsequent secure tunnel), the UAV flight time is impacted by 9.9%.

Applying the symmetric-key protocol presented by Podhradsky et al. (2017), the transmission of an authenticated and encrypted message adds a 4-ms delay, and increases the size of a typical message by 76% (37 bytes vs. 21 bytes).

In contrast, the group key agreement protocol of Semal et al. (2018) makes use of heavy asymmetric functions (pairing, operations on an elliptic curve). Two parties share a fresh session key in roughly 600 ms. This duration is proportional to the number of parties involved in the group key agreement (unless optimisations allow mutualising some computations).

Ozmen et al. (2018) use a combination of asymmetric algorithms (based on elliptic curve operations) to transport a fresh session key, and lightweight symmetric functions to protect the application message. Two platforms have been tested: 8-bit AVR ATmega 2560, and 32-bit ARM Cortex M4. With the AVR microcontroller, a message is processed in 422 ms before its transmission, and 962 ms after its reception. This translates respectively into an energy consumption of 42 mJ and 96 mJ. With the ARM microcontroller, a message is processed in 4 ms before its transmission, and 8 ms after its reception. This translates respectively into an energy consumption of 0.5 mJ and 1 mJ. These figures are obtained at the cost of the following memory usage: 41 Kbytes of precomputed data are necessary to process a message before its transmission (and 64 bytes to process a message upon reception).

While other security protocols would yield different results, this short excerpt highlights the gap between symmetric-key functions and asymmetric algorithms: the efficiency of the former is only reached with a hardware module powerful enough to implement the latter. In turn, public key cryptography provides functionalities that cannot be achieved with symmetric-key cryptography.

Note that despite the fact that the same criteria (security properties, functionalities) are used to compare all the proposals in Table 3, not all schemes aim at guaranteeing the corresponding properties and functionalities.

A focus is now made on the challenges related to the mitigation of threats for GNSS communications.

Mitigation of GNSS Spoofing Attacks

GNSS satellites including the GLObal Navigation Satellite System (GLONASS), GPS, or Galileo broadcast on their respective carrier frequencies located in three bands: L1, L2 and L5.

Several bands may be used by a given geolocation system. For instance, the GPS system, operated by the US Department of Defense (DoD) for both civilian and military use, broadcasts in all three bands.

While the use of multiple bands increases the resilience of a geolocation system, it does not in itself ensure that signals cannot be spoofed, and additional measures are required to guarantee authenticity. Unfortunately not all signals are protected today.

Considering the case of GPS: L1 is broadcast at 1,575.42 MHz, and modulated with two codes, C/A (Coarse and Acquisition code) for civilians, and P (Precise) for military use. L2 is broadcast at 1,227.60 MHz and modulated with the P code.

An anti-spoofing feature can be activated by the US DoD to prevent intentional deception of receivers. As a result, the P code is encrypted. This encrypted code is called the Y code (Carter, 1997). The code meant for civilian use on the other hand is not protected and is known to be easily spoofable using SDR tools such as version 1.0 of GPS-SDR-SIM (2018).

Additionally the drone may have to process geolocation data that is acquired both by itself and by its controller. For example in some cases the drone is controlled by a controller (e.g., smartphone) that sends its own geolocation data through radio link (e.g., WLAN) so that the drone can find its way back to the controller. If the GNSS signal acquired by the controller is spoofed, it will affect the trajectory of the drone even if the GNSS signal acquired on the drone is valid.

Detection-Only Countermeasures

Given the vulnerabilities of civilian GNSS, several studies have anticipated countermeasures for GNSS spoofing (Leccadito et al., 2018; O'Hanlon et al., 2012; Warner & Johnston, 2003; Wen et al., 2005).

An intuitive measure is to reject all signals above a given power level, since legitimate signals coming from as far as a satellite are weak. More complex measures also exist, most of them based on the analysis of different dimensions of the GNSS signals, both authentic and spoofed. They include monitoring suspicious deviations in the GNSS signal acquired over time, both at the physical layer (power and phase changes of the carriers) and logical layer (e.g., changes in time and geolocation data in the signal).

Such anti-spoofing methods can be processed in software without altering the GNSS receiver design. Therefore, in theory, such methods could be implemented as software-only solutions without any modification of the drone.

However, in practice, most current Commercial Off-the-Shelf (COTS) drones (leisure and/or low-cost commercial) are not compatible with such straightforward countermeasures without making deep modifications to the hardware. High computing capabilities may be not necessarily available or not compatible with the actual drone battery autonomy. Some countermeasures assume the use of signals from multiple bands at the level of the GNSS receiver. This feature is not always available on older GNSS or low-cost drones. To be implemented, some countermeasures require the drone to be equipped with *multi-antenna arrays*. Due to the form factor, weight, and array size, this makes difficult an implementation without compromising the drone's flying ability. Therefore, a software-only approach appears more suited to dedicated commercial drones or to be taken into account during the design stage of the drone life-cycle.

A promising approach for detection is based on *deep neural networks* (Xue et al., 2020). The main idea is to use deep learning in order to compare aerial photographs taken by the UAV with satellite imagery (drawn from a predefined dataset) corresponding to the area that the UAV is presumably flying over. A discrepancy between the two pictures denotes a spoofing attack. Results obtained from real-world experiments show that this strategy has a success rate of roughly 95% in detecting such an attack within 100 ms. This method does not require any modification on existing GPS infrastructure, structure of GPS signals, nor additional detection equipment. It is also worth noting that some UAVs (e.g., DJI Spark) can be equipped with neural computing accelerator modules (Intel, 2017).

Detection and Mitigation Countermeasures

Some countermeasures succeed in detecting and mitigating GNSS spoofing (Jafarnia-Jahromi et al., 2012). Some of them include vestigial signal detection (Humphreys et al., 2008), multi-antenna array (Daneshmand et al., 2012), and Receiver Autonomous Integrity Monitoring (RAIM) (Ledvina et al., 2001).

The most efficient mitigation technique requires *multi-antenna technology*. But this technique may be difficult to deploy on drones.

Another approach is *multi-sensor data fusion* to allow cross-checking mechanisms to avoid any integrity or availability loss (Leccadito et al., 2018). It implies sensors which communicate with each other, and a dedicated computation which may be complex and time consuming.

Discussion

It appears easier to detect GNSS spoofing rather than to mitigate it. Some results report a successful spoofing attack without triggering the GNSS receiver fault detector (Su et al., 2016). In case of unavailable GNSS during short term outages, the UAV may rely on *backup systems*, like an Inertial Navigation System (INS), a video analysis or a stationary reference point.

Apart from solutions relying on software processing (signal analysis) and antenna array (null steering technology and beamforming), the key countermeasure relies at least on authentication of the GNSS signal: *Selective Availability Anti-Spoofing Module (SAASM)* (National Research Council, 1995). This approach is available only for military applications, and relies on the encryption of the GNSS signal.

Authentication of the civilian GNSS signal cannot be practically deployed on existing constellations, as it assumes the modification of the civilian signal at the satellite level.

Galileo, the European GNSS system, plans to implement Navigation Message Authentication (NMA): users can verify that a navigation message comes from a Galileo satellite and not from a potentially malicious source. New GNSS receivers have to be developed to be compliant with the NMA signal. The European GNSS Agency (GSA) has launched funding opportunities to support the development, supply and testing of a Galileo Open Service authentication user terminal.

CHIMERA (CHips MEssage Robust Authentication) proposed by Scott technology is under testing by the Air Force Research Laboratory (AFRL) (Divis, 2019). CHIMERA involves encrypted, steganographic watermarks that are encoded into the signal by the satellite. AFRL is adding the experimental signal to the NTS-3 satellite (Navigation Technology Satellite 3), set to launch in 2022. GNSS receivers compliant with CHIMERA have also to be developed and largely deployed to ensure the success of this technology.

The many publications related to successful GPS spoofing attacks against civilian drones are proof of the absence of efficient COTS anti-spoofing module for civilian applications. Thus, GNSS spoofing remains a serious risk for service availability, confidentiality and safety.

Commercial implementations of efficient countermeasures are needed, but their deployment is probably restrained by the cost of such features and the lack of maturity of the ecosystem.

Commercial products are now available for detection, mitigation and reporting of GNSS spoofing attacks. For instance: Pyramid GNSS technology (Regulus), GPSdome (InfiniDome), and AIM+ (Advanced Interference Monitoring and Mitigation) technology (Septentrio).

Identification and Data Management

Drone identification, also known in the industry as UAS Remote Identification and tracking or UAS RID, is key to unlocking high-ROI (Return On Investment) Beyond Line of Sight (BLoS) operations. It is also the main bottleneck limiting progress on many high-priority policy goals. It should provide the ability for drone service providers to safely share the same airspace, for law enforcement officials to identify friends and foes and develop counter-drone technologies, and for populations to be assured that the drones flying near them are in compliance with local, national and supra-national laws.

Most entities involved in defining drone identification systems, such as airspace agencies, the standards body ASTM International (American Society of Testing and Materials International [ASTM], 2019) through the Committee F38, the IETF (Internet Engineering Task Force [IETF], 2020), or the GSMA (Global System for Mobile Communications [GSMA], 2018), agree with the need for both physical and electronic identifiers (ID):

- The *physical ID* is produced by the drone manufacturer at the production stage and engraved, printed or pasted directly on the drone (as a physical object).
- The *electronic ID* is obtained from the regulatory authorities when registering the drone and the pilot, for a given activity within a given airspace. This ID could also come from a UTM USS with authorization from the relevant Civil Aviation Authority. It should be electronically readable and be continuously available in near real-time during operating periods.

Two complementary approaches have been proposed for rendering the drone identifier available at any time, using remote identifiers (RID), the so-called *Broadcast RID* and *Network RID* systems.

- *Broadcast RID* refers to the information that is advertised locally directly by a drone (e.g., using Bluetooth, WLAN). The drone ID may be broadcast directly from an on-board transmitter and consumed by any party provided with adequate receiver capabilities and located in the vicinity of the flying drone. Such systems are one-direction only, with no specific destination or recipient, and do not depend on network coverage.
- *Network RID* refers to a set of information that populates dedicated remote servers, and is made globally available to any authorized third-party. The network RID approach involves transmitting the drone ID (directly from an on-board transmitter or via the GCS) over a pre-existing network infrastructure, to a server connected to the Internet, hosted in a public or private cloud infrastructure with certification by airspace authorities. This approach requires continuous connectivity, but allows parties granted access to the internet-based service to both consume and populate data (KittyHawk, 2019).

Legislation is still in progress, but tensions have already arisen between advocates of both solutions. Some drone service providers fear that the only way to resolve the situation could be to provide their drones with several ID transmission devices, thereby leading to cost, weight, and battery drainage implications. Also, remote drone identification schemes raise controversy when it comes to privacy.

In practice, the two methods are complementary and depend on the mission. Direct broadcast is appropriate for drones operating nearby, flying in visual line of sight or in a limited airspace, such as stadium or industrial campus. However, over long distances, with drones flying at higher altitude and with a greater velocity, broadcasting identification hardly makes sense. More investigation is thus required to assess to what extent RID tools can be usable without exposing private information.

Attestation

A key requirement for UAS security is to guarantee *trustworthiness* of the drone internal state, hardware and software, and of the UAV network. The objective is for instance to detect tampering on drone safety-critical systems such as the flight controller, or presence of a faulty or malicious UAV in the FANET. *Attestation* is a core primitive to meet such goals, jointly with other isolation and security mechanisms such as Trusted Execution Environments (TEE).

Some Definitions

An *attestation protocol* is a cryptographic protocol involving a target, an attester, an appraiser, and possibly other principals serving as trust proxies (Coker et al., 2011). It supplies evidence considered authoritative by the appraiser, while respecting the privacy goals of the target (or its owner).

For a dynamic fleet of drones, the GCS may be an *appraiser* and requires an *attestation* about the integrity state (the *claim)* of a new drone (the *target/attester*) before allowing it to integrate a swarm (*decision*).

Software-based attestation does not require any dedicated hardware (Gardner et al., 2009; Li et al., 2011; Seshadri et al., 2008). Such protocols are interesting for resource-constrained devices. They are subject to many attacks such as root-based attacks (i.e., a malicious program that allows a permanent and undetectable presence on a system) or compression attacks (i.e., an attacker can use available empty program memory), and usually have restrictive assumptions on adversarial capabilities (Castelluccia et al., 2009).

For drones, this class of attestation is interesting for interoperability and scalability due to hardware-independence. It still has many security vulnerabilities. The choice then depends on other parameters such as the use case (e.g., mission-critical – strict security – or entertainment – relaxed security).

Hardware-based attestation relies on specialized hardware (e.g., TPM) or on the availability of special CPU instructions to execute attestation code in a secure/trusted environment (Kovah et al., 2012; McCune et al., 2010). Such protocols provide better security guarantees, but are still vulnerable to hardware attacks (Kocher et al., 2019; Lipp et al., 2018). They also have limitations in terms of scalability and interoperability between technologies.

For drones, specialized hardware can provide enhanced security mechanisms such as secure/trusted boot, root of trust, secure storage for data and credentials, or secure cryptographic operations. It may also raise some barriers for large scale deployments. For instance:

- Can two drones using different hardware technologies securely communicate with each other?
- Are security solutions based on a given hardware technology compatible with other technologies?
- Can a GCS control a swarm where drones use different hardware technologies?

Many concerns are related to interoperability and scalability, making this type of attestation interesting, but only in small-medium drone deployments (typically for <10-50 nodes).

Hybrid attestation is based on software/hardware co-design. It provides attestation features while minimizing impact on underlying hardware. It minimizes the hardware security features required for enabling secure remote attestation. Such security features can be as simple as a ROM or MPU (Memory Protection Unit) (Brasser et al., 2015; Eldefrawy et al., 2012; Koeberl et al., 2014). It can also be a firmware-based TPM (fTPM) which provides a TPM implementation that does not require a dedicated hardware and leverages the existing trusted execution environment (Thom et al., 2011). Such solutions could have interest in large-scale deployments of drone-based services.

Attestation and Drones

Using attestation, a drone or a swarm of drones (target/attester) can prove some properties about its state to a GCS or a third party (appraiser).

A key number of properties are about *integrity attestation*:

- *Software integrity* proves the integrity of a given component/platform (European Telecommunications Standards Institute [ETSI], 2017). Integrity may be static (only on boot) (Eldefrawy et al., 2012; Kovah et al. 2012; Seshadri et al., 2008) or dynamic (anytime upon request, to detect run-time attacks).
- *Control flow attestation* attests the exact control-flow path of an executed program (Abera et al., 2016; Abera et al., 2019; Dessouky et al., 2018; Zeitouni et al. 2017). This can be used to dynamically attest the integrity of software and prevent code-reuse attacks.

- *Data integrity attestation* attests that the data has not been maliciously modified by compromised software (Abera et al., 2019). It is inherited from the integrity of the software that processed it.

More broadly, *geolocation attestation* and *proof of transit* are the ability of a particular component to assert its location (ETSI, 2017). Geolocation usually refers to geographic (physical) location. Logical location may also be an important issue to consider. For drones, a proof of transit would be the mechanism to safely prove that a given drone transited through specific/legitimate locations (e.g., delivery path).

Challenges

All attestation protocols, regardless of the claim or type of attestation, share the same challenges.

- **Efficiency**: all steps of an attestation protocol (e.g., cryptographic computation, exchanges between entities, data collection, and measurements) should have no impact: (1) on the target or attester: e.g., availability, downgrading the target service; (2) on the network: e.g., availability, overload, latency.
- **Security**: the attestation mechanism must be trustworthy to guarantee non-repudiation, provide protection against malicious forgery, and freshness of information. Secure storage of the attestation credentials and measurements should be guaranteed.
- **Privacy**: this implies trade-offs between comprehensive information and constrained disclosure.

FUTURE TRENDS

Drone security is rapidly developing. This section highlights a selection of key future trends such as: the convergence of drones with other verticals, focusing on connected and autonomous mobility, in terms of roadblocks, attack techniques, and defenses; the evolution of regulation; and impact on the Future Internet.

Convergence With Other Verticals Domains

Drone security shares roadblocks with several applications areas of mobile network infrastructures (e.g., IoT, smart cities, connected and autonomous vehicles, drones, robots). Examples of such roadblocks include device management, communication security or data protection.

Multiple technical synergies can also be identified in *managing drones and autonomous cars*. The city of Austin is conducting a series of experiments with drones (e.g., support to firemen, to first responders during massive shooting events). One of the objectives is to learn from drone-based missions to prepare the future introduction of autonomous cars in the smart city.

However, business ecosystems are not yet at the same level of maturity, drones being still at an early stage. Legal frameworks remain also significant barriers: *liability management* is more complex for autonomous vehicles that carry and strongly interact with human beings. However, some scenarios are already showing a convergence in use, e.g., to convey blood bags between hospitals in Belgium, where drones can be preferred to vehicles to avoid traffic jams (McCullough, 2019). Another prominent real-world application involving both drone and autonomous mobility ecosystems is the emergence of *air taxi services*, bringing to reality the long-standing dream of a "flying vehicle".

Using Drones to Attack Vehicles

Drones can be used to carry out *phantom attacks* against Advanced Driving Assistance Systems (ADAS) and autopilots of semi/fully autonomous cars. Vehicles, relying on sensor fusion, usually fail to validate the perceived environment as "real" from an external source. This can be exploited through the projection of *phantoms*, which are "flat" representations of a three-dimensional objects such as an obstacle, lane, or road sign. Such phantoms may be displayed on the road using a drone to trick the ADAS/autopilot into believing the obstacle is "real" (Nassi et al., 2020). The attack may trigger undesired or unsafe reactions such as emergency braking of the vehicle.

Towards Integrated Drone, Vehicular, and Space Defense

Current Vehicle-to-Everything (V2X) architectures face a number of challenges that prevent rapid deployment of smart and connected mobility technologies including: heterogeneous QoS requirements, to meet different levels of QoS imposed by various network scenarios, notably low to ultra-low latencies for safe UAS operations; unreliable connectivity, performance being degraded by low-quality links, weather conditions, network disconnections, or interferences; poor coverage, some regions being difficult to access; high mobility, to manage handoff efficiently; and interoperability to support seamless vehicular services among multiple heterogeneous standards, domains, networking technologies, and stakeholders.

While current drones do not operate in a V2X environment, integrating V2X architectures with other forms of connectivity such as drones or satellites may help meeting the aforementioned challenges – drones enhancing capacity for high-service demands, enabling regional coverage, and easy deployment, and satellites providing seamless coverage through broadcasting.

A first step is to design *integrated drone-vehicular network architectures*. For instance, cooperative vehicular aerial-ground architectures, with an aerial plane and a control plane (Zhou et al., 2015). Swarms of UAVs are grouped into an aerial sub-network that collects and transmits data from ground vehicles that form a separate vehicular sub-network. The UAV is dispatched from a ground vehicle that collects it when the mission is accomplished.

Those architectures are well adapted to search-and-rescue missions. They enhance network connectivity, as UAVs can behave as relays when ground infrastructures are no longer available. They simplify collection of information in difficult-to-reach areas, and enhance information delivery to vehicles to guide rescue teams.

Software-Defined Networking (SDN) techniques are pivotal to provide flexibility thanks to network programmability and a global, systemic, view of the network architecture and companion computation logic for proper resource allocation and dynamic policy enforcement schemes, e.g., OLSR (Optimized Link State Routing protocol, Clausen & Jacquet, 2003)-based routing policy instantiation for drone fleets. Model-driven approaches are particularly promising to mitigate the different classes of vulnerabilities from a secure routing standpoint in UAV Ad hoc Networks (UAANET), with the perspective to fully certify the communication architecture to enable commercial applications (Maxa et al., 2015).

One step further are *ground-aerial-space architectures*, with coordinated aerial (drones), space (satellites), and vehicular segments (Zhang et al., 2017). A typical hierarchical SDN-based architecture features three different data planes, one for each segment, managed by distinct SDN controllers, with also different scopes of granularity for control (e.g., local, regional, global). A second line of SDN controllers performs segment coordination to overcome data plane heterogeneity, providing seamless vehicular services and network management in the application layer.

Several challenges still remain, the first of which is security. Such SDN-based architectures are target to many threats against confidentiality, integrity, authenticity, and availability (Lacoste et al., 2019). Other challenges include ecosystem issues to reconcile business goals of various stakeholders, power consumption challenges, where trade-offs must be found between communications and flying control, regulatory barriers, and network architecture design.

Evolutions In The Regulatory Landscape

Although the future regulation is meant to be technology-agnostic, it is so far unclear how to achieve the same performance of security and safety and how to coordinate drone systems if based on radio technologies and infrastructures as different as WLAN, cellular, and satellite networks.

Many telecom vendors and operators are actively contributing to the UTM / U-Space implementation, through standardization, public-private consortia or research projects. Significant work has been achieved at the 3GPP since Release 15 to target 4G and 5G features able to support drone identification and tracking, to establish the necessary connectivity between each other and UTM – for both Visual Line of Sight (VLoS) and BVLoS, as well as to detect and to report unauthorized UAVs towards the UTM. A study on security aspects has just been started on UAS authorization, location information veracity, security of the Command and Control (C2) link and privacy. In 2020, the IETF launched a working group on drone identification, called DRIP for Drone Remote ID Protocol (Card et al., 2020). The GSMA, together with the Global UTM Association (GUTMA) launched a joint initiative to align mobile and aviation industries. Called ACJA, for Aerial Connectivity Joint Activity, this group aims to identify the potential capabilities and needs of cellular networks in unmanned traffic management and aviation, to coordinate efforts between aviation and cellular standardization, to specify minimum operational performance for drone connectivity and to design interfaces for data exchange between Mobile Network Operators (MNOs) and the UTM ecosystem.

Broader Impact on Future Internet Design

Drones are one of the key elements towards the Internet of the Future, whether for the services they provide or for extended cell coverage provisioning ("cells on wings"). Yet, *security and privacy issues* may lower the general public acceptance of drones. In particular, there is a crucial need for certification of elements of the resulting infrastructures by the competent authorities, as emphasized by the EASA (2020). A number of security issues may then result to be pretty similar to the protection of data in traditional servers or cloud infrastructures. UAVs open a number of opportunities for the "Internet of Everything (IoE)", notably for Beyond 5G networks, in terms of scalability, intelligence, and diversity, security being an intrinsic constraint that must be addressed (Liu et al., 2020).

On a more technical perspective, the following aspects deserve future research and development (Choudhary et al., 2018).

The overheads of drones in terms of memory, energy, and delays lead to several issues such as resource degradations and low efficiency. Therefore, supporting multiple tasks (in particular real-time capturing and processing of data, securing communications) with low overheads is an open challenge. In this regard dynamic load balancing can be considered as an effective solution, and a topic for further research.

Dynamic topologies and adaptive routing mechanisms facilitate on-demand and real-world applications. Such mechanisms are especially needed as fully automated systems are being increasingly developed. Likewise, one of the valuable features of drone technology, among many other, is the flexibility of deployment (Otto et al., 2018). Consequently, future research should work out dynamic planning schemes for a range of relevant drone operations.

The UAVs are particularly at risk since they are intended to evolve in a possibly adversarial environment. They must face risks of very different nature (logical, physical). Consequently the UAVs must keep their capabilities working as efficiently as possible even under attacks. The ability to keep operating in such a degraded state depends on the resilience and survivability of the UAVs (Biediger et al., 2019).

CONCLUSION

This chapter reviewed the security threats posed by drone technologies, and some protection challenges and available counter-measures for mitigation. Requirements are diverse in terms of security, privacy, infrastructure, and resource processing capabilities, depending on the wide range of existing drones.

Two broad classes of attacks may be distinguished: attacks on drones, and attacks using drones. In the former category, both professional and non-professional drones are impacted, several attacks coming from traditional IoT vulnerabilities. An acute class of threat is related to civilian *GNSS spoofing*, easy to perform at low-cost. So far, detection-only solutions are available, although some products have been emerging recently for mitigation. Overall, protection remains elementary, compared to the potential impact of threats. In the latter category, threats include spying or kinetic attacks, which may threaten critical infrastructures like data centers or network equipment. Many attacks exploit the vulnerabilities of radio protocols.

Drone security challenges are both design-time and run-time. Supply-chain attacks require revisiting contracts to avoid untrustworthy partnerships. A key end-to-end challenge is communication security in the drone system. Many cryptographic schemes are available to guarantee properties such as confidentiality, authentication, or anonymity, with hard trade-offs to find with efficiency, resource limitations, and real-time constraints. Similar trade-offs between hardware and software solutions must also be reached to guarantee the trustworthiness of the drone internal state. *Drone identification* is pivotal for safe co-existence of drones sharing a same airspace, with strong impact on regulation, public safety, and privacy.

Several challenges are common with other 5G verticals such as *connected and autonomous vehicles*. Despite different maturity levels, those two verticals increasingly share use cases. Drones are used to attack vehicles. Integrated ground-air-space SDN-based architectures are emerging for security management purposes. The regulatory framework is not definitive, but major players are highly active in public, private, and governmental sectors.

Despites threats, advances in drone technology provide new ways to collect, process, and share data, for a variety of use cases such as improving network connectivity, monitoring and maintaining network infrastructures, or for dedicated events such as crowd surveillance in sports competitions or artistic performance (e.g., drone light shows). Accordingly, the drone market has undergone sustained growth.

Key potential networking service areas include enhancing network operations for better quality of service, such as grafting a swarm of drones to a network to provide localized services, e.g., to extend network coverage or to guarantee service continuity against network failures. For security, foreseen service areas include mobile mitigation of DDoS attacks, on-site security audits and intrusion detection, GNSS spoofing mitigation, or more broadly system and network monitoring, data protection, and resilience.

A direction for deeper investigations is to better understand the relation between the drone and the connected and autonomous mobility vertical domains. Those verticals are increasingly interconnected, whether for attacks or mitigation, perhaps also extending to other forms of drones such as maritime drones.

Another direction is related to *cellular drones*, and to the specificities brought by mobile networks. So far, the drone ecosystem has remained almost exclusively centered on network topologies where all nodes are drones, controllers or GCS, using mostly WLAN technologies. Moving to a network where communications go through a trusted cellular base station independent from the drone manufacturer could bring significant benefits, e.g., for legal interception. How the challenges, solutions, and opportunities for drone security will evolve in this setting will be very interesting to monitor in the near future.

DEDICATION

In memory of our colleague Yvan, who passed away while he was contributing to this chapter.

REFERENCES

Abera, T., Asokan, N., Davi, L., Ekberg, J.-E., Nyman, T., Paverd, A., Sadeghi, A.-R., & Tsudik, G. (2016). C-FLAT: Control-Flow Attestation for Embedded Systems Software. *ACM SIGSAC Conference on Computer and Communications Security (CCS)*. 10.1145/2976749.2978358

Abera, T., Bahmani, R., Brasser, F., Ibrahim, A., Sadeghi, A.-R., & Schunter, M. (2019). DIAT: Data Integrity Attestation for Resilient Collaboration of Autonomous Systems. *Annual Network and Distributed System Security Symposium (NDSS)*. 10.14722/ndss.2019.23420

Akram, R. N., Markantonakis, K., Mayes, K., Habachi, O., Sauveron, D., Steyven, A., & Chaumette, S. (2017). Security, privacy and safety evaluation of dynamic and static fleets of drones. *IEEE/AIAA Digital Avionics Systems Conference (DASC)*.

Amazon Prime Air. (n.d.). Retrieved October 13, 2020, from https://www.amazon.com/Amazon-Prime-Air

American Society of Testing and Materials International. (2019). *Standard Specification for Remote ID and Tracking* (ASTM F3411-19). Author.

Ansys. (2019). *How to validate autonomous VTOL safety* (Ansys White Paper). Author.

Associated Press. (2015, April 22). Drone 'containing radiation' lands on roof of Japanese PM's office. *The Guardian*. https://www.theguardian.com/

Azhar, H. (2019). Challenges and Techniques in Drone Forensics. *International Conference on Cyber-Technologies and Cyber-Systems (CYBER)*.

BBC News. (2015, September 17). Warning over drone security threat to prisons. *BBC News*. https://www.bbc.com/news/

Best, K.L., Schmid, J., Tierney, S., Awan, J., Beyene, N., Holliday, M.A., Khan, R., & Lee, K. (2020). *How to Analyze the Cyber Threat from Drones: Background, Analysis Frameworks, and Analysis Tools.* RAND Corporation Research Report.

Biediger, D., Mahadev, A., & Becker, A. T. (2019). Investigating the survivability of drone swarms with flocking and swarming flight patterns using Virtual Reality. *International Conference on Automation Science and Engineering (CASE).* 10.1109/COASE.2019.8843173

Boyens, J., Paulsen, C., Moorthy, R., & Bartol, N. (2015). *Supply Chain Risk Management Practices for Federal Information Systems and Organizations.* NIST Special Publication 800-161.

Brasser, F., El Mahjoub, B., Sadeghi, A.-R., Wachsmann, C., & Koeberl, P. (2015). TyTAN: Tiny trust anchor for tiny devices. *ACM/EDAC/IEEE Design Automation Conference (DAC).* 10.1145/2744769.2744922

Brewster, T. (2019, November 5). Amazon Alexa Can Be Hacked By A Laser From 100 Meters—Is It Time To Hide Your Echo? *Forbes.* https://www.forbes.com/

Card, S. (Ed.). (2020). Drone Remote Identification Protocol (DRIP) Requirements (DRIP Internet-Draft). Academic Press.

Carter, C. (1997). *Principles of GPS: A Brief Primer on the Operation of the Global Positioning System.* Allen Osborne Associates.

Castelluccia, C., Francillon, A., Perito, D., & Soriente, C. (2009). On the difficulty of software-based attestation of embedded devices. *ACM Conference on Computer and Communications Security (CCS).* 10.1145/1653662.1653711

Čermák, M., Svorenčík, S., & Lipovský, R. (2020). *Kr00k - CVE-2019-15126 – Serious vulnerability deep inside your Wi-Fi encryption.* ESET Research White Paper.

Checkpoint Research. (2019). *Cyber Attack Trends: 2019 Mid-Year Report.* Author.

Choudhary, G., Sharma, S., Gupta, T., Kim, J., & You, I. (2018). *Internet of Drones (IoD): Threats, Vulnerability, and Security Perspectives.* CoRR abs/1808.00203.

Clausen, T. & Jacquet, P. (2003) *Optimized Link State Routing Protocol (OLSR)* (IETF RFC 3626).

Coker, G., Guttman, J., Loscocco, P., Herzog, A. L., Millen, J., O'Hanlon, B., Ramsdell, J. D., Segall, A., Sheehy, J., & Sniffen, B. T. (2011). Principles of remote attestation. *International Journal of Information Security, 10*(2), 63–81. doi:10.100710207-011-0124-7

Crawford, J. (2016, October 20). Report warns of ISIS developing drones for chemical attacks. *CNN Politics.* https://edition.cnn.com/politics

Daneshmand, S., Jafarnia-Jahromi, A., Broumandon, A., & Lachapelle, G. (2012). A Low-Complexity GPS Anti-Spoofing Method Using a Multi-Antenna Array. *International Technical Meeting of the Satellite Division of the Institute of Navigation (ION GNSS).*

Davidson, D., Wu, H., Jellinek, R., Singh, V., & Ristenpart, T. (2016). Controlling uavs with sensor input spoofing attacks. *USENIX Conference on Offensive Technologies (WOOT).*

De Clercq, G. (2018, July 3). Greenpeace crashes Superman-shaped drone into French nuclear plant. *Reuters*. https://www.reuters.com

DeDrone. (2020). *Worldwide Drone Incidents*. https://www.dedrone.com/resources/incidents/all

Department of Homeland Security, Cybersecurity and Infrastructure Security Agency. (2020). *Protecting Against the Threat of Unmanned Aircraft Systems (UAS): An Interagency Security Committee Best Practice*. Author.

Department of Homeland Security, Office of Cyber and Infrastructure Analysis. (2018). *Cybersecurity Risks Posed by Unmanned Aircraft Systems*. DHS Infrastructure Security Note.

Dessouky, G., Abera, T., Ibrahim, A., & Sadeghi, A.-R. (2018). LiteHAX: Lightweight Hardware-Assisted Attestation of Program Execution. *IEEE/ACM International Conference on Computer-Aided Design (ICCAD)*. 10.1145/3240765.3240821

Divis, D. A. (2019, June 3). New Chimera Signal Enhancement Could Spoof-Proof GPS Receivers. *Inside GNSS*. https://insidegnss.com/

Eldefrawy, K. M., Tsudik, G., Francillon, A., & Perito, D. (2012). SMART: Secure and Minimal Architecture for (Establishing Dynamic) Root of Trust. *Annual Network and Distributed System Security Symposium (NDSS)*.

Ericsson. (2018). *Drone and Networks Ensuring Safe and Secure Operations* (Ericsson White Paper No. GFMC-18:000526). Author.

European Telecommunications Standards Institute. (2017). *Report on Attestation Technologies and Practices for Secure Deployments* (ETSI GR NFV-SEC 007 V1.1.1 2017-10). Author.

European Union Aviation Safety Agency. (2020). *Opinion No 01/2020, High-level regulatory framework for the U-space* (RMT 02.30). Author.

Fotouhi, A., Qiang, H., Ding, M., Hassan, M., Giordano, L. G., García-Rodríguez, A., & Yuan, J. (2019). Survey on UAV Cellular Communications: Practical Aspects, Standardization Advancements, Regulation, and Security Challenges. *IEEE Communications Surveys and Tutorials*, 21(4), 3417–3442. doi:10.1109/COMST.2019.2906228

Frymann, N., & Manulis, M. (2019). *Securing Fleets of Consumer Drones at Low Cost*. ArXiv, abs/1912.05064.

Gardner, R., Garera, S., & Rubin, A. (2009). Detecting Code Alteration by Creating a Temporary Memory Bottleneck. *IEEE Transactions on Information Forensics and Security*, 4(4), 638–650. doi:10.1109/TIFS.2009.2033231

Global System for Mobile Communications. (2018). *Using Mobile Networks to Coordinate Unmanned Aircraft Traffic* (Report). Author.

GPS-SDR-SIM [Computer software]. (2018). *GPS-SDR-SIM documentation and source code (Version 1.0)*. https://github.com/osqzss/gps-sdr-sim

Gupta, L., Jain, R., & Vaszkun, G. (2016). Survey of Important Issues in UAV Communication Networks. *IEEE Communications Surveys and Tutorials, 18*(2), 1123–1152. doi:10.1109/COMST.2015.2495297

He, S., Wu, Q., Liu, J., Hu, W., Qin, B., & Li, Y. (2017). Secure Communications in Unmanned Aerial Vehicle Network. *Information Security Practice and Experience Conference (ISPEC)*. 10.1007/978-3-319-72359-4_37

Herrero, A. V., & Casey, N. (2018, August 4). Venezuelan President Targeted by Drone Attack, Officials Say. *The New York Times.* https://www.nytimes.com/

Humphreys, T., Ledvina, B., Psiaki, M. L., O'Hanlon, B. W., & Kintner, P. (2008). Assessing the Spoofing Threat: Development of a Portable GPS Civilian Spoofer. *International Technical Meeting of the Satellite Division of the Institute of Navigation (ION GNSS).*

InfiniDome. (n.d.). *GPSdome.* Retrieved October 13, 2020, from https://www.infinidome.com/

Intel. (2017, May 25). *Intel Movidius Myriad 2 VPU Enables Advanced Computer Vision and Deep Learning Features in Ultra-Compact DJI Spark Drone.* Retrieved January 14, 2021, from https://newsroom.intel.com

Internet Engineering Task Force. (n.d.). *Drone Remote ID Protocol (drip) Working Group.* Retrieved October 13, 2020, from https://datatracker.ietf.org/wg/drip/about/

Jafarnia-Jahromi, A., Broumandan, A., Nielsen, J., & Lachapelle, G. (2012). GPS Vulnerability to Spoofing Threats and a Review of Antispoofing Techniques. *International Journal of Navigation and Observation, 2012,* 1–16. doi:10.1155/2012/127072

Javaid, A., Sun, W., Devabhaktuni, V., & Alam, M. (2012). Cyber security threat analysis and modeling of an unmanned aerial vehicle system. *IEEE Conference on Technologies for Homeland Security (HST)* 10.1109/THS.2012.6459914

Joo, O. J. (2019). *Drones Everywhere on 5G.* GSMA IoT Innovation Summit.

Kaufman, C., Hoffman, P. Nir, Y., Eronen, P. & Kivinen, T. (2014) *Internet Key Exchange Protocol Version 2 (IKEv2).* IETF RFC 7296.

Kent, S. & Seo, K. (2005). *Security Architecture for the Internet Protocol.* IETF RFC 4301.

Key Reinstallation Attacks. (2017). Retrieved October 13, 2020, from https://www.krackattacks.com/

Khan, A. (2016). *Hacking the Drones.* Open Web Application Security Project. https://www.owasp.org/images/5/5e/OWASP201604_Drones.pdf

KittyHawk. (2019). *Remote ID & Commercial Drones: Enabling Identification and Transparency in the National Airspace.* KittyHawk White Paper.

KNOB Attack. (2019). Retrieved October 13, 2020, from https://knobattack.com/

Kocher, P., Genkin, D., Gruss, D., Haas, W., Hamburg, M., Lipp, M., Mangard, S., Prescher, T., Schwarz, M., & Yarom, Y. (2019). Spectre Attacks: Exploiting Speculative Execution. *IEEE Symposium on Security and Privacy.*

Koeberl, P., Schulz, S., Sadeghi, A.-R., & Varadharajan, V. (2014). TrustLite: a security architecture for tiny embedded devices. *EuroSys '14.*

Kopardekar, P., Rios, J., Prevot, T., Johnson, M., Jung, J., & Robinson, J. E. (2016). *Unmanned Aircraft System Traffic Management (UTM) Concept of Operations.* AIAA Aviation Technology, Integration, and Operations Conference.

Kovah, X., Kallenberg, C., Weathers, C., Herzog, A., Albin, M., & Butterworth, J. (2012). New Results for Timing-Based Attestation. *IEEE Symposium on Security and Privacy.*

Lacoste, M., Armand, D., L'Hereec, Prévost, F., Rafflé, Y., & Roché, S. (2019). Software-Defined Vehicular Networking Security: Threats & Security Opportunities for 5G. *Computer & Electronics Security Applications Rendez-vous (C&ESAR).*

Lasconjarias, G., & Maged, H. (2019) Fear the Drones: Remotely Piloted Systems and Non-State Actors in Syria and Iraq. *IRSEM Research Paper, 77*(4).

Leccadito, M. T., Bakker, T., Klenke, R., & Elks, C. (2018). A survey on securing UAS cyber physical systems. *IEEE Aerospace and Electronic Systems Magazine, 33*(10), 22–32. doi:10.1109/MAES.2018.160145

Ledvina, B., Bencze, W., Galusha, B. T., & Miller, I. (2010). An In-Line Anti-Spoofing Device for Legacy Civil GPS Receivers. *International Technical Meeting of the Institute of Navigation.*

Li, Y., McCune, J., & Perrig, A. (2011). VIPER: verifying the integrity of PERipherals' firmware. *ACM SIGSAC Conference on Computer and Communications Security (CCS).* 10.1145/2046707.2046711

Lipp, M., Schwarz, M., Gruss, D., Prescher, T., Haas, W., Fogh, A., Horn, J., Mangard, S., Kocher, P., Genkin, D., Yarom, Y., & Hamburg, M. (2018). Meltdown: Reading Kernel Memory from User Space. *USENIX Security Symposium.*

Liu, Y., Dai, H.-N., Wang, Q., Shukla, M.K., & Imram, M. (2020). *Unmanned Aerial Vehicle for Internet of Everything: Opportunities and Challenges.* ArXiv, abs/2003.13311.

Long, J. (2017, June 29). Kali Drones. Kali Drones, Portable CTF Builds, Raspberry Pi Craziness and More! *Kali Linux News.* https://www.kali.org/news/

Maxa, J.-A., Ben Mahmoud, M.-S., & Larrieu, N. (2015). Secure Routing Protocol Design for UAV Ad Hoc Networks. *IEEE/AIAA Digital Avionics Systems Conference (DASC).*

McCullough, E. (2019, August 13). New drone network service will transport blood and tissue between Belgian hospitals. *The Brussels Times.* https://www.brusselstimes.com/

McCune, J., Li, Y., Qu, N., Zhou, Z., Datta, A., Gligor, V., & Perrig, A. (2010). TrustVisor: Efficient TCB Reduction and Attestation. *IEEE Symposium on Security and Privacy.*

Murray, V. (2019). Legal Over-the-Air Spoofing of GPS and the Resulting Effects on Autonomous Vehicles. Academic Press.

Nassi, B., Nassi, D., Ben-Netanel, R., Mirsky, Y., Drokin, O., & Elovici, Y. (2020). Phantom of the ADAS: Phantom Attacks on Driver-Assistance Systems. *ACM SIGSAC Conference on Computer and Communications Security (CCS).*

Nassi, B., Shabtai, A., Masuoka, R., & Elovici, Y. (2019). *SoK - Security and Privacy in the Age of Drones: Threats, Challenges, Solution Mechanisms, and Scientific Gaps.* ArXiv, abs/1903.05155.

National Institute of Standards and Technology. (2016). *Cyber Supply Chain Best Practices (Best Practices in Cyber Supply Chain Risk Management Conference Materials).* Author.

National Institute of Standards and Technology. (2018). *Framework for Improving Critical Infrastructure Cybersecurity* (version 1.1). Author.

National Research Council. (1995). *The Global Positioning System: A Shared National Asset.* The National Academies Press. Retrieved from https://www.nap.edu/catalog/4920/the-global-positioning-system-a-shared-national-asset

O'Hanlon, B., Psiaki, M. L., Humphreys, T., & Bhatti, J. (2012). Real-Time Spoofing Detection Using Correlation Between two Civil GPS Receiver. *International Technical Meeting of the Satellite Division of the Institute of Navigation (ION GNSS).*

Otto, A., Agatz, N., Campbell, J., Golden, B., & Pesch, E. (2018). Optimization approaches for civil applications of unmanned aerial vehicles (UAVs) or aerial drones: A survey. *New Advances and Applications in Deterministic and Stochastic Network Optimization, 72*(4), 411–458. doi:10.1002/net.21818

Ozmen, M.O., Behnia, R., & Yavuz, A.A. (2019). *IoD-Crypt: A Lightweight Cryptographic Framework for Internet of Drones.* ArXiv, abs/1904.06829.

Podhradský, M., Coopmans, C., & Hoffer, N. (2017). Improving communication security of open source UAVs: Encrypting radio control link. *International Conference on Unmanned Aircraft Systems (ICUAS).* 10.1109/ICUAS.2017.7991460

Raja, Z. (2020). *Security specialists trick Tesla's Computer Vision algorithm with a drone and a projector.* Retrieved from https://www.talentometry.co.uk/blog/technology/security-specialists-trick-teslas-computer-vision-algorithm-with-a-drone-and-a-projector/

Regulus. (n.d.). *Pyramid GNSS.* Retrieved October 13, 2020, from https://www.regulus.com/solutions/pyramid-gnss/

Rescorla, E. (2018). *The Transport Layer Security (TLS) Protocol Version 1.3.* IETF RFC 8446.

Rodday, N. (2016). *Hacking a professional drone.* Black Hat Asia.

Russon, M.-A. (2016). *NASA Drone Hack Revealed.* https://www.uasvision.com/2016/02/02/nasa-drone-hack-revealed/

Rydén, H., Redhwan, S.B., & Lin, X. (2018). *Rogue Drone Detection: A Machine Learning Approach.* ArXiv, abs/1805.05138.

Scheffer, Y., Holz, R. & Saint-Andre, P. (2015). *Recommendations for Secure Use of Transport Layer Security (TLS) and Datagram Transport Layer Security (DTLS).* IETF RFC 7525)

Semal, B., Markantonakis, K., & Akram, R. (2018). A Certificateless Group Authenticated Key Agreement Protocol for Secure Communication in Untrusted UAV Networks. *IEEE/AIAA 37th Digital Avionics Systems Conference (DASC).*

Septentrio. (n.d.). *Advanced Interference Monitoring & Mitigation (AIM+)*. Retrieved October 13, 2020, from https://www.septentrio.com/en/advanced-interference-monitoring-mitigation-aim

Seshadri, A., Luk, M., & Perrig, A. (2011). SAKE: Software attestation for key establishment in sensor networks. *Ad Hoc Networks*, *9*(6), 1059–1067. doi:10.1016/j.adhoc.2010.08.011

Son, Y., Shin, H., Kim, D., Park, Y., Noh, J., Choi, K., Choi, J., & Kim, Y. (2015). Rocking Drones with Intentional Sound Noise on Gyroscopic Sensors. *USENIX Security Symposium.*

Su, J., He, J., Cheng, P., & Chen, J. (2016). A Stealthy GPS Spoofing Strategy for Manipulating the Trajectory of an Unmanned Aerial Vehicle. *IFAC-PapersOnLine*, *49*(22), 291–296. doi:10.1016/j.ifacol.2016.10.412

Tedeschi, P., Oligeri, G., & Di Pietro, R. (2020). Leveraging Jamming to Help Drones Complete Their Mission. *IEEE Access: Practical Innovations, Open Solutions*, *8*, 5049–5064. doi:10.1109/ACCESS.2019.2963105

Thales. (2018). *7 Key Factors for Enabling Trust in the Drone Ecosystem*. https://dis-blog.thalesgroup.com/iot/2018/03/08/7-key-factors-for-enabling-trust-in-the-drone-ecosystem/

Thom, S., Cox, J., Linsley, D., Nystrom, M., Raj, H., Robinson, D., Saroiu, S., Spiger, R., & Wolman, A. (2011). *Firmware-based trusted platform module for arm processor architectures and trustzone security extensions*. US Patent No. 8,375,221 B1. Washington, DC: U.S.

Vodafone. (2018). *The rise of drones*. Vodafone White Paper.

Warner, J. S., & Johnston, R. (2003). GPS Spoofing Countermeasures. *Homeland Security Journal*, *25*(2), 19–27.

Wen, H., Huang, P. Y., Dyer, J., Archinal, A., & Fagan, J. (2005). Countermeasures for GPS Signal Spoofing. *International Technical Meeting of the Satellite Division of the Institute of Navigation.*

Xue, N., Niu, L., Hong, X., Li, Z., Hoffaeller, L., & Pöpper, C. (2020). DeepSIM: GPS Spoofing Detection on UAVs using Satellite Imagery Matching. *Annual Computer Security Applications Conference (ACSAC)*. 10.1145/3427228.3427254

Yeung, P. (2016, August 7). Drone reports to UK police soar 352% in a year amid urgent calls for regulation. *The Independent*. https://www.independent.co.uk/

Zeitouni, S., Dessouky, G., Arias, O., Sullivan, D., Ibrahim, A., Jin, Y., & Sadeghi, A. (2017). ATRIUM: Runtime attestation resilient under memory attacks. *IEEE/ACM International Conference on Computer-Aided Design (ICCAD)*. 10.1109/ICCAD.2017.8203803

Zhang, N., Zhang, S., Yang, P., Alhussein, O., Zhuang, W., & Shen, X. (2017). Software Defined Space-Air-Ground Integrated Vehicular Networks: Challenges and Solutions. *IEEE Communications Magazine*, *55*(7), 101–109. doi:10.1109/MCOM.2017.1601156

Zhou, Y., Cheng, N., Lu, N., & Shen, X. (2015). Multi-UAV-Aided Networks: Aerial-Ground Cooperative Vehicular Networking Architecture. *IEEE Vehicular Technology Magazine*, *10*(4), 36–44. doi:10.1109/MVT.2015.2481560

ADDITIONAL READING

Cofer, D., Gacek, A., Backes, J. D., Whalen, M. W., Pike, L., Foltzer, A., Podhradský, M., Klein, G., Kuz, I., Andronick, J., Heiser, G., & Stuart, D. (2018). A Formal Approach to Constructing Secure Air Vehicle Software. *Computer, 51*(11), 14–23. doi:10.1109/MC.2018.2876051

Dey, V., Pudi, V., Chattopadhyay, A., & Elovici, Y. (2018). Security Vulnerabilities of Unmanned Aerial Vehicles and Countermeasures: An Experimental Study. *International Conference on VLSI Design and 2018 17th International Conference on Embedded Systems (VLSID)*. 10.1109/VLSID.2018.97

Du, S., Lu, T., Zhao, L., Xu, B. S., Guo, X., & Yang, H. (2013). Towards An Analysis of Software Supply Chain Risk Management. *World Congress on Engineering and Computer Science.*

Guerber, C., Larrieu, N., & Royer, M. (2019). Software defined network based architecture to improve security in a swarm of drones. *International Conference on Unmanned Aircraft Systems*. 10.1109/ICUAS.2019.8797834

Mansfield, K., Eveleigh, T., Holzer, T., & Sarkani, S. (2015). DoD Comprehensive Military Unmanned Aerial Vehicle Smart Device Ground Control Station Threat Model. *Defense Acquisition Research Journal, 22*, 240–273.

Secinti, G., Darian, P. B., Canberk, B., & Chowdhury, K. (2018). SDNs in the Sky: Robust End-to-End Connectivity for Aerial Vehicular Networks. *IEEE Communications Magazine, 56*(1), 16–21. doi:10.1109/MCOM.2017.1700456

Shi, W., Zhou, H., Li, J., Xu, W., Zhang, N., & Shen, X. (2018). Drone Assisted Vehicular Networks: Architecture, Challenges and Opportunities. *IEEE Network, 32*(3), 130–137. doi:10.1109/MNET.2017.1700206

KEY TERMS AND DEFINITIONS

Attestation: A security protocol enabling to guarantee trustworthiness of the drone internal state, hardware and software, and of the UAV network.

Broadcast Remote Identification: The information identifying a drone that is advertised locally directly by the drone itself.

Drone: An airborne device formed of an aerial node that may cooperate with a number of ground nodes used in civilian and military applications. *Synonyms:* Unmanned Aerial Vehicle (UAV).

Fleet of Drones: Multiple drones flying together to complete the same mission, usually coordinating through wireless communications. *Synonyms:* Network of UAVs, swarm of drones.

Global Navigation Satellite System Spoofing: An attack where the signal coming from satellite systems such as GPS for long distance guidance of drones is forged.

Network Remote Identification: The information identifying a drone made globally available to any authorized third-party and transmitted on network infrastructures to remote servers.

Secure Tunneling: A security protocol allowing entities in a drone system to exchange application-level messages with confidentiality and authenticity guarantees.

Supply Chain Attack: A design-time attack against drone software or hardware due to threats against untrustworthy suppliers, often less protected than device vendors.

UAS Traffic Management: The UTM is the minimal set of rules and services to enable safe and efficient low-altitude drone operations for all individuals and businesses. *Synonym:* U-Space, based upon the UTM but more ambitious.

ENDNOTE

[1]   Depending on the standardization organization, the specific terminology related to drones may vary. For instance, ICAO considers UAV as deprecated for Unmanned Aircraft (UA), as ICAO is aviation-oriented. ITU and 3GPP may still keep UAV, as those organizations have strong background in ground vehicles and consider how drones could become airborne.

Chapter 14
Security Risk Assessments and Shortfalls for Evaluating and Protecting Dynamic Autonomic Systems in Future Internet

Hamid Asgari

(iD) https://orcid.org/0000-0002-9317-7045

Thales UK Research, Technology, and Innovation, UK

ABSTRACT

Methodologically-sound security assessments are crucial for understanding a system in fulfilling the requirements, realizing its behavior, and identifying implications. A system is made resilient if and only if there is enduring confidence that it will function as expected. It is cyber secure if it displays this property in the face of an adversary. This chapter provides an explanation of various static security risk assessment methodologies (SSRAM) having long epochs for assessing and revisiting the risks and explains their strengths and weaknesses. The SSRAM will form the basis for elaborating on dynamic security risk assessment methodologies that must have very short epochs depending on the emergent threats and vulnerabilities to combat new or evolving threats. This is essential for handling cyber security of dynamic complex systems including future networks having a number of self-managing properties including self-protection for defending against malicious attacks.

INTRODUCTION

Security threats are associated to vulnerabilities of systems and networks that can be exploited by attackers. There are several types of attacks on communication networks including disrupting or blocking communications, intercepting, injecting fabricated packets, accessing and modifying the information. Any intrusion or attacks on the networks or information systems in order to exploit vulnerabilities may have undesirable consequences. Existing network security approaches do not provide tight integration of network/system functions and security controls to properly countermeasure the attacks. Therefore,

DOI: 10.4018/978-1-7998-7646-5.ch014

new innovative ways of protecting networks against attacks are required, i.e., by embedding the security functions in the fabric of network systems to address the shortcomings.

In any new network architecture designs, programmability, the ability to dynamically configure, control, and combine network and security functions in particular, is regarded as a key feature to create resilient network systems for preventing or reducing the impact of attacks. Here, a new network system refers to a system consists of many elements interacting with each other that enable communication among nodes occur. It includes existing functionality that a network has plus the functionality in adapting or reacting to the pattern these elements create or external environment trigger, could exhibit non-deterministic behavior, and may evolve. Methodologically sound security assessments are crucial for understanding a network system in fulfilling the needs, realizing its behavior, and identifying the possible implications. This is to identify run-time threats, assess the impact and likelihood of occurrence of attacks relevant to the threats, evaluate the design principles, and validate the built-in security enablers and the mitigation actions that are devised to combat such attacks. In general, the use of a structured methodological approach for identifying threats and assessing the associated risks in the network systems is crucial. Undertaking security risk assessment in a structured way means making more accurate design decisions about the resilience of a system's services and functions and avoiding costly security incidents during a system's operation. As a reminder, the three main security requirements specified for consideration in information systems are: to prevent unauthorized information disclosure (confidentiality) and improper malicious modifications of information (integrity), while ensuring access to authorized entities (availability).

The successful deployment of complex systems including network systems represents one of the most significant engineering challenges of our time. Cyber security of highly connected systems presents specific challenges than the security realized by conventional systems. This chapter provides a review of various Static Security Risk Assessment Methodologies (SSRAM) that are aimed at Information Communication Technology (ICT) systems and explains their strengths and weaknesses and their shortcomings towards assessing cyber security risks of these systems. These are called static as the security analysis is static, assumes that the system is built to a specification, and epochs for assessing and revisiting the risks are long (e.g., weeks, months).

However, for a dynamic or autonomic system, its behavior may evolve over time. This means that activities to assure an autonomic function cannot simply be performed once and remain valid for the operational lifetime of the system.

Autonomic computing was used first by IBM to describe computing systems that are self-managing or self-adaptive. Self-managing, refers to systems that will "maintain and adjust their operation in the face of changing components, workloads, demands and external conditions and in the face of hardware and software failures both non-intentional and malicious" (Kephart, 2003). Four main properties of self-management were established by IBM:

- Self-configuration: An autonomic system will alleviate challenges that are faced with by configuring itself according to high level goals automatically, e.g. new introduced components will blend in with the rest of the system and the systems will adapt to the presence of the new component.
- Self-optimisation: this aims at experimenting, identifying and selecting adequate tuning parameters to optimise the use of resources, hence increasing efficiency.
- Self-healing: it detects, diagnose and repair the root cause of failures, using knowledge about the system configuration and monitoring data.

- Self-protection: it detects, or even anticipates, and defends the system against malicious attacks or system failures uncorrected by the self-healing property.

A key aspect of self-managing/autonomic systems is that decisions are moved towards runtime to control behavior in response to dynamic stimuli. This is where dynamic risk assessment plays its role.

It is believed that Dynamic Security Risk Assessment Methodologies (DSRAM) are essential for handling cyber security of future connected systems that are composed of self-managing functions. Therefore, the objectives set for this chapter are:

- To introduce SSRAM standards and methodologies.
- To provide guidelines for the engineers/consultants in selecting a SSRAM methodology suitable for their context and application types.
- To provide a basis for further work on Dynamic Security Risk Assessment Methodology (DSRAM) that must have very short epochs depending on the emergent threats and vulnerabilities.

In this chapter, we provide an overview of risk assessment standards and methodologies/tools including their application areas. This chapter also provides the steps covered by risk assessment methodologies and compares and contrasts the introduced methodologies, in particular looking at the benefits of each and their applicability depending on the context/scenario. Finally, we look at the need for conducting DSRAM for high dynamic domains with systems that include autonomy functions.

Risk Assessment Types

Risk assessment can be quantitative, qualitative, or semi-quantitative as described below.

Qualitative assessment uses descriptive variables to express the probability of an event occurring and the consequences of risk. An immediate improvement can be realized using this approach and it does not require an accurate calculation of the network system's asset value or the cost of realizing the mitigation plans. The disadvantages are that the result is often inaccurate and it is difficult to calculate the cost effectiveness of the risk management process.

Quantitative assessment uses numerical variables to describe the probability of an event occurring and the loss that may be incurred. This has the advantage of being the most detailed approach and helps to calculate the cost effectiveness of the risk management process. The disadvantages are that it requires too much time and resources and the precision of impacts are unclear, requiring further interpretation.

Semi-quantitative assessment is a compromise between the previous two approaches, with numerical values to estimate risk and descriptive variables to interpret the results. This combination approach has the advantage of being able to classify the probability and consequence of risk using quantitative categories. The disadvantage is that the risk usually gets placed into broad categories.

SECURITY RISK ASSESSMENT STANDARDS

ISO/IEC Standards

The International Standards Organization (ISO) and International Electrotechnical Commission (IEC) jointly publish information security standards. The full ISO/IEC 27000-series standards list is available in (ISO, 2018). The most relevant standards for information security are listed below:

- ISO/IEC 27001: a framework for information security management (ISO, 2013). It is a general IT security standard rather than a specific cyber security standard.
- ISO/IEC 27002, 2017 revision: a code of practice for information security controls.
- ISO/IEC 27005: as part of the ISO 27000 family of standards is the information security risk management standard used commercially and in government organizations (ISO, 2018). ISO 27005 framework provides guidance for defining the scope and boundaries of the security risk management, and hence for the threat identification. ISO 27005 requires as input "*all information about the organization relevant to the context establishment*". While ISO 27005 provides a framework focusing on a single "organization" for establishment of the context, no method is defined by the standard. While the definition of organization can span different entities, the standard is typically applied within a context of a single organizational unit or the entire organization. ISO 27005 provides a systematic, structured risk assessment process, which defines the steps required without being prescriptive, allowing organizations to select their own approach to risk assessment. For example, it allows both qualitative and quantitative approaches for estimating risk. The first step of the process is identifying assets and classifying them into primary and supporting assets, followed by threat identification and profiling. The process then identifies existing controls, which are then taken into account in the assessment of vulnerabilities and consequences. The final step is risk estimation and evaluation. The standard also lacks a clear separation between the concepts of primary assets and supporting assets to be protected, feared events and threat scenarios.

A number of Codes of Practices (CoP) and guidelines are also published, e.g.:

- ISO/IEC 27017: a code of practice for 37 of the information security controls in ISO/IEC 27002, 2017 revision plus 7 new controls for cloud services (ISO, 2020).
- ISO/IEC 27018: a code of practice for protection of personally identifiable information (PII) in public clouds.
- ISO/IEC 27032; 2012 revision: guidelines for cyber security. This CoP document addresses Internet security issues and provides technical guidance for addressing common Internet security risks.
- ISO/IEC 31010 – Risk management — Risk assessment techniques: the standard that specifies 31 risk assessment techniques (ISO, 2019).

British Standards Institution (BSI)

The British Standards Institution (BSI) group has a role as the UK National Standards Body which extends to the international standards community to help industries in 182 countries worldwide in developing their own standards (BSI, 2020a). In (BSI, 2020b), a list of relevant BSI and ISO standards is given on the cyber security subject area including:

- BS 31111:2018 standard is about cyber risk and resilience and provides guidance for risk management professionals. It is to protect organizations and their stakeholders from the consequences of cyber-related failures and errors as well as malicious cyber-attacks.
- BS 7799-3:2017 standard describes information security management systems and provides guidelines for information security risk management.

Information Security Forum (ISF)

The Information Security Forum (ISF, 2020) is one of the world's leading authorities on cyber, information security and risk management. As well as conducting research and providing consultancy services they provide tools and methodologies which organizations can use to deploy their security and risk management strategies; ISF's IRAM2 tool is one such example that is described in the Risk Assessment Methodologies/Tools section.

National Institute of Standards and Technology (NIST)

NIST (National Institute of Standards and Technology) provides engineering principles for information technology security in its Technical Report 800-27 Revision A for establishing a security baseline (NIST, 2004) which was superseded by SP 800-160 in 2016. NIST Special Publication (SP) information security standard is NIST SP 800-39 (NIST, 2011). This provides guidance for managing information security risk to organizational operations, assets, individuals, other organizations, and the Nation resulting from operation and the use of federal information systems. NIST SP 800-39 is used to frame the risks, i.e., to establish the context, assess risk, respond to and monitor risk and is supplemented by a series of security standards and guidelines necessary for managing information security risk, as defined below:

- NIST SP 800-30 "Guide for Conducting Risk Assessments". It provides guidance relating to federal information systems organizations. NIST Special Publication (SP) 800-30 provides guidance for conducting risk assessments of an organization's information systems. It is the US government's preferred risk assessment methodology and is mandated for US government agencies. It is intended to be consistent with the ISO standards. NIST SP 800-30 provides a detailed step-by-step process that starts with establishing the context, scope, assumptions, and key information sources before performing the assessment and uses identified threats and vulnerabilities to determine likelihood, impact and risk. The steps are continued to communicate the results and to maintain the assessment, which includes monitoring the effectiveness of controls and verifying compliance. However, like other standards aimed at IT systems, NIST SP 800-30 does not provide additional guidance for safety-critical systems, such as connected automotive systems. As an example, a study looked at impact-oriented risk assessment of in-vehicle networks (Kelarestaghi, 2019) and incorporated the NIST SP 800-30 model. It suggests that NIST SP 800-30 is a suitable methodology for automotive cyber security.

Other relevant NIST publications are:

- NIST SP 800-37 Rev. 2, 2018 – Risk Management Framework for Information Systems and Organizations: A System Life Cycle Approach for Security and Privacy
- NIST SP 800-53A – Rev. 5, 2020, Security and Privacy Controls for Information Systems and Organizations.

Other Security Standards

Table 1 shows a list of some of the SSRAM security standards that have relevance to the topics in this chapter.

Table 1. A list of relevant standards

Standard Number	Title/Description
BSI: PAS 1192-5:2015	Specification for security-minded building information modeling – digital built environments and smart asset management
BS EN ISO/IEC 27042:2016	Information technology – Security techniques – Guidelines for the analysis and interpretation of digital evidence
BSI: PAS 1085:2018	Establishing and implementing a security-minded approach – Specification
BS EN IEC 62443: 2018	Security for industrial automation and control systems
BS 10754: 2018	Information technology – Systems trustworthiness – Governance and management specification
ISO/IEC 15026-2:2011	Systems and software engineering – Systems and software assurance – Part 2: Assurance case
ISO/IEC 27037: 2012	Information technology – Security techniques – Guidelines for identification, collection, acquisition and preservation of digital evidence
ISO/IEC TS 17961:2013	Information technology – Programming languages, their environments and system software interfaces – C secure coding rules
ISO/IEC TR 24772:2013	Information technology – Programming languages – Guidance to avoiding vulnerabilities in programming languages through language selection and use
ISO 55000: 2014	Asset management – Overview, principles and terminology
ISO/IEC/IEEE 15288:2015	Systems and software engineering – System life cycle processes
ISO/IEC 27035-1: 2016	Information technology – Security techniques – Information security incident management
ISO/IEC 29147:2018	Information technology – Security techniques – Vulnerability disclosure
ISO 22300:2018	Security and resilience – Vocabulary
NATO: AC/35-D/2005-REV3	The (NATO, 2015) document provides guidelines for security risk assessment and risk management processes that shall follow a structured approach (either carried out manually or using an automated tool). Qualitative Risk Assessment methodology is the approach that has been adopted by leading engineering organizations and possibly by NATO (Piper, 2020).

Risk Assessment Methodologies/Tools

The following sub-section identifies some known risk assessment methodologies that may be used in a security context. These risk assessment methodologies are aimed at any Critical Information Infrastructure (CII). CII is the computer and communication networks within a country's national critical infrastructures which enables various national sectors to function. CII is also referred to those computer resource, incapacitation or destruction of which, shall have debilitating on national security, public health or safety". The critical sectors include banking and financial sectors, telecom among others.

SecRAM (Security Risk Assessment Methodology)

SecRAM (SecRAM, 2017) is a well-defined risk assessment methodology based on the ISO 27005 developed by the SESAR program (SESAR, 2020) and is compatible with existing methodologies. SecRAM methodology requires establishing the context for defining the boundaries of what one wants to analyze; sets out the scope of the security analysis; and specifies the criteria that will be used to assess the risk, in order to provide consistent and defensible results. It facilitates integration of security from the beginning of the system development life-cycle including the architectural phase. Therefore, the SecRAM methodology's main principles can be applied by security risk assessment studies of different contexts, e.g., a network system, considering all its assets and their values to the network architecture. SecRAM process adheres to the following steps (Asgari, 2017). Some of the steps are further described in the following sections.

1. *Establish the context and an accurate scope*: describe the system that is the target of the study, boundaries, and the dependencies on other systems and infrastructure. SecRAM requires establishing the context for defining the boundaries of what one wants to analyze; sets out the scope of the security analysis; and specifies the criteria that will be used to assess the risk, in order to provide consistent and defensible results.
2. *Identify the assets*: there are two types of assets: Primary Asset (PA) and Supporting Asset (SA). PAs are the main resources that are the targets of attacks, i.e., functions, processes, activities, information, and services that need to be protected. PAs are valuable in the sense that a successful attack impairing them will mean harm to the system in terms of personnel, capacity, performance, etc. SAs are tangible entities that enable and support the existence of PAs. Entities involved in storing, processing, and/or transmitting PA are classified as SA. SAs have vulnerabilities that are exploitable by threats aiming at impairing PAs. All supporting assets and their links to PAs need to be identified.
3. *Impact assessment*: for each PA the required level of Confidentiality (C), Integrity (I), and Availability (A) must be identified. This evaluation is based on a scale ranging from 1 to 5 (defined in SecRAM) to be associated to each of the C, I, and A criteria related to each of the PA. To perform this assessment, the impact is evaluated due to the loss of C, I, and/or A for each of its PA on each of the impact areas (safety, performance, cost, environment, etc.).
4. *Evaluate the assets*: all PAs are linked with at least one SA, and all SAs are linked with at least one PA. They will inherit the C, I, and A levels of the PA they support.
5. *Identify the threats and threat scenarios*: A threat is a combination of an attacker and his/her resources, motivation and goal, regardless of the existing security measures or vulnerabilities in the system. The threat is the potential cause of an unwanted incident which may result in an impact on the system. This step is to identify and analyze all possible (or credible) threat sources and the related threat scenarios to highlight all routes through the system that an attacker may use to access an SA, i.e., tangible network entities. A number of example threats are: application attack, abuse of management interface, attacks on data links, subverted software, etc.

6. *Impact assessment:* This is to evaluate the impact of attacks, assessing the harm resulting from each SA being targeted by an attack, taking into account the value of the asset in terms of the C, I, and A pertinence of the threat.

7. *Evaluate the likelihood (probability) of each threat scenario*: estimate the chance that the threat occurs and that the threat scenario sequence is completed successfully.

8. *Assess the security risk*: evaluate the risk level associated to each combination of threat and threat scenario based on their likelihood and impact on the assets. Risk is defined as a function of the likelihood of a given threat source exercising an action on a particular potential vulnerability, and the resulting impact of that has an adverse effect on the network system.

9. *Verify the risk level against the security objective*: evaluate and verify the evaluated risk level against the defined security objectives as a measurable statement of intent relating to the protection of a PA. Security objectives correspond to the level of risk that a PA is prepared to accept on the C, I, or A criterion, before any action is deemed necessary to reduce it.

10. *Risk treatment*: define the action to take, which can be to accept or tolerate the risk, reduce the risk, avoid the risk by withdrawing from the activity, or transfer the risk to another party to manage it. If the action is to reduce the risk, the security analyst/manager needs to define a set of security controls and the associated requirements to reduce the risk to an acceptable level (i.e., within the risk appetite as the level of risk an organization is prepared to retain or take).

11. *Security controls*: implement and put in place the security controls and functions identified during the risk treatment step.

The SecRAM steps are depicted in Figure 1.

SecRAM - IMPACT ASSESSMENT

1. Impact Areas

SecRAM considers a number of critical Impact Areas (IA) to evaluate the impact on confidentiality, integrity, or availability of Primary Assets. The Impact Areas are categorized for different concerns: Personnel, Capacity, Performance, Economic, Branding, Regulatory, and Environment (SESAR, 2013). They are described below:

- **IA1 Personnel:** This impact criterion is directly linked with protecting people.
- **IA2 Capacity:** The capacity impact area is linked with the capacity of the system (e.g., Air Traffic Management (ATM)). For example, if a loss of integrity of a primary asset would lead to a loss of 10% of the capacity of the ATM system.
- **IA3 Performance:** Performance is a more generic criterion than capacity. It is used when a loss of CIA (Confidentiality, Integrity, and Availability) leads to a loss of performance of the system, but it would be difficult to evaluate it in terms of capacity, economics, or any other criteria.
- **IA4 Economic:** This criterion captures the loss of income (e.g., "Serious", "Large", and "Minor") and may vary from one system to another. The same basic rules still apply: a minor loss of income is only considered if the security event is likely to occur and serious or large loss of income will be considered for higher likelihood.

Figure 1. The steps in SecRAM process

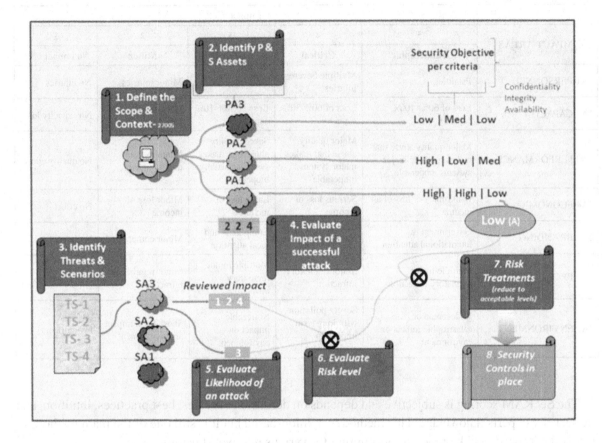

- **IA5 Branding:** This criterion captures the impact on the branding image of the system/company as well as trust, confidence of their users and stakeholders.
- **IA6 Regulatory:** This criterion is linked with possible regulation or standards violations that could occur after a security incident.
- **IA7 Environment:** This criterion relates to noise and emissions caused by compromising the system.

For each primary asset the required level of CIA required must be identified. The impact is calculated when the CIA for each of its primary assets is compromised. The impact is assessed for each of the SESAR Security Impact Areas described in Table 2.

Primary Asset Impact Evaluation

This is to assess the impact of CIA compromise on primary assets. For each threat, the impact on the CIA of PA is assessed according to the scales (1 to 5) defined in the Impact Areas. The Overall Impact is then calculated as the highest of the three impact values of C, I, and A (see the example for PA#01 in Table 3).

Table 2. SESAR Security Impact Areas

IMPACT AREAS	Impact				
	5	**4**	**3**	**2**	**1**
	Catastrophic	**Critical**	**Severe**	**Minor**	**No impact / NA**
IA1:PERSONNEL	Fatalities	Multiple Severe injuries	Severe injuries	Minor injuries	No injuries
IA2:CAPACITY	Loss of 60%- 100% capacity	Loss of 60%-30% capacity	Loss of 30%-10% capacity	Loss of up to 10% capacity	No capacity loss
IA3:PERFORMANCE	Major quality abuse that makes multiple major systems inoperable	Major quality abuse that makes major system inoperable	Severe quality abuse that makes systems partially inoperable	Minor system quality abuse	No quality abuse
IA4:ECONOMIC	Bankruptcy or loss of all income	Serious loss of income	Large loss of income	Minor loss of income	No effect
IA5:BRANDING	Government & international attention	National attention	Complaints and local attention	Minor complaints	No impact
IA6:REGULATORY	Multiple major regulatory infractions	Major regulatory infraction	Multiple minor regulatory infractions	Minor regulatory infraction	No impact
IA7:ENVIRONMENT	Widespread or catastrophic impact on environment	Severe pollution with long term impact on environment	Noticeable impact on environment	Short Term impact on environment	Insignificant

The SecRAM scoring is subjective and depends on definition of scales, best practices, intuition, and the security experts' knowledge. This method is opinion-based but it is still one of the main methods to access the impact and likelihood by accounting for various real-world parameters.

Threat Scenario Evaluation

The threat scenario evaluation is performed in accordance with the following steps. For each Supporting Asset:

- Relevant threats are identified.
- For each threat, the targeted criteria (CIA) are identified.

Table 3. Primary Asset Impact Evaluation

ID	Primary Asset	CIA	IA1	IA2	IA3	IA4	IA5	IA6	IA7	Threat Scenario (TC)	Overall Impact
PA#01	Com. service	C	1	1	1	1	1	1	1	**TC1**	1
		I	3	4	4	3	3	3	2	**TC2**	4
		A	5	5	3	3	3	4	2	**TC3**	5

The impact is valued and assessed according to the CIA for every PA linked to SAs. The SAs inherit the C, I, A values of their PAs. However, in the SecRAM process:

1. When one SA enables more than one PA, it will inherit the highest C, I, and A values of the PA in question.
2. When several SAs (interconnected or otherwise) enable one PA, the C, I, and A criteria associated with the relevant threat/s that is linked to each SA is evaluated individually.

The Overall Impact is then calculated as the highest (worst-case) of the three impact values of C, I, and A.

In Table 3, each of the rows corresponds to a threat scenario targeting a supporting asset, and indicating which of Confidentiality, Integrity and Availability are compromised by it.

2. Impact Evaluation

For each Supporting Asset as the example shown in Table 4, the impact of the threat scenarios are evaluated at two levels:

- *The Inherited Impact*: The inherited impact is a characteristic of threat scenarios. Each threat scenario uses as entry to the system a specific SA, which has a valuated impact on each CIA criteria of each supported PA. The inherited impact of a threat scenario is the maximum of all valuated impacts of the SA the scenario is using.
- *The Reviewed Impact*: The Reviewed Impact is an adjustment of the inherited impact due to existing or planned controls which will be in place to reduce the impact. These controls will relate to reducing the impact rather than reducing the likelihood of attack. The Reviewed Impact is always equal to or less than the Inherited Impact.

Table 4. Supporting Asset Impact Evaluation

SA ID	Supporting Asset	Threat	Impact		Justification
			Inherited	Reviewed	
SA#1	Wireless link	RF interference	5	3	Only severe because the effect is limited in time and area
		Wireless router physical damage	5	3	Only severe because redundancy and backup are available

SecRAM - Likelihood Evaluation

According to the SecRAM, the likelihood is built from a split into *exposure* or frequency of occurrence of the threat source and *potentiality* that, once the threat source occurs, the threat scenario sequence is completed successfully. Once both likelihood layers have been evaluated (see Table 5 example), the likelihood is obtained from the average of both values rounded up to the next integer.

Table 5. Likelihood Evaluation

SA ID	SA	Threat Scenario	Reviewed Impact	Exposure Level	Potentiality Level	Rationale for each parameter considered (The final value is the average value obtained from each parameter and rounding up to the next integer)
SA#1	Wireless link	RF interference	3	2	4	**Exposure Level**: Extent of Attention (3), Profit (2), Feeling of Impunity (1), History of Threats (2), Collateral Damage (2); *Parameter values for the Exposure Level Calculation e.g. for Collateral Damage are:* Certainty (5), high chance (4), fair chance (3), little chance (2) and no chance of Collateral Damage (1). **Potentiality Level**: Expertise/skills (4), Knowledge of the target (4), Means/Equipment (3), Window of opportunity - accessible time (5), chances of Detection (1); *Potentiality Level Calculation:* Might well expected (5), Quite possible (4), Only remotely possible (3), Conceivable but very unlikely (2), Practically impossible (1)
		Wireless router physical damage	3	1	5	Attention (1), Profit (1), Impunity (1), History (1), Collateral Damage (1); Expertise (5), Knowledge (4), Means (3), Opportunity (5), Detection (4)

The Likelihood of a threat scenario is practically realized according to the following scale:

- Scale 1: Very unlikely - Practically impossible
- Scale 2: Unlikely - Conceivable but unlikely
- Scale 3: Likely - Only somewhat possible
- Scale 4: Very likely - Quite possible
- Scale 5: Certain - Might well be expected.

Now that the exposure and potentiality level have been calculated, the likelihood evaluation can be processed (see Table 6 example).

Table 6. The reviewed Impact and Likelihood

SA ID	Supporting Asset	Threat	Reviewed Impact	Likelihood
SA#1	Wireless link	RF interference	3	3
		Wireless router physical damage	3	3

SecRAM – Risk Level Evaluation

Once the likelihood and impact of each threat have been assessed, the level of risk is calculated according to the SecRAM recommendation. For each Supporting Asset, the Risk Level of each threat scenario is evaluated using the Likelihood and Reviewed Impacts that have previously been evaluated. Risk Levels are Low, Medium, or High. See Table 7.

Table 7. Risk Evaluation

SA ID	Supporting Asset	Threat	Primary Asset	Reviewed Impact	Likelihood	Risk Level
SA#2	Wireless link	RF interference	PA#01 PA#02	3	3	Medium
		Wireless router physical damage	PA#01 PA#02	3	3	Medium

Security Objectives

Security Objectives (SO) are defined to protect primary assets. Security Objectives correspond to the *level of risk that a primary asset is prepared to accept* on each criterion (notably confidentiality, integrity, availability), before any action is deemed necessary to reduce it. The security objective level comes from the impact area definition. Table 8 defines the security objective level (or risk appetite) for the Performance Impact Area only. A security need is defined whether a risk needs to be treated or not; when the level of a risk is higher than the security objective of a Supporting Asset (i.e., the lowest security objective) it is targeting, a treatment shall be applied.

Table 8. Security Objective level (or risk appetite) for the Performance Impact Area

Security objective level	Low	Medium	High
Impact Impact Area	5 or 4	3	2 or 1
Performance	Major quality abuse making system inoperable	Severe quality abuse making system partially inoperable	Minor or No system quality abuse
Security objective level	Low	Medium	High
Impact Impact Area	5 or 4	3	2 or 1
Performance	Major quality abuse making system inoperable	Severe quality abuse making system partially inoperable	Minor or No system quality abuse

SO rating is the sum of points given to each criterion:

- High security objective: 1 point;
- Medium security objective: 2 points;
- Low security objective: 3 points.

From the above calculation, it is possible to have a ranking on the Primary Asset: the higher the value the more security protection on the primary asset is needed (see Table 9 example).

Table 9. Primary Asset ranking

PA ID	Primary Asset	C	I	A	Rating of SO
PA#01	Control and management communication service	High (1)	Low (3)	Low (3)	7
PA#02	Satellite managed service	High (1)	Medium (2)	Medium (2)	5

Risk Treatment Prioritization

The security assessment for each Threat scenario (T) should be done as shown in Table 9. The most feared and critical threat scenarios are the ones with most of evaluated risks are assessed to High (H) and with Low Security Objectives. The evaluator should decide to give a risk treatment prioritization. In Table 10, the values High, Medium and Low in the last column refer to the urgency for treatment.

Table 10. Risk Treatment Priority

Risk ID	Risk Level	Threat	SA	Related Primary Asset(s)	Security Criteria C	Security Criteria I	Security Criteria A	Security objective	Security need	Risk Treatment Priority
R1	H	T-No.1	SA#02	PA#01		X	X	Low	Risk should be treated	Medium
R3	H	T-No.2	SA#02	PA#01			X	Low	Risk should be treated	Low
R5	H	T-No.3	SA#03	PA#01, PA#02		X	X	Low	Risk should be treated	High

SecRAM - Security Control for Risk Treatment

Treatment actions or Security Controls are defined to protect Supporting Assets. They are a collection of measures for managing risks and to ensure the security objectives are met. They include, but are not limited to, procedures, policies, more robust technical solutions, and management actions. The security objective level comes from the definition of the Impact Areas. A security need is defined whether a risk needs to be treated or not; when the level of a risk is higher than the security objective of a Supporting Asset (i.e., the lowest security objective) it is targeting, a treatment shall be applied.

The risk treatment option should be selected from the actions, i.e. Tolerate, Reduce, Avoid, or Transfer. We can choose the "Tolerate" option for the threats with 'Low' risk level and the "Reduce" option in combating threats with 'Medium' and 'High' risk levels to meet security objective levels. In defining the Security Controls, it is important to take into account the three parameters (i.e., likelihood, impact, and risk-level). For example, if the likelihood has a high value and impact has a low value, but risk level is high, the Security Control should be primarily defined to counter the likelihood and it could overlook the impact.

Once the type of treatment is evaluated (e.g., for reduction of the risk), a strategy for protecting Supporting Assets is applied in order to choose the best set of Security Controls. The strategy proposed by SESAR offers two approaches for combined Security Control: "Defense in Depth" and "Strength of Control". Defense in depth relies on a multi-layered set of unrelated controls acting together to provide protection to a Supporting Asset. The multi-layered approach to controls means that if one control is compromised then another control should act as the next layer of defense. Strength of control relies on improving the performance of one 'type' of control (e.g., rigorous access control, strong authorization). This means an attacker needs more expertise, better tools, and more time to break through the control.

Therefore, we should identify and consider Security Controls for threats with a risk level of Medium and High. This is to reduce the risk level to the acceptable level that corresponds to the security objective of Supporting Assets. The most feared and critical threat scenarios are with the risks evaluated as High with low security objectives. These have high priority in treating them.

Use of SecRAM For Assesing Security Risks In Communication Networks

In this section, we provide three examples of applying SecRAM in assessing security risks in existing and clean-slate networking architectures.

GAMMA (Global ATM security management)

GAMMA was an European Commission (EC) *7th Framework Programme project* and was aimed at providing a holistic vision of ATM (Air Traffic Management) security. This is achieved by adhering to the above standards and addressing the gap in today's capabilities by identifying the security risks stemming from ATM system operation. It is reported in (Asgari, 2017) that the overall aim of the EC GAMMA project was to provide a concrete security solution for realization of capabilities such as self-protection and resilience of the ATM domain utilizing a rich set of heterogeneous systems and network infrastructures by embedding them into its System of Systems (SoS). Security issues related to the ATM domain have been already changing throughout the years, raising new challenges to be dealt with due to technological advances. The existing ATM SoS has vulnerabilities and security-related capability gaps and there is an urgent need to efficiently and consistently respond to attacks and to anticipate new attacks. Combining and interconnecting various systems on the same infrastructure as well as integrating the many communication means, could potentially open up the ATM SoS to more attacks, thereby increasing vulnerabilities and the overall security risks. This necessitates a security management solution to handle the challenges.

GAMMA project adopted the SecRAM methodology and MSSC (Minimum Set of Security Controls) [12] to address ATM security risk assessment. In this work, the scope and boundaries of the ATM SoS were defined and the context was established for defining the boundaries of what one wants to analyze; sets out the scope of the security analysis; and specified the criteria that was used to assess the risk, in order to provide consistent and defensible results. Overall, the security gaps and involved risks were addressed to protect the ATM SoS assets, and an inclusive security solution was proposed, demonstrated and validated through implementation of system prototypes.

Integrated Modular Communications (IMC) Platform

An integrated standalone on-board processing platform called Integrated Modular Communications (IMC) was designed to offer multi-radio off-board communication to/from different providers and on-board network connectivity for cockpit and passenger applications. In (Asgari, 2016), it is reported a risk assessment analysis was conducted for IMC using SecRAM where five categories of threats were identified i.e., on-board application attack, off-board application attack, subverted software or hardware, abuse of management interface, and jamming of data links. These threats have been mitigated using the mechanisms to be considered as built-in Security Controls/enablers for IMC, to satisfy the stated CIA security requirements. The Security Controls have been categorized as: user authentication of the IMC, controlling the access to the resources, cryptographic protection for confidentiality and integrity of assets and monitoring and controlling the relevant processes within the IMC. Risks can be reduced by the monitoring of activities to identify activities that are not expected and then take appropriate actions to mitigate emerging risks.

RINA (Recursive Internetwork Architecture)

In new network architecture designs, programmability, the ability to dynamically configure, control, and combine the security functions, are regarded as the key features to create resilient network systems for preventing or reducing the impact of attacks. RINA (recursive internetwork architecture) is a clean slate network architecture that recognizes the need for building security enablers into the network architecture and is aiming to provide the stated key design features.

In (Asgari, 2018), it is reported that the SecRAM is systematically applied to a new context for the first time, i.e., the RINA network architecture. SecRAM was intended for an ATM context and as such it is too heavyweight to apply it in full to a network system. The SecRAM methodology was tailored to apply it specifically to RINA.

Resulting from the risk assessment, specific measures were proposed to further improve cyber resiliency of the RINA, in securing its layers and components. In this work, the context was established and the scope was set out for the security analysis of the network architecture, assessing the risk levels, validating the necessary security enablers/controls that have been built into the architecture, and recommending some new enhancements. The enhancement prevails through the utilization of multi-layered security controls or the increase in their strength. It was also shown how programmable security controls can assist in tackling network attacks. For validation purposes, the defined security enablers/controls were checked against the stakeholders' security requirements and network security needs in order to meet them. Embedding security controls in the architecture for combating run-time threats is the key step towards the security-by-design concept enabling cyber resiliency and avoiding incremental updates and plug-ins. Cyber resiliency enablement allows the network systems to be resilient against persistent, stealthy attacks targeted at cyber assets. The way this risk assessment methodology was applied to an emerging network system (RINA) can inspire its use in other emerging network architecture settings. It was claimed this is the first work to systematically provide a complete description of the processes required for identifying the security threats and quantifying the risks, validating the need for built-in security functions, and proposing additional measures for reducing security risks to acceptable levels for improving cyber resiliency of a network system. These measures constitute the network system's self-protection, so that it is crucial to establish that the overall system design is resilient and reliable for large-scale use. This can also pave the way for applying it to other emerging network architecture settings.

Automated Risk and Utility Management (AURUM)

AURUM is a framework for supporting the risk management process defined in NIST SP 800-30 standard in the context of IT infrastructure (Ekelhart, 2009). It is divided into three main phases:

1. Risk assessment (identify potential risks and their impacts) in order to recommend risk-reducing countermeasures.
2. Risk mitigation: a) Prioritize identified risks b) Implement and maintain countermeasures.
3. Risk evaluation: Determine whether or not the implemented countermeasures are decreasing the risk to an acceptable level and if further controls are needed.

Compared to existing solutions, the AURUM methodology has the following benefits:

*   Specifying an ontological information security knowledge base that provides knowledge to the risk manager in a consistent and comprehensive way.
*   Modelling the organization's resources within the ontological framework to ensure consistency.
*   Existing best-practice guidelines and information security standards are used to ensure only widely accepted information security knowledge is used for threat/vulnerability identification and countermeasure/control recommendations.
*   Objectively determining a Bayesian threat likelihood Liu (2005), Poolappasit (2012), Chockalingam (2017).
*   Automatically calculating threat impacts.
*   Automatically offering risks reduction control measures.
*   Using interactive decision support to allow the risk manager to investigate various scenarios, to discover the characteristics of the underlying problem and ensure an efficient solution is selected.

The main disadvantage of a Bayesian risk assessment methodology like AURUM is the need for a potentially vast amount of training data (knowledge base) and the difficultly in being applied to new security context/situations.

CORAS Security Risk Analysis

CORAS is a UML (Unified Modelling Language) model-based risk analysis methodology used for information security of critical systems. It provides a customized language for threat and risk modeling, with guidelines on how the language should be used to capture and model relevant information (Dahl, 2008). The CORAS method uses a qualitative risk assessment approach and follows the following steps:

1. Introduction – Gathering information about target; Focus of the analysis (i.e., data security) and scope of the analysis (i.e., data security at work).
2. High level analysis – ensure analysts and the client have a common understanding of the target of analysis. Determine the assets relevant to the analysis.
3. Approval – Agree on target description. Decide acceptable risk levels for each asset.
4. Risk identification – Determine how threats may exploit vulnerabilities thus causing unwanted incidents that harm the assets.

5. Risk estimation – Estimate current risk level, assign likelihoods to each incident and consequences to each impact.
6. Risk evaluation – Evaluate which risks are acceptable and which are not.
7. Risk treatment – Provide overview of potential treatments of unacceptable risks.

CORAS uses open source tools and provides a graphical view of whom and what caused the risks and the vulnerabilities that caused them; it also assists with iterative communication between stakeholders. The effectiveness of the security controls is not included and the implementation of the method requires a thorough knowledge of various fields. There is also no risk monitoring.

CCTA Risk Analysis and Management Method (CRAMM)

CRAMM is a risk analysis method developed by the British government organization CCTA (Central Communication and Telecommunication Agency), now renamed as Office of Government Commerce (OGC) in 1987. CRAMM is used for IT infrastructure (CRAMM, 2020) and there is a tool having the same name which supports the method. There are three stages of CRAMM as listed below:

1) Establish the objectives:
    a. Define the scope/context in which the system operates.
    b. Identify and value the physical assets of the system.
    c. Determine the 'value' of data held by interviewing users about potential business impact that could arise from unavailability, destruction, disclosure or modification.
    d. Identify and value the software assets of the systems.
2) Assess the risks:
    a. Identify type and level of threats that may affect the system.
    b. Assess the system's vulnerabilities to identified threats.
    c. Combine threat and vulnerability assessment with asset values to calculate measures of risks.
3) Identify and select countermeasures that are in-line with the calculated measures of risks.

CRAMM provides a library containing detailed countermeasures and software for the implementation of the methodology. The efficiency of the security controls is not reviewed and there is no risk monitoring. Whilst CRAMM provides software to implement the method it is reported that the method is rather difficult to use without the tool.

Expression Des Besoins Et Identification des Objectifs de Sécurité (EBIOS)

EBIOS methodology was created by the French ANSSI (Agence Nationale de la Sécurité des Systémes d'Information) in 1995 and is used for IT infrastructure. EBIOS is used to analyze, evaluate and treat risks relating to information systems. EBIOS is open source, requiring a GNU license. The risks of information systems are assessed by specifying suitable security measures (Abbass, 2015). The process is described in (EBIOS, 2019) as: determine the context, determine the security requirements, perform a risk analysis, identify security goals, and determine security requirements. EBIOS is primarily used by government and commercial organizations, working with the French Ministry of Defence, that handle confidential or secret defense classified information. The updated version (EBIOS, 2010) is compatible with international standards including ISO/IEC 27005. EBIOS looks at all impact assessment areas IA1-IA7, as mentioned in Table 2.

The EBIOS methodology can adapt to the context of each organization, including its methodological tools and habits. EBIOS mandates a clear separation between the concepts of primary assets and feared events, and supporting assets and threat scenarios. ANSSI (National Cybersecurity Agency of France) also defines an EBIOS Risk Manager (EBIOS-RM) process, which is an agile enhancement to EBIOS 2010. An initial high level assessment can be performed via a small number of workshops with key stakeholders. The outputs can subsequently be refined incrementally through the development lifecycle of a solution or product. A number of tools embody the EBIOS and EBIOS-RM processes that facilitate the deployment of the process and present outputs in a consistent manner.

A lot of information is generated (Abbass, 2015) and much of the documentation only appears to be available in French, although the EBIOS-RM method is available in English. Referring to the process, like ISO/IEC 27005, the "study of the context" does not establish a compliance-based security baseline based on a business impact assessment. In general, EBIOS's view is that you should always follow best practice by default and then spend the effort analyzing what the residual risks are. The two points to consider are 1) to get some controls into the design early rather than having to delay design work for months while the security analysis concludes and 2) if there is infinite time, the analyst would start from an unprotected system and conduct a risk analysis based on a business impact. As there is no infinite time available and because an analyst must prioritize the efforts, apply best practice quickly (the baseline) and then analyze only residual risk. It is also viewed that many cyber design analysts and authorities are in favor of this approach, as they say that they do it subjectively anyway using security experts' knowledge and opinion. The important point is that nobody should stop there, but having it as a first step is a pragmatic approach. This may not necessarily extend to high assurance systems.

Information Risk Assessment Methodologies (IRAM/IRAM2)

IRAM is used for IT infrastructure security risk assessment. ISF's IRAM2 tool, provides an approach to performing business-focused risk assessments (IRAM2, 2020). The steps in the process include:

- Scoping: Develop a profile of the environment and scope for the assessment.
- Business impact assessment: Identify information assets and their business impact.
- Threat profiling: Populate threat landscape, prioritize threats, identify, and map the information assets impacted by each threat.
- Vulnerability assessment: Identify vulnerabilities and related controls and assess effectiveness of controls.
- Risk evaluation: Derive likelihood of success, residual likelihood and residual risk rating.
- Risk treatment: Evaluate each risk against risk appetite, create risk treatment plan, execute plan and validate results.

The IRAM2 tool only looks at the economic aspects as defined by IA4 in Table 2. IRAM2 is widely used in the industry but it is not fit for purpose in the contexts that look at security for safety purposes.

Information Security Assessment & Monitoring Method (ISAMM)

ISAMM (Harpes, 2007) uses mathematics in its quantitative risk assessment method and is a tool to assess both security risks and current compliance with respect to ISO 27002. Furthermore, it delivers an optimized action plan to address the identified risks. ISAMM recurs to the list of security measures of ISO 27002 and assigns to each security control some risk reduction properties. Based on estimates of current risks, on implementation costs of missing security controls, and on risk reduction factors, the economic benefit, the so-called Return on Security Investment (ROSI), is estimated. It is used to build an action list to improve security. ISAMM links the assessment of the security risks, expressed in monetary terms as an Annual Loss Expectancy (ALE), with security controls that can most economically contribute to a reduction of the risks. ISAMM recurs to a knowledge base with context-dependent risk reducing capabilities of security controls. The knowledge-base can be considered as a matrix containing each control objective and each of the generic threats (e.g., risk of internal data theft, accidental outages due to errors, bugs or bad practice). Thus, difference ΔALE of the ALE is derived before and after implementing a security control. Based thereon, the ROSI and relative ROSI are respectively defined as:

- ROSI = ΔALE$-$Cost and ROSI (Relative) = (ΔALE$-$Cost)/Cost

Both, ROSI and ROSI Relative are important indicators to identify the most effective controls (those having the greatest risk reduction capabilities, while having the lowest costs) and to prioritize certain controls. Both calculations are used to evaluate the monetary benefit of each single security control and provide an efficient ordering system for implementation priorities. ISAMM assessed risks are expressed through ALE which means it only looks at the SecRAM impact assessment area of IA4 "Economic".

Method For Harmonized Analysis of Risk (MEHARI)

MEHARI is a free open source, information systems and information processes risk analysis and management method (MEHARI, 2019). MEHARI was created by CLUSIF France in 1995 and uses a quantitative risk assessment approach. MEHARI has steadily evolved to support standards like ISO/IEC 27001, 27002, 27005 and NIST SP 800-30, combining a knowledge base with a suite of tools to allow:

1) Performing threat analysis based on an organization's activities and the potential issues that may impact those activities.
2) Determining organizational, human and technical assets based on the business processes.
3) Classifying the assets using the security CIA criteria.
4) Evaluating the likelihood/probability of the threat event types.
5) Assessing the intrinsic severity of risks using scenarios in the knowledge base.
6) Employing diagnostic questionnaires filled by users to help them determine if their existing security measures/controls are capable of mitigating risks.
7) Grouping organizational and technical security measures/controls into services to be discussed with the relevant managers.
8) Displaying the current severity level of each risk scenario.
9) Selecting action plans for the on-going management of the risks; these are based on the expected effectiveness of additional security measures and the timescales for their implementation.

The MEHARI methodology allows measurement of the maturity level of security through indicators like efficiency and resilience. The start of the risk analysis requires a complicated adaptation of the knowledge base. In addition, there is no risk monitoring by default.

Operationally Critical Threat, Asset and Vulnerability Evaluation (OCTAVE)

OCTAVE is a structured approach to evaluate the risks related to operational (business units) risks. OCTAVE was created by CERT USA in 1999, uses a qualitative risk assessment approach and is divided into three main phases covering similar aspects to the other methodologies stated in this chapter (Paulina, 2007):

1) Build Asset-based threat profiles: Evaluate the company's security strategy (current practices, organization vulnerabilities, and security requirements) and determine resources (assets, threats) by interviewing the employees.
2) Identify infrastructure vulnerabilities: Evaluate the information management system based on data gathered in phase 1. Technical (data protection) vulnerabilities are determined.
3) Develop security strategy and plans: Based on information gathered in phases 1 and 2, the risk of data compromise is assessed. The risk associated with the company's business activity is also assessed. The security (protection) strategy is developed. Attack types that may take place in the future can be determined. Mitigation plans are developed.

In OCTAVE, risks are assessed from an operational point of view and the methodology includes a variety of supporting documentation and tools. The method requires proprietary software and it does not provide risk monitoring. While the mitigation and acceptance of risk is considered, its avoidance is not (Paulina, 2007).

Quantitative Risk and Impact Assessment Framework (QUIRC)

QUIRC is used to assess the security risks associated with cloud computing platforms. QUIRC defines risk as a combination of the probability of a security threat event and its severity, measured as its impact (Saripalli, 2010). Six key Security Objectives (SO) are identified for cloud platforms and it is proposed that most of the typical attack vectors and events map to these six categories. The wide-band Delphi method is proposed as a scientific means to collect the information necessary for assessing security risks. Risk assessment knowledge bases could be developed specific to each industry vertical, which then serve as inputs for security risk assessment of cloud computing platforms.

QUIRC is a fully quantitative and iterative convergence approach, which enables stakeholders to comparatively assess the relative robustness of different cloud vendor offerings and approaches. It allows the relative robustness of different cloud vendor offerings and approaches to be compared by vendors, customers, etc. The approach is also helpful in reducing the Fear, Uncertainty and Doubt (FUD) associated with cloud platform security issues. The issue with QUIRC is that it requires a detailed collection of input data for determining probabilities of events.

System Theoretic Process Analysis –Security (STPA-Sec)

STPA is a safety/hazard analysis methodology formulated by MIT (Leveson, 2012). It is intended to provide an alternative to more traditional analysis techniques, such as Fault Tree Analysis (FTA, top-down), Failure Mode Effect Analysis (FMEA, bottom-up) or Hazard and Operability Analysis (HAZOP), that is more suitable for more complex and highly integrated systems, often with a socio-technical dimension. STPA is used to find new requirements to prevent accidents and losses. This approach treats safety as a control problem and asserts that accidents result from loss of control, not chains of failure events.

STPA-Sec (Lee, 2018), (Freiberg 2017) extends System-Theoretic Process Analysis from a safety to cyber security analysis, identifying system vulnerabilities and requirements for cyber and cyber-physical systems. STPA-Sec is focused on cyber security use cases whereas STPA-SafeSec attempts to address both safety and security using just one analysis.

STPA-Sec provides a means to clearly link security to the broader mission or business objectives – it enhances but does not replace standard security engineering approaches. This is also a more top-down approach to security (Young 2017) which is focused on outcomes as opposed to more bottom-up approaches (such as CHASSIS - Combined Harm Analysis of Safety and Security for Information Systems) which use threat vectors as the starting point. CHASSIS (Raspotnig, 2018) is a method for collaborative determination of requirements for safe and secure systems. STPA-Sec utilizes a causality model based on system theory to provide a more integrated approach to safety and security co-analysis. It is claimed that STPA is better at dealing with emergent properties by virtue of its top-down (as opposed to bottom-up) approach. STPA-Sec provides a means to clearly link security to the broader mission or business objectives – it enhances but does not replace standard security engineering approaches. This is also a more top-down approach to security which is focused on outcomes as opposed to more bottom-up approaches which use threat vectors as the starting point.

VULNERABILITY ASSESSMENT

Vulnerability assessment is just as vital as risk assessment. The ISO/IEC 27000 standard (ISO 2018) defines a vulnerability as a weakness of an asset or control that can be exploited by attackers. Vulnerability assessment in an ICT system involves a comprehensive scrutiny of assets to determine gaps that an entity or event can take advantage of — resulting in the realization of a threat. There are several steps involved in vulnerability assessment including:

1. *Context Definition and perform Initial Assessment*: Identify the context and assets and define the risks involved.
2. *Vulnerability Scan:* To use tools and techniques to identify and exploit vulnerabilities.
3. *Vulnerability Assessment Reporting:* To summarize the findings, including description of vulnerability, score, potential impact, and recommended mitigation.

There are standardization efforts for security vulnerability assessment, such as the Common Vulnerability Scoring System (CVSS, 2020). The CVSS is an open industry standard for assessing the severity of computer system security vulnerabilities. CVSS attempts to assign numerical severity scores to vulnerabilities, allowing prioritizing responses and resources according to the threat. The numerical score can then be translated into a qualitative representation (such as low, medium, high, and critical).

Network Mapper (Nmap)

Network Mapper (Nmap, 2020) is an open source tool designed to scan networks for vulnerabilities. The vulnerability scan reveals system hardening configuration issues and the services scan finds vulnerable software at the end-systems. Nmap also provides web directories' enumeration leading to deep information that can further reveal exploitability issues. It determines what hosts are available on the network, what services those hosts are offering, what operating systems they are running, what type of packet filters/firewalls are in use, and other characteristics. The output from Nmap is a list of scanned targets, with supplemental information (such as a ports table that includes port number, protocol, service name, and state) on each, depending on the options used. In addition to the ports table, Nmap can provide further information on targets, including reverse DNS names, operating system, device types, and MAC addresses.

NESSUS

Nessus (Nessus, 2020) is one of the vulnerability scanners used for vulnerability assessments and penetration testing. It provides fully automated scan comprising functionalities like, configuration audit, target profiling, malware detection, data discovery, etc. Automated scans provide the number of vulnerabilities ranging from unencrypted sensitive files at endpoint systems to the extent of systems without basic authentication and remote code execution prevention. NESSUS has a number of products that offer multiple services ranging from Web application scanning to mobile device scanning, cloud environment scanning, malware detection, control systems auditing (including supervisory control and data acquisition systems - SCADA and embedded devices) and configuration auditing and compliance checks.

Network Infrastructure Parser (NIPPER)

Nipper (Nipper, 2020) discovers vulnerabilities by scanning to determine and map vulnerabilities of network devices such as switches, routers, and firewalls. It works by parsing and analyzing the device configuration file. Nipper enables the user to dedicate the valuable resources for analyzing and prioritizing fixes by providing:

- Visibility of actual network vulnerabilities
- Automated risk prioritization
- Precise remediation with technical fixes
- Flexible and configurable reports

THE NEED FOR DYNAMIC RISK ASSESSMENT AND RUN-TIME MITIGATION

Many of the risk assessment techniques are concerned with risk identification and evaluation but do not provide insights into how to mitigate these risks once they have been identified, in order to improve security. Normally a domain expert would analyze these risks and subsequently propose changes (or any other appropriate mitigation plan) to the system/architecture to address them. The appropriate risk assessment methodology can then be invoked again in order to understand how the risk profile has changed and to identify residual risks. The main shortcomings of the traditional methods which are currently in use are:

(a)   They tend to be focused on more static systems whose properties and behaviors are fixed at the design time, and the system boundary is well-defined and static, and it does not change at run time.

(b)   They may not scale well to larger, more global, systems with more entities and more interconnections.

(c)   Because risks are evaluated at discrete time intervals, the methods are not suited to changing scenarios such as new environments or changing assets.

(d)   They are less likely to cope well with emergence of new threats as these are unknown in advance and are unlikely to be included in an analysis.

By contrast to SSRAM, Dynamic Security Risk Assessment Methodologies (DSRAM) techniques must be capable of continuously estimating risks by adapting to the dynamic nature of the environment (Mirzaei, 2018). In an autonomic system environment, the overall context is subjected to randomness and dynamism showing:

- Changes in assets: mainly addition, modification or removal of assets.
- Unknown/new threats and zero-day vulnerabilities.
- Evolution of already known threats.
- Changes in the concept of operations.
- New interconnections with other systems.

The epochs of re-assessing security could be much shorter than the traditional methodologies. Therefore, there is need for:

- *Dynamic Security Risk Assessment:* continuously monitoring, detecting, assessing and evolving security reasoning and incident reporting to provide through-life security assurance.
- *Dynamically design and implement or adapt relevant security controls/measures:* to prevent harming the assets and to influence the system's behavior.
- *Dynamic security case:* continuously have confidence in, and proactively update the reasoning about, the run-time security of on-going operations.

Despite the growing urgency in having such capability, the state of the art is very light in this area. The terms "Online Risk Assessment" and "Real Time Risk Assessment" are synonymous with "Dynamic Risk Assessment" in some literature, while all typically rely on a regular update of the risk assessment variables defining the information system and its environment. The following are notable works, but still remain a limited set of contributions to a very complex problem:

- In (Feth, 2018), an approach is described for the dynamic risk assessment (in the context of creating situation awareness regarding risk) of autonomous vehicles.
- In (Verhoogt, 2018), a static risk assessment framework is used as a starting point for a DSRAM (cyber) for military aircraft.

- On risk assessment in information systems, (Lopez, 2013) describes how in previous studies involving attack trees/graphs, like Bayesian Attack Graphs (Poolappasit 2012), DSRAM is an analysis of attack dynamics based on predefined scenarios.

AESIN cyber security workstream is currently working on DSRAM, which includes contributions from the ResiCAV project (ResiCAV, 2020), by creating and experimenting with a new STPA-Res (Resilient) methodology for dynamically assessing and managing cyber security risks raised by an connected autonomous vehicle. This work is still conceptual, i.e., the steps for a methodology are defined, but many of the steps need further detailed work to be realized. Zenzic are now also collating the results of many feasibility studies in this subject area (Zenzic, 2020).

CONCLUSION

We introduced a number of the static security risk assessment methodologies (SSRAM), standards and tools such as ISO 27005, NIST SP 800-30, SecRAM, CRAMM, CORAS, EBIOS, OCTAVE, etc., that all share a common requirement to conduct the assessment. This requirement is to have a detailed knowledge about the security context and the environment. The list of SSRAM methods and standards is not complete. Thus, an inventory of SSRAM is included in (ENSIA, 2020). We particularly focused on the use of a security risk assessment methodology (SecRAM) that can be used for network systems. We also introduced studies that identified and prioritized run-time threats to the emerging network environments. EBIOS also appears to be a well-rounded methodology that covers all of the impact assessment areas specified in SecRAM and includes risk monitoring, making it possibly suitable to contribute in forming a DSRAM.

DSRAM will not be achieved through small increments to SSRAM, as the level of automation of SSRAM remains low. Moreover, SSRAM do not address run-time risk treatment, which DSRAM would need to do in order to be of value (detecting vulnerabilities at a significantly higher rate than they can be addressed makes the system less secure rather than more secure).

A cyber-attack is a deliberate act performed by a threat agent against a system. When a complex system is released to market it will contain vulnerabilities. A system is resilient if, and only if, there is justifiable and enduring confidence that it will consistently function as expected, when expected. It is also cyber secure if it displays this property in the face of an adversary. The most promising work is being conducted by the AESIN cyber security workstream towards a DSRAM for autonomous vehicles (ResiCAV, 2020).

The vision for the future should be for designers now to move towards the concept of dynamic risk assessments and cyber resilience. They need to investigate new techniques for designing and analyzing complex systems and for those systems to resist and bounce back from cyber-attacks.

ACKNOWLEDGMENT

Work towards this chapter was partially funded by the Thales UK and Innovate UK. The author would like to thank his colleagues for their inputs and fruitful discussions and comments made in the development of work presented in this chapter.

REFERENCES

Abbass, W. (2015). Using EBIOS for risk management in critical information infrastructure. *5th World Congress on Information and Communication Technologies (WICT)*. 10.1109/WICT.2015.7489654

Asgari, H. (2016). Security Risk Assessment and Risk Treatment for Integrated Modular Communication. *International conference on Availability, Reliability, and Security (ARES), presented at ATMSec Workshop*. http://www.ares-conference.eu

Asgari, H., Haines, S., & Rysavy, O. (2018). Identification of threats and security risk assessments for recursive Internet architecture. *IEEE Systems Journal*, *12*(3), 2437–2448. doi:10.1109/JSYST.2017.2765178

Asgari, H., Stelkens-Kobsch, T. H., Montefusco, P., Abhaya, L., Koelle, R., Markarian, G., & D'Auria, G. (2017). Provisioning for a distributed ATM security management: The GAMMA approach. Featured Article. *IEEE Aerospace and Electronic Systems Magazine*, *32*(11), 5–21. doi:10.1109/MAES.2017.170037

BSI Document. (2020). *Understanding your Cyber security Risks*. https://www.bsigroup.com/contentassets/6466e375387a4ffa8ddbc64e535e27b0/understanding-your-cybersecurity-risk-bsi.pdf

BSI Group. (2020). https://www.bsigroup.com/en-GB/about-bsi/

Chockalingam, S. (2017). Bayesia Network models in Cyber Security: A systematic Review. *Proceeding of NORDIC Conference on Secure IT systems*, 105-122. 10.1007/978-3-319-70290-2_7

CORAS. (2015). *The CORAS Method*. http://coras.sourceforge.net/

CRAMM. (2020). *Wikipedia page*. https://en.wikipedia.org/wiki/CRAMM

CVSS. (2020). *Common Vulnerability Scoring System version 3.1: Specification Document - CVSS Version 3.1 Release*. https://www.first.org/cvss/specification-document

Dahl, H. E. I. (2008). *The CORAS method for security risk analysis*. http://coras.sourceforge.net/documents/080828TheCORASMethod.pdf

EBIOS. (2010). In *Wikipedia*. https://en.wikipedia.org/wiki/EBIOS

Ekelhart, A. (2009). AURUM: A Framework for Information Security Risk Management. *42nd Hawaii International Conference on System Sciences*.

ENISA. (2020). Inventory of Risk Management / Risk Assessment Method. *European Union Agency for Cyber Security*. https://www.enisa.europa.eu/topics/threat-risk-management/risk-management/current-risk/risk-management-inventory/rm-ra-methods

Feth, P. (2018). *Dynamic Risk Assessment for Vehicles of Higher Automation Levels by Deep Learning*. Fraunhofer Institute for Experimental Software Engineering & DFKI – German Research Centre for Artificial Intelligence. doi:10.1007/978-3-319-99229-7_48

Freiberg, I. (2017). STPA-SafeSec: Safety and Security Analysis for Cyber-Physical Systems. *Elsevier Journal of Information Security and Applications, 34*(Part 2), 183–196.

Harpes, C. (2007). *Quantitative Risk Assessment with ISAMM on ESA's Operations Data System*. Telindus S.A., Security, Audit and Governance Services, Luxembourg. https://www.itrust.lu/wp-content/uploads/2007/09/publications_TTC_2007_abstract_risk_assessment_with_ISAMM.pdf

IRAM2. (2020). *IRAM2 summary on ISF homepage*. https://www.securityforum.org/tool/information-risk-assessment-methodology-iram2/

ISF homepage. (2020). https://www.securityforum.org/

ISO/IEC 27000. (2018). *An introduction to 27000-series (27001-27006)*. https://standards.iso.org/ittf/PubliclyAvailableStandards/

ISO/IEC 27001. (2013). *Information technology—Security techniques—Information security management systems—Requirements. Standard*. https://www.iso.org/iso/iso27001

ISO/IEC 27005. (2018). *Information Technology – Security Techniques _Information Security Risk Management; Guidance for establishing the context*. ISO.

ISO/IEC 27017. (2015). *Information technology -- Security techniques -- Code of practice for information security controls based on ISO/IEC 27002 for cloud services*. https://www.iso.org/standard/43757.html

ISO/IEC 31010. (2019). *Risk management — Risk assessment techniques*. https://www.iso.org/standard/72140.html

Kelarestaghi, K. B. (2019). *Intelligent Transportation System Security: Impact-Oriented Risk Assessment of in-Vehicle Networks. IEEE Intelligent Transportation Systems Magazine*.

Kephart, J., & Chess, D. (2003). The vision of autonomic computing. *Computer, 36*(1), 41–50. https://ieeexplore.ieee.org/document/1160055/

Lee, C., & Madnick, S. (2018). *A Systems Theoretic Approach to Cyber security Risk Analysis and Mitigation for Autonomous Passenger Vehicles*. MIT Management Sloan School.

Leveson, N. (2012). *Engineering a Safer World - Systems Thinking Applied to Safety*. MIT Press.

Liu, Y., & Man, H. (2005). *Network vulnerability assessment using Bayesian networks*. Proceeding of SPIE, 61-71.

Lopez, D. (2013). Dynamic Risk Assessment in Information Systems: State-of-the-art. *The 6th International Conference on Information Technology (ICIT)*.

MEHARI. (2019). In *Wikipedia*. https://en.wikipedia.org/wiki/MEHARI

Mirzaei, O. (2018). Dynamic Risk Assessment in IT Environments: A Decision Guide. In Z. Fields (Ed.), *Handbook of Research on Information and Cyber Security in the Fourth Industrial Revolution* (pp. 234–263). IGI Global.

NATO. (2015). *Management Directive on CIS Security*. https://www.nbu.cz/download/pravni-predpisy---nato/AC_35-D_2005-REV3.pdf

Nessus. (2020). *Tenable Security Ltd.* https://resources.infosecinstitute.com/a-brief-introduction-to-the-nessus-vulnerability-scanner/

Nipper. (2020). *TITANIA*. https://www.titania.com/products/nipper/

NIST 800-27. (2004). *Engineering Principles for Information Technology Security (ABaseline for Achieving Security), Revision A. superseded by SP 800-160 (November 2016)*. https://nvlpubs.nist.gov/nistpubs/Legacy/SP/nistspecialpublication800-27ra.pdf

NIST 800-30. (2012). Special Publication 800-30, Guide for Conducting Risk Assessments. *U.S. Department of Commerce.* https://nvlpubs.nist.gov/nistpubs/Legacy/SP/nistspecialpublication800-30r1.pdf

NIST 800-39. (2011). *NIST Special Publication 800-39, Managing Information Security Risk – Organization, Mission and Information System View.* U.S. Department of Commerce.

Nmap. (2020). *Network Mapper*. https://nmap.org/

Paulina, J. (2007). Designing a Security Policy According to BS 7799 Using the OCTAVE Methodology. *The Second International Conference on Availability, Reliability and Security (ARES'07).*

Piper, J. (2020). *Risk Management Framework: Qualitative Risk Assessment through Risk Scenario Analysis*. Technical Report, STO-MP-IST-166.

Poolappasit, N., Dewri, R., & Ray, I. (2012). Dynamic security risk assessment using bayesian attack graphs. *IEEE Transactions on Dependable and Secure Computing, 9*, 61–74.

Raspotnig, C. (2018). Combined Assessment of Software Safety and Security Requirements: An Industrial Evaluation of the CHASSIS Method. *Journal of Cases on Information Technology, 20*(1).

ResiCAV. (2020). *Economic and Technological Feasibility of CyRes Methodology*. Thales Technical report.

Saripalli, P. (2010). QUIRC: A Quantitative Impact and Risk Assessment Framework for Cloud Security. *IEEE 3rd International Conference on Cloud Computing.*

SecRAM. (2017). *SecRAM 2.0 Security Risk Assessment methodology for SESAR 2020*. https://www.sesarju.eu/sites/default/files/documents/transversal/SESAR%202020%20-%20Security%20Reference%20Material%20Guidance.pdf

SESAR. (2020). *Single European Sky ATM Research programme*. http://www.sesarju.eu/

Verhoogt, T. (2018). *Towards Dynamic Cyber Security Risk Assessment of Military Aircraft*. NATO Science and Technology Organization (SCO). Reference: STO-MP-SCI-300.

Young, W. (2017). System-Theoretic Process Analysis for Security (STPA-SEC): Cyber Security and STPA. *STAMP Conference.* http://psas.scripts.mit.edu/home/wp-content/uploads/2017/04/STAMP_2017_STPA_SEC_TUTORIAL_as-presented.pdf

Zenzic. (2020). *Zenzic's published work on Cyber Feasibility Studies for CAVs, in partnership with CCAV.* https://zenzic.io/cybersecurity/

APPENDIX I.

Threat Scenario

T-IMC No.3	
Target and impact description	
Targeted Supporting asset	SA#02 Computing device
Impact on targeted supporting asset	Could cause leakage or unauthorized modification of data within the device, and could cause reduced availability or even complete failure of the device.
Targeted Primary asset	PA#01
Impact on targeted supporting asset — Confidentiality	Yes
Impact on targeted supporting asset — Integrity	Yes
Impact on targeted supporting asset — Availability	Yes
Type of attack against asset	Yes, to device development environment, or to device during software or hardware update.
Adversary description	
Has an Internal access to the system	No to device, but access to an on-board application is required
Skills required	High knowledge and engineering skills
Tangible resources required	None
Motivation	To disrupt applications or to obtain their data.
Threat scenario description	
Define the pre-conditions of the threat	There needs to be vulnerability in the development environment that allows malicious or erroneous software or hardware to be introduced and accepted as valid, or in the software/hardware update process that allows unauthenticated updates. Other flaws or weaknesses in the device implementation may make such attacks easier, such as lack of authentication and separation of internal data and processes, but may not be necessary.
Define the main steps of the threat	Either insert malicious or erroneous software or hardware during development, or get maintainer to install unauthenticated malicious software or hardware updates. During operation of the device, this malicious functionality may then modify, delete, replay, read, etc. other applications' data.

Compilation of References

GPP – 3rd Generation Partnership Project. (2017). System Architecture for 5G System, Stage 2, 3GPP TS 23.501 v2.0.1.

GPP – 3rd Generation Partnership Project. (2018). TR 22.804, Technical Specification Group Services and System Aspects, Study on Communication for Automation in Vertical Domains (Release 16).

GPP. (2020a). *3GPP Technologies Home*. Retrieved November 28, 2020 from http://www.3gpp.org/technologies/technologies

GPP. (2020b). *Digital cellular telecommunications system (Phase 2+); (GSM);Universal Mobile Telecommunications System (UMTS); General Packet Radio Service (GPRS); GPRS Tunnelling Protocol (GTP) across the Gn and Gp interface (3GPP TS 29.060 version 16.0.0 Release 16)*. ETSI TS 129 060 V16.0.0 (2020-11). Retrieved December 28, 2020 from https://www.etsi.org/deliver/etsi_ts/129000_129099/129060/16.00.00_60/ts_129060v160000p.pdf

GPP. (2020c). *LTE; Evolved Universal Terrestrial; Radio Access Network (E-UTRAN); General aspects and principles for interfaces supporting Multimedia Broadcast Multicast Service (MBMS) within E-UTRAN (3GPP TS 36.440 version 16.0.0 Release 16)*. ETSI TS 136 440 V16.0.0 (2020-07). Retrieved October 23, 2020 from https://www.etsi.org/deliver/etsi_ts/136400_136499/136440/16.00.00_60/ts_136440v160000p.pdf

GPP. (2020d). *3rd Generation Partnership Project; Technical Specification Group Services and System Aspects; Multimedia Broadcast/Multicast Service (MBMS); Protocols and codecs (Release 16). 3GPP TS 26.346 V16.6.1 (2020-10).*

GPP. (2021). *Universal Mobile Telecommunications System (UMTS); LTE; 5G; 3GPP Evolved Packet System (EPS); Evolved General Packet Radio Service (GPRS) Tunnelling Protocol for Control plane (GTPv2-C); Stage 3 (3GPP TS 29.274 version 16.6.0 Release 16). ETSI TS 129 274 V16.6.0 (2021-01).* Retrieved February 12, 2021 from https://www.etsi.org/deliver/etsi_ts/129200_129299/129274/16.06.00_60/ts_129274v160600p.pdf

GPP-VES. (2020). 5G; Management and orchestration; Generic management services. *ETSI TS, 128*, 532.

3rd Generation Partnership Project, Interface between the Control Plane and the User Plane Nodes v16.6.0. (2020). *Stage 3, Release 16*. 3GPP.

3rd Generation Partnership Project, System architecture for the 5G System v16.6.0. (2020). *Stage 2, Release 16*. 3GPP.

GAA – 5G Automotive Association. (2017). Toward fully connected vehicles: Edge computing for advanced automotive communications (White Paper).

GACIA – 5G Alliance for Connected Industries and Automation. (2020). Key 5G Use Cases and Requirements (White Paper).

PPP Architecture Working Group. View on 5G Architecture. (2020). *Version 3.0*. https://5g-ppp.eu/wp-content/uploads/2020/02/5G-PPP-5G-Architecture-White-Paper_final.pdf

Abbas, M. T., Muhammad, A., & Song, W. C. (2020). SD-IoV: SDN enabled routing for internet of vehicles in road-aware approach. *Journal of Ambient Intelligence and Humanized Computing*, *11*(3), 1265–1280. doi:10.100712652-019-01319-w

Abbass, W. (2015). Using EBIOS for risk management in critical information infrastructure. *5th World Congress on Information and Communication Technologies (WICT)*. 10.1109/WICT.2015.7489654

Abboud, K., Omar, H. A., & Zhuang, W. (2016). Interworking of DSRC and cellular network technologies for V2X communications: A survey. *IEEE Transactions on Vehicular Technology*, *65*(12), 9457–9470. doi:10.1109/TVT.2016.2591558

Abera, T., Asokan, N., Davi, L., Ekberg, J.-E., Nyman, T., Paverd, A., Sadeghi, A.-R., & Tsudik, G. (2016). C-FLAT: Control-Flow Attestation for Embedded Systems Software. *ACM SIGSAC Conference on Computer and Communications Security (CCS)*. 10.1145/2976749.2978358

Abera, T., Bahmani, R., Brasser, F., Ibrahim, A., Sadeghi, A.-R., & Schunter, M. (2019). DIAT: Data Integrity Attestation for Resilient Collaboration of Autonomous Systems. *Annual Network and Distributed System Security Symposium (NDSS)*. 10.14722/ndss.2019.23420

Abgrall, D. (2011). *Virtual Home Gateway: How can Home Gateway virtualization be achieved?* EURESCOM Study Report P2055 D1.

ABI. (2020). *ABI Research. Cord-cutting driving decline in set-top box soc market from US$2.4 billion in 2019 to US$2 billion in 2023. April 4, 2019.* Retrieved October 30, 2020 from https://www.abiresearch.com/press/cord-cutting-driving-decline-set-top-box-soc-market-us2-billion-2023/

Abugabah, A., Alzubi, A. A., Alfarraj, O., Al-Maitah, M., & Alnumay, W. S. (2020). Intelligent Traffic Engineering in Software-Defined Vehicular Networking Based on Multi-Path Routing. *IEEE Access: Practical Innovations, Open Solutions*, *8*, 62334–62342. doi:10.1109/ACCESS.2020.2983204

Agarwal, K., Rozner, E., Dixon, C., & Carter, J. (2014). SDN traceroute: Tracing SDN forwarding without changing network behavior. In *Proceedings of the third workshop on Hot topics in software defined networking* (pp. 145-150). Academic Press.

Ahmad, A., Harjula, E., Ylianttila, M., & Ahmad, I. (2020). Evaluation of Machine Learning Techniques for Security in SDN. In *IEEE Global Communications Conference, GLOBECOM 2020*. IEEE Institute of Electrical and Electronic Engineers.

Akamai. (2012). *Press Release. November 20, 2012. Orange and Akamai form Content Delivery Strategic Alliance.* Retrieved October 23, 2020 from https://www.prnewswire.com/news-releases/orange-and-akamai-form-content-delivery-strategic-alliance-180145801.html

Akamai. (2020a). *Akamai IP Application Accelerator Web Page*. Retrieved October 30, 2020 from https://www.akamai.com/us/en/products/performance/ip-application-accelerator.jsp

Akamai. (2020b). *Visualizing Akamai Web Page*. Retrieved October 30, 2020 from https://www.akamai.com/us/en/resources/visualizing-akamai/

Akamai. (2020c). *Visualizing Akamai Web Page, Enterprise Threat Monitor*. Retrieved October 30, 2020 from https://www.akamai.com/us/en/resources/visualizing-akamai/enterprise-threat-monitor.jsp

Akamai. (2020d). *Akamai State of the Internet Report, Security Report Web Page*. Retrieved October 30, 2020 from https://www.akamai.com/us/en/resources/our-thinking/state-of-the-internet-report/global-state-of-the-internet-security-ddos-attack-reports.jsp

Akamai. (2020e). *Akamai Web Attack Visualization Web Page*. Retrieved October 30, 2020 from https://www.akamai.com/us/en/resources/our-thinking/state-of-the-internet-report/web-attack-visualization.jsp

Akamai. (2020f). *Akamai Security Web Page*. Retrieved October 30, 2020 from https://www.akamai.com/us/en/security.jsp

Akamai. (2020g). *Press Release. July 28, 2020. Akamai Reports Second Quarter 2020 Financial Results*. Retrieved October 30, 2020 from https://www.akamai.com/us/en/about/news/press/2020-press/akamai-reports-second-quarter-2020-financial-results.jsp

Akamai. (2020h). *Akamai Customer Identity and Access Management Web Page*. Retrieved October 30, 2020 from https://www.akamai.com/us/en/solutions/security/customer-identity-and-access-management.jsp

Akamai. (2020i). *Akamai Customer Identity Cloud Web Page*. Retrieved October 30, 2020 from https://www.akamai.com/us/en/products/security/identity-cloud.jsp

Akamai. (2020j). *Akamai IoT Edge Cloud Products Web Page*. Retrieved October 30, 2020 from https://www.akamai.com/us/en/solutions/iot-edge-cloud/

Akamai. (2020k). *Akamai API Gateway Web Page*. Retrieved October 30, 2020 from https://developer.akamai.com/akamai-api-gateway/

Akamai. (2020l). *Akamai Global Traffic Management Web Page*. Retrieved October 30, 2020 from https://www.akamai.com/us/en/products/performance/global-traffic-management.jsp

Akamai. (2020m). *Akamai EdgeWorkers Web Page*. Retrieved October 30, 2020 from https://developer.akamai.com/akamai-edgeworkers-overview/

Akamai. (2020n). *Akamai Cloulets Web Page*. Retrieved October 30, 2020 from https://www.akamai.com/us/en/products/performance/cloudlets/

Akhtar, N., Matta, I., Raza, A., Goratti, L., Braun, T., & Esposito, F. (2018, June). Virtual function placement and traffic steering over 5g multi-technology networks. In *2018 4th IEEE Conference on Network Softwarization and Workshops (NetSoft)* (pp. 114-122). IEEE.

Akhunzada, A., & Khan, M. K. (2017). Toward secure software defined vehicular networks: Taxonomy, requirements, and open issues. *IEEE Communications Magazine*, *55*(7), 110–118. doi:10.1109/MCOM.2017.1601158

Akram, R. N., Markantonakis, K., Mayes, K., Habachi, O., Sauveron, D., Steyven, A., & Chaumette, S. (2017). Security, privacy and safety evaluation of dynamic and static fleets of drones. *IEEE/AIAA Digital Avionics Systems Conference (DASC)*.

Alalmaei, S., Elkhatib, Y., Bezahaf, M., Broadbent, M., & Race, N. (2020). SDN Heading North: Towards a Declarative Intent-based Northbound Interface. In *2020 16th International Conference on Network and Service Management (CNSM)* (pp. 1-5). IEEE.

Aldrin, A., Pignataro, C., Kumar, N., Krishnan, R., & Ghanwani, A. (2020). S*ervice Function Chaining (SFC) Operations, Administration, and Maintenance (OAM) Framework*. RFC 8924. Available: https://tools.ietf.org/html/rfc8924

Alioua, A., Senouci, S. M., Moussaoui, S., Sedjelmaci, H., & Boualouache, A. (2017, October). Software-Defined heterogeneous vehicular networks: Taxonomy and architecture. In *2017 Global Information Infrastructure and Networking Symposium (GIIS)* (pp. 50-55). IEEE. 10.1109/GIIS.2017.8169805

Alter, C. (2014). *Broadband Forum Work on "Network Enhanced Residential Gateway" (WT-317) and "Virtual Business Gateway" (WT-328)*. Broadband Forum's liaison letter to the IETF.

Alter, C., & Daowood, S. (2014). *Broadband Forum Work on Flexible Service Chaining (SD-326).* Broadband Forum's liaison letter to the IETF.

Amazon Prime Air. (n.d.). Retrieved October 13, 2020, from https://www.amazon.com/Amazon-Prime-Air

Amazon. (2020). *Amazon Route53 Web Page.* Retrieved October 30, 2020 from https://aws.amazon.com/route53/

American Society of Testing and Materials International. (2019). *Standard Specification for Remote ID and Tracking (ASTM F3411-19).* Author.

Amjid, A., Khan, A., & Shah, M. A. (2020). VANET-Based Volunteer Computing (VBVC): A Computational Paradigm for Future Autonomous Vehicles. *IEEE Access: Practical Innovations, Open Solutions, 8,* 71763–71774. doi:10.1109/ACCESS.2020.2974500

Ananth, M. D., & Sharma, R. (2016, December). Cloud management using network function virtualization to reduce capex and opex. In *2016 8th International Conference on Computational Intelligence and Communication Networks (CICN)* (pp. 43-47). IEEE. 10.1109/CICN.2016.17

Ananth, M. D., & Sharma, R. (2017, January). Cost and performance analysis of network function virtualization based cloud systems. In *2017 IEEE 7th International Advance Computing Conference (IACC)* (pp. 70-74). IEEE. 10.1109/IACC.2017.0029

Anderson, J., Hu, H., Agarwal, U., Lowery, C., Li, H., & Apon, A. (2016). Performance considerations of network functions virtualization using containers. In *2016 International Conference on Computing, Networking and Communications (ICNC)* (pp. 1–7). 10.1109/ICCNC.2016.7440668

Andromeda, S., & Gunawan, D. (2020). Techno-economic analysis from implementing sd-wan with 4g/lte, a case study in xyz company. In *2020 International Seminar on Intelligent Technology and Its Applications (ISITIA)* (pp. 345-351). IEEE.

Ansys. (2019). *How to validate autonomous VTOL safety* (Ansys White Paper). Author.

Apache Thrift. (n.d.). https://thrift.apache.org/

Apache ThriftI. D. L. (n.d.). https://thrift.apache.org/docs/idl

Arif, M., Wang, G., Geman, O., Balas, V. E., Tao, P., Brezulianu, A., & Chen, J. (2020). SDN-based VANETs, Security Attacks, Applications, and Challenges. *Applied Sciences (Basel, Switzerland), 10*(9), 3217. doi:10.3390/app10093217

Arijs, P. (n.d.). *Docker Usage Stats: Adoption Up in the Enterprise and Production.* https://dzone.com/articles/docker-usage-statistics-increased-adoption-by-ente

Asgari, H. (2016). Security Risk Assessment and Risk Treatment for Integrated Modular Communication. *International conference on Availability, Reliability, and Security (ARES), presented at ATMSec Workshop.* http://www.ares-conference.eu

Asgari, H., Haines, S., & Rysavy, O. (2018). Identification of threats and security risk assessments for recursive Internet architecture. *IEEE Systems Journal, 12*(3), 2437–2448. doi:10.1109/JSYST.2017.2765178

Asgari, H., Stelkens-Kobsch, T. H., Montefusco, P., Abhaya, L., Koelle, R., Markarian, G., & D'Auria, G. (2017). Provisioning for a distributed ATM security management: The GAMMA approach. Featured Article. *IEEE Aerospace and Electronic Systems Magazine, 32*(11), 5–21. doi:10.1109/MAES.2017.170037

ASHRAE Technical Committee. (2016). *Data Center Power Equipment Thermal Guidelines and Best Practices.* https://ecoinfo.cnrs.fr/wp-content/uploads/2016/08/ashrae_2011_thermal_guidelines_data_center.pdf

Aslan, J., Mayers, K., Koomey, J. G., & France, C. (2017). Electricity intensity of internet data transmission: Untangling the estimates. *Journal of Industrial Ecology, 22*(4), 785–798. doi:10.1111/jiec.12630

Associated Press. (2015, April 22). Drone 'containing radiation' lands on roof of Japanese PM's office. *The Guardian.* https://www.theguardian.com/

ATIS. (2013). *Operational Opportunities and Challenges of SDN/NFV Programmable Infrastructure.* October 2013, Report.

Awduche, D., Berger, L., Gan, D., Li, T., Srinivasan, V., & Swallow, G. (2001). RSVP-TE: Extensions to RSVP for LSP Tunnels. *IETF.* Retrieved December 09, 2020, from https://tools.ietf.org/html/rfc3209

Awduche, D., Chiu, A., Elwalid, A., Widjaja, I., & Xiao, X. (2002). *Overview and principles of internet traffic engineering.* IETF RFC 3272.

Azhar, H. (2019). Challenges and Techniques in Drone Forensics. *International Conference on Cyber-Technologies and Cyber-Systems (CYBER).*

Baktir, A. C., Ozgovde, A., & Ersoy, C. (2017). How can edge computing benefit from software-defined networking: A survey, use cases, and future directions. *IEEE Communications Surveys and Tutorials, 19*(4), 2359–2391.

Baldoni, G., Cruschelli, P., Paolino, M., Meixner, C. C., Albanese, A., Papageorgiou, A., & Simeonidou, D. (2018, November). Edge Computing Enhancements in an NFV-based Ecosystem for 5G Neutral Hosts. In *2018 IEEE Conference on Network Function Virtualization and Software Defined Networks (NFV-SDN)* (pp. 1-5). IEEE.

Barguil, S., de Dios, O. G., Boucadair, M., Munoz, L., Jalil, L., & Ma, J. (2021a). *A Layer 2 VPN Network YANG Model.* IETF draft-ietf-opsawg-l2nm.

Barguil, S., Gonzalez de Dios, O., Lopez, V. Gagliano, R., & Carretero, I. (2020). *Experimental validation of L3 VPN Network Model for improving VPN Service design and Provisioning.* CNSM 2020.

Barguil, S., O, G. d. D., Boucadair, M., Munoz, L., & Aguado, A. (2021b*). A Layer 3 VPN Network YANG Model.* IETF draft-ietf-opsawg-l3sm-l3nm.

Barham, P., Dragovic, B., Fraser, K., Hand, S., Harris, T., Ho, A., Neugebauer, R., Pratt, I., & Warfield, A. (2003). Xen and the art of virtualization. *SIGOPS Oper. Syst. Rev., 37*(5), 164-177. doi:10.1145/1165389.945462

Barmpounakis, S., Maroulis, N., Papadakis, M., Tsiatsios, G., Soukaras, D., & Alonistioti, N. (2020). Network slicing-enabled RAN management for 5G: Cross layer control based on SDN and SDR. *Computer Networks, 166*, 106987.

Basak, D., Toshniwal, R., Maskalik, S., & Sequeira, A. (2010). Virtualizing networking and security in the cloud. *SIGOPS Oper. Syst. Rev., 44*(4), 86-94. https://doi.acm.org/10.1145/1899928.1899939 doi:10.1145/1899928.1899939

Basta, A., Kellerer, W., Hoffmann, M., Hoffmann, K., & Schmidt, E. D. (2013). A Virtual SDN-enabled LTE EPC Architecture: a case study for S-/P-Gateways functions. In *Future Networks and Services (SDN4FNS), 2013 IEEE SDN for* (pp. 1–7). IEEE.

Basta, A., Kellerer, W., Hoffmann, M., Morper, H. J., & Hoffmann, K. (2014). Applying NFV and SDN to LTE Mobile Core Gateways, the Functions Placement Problem. In *Proceedings of the 4th workshop on all things cellular: Operations, applications, & challenges* (pp. 33–38). New York, NY: ACM. 10.1145/2627585.2627592

Batool, R. (2019). Review, Analysis of SDN and Difficulties in Adoption of SD. *Journal of Information & Communication Technology, 13*(1).

Bazzi, A., & Onozato, Y. (2011). Feasibility Study of Security Virtual Appliances for Personal Computing. *IPSJ Journal of Information Processing, 19.*

BBC News. (2015, September 17). Warning over drone security threat to prisons. *BBC News*. https://www.bbc.com/news/

BBF MR-430. (2018). *Broadband Forum MR-430: Cloud Central Office (CloudCO)*. Retrieved September 2020 https://www.broadband-forum.org/marketing/download/MR-430.pdf

Bcom. (2020). *Wireless Edge Factory*. https://b-com.com/fr/bcom-wireless-edge-factory

Bemby, S., Lu, H., Zadeh, K. H., Bannazadeh, H., & Leon-Garcia, A. (2015). Vino: SDN overlay to allow seamless migration across heterogeneous infrastructure. In *2015 IFIP/IEEE International Symposium on Integrated Network Management (IM)*, (pp. 782–785). IEEE. 10.1109/INM.2015.7140375

Benalia, E., Bitam, S., & Mellouk, A. (2020). Data dissemination for Internet of vehicle based on 5G communications: A survey. *Transactions on Emerging Telecommunications Technologies*, *31*(5), e3881. doi:10.1002/ett.3881

Bentaleb, A., Taani, B., Begen, A., Timmermer, C., & Zimmermann, R. (2018). A Survey on Bitrate Adaptation Schemes for Streaming Media over HTTP. IEEE Communications Surveys & Tutorials (IEEE COMST), 1(1).

Berde, P., Gerola, M., Hart, J., Higuchi, Y., Kobayashi, M., Koide, T., Lantz, B., O'Connor, B., Radoslavov, P., Snow, W., & Parulkar, G. (2014). ONOS: towards an open, distributed SDN OS. In *Proceedings of the third workshop on Hot topics in software defined networking* (pp. 1-6). Academic Press.

Berde, P., Gerola, M., Hart, J., Higuchi, Y., Kobayashi, M., Koide, T., ... Parulkar, G. (2014). ONOS: Towards an Open, Distributed SDN OS. In *Proceedings of the Third Workshop on Hot Topics in Software Defined Networking* (pp. 1–6). New York, NY: ACM. 10.1145/2620728.2620744

Bergkvist, A., Burnett, D. C., Jennings, C., & Narayanan, A. (2013). WebRTC 1.0: Real-time Communication Between Browsers. *World Wide Web Consortium*. Retrieved December 09, 2020, from www.w3.org/TR/webrtc/

Bernardos, C. J., de la Oliva, A., Serrano, P., Banchs, A., Contreras, L. M., Jin, H., & Zúñiga, J. C. (2014, June). An Architecture for Software Defined Wireless Networking. IEEE Wireless Communications Magazine.

Bertrand, G., Stephan, E., Burbridge, T., Eardley, P., Ma, K., & Watson, G. (2012). Use Cases for Content Delivery Network Interconnection. *IETF*. Retrieved December 09, 2020, from https://tools.ietf.org/html/rfc6770

Best, K.L., Schmid, J., Tierney, S., Awan, J., Beyene, N., Holliday, M.A., Khan, R., & Lee, K. (2020). *How to Analyze the Cyber Threat from Drones: Background, Analysis Frameworks, and Analysis Tools*. RAND Corporation Research Report.

Bhatia, A., Haribabu, K., Gupta, K., & Sahu, A. (2018, January). Realization of flexible and scalable VANETs through SDN and virtualization. In *2018 International Conference on Information Networking (ICOIN)* (pp. 280-282). IEEE. 10.1109/ICOIN.2018.8343125

Bianchi, G., Bianco, C., Boldi, M., Bolla, R., Le Grand, O., Meo, M., Penhoat, J. & Renga, D. (2019). Sustainability, a key issue of 5G network ecosystem. *The 5G Italy Book 2019: a Multiperspective View of 5G.*

Bianchini, R., Fontoura, M., Cortez, E., Bonde, A., Muzio, A., Constantin, A. M., ... Russinovich, M. (2020). Toward ML-centric cloud platforms. *Communications of the ACM*, *63*(2), 50–59.

Biediger, D., Mahadev, A., & Becker, A. T. (2019). Investigating the survivability of drone swarms with flocking and swarming flight patterns using Virtual Reality. *International Conference on Automation Science and Engineering (CASE)*. 10.1109/COASE.2019.8843173

Bierman, A., Bjorklund, M., & Watsen, K. (2017). *RESTCONF protocol*. IETF RFC 8040.

Bierman, A., Bjorklund, M., & Watsen, K. (2017). *RESTCONF Protocol*. IETF RFC 8040.

Birk, M., Choudhury, G., Cortez, B., Goddard, A., Padi, N., Raghuram, A., Tse, K., Tse, S., Wallace, A., & Xi, K. (2016). Evolving to an SDN-enabled ISP Backbone: Key Technologies and Applications. *IEEE Communications Magazine, 54*(10), 129–135. doi:10.1109/MCOM.2016.7588281

Bishop, M. (2020). *Hypertext Transfer Protocol Version 3 (HTTP/3). draft-ietf-quic-http-32.* Retrieved October 30, 2020 from https://tools.ietf.org/html/draft-ietf-quic-http-32

Biswas, J., Lazar, A. A., Huard, J. F., Lim, K., Mahjoub, S., Pau, L. F., ... Weinstein, S. (1998). The IEEE P1520 standards initiative for programmable network interfaces. *Communications Magazine, IEEE, 36*(10), 64–70.

Bjorklund, M. (2010). *YANG – A Data Modeling Language for the Network Configuration Protocol (NETCONF).* IETF RFC 6020.

Bjorklund, M. (2010). *YANG-a data modeling language for the network configuration protocol (NETCONF).* IETF RFC6020.

Bjorklund, M. (2016). *The YANG 1.1 Data Modeling Language.* IETF RFC 7950.

Bjorklund, M. (Ed.). (2016). *The YANG 1.1 Data Modeling Language.* IETF. RFC 7950. Retrieved October 09, 2020, from https://tools.ietf.org/html/rfc7950

Bjorklund, M., Schoenwaelder, J., Shafer, P., Watsen, K., & Wilton, R. (2018). *Network Management Datastore Architecture (nmda).* IETF RFC, RFC 8342.

Blackford, J., & Digdon, M. (2013). *Broadband Forum, "TR-069 – CPE WAN Management Protocol", Issue 1, Amendment 5, November 2013.*

Blake, S., Black, D., Carlson, M., Davies, E., Wang, Z., & Weiss, W. (1998). *An Architecture for Differentiated Services.* IETF RFC 2475.

Blengini, G. A., Latunussa, E. L. C., Eynard, U., de Matos, C. T., Wittmer, D., Georgitzikis, K., Pavel, C., Carrara, S., Mancini, L., Unguru, M., Blagoeva, D., Mathieux, F., & Pennington, D. (2020). *Study on the EU's list of Critical Raw Materials (2020) Final Report.* European Commission Technical Report.

Bolla, R., Bruschi, R., Davoli, F., & Lombardo, C. (2015). Fine-Grained Energy-Efficient Consolidation in SDN Networks and Devices. *IEEE eTransactions on Network and Service Management, 12*(5), 132–145. doi:10.1109/TNSM.2015.2431074

Boman, D., Deering, S., & Hinden, R. (1999). *IPv6 Jumbograms.* IETF RFC 2675.

Bonafiglia, R., Cerrato, I., Ciaccia, F., Nemirovsky, M., & Risso, F. (2015). Assessing the Performance of Virtualization Technologies for NFV: A Preliminary Benchmarking. In *Software Defined Networks (EWSDN), 2015 Fourth European Workshop on* (pp. 67–72). 10.1109/EWSDN.2015.63

Bonomi, F., Milito, R., Zhu, J., & Addepalli, S. (2012). Fog computing and its role in the internet of things. In *Proceedings of the first edition of the mcc workshop on mobile cloud computing* (pp. 13–16). New York, NY: ACM. 10.1145/2342509.2342513

Bordage, F. (2019). *The environmental footprint of the digital world.* https://www.greenit.fr/wp-content/uploads/2019/11/GREENIT_EENM_etude_EN_accessible.pdf

Bosshart, P., Daly, D., Izzard, M., McKeown, N., Rexford, J., Talayco, D., ... Walker, D. (2013). *Programming protocol-independent packet processors.* arXiv preprint arXiv:1312.1719.

Bosshart, P., Daly, D., Gibb, G., Izzard, M., McKeown, N., Rexford, J., Schlesinger, C., Talayco, D., Vahdat, A., Varghese, G., & Walker, D. (2014, July 28). P4: Programming protocol-independent packet processors. *Computer Communication Review, 44*(3), 87–95.

Boualouache, A., Soua, R., & Engel, T. (2020, May). SDN-based Misbehavior Detection System for Vehicular Networks. In *2020 IEEE 91st Vehicular Technology Conference (VTC2020-Spring)* (pp. 1-5). IEEE. 10.1109/VTC2020-Spring48590.2020.9128604

Boubendir, A., Bertin, E., & Simoni, N. (2017, March). A VNF-as-a-service design through micro-services disassembling the IMS. In *2017 20th Conference on Innovations in Clouds, Internet and Networks (ICIN)* (pp. 203-210). IEEE.

Boucadair, M. & Jacquenet, C. (2014). *Software-defined Networking: A Perspective from within a Service Provider Environment.* IETF RFC 7149.

Boucadair, M. (Ed.). (2020). *Distributed Denial-of-Service Open Threat Signaling (DOTS) Data Channel Specification.* IETF. RFC 8783. Retrieved October 09, 2020, from https://www.rfc-editor.org/rfc/rfc8783.pdf

Boucadair, M. (Ed.). (2020). *Distributed Denial-of-Service Open Threat Signaling (DOTS) Telemetry.* IETF. Retrieved October 09, 2020, from https://datatracker.ietf.org/doc/draft-ietf-dots-telemetry/

Boucadair, M., & Jacquenet, C. (2014). Software-Defined Networking: A Perspective from within a Service Provider Environment. *IETF.* Retrieved December 09, 2020, from https://tools.ietf.org/html/rfc7149

Boucadair, M., & Jacquenet, C. (2014). *Software-Defined Networking: A Perspective from within a Service Provider Environment.* IETF. RFC 7149. Retrieved October 09, 2020, from https://tools.ietf.org/html/rfc7149

Boucadair, M., Jacquenet, C., & Wang, N. (2014). IP Connectivity Provisioning Profile (CPP). *IETF.* Retrieved December 09, 2020, from https://tools.ietf.org/html/rfc7297

Boucadair, M., Jacquenet, C., & Wang, N. (2014). *IP Connectivity Provisioning Profile (CPP).* IETF. RFC 7297. Retrieved October 09, 2020, from https://tools.ietf.org/html/rfc7297

Boucadair, M., Jacquenet, C., Jiang, Y., Parker, R., Pignataro, C., & Naito, K. (2014). *Requirements for Service Function Chaining (SFC) (draft-boucadair-sfc-requirements-05).* IETF Internet Draft.

Boucadair, M., Jacquenet, C., Parker, R., & Dunbar, L. (2014). *Service Function Chaining: Design Considerations, Analysis & Recommendations* (draft-boucadair-sfc-design-analysis-02). IETF Internet Draft.

Boucadair, M., Jacquenet, C., Zhang, D., & Georgatsos, P. (2020a). *Dynamic Service Negotiation.* IETF. RFC 8921. Retrieved October 09, 2020, from https://tools.ietf.org/html/rfc8921

Boukerche, A., & Robson, E. (2018). Vehicular cloud computing: Architectures, applications, and mobility. *Computer Networks, 135,* 171–189. doi:10.1016/j.comnet.2018.01.004

Bouras, C., Kollia, A., & Papazois, A. (2017), March. SDN & NFV in 5G: Advancements and challenges. In *2017 20th Conference on innovations in clouds, internet and networks (ICIN)* (pp. 107-111). IEEE.

Boyens, J., Paulsen, C., Moorthy, R., & Bartol, N. (2015). *Supply Chain Risk Management Practices for Federal Information Systems and Organizations.* NIST Special Publication 800-161.

Bozkaya, E., & Canberk, B. (2015, December). QoE-based flow management in software defined vehicular networks. In *2015 IEEE Globecom Workshops (GC Wkshps)* (pp. 1-6). IEEE.

Braden, R., Zhang, L., Herzog, S., Berson, S., & Jamin, S. (1997). Resource ReSerVation Protocol (RSVP). *IETF.* Retrieved December 09, 2020, from https://tools.ietf.org/html/rfc2205

Brasser, F., El Mahjoub, B., Sadeghi, A.-R., Wachsmann, C., & Koeberl, P. (2015). TyTAN: Tiny trust anchor for tiny devices. *ACM/EDAC/IEEE Design Automation Conference (DAC)*. 10.1145/2744769.2744922

Brewster, T. (2019, November 5). Amazon Alexa Can Be Hacked By A Laser From 100 Meters—Is It Time To Hide Your Echo? *Forbes*. https://www.forbes.com/

BroadPeak. (2020a). *Broadpeak Web Portal Page*. Retrieved October 30, 2020 from http://www.broadpeak.tv/

BroadPeak. (2020b). *Broadpeak Press Release. April 5, 2016. Broadpeak Launches CDN Diversity, Dramatically Improving Live/VOD Content Delivery and QoE*. Retrieved October 30, 2020 from https://broadpeak.tv/newsroom/broadpeak-launches-cdn-diversity-dramatically-improving-livevod-content-delivery-and-qoe/

Brockners, F., Bhandari, S., & Mizrahi, T. (2020). *Data Fields for In-situ OAM*. IETF draft-ietf-ippm-iom-data.

Brodkin, J. (2020). AT&T kills DSL, leaves tens of millions of homes without fiber Internet. *ARS Technica*. Available at: https://arstechnica.com/tech-policy/2020/10/life-in-atts-slow-lane-millions-left-without-fiber-as-company-kills-dsl/

Brooks, M. (2020). *Introduction to Citrix Intelligent Traffic Management*. Retrieved October 30, 2020 from https://docs.citrix.com/en-us/tech-zone/learn/tech-briefs/itm.html#intelligent-traffic

Bryant, S., & Pate, P. (2005). *Pseudo Wire Emulation Edge-to-Edge (PWE3) Architecture*. IETF RFC 3985.

BSI Document. (2020). *Understanding your Cyber security Risks*. https://www.bsigroup.com/contentassets/6466e3753 87a4ffa8ddbc64e535e27b0/understanding-your-cybersecurity-risk-bsi.pdf

BSI Group. (2020). https://www.bsigroup.com/en-GB/about-bsi/

Bushaus, D. (2017). *Telefónica 'gets its hands dirty' with new OnLife Network*. Retrieved September 2020 from https://inform.tmforum.org/news/2017/05/telefonica-gets-hands-dirty-new-platform-architecture/

CableLabs, Inc. (2014). *DOCSIS 3.1 Physical Specification*. CableLabs.

CableLabs, Inc. (2020). *DOCSIS 4.0 Physical Specification*. CableLabs. Available at: https://www.cablelabs.com/technologies/docsis-4-0-technology

Caesar, M., Caldwell, D., Feamster, N., Rexford, J., Shaikh, A., & van der Merwe, J. (2005). Design and implementation of a routing control platform. In *Proceedings of the 2nd conference on Symposium on Networked Systems Design & Implementation-Volume 2* (pp. 15-28). USENIX Association.

Cain, B., Deering, S., Kouvelas, I., Fenner, B., & Thyagarajan, A. (2002). *Internet Group Management Protocol, Version 3*. IETF Standard RFC 3376.

Campanella, A., Okui, H., Mayoral, A., Kashiwa, D., de Dios, O. G., Verchere, D., Van, Q. P., Giorgetti, A., Casellas, R., & Morro, R. (2019). ODTN: Open disaggregated transport network. Discovery and control of a disaggregated optical network through open source software and open APIs. In 2019 OpticalFiber Communications Conference and Exhibition (OFC), (pp. 1–3). IEEE.

Campbell, A. T., De Meer, H. G., Kounavis, M. E., Miki, K., Vicente, J. B., & Villela, D. (1999). A survey of programmable networks. *Computer Communication Review*, 29(2), 7–23.

Campolo, C., Molinaro, A., & Scopigno, R. (2015). From today's VANETs to tomorrow's planning and the bets for the day after. *Vehicular Communications*, 2(3), 158–171. doi:10.1016/j.vehcom.2015.06.002

Camunda. (2020). *Reinventing Process Automation for the Digital Enterprise*. https://camunda.com/

Cantó Palancar, R., López da Silva, R. A., Folgueira Chavarría, J. L., López, D. R., Elizondo Armengol, A. J., Gamero Tinoco, R., ... Gamero Tinoco, R. (2015). Virtualization of residential customer premise equipment. Lessons learned in Brazil vCPE trial. *IT - Information Technology, 57*(5), 285–294. . doi:10.1515/itit-2015-0028

Cao, S., Wang, Z., Chen, Y., Jiang, D., Yan, Y., & Chen, H. (2020). Research on Design and Application of Mobile Edge Computing Model Based on SDN. In *2020 29th International Conference on Computer Communications and Networks (ICCCN)* (pp. 1-6). IEEE.

Cao, Y., Zhao, Y., Wang, J., Yu, X., Ma, Z., & Zhang, J. (2019, March). SDQaaS: Software-defined networking for quantum key distribution as a service. *Optics Express, 27*(5), 6892. Advance online publication. doi:10.1364/OE.27.006892 PMID:30876265

Card, S. (Ed.). (2020). Drone Remote Identification Protocol (DRIP) Requirements (DRIP Internet-Draft). Academic Press.

Carey, J(2015). *Component Objects for CWMP, TR-157 Issue 1 Amendment 10*. Broadband Forum Tech. Report. Retrieved August 2020 from https://www.broadband-forum.org/download/TR-157.pdf

Carey, T., Thorne, D., & Allan, D. (2016). *Broadband Forum TR-359: A Framework for Virtualization, Issue 1*. Broadband Forum. Retrieved September 2020 from https://www.broadband-forum.org/download/TR-359.pdf

Carter, C. (1997). *Principles of GPS: A Brief Primer on the Operation of the Global Positioning System*. Allen Osborne Associates.

Casado, M., Freedman, M. J., Pettit, J., Luo, J., McKeown, N., & Shenker, S. (2007). Ethane: Taking control of the enterprise. *Computer Communication Review, 37*(4), 1–12.

Casado, M., Koponen, T., Shenker, S., & Tootoonchian, A. (2012, August). Fabric: a retrospective on evolving SDN. In *Proceedings of the first workshop on Hot topics in software defined networks* (pp. 85-90). 10.1145/2342441.2342459

Castelluccia, C., Francillon, A., Perito, D., & Soriente, C. (2009). On the difficulty of software-based attestation of embedded devices. *ACM Conference on Computer and Communications Security (CCS)*. 10.1145/1653662.1653711

Catchpoint. (2020). *Catchpoint Web Portal Page*. Retrieved October 30, 2020 from https://www.catchpoint.com/

CDNetworks. (2020). *CDNetworks Web Portal Page*. Retrieved October 30, 2020 from https://www.cdnetworks.com/

Čermák, M., Svorenčík, S., & Lipovský, R. (2020). *Kr00k - CVE-2019-15126 – Serious vulnerability deep inside your Wi-Fi encryption*. ESET Research White Paper.

Cerrato, I., Annarumma, M., & Risso, F. (2014). Supporting Fine-Grained Network Functions through Intel DPDK. In *Software Defined Networks (EWSDN), 2014 Third European Workshop on* (pp. 1–6). 10.1109/EWSDN.2014.33

Chahal, M., Harit, S., Mishra, K. K., Sangaiah, A. K., & Zheng, Z. (2017). A survey on software-defined networking in vehicular ad hoc networks: Challenges, applications and use cases. *Sustainable Cities and Society, 35*, 830–840. doi:10.1016/j.scs.2017.07.007

Channegowda, M., Nejabati, R., & Simeonidou, D. (2013). Software-defined optical networks technology and infrastructure: enabling software-defined optical network operations. *Optical Communications and Networking, IEEE/OSA Journal of, 5*(10), A274-A282.

Check Point 2020 Cyber Security Report. (2020). Retrieved February 01, 2021, from https://www.ntsc.org/assets/pdfs/cyber-security-report-2020.pdf

Checkpoint Research. (2019). *Cyber Attack Trends: 2019 Mid-Year Report*. Author.

Chekired, D. A., Togou, M. A., Khoukhi, L., & Ksentini, A. (2019). 5G-slicing-enabled scalable SDN core network: Toward an ultra-low latency of autonomous driving service. *IEEE Journal on Selected Areas in Communications*, *37*(8), 1769–1782.

Chiosi, M. (2012). *Network Functions Virtualization – An Introduction, Benefits, Enablers, Challenges & Call for Action. Issue 1*. ETSI White Paper. Retrieved September 2020 from https://portal.etsi.org/NFV/NFV_White_Paper.pdf

Chiosi, M. (2014). *Network Functions Virtualization – Network Operator Perspectives on Industry Progress. Issue 1*. ETSI White Paper. Retrieved September 2020 from https://portal.etsi.org/Portals/0/TBpages/NFV/Docs/NFV_White_Paper3.pdf

Chiosi, M., Clarke, D., Willis, P., Reid, A., López, D., ... A. M. (2012, October). *Network Functions Virtualisation. An Introduction, Benefits, Enablers, Challenges and Call for Action.* https://portal.etsi.org/NFV/NFV_White_Paper.pdf

Chockalingam, S. (2017). Bayesia Network models in Cyber Security: A systematic Review. *Proceeding of NORDIC Conference on Secure IT systems*, 105-122. 10.1007/978-3-319-70290-2_7

Choudhary, G., Sharma, S., Gupta, T., Kim, J., & You, I. (2018). *Internet of Drones (IoD): Threats, Vulnerability, and Security Perspectives.* CoRR abs/1808.00203.

Chowdhury, S. R., Salahuddin, M. A., Limam, N., & Boutaba, R. (2019). Re-architecting NFV ecosystem with microservices: State of the art and research challenges. *IEEE Network*, *33*(3), 168–176.

Chunduri, U., Clemm, A., & Li, R. (2018). Preferred path routing – A next-generation routing framework beyond segment routing. IEEE GLOBECOM 2018.

Cianfrani, A., Eramo, V., Listanti, M., Polverini, M., & Vasilakos, A. V. (2012). An OSPF-Integrated Routing Strategy for QoS-Aware Energy Saving in IP Backbone Networks. *IEEE eTransactions on Network and Service Management*, *9*(3), 254–267. doi:10.1109/TNSM.2012.031512.110165

Cisco. (2018). *Intent-Based Networking: Building the bridge between business and IT.* https://www.cisco.com/c/dam/en/us/solutions/collateral/enterprise-networks/digital-network-architecture/nb-09-intent-networking-wp-cte-en.pdf

Cisco. (2019a). *Cisco Visual Networking Index: Global IP Forecast, 2017–2022.* Retrieved October 30, 2020 from https://www.cisco.com/c/en/us/solutions/collateral/service-provider/visual-networking-index-vni/white-paper-c11-741490.html

Cisco. (2019b). *Cisco Visual Networking Index: Mobile Forecast Highlights, 2017–2022.* Retrieved October 30, 2020 from https://www.cisco.com/c/dam/assets/sol/sp/vni/forecast_highlights_mobile/pdf/Global_2022_Forecast_Highlights.pdf

Cisco. (2020). *Cisco Annual Internet Report (2018–2023).* https://www.cisco.com/c/en/us/solutions/collateral/executive-perspectives/annual-internet-report/white-paper-c11-741490.html

Clausen, T. & Jacquet, P. (2003) *Optimized Link State Routing Protocol (OLSR)* (IETF RFC 3626).

Clemm, A. (2007). Network Management Fundamentals. Cisco Press.

Clemm, A., Ciavaglia L., Granville L., Tantsure J. (2020). *Intent-Based Networking – Concepts and Definitions.* IRTF draft, draft-irtf-nmrg-ibn-concepts-definitions.

Clemm, A., Medved, J., Varga, R., Bahadur, N., Ananthakrishnan, H., & Liu, X. (2018). *A yang data model for network topologies.* IETF RFC 8345.

Clemm, A., & Chunduri, U. (2019). Network-programmable operational flow profiling. *IEEE Communications Magazine*, *47*(7), 72–77.

Clemm, A., & Eckert, T. (2020). High-Precision Latency Forwarding over Packet- Programmable Networks. *IEEE/IFIP Network Operations and Management Symposium (NOMS 2020).*

Clemm, A., Torres Vega, M., Ravuri, H. K., Wauters, T., & De Turck, F. (2020). Toward truly immersive holographic-type communication: Challenges and solutions. *IEEE Communications Magazine, 58*(1), 93–99.

Cloudflare. (2020a). *What is the Difference Between Routing and Smart Routing?* Retrieved October 30, 2020 from https://www.cloudflare.com/en-gb/learning/performance/routing-vs-smart-routing/

Cloudflare. (2020b). *Cloudflare DNS Web Page.* Retrieved October 30, 2020 from https://www.cloudflare.com/dns/

Cloudflare. (2020c). *Cloudflare DDoS Web Page.* Retrieved October 30, 2020 from https://www.cloudflare.com/en-gb/ddos/

Cloudflare. (2020d). *Cloudflare Web Page.* Retrieved October 30, 2020 from https://www.cloudflare.com/

CMAF. (2020). *ISO/IEC 23000-19:2020. Information technology - Multimedia application format (MPEG-A) - Part 19: Common media application format (CMAF) for segmented media. Publication date: 2020-03.* Retrieved October 30, 2020 from https://www.iso.org/standard/79106.html

CNCF. (2019). *Cloud Native Computing Foundation Annual Report 2019.* Retrieved October 30, 2020 from https://www.cncf.io/cncf-annual-report-2019/

Cncf. (2021). *Building sustainable ecosystems for cloud native software.* https://www.cncf.io/

Coker, G., Guttman, J., Loscocco, P., Herzog, A. L., Millen, J., O'Hanlon, B., Ramsdell, J. D., Segall, A., Sheehy, J., & Sniffen, B. T. (2011). Principles of remote attestation. *International Journal of Information Security, 10*(2), 63–81. doi:10.100710207-011-0124-7

Coles, H. C. (2014). *Demonstration of Rack-Mounted Computer Equipment Cooling Solutions, Environmental Energy technologies division.* Ernest Orlando Lawrence Berkeley National Laboratory. https://eta.lbl.gov/sites/default/files/publications/demo_of_rack-mounted_computer_equip_cooling_solutions.pdf

Colmant, M., Rouvoy, R., Kurpicz, M., Sobe, A., Felber, P., & Seinturier, L. (2018). The next 700 CPU power models. *Journal of Systems and Software, 144*, 382–396. doi:10.1016/j.jss.2018.07.001

Confluent. (2021). *Cloud-native reliability for Apache Kafka.* https://www.confluent.io/

Cong, G., & Wen, H. (2013). (2013). Mapping Applications for High Performance on Multithreaded, NUMA Systems. In *Proceedings of the ACM international conference on computing frontiers* (pp. 7:1–7:4). New York, NY: ACM.

Contreras, LM., Bernardos, CJ., Lopez, D., Boucadair, M., & Iovanna, P. (2019). *Cooperating Layered Architecture for Software-Defined Networking (CLAS).* IETF RFC 8579.

Contreras, L., Gonzalez de Dios, O., Lopez, V., Fernandez-Palacios, J., & Folgueira, J. (2019). iFUSION: Standards-based SDN Architecture for Carrier Transport Network. In *2019 IEEE Conference on Standards for Communications and Networking (CSCN)*, (pp. 1–7). IEEE. 10.1109/CSCN.2019.8931386

Conviva. (2020). *Conviva Web Portal Page.* Retrieved October 30, 2020 from https://www.conviva.com/

CORAS. (2015). *The CORAS Method.* http://coras.sourceforge.net/

Correia, S., & Boukerche, A. (2017, December). Toward a scalable software-defined vehicular network. In *GLOBECOM 2017-2017 IEEE Global Communications Conference* (pp. 1-6). IEEE. 10.1109/GLOCOM.2017.8254519

Correia, S., Boukerche, A., & Meneguette, R. I. (2017). An architecture for hierarchical software-defined vehicular networks. *IEEE Communications Magazine, 55*(7), 80–86. doi:10.1109/MCOM.2017.1601105

Cox, C. (2012). *An Introduction to LTE: LTE, LTE-Advanced, SAE and 4G Mobile Communications.* John Wiley & Sons. doi:10.1002/9781119942825

CRAMM. (2020). *Wikipedia page.* https://en.wikipedia.org/wiki/CRAMM

Crawford, J. (2016, October 20). Report warns of ISIS developing drones for chemical attacks. *CNN Politics.* https://edition.cnn.com/politics

Cruz, T., Simões, P., & Monteiro, E. (2015). Optimizing the Delivery of Services Supported by Residential Gateways: Virtualized Residential Gateways. Handbook of Research on Redesigning the Future of Internet Architectures, 432–473.

Cruz, T., Simões, P., Reis, N., Monteiro, E., Bastos, F., & Laranjeira, A. (2013). An architecture for virtualized home gateways. In *Integrated Network Management (IM 2013), 2013 IFIP/IEEE International Symposium on* (pp. 520–526). IEEE.

Cui, A., Hertoghs, Y. (2012). *TR-145: Multi-service Broadband Network Functional Modules and Architecture, Issue 1.* Broadband Forum Technical Report.

CVSS. (2020). *Common Vulnerability Scoring System version 3.1: Specification Document - CVSS Version 3.1 Release.* https://www.first.org/cvss/specification-document

Cziva, R., & Pezaros, D. P. (2017, May). On the latency benefits of edge NFV. In *2017 ACM/IEEE Symposium on Architectures for Networking and Communications Systems (ANCS)* (pp. 105-106). ACM.

Da Silva, R., Fernandez, M., Gamir, L., & Perez, M. (2011). Home routing gateway virtualization: An overview on the architecture alternatives. Future Network & Mobile Summit (FutureNetw), 1-9.

Dahl, H. E. I. (2008). *The CORAS method for security risk analysis.* http://coras.sourceforge.net/documents/080828TheCORASMethod.pdf

Daneshmand, S., Jafarnia-Jahromi, A., Broumandon, A., & Lachapelle, G. (2012). A Low-Complexity GPS Anti-Spoofing Method Using a Multi-Antenna Array. *International Technical Meeting of the Satellite Division of the Institute of Navigation (ION GNSS).*

DASH. (2019). *ISO/IEC 23009-1:2019/DAmd.1:2020. Information technology - Dynamic adaptive streaming over HTTP (DASH) — Part 1: Media presentation description and segment. Publication date: 2019-12.*

Davidson, D., Wu, H., Jellinek, R., Singh, V., & Ristenpart, T. (2016). Controlling uavs with sensor input spoofing attacks. *USENIX Conference on Offensive Technologies (WOOT).*

De Clercq, G. (2018, July 3). Greenpeace crashes Superman-shaped drone into French nuclear plant. *Reuters.* https://www.reuters.com

De la Oliva. (n.d.). *5G Coral: a 5G Convergent Virtualized RAN living at the edge.* http://5g-coral.eu

DeLauretis, L. (2019, October). From Monolithic Architecture to Microservices Architecture. In *2019 IEEE International Symposium on Software Reliability Engineering Workshops (ISSREW)* (pp. 93-96). IEEE.

De Oliveira, B. T., Gabriel, L. B., & Margi, C. B. (2015). TinySDN: Enabling multiple controllers for software-defined wireless sensor networks. *IEEE Latin America Transactions, 13*(11), 3690–3696.

Debeau, E., & Al-Hakim, C. (2019). Retrieved 02 March 2021 from, https://events19.linuxfoundation.org/wp-content/uploads/2018/07/ONS2019-SDWAN-POC-Orange-Huawei-Final-LFN.pdf

DeDrone. (2020). *Worldwide Drone Incidents.* https://www.dedrone.com/resources/incidents/all

Deering, S. (1992). *Simple Internet Protocol (SIP) Specification*. Retrieved February 2021, from https://tools.ietf.org/html/draft-deering-sip-00

Dely, P., Kassler, A., & Bayer, N. (2011). Openflow for wireless mesh networks. In *Computer Communications and Networks (ICCCN), 2011 Proceedings of 20th International Conference on* (pp. 1-6). IEEE.

Demchenko, Y., Filiposka, S., de Vos, M., Regvart, D., Karaliotas, T., Grosso, P., & de Laat, C. (2016). Zerotouch provisioning (ZTP) model and infrastructure components for multi-provider cloud services provisioning. In *2016 IEEE International Conference on Cloud Engineering Workshop (IC2EW),* (pp. 184–189). IEEE.

Demestichas, P., Georgakopoulos, A., Karvounas, D., Tsagkaris, K., Stavroulaki, V., Lu, J., Xiong, C., & Yao, J. (2013). 5G on the horizon: Key challenges for the radio-access network. *IEEE Vehicular Technology Magazine, 8*(3), 47–53.

Department of Homeland Security, Cybersecurity and Infrastructure Security Agency. (2020). *Protecting Against the Threat of Unmanned Aircraft Systems (UAS): An Interagency Security Committee Best Practice.* Author.

Department of Homeland Security, Office of Cyber and Infrastructure Analysis. (2018). *Cybersecurity Risks Posed by Unmanned Aircraft Systems.* DHS Infrastructure Security Note.

Department of the Interior. (2018). Final List of Critical Minerals 2018. *Federal Register, 83*(97). https://www.govinfo.gov/content/pkg/FR-2018-05-18/pdf/2018-10667.pdf

Desbureaux, S., & Richomme, M. (2020). *Introduction to ONAP python SDK.* Academic Press.

Dessouky, G., Abera, T., Ibrahim, A., & Sadeghi, A.-R. (2018). LiteHAX: Lightweight Hardware-Assisted Attestation of Program Execution. *IEEE/ACM International Conference on Computer-Aided Design (ICCAD).* 10.1145/3240765.3240821

Dey, K. C., Rayamajhi, A., Chowdhury, M., Bhavsar, P., & Martin, J. (2016). Vehicle-to-vehicle (V2V) and vehicle-to-infrastructure (V2I) communication in a heterogeneous wireless network–Performance evaluation. *Transportation Research Part C, Emerging Technologies, 68*, 168–184. doi:10.1016/j.trc.2016.03.008

Di Renzo, M., Debbah, M., Phan-Huy, D.-T., Zappone, A., Alouini, M.-S., Yuen, C., & Sciancalepore, V. (2019). Smart radio environments empowered by reconfigurable AI meta-surfaces: An idea whose time has come. *EURASIP Journal on Wireless Communications and Networking, 2019*(1), 129. doi:10.118613638-019-1438-9

Di Renzo, M., Ntontin, K. S., Song, J., Danufane, F. H., Qian, X., Lazarakis, F., De Rosny, J., Phan-Huy, D.-T., Simeone, O., Zhang, R., Debbah, M., Lerosey, G., Fink, M., Tretyakov, S., & Shamai, S. (2020). Reconfigurable Intelligent Surfaces vs. Relaying: Differences, Similarities, and Performance Comparison. *IEEE Open Journal of the Communications Society, 1*, 798–807. doi:10.1109/OJCOMS.2020.3002955

Dierks, T., & Rescorla, E. (2008). The Transport Layer Security (TLS) Protocol Version 1.2. *IETF.* Retrieved December 09, 2020, from https://tools.ietf.org/html/rfc5246

Dillon, M., & Winters, T. (2014). Virtualization of Home Network Gateways. *Computer, 47*(11), 62–65. doi:10.1109/MC.2014.338

Din, S., Paul, A., Ahmad, A., Ahmed, S. H., Jeon, G., & Rawat, D. B. (2018, April). Hierarchical architecture for 5g based software-defined intelligent transportation system. In *IEEE INFOCOM 2018-IEEE Conference on Computer Communications Workshops (INFOCOM WKSHPS)* (pp. 462-467). IEEE.

Divis, D. A. (2019, June 3). New Chimera Signal Enhancement Could Spoof-Proof GPS Receivers. *Inside GNSS.* https://insidegnss.com/

DLNA. (2016). *DLNA Networked Device Interoperability Guidelines*. DLNA Consortium Guidelines. Retrieved September 2020 from: https://spirespark.com/dlna/guidelines

Dnsperf. (2020). *Dnsperf Web Page*. Retrieved October 27, 2020 from www.dnsperf.com/

Docker. (2020). *Developing with Docker*. https://www.docker.com/why-docker

Docker. (2020). *Docker Homepage*. Retrieved September 2020 from https://www.docker.com/

Dong, L., & Li, R. (2019). Big Packet Protocol: Advances the Internet with In-Network Services and Functions. MMTC Communications – Frontiers, 14(5).

Dong, L., & Li, R. (2019). In-Packet Network Coding for Effective Packet Wash and Packet Enrichment. *IEEE GLOBECOM 2019 Workshop on Future Internet Architecture, Technologies and Services for 2030 and Beyond.*

Dong, L., & Li, R. (2020). Packet Level In-Time Guarantee: Algorithm and Theorems. IEEE GLOBECOM 2020.

Dong, L., Han, L., & Li, R. (2020). Support Precise Latency for Network Based AR/VR Applications with New IP. EAI Mobimedia 2020.

Dong, L., & Han, L. (2021). New IP Enabled In-Band Signaling for Accurate Latency Guarantee Service. *IEEE Wireless Communications and Networking Conference (WCNC 2021).*

Dong, L., Makhijani, K., & Li, R. (2020). Qualitative Communication Via Network Coding and New IP. In *IEEE High-Performance Switching and Routing*. HPSR.

Douchet, F., Nortershauser, D., Le Masson, S., & Glouannec, P. (2015). Experimental and numerical study of water-cooled datacom equipment. *Applied Thermal Engineering*, *84*, 350–359. doi:10.1016/j.applthermaleng.2015.03.030

Dustzadeh, J. (2013). *SDN: Time to Accelerate the Pace*. Keynote presentation at the Open Networking Summit 2013, Santa Clara, CA. Retrieved July 2020 from https://www.slideshare.net/opennetsummit/ons2013-justin-joubine-dustzadehhuawei

DVB. (2018). *Adaptive media streaming over IP Multicast. DVB Document A176. March 2018*. Retrieved October 30, 2020 from https://www.dvb.org/resources/public/standards/a176_adaptive_media_streaming_over_ip_multicast_2018-02-16_draft_bluebook.pdf

DVB. (2020). *Adaptive media streaming over IP Multicast. DVB Document A176 (Second edition). March 2020*. Retrieved October 30, 2020 from https://dvb.org/wp-content/uploads/2020/03/A176_Adaptive-Media-Streaming-over-IP-Multicast_Mar-2020.pdf

Dynatrace. (2020). *Dynatrace Web Portal Page*. Retrieved October 30, 2020 from https://www.dynatrace.fr/

EBIOS. (2010). In *Wikipedia*. https://en.wikipedia.org/wiki/EBIOS

Edelman, J., Lowe, S. S., & Oswalt, M. (2018). *Network Programmability and Automation: Skills for the Next-Generation Network Engineer*. O'Reilly Media, Inc.

Egi, N., Greenhalgh, A., Handley, M., Hoerdt, M., Huici, F., Mathy, L., & Papadimitriou, P. (2010). A platform for high performance and flexible virtual routers on commodity hardware. *SIGCOMM Computer Communications Review, 40*(1), 127-128. https://doi.acm.org/10.1145/1672308.1672332 doi:10.1145/1672308.1672332

Egi, N., Greenhalgh, A., Handley, M., Hoerdt, M., Mathy, L., & Schooley, T. (2007). Evaluating Xen for Router Virtualization. *Computer Communications and Networks, 2007. ICCCN 2007. Proceedings of 16th International Conference on*, 1256-1261. 10.1109/ICCCN.2007.4317993

Ekelhart, A. (2009). AURUM: A Framework for Information Security Risk Management. *42nd Hawaii International Conference on System Sciences.*

Eldefrawy, K. M., Tsudik, G., Francillon, A., & Perito, D. (2012). SMART: Secure and Minimal Architecture for (Establishing Dynamic) Root of Trust. *Annual Network and Distributed System Security Symposium (NDSS).*

Enghardt, T., & Kraehenbuehl, C. (2020). *IRTF.* Retrieved October 07, 2020, from https://datatracker.ietf.org/doc/draft-irtf-panrg-path-properties/

ENISA. (2020). Inventory of Risk Management / Risk Assessment Method. *European Union Agency for Cyber Security.* https://www.enisa.europa.eu/topics/threat-risk-management/risk-management/current-risk/risk-management-inventory/rm-ra-methods

Enns, R., Bjorklund, M., Schoenwaelder, J., & Bierman, A. (2011). Network Configuration Protocol (NETCONF). *IETF.* Retrieved December 09, 2020, from https://tools.ietf.org/html/rfc6241

Enns, R., Bjorklund, M., Schoenwaelder, J., & Bierman, A. (2011). *Network Configuration Protocol.* IETF RFC 6020.

Erickson, D. (2013). The beacon openflow controller. In *Proceedings of the second ACM SIGCOMM workshop on Hot topics in software defined networking* (pp. 13-18). ACM.

Ericsson. (2014). *Virtual CPE and Software Defined Networking.* Whitepaper. Retrieved September 2020 from https://www.ericsson.com/res/docs/2014/virtual-cpe-and-software-defined-networking.pdf

Ericsson. (2018). *Drone and Networks Ensuring Safe and Secure Operations* (Ericsson White Paper No. GFMC-18:000526). Author.

ETSI ES 203 237. (2014). *Environmental Engineering (EE); Green Abstraction Layer (GAL); Power management capabilities of the future energy telecommunication fixed network nodes.* ETSI. https://www.etsi.org/deliver/etsi_es/2032 00_203299/203237/01.01.01_60/es_203237v010101p.pdf

ETSI ES 203 682. (2019). *Environmental Engineering (EE); Green Abstraction Layer (GAL); Power management capabilities of the future energy telecommunication fixed network nodes; Enhanced Interface for power management in Network Function Virtualisation (NFV) environments.* https://www.etsi.org/deliver/etsi_es/203600_203699/203682/01.01.00_50/es_203682v010100m.pdf

ETSI GS NFV 002. (2013). *Network Functions Virtualisation (NFV); Architectural Framework.* https://www.etsi.org/deliver/etsi_gs/NFV/001_099/002/01.01.01_60/gs_NFV002v010101p.pdf

ETSI NFV 001. (2017). *Network Functions Virtualization (NFV); Use Cases, version 1.2.1.* ETSI. Retrieved September 2020 from https://www.etsi.org/deliver/etsi_gr/nfv/001_099/001/01.02.01_60/gr_nfv001v010201p.pdf

ETSI NFV 002. (2014). *Network Functions Virtualization (NFV); Architectural Framework, version 1.2.1.* ETSI.

ETSI NFV ISG. (n.d.). https://www.etsi.org/about/how-we-work/industry-specification-groups

ETSI OSM. (2016). *ONF OSM Open Source Mano.* Retrieved September 2020 from https://osm.etsi.org/

ETSI. (2013). *CDN Interconnection Architecture. ETSI TS 182 032 V1.1.1 (2013-04).* Retrieved October 23, 2020 from http://www.etsi.org/deliver/etsi_ts/182000_182099/182032/01.01.01_60/ts_182032v010101p.pdf

ETSI. (2020). *Digital Video Broadcasting (DVB); Adaptive media streaming over IP Multicast. ETSI TS 103 769 V1.1.1 (2020-11).* Retrieved October 30, 2020 from https://www.etsi.org/deliver/etsi_ts/103700_103799/103769/01.01.01_60/ts_103769v010101p.pdf

ETSI-GS-ZSM. (2019). *Zero-touch network and Service Management (ZSM); Reference Architecture.* ETSI GS ZSM 002 V1.1.1

ETSI-NFV. (2013). *Network Functions Virtualization (NFV) Architectural Framework.* ETSI GS NFV 002 V1.1.1.

ETSI-NFV-ISG. (2014). *Network Functions Virtualisation (NFV); Architectural Framework* (Tech. Rep.). ETSI. https://www.etsi.org/deliver/etsi_gs/NFV/001_099/002/01.02.01_60/gs_NFV002v010201p.pdf

ETSI-NFV-ISG. (2014a). *Network Functions Virtualisation (NFV); NFV Performance & Portability Best Practises* (Tech. Rep.). ETSI. https://www.etsi.org/deliver/etsi_gs/NFV-PER/001_099/001/01.01.01_60/gs_NFV-PER001v010101p.pdf

ETSI-NFV-ISG. (2014b). *Network Functions Virtualisation (NFV); NFV Security; Problem Statement* (Tech. Rep.). ETSI. https://www.etsi.org/deliver/etsi_gs/NFV-SEC/001_099/001/01.01.01_60/gs_NFV-SEC001v010101p.pdf

ETSI-NFV-ISG. (2015). *Network Function Virtualisation (NFV); Resiliency Requirements* (Tech. Rep.). ETSI. https://www.etsi.org/deliver/etsi_gs/NFV-REL/001_099/001/01.01.01_60/gs_NFV-REL001v010101p.pdf

ETSI-NFV-ISG. (2017). *Network Functions Virtualisation (NFV); Use Cases* (Tech. Rep.). ETSI. https://www.etsi.org/deliver/etsi_gr/NFV/001_099/001/01.02.01_60/gr_NFV001v010201p.pdf

ETSI-NFV-MAN. (2014). *Network Functions Virtualization (NFV) Management and Orchestration.* ETSI GS NFV-MAN 001 V1.1.1.

European Commission. (2020). *Communication from the commission to the European parliament, the council, the European economic and social committee and the committee of the regions, Critical Raw Materials Resilience: Charting a Path towards greater Security and Sustainability.* https://eur-lex.europa.eu/legal-content/EN/TXT/?uri=CELEX:52020DC0474

European Telecommunications Standards Institute. (2012). *Network Functions Virtualisation, white paper.* Retrieved February 09, 2021, from https://portal.etsi.org/NFV/NFV_White_Paper.pdf

European Telecommunications Standards Institute. (2015). *Report on SDN Usage in NFV Architectural Framework, white paper.* Retrieved February 09, 2021, from https://www.etsi.org/deliver/etsi_gs/NFV-EVE/001_099/005/01.01.01_60/gs_NFV-EVE005v010101p.pdf

European Telecommunications Standards Institute. (2017). *Report on Attestation Technologies and Practices for Secure Deployments* (ETSI GR NFV-SEC 007 V1.1.1 2017-10). Author.

European Union Aviation Safety Agency. (2020). *Opinion No 01/2020, High-level regulatory framework for the U-space* (RMT 02.30). Author.

Evens, J. (2015). *A comparison of containers and virtual machines for use with NFV* (M.Sc. Thesis). Retrieved September 2020 from http://hdl.handle.net/1942/19367

Facca, F. M., Salvadori, E., Karl, H., López, D. R., Gutiérrez, P. A. A., Kostic, D., & Riggio, R. (2013). NetIDE: First steps towards an integrated development environment for portable network apps. In *Software Defined Networks (EWSDN), 2013 Second European Workshop on* (pp. 105-110). IEEE.

Fang, Y., & Lu, Y. (2020). Real-Time Verification of Network Properties Based on Header Space. *IEEE Access: Practical Innovations, Open Solutions, 8,* 36789–36806.

Fara, R., Phan-Huy, D.-T., Ourir, A., Di Renzo, M., & De Rosny, J. (2020b). Robust Ambient Backscatter Communications with Polarization Reconfigurable Tags. *IEEE 31st Annual International Symposium on Personal. Indoor and Mobile Radio Communications.*

Fara, R., Bel-Haj-Maati, N., Phan-Huy, D.-T., Malhouroux, N., & Di Renzo, M. (2020c). First Experimental Evaluation of Ambient Backscatter Communications with Massive MIMO Reader. *31st International Symposium on Personal, Indoor and Mobile Radio Communications.*

Fara, R., Phan-Huy, D.-T., Ourir, A., Prevotet, J.-C., Hélard, M., Di Renzo, M., & De Rosny, J. (2020a). *Polarization-Based Reconfigurable Tags for Robust Ambient Backscatter Communications. IEEE Open Journal of the Communications Society.*

Fara, R., Phan-Huy, D.-T., & Renzo, M. D. (2020). Ambient backscatters-friendly 5G networks: creating hot spots for tags and good spots for readers. *IEEE Wireless Communications and Networking Conference*, 1-7. 10.1109/WCNC45663.2020.9120781

Farrel, A., Vasseur, J. P., & Ash, J. (2006). *A Path Computation Element (PCE)-based Architecture.* IETF RFC 4655

Fazio, P., De Rango, F., & Sottile, C. (2015). A predictive cross-layered interference management in a multichannel MAC with reactive routing in VANET. *IEEE Transactions on Mobile Computing*, *15*(8), 1850–1862. doi:10.1109/TMC.2015.2465384

Feamster, N., Rexford, J., Shenker, S., Clark, R., Hutchins, R., Levin, D., & Bailey, J. (2013). *SDX: A software-defined internet exchange.* Open Networking Summit.

Feamster, N., Rexford, J., & Zegura, E. (2013). The road to SDN. *Queue*, *11*(12), 20.

Feth, P. (2018). *Dynamic Risk Assessment for Vehicles of Higher Automation Levels by Deep Learning.* Fraunhofer Institute for Experimental Software Engineering & DFKI – German Research Centre for Artificial Intelligence. doi:10.1007/978-3-319-99229-7_48

Fieau, F., Stephan, E., & Mishra, S. (2020). *CDNI extensions for HTTPS delegation, draft-ietf-cdni-interfaces-https-delegation-04.* Retrieved October 23, 2020 from https://tools.ietf.org/html/draft-ietf-cdni-interfaces-https-delegation-04

Fielding, R., & Reschke, J. (2014). Hypertext Transfer Protocol (HTTP/1.1): Message Syntax and Routing. Internet Engineering Task Force RFC 7230. Retrieved from https://tools.ietf.org/html/rfc7230

Filsfils, C., Previdi, S., Decraene, B., Litkowski, S., Horneffer, H., Milojevic, I., Shakir, R., Ytti, S., Henderickx, W., Tantsura, J., & Crabbe, E. (2018). Segment Routing Architecture. *IETF.* Retrieved December 09, 2020, from https://tools.ietf.org/html/rfc8402

Finkelman, O., Devabhaktuni, J., & Stock, M. (2017). *Open Caching Content Management Operations Specification. Version 1.0 (November, 2017).* Retrieved October 21, 2020 from https://www.streamingvideoalliance.org/document/open-caching-content-management-operations-specification/

Finn, N., Thubert, P., Varga, B., & Farkas, J. (2019). *Deterministic Networking Architecture.* IETF RFC 8655.

Floodlight, S. D. N. (n.d.). *OpenFlow Controller.* Retrieved February 09, 2021, from https://github.com/floodlight/floodlight

Flores Moyano, R., Fernández, D., Bellido, L., & González, C. (2017). A software-defined networking approach to improve service provision in residential networks. *International Journal of Network Management*, *27*(6), 1–19. doi:10.1002/nem.1984

Fontes, R. D. R., Campolo, C., Rothenberg, C. E., & Molinaro, A. (2017). From theory to experimental evaluation: Resource management in software-defined vehicular networks. *IEEE Access: Practical Innovations, Open Solutions*, *5*, 3069–3076. doi:10.1109/ACCESS.2017.2671030

FORCES. (n.d.). *IETF Forwarding and Control Element Separation (forces) Working Group Website*. Retrieved November 2020 from: https://datatracker.ietf.org/wg/forces/charter/

Foster, N., Harrison, R., Freedman, M. J., Monsanto, C., Rexford, J., Story, A., & Walker, D. (2011). Frenetic: A network programming language. *ACM SIGPLAN Notices, 46*(9), 279–291.

Foster, N., McKeown, N., Rexford, J., Parulkar, G., Peterson, L., & Sunay, O. (2020). Using deep programmability to put network owners in control. *Computer Communication Review, 50*(4), 82–88.

Fotouhi, A., Qiang, H., Ding, M., Hassan, M., Giordano, L. G., García-Rodríguez, A., & Yuan, J. (2019). Survey on UAV Cellular Communications: Practical Aspects, Standardization Advancements, Regulation, and Security Challenges. *IEEE Communications Surveys and Tutorials, 21*(4), 3417–3442. doi:10.1109/COMST.2019.2906228

Foukas, X., Patounas, G., Elmokashfi, A., & Marina, M. K. (2017). Network slicing in 5G: Survey and challenges. *IEEE Communications Magazine, 55*(5), 94–100.

Fragouli, C., Boudec, J. Y. L., & Widmer, J. (2006). Network coding: An instant primer. *Computer Communication Review, 36*(1), 63–68.

Francis, P. (1994). *Pip Header Processing*. IETF RFC 1622.

Francois, J., Clemm, A., Maintenant, V., & Tabor, S. (2020). BPP over P4: Exploring Frontiers and Limits in Programmable Packet Processing. *IEEE Global Communications Conference (GLOBECOM)*.

Frank, A. (2016). *Pokémon Go Plus: Everything you need to know*. Polygon. Vox Media.

Freiberg, I. (2017). STPA-SafeSec: Safety and Security Analysis for Cyber-Physical Systems. *Elsevier Journal of Information Security and Applications, 34*(Part 2), 183–196.

Frymann, N., & Manulis, M. (2019). *Securing Fleets of Consumer Drones at Low Cost*. ArXiv, abs/1912.05064.

Future Internet REsearch (FIRE). (n.d.). Retrieved February 09, 2021, from https://ec.europa.eu/digital-single-market/en/future-internet-research-and-experimentation-fire

Gardner, R., Garera, S., & Rubin, A. (2009). Detecting Code Alteration by Creating a Temporary Memory Bottleneck. *IEEE Transactions on Information Forensics and Security, 4*(4), 638–650. doi:10.1109/TIFS.2009.2033231

Gati, A., Salem, F. E., Galindo-Serrano, A. M., Marquet, D., Le Masson, S., Rivera, T., Phan-Huy, D.-T., Altman, Z., Landre, J.-B., Simon, O., Le Rouzic, E., Bourgart, F., Gosselin, S., Vautier, M., Gourdin, E., En-Najjary, T., El-Tabach, M., Indre, R.-M., Gerard, G., & Delsart, G. (2019). (Submitted to). Key technologies to accelerate the ict green evolution: An operators point of view. *IEEE Communications Surveys and Tutorials*. https://arxiv.org/abs/1903.09627

Gerő, B., Jocha, D., Szabó, R., Czentye, J., Haja, D., Németh, B., & Murillo, L. M. C. (2017). The orchestration in 5G exchange—A multi-provider NFV framework for 5G services. In *2017 IEEE Conference on Network Function Virtualization and Software Defined Networks (NFV-SDN)* (pp. 1-2). IEEE.

Ghafoor, H., & Koo, I. (2017). CR-SDVN: A cognitive routing protocol for software-defined vehicular networks. *IEEE Sensors Journal, 18*(4), 1761–1772. doi:10.1109/JSEN.2017.2788014

Gharbaoui, M., Contoli, C., Davoli, G., Cuffaro, G., Martini, B., Paganelli, F., ... Castoldi, P. (2018, November). Demonstration of Latency-Aware and Self-Adaptive Service Chaining in 5G/SDN/NFV infrastructures. In *2018 IEEE Conference on Network Function Virtualization and Software Defined Networks (NFV-SDN)* (pp. 1-2). IEEE.

Giorgetti, A., Sgambelluri, A., Casellas, R., Morro, R., Campanella, A., & Castoldi, P. (2019). Control of open and disaggregated transport networks using the Open Network Operating System (ONOS). *Journal of Optical Communications and Networking, 12*(2), A171–A181.

Global Environment for Network Innovations (GENI). (n.d.). Retrieved February 09, 2021, from https://www.geni.net/

Global System for Mobile Communications. (2018). *Using Mobile Networks to Coordinate Unmanned Aircraft Traffic* (Report). Author.

Google Protobufs. (n.d.). https://developers.google.com/protocol-buffers

GoogleR. P. C. (n.d.). https://grpc.io/

Gos, K., & Zabierowski, W. (2020, April). The Comparison of Microservice and Monolithic Architecture. In *2020 IEEE XVIth International Conference on the Perspective Technologies and Methods in MEMS Design (MEMSTECH)* (pp. 150-153). IEEE.

Gouareb, R., Friderikos, V., & Aghvami, A.-H. (2018). Virtual network functions routing and placement for edge cloud latency minimization. *IEEE Journal on Selected Areas in Communications, 36*(10), 2346–2357.

GPS-SDR-SIM [Computer software]. (2018). *GPS-SDR-SIM documentation and source code (Version 1.0).* https://github.com/osqzss/gps-sdr-sim

Greenberg, A., Hjalmtysson, G., Maltz, D. A., Myers, A., Rexford, J., Xie, G., ... Zhang, H. (2005). A clean slate 4D approach to network control and management. *Computer Communication Review, 35*(5), 41–54.

Gringeri, S., Bitar, N., & Xia, T. J. (2013). Extending software defined network principles to include optical transport. *Communications Magazine, IEEE, 51*(3), 32–40.

Grossman, E. (2019). Deterministic Networking Use Cases. *IETF.* Retrieved October 07, 2020, from https://www.rfc-editor.org/info/rfc8578

GSMA. (2019). *GSMA EMF Policy.* https://www.gsma.com/publicpolicy/consumer-affairs/emf-and-health/emf-policy

GSMA. (2019a). *The Mobile Economy.* https://data.gsmaintelligence.com/api-web/v2/research-file-download?id=39256194&file=2712-250219-ME-Global.pdf

GSMA. (2020). *Mobile Telecommunications Security Threat Landscape.* January 2020. Retrieved October 21, 2020 from https://www.gsma.com/security/wp-content/uploads/2020/02/2020-SECURITY-THREAT-LANDSCAPE-REPORT-FINAL.pdf/

GSMA. (2020). *Position paper on the European Green Deal.* https://www.gsma.com/gsmaeurope/wp-content/uploads/2020/06/GSMA-position-paper-on-Green-Deal-June_2020.pdf

GSMA. (2021). *5G Network Slicing.* https://www.gsma.com/futurenetworks/ip_services/understanding-5g/network-slicing/

GSMA. (2021). *European EMF and antenna siting policy.* https://www.gsma.com/publicpolicy/european-emf-and-antenna-siting-policy

Gude, N., Koponen, T., Pettit, J., Pfaff, B., Casado, M., McKeown, N., & Shenker, S. (2008). NOX: Towards an operating system for networks. *Computer Communication Review, 38*(3), 105–110.

Guha, A., Reitblatt, M., & Foster, N. (2013). *Formal Foundations For Software Defined Networks.* Open Net Summit.

Gunn, G. (2014). Critical Metals Handbook. John Wiley & Sons, Ltd. doi:10.1002/9781118755341

Guo, L., Pang, J., & Walid, A. (2016, November). Dynamic service function chaining in SDN-enabled networks with middleboxes. In *2016 IEEE 24th International Conference on Network Protocols (ICNP)* (pp. 1-10). IEEE.

Guo, Y., Wang, S., Zhou, A., Xu, J., Yuan, J., & Hsu, C. H. (2020). User allocation-aware edge cloud placement in mobile edge computing. *Software, Practice & Experience, 50*(5), 489–502.

Gupta, L., Jain, R., & Vaszkun, G. (2016). Survey of Important Issues in UAV Communication Networks. *IEEE Communications Surveys and Tutorials, 18*(2), 1123–1152. doi:10.1109/COMST.2015.2495297

Gysel, M., Kölbener, L., Giersche, W., & Zimmermann, O. (2016, September). Service cutter: A systematic approach to service decomposition. In *European Conference on Service-Oriented and Cloud Computing* (pp. 185-200). Springer.

Hai, D., Dobrowski, G., Cornaglia, B., Hertoghs, Y., & Zong, N. (2020). *Broadband Forum TR-408: Cloud CO Migration and Coexistence, Issue 1*. Broadband Forum. Retrieved October 2020 from https://www.broadband-forum.org/technical/download/TR-408.pdf

Hakiri, A., Gokhale, A., Berthou, P., Schmidt, D. C., & Thierry, G. (2014). Software-defined Networking: Challenges and Research Opportunities for Future Internet. *Computer Networks.*

Haleplidis, E., Pentikousis, K., Denazis, S., Salim, J. H., Meyer, D., & Koufopavlou, O. (2015). *Software-defined networking (SDN): Layers and architecture terminology.* IETF RFC 7426.

Haleplidis, E., Joachimpillai, D., Salim, J. H., Lopez, D., Martin, J., Pentikousis, K., Denazis, S., & Koufopavlou, O. (2014). ForCES applicability to SDN-enhanced NFV. In *2014 Third European Workshop on Software Defined Networks* (pp. 43-48). IEEE.

Haleplidis, E., Pentikousis, K., Denazis, S., Salim, J. H., Meyer, D., & Koufopavlou, O. (2014). *RFC 7426 Software Defined Networking: Layers and Architecture Terminology.* IRTF SDNRG.

Haleplidis, E., Salim, J. H., Denazis, S., & Koufopavlou, O. (2014). Towards a Network Abstraction Model for SDN. *Journal of Network and Systems Management,* 1–19.

Halpern, J., & Pignataro, C. (2015). *Service Function Chaining (SFC) Architecture.* IETF. Retrieved from https://www.ietf.org/rfc/rfc7665.txt

Halpern, J., & Pignataro, C. (2015). *Service Function Chaining (SFC) Architecture.* IETF. RFC 7665. Retrieved October 09, 2020, from https://tools.ietf.org/html/rfc7665

Hamdi, M. M., Audah, L., Rashid, S. A., Mohammed, A. H., Alani, S., & Mustafa, A. S. (2020, June). A review of applications, characteristics and challenges in vehicular ad hoc networks (VANETs). In *2020 International Congress on Human-Computer Interaction, Optimization and Robotic Applications (HORA)* (pp. 1-7). IEEE.

Han, L., Qu, Y., Dong, L., & Li, R. (2020). A Framework for Bandwidth and Latency Guaranteed Service in New IP Network. *IEEE INFOCOM 2020 Workshop on New IP.*

Han, B., Gopalakrishnan, V., Ji, L., & Lee, S. (2015). Network function virtualization: Challenges and opportunities for innovations. *Communications Magazine, IEEE, 53*(2), 90–97. doi:10.1109/MCOM.2015.7045396

Handigol, N., Heller, B., Jeyakumar, V., Maziéres, D., & McKeown, N. (2012). Where is the debugger for my software-defined network? In *Proceedings of the first workshop on Hot topics in software defined networks* (pp. 55-60). Academic Press.

Handigol, N., Heller, B., Jeyakumar, V., Mazières, D., & McKeown, N. (2012). Where is the debugger for my software-defined network? In *Proceedings of the first workshop on Hot topics in software defined networks*(pp. 55-60). ACM.

Harpes, C. (2007). *Quantitative Risk Assessment with ISAMM on ESA's Operations Data System.* Telindus S.A., Security, Audit and Governance Services, Luxembourg. https://www.itrust.lu/wp-content/uploads/2007/09/publications_TTC_2007_abstract_risk_assessment_with_ISAMM.pdf

Hartenstein, H., & Laberteaux, L. P. (2008). A tutorial survey on vehicular ad hoc networks. *IEEE Communications Magazine, 46*(6), 164–171. doi:10.1109/MCOM.2008.4539481

Hasan, S., King, Z., Hafiz, M., Sayagh, M., Adams, B., & Hindle, A. (2016). Energy Profiles of Java Collections Classes. *38th International Conference on Software Engineering,* 225-236.

Helm. (2020). *The package manager for Kubernetes.* https://helm.sh/

Hemid, A. (2017). Facilitation of The OpenDaylight Architecture. *The 4th Computer Science Conference for University of Bonn Students.*

Herbaut, N., Negru, D., Xilouris, G., & Chen, Y. (2015). Migrating to a NFV-based Home Gateway: Introducing a Surrogate vNF approach. In *Network of the Future (NOF), 2015 6th International Conference on the* (pp. 1–7). 10.1109/NOF.2015.7333284

Hernando, G., A. B., Da Silva Farina, A., Bellido Triana, L., Ruiz Pinar, F. J., & Fernandez Cambronero, D. (2017). Virtualization of residential IoT functionality by using NFV and SDN. *2017 IEEE International Conference on Consumer Electronics, ICCE 2017,* 86–87. 10.1109/ICCE.2017.7889240

Herrero, A. V., & Casey, N. (2018, August 4). Venezuelan President Targeted by Drone Attack, Officials Say. *The New York Times.* https://www.nytimes.com/

He, S., Wu, Q., Liu, J., Hu, W., Qin, B., & Li, Y. (2017). Secure Communications in Unmanned Aerial Vehicle Network. *Information Security Practice and Experience Conference (ISPEC).* 10.1007/978-3-319-72359-4_37

He, Z., Cao, J., & Liu, X. (2016). SDVN: Enabling rapid network innovation for heterogeneous vehicular communication. *IEEE Network, 30*(4), 10–15. doi:10.1109/MNET.2016.7513858

Hickey, P. (2019). *Announcing Lucet: Fastly's native WebAssembly compiler and runtime.* Retrieved October 23, 2020 from https://www.fastly.com/blog/announcing-lucet-fastly-native-webassembly-compiler-runtime

Hoffman, P., & McManus, P. (2018). *DNS Queries over HTTPS (DoH).* Internet Engineering Task Force RFC 8484. Retrieved from https://tools.ietf.org/html/rfc8484

Hootsuite & We Are Social. (2021). *Digital 2021 Global Digital Overview.* Retrieved 11 March 2020 from, https://datareportal.com/reports/digital-2021-global-digital-overview

HTTP Adaptive Streaming. (n.d.). *Wikipedia.* Retrieved December 09, 2020, from https://en.wikipedia.org/wiki/Adaptive_bitrate_streaming

Huang, N.-F., Li, C.-H., Chen, C.-C., Hsu, I.-H., Li, C.-C., & Chen, C.-H. (2017). A Novel vCPE Framework for Enabling Virtual Network Functions with Multiple Flow Tables Architecture in SDN Switches. In *2017 19th Asia-Pacific Network Operations and Management Symposium (APNOMS)* (pp. 64–69). 10.1109/APNOMS.2017.8094180

Huang, C. M., Chiang, M. S., Dao, D. T., Pai, H. M., Xu, S., & Zhou, H. (2017). Vehicle-to-Infrastructure (V2I) offloading from cellular network to 802.11 p Wi-Fi network based on the Software-Defined Network (SDN) architecture. *Vehicular Communications, 9,* 288–300. doi:10.1016/j.vehcom.2017.03.003

Huang, C. M., Chiang, M. S., Dao, D. T., Su, W. L., Xu, S., & Zhou, H. (2018). V2V data offloading for cellular network based on the software defined network (SDN) inside mobile edge computing (MEC) architecture. *IEEE Access: Practical Innovations, Open Solutions*, 6, 17741–17755.

Huang, Y., Chen, B., Shih, M., & Lai, C. (2012). Security Impacts of Virtualization on a Network Testbed. *2012 IEEE Sixth International Conference on Software Security and Reliability*, 71-77. 10.1109/SERE.2012.17

Huawei Technologies Co. Ltd. (2010). *SmartAX MA5600T Series Product Website*. Retrieved October 2014 from: http://enterprise.huawei.com/en/products/network/access-network/olt/en_ma5600t.htm

Huawei. (2016). *News report: Telefonica and Huawei Announce Industry's First SDN IP+Optical Field Trial with Commercial Traffic in Peru*. Accessed 13/01/2021 from https://www.huawei.com/en/news/2016/2/industry-first-sdn-ip

Humphreys, T., Ledvina, B., Psiaki, M. L., O'Hanlon, B. W., & Kintner, P. (2008). Assessing the Spoofing Threat: Development of a Portable GPS Civilian Spoofer. *International Technical Meeting of the Satellite Division of the Institute of Navigation (ION GNSS)*.

Huynh, L. N., Lee, Y., & Balan, R. K. (2017, June). Deepmon: Mobile gpu-based deep learning framework for continuous vision applications. In *Proceedings of the 15th Annual International Conference on Mobile Systems, Applications, and Services* (pp. 82-95). Academic Press.

IEEE 802.1Q. (2011). *IEEE Standard 802.1Q-2011, Media Access Control Bridges and Virtual Bridged Local Area Networks*. IEEE 802.1 Working Group.

IETF SFC WG. (n.d.). https://datatracker.ietf.org/wg/sfc/documents

IETF SFC working group. (n.d.). Retrieved September 01, 2020, from https://datatracker.ietf.org/wg/sfc/charter/

IETF. (2020). *Cdni Status Pages*. Retrieved October 23, 2020 from http://tools.ietf.org/wg/cdni/

IETF. (2020, Nov). *Service Function Chaining Charter* (Tech. Rep.). IETF. https://datatracker.ietf.org/wg/sfc/charter

IETF. (2021). *A framework for Automating Service and Network Management with YANG*. IETF RFC 8969.

Imani, A., Keshavarz-Haddad, A., Eslami, M., & Haghighat, J. (2018). Security Challenges and Attacks in M2M Communications. *9th International Symposium on Telecommunications*. 10.1109/ISTEL.2018.8661044

Industrial Internet Consortium. (2017). *Smart Factory Applications in Discrete Manufacturing*. Retrieved February 2021, from https://www.iiconsortium.org/pdf/Smart_Factory_Applications_in_Discrete_Mfg_white_paper_20170222.pdf

InfiniDome. (n.d.). *GPSdome*. Retrieved October 13, 2020, from https://www.infinidome.com/

Insler, R. (2017). *Broadband Forum TR-328: Virtual Business Gateway, Issue 1*. Broadband Forum. Retrieved August 2020 from https://www.broadband-forum.org/download/TR-328.pdf

Intel. (2017, May 25). *Intel Movidius Myriad 2 VPU Enables Advanced Computer Vision and Deep Learning Features in Ultra-Compact DJI Spark Drone*. Retrieved January 14, 2021, from https://newsroom.intel.com

Internet Engineering Task Force. (n.d.). *Drone Remote ID Protocol (drip) Working Group*. Retrieved October 13, 2020, from https://datatracker.ietf.org/wg/drip/about/

IRAM2. (2020). *IRAM2 summary on ISF homepage*. https://www.securityforum.org/tool/information-risk-assessment-methodology-iram2/

ISF homepage. (2020). https://www.securityforum.org/

ISO/IEC 23009-1. (2019). Information technology – Dynamic adaptive streaming over HTTP (DASH) – Part 1: Media presentation description and segment formats.

ISO/IEC 27000. (2018). *An introduction to 27000-series (27001-27006).* https://standards.iso.org/ittf/PubliclyAvailableStandards/

ISO/IEC 27001. (2013). *Information technology—Security techniques—Information security management systems—Requirements. Standard.* https://www.iso.org/iso/iso27001

ISO/IEC 27005. (2018). *Information Technology – Security Techniques _Information Security Risk Management; Guidance for establishing the context.* ISO.

ISO/IEC 27017. (2015). *Information technology -- Security techniques -- Code of practice for information security controls based on ISO/IEC 27002 for cloud services.* https://www.iso.org/standard/43757.html

ISO/IEC 31010. (2019). *Risk management — Risk assessment techniques.* https://www.iso.org/standard/72140.html

Isolani, P. H., Haxhibeqiri, J., Moerman, I., Hoebeke, J., Marquez-Barja, J. M., Granville, L. Z., & Latré, S. (2020). An SDN-based framework for slice orchestration using in-band network telemetry in IEEE 802.11. In *2020 6th IEEE Conference on Network Softwarization (NetSoft)* (pp. 344-346). IEEE.

ITU-T FG-NET2030 Focus Group on Technologies for Network 2030. (2019). New Services and Capabilities for Network 2030: Description, Technical Gap and Performance Target Analysis.

ITU-T FG-NET2030 Focus Group on Technologies for Network 2030. (2020). Gap Analysis of Network 2030 New Services, Capabilities and Use Cases (NET2030-O-039).

ITU-T Study Group 13. (2014). *Y.3300, Framework of software-defined networking.* Retrieved February 09, 2021, from https://www.itu.int/ITU-T/recommendations/rec.aspx?rec=12168

ITU-T. (2010). The international public telecommunication numbering plan (E-164).

Jaballah, W. B., Conti, M., & Lal, C. (2019). *A survey on software-defined VANETs: benefits, challenges, and future directions.* arXiv preprint arXiv:1904.04577.

Jafarnia-Jahromi, A., Broumandan, A., Nielsen, J., & Lachapelle, G. (2012). GPS Vulnerability to Spoofing Threats and a Review of Antispoofing Techniques. *International Journal of Navigation and Observation, 2012,* 1–16. doi:10.1155/2012/127072

Jagroep, E., Procaccianti, G., Werf, J. M. V. D., Brinkkemper, S., Blom, L. & Vliet, R. (2017). Energy efficiency on the product roadmap: An empirical study across releases of a software product. *Journal of Software: Evolution and Process, 29.*

Jain, S., Kumar, A., Mandal, S., Ong, J., Poutievski, L., Singh, A., ... Vahdat, A. (2013). B4: Experience with a globally-deployed software defined WAN. In *Proceedings of the ACM SIGCOMM 2013 conference on SIGCOMM* (pp. 3-14). ACM.

Jain, S., Kumar, A., Mandal, S., Ong, J., Poutievski, L., Singh, A., Venkata, S., Wanderer, J., Zhou, J., Zhu, M., Zolla, J., Hölzle, U., Stuart, S., & Vahdat, A. (2013). B4: Experience with a globally-deployed software defined wan. *Computer Communication Review, 43*(4), 3–14. doi:10.1145/2534169.2486019

Jalodia, N., Henna, S., & Davy, A. (2019, November). Deep Reinforcement Learning for Topology-Aware VNF Resource Prediction in NFV Environments. In *2019 IEEE Conference on Network Function Virtualization and Software Defined Networks (NFV-SDN)* (pp. 1-5). IEEE.

Jammal, M., Singh, T., Shami, A., Asal, R., & Li, Y. (2014). *Software-Defined Networking: State of the Art and Research Challenges.* arXiv preprint arXiv:1406.0124.

Jang, C., & Lee, J. H. (2010, September). *Path selection algorithms for multi-hop VANETs. In 2010 IEEE 72nd Vehicular Technology Conference-Fall.* IEEE.

Javaid, A., Sun, W., Devabhaktuni, V., & Alam, M. (2012). Cyber security threat analysis and modeling of an unmanned aerial vehicle system. *IEEE Conference on Technologies for Homeland Security (HST)* 10.1109/THS.2012.6459914

Jenkins. (2020). *Jenkins, an open source automation server.* http://www.jenkins.io

Jia, Y., Chen, Z., & Jiang, S. (2020). *Flexible IP: An Adaptable IP Address Structure.* IETF draft-jia-flex-ip-address-structure.

Jia, Y., Li, G., & Jiang, S. (2020). *Scenarios for Flexible Address Structure.* IETF draft-jia-scenarios-flexible-address-structure.

Jiang, D., & Delgrossi, L. (2008, May). IEEE 802.11 p: Towards an international standard for wireless access in vehicular environments. In VTC Spring 2008-IEEE Vehicular Technology Conference (pp. 2036-2040). IEEE.

Jiang, W., Strufe, M., & Schotten, H. (2017). Experimental Results for Artificial Intelligence-based Self-Organized 5G Networks. *2017 IEEE 28th Annual International Symposium on Personal, Indoor and Mobile Radio Communications (PIMRC).* 10.1109/PIMRC.2017.8292532

Jiang, Y., & Li, H. (2014). *An Architecture of Service Function Chaining* (draft-jiang-sfc-arch-01.txt). IETF Internet Draft.

Jiang, C., Wang, Y., Ou, D., Li, Y., Zhang, J., Wan, J., Luo, B., & Shi, W. (2019). Energy efficiency comparison of hypervisors. *Sustainable Computing: Informatics and Systems, 22*, 311–321.

Jindal, A., Aujla, G. S., Kumar, N., Chaudhary, R., Obaidat, M. S., & You, I. (2018). SeDaTiVe: SDN-enabled deep learning architecture for network traffic control in vehicular cyber-physical systems. *IEEE Network, 32*(6), 66–73. doi:10.1109/MNET.2018.1800101

Ji, X., Yu, H., Fan, G., & Fu, W. (2016, December). SDGR: An SDN-based geographic routing protocol for VANET. In *2016 IEEE International Conference on Internet of Things (iThings) and IEEE Green Computing and Communications (GreenCom) and IEEE Cyber, Physical and Social Computing (CPSCom) and IEEE Smart Data (SmartData)* (pp. 276-281). IEEE. 10.1109/iThings-GreenCom-CPSCom-SmartData.2016.70

John, W., Pentikousis, K., Agapiou, G., Jacob, E., Kind, M., Manzalini, A., & Meirosu, C. (2013, November). Research directions in network service chaining. In *Future Networks and Services (SDN4FNS), 2013 IEEE SDN for* (pp. 1–7). IEEE.

Jones, N. (2018). How to stop data centers from gobbling up the world's electricity. *Nature, 561*(7722), 163–166. doi:10.1038/d41586-018-06610-y PMID:30209383

Jonker, M., King, A., Krupp, J., Rossow, C., Sperotto, A., & Dainotti, A. (2017). Millions of Targets under Attack: a Macroscopic Characterization of the DoS Ecosystem. *Proceedings of IMC'17.* Retrieved February 01, 2021, from https://dl.acm.org/doi/10.1145/3131365.3131383

Joo, O. J. (2019). *Drones Everywhere on 5G.* GSMA IoT Innovation Summit.

Jouppi, N. P., Young, C., Patil, N., & Patterson, D. (2017). In-Datacenter Performance Analysis of a Tensor Processing UnitTM. *Proceedings of the 44th International Symposium on Computer Architecture.* 10.1145/3079856.3080246

Kablan, M., Alsudais, A., Keller, E., & Le, F. (2017). Stateless network functions: Breaking the tight coupling of state and processing. In *14th {USENIX} Symposium on Networked Systems Design and Implementation ({NSDI} 17)* (pp. 97-112). USENIX.

Kadhim, A. J., & Seno, S. A. H. (2019). Energy-efficient multicast routing protocol based on SDN and fog computing for vehicular networks. *Ad Hoc Networks, 84*, 68–81. doi:10.1016/j.adhoc.2018.09.018

Kafka. (2021). *Introduction to Kafka.* https://docs.confluent.io/home/kafka-intro.html

Kaljic, E., Maric, A., Njemcevic, P., & Hadzialic, M. (2019). A Survey on Data Plane Flexibility and Programmability in Software-Defined Networking. *IEEE Access: Practical Innovations, Open Solutions, 7*, 47804–47840. doi:10.1109/ACCESS.2019.2910140

Karagiannis, G., Hai, D., Dobrowski, G., Croot, C., Hertoghs, Y., & Zong, N. (2018a). *Broadband Forum TR-384: Cloud Central Office Reference Architectural Framework, Issue 1.* Broadband Forum. Retrieved September 2020 from https://www.broadband-forum.org/download/TR-384.pdf

Karagiannis, G., Hai, D., Dobrowski, G., Croot, C., Hertoghs, Y., & Zong, N. (2018b). *Broadband Forum TR-416: CloudCO Use Cases and Scenarios, Issue 1. Broadband Forum.* Retrieved September 2020 from https://www.broadband-forum.org/download/TR-384.pdf

Karmel, A., Chandramouli, R., & Iorga, M. (2016). Nist definition of microservices, application containers and system virtual machines (No. NIST Special Publication (SP) 800-180 (Draft)). National Institute of Standards and Technology.

Kaufman, C., Hoffman, P. Nir, Y., Eronen, P. & Kivinen, T. (2014) *Internet Key Exchange Protocol Version 2 (IKEv2).* IETF RFC 7296.

Kazemian, P., Varghese, G., & McKeown, N. (2012). Header space analysis: Static checking for networks. In *9th USENIX Symposium on Networked Systems Design and Implementation (NSDI 12)* (pp. 113-126). USENIX.

Kelarestaghi, K. B. (2019). *Intelligent Transportation System Security: Impact-Oriented Risk Assessment of in-Vehicle Networks. IEEE Intelligent Transportation Systems Magazine.*

Kent, S. & Seo, K. (2005). *Security Architecture for the Internet Protocol.* IETF RFC 4301.

Kepes, B. (2014). *SDN meets the real-world: Implementation benefits and challenges.* GIGAOM RESEARCH, Giga Omni Media, Inc.

Kephart, J., & Chess, D. (2003). The vision of autonomic computing. *Computer, 36*(1), 41–50. https://ieeexplore.ieee.org/document/1160055/

Key Reinstallation Attacks. (2017). Retrieved October 13, 2020, from https://www.krackattacks.com/

Khan, A. (2016). *Hacking the Drones.* Open Web Application Security Project. https://www.owasp.org/images/5/5e/OWASP201604_Drones.pdf

Khelifi, H., Luo, S., Nour, B., Moungla, H., Faheem, Y., Hussain, R., & Ksentini, A. (2019). Named data networking in vehicular ad hoc networks: State-of-the-art and challenges. *IEEE Communications Surveys and Tutorials, 22*(1), 320–351. doi:10.1109/COMST.2019.2894816

Kirkpatrick, K. (2013). Software-defined networking. *Communications of the ACM, 56*(9), 16–19. doi:10.1145/2500468.2500473

Kirksey, H. (2017). *TR-140 – TR-069 Data Model for Storage Service Enabled Devices, Issue: 1 Amendment 3, April 2017.* Academic Press.

KittyHawk. (2019). *Remote ID & Commercial Drones: Enabling Identification and Transparency in the National Airspace.* KittyHawk White Paper.

Klein, E., Gressel, Y., & Biran, S. (2020). *Open Caching Relayed Token Authentication.* Streaming Video Alliance Technical Publication. Retrieved October 21, 2020 from https://www.streamingvideoalliance.org/document/open-caching-relayed-token-authentication/

KNOB Attack. (2019). Retrieved October 13, 2020, from https://knobattack.com/

Kocher, P., Genkin, D., Gruss, D., Haas, W., Hamburg, M., Lipp, M., Mangard, S., Prescher, T., Schwarz, M., & Yarom, Y. (2019). Spectre Attacks: Exploiting Speculative Execution. *IEEE Symposium on Security and Privacy.*

Koeberl, P., Schulz, S., Sadeghi, A.-R., & Varadharajan, V. (2014). TrustLite: a security architecture for tiny embedded devices. *EuroSys '14.*

Kohler, E., Morris, R., Chen, B., Jannotti, J., & Kaashoek, M. F. (2000). The Click modular router. *ACM Transactions on Computer Systems*, *18*(3), 263–297.

Kokar, Y., Phan-Huy, D.-T., Fara, R., Rachedi, K., Ourir, A., De Rosny, J., Di Renzo, M., Prévotet, J.-C., & Hélard, M. (2019). First experimental ambient backscatter communication using a compact reconfigurable tag antenna. *IEEE Global Communications Conference.* 10.1109/GCWkshps45667.2019.9024698

Kopardekar, P., Rios, J., Prevot, T., Johnson, M., Jung, J., & Robinson, J. E. (2016). *Unmanned Aircraft System Traffic Management (UTM) Concept of Operations.* AIAA Aviation Technology, Integration, and Operations Conference.

Kourtis, M.-A., Xilouris, G., Riccobene, V., McGrath, M. J., Petralia, G., Koumaras, H., . . . Liberal, F. (2015). Enhancing VNF performance by exploiting SR-IOV and DPDK packet processing acceleration. In *Network Function Virtualization and Software Defined Network (NFV-SDN), 2015 IEEE Conference on* (pp. 74–78). 10.1109/NFV-SDN.2015.7387409

Kovah, X., Kallenberg, C., Weathers, C., Herzog, A., Albin, M., & Butterworth, J. (2012). New Results for Timing-Based Attestation. *IEEE Symposium on Security and Privacy.*

Kreutz, D., Ramos, F., & Verissimo, P. (2013). Towards secure and dependable software-defined networks. In *Proceedings of the second ACM SIGCOMM workshop on Hot topics in software defined networking* (pp. 55-60). ACM.

Ku, I., Lu, Y., Gerla, M., Gomes, R. L., Ongaro, F., & Cerqueira, E. (2014, June). Towards software-defined VANET: Architecture and services. In *2014 13th annual Mediterranean ad hoc networking workshop (MED-HOC-NET)* (pp. 103-110). IEEE.

Kubernetes. (2020). *Kubernetes - Production-Grade Container Orchestration Homepage - v1.19.1.* Retrieved September 2020 from https://kubernetes.io/

Kumar, M., Rajewski, L., & Banka, K. (2020). *NFO – Guilin CNF Improvement Overview.* Retrieved 02 March 2021 from, https://wiki.lfnetworking.org/spaces/flyingpdf/pdfpageexport.action?pageId=46105100

Kumar, M., Li, Y., & Shi, W. (2017). Energy consumption in Java: An early experience. *Eighth International Green and Sustainable Computing Conference*, 1-8. 10.1109/IGCC.2017.8323579

Lacoste, M., Armand, D., L'Hereec, Prévost, F., Rafflé, Y., & Roché, S. (2019). Software-Defined Vehicular Networking Security: Threats & Security Opportunities for 5G. *Computer & Electronics Security Applications Rendez-vous (C&ESAR).*

Laghrissiand, A., & Taleb, T. (2019). A survey on the placement of virtual resources and virtual network functions. *IEEE Commun. Surveys Tuts.*, *21*(2), 1409–1434.

Lai, C. F., Chang, Y. C., Chao, H. C., Hossain, M. S., & Ghoneim, A. (2017). A buffer-aware QoS streaming approach for SDN-enabled 5G vehicular networks. *IEEE Communications Magazine*, *55*(8), 68–73. doi:10.1109/MCOM.2017.1601142

Lasconjarias, G., & Maged, H. (2019) Fear the Drones: Remotely Piloted Systems and Non-State Actors in Syria and Iraq. *IRSEM Research Paper, 77*(4).

Latif, Z., Sharif, K., Li, F., Karim, M. M., Biswas, S., & Wang, Y. (2020). A comprehensive survey of interface protocols for software defined networks. *Journal of Network and Computer Applications, 156*(January), 102563. doi:10.1016/j.jnca.2020.102563

Leach, S. (2020). *Performance matters: why Compute@Edge does not yet support JavaScript.* Retrieved October 23, 2020 from https://www.fastly.com/blog/why-edge-compute-does-not-yet-support-javascript

Leccadito, M. T., Bakker, T., Klenke, R., & Elks, C. (2018). A survey on securing UAS cyber physical systems. *IEEE Aerospace and Electronic Systems Magazine, 33*(10), 22–32. doi:10.1109/MAES.2018.160145

Ledvina, B., Bencze, W., Galusha, B. T., & Miller, I. (2010). An In-Line Anti-Spoofing Device for Legacy Civil GPS Receivers. *International Technical Meeting of the Institute of Navigation.*

Lee, Y., & Ghai, R. (2014). *Problem Statements of Virtualizing Home Services* (draft-lee-vhs-ps-00). IETF Internet Draft.

Lee, Y., & Xie, C. (2014). *Virtualizing Home Services Use Cases* (draft-lee-vhs-usecases-00). IETF Internet Draft.

Lee, C., & Madnick, S. (2018). *A Systems Theoretic Approach to Cyber security Risk Analysis and Mitigation for Autonomous Passenger Vehicles.* MIT Management Sloan School.

Lemke, A. (2015). *Alcatel Lucent - Why service providers need an NFV platform: Strategic White Paper.* Academic Press.

Lengdell, M., Pavon, J., Wakano, M., Chapman, M., & Kawanishi, M. (1996). The TINA network resource model. *IEEE Communications Magazine, 34*(3), 74–79.

Letaief, K. B., Chen, W., Shi, Y., Zhang, J., & Zhang, Y. J. A. (2019). The roadmap to 6G: AI empowered wireless networks. *IEEE Communications Magazine, 57*(8), 84–90.

Leveson, N. (2012). *Engineering a Safer World - Systems Thinking Applied to Safety.* MIT Press.

LFAI. (2020). *Linux Foundation Artificial Intelligence.* https://lfaidata.foundation/

LFN Analytics. (2020). https://insights.lfx.linuxfoundation.org/projects/lfn/onap/dashboard

LFN. (2021). *CNTT.* https://www.lfnetworking.org/about/cntt/

Li, H., Ota, K., & Dong, M. (2016, September). Network virtualization optimization in software defined vehicular ad-hoc networks. In *2016 IEEE 84th Vehicular Technology Conference (VTC-Fall)* (pp. 1-5). IEEE. 10.1109/VTCFall.2016.7881106

Li, L. E., Mao, Z. M., & Rexford, J. (2012). Toward software-defined cellular networks. In *2012 European workshop on software defined networking* (pp. 7-12). IEEE.

Li, X., Wang, X., Liu, F., & Xu, H. (2018). DHL: Enabling flexible software network functions with FPGA acceleration. *Proceedings - International Conference on Distributed Computing Systems,* 1–11. 10.1109/ICDCS.2018.00011

Li, Z., Peng, S., Voyer, D., Xie, C., Liu, P., Qin, Z., Ebisawa, K., Previdi, S., & Guichard. J. (n.d.). Application-aware Networking (APN) Framework. *IETF.* Retrieved October 07, 2020, from https://datatracker.ietf.org/doc/draft-li-apn-framework/

Libes, D. (1995). *Exploring Expect: a Tcl-based toolkit for automating interactive programs.* O'Reilly Media, Inc.

Li, D., & Halfond, W. G. J. (2014). An investigation into energy-saving programming practices for Android smartphone app development. *Proceedings of the 3rd International Workshop on Green and Sustainable Software*, 46–53. 10.1145/2593743.2593750

Li, L., Qiao, X., Lu, Q., Ren, P., & Lin, R. (2020). Rendering Optimization for Mobile Web 3D Based on Animation Data Separation and On-Demand Loading. *IEEE Access: Practical Innovations, Open Solutions*, 8, 88474–88486.

Limelight. (2019). *Limelight Networks Market Research. The State of Online Video 2019*. Retrieved October 30, 2020 from https://fr.limelight.com/resources/white-paper/state-of-online-video-2019/

Linares-Vásquez, M., Bavota, G., Bernal-Cárdenas, C., Oliveto, R., Di Penta, M., & Poshyvanyk, D. (2014). Mining energy-greedy API usage patterns in Android apps: an empirical study. *Proceedings of the 11th Working Conference on Mining Software Repositories*, 2–11. 10.1145/2597073.2597085

Lipp, M., Schwarz, M., Gruss, D., Prescher, T., Haas, W., Fogh, A., Horn, J., Mangard, S., Kocher, P., Genkin, D., Yarom, Y., & Hamburg, M. (2018). Meltdown: Reading Kernel Memory from User Space. *USENIX Security Symposium*.

Li, R., Clemm, A., Chunduri, U., Dong, L., & Makhijani, K. (2018). A New Framework and Protocol for Future Networking Applications. *ACM Sigcomm Workshop on Networking for Emerging Applications and Technologies (NEAT 2018)*, 637–648.

Li, R., Makhijani, K., & Dong, L. (2020). New IP: A Data Packet Framework to Evolve the Internet. *Proceedings of IEEE HPSR 2020*.

Li, R., Makhijani, K., Yousefi, H., Westphal, C., Dong, L., Wauters, T., & De Turck, F. (2019). A Framework for Qualitative Communications Using Big Packet Protocol. *Proceedings of the 2019 ACM Sigcomm Workshop on Networking for Emerging Applications and Technologies (NEAT 2019)*, 22–28.

Liu, F., Li, P., Gao, S., Wan, X., & An, W. (2019, December). Optimized Service Function Path Scaling in SDN/NFV Networks. In *Proceedings of the 2019 5th International Conference on Systems, Control and Communications* (pp. 27-32). Academic Press.

Liu, L., Li, H., & Gruteser, M. (2019, August). Edge assisted real-time object detection for mobile augmented reality. In *The 25th Annual International Conference on Mobile Computing and Networking* (pp. 1-16). Academic Press.

Liu, Q., & Han, T. (2018, September). Dare: Dynamic adaptive mobile augmented reality with edge computing. In *2018 IEEE 26th International Conference on Network Protocols (ICNP)* (pp. 1-11). IEEE.

Liu, Q., Huang, S., Opadere, J., & Han, T. (2018, April). An edge network orchestrator for mobile augmented reality. In *IEEE INFOCOM 2018-IEEE Conference on Computer Communications* (pp. 756-764). IEEE.

Liu, W., Xie, C., Strassner, J., Karagiannis, G., Klyus, M., Bi, J., Cheng, Y., & Zhang, D. (2018). *Policy-Based Management Framework for the Simplified Use of Policy Abstractions (SUPA)*. IETF. RFC 8328. Retrieved October 09, 2020, from https://tools.ietf.org/html/rfc8328

Liu, W., Xie, C., Strassner, J., Karagiannis, G., Klyus, M., Bi., J, Cheng, Y., & Zhang, D. (2018). *Policy-Based Management Framework for the Simplified Use of Policy Abstractions (SUPA)*. IETF RFC 8328.

Liu, Y., Dai, H.-N., Wang, Q., Shukla, M.K., & Imram, M. (2020). *Unmanned Aerial Vehicle for Internet ofEverything: Opportunities and Challenges*. ArXiv, abs/2003.13311.

Liu, V., Parks, A. N., Talla, V., Gollakota, S., Wetherall, D. J., & Smith, J. R. (2013). Ambient backscatter: wireless communication out of thin air. *Proceedings of the ACM SIGCOMM 2013 conference on SIGCOMM*, 39–50. 10.1145/2486001.2486015

Liu, Y., & Man, H. (2005). *Network vulnerability assessment using Bayesian networks.* Proceeding of SPIE, 61-71.

Li, Y. J. (2010, November). An overview of the DSRC/WAVE technology. In *International Conference on Heterogeneous Networking for Quality, Reliability, Security and Robustness* (pp. 544-558). Springer.

Li, Y., McCune, J., & Perrig, A. (2011). VIPER: verifying the integrity of PERipherals' firmware. *ACM SIGSAC Conference on Computer and Communications Security (CCS).* 10.1145/2046707.2046711

Liyanage, K. S. K., Ma, M., & Chong, P. H. J. (2018). Controller placement optimization in hierarchical distributed software defined vehicular networks. *Computer Networks, 135,* 226–239. doi:10.1016/j.comnet.2018.02.022

Lockwood, J. W., McKeown, N., Watson, G., Gibb, G., Hartke, P., Naous, J., . . . Luo, J. (2007). NetFPGA--An Open Platform for Gigabit-Rate Network Switching and Routing. In *Microelectronic Systems Education, 2007. MSE'07. IEEE International Conference on* (pp. 160-161). IEEE.

Long, J. (2017, June 29). Kali Drones. Kali Drones, Portable CTF Builds, Raspberry Pi Craziness and More! *Kali Linux News.* https://www.kali.org/news/

Lopez, D. (2013). Dynamic Risk Assessment in Information Systems: State-of-the-art. *The 6th International Conference on Information Technology (ICIT).*

Lopez, V., Vilalta, R., Uceda, V., Mayoral, A., Casellas, R., Martinez, R., Munoz, R., & Palacios, J. P. F. (2016). Transport API: A solution for SDN in Carriers Networks. In *ECOC 2016; 42nd European Conference on Optical Communication,* (pp. 1–3). VDE.

Loukides, M. (2012). *What is DevOps? Infrastructure as Code.* O'Reilly Media.

Lucet. (2020). *GitHub Repository of Lucet Project from Fastly.* Retrieved October 23, 2020 from https://github.com/fastly/lucet/

Luo, T., Tan, H. P., & Quek, T. Q. (2012). Sensor OpenFlow: Enabling software-defined wireless sensor networks. *IEEE Communications Letters, 16*(11), 1896–1899.

Mahmood, A., Zhang, W. E., & Sheng, Q. Z. (2019). Software-defined heterogeneous vehicular networking: The architectural design and open challenges. *Future Internet, 11*(3), 70. doi:10.3390/fi11030070

Mahy, R., Matthews, P., & Rosenberg, J. (2020). Traversal Using Relays around NAT (TURN): Relay Extensions to Session Traversal Utilities for NAT (STUN). *IETF.* Retrieved December 09, 2020, from https://tools.ietf.org/html/rfc8656

Manotas, I., Bird, C., Zhang, R., Shepherd, D., Jaspan, C., Sadowski, C., Pollock, L., & Clause, J. (2016). An empirical study of practitioners' perspectives on green software engineering. *Proceedings of the 38th International Conference on Software Engineering,* 237–248. 10.1145/2884781.2884810

Margi, C. B., Alves, R. C., Segura, G. A. N., & Oliveira, D. A. (2018). Software-defined wireless sensor networks approach: Southbound protocol and its performance evaluation. *Open Journal of Internet Of Things, 4*(1), 99–108.

Masson-Delmotte, V., Zhai, P., Pörtner, H.-O., Roberts, D., Skea, J., Shukla, P. R., Pirani, A., Moufouma-Okia, W., Péan, C., Pidcock, R., Connors, S., Matthews, J. B. R., Chen, Y., Zhou, X., Gomis, M. I., Lonnoy, E., Maycock, T., Tignor, M., & Waterfield, T. (2018). *Summary for Policymakers, In: Global Warming of 1.5°C. An IPCC Special Report on the impacts of global warming of 1.5°C above pre-industrial levels and related global greenhouse gas emission pathways, in the context of strengthening the global response to the threat of climate change, sustainable development, and efforts to eradicate poverty.* https://www.ipcc.ch/site/assets/uploads/sites/2/2019/05/SR15_SPM_version_report_LR.pdf

Maxa, J.-A., Ben Mahmoud, M.-S., & Larrieu, N. (2015). Secure Routing Protocol Design for UAV Ad Hoc Networks. *IEEE/AIAA Digital Avionics Systems Conference (DASC).*

McCullough, E. (2019, August 13). New drone network service will transport blood and tissue between Belgian hospitals. *The Brussels Times.* https://www.brusselstimes.com/

McCune, J., Li, Y., Qu, N., Zhou, Z., Datta, A., Gligor, V., & Perrig, A. (2010). TrustVisor: Efficient TCB Reduction and Attestation. *IEEE Symposium on Security and Privacy.*

McKeown, N., & Rexford, J. (2016). *Clarifying the differences between P4 and OpenFlow.* Retrieved September 2020 from https://p4.org/p4/clarifying-the-differences-between-p4-and-openflow.html

McKeown, N., Anderson, T., Balakrishnan, H., Parulkar, G., Peterson, L., Rexford, J., & Turner, J. (2008). OpenFlow: Enabling innovation in campus networks. *Computer Communication Review, 38*(2), 69–74. doi:10.1145/1355734.1355746

Medved, J., Varga, R., Tkacik, A., & Gray, K. (2014). OpenDaylight: Towards a Model-Driven SDN Controller architecture. In *A World of Wireless, Mobile and Multimedia Networks (WoWMoM), 2014 IEEE 15th International Symposium on* (pp. 1-6). IEEE.

Medved, J., Varga, R., Tkacik, A., & Gray, K. (2014). Opendaylight: Towards a model-driven sdn controller architecture. In *Proceeding of IEEE International Symposium on a World of Wireless, Mobile and Multimedia Networks 2014* (pp. 1-6). IEEE.

MEF. (2018). *Orange is designing standardized APIs to facilitate the interoperability of Ethernet services from operators to businesses.* Retrieved 02 March 2021 from, https://hellofuture.orange.com/en/orange-designing-standardised-apis-facilitate-interoperability-ethernet-services-operators-businesses/

MEF. (2021). *Empowering Digital Transformation.* https://www.mef.net/

MEHARI. (2019). In *Wikipedia.* https://en.wikipedia.org/wiki/MEHARI

Mell, P., & Grance, T. (2011). *The NIST Definition of Cloud Computing* (Special Publication No. 800-145). Computer Security Division, Information Technology Laboratory, National Institute of Standards and Technology. https://csrc.nist.gov/publications/nistpubs/800-145/SP800-145.pdf

Members. (2021). Available at https://www.lfnetworking.org/membership/members/

Mendonca, M., Nunes, B. A. A., Nguyen, X. N., Obraczka, K., & Turletti, T. (2013). *A Survey of software-defined networking: past, present, and future of programmable networks.* hal-00825087.

Meneses, F., Fernandes, M., Vieira, T., Corujo, D., Figueiredo, S., Neto, A., & Aguiar, R. L. (2019b). Traffic-aware Live Migration in Virtualized CPE Scenarios. In *IEEE Conference on Network Function Virtualization and Software Defined Networks, NFV-SDN 2019 - Proceedings.* Institute of Electrical and Electronics Engineers Inc. 10.1109/NFV-SDN47374.2019.9039975

Meneses, F., Fernandes, M., Vieira, T., Corujo, D., Neto, A., & Aguiar, R. L. (2019a). Dynamic Modular vCPE Orchestration in Platform as a Service Architectures. In *Proceeding of the 2019 IEEE 8th International Conference on Cloud Networking, CloudNet 2019.* Institute of Electrical and Electronics Engineers Inc. 10.1109/CloudNet47604.2019.9064147

Meng, H., Zheng, K., Chatzimisios, P., Zhao, H., & Ma, L. (2015, June). A utility-based resource allocation scheme in cloud-assisted vehicular network architecture. In *2015 IEEE International Conference on Communication Workshop (ICCW)* (pp. 1833-1838). IEEE. 10.1109/ICCW.2015.7247447

Mijumbi, R., Serrat, J., Gorricho, J., Latré, S., Charalambides, M., & Lopez, D. (2016). *Management and orchestration challenges in network functions virtualization.* Academic Press.

Mijumbi, R., Serrat, J., Gorricho, J. L., Bouten, N., De Turck, F., & Boutaba, R. (2015). Network function virtualization: State-of-the-art and research challenges. *IEEE Communications Surveys and Tutorials, 18*(1), 236–262.

MiniZinc. (2020). *A free and open-source constraint modeling language.* https://www.minizinc.org/

Minodier, D. (2016). *Broadband Forum TR-317: Network Enhanced Residential Gateway, Issue 1.* Broadband Forum. Retrieved August 2020 from https://www.broadband-forum.org/download/TR-317.pdf

Mirzaei, O. (2018). Dynamic Risk Assessment in IT Environments: A Decision Guide. In Z. Fields (Ed.), *Handbook of Research on Information and Cyber Security in the Fourth Industrial Revolution* (pp. 234–263). IGI Global.

Mitola, J. (1993). Software radios: Survey, critical evaluation and future directions. *IEEE Aerospace and Electronic Systems Magazine, 8*(4), 25–36.

Mittal, R., Kansal, A., & Chandra, R. (2012). Empowering developers to estimate app energy consumption. *Proceedings of the 18th annual international conference on Mobile computing and networking,* 317–328. 10.1145/2348543.2348583

Mittal, V., Nautiyal, L., & Mittal, M. (2017). *Cloud testing-the future of contemporary software testing.* In *2017 International Conference on Next Generation Computing and Information Systems (ICNGCIS),* (pp. 131–136). IEEE. 10.1109/ICNGCIS.2017.11

Modig, D., & Ding, J. (2016). Performance impacts on container based virtualization in virtualized residential gateways. In *2016 39th International Conference on Telecommunications and Signal Processing (TSP)* (pp. 27–32). 10.1109/TSP.2016.7760823

Monsanto, C., Reich, J., Foster, N., Rexford, J., & Walker, D. (2013). Composing Software Defined Networks. In NSDI (pp. 1-13). Academic Press.

Monsanto, C., Foster, N., Harrison, R., & Walker, D. (2012). A compiler and run-time system for network programming languages. *ACM SIGPLAN Notices, 47*(1), 217–230.

Morabito, R., Kjällman, J., & Komu, M. (2015). Hypervisors vs. Lightweight Virtualization: a Performance Comparison. *IEEE International Conference on Cloud Engineering.*

Morabito, R. (2015). Power Consumption of Virtualization Technologies: an Empirical Investigation. *8th IEEE/ACM International Conference on Utility and Cloud Computing.*

Morgan, Y. L. (2010). Notes on DSRC & WAVE standards suite: Its architecture, design, and characteristics. *IEEE Communications Surveys and Tutorials, 12*(4), 504–518. doi:10.1109/SURV.2010.033010.00024

Mozilla. (2020a). *Firefox DNS over HTTPs Web Page.* Retrieved October 30, 2020 from https://support.mozilla.org/en-US/kb/firefox-dns-over-https/

Mozilla. (2020b). *Mozilla's Service Worker API Web Page.* Retrieved October 30, 2020 from https://developer.mozilla.org/fr/docs/Web/API/Service_Worker_API

Munaf, R. M., Ahmed, J., Khakwani, F., & Rana, T. (2019, March). Microservices Architecture: Challenges and Proposed Conceptual Design. In *2019 International Conference on Communication Technologies (ComTech)* (pp. 82-87). IEEE.

Muqaddas. (2020). *Field Trial of Multi-Layer Slicing Over Disaggregated Optical Networks Enabling End-to-End Crowdsourced Video Streaming.* ECOC 2020.

Murray, V. (2019). Legal Over-the-Air Spoofing of GPS and the Resulting Effects on Autonomous Vehicles. Academic Press.

Nadal, L., Fabrega, J. M., Moreolo, M. S., Casellas, R., Muñoz, R., Rodríguez, L., Vilalta, R., Vílchez, F. J., & Martínez, R. (2019). SDN-enabled sliceable transceivers in disaggregated optical networks. *Journal of Lightwave Technology*, *37*(24), 6054–6062.

Nadjahi, C., Louahlia-Gualous, H., & Le Masson, S. (2020). Experimental study and analytical modeling of thermosyphon loop for cooling data center racks. *Heat and Mass Transfer*, *56*(1), 121–142. doi:10.100700231-019-02695-x

Nakao, A. (2012). *Flare: Open deeply programmable network node architecture.* Academic Press.

Nassi, B., Shabtai, A., Masuoka, R., & Elovici, Y. (2019). *SoK - Security and Privacy in the Age of Drones: Threats, Challenges, Solution Mechanisms, and Scientific Gaps.* ArXiv, abs/1903.05155.

Nassi, B., Nassi, D., Ben-Netanel, R., Mirsky, Y., Drokin, O., & Elovici, Y. (2020). Phantom of the ADAS: Phantom Attacks on Driver-Assistance Systems. *ACM SIGSAC Conference on Computer and Communications Security (CCS)*.

Nath, S. B., Chattopadhyay, S., Karmakar, R., Addya, S. K., Chakraborty, S., & Ghosh, S. K. (2019, December). PTC: Pick-Test-Choose to Place Containerized Micro-Services in IoT. In *2019 IEEE Global Communications Conference (GLOBECOM)* (pp. 1-6). IEEE.

National Institute of Standards and Technology. (2016). *Cyber Supply Chain Best Practices (Best Practices in Cyber Supply Chain Risk Management Conference Materials)*. Author.

National Institute of Standards and Technology. (2018). *Framework for Improving Critical Infrastructure Cybersecurity* (version 1.1). Author.

National Minerals Information Center. (2020). *Mineral Commodity Summaries.* https://www.usgs.gov/centers/nmic/mineral-commodity-summaries

National Research Council. (1995). *The Global Positioning System: A Shared National Asset.* The National Academies Press. Retrieved from https://www.nap.edu/catalog/4920/the-global-positioning-system-a-shared-national-asset

NATO. (2015). *Management Directive on CIS Security.* https://www.nbu.cz/download/pravni-predpisy---nato/AC_35-D_2005-REV3.pdf

NEC. (2016). *NEC Advances World's First Virtual Customer Premises Equipment Trial In Brazil.* Retrieved September 2020 from https://www.nec.com/en/press/201606/global_20160622_01.html

Nessus. (2020). *Tenable Security Ltd.* https://resources.infosecinstitute.com/a-brief-introduction-to-the-nessus-vulnerability-scanner/

Netflix. (2020). *Netflix Open Connect Program.* Retrieved October 30, 2020 from https://openconnect.netflix.com/

Nipper. (2020). *TITANIA.* https://www.titania.com/products/nipper/

NIST 800-27. (2004). *Engineering Principles for Information Technology Security (ABaseline for Achieving Security), Revision A. superseded by SP 800-160 (November 2016).* https://nvlpubs.nist.gov/nistpubs/Legacy/SP/nistspecialpublication800-27ra.pdf

NIST 800-30. (2012). Special Publication 800-30, Guide for Conducting Risk Assessments. *U.S. Department of Commerce.* https://nvlpubs.nist.gov/nistpubs/Legacy/SP/nistspecialpublication800-30r1.pdf

NIST 800-39. (2011). *NIST Special Publication 800-39, Managing Information Security Risk – Organization, Mission and Information System View.* U.S. Department of Commerce.

Niu, L., Li, H., Jiang, Y., Yong, L. (2014). *A Service Function Chaining Header and Forwarding Mechanism* (draft-niu-sfc-mechanism-01.txt). IETF Internet Draft.

Nmap. (2020). *Network Mapper.* https://nmap.org/

Nobre, J., Rosario, D., Both, C., Cerqueira, E., & Gerla, M. (2016). Toward software-defined battlefield networking. *IEEE Communications Magazine, 54*(10), 152–157.

NS1. (2020a). *NS1 Multi-CDN Web Page.* Retrieved October 30, 2020 from https://ns1.com/multi-cdn/

NS1. (2020b). *NS1 Web Portal Page.* Retrieved October 30, 2020 from https://ns1.com/

O'Hanlon, B., Psiaki, M. L., Humphreys, T., & Bhatti, J. (2012). Real-Time Spoofing Detection Using Correlation Between two Civil GPS Receiver. *International Technical Meeting of the Satellite Division of the Institute of Navigation (ION GNSS).*

OAI. (2020). *Open Air Interface.* https://www.openairinterface.org/

OCN. (2021). *Open Core Network.* https://telecominfraproject.com/open-core-network/

OF-CONFIG. (2013). *OpenFlow Configuration and Management Protocol.* ONF. https://www.opennetworking.org/standards/of-config

Olsson, M., Rommer, S., Mulligan, C., Sultana, S., & Frid, L. (2009). *SAE and the Evolved Packet Core: Driving the mobile broadband revolution.* Academic Press.

OMG. (2021). https://www.omg.org/spec/BPMN/

ONAP Courses. (2021). *Introduction to ONAP: Complete Network Automation.* https://training.linuxfoundation.org/training/introduction-to-onap-complete-network-automation/

ONAP Wiki. (2018a). *Homing 5G RAN VNFs.* https://wiki.onap.org/display/DW/Homing+5G+RAN+VNFs

ONAP Wiki. (2018b). *vCPE Homing Use Case.* https://wiki.onap.org/display/DW/vCPE+Homing+Use+Case

ONAP Wiki. (2021). https://wiki.onap.org/

ONAP. (2018a). *ONAP vCPE Use Case.* Retrieved September 2020 from https://docs.onap.org/en/casablanca/submodules/integration.git/docs/docs_vCPE.html

ONAP. (2018b). *ONAP vCPE Blueprint Overview.* Retrieved September 2020 from https://www.onap.org/wp-content/uploads/sites/20/2018/11/ONAP_CaseSolution_vCPE_112918FNL.pdf

ONAP. (2019). *Harmonizing Open Source and Standards: Progress of ONAP.* Retrieved September 2020 from https://www.onap.org/wp-content/uploads/sites/20/2019/04/ONAP_HarmonizingOpenSourceStandards_032719.pdf

ONAP. (2021a). *Offered APIs.* https://docs.onap.org/projects/onap-externalapi-nbi/en/latest/offeredapis/offeredapis.html#offeredapis

ONAP. (2021b). *ONAP documentation.* https://docs.onap.org/en/latest/

ONAP. (2021c). *Service: VES Event Listener 7.1.1.* https://docs.onap.org/projects/onap-vnfrqts-requirements/en/latest/Chapter8/ves7_1spec.html#datatype-commoneventheader

ONAP. (2021d). *TOSCA Policy Primer*. Retrieved 02 March 2021 from, https://docs.onap.org/en/elalto/submodules/policy/parent.git/docs/architecture/tosca-policy-primer.html

OneAPI. (n.d.). *GSM Association*. Retrieved December 09, 2020, from https://www.gsma.com/identity/api-exchange

ONF TR-502. (2014). *The SDN architecture, issue 1.0*. Available online at https:www.opennetworking.orgimagesstoriesdownloadssdn-resourcestechnical-reportsTR_SDN_ARCH_1.0_06062014.pdf

ONF TR-526. (2016). *Applying SDN Architecture to 5G Slicing*. Academic Press.

ONF. (2014). *Openflow-enabled SDN and Network Functions Virtualization*. ONF Solution Brief, Open Networking Foundation.

ONF. (2015). *OpenFlow Switch Specification, version 1.5.1* (Wire Protocol 0x06). Open Networking Foundation. Retrieved July 2020 from https://opennetworking.org/wp-content/uploads/2014/10/openflow-switch-v1.5.1.pdf

Open Networking Foundation. (2009). *OpenFlow Switch Specification v1.0.0*. Retrieved August 20, 2020, from https://opennetworking.org/wp-content/uploads/2013/04/openflow-spec-v1.0.0.pdf

Open Networking Foundation. (2012). *Software-Defined Networking: The New Norm for Networks*. ONF White Paper.

Open Networking Foundation. (2013). *SDN Architecture Overview*. Retrieved February, 2021, from https://opennetworking.org/wp-content/uploads/2014/11/TR_SDN-ARCH-1.0-Overview-12012016.04.pdf

Open Networking Foundation. (2014). *OpenFlow Table Type Patterns Version 1.0*. Retrieved February 09, 2021, from https://opennetworking.org/wp-content/uploads/2013/04/OpenFlow%20Table%20Type%20Patterns%20v1.0.pdf

Open Networking Foundation. (2014). *SDN Architecture, Issue 1*. Retrieved February 2021 from https://opennetworking.org/wp-content/uploads/2014/10/TR-521_SDN_Architecture_issue_1.1.pdf

OpenConfig data models. (n.d.). https://www.openconfig.net/projects/models/

OpenConfig. (n.d.). www.openconfig.net

OpenCord. (2017a). *AT&T and R-CORD*. Retrieved September 2020 from https://wiki.opencord.org/pages/viewpage.action?pageId=1966449

OpenCord. (2017b). *NTT and R-CORD*. Retrieved September 2020 from https://wiki.opencord.org/display/CORD/NTT+and+R-CORD

OpenCord. (2020). *Telefónica and R-CORD*. Retrieved September 2020 from https://wiki.opencord.org/pages/viewpage.action?pageId=1967521

OpenFlow. (2014). OpenFlow Switch Specification Version 1.4. *OpenNetworking Foundation*. Retrieved December 09, 2020, from http://opennetworking.wpengine.com/wp-content/uploads/2014/10/openflow-spec-v1.4.0.pdf

OpenLab. (2018). *The 1st Orange ONAP OpenLab platform*. Retrieved 02 March 2021 from, https://www.lfnetworking.org/wp-content/uploads/sites/55/2018/09/Orange-OpenLab_ONS-EU-vf-.pdf

OPNFV. (2021). *OPNFV*. https://www.opnfv.org/

O-RAN. (2020). *Operator Defined Open and Intelligent Radio Access networks*. https://www.o-ran.org/

Orange. (2020). *5G: energy efficiency by design. Orange*. https://hellofuture.orange.com/en/5g-energy-efficiency-by-design/

Ordonez-Lucena, J., Ameigeiras, P., Lopez, D., Ramos-Munoz, J. J., Lorca, J., & Folgueira, J. (2017). Network slicing for 5G with SDN/NFV: Concepts, architectures, and challenges. *IEEE Communications Magazine, 55*(5), 80–87.

OSGi. (2018). *OSGI Service Compendium, Release 7.* OSGi Alliance Specification. Retrieved July 2020 from: http://www.osgi.org /Specifications/HomePage

OSM. (2020). *Open Source Mano.* https://osm.etsi.org/

OSM. (2020). *OSM Scope and Functionality.* Retrieved September 2020 from https://osm.etsi.org/wikipub/index.php/OSM_Scope_and_Functionality

Otto, A., Agatz, N., Campbell, J., Golden, B., & Pesch, E. (2018). Optimization approaches for civil applications of unmanned aerial vehicles (UAVs) or aerial drones: A survey. *New Advances and Applications in Deterministic and Stochastic Network Optimization, 72*(4), 411–458. doi:10.1002/net.21818

Ournani, Z., Rouvoy, R., Rust, P., & Penhoat, J. (2020). On Reducing the Energy Consumption of Software: From Hurdles to Requirements. *Proceedings of the 14th ACM / IEEE International Symposium on Empirical Software Engineering and Measurement,* 1–12.

Ozmen, M.O., Behnia, R., & Yavuz, A.A. (2019). *IoD-Crypt: A Lightweight Cryptographic Framework for Internet of Drones.* ArXiv, abs/1904.06829.

P4 API working group. (2020). *P4Runtime Specification.* https://p4.org/p4runtime/spec/master/P4Runtime-Spec.html

P4. (2019). *P4 Language Specification v1.2.0.* Retrieved June 2020 from https://p4.org/p4-spec/docs/P4-16-v1.2.0.html

Panda, A., Scott, C., Ghodsi, A., Koponen, T., & Shenker, S. (2013). CAP for Networks. In *Proceedings of the second ACM SIGCOMM workshop on Hot topics in software defined networking* (pp. 91-96). ACM.

Parniewicz, D., Doriguzzi Corin, R., Ogrodowczyk, L., Rashidi Fard, M., Matias, J., Gerola, M., ... Pentikousis, K. (2014). Design and implementation of an OpenFlow hardware abstraction layer. In *Proceedings of the 2014 ACM SIGCOMM workshop on Distributed cloud computing* (pp. 71-76). ACM.

Paulina, J. (2007). Designing a Security Policy According to BS 7799 Using the OCTAVE Methodology. *The Second International Conference on Availability, Reliability and Security (ARES'07).*

PCI-SIG. (2010). *Peripheral Component Interconnect Special Interest - Special Interest Group Homepage.* Retrieved from https://pcisig.com/

Peng, H., Ye, Q., & Shen, X. S. (2019). SDN-based resource management for autonomous vehicular networks: A multi-access edge computing approach. *IEEE Wireless Communications, 26*(4), 156–162. doi:10.1109/MWC.2019.1800371

Penno, R., Reddy, T., Boucadair, M., & Wing, D. (2013). Application Enabled SDN (A-SDN). *IETF.* Retrieved December 09, 2020, from https://tools.ietf.org/html/draft-penno-pcp-asdn-00

Pentikousis, K., Wang, Y., & Hu, W. (2013). Mobileflow: Toward software-defined mobile networks. Communications Magazine, IEEE, 51(7).

Pereira, R., Couto, M., Ribeiro, F., Rua, R., Cunha, J., Fernandes, J. P., & Saraiva, J. (2017). Energy efficiency across programming languages: how do energy, time, and memory relate? *Proceedings of the 10th ACM SIGPLAN International Conference on Software Language Engineering,* 256–267. 10.1145/3136014.3136031

Pérez-Caparrós, D., Al-Hakim, C., & Carey, T. (2019). *BBS: Broadband Services Orchestration with ONAP.* Retrieved 02 March 2021 from, https://events19.linuxfoundation.org/wp-content/uploads/2018/07/ONS2019_BBS_Broadband_Services_Orchestration_with_ONAP.pdf

Personè, V. D. N., & Grassi, V. (2019, July). Architectural Issues for Self-Adaptive Service Migration Management in Mobile Edge Computing Scenarios. In *2019 IEEE International Conference on Edge Computing (EDGE)* (pp. 27-29). IEEE.

Peterson, L., Al-Shabibi, A., Anshutz, T., Baker, S., Bavier, A., Das, S., Hart, J., Palukar, G., & Snow, W. (2016). Central office re-architected as a data center. *IEEE Communications Magazine, 54*(10), 96–101. doi:10.1109/MCOM.2016.7588276

Pham, M., & Hoang, D. B. (2016). *SDN applications-The intent-based Northbound Interface realisation for extended applications. In 2016 IEEE NetSoft Conference and Workshops (NetSoft)*. IEEE.

Phan-Huy, D.-T., Wesemann, S., Bjoersell, J., & Sternad, M. (2018). Adaptive Massive MIMO for fast moving connected vehicles: It will work with Predictor Antennas! *22nd International ITG Workshop on Smart Antennas*, 1-8.

Phan-Huy, D.-T., Wesemann, S., & Sehier, P. (2019). How Wireless Dumb Devices Could Attain High Data Rates Thanks to Smart Massive MIMO Networks. *23rd International ITG Workshop on Smart Antennas*, 1-8.

Piper, J. (2020). *Risk Management Framework: Qualitative Risk Assessment through Risk Scenario Analysis*. Technical Report, STO-MP-IST-166.

Pisa, P., Moreira, M., Carvalho, H., Ferraz, L., & Duarte, O. (2010). Migrating Xen Virtual Routers with No Packet Loss. *Proceedings of the First Workshop on Network Virtualization and Intelligence For Future Internet (WNetVirt'10)*.

Planning, V. N. I. (2016). SDN-NFV reference architecture. *Version, 1*, 8–34.

Podhradský, M., Coopmans, C., & Hoffer, N. (2017). Improving communication security of open source UAVs: Encrypting radio control link. *International Conference on Unmanned Aircraft Systems (ICUAS)*. 10.1109/ICUAS.2017.7991460

Poolappasit, N., Dewri, R., & Ray, I. (2012). Dynamic security risk assessment using bayesian attack graphs. *IEEE Transactions on Dependable and Secure Computing, 9*, 61–74.

Pradel, M., Garcia, J., & Vaija, M. S. (2021). A framework for good practices to assess abiotic mineral resource depletion in Life Cycle Assessment. *Journal of Cleaner Production, 219*, 123296. doi:10.1016/j.jclepro.2020.123296

Pratt, A., Kumar, P., & Aldridge, T. V. (2007). Evaluation of 400V DC distribution in telco and data centers to improve energy efficiency. *29th International Telecommunications Energy Conference*, 32-39. 10.1109/INTLEC.2007.4448733

Proença, J., Cruz, T., Simões, P., Gaspar, G., Parreira, B., Laranjeira, A., & Bastos, F. (2017). Building an NFV-Based vRGW: lessons learned. *14th IEEE Consumer Communications and Networking Conference (CCNC 2017)*.

Proença, J., Cruz, T., Simões, P., & Monteiro, E. (2019). Virtualization of Residential Gateways: A Comprehensive Survey. *IEEE Communications Surveys and Tutorials, 21*(2), 1462–1482. doi:10.1109/COMST.2018.2874827

Pronto. (2021). Retrieved 13 January 2021, from https://prontoproject.org/

Puopolo, S., Latouche, M., Le Faucheur, F., & Defour, J. (2011). *Cisco white paper. Content Delivery Network (CDN) Federations. How SPs Can Win the Battle for Content-Hungry Consumers*. Retrieved October 30, 2020 from https://www.cisco.com/c/dam/en/us/products/collateral/video/videoscape-distribution-suite-service-broker/cdn_vds_sb_white_paper.pdf

Qiao, X., Ren, P., Dustdar, S., Liu, L., Ma, H., & Chen, J. (2019). Web AR: A promising future for mobile augmented reality—State of the art, challenges, and insights. *Proceedings of the IEEE, 107*(4), 651–666. doi:10.1109/JPROC.2019.2895105

Qiao, X., Ren, P., Nan, G., Liu, L., Dustdar, S., & Chen, J. (2019). Mobile web augmented reality in 5G and beyond: Challenges, opportunities, and future directions. *China Communications, 16*(9), 141–154. doi:10.23919/JCC.2019.09.010

Qin, Z., Denker, G., Giannelli, C., Bellavista, P., & Venkatasubramanian, N. (2014) A Software Defined Networking Architecture for the Internet-of-Things. In *Network Operations and Management Symposium (NOMS)*. IEEE.

Quinn, P., & Nadeau, T. (2014). *Service Function Chaining Problem Statement* (draft-ietf-sfc-problem-statement-07. txt). IETF Internet Draft.

Quintuna, V., Corbel, R., Guillemin, F., & Ferrieux, A. (2020b). Cloud-RAN Factory: Instantiating virtualized mobile networks with ONAP. *2020 11th International Conference on Network of the Future (NoF)*.

Quintuna, V., Guillemin, F., & Boubendir, A. (2020a). 5G E2E Network Slicing Management with ONAP. 2020 23rd Conference on Innovation in Clouds. *Internet and Networks and Workshops (ICIN)*.

Quintuna, V., & Guillemin, F. (2019). *End-to-end virtual mobile network deployment on ONAP Onboarding. Distributing and instantiating the Wireless Edge Factory (WEF)*. NASA Deliverable.

Quintuna, V., Guillemin, F., & Boubendir, A. (2019). Automating the deployment of 5G Network Slices using ONAP. *10th International Conference on Networks of the Future (NoF)*.

Qu, L., Assi, C., & Shaban, K. (2016). Delay-aware scheduling and resource optimization with network function virtualization. *IEEE Transactions on Communications*, *64*(9), 3746–3758.

Rachedi, K., Phan-Huy, D.-T., Ourir, A., & De Rosny, J. (2019). Spatial characterization of the ambient backscatter communication performance in line-of-sight. *IEEE International Symposium on Antennas and Propagation and USNC-URSI Radio Science Meeting*. 10.1109/APUSNCURSINRSM.2019.8889046

Rachedi, K., Phan-Huy, D.-T., Selmene, N., Ourir, A., Gautier, M., Gati, A., Galindo-Serrano, A. M., Fara, R., & De Rosny, J. (2019). Demo abstract: *Real-Time Ambient Backscatter Demonstration. IEEE International Conference on Computer Communications*.

Raja, Z. (2020). *Security specialists trick Tesla's Computer Vision algorithm with a drone and a projector*. Retrieved from https://www.talentometry.co.uk/blog/technology/security-specialists-trick-teslas-computer-vision-algorithm-with-a-drone-and-a-projector/

Raspotnig, C. (2018). Combined Assessment of Software Safety and Security Requirements: An Industrial Evaluation of the CHASSIS Method. *Journal of Cases on Information Technology*, *20*(1).

Rawlins, D., Kulkarni, A., Chan, K., Bokaemper, M., & Dutt, C. (2003). *Framework Policy Information Base for Usage Feedback*. IETF. RFC 3571. Retrieved October 09, 2020, from https://tools.ietf.org/html/rfc3571

R-CORD. (n.d.). *Residential CORD*. Retrieved September 2020 from https://wiki.opencord.org/display/CORD/Residential+CORD

Reddy, T. (Ed.). (2020). *Distributed Denial-of-Service Open Threat Signaling (DOTS) Signal Channel Specification*. IETF. RFC 8782. Retrieved October 09, 2020, from https://www.rfc-editor.org/rfc/rfc8782.pdf

Regulus. (n.d.). *Pyramid GNSS*. Retrieved October 13, 2020, from https://www.regulus.com/solutions/pyramid-gnss/

Reich, J., Monsanto, C., Foster, N., Rexford, J., & Walker, D. (2013). Modular SDN Programming with Pyretic. *USENIX*, *38*(5), 128-134.

Rescoria, E., & Modadugu, N. (2012). *Datagram transport Layer Security Version 1.2*. IETF RFC 6347. Retrieved October 09, 2020, from https://tools.ietf.org/html/rfc6347

Rescorla, E. (2018). *The Transport Layer Security (TLS) Protocol Version 1.3*. IETF RFC 8446.

Rescorla, E. (2018). *The Transport Layer Security (TLS) Protocol Version 1.3.* IETF RFC 8446. Retrieved October 09, 2020, from https://tools.ietf.org/html/rfc8446

Research and Markets. (2020). *$32+ Billion Worldwide Software-Defined Networking Market to 2025 - Featuring Cisco, Huawei & VMware Among Others.* Retrieved 10 March 2021 from, https://www.globenewswire.com/news-release/2020/08/18/2079769/0/en/32-Billion-Worldwide-Software-Defined-Networking-Market-to-2025-Featuring-Cisco-Huawei-VMware-Among-Others.html

ResiCAV. (2020). *Economic and Technological Feasibility of CyRes Methodology.* Thales Technical report.

Reynaud, F., Aguessy, F. X., Bettan, O., Bouet, M., & Conan, V. (2016, June). Attacks against network functions virtualization and software-defined networking: State-of-the-art. In *2016 IEEE NetSoft Conference and Workshops (NetSoft)* (pp. 471-476). IEEE.

Richomme, M., & Desbureaux, S. (2020). *Gating retrospective.* Retrieved 02 March 2021 from, https://wiki.lfnetworking.org/download/attachments/25364127/gating_retrospective_final.pptx?version=1&modificationDate=1579086074000&api=v2

Rinki, S. (2014). *Simulation studies on effects of dual polarisation and directivity of antennas on the performance of MANETs* (Doctoral dissertation). Coventry University.

Robert, R. (2019). *Service Resolver.* https://gitlab.com/Orange-OpenSource/lfn/onap/service-resolver

Roberts, J., (2009). The clean-slate approach to future Internet design: a survey of research initiatives. *Annals of Telecommunications-Annales des Télécommunications, 64*(5-6), 271-276.

Rodday, N. (2016). *Hacking a professional drone.* Black Hat Asia.

Rogelj, J., Shindell, D., Jiang, K., Fifita, S., Forster, P., Ginzburg, V., Handa, C., Kheshgi, H., Kobayashi, S., Kriegler, E., Mundaca, L., Séférian, R., & Vilariño, M. V. (2018). *Mitigation Pathways Compatible with 1.5°C in the Context of Sustainable Development, In: Global Warming of 1.5°C. An IPCC Special Report on the impacts of global warming of 1.5°C above pre-industrial levels and related global greenhouse gas emission pathways, in the context of strengthening the global response to the threat of climate change, sustainable development, and efforts to eradicate poverty.* https://www.ipcc.ch/site/assets/uploads/sites/2/2019/02/SR15_Chapter2_Low_Res.pdf

Rooney, S., van der Merwe, J. E., Crosby, S. A., & Leslie, I. M. (1998). The Tempest: A framework for safe, resource assured, programmable networks. *Communications Magazine, IEEE, 36*(10), 42–53.

Rosemberg, J. (2002). *SIP: Session Initiation Protocol.* IETF Internet Standard. RFC 3261.

Rosenberg, J., Mahy, R., & Wing, D. (2008). Session Traversal Utilities for NAT (STUN). *IETF.* Retrieved December 09, 2020, from https://tools.ietf.org/html/rfc5389

Rotter, C., Farkas, L., Nyiri, G., Csatári, G., Jánosi, L., & Springer, R. (2016). *Using Linux Containers in Telecom Applications. Innovations in Clouds, Internet and Networks.* ICIN.

Royon, Y. (2007). *Environments d'exécution pour paserelles domestiques* (PhD thesis). Institut National des Sciences Apliquées (INSA/INRIA).

Rusek, F., Persson, D., Lau, B. K., Larsson, E. G., Marzetta, T. L., Edfors, O., & Tufvesson, F. (2013). Scaling Up MIMO: Opportunities and Challenges with Very Large Arrays. *IEEE Signal Processing Magazine, 30*(1), 40–60. doi:10.1109/MSP.2011.2178495

Rusek, K., Suárez-Varela, J., Almasan, P., Barlet-Ros, P., & Cabellos-Aparicio, A. (2020). RouteNet: Leveraging Graph Neural Networks for network modeling and optimization in SDN. *IEEE Journal on Selected Areas in Communications*, *38*(10), 2260–2270.

Russon, M.-A. (2016). *NASA Drone Hack Revealed*. https://www.uasvision.com/2016/02/02/nasa-drone-hack-revealed/

Rydén, H., Redhwan, S.B., & Lin, X. (2018). *Rogue Drone Detection: A Machine Learning Approach*. ArXiv, abs/1805.05138.

Saad, T., Gandhi, R., Liu, X., Beeram, V., & Bryskin, I. (2021). *A YANG Data Model for Traffic Engineering Tunnels, Label Switched Paths and Interfaces*. IETF Draft, draft-ietf-teas-yang-te-25.

Saint-Andre, P. (2011). Extensible Messaging and Presence Protocol (XMPP): Core. *IETF*. Retrieved December 09, 2020, from https://tools.ietf.org/html/rfc6120

Salahuddin, M. A., Al-Fuqaha, A., & Guizani, M. (2014). Software-defined networking for rsu clouds in support of the internet of vehicles. *IEEE Internet of Things Journal*, *2*(2), 133–144. doi:10.1109/JIOT.2014.2368356

Salameh, M. G. (2013). *The United States' Shale Oil Revolution in Perspective*. USAEE Working Paper No. 13-099. doi:10.2139srn.2201990

Salem, F. E., Gati, A., Altman, Z., & Chahed, T. (2017). Advanced Sleep Modes and Their Impact on Flow-Level Performance of 5G Networks. *IEEE 86th Vehicular Technology Conference (VTC-Fall)*.

Salman, O., Elhajj, I. H., Kayssi, A., & Chehab, A. (2016), April. SDN controllers: A comparative study. In *2016 18th Mediterranean Electrotechnical Conference (MELECON)* (pp. 1-6). IEEE.

Saripalli, P. (2010). QUIRC: A Quantitative Impact and Risk Assessment Framework for Cloud Security. *IEEE 3rd International Conference on Cloud Computing*.

Sato, Y., Fukuda, I., & Tomonori, F. (2013, December). Deployment of OpenFlow/SDN Technologies to Carrier Services. *IEICE Transactions*, *96-B*(12), 2946–2952. doi:10.1587/transcom.E96.B.2946

Satyanarayanan, M. (2017). The emergence of edge computing. *IEEE Computer*, *50*(1), 30–39.

Scheffer, Y., Holz, R. & Saint-Andre, P. (2015). *Recommendations for Secure Use of Transport Layer Security (TLS) and Datagram Transport Layer Security (DTLS)*. IETF RFC 7525)

Schoenwaelder, J. (2003). *Overview of the 2002 IAB Network Management Workshop*. IETF RFC 3535.

Schwarz, S., Preda, M., Baroncini, V., Budagavi, M., Cesar, P., Choud, P., Cohen, R., Krivokuca, M., Lasserre, S., Li, Z., Llach, J., Mammou, K., Mekuria, R., Nakagami, O., Siahaan, E., Tabatabai, A., Tourapis, A., & Zahkarchenko, V. (2019). Emerging MPEG Standards for Point Cloud Compression. *IEEE Journal on Emerging and Selected Topics in Circuits and Systems*, *9*(1), 133–148.

Science-based Targets. (2020). *Science-based Targets*. https://sciencebasedtargets.org/

SecRAM. (2017). *SecRAM 2.0 Security Risk Assessment methodology for SESAR 2020*. https://www.sesarju.eu/sites/default/files/documents/transversal/SESAR%202020%20-%20Security%20Reference%20Material%20Guidance.pdf

Seedorf, J., Peterson, J., Previdi, S., van Brandenburg, R., & Ma, K. (2016). *Content Delivery Network Interconnection (CDNI) Request Routing: Footprint and Capabilities Semantics*. Internet Engineering Task Force RFC 8008. Retrieved from https://tools.ietf.org/html/rfc8008

Selmadji, A., Seriai, A. D., Bouziane, H. L., Mahamane, R. O., Zaragoza, P., & Dony, C. (2020, March). From Monolithic Architecture Style to Microservice one Based on a Semi-Automatic Approach. In *2020 IEEE International Conference on Software Architecture (ICSA)* (pp. 157-168). IEEE.

Semal, B., Markantonakis, K., & Akram, R. (2018). A Certificateless Group Authenticated Key Agreement Protocol for Secure Communication in Untrusted UAV Networks. *IEEE/AIAA 37th Digital Avionics Systems Conference (DASC).*

Septentrio. (n.d.). *Advanced Interference Monitoring & Mitigation (AIM+).* Retrieved October 13, 2020, from https://www.septentrio.com/en/advanced-interference-monitoring-mitigation-aim

SESAR. (2020). *Single European Sky ATM Research programme.* http://www.sesarju.eu/

Seshadri, A., Luk, M., & Perrig, A. (2011). SAKE: Software attestation for key establishment in sensor networks. *Ad Hoc Networks, 9*(6), 1059–1067. doi:10.1016/j.adhoc.2010.08.011

Sezer, S., Scott-Hayward, S., Chouhan, P. K., Fraser, B., Lake, D., Finnegan, J., . . . Rao, N. (2013). Are we ready for SDN? Implementation challenges for software-defined networks. Communications Magazine, IEEE, 51(7).

Sharma, G. P., Tavernier, W., Colle, D., & Pickavet, M. (2019). VNF-AAP: Accelerator-aware Virtual Network Function Placement. *IEEE Conference on Network Function Virtualization and Software Defined Networks, NFV-SDN 2019 - Proceedings,* 25–28. 10.1109/NFV-SDN47374.2019.9040061

Sharma, R., & Reddy, H. (2019, December). Effect of Load Balancer on Software-Defined Networking (SDN) based Cloud. In *2019 IEEE 16th India Council International Conference (INDICON)* (pp. 1-4). IEEE.

Sharma, R., Kadambi, G. R., Vershinin, Y. A., & Mukundan, K. N. (2015, April). Multipath Routing Protocol to Support Dual Polarised Directional Communication for Performance Enhancement of MANETs. In *2015 Fifth International Conference on Communication Systems and Network Technologies* (pp. 258-262). IEEE. 10.1109/CSNT.2015.105

Sharma, R., Kadambi, G., Vershinin, Y. A., & Mukundan, K. N. (2016). A survey of MAC layer protocols to avoid deafness in wireless networks using directional antenna. In Mobile Computing and Wireless Networks: Concepts, Methodologies, Tools, and Applications (pp. 1758-1797). IGI Global.

Sharma, R., Kadambi, G. R., Vershinin, Y. A., & Mukundan, K. N. (2015, April). Dual Polarised Directional Communication based Medium Access Control Protocol for Performance Enhancement of MANETs. In *2015 Fifth International Conference on Communication Systems and Network Technologies* (pp. 185-189). IEEE. 10.1109/CSNT.2015.104

Shea, R., Sun, A., Fu, S., & Liu, J. (2017, June). Towards fully offloaded cloud-based AR: Design, implementation and experience. In *Proceedings of the 8th ACM on Multimedia Systems Conference* (pp. 321-330). ACM.

Shenker, S., Partridge, C., & Guerin, R. (1997). *Specification of Guaranteed Quality of Service.* IETF RFC 2212.

Sherwood, R., Gibb, G., Yap, K. K., Appenzeller, G., Casado, M., McKeown, N., & Parulkar, G. (2009). *Flowvisor: A network virtualization layer.* OpenFlow Switch Consortium, Tech. Rep.

Sherwood, R., Chan, M., Covington, A., Gibb, G., Flajslik, M., Handigol, N., Huang, T. Y., Kazemian, P., Kobayashi, M., Naous, J., & Seetharaman, S. (2010, January 7). Carving research slices out of your production networks with OpenFlow. *Computer Communication Review, 40*(1), 129–130.

Shin, Y. Y., Kang, S. H., Kwak, J. Y., & Yang, S. H. (2015). iNaaS: OpenStack and SDN/OpenFlow based network virtualization with OpenIRIS. In *2015 17th International Conference on Advanced Communication Technology (ICACT)* (pp. 517-520). IEEE.

Shu, Z., Wan, J., Lin, J., Wang, S., Li, D., Rho, S., & Yang, C. (2016). Traffic engineering in software-defined networking: Measurement and management. *IEEE Access: Practical Innovations, Open Solutions, 4*, 3246–3256. doi:10.1109/ACCESS.2016.2582748

Smedt, A., Balemans, H., Onnegren, J., & Haeseleer, S. (2006). The multi-play service enabled Residential Gateway. Proc. of Broadband Europe 2006.

Smida, K., Tounsi, H., Frikha, M., & Song, Y. Q. (2019, June). Software defined Internet of Vehicles: A survey from QoS and scalability perspectives. In 2019 15th International Wireless Communications & Mobile Computing Conference (IWCMC) (pp. 1349-1354). IEEE. doi:10.1109/IWCMC.2019.8766647

Smith, M., Dvorkin, M., Laribi, Y., Pandey, V., Garg, P. & Weidenbacher, N. (2016). *OpFlex Control Protocol.* IETF individual draft, draft-smith-opflex-03.

Sokolov, V., Alekseev, I., Mazilov, D., & Nikitinskiy, M. (2014). A network analytics system in the SDN. In *2014 International Science and Technology Conference (Modern Networking Technologies) (MoNeTeC)* (pp. 1-3). IEEE.

Song, H. (2020). Adaptive Addresses for Next Generation IP Protocol in Hierarchical Networks. *IEEE 28th International Conference on Network Protocols (ICNP).*

Song, H. (2013). Protocol-oblivious forwarding: Unleash the power of SDN through a future-proof forwarding plane. In *Proceedings of the second ACM SIGCOMM workshop on Hot topics in software defined networking* (pp. 127-132). ACM.

Son, Y., Shin, H., Kim, D., Park, Y., Noh, J., Choi, K., Choi, J., & Kim, Y. (2015). Rocking Drones with Intentional Sound Noise on Gyroscopic Sensors. *USENIX Security Symposium.*

Soua, R., Kalogeiton, E., Manzo, G., Duarte, J. M., Palattella, M. R., Di Maio, A., & Rizzo, G. A. (2017). SDN coordination for CCN and FC content dissemination in VANETs. In *Ad Hoc Networks* (pp. 221–233). Springer. doi:10.1007/978-3-319-51204-4_18

Stiemerling, M., Schulzrinne, H., Rao, A., Lanphier, R., & Westerlund, M. (2016). *Real-Time Streaming Protocol Version 2.0.* Internet Engineering Task Force RFC 7826. Retrieved from https://tools.ietf.org/html/rfc7826

Storck, C. R., & Duarte-Figueiredo, F. (2020). A Survey of 5G Technology Evolution, Standards, and Infrastructure Associated With Vehicle-to-Everything Communications by Internet of Vehicles. *IEEE Access: Practical Innovations, Open Solutions, 8*, 117593–117614. doi:10.1109/ACCESS.2020.3004779

Sudheer, K. K., Ma, M., & Chong, P. H. J. (2017, December). Link dynamics based packet routing framework for software defined vehicular networks. In *GLOBECOM 2017-2017 IEEE Global Communications Conference* (pp. 1-6). IEEE. 10.1109/GLOCOM.2017.8254597

Sudheera, K. L. K., Ma, M., & Chong, P. H. J. (2019). Link stability based optimized routing framework for software defined vehicular networks. *IEEE Transactions on Vehicular Technology, 68*(3), 2934–2945. doi:10.1109/TVT.2019.2895274

Su, J., He, J., Cheng, P., & Chen, J. (2016). A Stealthy GPS Spoofing Strategy for Manipulating the Trajectory of an Unmanned Aerial Vehicle. *IFAC-PapersOnLine, 49*(22), 291–296. doi:10.1016/j.ifacol.2016.10.412

Sultana, N., Chilamkurti, N., Peng, W., & Alhadad, R. (2019). Survey on SDN based network intrusion detection system using machine learning approaches. *Peer-to-Peer Networking and Applications, 12*(2), 493–501.

Sultan, S., Ahmad, I., & Dimitriou, T. (2019). Container security: Issues, challenges, and the road ahead. *IEEE Access: Practical Innovations, Open Solutions, 7*, 52976–52996. doi:10.1109/ACCESS.2019.2911732

Sun, P., AlJeri, N., & Boukerche, A. (2020). *DACON: A Novel Traffic Prediction and Data-Highway-Assisted Content Delivery Protocol for Intelligent Vehicular Networks. IEEE Transactions on Sustainable Computing.*

Sun, S., Gong, L., Rong, B., & Lu, K. (2015). An intelligent SDN framework for 5G heterogeneous networks. *IEEE Communications Magazine, 53*(11), 142–147.

SVA. (2020). *Web Portal of the Open Caching Working Group from the Streaming Video Alliance.* Retrieved October 30, 2020 from https://www.streamingvideoalliance.org/working-group/open-caching/

Taleby Ahvanooey, M., Li, Q., Rabbani, M., & Rajput, A. R. (2017). A Survey on Smartphones Security: Software Vulnerabilities, Malware, and Attacks. *International Journal of Advanced Computer Science and Applications., 8*(10), 2017.

Tang, J., Zhang, W., Gong, X., Li, G., Yu, D., Tia, Y., Liu, B., & Zhao, L. (2020). A Flexible Hierarchical Network Architecture with Variable-Length IP Address. *IEEE Conference on Computer Communications Workshop on New IP: The Next Step*, 267-272.

Tang, F., Kawamoto, Y., Kato, N., & Liu, J. (2019). Future intelligent and secure vehicular network toward 6G: Machine-learning approaches. *Proceedings of the IEEE, 108*(2), 292–307. doi:10.1109/JPROC.2019.2954595

Tang, Y., Cheng, N., Wu, W., Wang, M., Dai, Y., & Shen, X. (2019). Delay-minimization routing for heterogeneous VANETs with machine learning based mobility prediction. *IEEE Transactions on Vehicular Technology, 68*(4), 3967–3979. doi:10.1109/TVT.2019.2899627

Tedeschi, P., Oligeri, G., & Di Pietro, R. (2020). Leveraging Jamming to Help Drones Complete Their Mission. *IEEE Access: Practical Innovations, Open Solutions, 8*, 5049–5064. doi:10.1109/ACCESS.2019.2963105

Telecom Infra Project. (2019). *CANDI First Experimental Demonstration.* Available online at https://www.ntt.co.jp/topics_e/tip2019/pdf/TIP_CANDI_1st_Experimental_Demonstration.pdf

Telecom Intra Project. (2020). *Open Transport SDN Whitepaper.* Available online at https://cdn.brandfolder.io/D8DI15S7/at/jh6nnbb6bjvn7w7t5jbgm5n/OpenTransportArchitecture-Whitepaper_TIP_Final.pdf

Telecommunication Standardization sector of ITU. (1990). *CCITT Recommendation 1.361, B-ISDN ATM Layer Specification.* Geneva, Switzerland: ITU.

Telecommunication Standardization sector of ITU. (1993). *ITU, Q.700: Introduction to CCITT Signalling System No. 7.* Geneva, Switzerland: ITU.

Telstra. (2018). *Press Release. Telstra deploys Australia's first LTE-Broadcast technology to support sports streaming. July 11, 2018.* Retrieved October 23, 2020 from https://www.telstra.com.au/aboutus/media/media-releases/Telstra-deploys-Australias-first-LTE-Broadcast-technology-to-support-sports-streaming

Tennenhouse, D. L., Smith, J. M., Sincoskie, W. D., Wetherall, D. J., & Minden, G. J. (1997). A survey of active network research. *Communications Magazine, IEEE, 35*(1), 80–86.

Terraform. (2020). *Terraform Registry of Fastly Provider.* Retrieved October 23, 2020 from https://registry.terraform.io/providers/fastly/fastly/latest/

Thales. (2018). *7 Key Factors for Enabling Trust in the Drone Ecosystem.* https://dis-blog.thalesgroup.com/iot/2018/03/08/7-key-factors-for-enabling-trust-in-the-drone-ecosystem/

Thom, S., Cox, J., Linsley, D., Nystrom, M., Raj, H., Robinson, D., Saroiu, S., Spiger, R., & Wolman, A. (2011). *Firmware-based trusted platform module for arm processor architectures and trustzone security extensions.* US Patent No. 8,375,221 B1. Washington, DC: U.S.

Thriveni, H. B., Kumar, G. M., & Sharma, R. (2013, April). Performance evaluation of routing protocols in mobile ad-hoc networks with varying node density and node mobility. In *2013 International Conference on Communication Systems and Network Technologies* (pp. 252-256). IEEE. 10.1109/CSNT.2013.60

Time-Sensitive Networking (TSN) Task Group. (2020). Available from https://1.ieee802.org/tsn/

TIP. (2020). *Telecom Infra Project*. https://telecominfraproject.com/

TMF. (2020). *Open Digital Architecture. A blueprint for success in the digital markets of tomorrow*. https://www.tm-forum.org/oda/

Tombes, J. (2019). *White Paper. Multicast ABR, Low-Latency CMAF, CTE, and Optimized Video Playback. Reducing Latency in Live Online Video*. Retrieved October 30, 2020 from https://www.theoplayer.com/whitepaper-abr-cmaf-low-latency/

Tootaghaj, D. Z., Ahmed, F., Sharma, P., & Yannakakis, M. (2020). Homa: An Efficient Topology and Route Management Approach in SD-WAN Overlays. In *IEEE INFOCOM 2020-IEEE Conference on Computer Communications* (pp. 2351-2360). IEEE.

TPM Main Specification. (2011, March). https://www.trustedcomputinggroup.org/resources/tpm_main_specification

Trammell, B. (2020). Current Open Questions in Path Aware Networking. *IRTF*. Retrieved October 07, 2020, from https://datatracker.ietf.org/doc/draft-irtf-panrg-questions/

Troan, O., & Droms, R. (2003). *IPv6 Prefix Options for Dynamic Host Configuration Protocol (DHCP) version 6*. IETF Internet Standard RFC3633.

Troia, S., Zorello, L. M. M., Maralit, A. J., & Maier, G. (2020). SD-WAN: An Open-Source Implementation for Enterprise Networking Services. In *2020 22nd International Conference on Transparent Optical Networks (ICTON)* (pp. 1-4). IEEE.

Truong, N. B., Lee, G. M., & Ghamri-Doudane, Y. (2015, May). Software defined networking-based vehicular adhoc network with fog computing. In *2015 IFIP/IEEE International Symposium on Integrated Network Management (IM)* (pp. 1202-1207). IEEE. 10.1109/INM.2015.7140467

United Nations. (2020). *Sustainable Development Goals*. https://www.un.org/sustainabledevelopment/

UptimeInstitute. (2020). *10th annual Data Center Industry Survey Results*. https://uptimeinstitute.com/2020-data-center-industry-survey-results

Vaija, M. S., & Philipot, E. (2020). L'importance des métaux rares pour le secteur des technologies de l'information et de la communication, le cas d'Orange. *Responsabilité & Environnement, 99*. http://annales.org/re/2020/re99/2020-07-4.pdf

Valadarsky, A., Schapira, M., Shahaf, D., & Tamar, A. (2017). A Machine Learning Approach to Routing, Cornell University. https://arxiv.org/abs/1708.03074

van Brandenburg, R., Leung, K., & Sorber, P. (2020). *URI Signing for CDN Interconnection (CDNI), draft-ietf-cdni-uri-signing-19*. Retrieved October 23, 2020 from https://tools.ietf.org/html/draft-ietf-cdni-uri-signing-19

van Brandenburg, R., van Deventer, O., Le Faucheur, F., & Leung, K. (2013). *Models for HTTP-Adaptive-Streaming-Aware Content Distribution Network Interconnection (CDNI)*. Internet Engineering Task Force RFC 6983. Retrieved from https://tools.ietf.org/html/rfc6983

Van Huynh, N., Hoang, D. T., Lu, X., Niyato, D., Wang, P., & Kim, D. I. (2018). Ambient Backscatter Communications: A Contemporary Survey. *IEEE Communications Surveys and Tutorials, 20*(4), 2889–2922. doi:10.1109/COMST.2018.2841964

Van Oers, L., De Koning, A., Guinée, J. B., & Huppes, G. (2002). *Abiotic resource depletion in LCA Improving characterisation factors for abiotic resource depletion as recommended in the new Dutch LCA Handbook.* https://www.leidenuniv.nl/cml/ssp/projects/lca2/report_abiotic_depletion_web.pdf

Van Oers, L., Guinée, J. B., & Heijungs, R. (2020). Abiotic resource depletion potentials (ADPs) for elements revisited - updating ultimate reserve estimates and introducing time series for production data. *The International Journal of Life Cycle Assessment, 25*(2), 309–310. doi:10.100711367-019-01709-4

Van Tu, N., Hyun, J., & Hong, J. W. K. (2017). Towards onos-based sdn monitoring using in-band network telemetry. In *2017 19th Asia-Pacific Network Operations and Management Symposium (APNOMS)* (pp. 76-81). IEEE.

Venkatramana, D. K. N., Srikantaiah, S. B., & Moodabidri, J. (2017). SCGRP: SDN-enabled connectivity-aware geographical routing protocol of VANETs for urban environment. *IET Networks, 6*(5), 102–111. doi:10.1049/iet-net.2016.0117

Verhoogt, T. (2018). *Towards Dynamic Cyber Security Risk Assessment of Military Aircraft.* NATO Science and Technology Organization (SCO). Reference: STO-MP-SCI-300.

Verizon. (2018). *Embracing the disruptive power of software-defined networking.* Report.

Virtualisation, E. N. F. (2015). Ecosystem; report on SDN usage in NFV architectural framework. *ETSI Netw. Funct. Virtualisat. Ind. Specif. Group GS NFV-EVE, 5,* V1.

Vissicchio, S., Vanbever, L., & Bonaventure, O. (2014). Opportunities and research challenges of hybrid software defined networks. *Computer Communication Review, 44*(2), 70–75. doi:10.1145/2602204.2602216

Vodafone. (2018). *The rise of drones.* Vodafone White Paper.

Voellmy, A., Kim, H., & Feamster, N. (2012). Procera: a language for high-level reactive network control. In *Proceedings of the first workshop on Hot topics in software defined networks* (pp. 43-48). ACM.

Vollbrecht, J., Calhoun, P., Farrell, S., Gommans, L., Gross, G., de Bruijn, B., & Spence, D. (2000, August). *AAA Authorization Framework* (Tech. Rep. No. 2904). IETF. RFC 2904.

W3.org. (2020). *W3.org WASM Web Page.* Retrieved October 27, 2020 from https://www.w3.org/wasm/

Wang, G., Estrada, Z., Pham, C., Kalbarczyk, Z., & Iyer, R. (2015).Hypervisor Introspection: A Technique for Evading Passive Virtual Machine Monitoring. *9th USENIX Workshop on Offensive Technologies (WOOT15).*

Wang, S., Urgaonkar, R., He, T., Chan, K., Zafer, M., & Leung, K. K. (2016). Dynamic service placement for mobile micro-clouds with predicted future costs. *IEEE Transactions on Parallel and Distributed Systems, 28*(4), 1002–1016.

Wang, X., Mao, S., & Gong, M. X. (2017). An overview of 3GPP cellular vehicle-to-everything standards. *GetMobile: Mobile Computing and Communications, 21*(3), 19–25. doi:10.1145/3161587.3161593

Warner, J. S., & Johnston, R. (2003). GPS Spoofing Countermeasures. *Homeland Security Journal, 25*(2), 19–27.

Webassembly.org. (2020). *Webassembly.org Web Page.* Retrieved October 27, 2020 from https://webassembly.org/

Wen, B., Fioccola, G., Xie, C., & Jalil, L. (2018). *A YNAG Data Model for Layer 2 Virtual Private Network (l2vpn) Service Delivery.* IETF RFC 8466.

Wen, H., Huang, P. Y., Dyer, J., Archinal, A., & Fagan, J. (2005). Countermeasures for GPS Signal Spoofing. *International Technical Meeting of the Satellite Division of the Institute of Navigation.*

Wetherall, D. J., Guttag, J. V., & Tennenhouse, D. L. (1998). ANTS: A toolkit for building and dynamically deploying network protocols. In Open Architectures and Network Programming, 1998 IEEE (pp. 117-129). IEEE.

Weyns, D., Schmerl, B., Grassi, V., Malek, S., Mirandola, R., Prehofer, C., & Göschka, K. M. (2013). On patterns for decentralized control in self-adaptive systems. In *Software Engineering for Self-Adaptive Systems II* (pp. 76–107). Springer.

Wikipedia. (2021). *Lindbergh operation.* Available from https://en.wikipedia.org/wiki/Lindbergh_operation

Wing, D., Cheshire, S., Boucadair, M., Penno, R., & Selkirk, P. (2013). Port Control Protocol (PCP). *IETF.* Retrieved December 09, 2020, from https://tools.ietf.org/html/rfc6887

Wing, D., Penno, R., Reddy, T., & Selkirk, P. (2013). PCP Flowdata Option. *IETF.* Retrieved December 09, 2020, from https://tools.ietf.org/html/draft-wing-pcp-flowdata-00

Wroclawski, J. (1997). *Specification of the Controlled-Load Network Element Service.* IETF RFC 2211.

Wu, C. C., Tung, L. P., Lin, C. Y., Lin, B. S. P., & Tseng, Y. C. (2014, June). On local cache management strategies for Mobile Augmented Reality. In *Proceeding of IEEE International Symposium on a World of Wireless, Mobile and Multimedia Networks 2014* (pp. 1-3). IEEE.

Wu, Q., Boucadair, M., Lopez, D., Xie, C., & Geng, L. (2021). *A Framework for Automating Service and Network Management with YANG.* IETF RFC 8969.

Wu, Q., Litkowski, S., Tomotaki, L., & Ogaki, K. (2018). *YANG Data Model for L3VPN Service Delivery.* IETF RFC 8299.

Wu, Q., Liu, W., & Farrel, A. (2018). *Service Models Explained.* IETF RFC 8309.

Xia, L., Wu, Q., & King, D. (2013). *Use cases and Requirements for Virtual Service Node Pool Management* (draft-xia-vsnpool-management-use-case-01). IEFT Internet Draft.

Xie, J., Yu, F. R., Huang, T., Xie, R., Liu, J., Wang, C., & Liu, Y. (2018). A survey of machine learning techniques applied to software defined networking (SDN): Research issues and challenges. *IEEE Communications Surveys and Tutorials,* *21*(1), 393–430. doi:10.1109/COMST.2018.2866942

Xu, C., Rajamani, K., & Felter, W. (2018). Nbwguard: Realizing network qoS for kubernetes. In *Proceedings of the 19th International Middleware Conference Industry* (pp. 32-38). Academic Press.

Xue, N., Niu, L., Hong, X., Li, Z., Hoffaeller, L., & Pöpper, C. (2020). DeepSIM: GPS Spoofing Detection on UAVs using Satellite Imagery Matching. *Annual Computer Security Applications Conference (ACSAC).* 10.1145/3427228.3427254

Xu, K., Wang, X., Wei, W., Song, H., & Mao, B. (2016). Toward software defined smart home. *IEEE Communications Magazine,* *54*(5), 116–122.

Xu, X., Pan, Y., Lwin, P. P. M. Y., & Liang, X. (2011). 3D holographic display and its data transmission requirement. *2011 International Conference on Information Photonics and Optical Communications.*

Yahiatene, Y., Rachedi, A., Riahla, M. A., Menacer, D. E., & Nait-Abdesselam, F. (2019). A blockchain-based framework to secure vehicular social networks. *Transactions on Emerging Telecommunications Technologies,* *30*(8), e3650. doi:10.1002/ett.3650

YANG Catalog. (2021). Available at https://yangcatalog.org/

Yang, Z., Cui, Y., Li, B., Liu, Y., & Xu, Y. (2019). Software-defined wide area network (SD-WAN): Architecture, advances and opportunities. In *2019 28th International Conference on Computer Communication and Networks (ICCCN)* (pp. 1-9). IEEE.

Yang, K., Zhang, J., Xu, Y., & Chao, J. (2020).DDoS Attacks Detection with AutoEncoder. *2020 IEEE/IFIP Network Operations and Management Symposium.* 10.1109/NOMS47738.2020.9110372

Yan, S., Aguado, A., Ou, Y., Wang, R., Nejabati, R., & Simeonidou, D. (2017). Multilayer network analytics with SDN-based monitoring framework. *Journal of Optical Communications and Networking, 9*(2), A271–A279.

Yap, K. K., Kobayashi, M., Sherwood, R., Huang, T. Y., Chan, M., Handigol, N., & McKeown, N. (2010). OpenRoads: Empowering research in mobile networks. *Computer Communication Review, 40*(1), 125–126.

Yap, K. K., Motiwala, M., Rahe, J., Padgett, S., Holliman, M., Baldus, G., ... Vahdat, A. (2017, August). Taking the edge off with espresso: Scale, reliability and programmability for global internet peering. In *Proceedings of the Conference of the ACM Special Interest Group on Data Communication* (pp. 432-445). 10.1145/3098822.3098854

Yaqoob, I., Ahmad, I., Ahmed, E., Gani, A., Imran, M., & Guizani, N. (2017). Overcoming the key challenges to establishing vehicular communication: Is SDN the answer? *IEEE Communications Magazine, 55*(7), 128–134. doi:10.1109/MCOM.2017.1601183

Yavatkar, R., Pendarakis, D., & Guerin, R. (2000). A Framework for Policy-based Admission Control. *IETF*. Retrieved December 09, 2020, from https://tools.ietf.org/html/rfc2753

Ye, Q., Zhuang, W., Li, X., & Rao, J. (2019). End-to-end delay modeling for embedded VNF chains in 5G core networks. *IEEE Internet Things J., 6*(1), 692–704.

Yeung, P. (2016, August 7). Drone reports to UK police soar 352% in a year amid urgent calls for regulation. *The Independent.* https://www.independent.co.uk/

Young, W. (2017). System-Theoretic Process Analysis for Security (STPA-SEC): Cyber Security and STPA. *STAMP Conference.* http://psas.scripts.mit.edu/home/wp-content/uploads/2017/04/STAMP_2017_STPA_SEC_TUTORIAL_as-presented.pdf

Yousaf, F. Z., Bredel, M., Schaller, S., & Schneider, F. (2017). NFV and SDN—Key technology enablers for 5G networks. *IEEE Journal on Selected Areas in Communications, 35*(11), 2468–2478.

Zaballa, E. O., Franco, D., Aguado, M., & Berger, M. S. (2020). Next-generation SDN and fog computing: A new paradigm for SDN-based edge computing. In *2nd Workshop on Fog Computing and the IoT* (pp. 9-1). Schloss Dagstuhl-Leibniz-Zentrum fur Informatik GmbH, Dagstuhl Publishing.

Zazo, J. F., Lopez-Buedo, S., Audzevich, Y., & Moore, A. W. (2015). A PCIe DMA engine to support the virtualization of 40 Gbps FPGA-accelerated network appliances. In *ReConFigurable Computing and FPGAs (ReConFig), 2015 International Conference on* (pp. 1–6). 10.1109/ReConFig.2015.7393334

Zeitouni, S., Dessouky, G., Arias, O., Sullivan, D., Ibrahim, A., Jin, Y., & Sadeghi, A. (2017). ATRIUM: Runtime attestation resilient under memory attacks. *IEEE/ACM International Conference on Computer-Aided Design (ICCAD).* 10.1109/ICCAD.2017.8203803

Zeng, S., & Hao, Q. (2009). Network I/O Path Analysis in the Kernel-based Virtual Machine Environment through Tracing. *Proceedings of the 1st Int. Conf. on Information Science and Engineering (ICISE) 2009.*

Zeng, X., Cao, K., & Zhang, M. (2017, June). MobileDeepPill: A small-footprint mobile deep learning system for recognizing unconstrained pill images. In *Proceedings of the 15th Annual International Conference on Mobile Systems, Applications, and Services* (pp. 56-67). Academic Press.

Zenzic. (2020). *Zenzic's published work on Cyber Feasibility Studies for CAVs, in partnership with CCAV.* https://zenzic.io/cybersecurity/

Zepf, V., Simmons, J., Reller, A., Rennie, C., Ashfield, M., & Achzet, B. (2014). *Materials Critical to the Energy Industry: An Introduction* (2nd ed.). BP Plc.

Zeydan, E., & Turk, Y. (2020). Recent advances in intent-based networking: A survey. In *2020 IEEE 91st Vehicular Technology Conference (VTC2020-Spring)* (pp. 1-5). IEEE.

Zhang, W., Han, B., Hui, P., Gopalakrishnan, V., Zavesky, E., & Qian, F. (2018, February). CARS: Collaborative augmented reality for socialization. In *Proceedings of the 19th International Workshop on Mobile Computing Systems & Applications* (pp. 25-30). Academic Press.

Zhang, W., Hwang, J., Rajagopalan, S., Ramakrishnan, K. K., & Wood, T. (2016, December). Flurries: Countless fine-grained nfs for flexible per-flow customization. In *Proceedings of the 12th International on Conference on emerging Networking Experiments and Technologies* (pp. 3-17). Academic Press.

Zhang, N., Zhang, S., Yang, P., Alhussein, O., Zhuang, W., & Shen, X. (2017). Software Defined Space-Air-Ground Integrated Vehicular Networks: Challenges and Solutions. *IEEE Communications Magazine, 55*(7), 101–109. doi:10.1109/MCOM.2017.1601156

Zhang, Y., Zhang, H., Long, K., Zheng, Q., & Xie, X. (2018). Software-defined and fog-computing-based next generation vehicular networks. *IEEE Communications Magazine, 56*(9), 34–41. doi:10.1109/MCOM.2018.1701320

Zhao, L., Al-Dubai, A., Zomaya, A. Y., Min, G., Hawbani, A., & Li, J. (2020). Routing schemes in software-defined vehicular networks: Design open issues and challenges. *IEEE Intell. Transp. Syst. Mag.*

Zheng, K., Zheng, Q., Chatzimisios, P., Xiang, W., & Zhou, Y. (2015). Heterogeneous vehicular networking: A survey on architecture, challenges, and solutions. *IEEE Communications Surveys and Tutorials, 17*(4), 2377–2396. doi:10.1109/COMST.2015.2440103

Zhou, Y., Cheng, N., Lu, N., & Shen, X. (2015). Multi-UAV-Aided Networks: Aerial-Ground Cooperative Vehicular Networking Architecture. *IEEE Vehicular Technology Magazine, 10*(4), 36–44. doi:10.1109/MVT.2015.2481560

Zhu, H., & Huang, C. (2018). VNF-B&B: Enabling Edge-based NFV with CPE resource sharing. In *IEEE International Symposium on Personal, Indoor and Mobile Radio Communications, PIMRC* (pp. 1–5). Institute of Electrical and Electronics Engineers Inc. 10.1109/PIMRC.2017.8292421

Zhu, L., Karim, M. M., Sharif, K., Li, F., Du, X., & Guizani, M. (2019). *SDN controllers: Benchmarking & performance evaluation.* arXiv preprint arXiv:1902.04491.

Zhu, M., Cai, Z. P., Xu, M., & Cao, J. N. (2015). Software-defined vehicular networks: Opportunities and challenges. In Energy Science and Applied Technology. CRC Press.

Zhu, M., Cao, J., Cai, Z., He, Z., & Xu, M. (2016). Providing flexible services for heterogeneous vehicles: An NFV-based approach. *IEEE Network, 30*(3), 64–71. doi:10.1109/MNET.2016.7474346

Zhu, M., Cao, J., Pang, D., He, Z., & Xu, M. (2015, August). SDN-based routing for efficient message propagation in VANET. In *International Conference on Wireless Algorithms, Systems, and Applications* (pp. 788-797). Springer. 10.1007/978-3-319-21837-3_77

Zhu, T., Chen, X., Chen, L., Wang, W., & Wei, G. (2020). GCLR: GNN-Based Cross Layer Optimization for Multipath TCP by Routing. *IEEE Access: Practical Innovations, Open Solutions, 8*, 17060–17070.

ZigBee Alliance. (2015). *ZigBee Specification* (ZigBee Document 05-3474-21). Author.

Zuo, Y., Wu, Y., Min, G., & Cui, L. (2019). Learning-based network path planning for traffic engineering. *Future Generation Computer Systems, 92*, 59–67.

About the Contributors

Mohamed Boucadair is an IP Networking Strategist within "Strategies for IP Networking" team part of the Wireline Technical Strategy Directorate, which is part of Orange. In charge of novel IP techniques activity within "Strategies for IP Networking" team. Contributes to the definition of strategies for fixed networks, based upon the integration of IPv6, intra and inter-domain routing, Policy-based management, SDN (Softwire-Defined Networking), Network Automation, Service Function Chaining (SFC), Power-Aware Networking, Multipath TCP, Dynamic Service Negotiation & Provisioning, Performance-based Routing, Multicast, Denial of Service, transport protocols evolution, autonomous networking, multi-homing and traffic engineering techniques, including an active contribution to the IETF standardization (+50 IETF RFCs) and patent deposits.

Christian Jacquenet graduated from the Ecole Nationale Supérieure de Physique de Marseille, a French school of engineers. He joined Orange in 1989, and he's currently the Referent Expert of the "Networks of the Future" Orange Expert community. Until March 2017, he was the Director of the Strategic Program Office for advanced IP networking within Orange Labs. He is also the head of Orange's IPv6 Program that aims at defining and driving the enforcement of the Group's IPv6 strategy. He conducts development activities in the areas of Software-Defined Networking (SDN), IP networking, automated service delivery procedures, including service function chaining techniques. He authored and co-authored several Internet standards in the areas of dynamic routing protocols and resource allocation techniques, as well as numerous papers and books in the areas of IP multicast, traffic engineering and automated IP service delivery techniques. He also holds several patents in the areas of advanced home and IP networking techniques.

* * *

Abdol-Hamid Aghvami was promoted to a Reader, in 1989, and in 1993, he was promoted to a Professor in telecommunications engineering. He was a Visiting Professor at NTT Radio Communication Systems Laboratories in 1990, a Senior Research Fellow at BT Laboratories from 1998 to 1999, and was an Executive Advisor to Wireless Facilities Inc., USA, from 1996 to 2002. He joined the Academic Staff at King's College London in 1984. He is currently the Founder of the Centre for Telecommunications Research, King's College London. He is also a Visiting Professor of Imperial College. He was the Director of the Centre from 1994 to 2014. He carries out consulting work on Digital Radio Communications Systems for British and International companies; he has published over 600 technical journal and conference papers, filed over 30 patents, and given invited talks and courses the world over on various aspects of Mobile Radio Communications. He is the Chairman of Advanced Wireless Technology Group Ltd. He is also the Managing Director of Wireless Multimedia Communications Ltd., his own consultancy company. He leads an active research team involved in numerous mobile and personal communications projects for Fourth and fifth generation networks; these projects are supported both by government and industry. He was a member of the Board of Governors of the IEEE Communications Society from 2001 to 2003, was a Distinguished Lecturer of the IEEE Communications Society from 2004 to 2007, and has been a member, the Chairman, and the ViceChairman of the technical programme and organizing committees of a large number of international conferences. He is also a Founder of the International Symposium on Personal Indoor and Mobile Radio Communications, a major yearly conference attracting some 1,000 attendees. He is a fellow of the Royal Academy of Engineering and IET. He received the IEEE Technical Committee on Personal Communications Recognition Award in 2005 for his outstanding technical contributions to the communications field, and for his service to the scientific and engineering communities. In 2009, he also received a Fellowship of the Wireless World Research Forum in recognition of his personal contributions to the wireless world, and for his research achievements as the Director with the Centre for Telecommunications Research, King's College London.

Pedro A. Aranda Gutiérrez holds a Telecommunications Engineer title from the Universidad Politécnica de Madrid (1988) and a PhD in Informatics from the University of Paderborn (2013). He worked between 1991 and 2016 for Telefónica, Investigación y Desarrollo in different Networking Areas and projects. During this time he participated in different EU funded research projects in Networking and Software Defined Networks, including the NetIDE project, where he was Technical Manager. Simultaneously, he started lecturing activities with the Universidad Carlos III de Madrid in 2015. He is currently coordinating the Virtualisation and the Advanced SDN and NFV Laboratory courses in its SDN/NFV Specialist and Master Programme in the University. His lecturing activities also include Networking and Software Networks in the Bachelors level.

Ghada Arfaoui (Eng, PhD) is a research engineer working on services and networks security at Orange Labs, France. She received her Telecommunications Engineer degree from Télécom SudParis, Institut Mines-Télécom, in 2011. In 2015, she received her PhD in Computer Science from University of Orléans, INSA Centre Val de Loire, France. She contributed to French and European research projects and presented in national and international conferences and meetings. Her main research interests encompass 5G Security, Future Network Security, Mobile Network Infrastructure Security, Trusted Computing, Cryptography, and Privacy.

David Armand is a security expert at Orange Labs, and is specialized in embedded systems. From 2009 to 2015 he was in charge of design and validation of security features in Orange Set-Top-Boxes. Most of his work now consists in pentesting of gateways and connected devices, as well as evaluation of new technologies.

Hamid Asgari is Thales Expert and a visiting professor at King's College London. He is currently leading both Verification &Validation and Network activities at Thales UK Research, Technology, & Innovation (RTI). He is a highly experienced in leading large collaborative R&D teams, a technical expert in Network & Cyber Security Architectures and concepts, Safety and Security Risk Management, Verification, Validation and Performance Evaluations of complex systems. Hamid has a proven track record and published more than 65 book chapters and papers in the most respected scientific journals and peer reviewed conferences. Hamid is IET fellow, Senior Member of IEEE and ACM. For full list of publication please visit: https://scholar.google.co.uk/citations?user=Mj_zIOEAAAAJ&hl=en.

Samier Barguil (M.Sc. 2018). PhD Candidate from the Universidad Autonoma de Madrid. Electronic Engineer from the District University of Bogota Francisco José de Caldas and Master in Science in Industrial Automation of the Universidad Nacional de Colombia. Currently, Samier is the IP SDN Technical Leader at Wipro Technologies Ltd.

Valéry Bastide obtained a degree level of telecommunication from Lille 1 University in 1987. He started as technical team manager on voice telephony and cable network in France Telecom. He worked during 5 years in Orange Labs on broadband access server and IP ADSL Networks. For fifteen years, he has been working on Content delivery activities for Orange Labs and he is currently in charge of integration and validation activities on Content Delivery Networks.

Nicolas Bihannic is currently Orange expert on "Network of the Future" in Orange Labs. He received his Master's degree in Electronics and Telecommunication from the "Institut Supérieur d'Electronique et du Numérique" (ISEN group) in 2000. His current research interests are on business model evolution for telcos in 5G networks and beyond. Nicolas leads several co-innovation projects on both B2B and wholesale markets.

Yiping Chen prepared his PhD in Computer Science between 2006 and 2010 at Telecom Bretagne and Technicolor Research France, on the topic of locality-awareness of Peer-to-Peer applications. After graduation, He worked at CNRS-LaBRI on the EU FP7 project Alicante. The project aims at the deployment of networked "Media Ecosystem", built on top of the Content-Aware Network and virtual home-box overlays. He then joined Orange Labs, and works on content delivery optimization and cloud infrastructure.

Uma S. Chunduri is a Distinguished Engineer at Future networks Chief Architect office, Futurewei Technologies in Santa Clara, California. He is an IP routing expert with 20+ years of extensive R&D background and expertise in service provider networks, enterprise, cellular backhaul and broadband access networks. He is currently focusing on enabling network services for various industry verticals with stringent network requirements, 5G/B5G network strategy, standardization, and deployment. He is an active contributor at IETF in Routing, Internet, and Security areas with 10 published RFCs and numerous Internet Drafts, as well as 50+ patents. Uma served as TPC Co-Chair of IEEE CSNM/HipNET 2018, 2019, IEEE/IFIP IM 2019 and organizer of several workshops. He served as a rapporteur of ETSI NGP's Integrated Routing and TE-architecture for next generation networks. Prior to Futurewei, Uma was with Kineto Wireless, NXP Semiconductors and was a Principal Engineer at Ericsson R&D, USA.

Alexander Clemm is a Distinguished Engineer at Futurewei Technologies in Santa Clara, California. His current research interests include high-precision networks, future networking services, network analytics, intent, manageability, and telemetry. Alex serves regularly on the Organizing Committees of many highly rated conferences, including IM/NOMS, CNSM, and Netsoft. In addition to papers and patents, he has authored 12 RFCs and several books including "Network Management Fundamentals".

He is the recipient of the 2020 Salah Aidarous Award given by IEEE CNOM and IFIP TC6.6 "to an individual who has provided unremitting service and dedication to the IT and Telecommunications Network Operations and Management community".

Tiago Cruz received the Ph.D. degree in informatics engineering from the University of Coimbra in 2012, where he has been an Assistant Professor with the Department of Informatics Engineering, since 2013. His research interests cover areas such as management systems for communications infrastructures and services, critical infrastructure security, broadband access network device and service management, Internet of Things, software defined networking, and network function virtualization.

Eric Debeau has 20 years of experience in the telecommunications area with a particular focus on the adoption of IT techniques in networks and OSS domains. Through his broad experience as network architect (SDH, VoIP, IMS), he has been recognized as Orange Expert in Future Networks. He is currently Head of the Network Automation Team which mainly address the core network evolution while considering NFV and network data analytics. His team has a strong involvement in opensource communities as OPNFV and now ONAP. Eric Debeau is himself ONAP TSC member and responsible of Orange contributions in the ONAP project. In addition, he has published various technical papers and holds several patents.

Gwenaelle Delsart is currently Edge computing and Smart Content Delivery Program Director for Orange Technology and Global Innovation. She previously coordinated the Celtic European SooGREEN research project, focused on Service-oriented optimization of Green Mobile Networks, within Orange Labs Networks. Before joining Orange in 2014, she worked for eighteen years in Alcatel-Lucent with skill in speech recognition, text to speech, mobile TV, project management and procurement. She holds an engineering degree in communication systems and networks from "INSA Rennes".

Spyros Denazis is an Associate Professor of the Electrical & Computer Engineering Department, in University of Patras, Greece. He received his B.Sc in Mathematics from the University of Ioannina, Greece, in 1987, and his PhD in Computer Science from the University of Bradford, UK, in 1993. In 1996, he joined the R&D Department of Intracom SA in Athens as Project Coordinator, and in 1998, he joined the Information Technology Laboratory of Hitachi Europe in Cambridge UK, as a Senior Research Engineer while serving for 3 years (1998- 2001) as an Industrial Research Fellow in the Centre for Communications Systems Research, of Cambridge University, UK. For the period 2003-2010 he had also been a Consultant for the Hitachi Europe Sophia Antipolis Laboratory, in France; during this period, he has collaborated in a number of research projects both internal and European. Currently, Prof. Denazis leads a quite active research group, the Network Architecture & Management Group (NAM) where he coordinates a range of research activities in the areas of P2P Live Streaming, Future Internet Research Experimentation, 5G/NFV/SDN, Cybersecurity and IoT. The NAM Group has deployed and operates an IoT network (LoRa based) across the city of Patras which is also part of the TheThingsNetwork community (https://www.thethingsnetwork.org/community/patras/). He has published over 70 papers in journals and conferences, and served as chair and member of a large number of conferences and workshops. He is the owner of one patent and he has contributed to various standardization bodies, IETF, IEEE and ETSI. He has been involved in many EU projects since 1996 acting also as Project Coordinator. He currently serves as the Technical Coordinator of the H2020 project 5GinFIRE (https://5ginfire.eu/). He has also served as a reviewer in European and national projects. He is one of the authors of the book "Programmable Networks for IP Service Deployment ", Artech House, and the owner of one patent. More information may be found in http://nam.ece.upatras.gr/denazis.

Mischa Dohler is full Professor in Wireless Communications at King's College London, driving cross-disciplinary research and innovation in technology, sciences and arts. He is a Fellow of the IEEE, the Royal Academy of Engineering, the Royal Society of Arts (RSA), the Institution of Engineering and Technology (IET); and a Distinguished Member of Harvard Square Leaders Excellence. He is a serial entrepreneur with 5 companies; composer & pianist with 5 albums on Spotify/iTunes; and fluent in 6 languages. He acts as policy advisor on issues related to digital, skills and education. He has had ample coverage by national and international press and media. He is a frequent keynote, panel and tutorial speaker, and has received numerous awards. He has pioneered several research fields, contributed to numerous wireless broadband, IoT/M2M and cyber security standards, holds a dozen patents, organized and chaired numerous conferences, was the Editor-in-Chief of two journals, has more than 300 highly-cited publications, and authored several books. He was the Director of the Centre for Telecommunications Research at King's from 2014-2018. He is the Cofounder of the Smart Cities pioneering company Worldsensing, where he was the CTO from 2008-2014. He also worked as a Senior Researcher at Orange/ France Telecom from 2005-2008.

Lijun Dong is a Research Architect at Futurewei Technologies, USA. She has broad and in-depth researches in the areas of Internet of Things, Machine-to-Machine communications, Information-Centric Networking, High Precision Networks and Future Internet services for more than a decade. She has served for many international conferences: industry program chair of ICNC 2020; publicity chair of CSCN 2016; TPC co-chair of ICNC 2017, etc. She was one of the board members of the WOCC conference for the year 2016-2018. She won the travel grant of Globecom 2009, InterDigital Innovation's Awards in 2013, best paper awards in MobiMedia 2020, WOCC 2018, and AFIN 2018. She is the major inventor to 50+ granted patents. She has 60+ publications and several book chapters. She is a senior member of the IEEE.

Gilles Dretsch is a French telecom engineer working for the innovation department of Orange. His main field of interest are energy efficiency and circular economy applied to the telecom industry to reduce its carbon footprint.

Loïc Ferreira is a research engineer at Orange Labs in Caen (France). He is a member of the Applied Cryptography Group. He studied at the University of Lyon (France) where he received a Bachelor degree in Mathematics, and a Master's degree in Applied Mathematics. He holds a Ph.D. in Computer Science (cryptography) from INSA Rennes. His main research topics focus on the security protocols for low-resource objects, and post-quantum cryptography.

Frédéric Fieau is a Telecom and Networks engineer and is currently a delegate at the IETF.

Quentin Fousson holds a telecommunications engineering degree and a master's degree in sustainable development. During his career with various telecom operators and equipment manufacturers, he was notably project manager for Green RAN (Radio Access Network) within the Orange group between

2017 and 2020. As such, he participated in the 5G program in order to anticipate and control the consumption of these new networks.

Vasilis Friderikos has been a Visiting Researcher with the WIN Lab, Rutgers University, NJ, USA, and in 2010, taught advanced mobility management protocols for the future Internet at the Institut Supérieur de lElectronique et du Numérique, France. He is currently a Reader with the Department of Engineering at King's College London, U.K. He has authored over 200 research papers in flagship IEEE, Elsevier, Springer journals, international conferences, and book chapters, and also holds patents. His research interests lie broadly within the closely overlapped areas of wireless networking, mobile computing, and architectural aspects of the future Internet. The emphasis of his research is the design and analysis of algorithms for network optimization in virtualized 6G networks with focus on the amalgamation of AI with model-based optimization techniques. He is a member of IET and the INFORMS section on telecommunications. He was a recipient of the British Telecom Fellowship Award in 2005. He received the Best Paper Award from the IEEE ICC 2010 Conference and the WWRF 10 Conference.

Ivan Froger is a network architect within Orange.

Guillaume Gerard is a senior green datacenter Engineer working at Orange Corporate and in European standardization bodies related to green ICT, datacenters and related operational KPIs, namely ETSI, AFNOR, CENELEC and NGO eG4U. He is mostly interested in operational sustainability and IT service continuity.

Óscar González de Dios received his M.S. degree in telecommunications engineering and Ph.D. degree (Hons.) from the University of Valladolid, Spain. He has 21 years of experience in Telefonica, where he has been involved in a number of European research and development projects (recently, STRONGEST, ONE, IDEALIST, Metro-Haul and now Teraflow). He has coauthored over 100 research papers and 17 IETF RFCs. He is currently the head of SDN Deployments for Transport Networks, called iFUSION in Telefonica Global CTIO. His main research interests include photonic networks, flexi-grid, interdomain routing, PCE, automatic network configuration, end-to-end MPLS, performance of transport protocols, and SDN. He is currently active in several IETF Working Groups such as OPSAWG and TEAS and is the Co-Chair of CANDI WG in OOPT Telecom Infra Project.

Yvon Gourhant acquired his Ph.D in Computer Science at INRIA in 1991. After 15 months in the DSG group at Trinity College Dublin, he joined the R&D division of France Telecom in Lannion (Brittany in France) in 1993, still working in distributed systems. From 1998 to 2009, he was leading a R&D team on programmable and adaptable networks. In 2007 and 2008, he was also leading and acting in a R&D program on Light Infrastructure Networks that encompass ad hoc/mesh networks, self-organized sensor networks, and vehicular networks. Since mid 2009, he is leading and acting in a research program on network coverage extension for multiple use cases: rural Africa, maritime, and UAV/drones.

Evangelos Haleplidis received his diploma in Electrical Engineering from the University of Patras in 2002. He received his Ph.D. from the Department of Electrical and Computer Engineering in the University of Patras in 2016 with the title Design, Model and implement Open Programmable Networks. He has taken part in the successful IST projects FlexiNET and IST Phosphorus. He is the main author of several RFCs, co-author of several drafts in the IETF's ForCES working group and also has submitted as main author four individual internet draft submissions in regards to the ForCES architecture and one of the authors of RFC7426 from the SDNRG IRTF research group. His main field of interest is network protocols, modeling and modeling languages for abstractions and network services. He has around 12 publication in journals, book chapters and conference papers related with his research interests.

Zhaohui Huang is now a PhD student of Telecommunications at King's College London, focusing on the routing problems of 5G or beyond 5G networks. Zhaohui previously graduated from the University of Sheffield and got his Master's degree in Software Systems and Internet Technology.

Tirumaleswar Reddy Konda is a Principal Engineer at McAfee. He has expertise in network and IoT/endpoint security, architecting, and developing security products and solutions. He has a proven track record of developing security and privacy standards for the Internet. He is currently chair of the TEEP WG and member of the "security area" review team at IETF. He has co-authored 22 RFC and is an active contributor in several working groups. He has 47 patents approved and 50 patents filed in USPTO. His recent work and interests include IoT Security, Service Function Chaining, DDoS mitigation, and Encrypted DNS.

Odysseas Koufopavlou received the Diploma of Electrical Engineering in 1983 and the Ph.D. degree in Electrical Engineering in 1990, both from University of Patras, Greece. From 1990 to 1994 he was at the IBM Thomas J. Watson Research Center, Yorktown Heights, NY, USA. He is currently Professor with the Department of Electrical and Computer Engineering, University of Patras. His research interests include computer networks, high performance communication subsystems architecture and implementation, VLSI low power design, and VLSI crypto systems. He served as conference General Chair of the ICECS 1999, SEAA 2009, DSD 2009. He was member of organizing and technical program committees of many major conferences. He leads several projects funded by the European Commission, the Greek government, and major companies. He has also been a consultant for several companies. Dr. Koufopavlou has published more than 200 technical papers and received patents and inventions. He is a member of IEEE, the IFIP 10.5 WG, Euromicro Society and the Technical Chamber of Greece.

Nathalie Labidurie Omnes obtained a PhD in mathematics applied to network dimensioning in 2001. She then joined Mitsubishi Electric ITE TCL in Rennes, to work on the QoS (Quality of Service) of HyperLAN2 wireless local networks. In 2007, she started working on Content Delivery architectures and joined devoteam. In 2010, she joined Orange Labs for studying end-to-end architectures for content services. She is now a leading architect studying the extension of the operator's infrastructure at the edge.

Marc Lacoste is a Senior Scientist in the Security Department of Orange Labs. His research focuses on security of virtualized systems (e.g., cloud infrastructures, autonomous vehicular networks, drone architectures), notably isolation and trusted execution environments. He is Orange research-lead on vehicular security. He was also Technical Leader of H2020 SUPERCLOUD on user-centric multi-cloud security. He holds engineering degrees from Ecole Polytechnique and Télécom ParisTech, and a PhD in Computer Science from the University of Grenoble, France.

Yannick Le Louédec holds an engineering degree in telecommunications from the "Ecole Nationale Supérieure des Telecommunications de Bretagne". He has been working for Orange Labs for nineteen years where he has been successively in charge of research activities on Optical Networks, IP Networks and Content Delivery Networks.

Richard Li is Chief Scientist and Vice President of Network Technologies at Futurewei, USA. Richard also served as the Chairman of the ITU-T FG Network 2030 from 2018 to 2020, and as the Vice Chairman of the Europe ETSI ISG NGP (Next-Generation Protocols) from 2016 to 2019. He has also served as Chair of steering committees and technical program committees of some academic and industrial conferences. Richard is extremely passionate about advancing ICT infrastructure technologies and solving problems in their entirety, thus creating a bigger and long-term impact on the networking industry. During his career, Richard spearheaded network technology innovation and development in Routing and MPLS, Mobile Backhaul, Metro and Core Networks, Data Center, Cloud and Virtualization. Currently he leads a team of scientists and engineers to develop technologies for next-generation network architectures, protocols, algorithms, and systems in the support of forward-looking applications and industry verticals in the context of New IP and Network 2030.

Diego R. Lopez joined Telefonica I+D in 2011 as a Senior Technology Expert on network middleware and services. He is currently in charge of the Technology Exploration activities within the GCTO Unit of Telefónica I+D. Before joining Telefónica he spent some years in the academic sector, dedicated to research on network service abstractions and the development of APIs based on them. During this period he was appointed as member of the High Level Expert Group on Scientific Data Infrastructures by the European Commission. Diego is currently focused on identifying and evaluating new opportunities in technologies applicable to network infrastructures, and the coordination of national and international collaboration activities. His current interests are related to network virtualization, infrastructural services, network mamagement, new network architectures, and network security. Diego is actively participating in the ETSI ISG on Network Function Virtualization (chairing its Network Operator Council), the IETF WGs connected to these activities, and several related open-source projects. Apart from this, Diego is a more than acceptable Iberian ham carver, and extremely fond of seeking and enjoying comics, wines, and cheeses.

Víctor López (M.Sc. 2005 - Ph.D. 2009) is a Technology Expert at Systems and Network Global Direction in Telefónica gCTIO. He works on the global IP and transport processes of the Telefonica group. Moreover, he is involved in the research projects as well as in the definition of the Telefonica network guidelines for IP and transport networks. He serves as co-chair at the Open Optical Packet Transport group in the Telecom Infra Project. He started his carrier in Telefónica I+D as a researcher (2004). He moved to Universidad Autonoma de Madrid in 2006, where he obtained the Ph.D. He became an Assistant Professor at UAM (2009), working on metro-backbone evolution projects (BONE, MAINS). In 2011, he joined Telefonica I+D as a Technology specialist working on funded research projects from the Telefonica group and the European Commission. He has co-authored more than 200 publications, six patents and contributed to IETF and ONF. Moreover, he is the editor of the book Elastic Optical Networks: Architectures, Technologies, and Control (308 pages, Springer 2016). His research interests include the integration of Internet services over IP/MPLS and optical networks and control plane technologies (PCE, SDN, GMPLS).

Edmundo Monteiro is a Full Professor at the University of Coimbra (UC), Portugal, from where he graduated in Electrical Engineering (Informatics Specialty) in 1984, received the PhD in Electrical Engineering (Computer Communications), and the Habilitation in Informatics Engineering, in 1996 and 2007 respectively. He is currently the Head of the Informatics Engineering Department. He is a Senior Researcher at the Centre for Informatics and Systems (CISUC). He has more than 30 years of research and industry experience in the fields of Communication Infrastructures, Cybersecurity, Critical Infrastructure Protection, Cloud Networking, and Internet of Things. He participated in many Portuguese and International research projects and initiatives. HE published more than 200 papers in international refereed journals and conferences. He is also co-author of 9 international patents. He is member of the Editorial Board of Springer Wireless Networks and ITU Journal on Future and Evolving Technologies journals. Edmundo Monteiro is member of Ordem dos Engenheiros, and Senior Member of IEEE Communication Society and ACM SIGCOMM.

Dominique Nussbaum is a SUPELEC engineer and doctor in signal processing from the University of Rennes. Between April 1999 and February 2017 he worked as a project manager at EURECOM, Sophia Antipolis, on the design and development of the OpenAirInterface software radio platform, in particular in charge of the development and the integration of the material parts (digital parts, Radio Frequency and Antennas). Since February 2017, he is a Project Manager at Orange on the deployment of massive MIMO 5G antennas (antenna performance, deployment issues, EMF, 2G / 3G / 4G / 5G hybrid systems) and an expert for OpenAirInterface, antennas active, 5G solutions.

Zakaria Ournani is a PhD computer scientist at Orange S.A. and INRIA Lille nord-europe. His research interest mainly include assessing and reducing software energy consumption.

Kellow Pardini received the M.S. degree in telecommunications engineering from the INATEL National Institute of Telecommunications, Minas Gerais, Brazil. He has more than 15 years of professional in the network industry, acting in the design, planning, implementation, support, and optimization of complex network environments of service providers. He is the author of 3 internet of things research articles published in the IEEE and MDPI and his main research interests include photonic networks, flexi-grid, interdomain routing, PCE, automatic network configuration, end to end MPLS, performance of transport protocols, and SDN.

Fanny Parzysz received the Ph.D. degree from the Ecole de Technologie Supérieure, Montreal, Canada, in 2015, and the M.Sc.Eng. degree from Telecom ParisTech, France, in 2009. From 2015 to 2018, she worked as a Post-Doctoral Fellow at the University of Barcelona, at the Universitat Pompeu Fabra, Barcelona, Spain, and at Orange Labs, Lannion, France. She is now Researcher at Orange Labs. Her research interests cover various aspects of future connectivity infrastructures for 5G vertical services, including Industry 4.0, drones, and energy-efficient communications.

Joël Penhoat holds a master degree in network security from Telecom Paris and a PhD in mobile networks from Rennes University. For more then thirty years, he is working on data center and network energy consumption. He teaches network energy consumption efficiency at Telecom Paris.

Dinh-Thuy Phan Huy received her degree in engineering from Supelec, in 2001, and her Ph.D. degree in electronics and telecommunications from the National Institute of Applied Sciences of Rennes, France, in 2015. In 2001, she joined France Telecom (now Orange), France. She led the national French collaborative research projects TRIMARAN (2011-2014) and SpatialModulation (2016-2019). She participated to the European projects on 5G METIS, Fantastic 5G, mmMAGIC and 5GCAR. She holds more than 40 patents and has co-authored more than 40 papers. She is the recipient of the 2016 Economical Impact Prize from the French National Research Agency, the 2018 General Ferrié Prize from the French Society of Electricity, Electronics and Information and Communication Technologies and the 2018 Irène Joliot-Curie Prize (Women-Research-Business) from the French Ministry of Education and Research. Her research interests include wireless communications, beamforming, time reversal, spatial modulation, predictor antenna, backscattering and intelligent reflecting surfaces.

Jorge Proença is a PhD candidate in Information Science and Technology at the University of Coimbra. He received his M.Sc. degree from the same institution in 2012. Since then he is a junior researcher in the Centre for Informatics and Systems of the University of Coimbra (CISUC), where he has participated in several research projects in the fields of network virtualization, telecom networks, security and critical infrastructure protection.

Veronica Quintuna-Rodriguez is a future network expert at Orange Labs, France. She received the Ph.D. degree from the Sorbonne University in 2018. Her research activity is focused on the performance analysis of virtualized network functions, exploiting cloud technologies and joining the IT and Telecom worlds to achieve flexible network architectures. She has authored more than 25 papers and patents and has gotten several awards for outstanding works.

Yvan Rafflé, deceased, was a Senior Security Expert in the Security Department of Orange Labs. He had received a PhD from the University of Lille in Electronics, and was very active in multiple areas of computer and network security, such as security of virtualized infrastructures, connected and autonomous mobility, mobile payment systems, and drones. Recently, he had notably co-authored papers at VNC 2019 on practical anonymous attestation-based pseudonym schemes, and at C&ESAR 2019 on vehicular software networking security. He passed away in 2020.

Sebastien Roché has a Master's degree in Telecommunications and Computer Science. Acting as Corporate Internal Auditor within Orange, he is specialized on mobile and banking threats and focuses on cyber rating trends.

Rinki Sharma has over 15 years of experience in teaching and research. She has over 20 publications in reputed journals, conferences, and books. She has been granted five international patents. Her areas of research are communication networks, wireless communication, vehicular communication networks and protocols, software defined networking and Internet of Things.

Paulo Simões is Associate Professor at the Department of Informatics Engineering of the University of Coimbra, Portugal, from where he obtained his doctoral degree in 2002. He is also senior researcher at the Centre for Informatics and Systems of the University of Coimbra and regularly collaborates with Instituto Pedro Nunes as senior consultant, leading technology transfer projects for industry partners such as telecommunications operators and energy utilities. He has been involved in many European research projects, with technical and managerial duties. His research interests include Future Internet, Network and Infrastructure Management, Security, Critical Infrastructure Protection and Virtualization of Networking and Computing Resources. He has over 150 publications in refereed journals and conferences, and he regularly serves on program committees of international conferences of these areas. He is Senior Member of the IEEE Communications Society.

Vincent Thiebaut, with an engineering diploma in 1995, experienced integration and testing on multiple network technologies (ATM, ISDN, PABX, Wireless access, IPTV, CDN) for different companies. Since 2008, he's been a project leader for IPTV and CDN inside orange Labs, in order to deploy new features in Orange footprint. He is now in charge of automation tools in the context of 5G programmable networks, in order to optimize integration and testing cycles.

Christos Tranoris is a Senior Researcher, he received his Diploma degree in 1999 and since 2006 he holds also a Ph.D. from the Electrical and Computer Engineering of University of Patras in the area of software processes in the modelling and design of industrial applications. Since 1995 he has worked in the private sector as a software engineer. During his Ph.D. worked for and founded several ICT companies. In 2001 he co-founded the software company Instance Ltd. After 2006 he worked as Software Tech. Lead QE in Bytemobile's European Development Centre. He is currently a Research Fellow at the Department of Electrical and Computer Engineering at the University of Patras. He has published over 30 papers in journals and conferences and holds one patent, is a member of IEEE, ACM and the Technical Chamber of Greece. Since 2008 he has participated in several FIRE projects (AutoI, Panlab-PII, Openlab, INFINITY-Tender, FORGE, 5GinFIRE). He has significant experience in the development of experimentation infrastructures and tools.

Mikko Samuli Vaija is one of Orange's lead analysts within the fields of life cycle assessment, eco-design and circular economy. He has been involved in the ITU-T standardisation effort on recommendations such as the recent L.1023 "Assessment method for circular scoring" and the European project on Product Environmental Footprint (PEF) on environmental labelling.

Marc Vautier is in charge of the Energy and Environment Orange Expert community made of around 60 persons coming from different Orange countries with different skill. The Objective of the community is to help Orange Group to improve it skills in energy and environment to reduce operational expenditure and carbon dioxide emissions. Between 2010 and 2017, he has been involved in Corporate Orange marketing entity to promote eco-design approach to marketing teams to reduce environmental impacts of product and services. Between 2008 and 2010, he has been involved in Technical Environment within Orange Lab R&D as a program manager.

Ricard Vilalta graduated in 2007 and received a Ph.D. degree in telecommunications in 2013, both from the UPC. He is a senior researcher at CTTC, in the Optical Networks and Systems Department. He is an active contributor in several standardization bodies such as ONF, ETSI and IETF. He is also a member of the technical steering team of Open Transport Configuration & Control in ONF. He has been involved in several international, EU, national and industrial research projects: INSPIRE-5Gplus, 5GCroCo, 5GTANGO, 5GCAR, BlueSPACE, 5G-Crosshaul, EU-Japan STRAUSS, ICT IDEALIST, ICT

COMBO, ICT STRONGEST, ICT OFELIA, FP6 E-Cab. Moreover, he led 5GTANGO impact activities (WP leader). He led experimental validation WP leader of 5GPPP phase 3 project INSPIRE-5Gplus and Project Coordinator of 5GPPP TeraFlow project.

Gaëlle Yven is managing an Orange Labs' team on content delivery optimization topics.

Index

O

P

Q

R

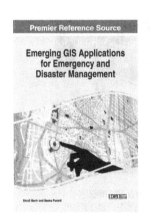
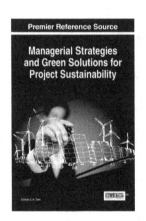

Printed in the United States
by Baker & Taylor Publisher Services